**(Continued on back endsheets)**

Dictionary of Literary Biography® • Volume One Hundred Thirty-Four

# Twentieth-Century Spanish Poets
## Second Series

# Twentieth-Century Spanish Poets
## Second Series

Edited by
Jerry Phillips Winfield
*Mercer University*

A Bruccoli Clark Layman Book
Gale Research Inc.
Detroit, Washington, D.C., London

Printed in the United States of America

Published simultaneously in the United Kingdom
by Gale Research International Limited
(An affiliated company of Gale Research Inc.)

The paper used in this publication meets the minimum requirements
of American National Standard for Information Sciences–Permanence
Paper for Printed Library Materials, ANSI Z39.48-1984. ∞ ™

Library of Congress Catalog Card Number 93-26861
ISBN 0-8103-5393-8

I(T)P

The trademark ITP is used under license.

10 9 8 7 6 5 4 3 2 1

# Contents

# Plan of the Series

The advisory board, the editors, and the publisher of the *Dictionary of Literary Biography* are joined in endorsing Mark Twain's declaration. The literature of a nation provides an inexhaustible resource of permanent worth. We intend to make literature and its creators better understood and more accessible to students and the reading public, while satisfying the standards of teachers and scholars.

To meet these requirements, *literary biography* has been construed in terms of the author's achievement. The most important thing about a writer is his writing. Accordingly, the entries in *DLB* are career biographies, tracing the development of the author's canon and the evolution of his reputation.

The purpose of *DLB* is not only to provide reliable information in a convenient format but also to place the figures in the larger perspective of literary history and to offer appraisals of their accomplishments by qualified scholars.

The publication plan for *DLB* resulted from two years of preparation. The project was proposed to Bruccoli Clark by Frederick C. Ruffner, president of the Gale Research Company, in November 1975. After specimen entries were prepared and typeset, an advisory board was formed to refine the entry format and develop the series rationale. In meetings held during 1976, the publisher, series editors, and advisory board approved the scheme for a comprehensive biographical dictionary of persons who contributed to North American literature. Editorial work on the first volume began in January 1977, and it was published in 1978. In order to make *DLB* more than a reference tool and to compile volumes that individually have claim to status as literary history, it was decided to organize vol-

umes by topic, period, or genre. Each of these free-standing volumes provides a biographical-bibliographical guide and overview for a particular area of literature. We are convinced that this organization — as opposed to a single alphabet method — constitutes a valuable innovation in the presentation of reference material. The volume plan necessarily requires many decisions for the placement and treatment of authors who might properly be included in two or three volumes. In some instances a major figure will be included in separate volumes, but with different entries emphasizing the aspect of his career appropriate to each volume. Ernest Hemingway, for example, is represented in *American Writers in Paris, 1920–1939* by an entry focusing on his expatriate apprenticeship; he is also in *American Novelists, 1910–1945* with an entry surveying his entire career. Each volume includes a cumulative index of the subject authors and articles. Comprehensive indexes to the entire series are planned.

With volume ten in 1982 it was decided to enlarge the scope of *DLB*. By the end of 1986 twenty-one volumes treating British literature had been published, and volumes for Commonwealth and Modern European literature were in progress. The series has been further augmented by the *DLB Yearbooks* (since 1981) which update published entries and add new entries to keep the *DLB* current with contemporary activity. There have also been *DLB Documentary Series* volumes which provide biographical and critical source materials for figures whose work is judged to have particular interest for students. One of these companion volumes is entirely devoted to Tennessee Williams.

We define literature as the *intellectual commerce of a nation:* not merely as belles lettres but as that ample and complex process by which ideas are generated, shaped, and transmitted. *DLB* entries are not limited to "creative writers" but extend to other figures who in their time and in their way influenced the mind of a people. Thus the series encompasses historians, journalists, publishers, and screenwriters. By this means readers of *DLB* may be aided to perceive literature not as cult scripture in the keeping of intellectual high priests but firmly positioned at the center of a nation's life.

DLB includes the major writers appropriate to each volume and those standing in the ranks immediately behind them. Scholarly and critical counsel has been sought in deciding which minor figures to include and how full their entries should be. Wherever possible, useful references are made to figures who do not warrant separate entries.

Each DLB volume has a volume editor responsible for planning the volume, selecting the figures for inclusion, and assigning the entries. Volume editors are also responsible for preparing, where appropriate, appendices surveying the major periodicals and literary and intellectual movements for their volumes, as well as lists of further readings. Work on the series as a whole is coordinated at the Bruccoli Clark Layman editorial center in Columbia, South Carolina, where the editorial staff is responsible for accuracy of the published volumes.

One feature that distinguishes DLB is the illustration policy – its concern with the iconography of literature. Just as an author is influenced by his surroundings, so is the reader's understanding of the author enhanced by a knowledge of his environment. Therefore DLB volumes include not only drawings, paintings, and photographs of authors, often depicting them at various stages in their careers, but also illustrations of their families and places where they lived. Title pages are regularly reproduced in facsimile along with dust jackets for modern authors. The dust jackets are a special feature of DLB because they often document better than anything else the way in which an author's work was perceived in its own time. Specimens of the writers' manuscripts are included when feasible.

Samuel Johnson rightly decreed that "The chief glory of every people arises from its authors." The purpose of the *Dictionary of Literary Biography* is to compile literary history in the surest way available to us – by accurate and comprehensive treatment of the lives and work of those who contributed to it.

The *DLB* Advisory Board

# Introduction

"Sólo el poeta puede
mirar lo que está lejos
dentro del alma en turbio
y mago sol envuelto."

(Only the poet can
see what is far away
inside of the soul, enclosed
in a magical and misty sun.)

– Antonio Machado, "Introduccíon" ("Galerías")

The twentieth century has produced some of Spain's best literature and has been described as a second Golden Age, recalling the magnificent literature of the years 1492–1650. The term *Golden Age* evokes the achievements of the era when Ferdinand and Isabella, Charles V, and Phillip II reigned and the great literary figures of Lope de Vega, Calderón de la Barca, Tirso de Molina, San Juan de la Cruz, Fray Luis de León, Santa Teresa de Avila, Luis de Góngora, Francisco de Quevedo, and Miguel de Cervantes created masterpieces of world literature. Spain then was at the forefront of European politics and culture. In the twentieth century another rebirth has occurred, especially in lyric poetry, which may well represent the most significant genre of Spain's contemporary literary contribution. Poets such as Antonio Machado, Juan Ramón Jiménez, Federico García Lorca, Vicente Aleixandre, Jorge Guillén, Rafael Alberti, and Luis Cernuda deserve to be included among the most original, talented, and profound artists of the century.

Yet, Spain entered the twentieth century burdened by defeat and doubt. It was to witness the end of four hundred years of colonial empire and a continual cycle of political and social spasms which ended the monarchy and ultimately engendered the violence and horror of the Spanish Civil War. The depth of the national crisis became apparent in the loss of Cuba, Puerto Rico, the Phillipines, and Guam following defeat in the Spanish-American War. Alienation, decadence, and disillusionment gave energy to the plaintive verses of Antonio Machado in his poem "A Orillas del Duero" (On the Banks of the Duero), collected in *Campos de Castilla* (Fields of Castile, 1912): "Castilla miserable, ayer dominadora, / envuelta en sus andrajos desprecia cuanto ignora." (Miserable Castile, yesterday dominant, / now wrapped in rags, despises all that it does not know.)

Around 1900 two movements appeared which continue to be confusing in the critical attempt to differentiate them. *Modernismo* began in Hispanic America and is associated with its principal proponent, the Nicaraguan poet Rubén Darío, who traveled to Spain, bringing the influence of the movement. In general terms *modernismo* followed the aesthetics of the nineteenth century, particularly the French symbolist poets such as Charles Baudelaire, Paul Verlaine, Stéphane Mallarmé, and Arthur Rimbaud as well as the American Edgar Allan Poe. Parallel to *modernismo* a group of writers who were to become known as the Generation of 1898 were led by Miguel de Unamuno, Angel Ganivet, and Antonio Machado. These writers and poets, in an effort of national renovation, searched for the authentic essence of Spain – in its soul, conscious of the continuing cultural, social, and political decline. The "question of Spain" led them in different directions; however, they agreed that to renew itself Spain must discover its values and identity. While *modernismo* is more often identified with aesthetics, technique, and form, the Generation of 1898 emphasized spiritual, moral, and existential questions.

Essentially *modernismo* was a reaction against the romanticism of the nineteenth century and the later stages of realism. The *modernista* poets were desperately attempting to escape a literature that had become shallow in meaning and trite and stagnant in form and style. Increasingly sensitive to the currents of western Europe, they found inspiration in the French Parnassian and symbolist schools. The Parnassian poets included Verlaine and Mallarmé, both of whom later moved toward symbolist poetry. They envisioned a cult of formal artistic perfection evading the imaginative and passionate elements of Romanticism. Verlaine indeed viewed poetry as the creation of music. Inspired by Baudelaire, Mallarmé, Verlaine, and Rimbaud, they completed the poetic circle of the symbolist movement and sought to create beauty through intuition, offering the genesis of a pure concept of art grounded in symbol and separate from everyday reality. In a rarefied atmosphere of exoticism, mystery, and sensuality the *modernista* poets created poetry of refined and elegant melancholy. In their technical innovations the *modernistas* practiced an extensive repertoire of rhetorical figures, neologisms, unusual metrical forms, and remarkable metaphors. Like the Romantics of the previous century, many of these poets were drawn to the subjective world of the oneiric – a poetic realm of dream and shadow. Darío, the great voice of *modernismo* from Nicaragua, made two visits to Spain and met with Unamuno, Machado, and Jiménez. The influence of the movement, however, was more pronounced in Hispanic America than of lasting and direct impression in Spain. Clearly the early works of Ramón del Valle-Inclán, Machado, Unamuno, and Jiménez embraced the tendencies of the modernist revolution, as did a considerable body of the verse of the brother of Antonio Machado, Manuel Machado. Yet as did the poetry of their mentor Darío, their verse evolved into distinct and original forms. The latter stages of modernism returned to a more traditional representation of social and spiritual values in contrast to the abstract, evasive, and often artificial themes of its beginnings.

The second significant literary current of the beginning of the twentieth century in Spain is identified with the group of writers known as the Generation of 1898 and includes the poetry of Antonio Machado and Unamuno as well as the narrative works of Ganivet, Pío Baroja, and José Martínez Ruiz (who wrote as Azorín). The year 1898 saw the disastrous defeat of Spain in the Spanish-American War. These writers envisioned not the creation of a new Spain, but one emerging from an interior sociohistorical and cultural reality which embraced the spiritual and mystical nature of its people. While contemporaneous to modernism, the Generation of 1898 was more concerned with ethical reform and ideology rather than technical and aesthetic forms. Principally Castilian in its focus, the poetry of the generation utilized a natural language grounded in reality and an open style exemplified by the latter poetry of Jiménez. This Nobel laureate represented one of the most powerful and gifted voices of the first part of the century and, while often included in the Generation of 1898, is best seen as a transitional poet difficult to place in any particular movement. The poetry of the master Jiménez has continued to influence aesthetics and creative form throughout the century.

Finally, at the end of the nineteenth century and early in the twentieth century, European ideas began to penetrate the closed circle of Spanish Catholicism and traditionalism. Although not of profound persuasion, the political philosophy of Karl Marx and the theories of evolution proposed by Charles Darwin challenged a moral and religious system of beliefs which appeared immutable. Friedrich Nietzsche, the German philosopher, announced the coming death of God and demanded the revaluation of all values. Unamuno was profoundly moved by the tortured search of the Dane Søren Kierkegaard to discover and believe in God – an agonizing thirst for immortality portrayed in Unamuno's philosophical work *La agonía del Cristianismo* (The Agony of Christianity, 1931) and in the existential struggle of his *Poesías* (Poems, 1907).

The Generation of 1927 has also been referred to as the Generation of 1925, although most of its members began to write before that time. It represents the superior poetry written between the end of World War I and the beginning of the civil war in Spain. Moreover, it is a period in which the great poets of the previous generation achieved full and mature expression. The movement includes some of the most distinguished poets of the century as Pedro Salinas, Jorge Guillén, Gerardo Diego, Federico García Lorca, Rafael Alberti, Vicente Aleixandre, and Luis Cernuda. Also worthy of mention are Dámaso Alonso, Emilio Prados, and Angela Aymerich Figuera. The year 1927 saw the tricentennial of the death of the great baroque poet Luis de Góngora, whose prestige these new poets attempted to restore as well as to offer with new clarity an interpretation of his poetry. Certainly the elegance and search for perfection of Jiménez continued to influence and inspire, as did the humanistic and philosophical questions of Machado and Unamuno in the later progressions of the movement. Although the poets of the generation demonstrated a continuity of defined traditions within Spanish poetry, these traditions were abruptly subjected to a cycle of avant-garde aesthetic currents from outside. Essentially hermetic, these literary movements stressed a depersonalized and pure lyric somewhat reminiscent of the aesthetic philosophy of José Ortega y Gasset in such works as *La deshumanización del arte e ideas sobre la novela* (The Dehumanization of Art and Ideas About the Novel, 1925). In the years following World War I these ideologies, with varying degrees of influence, challenged prevailing models of literary structure and art. Dadaism, of French origin, endured only a brief moment with its use of collage and nonsensical approach to meaning. Ultraism, also French, attempted to distill and define poetry by reducing it to the most fundamental elements of simile, image, and, above all, metaphor while purging poetry of narrative and a personal and anecdotal presence. Ultraism appeared in Spain as *creacionismo* (creationism), so named by the Chilean poet Vicente Huidobro. For the *creacionistas,* such as Diego, the poet was capable of creating a distinct reality in the poetic work in itself. Surrealism, whose doctrine had been proposed by André Bretón in France in 1924, exerted a more significant and enduring effect. Demanding in an intransigent and angry voice freedom from ideological and ethical concerns, it sought disengagement from aesthetic strictures through irrational symbols, the technique of "automatic writing," and the Freudian subconscious revealed in dreams and free association. To some degree all the poets of the Generation of 1927 were affected by surrealism, which is especially apparent in the poetry of Lorca, Alberti, and Aleixandre.

The poets of the Generation of 1927, for the most part, perceived poetry as autonomous and formalistic – a creative entity independent of its subject and separated from the everyday experience of its creators. Aspiring to an ideal of artistic perfection, they wrote in the atmosphere of the intellect – freed in the fantasy of imagination. Much of the poetry is demanding and not easily accessible by the reader because of its complexity and intimacy. Yet these poets do succeed in communicating a universal reality of human experience and form bonds in the relation of reader and work. Each poet remained an individual, integrating the prevailing currents in a distinct style. Moreover, as the generation advanced, intellectualized and formal preoccupations were tempered by a more emotive and humanized return to traditional themes of love, life, death, and the bonds of human existence. Perceptively, Carl W. Cobb, in *Contemporary Spanish Poetry (1898–1963)* (1976), has distinguished two groups within the generation. Poets of affirmation include Salinas, Guillén, and Diego, while others remain displaced and rebellious – the *poetas desarraigadas* (uprooted poets), whom Alonso said included Alberti, Aleixandre, and Cernuda. As Cobb indicates, all except Diego evidenced an anguished struggle in the loss of their Catholic faith as had their predecessors of the Generation of 1898.

In July 1936, with the outbreak of national revolt led by Generalissimo Francisco Franco, Spain entered a nightmarish world of violence, cruelty, and inhumanity which was to last three years. The totalitarian dictatorship of Franco which followed continued to erode and paralyze the artistic and intellectual will of the nation. In the tragic convulsion of the war and its immediate aftermath, Lorca was assassinated by Nationalist soldiers in Viznar, while the poets Alberti, Guillén, Cernuda, Machado, León Felipe, Salinas, and Jiménez were forced into exile. The voice of the great poet Miguel Hernández, who had supported the Republican forces against Franco, was silenced by his death in prison. Spanish literature suffered not only from the absence of its great writers but as well from the lack of published texts and the corrosive nature of censorship. Spain was trapped within itself, separated and alienated from outside cultural influences. After the war many artists returned; others such as Cernuda, Salinas, and Jiménez died in exile without seeing again the land and the people of their inspiration. The poet Juan Gil-Albert withdrew into his own interior exile. However, some of these poets produced memorable works of exceptional quality, such as the *Cántico* (Canticle) of Guillén, published in several editions between 1928 and 1950, and *Dios deseado y deseante* (God Desired and Desiring) by Jiménez (1964). Nonetheless, with the great figures of *modernismo* now gone, and most of the Generation of 1927 deceased or in exile, and amidst political and cultural orthodoxy, the future for Spanish poetry appeared bleak and threatened, especially for the younger poets. Yet the decades that followed would fortunately prove this untrue.

Until fairly recently in literary history, the poets of this moment were designated as the Generation of 1936, a year which coincided with the outbreak of the civil war and marked the four hundredth anniversary of the death of the poet Garcilaso de la Vega. Among these poets of the 1940s and 1950s are Carmen Conde, Leopoldo Panero, Luis Rosales, Gabriel Celaya, Dionisio Ridruejo, Hernández, Gil-Albert, Blas de Otero, Gloria Fuertes, José Hierro, and Carlos Bousoño, as well as two representatives of the Generation of 1927, Alonso and Aleixandre. These poets did share a common experience in the tragedy of the civil war, and their poetry is more personal and human as opposed to the intellectualized and formalistic poetry of the preceding generation. Many returned to traditional themes of love and religion, while others pursued existential and social themes emphasizing the relation of historical and individual circumstance. Yet since the mid 1960s criticism has called into question the very nature of the generational approach to literary history, especially regarding post-civil-war poetry. The generational scheme has been challenged by scholars such as José Olivio Jiménez, Bousoño, Dionisio Cañas, and Andrew P. Debicki. The generational approach creates confusion in grouping together poets who differ demonstrably in thematics, style, and use of language. Poets considerably differing in age exhibited similarities, while others who were contemporary seem directly opposing in their poetic credos. Moreover, as Debicki has noted, the concept of generation creates an arbitrary separation of Spanish literature from European currents such as postmodernism, precisely when an integration of the two has increased. Several critics have used the term *promoción* attempting to group movements of poetry exhibiting similarities of language, theme, and poetics, rather than a generalized chronological method. A clear solution to the question of classification continues to be problematic.

It is clear that the most significant change in the poetry that followed the civil war was the movement from art for art's sake to a dialectic between art and society. The hermetic and stylized poetry evident in the works of the Generation of 1927 was abandoned as a model in a new concentration on more clear and personal poetry centering the individual in historical circumstance. In this first *promoción* following the war, two significant movements appeared as the role of the poetic journal assumed increasing significance. One group identified with the review *Garcilaso*, founded by José García Nieto and others in 1943, supported a neoclassic line of serenity and composure inspired by the poet Garcilaso de la Vega, and often wrote of the themes of God, love, and family. These young poets assumed the identity of *juventud creadora* (creative youth) from a journal of the period named *Juventud*. In truth, these poets exhibited considerable diversity without any clear ideology or definitive poetic creed. In direct opposition, those poets who supported the journal *Espadaña*, founded in 1944 by Victoriano Crémer and Eugenio de Nora, offered a poetic vision focused on social needs and the common man. Poets as Blas de Otero, José Hierro, and Gabriel Celaya produced social poetry of enduring quality and meaning. In the ordinary language of the people, they indicted a society which ignored misery and injustice. Some of the social poetry revealed the technique of *tremendismo*, with its emphasis on anguish, violence, and brutality.

Two works written by poets usually associated with the Generation of 1927 exerted a singular and powerful presence in the poetry written after the civil war when they appeared in 1944. Alonso, in *Hijos de la ira* (1944; translated as *Children of Wrath*, 1970), plead for a God who might not exist to reveal himself in a age of cruelty, destruction, and death. In a portrait of human anguish he created one of the most memorable lines of contemporary verse: "Madrid es  una ciudad de más de un millón de cadáveres (según las últimas estadísticas)" (Madrid is a city of more than one million corpses [according to the latest statistics]) is a verse which voices the rage and pain of a poet witnessing a dehumanized world gone mad. With *poesía desarraigada*, Alonso stretched the limits of metaphor and image in creating unusual forms of expression. In the same year (1944) the Nobel laureate Aleixandre published *Sombra del paraíso* (Shadow of Paradise), grounded in the irrational nature of language, use of new techniques in free verse, and search for meaning.

This work continues to exert influence in Spanish poetry, as it did on the young poets of the time.

Each of the poets of the "generation," however, spoke with his own distinct voice. Otero and Rosales particularly were drawn to the search for God and religion. In their concern with individual experience, several of these poets, notably Bousoño and Hierro, increasingly emphasized the existential pain of the human condition. If Jiménez symbolized the ideal of poetry for the Generation of 1927, these poets looked to Antonio Machado as currents of social and existential concerns emerged and grew stronger. Often overlooked in a critical emphasis on realism and social concerns were the innovations of the *postismo* (after "isms") movement. The imaginative power of the word gave impulse to a search for formal beauty and total poetic freedom in the poetry of Miguel Labordeta and Carlos Edmundo de Ory. Centered in variances of surrealism, the vanguardist group of *postismo* evoked the erotic and subconscious often with a playful tone of satire regarding the social currents of the time.

The poets of the second postwar generation are also often designated as the Generation of 1950 and even the *promoción* of the 1960s. The difficulty of grouping such disparate thematics and poetic techniques results in a somewhat ambiguous classification. The majority of these poets began to publish in the journals of the 1940s and presented major works in the 1950s and 1960s with considerable diversity in their backgrounds, aesthetics, and definition of what poetry is. Continuing political consciousness and existential elements of the previous group, these poets progressed toward a more global vision of humankind in historical circumstance. They offered a new definition of language in itself as the power and essence of poetry as well as a new realism of the word. Included in this group among others are Angel González, José Angel Valente, Jaime Gil de Biedma, Claudio Rodríguez, José María Valverde, Eladio Cabañero, Carlos Sahagún, Angel Crespo, José Manuel Caballero Bonald, Carlos Barral, and José Agustín Goytisolo. The social poetry which dominated the 1950s had calcified, becoming stagnant and dogmatic, and the poets of the second postwar group sought to elevate social concern to a moral and ethical questioning in which poetry, not message, was primary. Because of their ages, many did not have a direct personal experience of the civil war and viewed the individual and society in a more universal context. Significantly, almost all interrogated the function of poetry itself.

Bousoño and Aleixandre accentuated the operation of poetry as *comunicación* (communication); the younger poets of the 1950s and 1960s stressed *conocimiento* (knowledge). From their viewpoint, the writing of poetry is an art and forms a reality apart from experience. Particularly Valente and González felt that the poet does not bring a fixed reality to the creative act but instead synthesizes a new reality in writing that is distinct from structure and words. Because the poet enters the conflict between the perception and experience of reality – new linguistic reality – there exists the probability of self-knowledge. These poets, in the nature of their works, invite the reader to participate in this *process* of poetry, evident especially in the verse of Sahagún, González, and Rodríguez. A new faith in poetry as language offered innovations of theme and aesthetics which will be integrated into the poetry of the 1970s. In several studies, including his introduction to *Spanish Contemporary Poetry* (1992), Debicki discovers a more substantial change in the poetry of this period than traditional criticism has indicated and designates a movement toward the western European current of postmodernism. The poets of this group offered a new focus upon syntax, lexicon, and the participatory role of the reader. They also employed an increased intertextuality – the poetic integration of past literary works and other works by the same author. Finally, it must be remembered that poets such as Aleixandre, Bousoño, Otero, and others who are generally associated with earlier movements continued to create lyrics of considerable artistic merit in these years.

In the mid 1960s another movement of poetry emerged including that group of poets born approximately in the years between 1939 and 1948. Several confusing designations have been proffered, including the *generación marginada* (marginal generation) suggested by Bousoño, the Generation of 1970, and the Generation of 1968. The most prevalent designation has been that of the *novísimos,* derived from the title of the controversial anthology of José M. Castellet, *Nueve novísimos poetas españoles* (Nine of the Newest Spanish Poets), published in 1970. Castellet specified nine poets whom he believed evidenced a poetic renewal of change in their rejection of traditional forms, their usage of cultural references from the past and emphasis on culture (*culturalismo*), and their recognition of poetry as an autonomous and self-sufficient form. These values were also given momentum by the poet Père (Pedro) Gimferrer (who later was to abandon Castilian for Catalan) in his celebrated work of 1966, *Arde El Mar* (The Sea is Burning), with its *culturalista* tones, surrealism, and exercise of automatic writing. Castellet included in his work Manuel Vázquez Montalbán, Antonio Martínez Sarrión, José María

Alvarez, Felix de Azúa, Gimferrer, Vicente Molina-Foix, Jaime Siles, Guillermo Carnero, Ana María Moix, and Leopoldo M. Panero, the son of Leopoldo Panero of the Generation of 1936. Another anthology, *Joven poesía española* (Young Spanish Poets), edited by Concepcíon G. Moral and Rosa María Pereda in 1979, included most of the poets selected by Castellet, as well as others, including Antonio Colinas and Luis Antonio de Villena.

In the beginning of this movement, a distinct rupture from the immediate previous generations was apparent, as the poets of this group returned for inspiration to the Generation of 1927, and the poetry of Aleixandre, Cernuda, and Lorca. Social and religious themes were disparaged. However, this return is not characteristic of such mature poets of previous movements as Bousoño, Francisco Brines, Gil de Biedma, and Rodríguez. Proclaiming the autonomy of the work of art and projecting what Bousoño has seen as a loss of faith in the capacity of language to mirror experiential reality, these younger poets defined poetry within its creation. As Debicki has noted in "New Poetics, New Works, New Approaches: Recent Spanish Poetry" in the journal *Siglo XX/20th Century,* this self-conscious element of poetry presents an indeterminate and open set of meanings which invite the involvement of the reader and which was already evidenced in the Generation of the 1950s in the poetry of Valente and Rodríguez. The attempt to define the poetic act within poetry (metapoetry), as seen in the brilliant work of Bousoño titled *Oda en la Ceniza* (Ode in the Ashes, 1975), is also related to an increasing intertextuality. Several of these poets extended their references to painting and music as well as literature. Drawn to the cosmopolitan, the exotic, and the hermetic, many were inspired by foreign writers such as the Marquis de Sade, T. S. Eliot, Saint-John Perse, Ezra Pound, Jorge Luis Borges, and Octavio Paz. These new Spanish poets fused their poetry with seemingly antithetical currents of the mass media, television, movies, and popular culture. Resisting what they felt as repression within art and society, some wrote of the human body, eroticism, homosexuality, and turned to themes of decadentism.

Lacking the perspective of time, it is almost impossible to identify and describe the most recent poetic movements in Spain. A multiplicity of themes and styles seems apparent – a diversity itself indicative of postmodernity. Prominent anthologies such as *Florilegium* (Collection of Flowers, 1982), edited by Elena de Jongh Rossel, and the *Postnovísimos* of Luis Antonio de Villena (1986) do not establish any clear orientation. Some have referred to these younger poets as the *postnovísimos*; yet there is no clear relation of their work to the *novísimos* discussed above. The most accurate term might be the simplest – "the poets of the 1980s." Obviously these poets are still maturing in their role as artists and it may well be that from this group and the *novísimos* will emerge yet another Spanish poet of greatness. A very restricted list of this group would include José Gutiérrez, Julio Alonso Llamazares, Blanca Andreu, Ana Rosetti, and Fanny Rubio. The poets of previous generations, such as Bousoño, Siles, and Villena, among others, continue to offer poetry of distinction. A tentative characterization of these younger poets might include a continued faith in the autonomy of poetry and emphasis on language, although the currents of culturalism and metapoetry seem to have lost some of their force. There is an increased lyricism and clarity in the desire to unify poetry with real and immediate experience in contrast with pure aestheticism. Significantly, the women poets have discovered a new freedom and identity in the voices of Andreu, Rosetti, and Rubio. The integration of contemporary poetry with that of preceding movements is clear, especially regarding the poetry of Jiménez, the Generation of 1927, the poets of the 1950s, and the vanguardists.

This volume also includes two outstanding Catalan poets, Salvador Espriu and J. V. Foix, in addition to those like Gimferrer who have written in Spanish and Catalan. Despite the artistic contributions of Catalonia in the visual arts (Salvador Dalí, Joan Miró, and Antonio Tàpies), architecture (Antoní Gaudí), and sculpture (Juli Gonzàlez), only recently has Catalan literature begun to receive the critical attention it deserves. This recognition is due in great part to the devoted work of scholars like David H. Rosenthal, who says in his work *Postwar Catalan Poetry* (1991) that "Catalan poetry ranks with the world's best but remains unknown to most English-speaking readers." The Spanish Civil War was particularly devastating to the Catalans, and following the bloody tragedy the Catalan language was banned. Indeed the very existence of Catalan culture faced extinction if not for the courageous resistance to the Fascists. Today, however, the poetry of Catalonia reveals the richness of its cultural heritage, which has opened itself to the currents of Spain and Europe while maintaining its distinctive identity.

It has been said that Spain is a nation of poets; clearly, in the twentieth century it is a nation which has produced great poets. This volume bears witness to an artistic rebirth which overcame the defeat of Spain in the Spanish-American War, the bloody struggle of the Spanish Civil War, and the closed totalitarian society of the Franco dictatorship. This volume is also a very limited attempt to portray the distinct contribution of Spanish poetry to contemporary world literature.

*– Jerry Phillips Winfield*

## ACKNOWLEDGMENTS

This book was produced by Bruccoli Clark Layman, Inc. Karen L. Rood is senior editor for the *Dictionary of Literary Biography* series. Jack Turner and Sam Bruce were the in-house editors.

Photography editors are Edward Scott and Timothy C. Lundy. Layout and graphics supervisor is Penney L. Haughton. Copyediting supervisor is Bill Adams. Typesetting supervisor is Kathleen M. Flanagan. Darren Harris-Fain and Julie E. Frick are editorial associates. Systems manager is George F. Dodge. The production staff includes Rowena Betts, Steve Borsanyi, Barbara Brannon, Ann M. Cheschi, Patricia Coate, Rebecca Crawford, Margaret McGinty Cureton, Denise Edwards, Sarah A. Estes, Joyce Fowler, Robert Fowler, Laurel M. Gladden, Jolyon M. Helterman, Tanya D. Locklair, Ellen McCracken, Kathy Lawler Merlette, John Morrison Myrick, Pamela D. Norton, Thomas J. Pickett, Patricia Salisbury, Maxine K. Smalls, Deborah P. Stokes, William L. Thomas, Jr., Jennifer Carroll Jenkins Turley, and Wilma Weant.

Walter W. Ross and Brenda Gross did library research. They were assisted by the following librarians at the Thomas Cooper Library of the University of South Carolina: Linda Holderfield and the interlibrary-loan staff; reference librarians Gwen Baxter, Daniel Boice, Faye Chadwell, Cathy Eckman, Gary Geer, Qun "Gerry" Jiao, Jean Rhyne, Carol Tobin, Carolyn Tyler, Virginia Weathers, Elizabeth Whiznant, and Connie Widney; circulation-department head Thomas Marcil; and acquisitions-searching supervisor David Haggard.

# Twentieth-Century Spanish Poets
## Second Series

# Dictionary of Literary Biography

# Blanca Andreu
## (1959 – )

Sylvia R. Sherno
*University of California, Los Angeles*

BOOKS: *De una niña de provincias que se vino a vivir en un Chaguall* (Madrid: Rialp/Adonais, 1981);
*Báculo de Babel* (Madrid: Hiperión, 1983);
*Elphistone* (Madrid: Visor, 1988).

OTHER: "Poética," in *Postnovísimos,* edited by Luis Antonio de Villena (Madrid: Visor, 1986), pp. 90–91.

Blanca Andreu's sparse but striking oeuvre has made her a key figure in recent Spanish poetry, especially among the so-called *postnovísimos* (those after the "very new ones"), the wave of young poets whose work began to be published in the late 1970s and early 1980s. Andreu has been the object of public notoriety for her provocative themes and daring imagery; she has also been the recipient of critical accolades for a sophisticated poetic style that belies her years and for a depth of vision that reconnects with the Spanish mystic tradition. The emotional nakedness and intensity of her voice signal a new intimacy in Spanish poetry, after the highly refined and somewhat depersonalized aesthetics favored by the *novísimos* (very new ones), the poets immediately preceding Andreu's generation. Yet her poetry transcends the expression of personal feelings and concerns, for it represents a larger vision embracing the truths and meanings beneath the surface of words and language. Still at an early stage in her poetic evolution, Andreu resists facile literary categorization and has elected not to conform to any one theory of poetry. Rather, between her debut collection and her most recent work, she draws on a wide variety of models and sources while exploring diverse modalities ranging from the oneiric lyricism and fragmented syntax reminiscent of the surrealists to

the less consciously refined patterns of ancient oral poetry.

Born in La Coruña in 1959, Blanca Andreu has lived not only in her native province of Galicia but also in Alicante and Murcia. She began studies at the University of Madrid in philosophy and journalism but did not finish her degree programs. She currently resides in Madrid and was married to the novelist Juan Benet, now deceased. Andreu fondly remembers idyllic Galician summers in a fifteenth-century estate belonging to her mother's family. In Galicia, Andreu was surrounded by the animals, especially horses, which she describes most notably in her earliest verses. During these summers spent in the Galician countryside, the young girl's rebellious spirit was given free rein. This freedom was partially reinforced during the rest of the year, spent in the town of Orihuela, in southeastern Spain. With her father's family, who participated in artistic and musical pursuits, Andreu enjoyed a relaxed and agreeable home environment. Yet circumstances outside the home may explain why, as she told interviewer Sharon Keefe Ugalde, her childhood was emotionally "catastrophic" and why, in her adolescence, she suffered bouts of insomnia and anorexia. Orihuela, like many other provincial Spanish towns, was dominated by the Catholic church. So, too, was the traditional boarding school Andreu attended, with its severe disciplinary practices and rigidly enforced Catholicism. Andreu has compared the stringently religious climate of this area of Spain to the oppressive and prisonlike milieu dramatized by Federico García Lorca in *La casa de Bernarda Alba* (1944; translated as *The House of Bernarda Alba,* in *Three Tragedies of Federico García Lorca,* 1947). The young Andreu displayed a profound sensitivity and

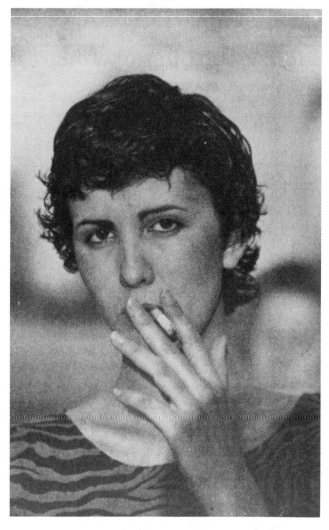

*Blanca Andreu*

resistance to the rigors of ceremonial religion and was inevitably labeled as "bad" or "guilty." This dread regarding religion infuses some of her strongest verses, as is evidenced in the intermingled strands of eroticism and terror running through *De una niña de provincias que se vino a vivir en un Chaguall* (About a Girl from the Provinces Who Went to Live in a Chaguall, 1981). At the same time, the obsession with evil and sin that was part of Andreu's Catholic childhood, abetted by her readings of works by Charles Baudelaire, Arthur Rimbaud, and others, is reflected in the persona of the traditional *poète maudit* (damned poet), vividly limned in her debut collection.

Andreu's first volume of poetry, mostly written when she was twenty-one, was at one point about to be thrown away by the discouraged young poet. But it was rescued by a friend who subsequently submitted the verses to the jury of Spain's distinguished Adonais Prize. Andreu has since

hinted that the good reception of the book has been due in part to its eye-catching title, one she dismisses now as outlandish and grammatically incorrect. With her provocative and insistent allusions in the poetry to alcohol, drugs, and ambiguous sexual activity, articulated in a youthful voice well versed in the manifestations of popular culture, *De una niña* seems to express with all the urgency of youth the unresolved longings and restlessness particular to adolescence. Furthermore, the repeated drug references call to mind poets such as Rimbaud and Baudelaire, who sought in poetry a continuation of the intense experiences, both ecstatic and anguished, induced by narcotic substances. The stunning imagery in *De una niña,* as well as the tortured syntax and general hallucinatory use of language, is evocative of the dreamlike lyricism of the surrealists and of two other poets Andreu has singled out as influential: Lorca and Pablo Neruda.

The poems of *De una niña* are autobiographical, if only in their original inspiration (at nineteen Andreu left the provinces for Madrid). The verses constitute a particularly intense portrait of the artist as a young girl. In a less somber moment the speaker looks back in almost heroic fashion to the feelings that defined her younger self: "Así, en pretérito pluscuamperfecto y futuro absoluto / voy hablando del trozo de universo que yo era" (Thus, in past pluperfect and absolute future / I am speaking of the piece of universe that I was). The speaker's life is like a saga, a journey back through time and over harrowing emotional terrain, and a process of growth toward illumination and inspiration.

*De una niña* conjures up anguished memories of a provincial girl — her painful adolescence, her fears of an uncomprehending and incomprehensible world, and her desire to escape by means of art. In the poem "Así morirán mis manos oliendo a espliego falso" (Thus my hands will die smelling of false lavender), she suffers the anguish of her changing physical being: "mis senos gramaticalmente elípticos / o las anchas caderas que tanto me hicieron llorar" (my grammatically elliptical breasts / or the wide hips that made me cry so much). She is acutely aware of time rushing by and of every effect left by time on her body. She conceives of her body in a state of ongoing decomposition, which mirrors the devastation of various cultures (Greece, Babylonia, and the medieval world) by time and history.

The girl suffers obsessions and fears of a newly discovered sexuality, and she is alternately attracted to and repelled by the objects of her love. She is pursued in her imagination by vampires, monstrous but also fascinating in their erotic power. In a poem titled "Cinco poemas para abdicar" (Five Poems to Abdicate) she assumes a series of masks that suggest the female roles blessed by society: those of a sacrificial virgin; a floating bride out of a Marc Chagall painting; Ophelia from *Hamlet;* a biblical foolish virgin; and a mystic bride. In the end, however, she refuses to succumb to the calcified values, norms, codes, roles, and institutions of the past.

A *rara avis*, the young woman recognizes herself in the bizarre and anomalous fauna, variously fearsome and vulnerable, that inhabit her imagination: withering doves, benign buffaloes, suicidal magpies, storks, and other long-legged birds such as those that appear in the paintings of Chagall. Horses, especially Gilda, a mare remembered from Andreu's Galician summers, represent the girl's desire for absolute freedom and appear unrestrained by harnesses, reins, or bridles. In her strange, non-conformist ways the girl identifies with the female figures created by Chagall but also finds refuge in the rebellious writings of Tom Wolfe. Hence she somewhat incongruously calls herself "la niña rusa / que comulgaba reno asado / . . . la niña rusa que leía a Tom Wolfe" (the Russian girl / whose communion was roasted reindeer / . . . the Russian girl who read Tom Wolfe).

Andreu's verses paint a picture of the claustrophobic atmosphere that weighs heavily on the schoolgirl as she dreams of a life in art. Images of drowning and enclosure are frequent, and the speaker feels asphyxiated by the "doscientos días de historia" (two hundred days of history), remnants of the past so revered in the schoolroom, where time stretches tediously before her like an "eternidad de tiza" (eternity of chalk). Similarly she is circumscribed by walls, balconies, towers, and other architectural structures that denote power, societal conventions, and the fixtures of culture. She senses everywhere the meddlesome and close-minded attitudes of her hometown. While Andreu has professed that "no me considero, ni me he considerado nunca, exactamente una mujer" (I do not consider myself, nor have I ever considered myself, exactly a woman), and while she expresses a distaste for "women's" poetry as a distinct category, the protagonist of *De una niña* is defiant in the face of the constricting roles and patterns women have traditionally been destined to fulfill and in which they have often been subsumed.

To escape from such a stultifying milieu, the provincial girl in the poems turns to the world of drugs and alcohol. *De una niña* abounds in references, both direct and indirect, to marijuana, amphetamines, opium, barbiturates, wine, and cognac. Like Paul Verlaine, Baudelaire, and Rimbaud, the incipient artist finds in these substances a way to rebel against the strictures of bourgeois conformity. Moreover, narcotics and alcohol promise the possibility of altering perceptions of reality. The hallucinatory superreality to which Andreu's speaker aspires is matched, however, by a sense of numbing oblivion. Allusions to poisons of all kinds (vitriol, strychnine, arsenic, and others) convey the degradation that is the other face of the narcotic experience. Yet, as did the French *poètes maudits* who inspire her, Andreu glimpses beauty in the devastation and ugliness wreaked by drugs. By means of drugs, her speaker makes an audacious "salto al vacío" (leap into the void) and thereby arrives at a newly illuminated vision of herself and the world.

It is this desire for illumination that moves *De una niña* beyond autobiographical roots. One of the

*Cover for Andreu's 1983 collection of prose poems, which shows the
influence of Arthur Rimbaud*

most important themes is the poet's quest for spiritual experience through her chosen art. Drugs, providing access to dreams, beauty, and even spiritual transcendence, are thus merely a metaphor for the knowledge and vision gained through the poetic process itself. Paradoxically, Andreu also invokes the vocabulary of mysticism to represent figuratively the various stages of discovery and awareness achieved through the process of creating poetry. Poetry for her is a state of grace, a faith, and a perfection not attainable in quotidian reality: "algo falta y hay que . . . creer en la poesía, y en la intolerancia de la poesía" (something is lacking . . . you have to believe in poetry, and in the intolerance of poetry). That is why the speaker, like a vampire, shuns the light of imperfect day. Instead she longs for night and darkness, the time of fear but also of fantasy.

Andreu's protagonist yearns for unmitigated darkness, since black not only conceals marred reality but is "el color de los sueños" (the color of dreams).

Like San Juan de la Cruz emerging from the darkest night, the young girl passes from darkness into the next stage of mystic progress, the stage in which the soul is cleansed. Fire is the medium by which the speaker readies herself for the illumination promised by poetry. She is purged and transformed, as if alchemically, like "algún metal en llamas" (some metal in flames). *De una niña* reverses the last two phases of traditional mystic experience, the illuminative and the unitive. During the unitive state the initiate in Andreu's poetry envisions her art as a sacrament in which sacrificial blood and wine are conjoined in a new configuration that dissolves the distinctions between good and evil:

"Amor de los incendios y de la perfección, amor entre la gracia y el crimen" (love of fires and of perfection, love between grace and crime). Illumination constitutes the culmination of her search for poetry. In this final stage the speaker leaves behind the "niña pluscuamperfecta, niña que nunca fuimos" (pluperfect girl, girl that we never were). That younger self is consigned to the dead past, but it is through death that she is illuminated by a new awareness. Death itself "se me vuelve radiante" (becomes radiant to me), shedding light on "los verbos claros" (clear words) from which her poetry will emerge. In "Para Olga" (For Olga) the final (and most optimistic) poem of the collection, Andreu's counterpart rises through "el verso vertical" (vertical verse) to meet "el desastre, luz quebrantahuesos" (disaster, bone-breaking light), a light capable of transfiguring and shattering reality.

*De una niña* charts a young woman's liberation from oppressive reality by means of fantasy and the imagination – in short, through the metamorphoses permitted by art and poetry. Significantly the transformation and the evasion of mundane reality are effected by the poet's use of language. Disjoined syntax and fragmented sentence structures, images without apparent logical referents in the external world, and abrupt and unexplained subject changes produce a discourse, evocative of surrealism, in which incoherence draws attention away from the phenomenal world and toward the text itself. *De una niña* underscores the centrality of the poetic text, making the outside world not only irrelevant but nonexistent – that is, devoid of true reality. The physical world is ephemeral; the body will not endure. The only reality, Andreu implies in this remarkable work, is that of poetry and language.

Andreu's second published work, *Báculo de Babel* (Staff of Babel, 1983), marks another step in her evolution as a writer and exemplifies her continuing desire to liberate herself from previous artistic values. The majority of the enigmatic pieces that make up this book are prose poems, reminiscent of works by Rimbaud. Just as Rimbaud does in his *Illuminations* (1886), Andreu imbues each fragment with a high degree of lyricism based on synesthesia and dreamlike, often violent, imagery. In this brief but intense collection Andreu is concerned with the origins of language and poetry and with the possibilities of discovering within her art new understandings of reality. The title, inspired by the biblical story of Babel, suggests that poetry is at once a sign with which to decipher the chaos of language and a guide through the labyrinth of the world.

Steeped in lyrical tones, associative rhythms, and incantatory repetitions, *Báculo de Babel* has the flavor of mythology. Indeed, like many ancient myths, it deals with creation and destruction – origins and ends – the ultimate mysteries Andreu links to the essential nature of poetry as an expression of human existence and destiny.

The first section of *Báculo de Babel* recalls the style of *De una niña*. The verses are long and enumerative; the language is obscure and ambiguous, as if generated directly by the unconscious. The initial verses feature unicorns and other fabulous or allegorical creatures, such as hares that "inventaban el fuego" (invented fire), as in the Promethean myth of creation. At the opposite end of the trajectory is death. Whether in the guise of a colt neighing silent arias or a docile dove, death is largely a favorable presence, a ceremonial figure invested with the power to enlighten and heal.

These illuminative and curative powers are the same ones Andreu ascribes to poetry in the poem "Sólo la muerte" (Only Death): "hay claraboyas nuevas en la lírica muerte, y hay farmacias" (there are new skylights in lyrical death, and there are pharmacies). Here is a vocation exercised in the cause of enlightenment, and she wields her pen like an "estrella espada" (star sword), a weapon wrought from a particularly luminous steel. Images of blood and fire in "Y corría la sangre" (And Blood Flowed) call to mind rites of sacrifice and purification: "fue la sangre pureza potencial, / dolor, ciencia y heráldica violenta" (the blood was potential purity, / pain, knowledge and violent heraldry). Andreu's intention in the book is to explore the nature of poetry as a receptacle of truth and knowledge, a window onto time and history, and a medium of spiritual discovery. Ultimately, as she says in "Muerte, paloma, dócil" (Death, Dove, Docile), her purpose is to retrieve "las palabras como rudas fuentes" (words like rough founts), to return to the source of words and language, and, in so doing, to encounter a higher reality.

The central portion of *Báculo de Babel* comprises eleven prose poems in the iterative style of litanies and other forms of ritualistic discourse. Although the syntax is disordered, made nearly incoherent by the lack of punctuation, the book is unified by Andreu's vision of poetry. The repeated references to vigils, psalms, and anointments highlight the aura of a ceremony whose purpose is not only artistic elevation but spiritual transcendence. Visible and invisible angels are invoked, as is a bitter god, in the speaker's prayers for understanding and enlightenment. She envisions herself as a Gothic ed-

*Andreu in 1984*

ifice or an aging temple; she is also the victim of sacrificial rites. Such rites are suffered in the name of
purification and illumination: "Sangro de veras
sangro luz" (I Bleed Truly I Bleed Light) is the title
of one poem.

Guided by her "staff of Babel," the speaker
gropes her way through the maze of paradoxes that
make up language and reality. She determines, for
example, to exorcise the spirit of the past in order,
paradoxically, to return to the past – to some primitive condition in which language is as yet unbur-
dened by meanings and associations imposed by
time. Through her "antífono de la eliminación"
(song of elimination), chanted in "Yo sola oscura
por azoteas" (I alone dark on rooftops), she resolves
to cast off "los padres y las madres que alzan hacia
mí las nomenclaturas" (the fathers and mothers
who raise to me their nomenclatures) and establish
herself as a generation of one alone. In this way she
will distill her language to its essence by removing
the strata of history that intervene between words
and the reality they represent. Assuming an almost
priestly function, she presides like Vulcan over
foundries where she will forge a language termed alternately "mi lengua micénica" (my Mycenic lan-

guage) and "mi lengua reciente" (my recent language).

Yet to arrive at the heart of her contradictory
idiom she must first uncover its messages, symbols,
secret inscriptions, angles, and letters: "recursos
clandestinos" (clandestine recourses) remain buried
within layers of "cieno arcaico virginal" (archaic
virginal mire). The task of discovery is described as
a descent through time and space; poetry is presented as a vertical construct. Thus, in "Di tú ángel
adelgazado" (Speak Slim Angel), she descends into
the "olvido favorable y lineal . . . en cinco longi-
tudes" (favorable and linear oblivion . . . in five lon-
gitudes) that constitutes the geology of time, in
order to unearth her language and restore to her
words the purity and naturalness of their primeval
state.

The third and final section of *Báculo de Babel*
corresponds to the completion of Andreu's prayer,
the consummation of the poetic act. The epigraph
from T. S. Eliot's *Four Quartets* (1943) "consumed by
the fire or the other fire" introduces an important
concept: the painful path toward perfection imperfectly mirrors the fires of devine perfection. At
the end of *Báculo de Babel* the speaker is in fact spent,

consumed by the fiery rituals, yet cleansed and therefore joyfully transformed: "río mi salvación" (I laugh my salvation). Images of absence and unreality are not meant to suggest negativity or emptiness but rather the innocence that is Andreu's dream of poetry: "Mi idioma busca un siglo salvaje, una ausencia de signos" (My language seeks a savage age, an absence of signs). Although such aspirations are inevitably thwarted – "no hay inocencia" (there is no innocence) – the sense of impossibility that marks the end of *Báculo de Babel* does not detract from the book's profound spiritual center. The search for a language in which words and meanings are joined is consonant with Andreu's vision of unity between the material world and a higher reality; between "un objeto que es mentira" (an object that is a lie) and the truths concealed behind appearances; and, finally, between human imperfection and divine perfection. Andreu's exploration of the unifying potential within language, and by extension within poetry, is the main reason *Báculo de Babel* was honored with the 1982 Fernando Rielo Prize for Mystic Poetry.

The inspiration for Andreu's third volume, *Elphistone* (1988), was her fascination with the name (a variant spelling of the last name of an eighteenth-century English admiral, George Keith Elphinstone) inscribed on a small desk that happened her way. Her interest in Elphinstone was further sparked when her husband (to whom *Elphistone* is dedicated) bought a poster announcing the auction of a Spanish ship that had been captured by the same man, then the captain of an English warship. Elphinstone is a well-known name in the annals of British naval history: Admiral Elphinstone was only one of the seamen in the family. In Andreu's book various historical personages are consolidated into a single fictitious character. Andreu's character Elphistone takes on a mythic air, even though he is not the noble hero celebrated in myths but rather a pirate, a slave trader, and a thief.

In important ways *Elphistone* represents a radical departure from Andreu's earlier poetry. It is more narrative than lyric, recounting a mysterious sea voyage of the title character. The unidentified narrator assumes the manner of an ancient bard, speaks lines that call to mind ancient epics, and insists on his credibility as a narrator. Stylistically the language is much more accessible than that of either of Andreu's previous works: the syntax and diction are more straightforward, and the imagery is less surreal.

Still, certain aspects of *Elphistone* unite this book with Andreu's other works. Whereas in her earlier poetry the language is distinctly ambiguous, here the ambiguity derives from the situations recounted. The pirate Elphistone is an obscure figure of unexplained origin and of disputed honor. More significant in terms of the cohesiveness with Andreu's body of work are the theme of illumination through poetry and the implication that language and therefore poetry are the means, however imperfect, for joining human existence with a more transcendent reality.

*Elphistone* is perhaps Andreu's most tightly woven unit of poems, due undoubtedly to the ominous but charismatic presence of the pirate captain. Repeatedly associated with cosmic forces, he is described as "dios de nada" (god of nothingness) and "señor de las noches" (master of the night). He possesses the power and knowledge of superior beings. This knowledge includes secrets lost to lesser mortals through the ravages of time and history and remaining only in the form of traces, ruins, and rubble. Embodied by "funestas cábalas" (fatal divinations), this information embraces the mysteries of existence and humanity's dreams of immortality. A complex character of many facets, Elphistone is depicted as nearly savage and at once diabolical and divine – "ángel y búho, en secreto concierto" (angel and owl, in secret concert). He is a fiery-eyed tiger, stallion, or minotaur in the same vein as Jorge Luis Borges's and William Blake's imaginary beasts. On the one hand, when he is compared to Neptune, Andreu's pirate is master of the ocean; his figurative domain is the unconscious, the imagination, and creativity. On the other hand, Elphistone appears encircled by fire and ashes and is implicitly analogous to Prometheus, thief of fire and of the gods' special knowledge.

Recalling the elusive language of the invocations in *Báculo de Babel,* Elphistone's is clearly the lost language of poetry: "un lenguaje desconocido, más misterioso que el sueco" (an unknown language, more mysterious than Swedish). In Andreu's poetic conception (as in Borges's and in Vladimir Nabokov's as well) the source of poetry resides in the ancient runes, primitive forms that reveal the eternal truths no longer a part of human memory. In her poem "Pale Fire," named after Nabokov's 1962 novel of the same title, Andreu suggests that the "sueños de verdad y de muerte" (dreams of truth and death) will remain undisclosed, and, thus, "tu solamente reino es el mundo" (your only kingdom is the world). Human destiny is unavoidably mortal, a "débil llama" (weak flame) alongside divine immortality, a moon overshadowed by the sun. *Elphistone,* much like *Báculo de Babel,* closes on a note of futility, as the answers to the speaker's questions recede in the same way that the pirate's ship sinks into the depths of the sea.

In view of the impossibility of Andreu's philosophical aspirations, it is not surprising that a sense of disillusionment or frustration regarding poetry and its practitioners creeps into the declaration of her poetics (in her 1986 essay "Poetica"). Poets, she states, are "arquitectos de nada, artífices de lo fugitovo . . . nobles o sórdidos constructores de espejos" (architects of nothing, artisans of the fugitive . . . noble or sordid constructors of mirrors). Likewise she adds, in words that resemble those of *Elphistone*, "el caballo de la poesía rapta novicios y se burla de sus fieles" (the horse of poetry abducts novices and mocks its faithful). Poetry is often a heartless master, one to whom Andreu, by her own acknowledgment, is unlikely to dedicate herself exclusively. Critical and popular attention to Andreu's brief literary career has so far been favorable. The interest on the part of Spanish readers in the twenty-one-year-old female author of *De una niña* tended to favor extraliterary matters over the deeper issues addressed by Andreu's verses. Meanwhile, although that initial effort is still the primary focus of critical studies about Andreu, her oeuvre has begun to be recognized because of her exploration of serious questions about poetry, language, and the nature of reality. While it is still too soon to predict what shape her future work will take, what seems certain is the originality of Blanca Andreu's poetic voice and the authenticity of her concern for the ethical imperatives she finds inherent in language and poetry.

**Interview:**

Sharon Keefe Ugalde, "Conversación con Blanca Andreu," in her *Conversaciones y poemas: La nueva poesía femenina española en castellano* (Madrid: Siglo XXI de España, 1991).

**References:**

Emilio Miró, "Dos premios para dos nuevas voces: Blanca Andreu y Ana Rossetti," *Insula,* 36 (September 1981): 6;

Candelas Newton, "La reflexión sobre el signo en la poesía de Blanca Andreu," *Letras Peninsulares* (Fall 1989): 193–209;

Sharon Keefe Ugalde, "The Feminization of Female Figures in Spanish Women's Poetry of the 1980s," *Studies in 20th Century Literature,* 16 (Winter 1992): 165–184;

Francisco Umbral, Prologue to Andreu's *De una niña de provincias que se vino a vivir en un Chagall* (Madrid: Adonais, 1981), pp. 7–10;

Luis Antonio de Villena, ed., *Postnovísimos* (Madrid: Visor, 1986);

John C. Wilcox, "Blanca Andreu: A 'poeta maldita' of the 1980s," *Siglo XX / Twentieth Century,* 7 (1989–1990): 29–34;

Wilcox, "Visión y revisión en algunas poetas contemporáneas: Amparo Amorós, Blanca Andreu, Luisa Castro y Almudena Guzmán," in *Novísimos postnovísimos clásicos: La poesía de los 80 en España,* edited by Biruté Ciplijauskaité (Madrid: Orígenes, 1990), pp. 95–113.

# Carlos Barral

## (2 June 1928 – 12 December 1989)

### Mary Makris
#### University of Louisville

BOOKS: *Las aguas retiradas* (Barcelona: Publicaciones de la Revista *Laye*, 1952);

*Metropolitano* (Torrelavega: Cantalapiedra, 1957); enlarged as *Metropolitano y poemas, 1973–1975* (Barcelona: Ambito, 1976);

*Diecinueve figuras de mi historia civil* (Barcelona: Literaturasa, 1961);

*Usuras* (Madrid: Poesía para Todos, 1965);

*Figuración y fuga* (Barcelona: Seix Barral, 1966);

*Informe personal sobre el alba y acerca de algunas auroras particulares* (Barcelona: Lumen, 1970);

*Usuras y figuraciones: Poesía 1952–1972* (Las Palmas: Inventarios Provisionales, 1973; enlarged edition, Barcelona: Lumen, 1979);

*Años de penetencia* (Madrid: Alianza, 1975); enlarged as *Años de penetencia; Precedido de dos capitulos ineditos de Memorias de infancia* Barcelona: Tusquets, 1990);

*Los años sin excusa* (Barcelona: Barral, 1978);

*Pel car de fora: Catalunya des del mar* (Barcelona: Ediciones 62, 1982);

*Penúltimos castigos* (Barcelona: Seix Barral, 1983);

*Diez poemas para el nieto Malcolm* (Barcelona, 1984);

*Catalunya a vol d'ocell* (Barcelona: Ediciones 62, 1985);

*Roca-Sastre* (Barcelona: Ambit, 1985);

*Lecciones de cosas: Veinte poemas para el nieto Malcolm* (Barcelona: Ediciones 62, 1986);

*Cuando las horas veloces* (Barcelona: Tusquets, 1988);

*Diario de "Metropolitano,"* edited by Luis García Montero (Granada: Excma, 1989);

*Antología poética,* edited by Juan García Hortelano (Madrid: Alianza, 1989);

*Poesía,* edited by Carme Riera (Madrid: Cátedra, 1991).

OTHER: "Poesía no es comunicación," in *Poéticas españolas contemporáneas: La generación del 50,* edited by Pedro Provencio (Madrid: Libros Hiperión, 1988), pp. 64–68;

Yvonne Hortet, trans., "Debate con Carlos Barral (Coloquio Internacional de la Universidad de Provenza)," *Revista de Occidente,* 110–111 (July–August 1990): 148–160.

SELECTED PERIODICAL PUBLICATIONS – UNCOLLECTED: "Memoria de un poema," *Papeles de Son Armadans,* 11 (November–December 1958): 394–400;

"Reflexiones acerca de las aventuras del estilo en la penúltima literatura española," *Cuadernos para el Diálogo,* 14 (1969).

Carlos Barral was perhaps the most important Spanish publisher and editor during the second half of the twentieth century; he also translated the poems of Rainer Maria Rilke into Spanish and wrote three volumes of memoirs, a novel, travel books, and several articles and essays on literary topics. However, Barral considered himself, above all, a poet. Along with the poets Jaime Gil de Biedma and José Agustín Goytisolo and the critic José María Castellet, he formed the nucleus of the literary group known as the Escuela de Barcelona (Barcelona School). Barral was also an important poetic voice of the Generación del 50 (Generation of 1950), whose members include Angel González, José Angel Valente, Francisco Brines, and Gloria Fuertes.

Barral was born on 2 June 1928 into a middle-class Catalonian family in Barcelona, where he lived and worked for his entire life. He received a degree in law from the University of Barcelona in 1950. Barral's talent for modifying nouns, which is a key stylistic aspect of his poetry, surfaced during his university career, in a course on administrative law. As his friend Alberto Oliart recounts, Barral received a "matrícula de honor" (pass with honors) in the class because of the final exam, in which the students were asked to write adjectives to describe ten world cities. According to Oliart, Barral's exam was "un prodigio de ingenio, de precisión y de acierto" (a wonder of genius, of precision, and of success). After completing his studies, which he had pursued with little interest and at the insistence of his family,

*Carlos Barral*

Barral intended to enter the diplomatic service but never sat for the entrance exam. He joined the publishing house Seix Barral in 1951, and in 1970 he founded Barral Editores. Often defying censorship laws, Barral introduced Spanish readers to European and American writers such as Alain Robbe-Grillet, Marguerite Duras, Doris Lessing, and Henry Miller, and Hispanic authors such as Juan García Hortelano, Juan Marsé, Carlos Fuentes, and Mario Vargas Llosa. From 1982 to 1988, as a candidate of PSOE, the Partido Socialista Obrero Español (Spanish Socialist Worker Party), he served in the senate, representing Tarragona. Under the auspices of PSOE, Barral also became a member of the European parliament. After losing his bid for reelection to a third term in the senate, Barral directed his energies toward his creative writing and preparing editions of his essays and work diaries for eventual publication.

He died soon after an internal hemorrhage on 12 December 1989.

Barral began writing poetry around 1942, the date Carmen Riera assigns to the poems collectively titled "Fósiles" (Fossils) in her edition of Barral's *Poesía* (1991). These early poems, discovered in Barral's personal files, bore the annotation "romanticized epoch of Tonia." Riera believes that this note may allude to the young girl that inspired them and of whom Barral was enamored. In 1952 Barral's first published poem, "Las aguas retiradas" (Secluded Waters), appeared in the journal *Laye*. Later that same year *Laye* published the poem as a booklet, which Barral distributed to his friends. This long poem, consisting of various sections, contains elements and tendencies, such as the use of epithets, that also characterize his later poetry.

In 1953 Barral published the essay "Poesía no es comunicación" (Poetry Is Not Communication) in *Laye*. He wrote the essay in order to dispute poet Carlos Bousoño's assertion in his *Teoría de la expresión poética* (Theory of Poetic Expression, 1952) that poetry is communication. In "Poesía no es comunicación," a defense of the aesthetic autonomy of each poem, Barral distinguishes between pre- and postsymbolist poetry and relegates those who pretend to communicate something in poetry, either an intimate or collective message, to the realm of the superficial. Barral also outlines the basic differences between poetry as a reflection of a specific reality or experience and poetry as a kind of linguistic laboratory. He criticizes the then-dominant trends of poetry (the use of anecdote and colloquial language, for example) because, in his view, they imply "la existencia de una serie de fantasmas teóricos: el mensaje, la comunicación, la asequibilidad a la mayoría, temas de nuestro tiempo que coartan la vocación creativa" (the existence of a series of theoretical ghosts: the message, communication, the accessibility to the majority, themes of our time that limit the creative vocation). Finally Barral draws an analogy between reading a poem and writing one: reading consists of a true poetic act similar to that of the poet; and just as there exists what Barral calls sterility of reading, so too there exists sterility of creativity. "Poesía no es comunicación" is the basis of his poetics.

Barral's concept of poetry as a linguistic laboratory manifests itself in *Metropolitano* (Metropolitan, 1957), his first collection of poems. The title refers to both the city and the subway, thereby underscoring Barral's tendency to incorporate semantic ambiguities into his poetry. The poems, most of them composed between 1955 and 1956, are dramatic monologues in which the use of different typefaces alerts the reader to a plurality of poetic voices. Despite the varied thematic content of *Metropolitano* and the use of multiple speakers, Barral observes the unities of time, action, and place. He situates the poems within a purely urban environment; he focuses on the inhabitants, sights, and sounds; and he plays with perceptions. For example, in "Ciudad mental" (Mental City) an emphasis on vertical lines suggests the construction of the city, while an emphasis on horizontal lines implies its eventual destruction and ruin. "Portillo automático" (Automatic Door) alludes to temporal perceptions and distortions one may experience underwater. In "Mendigo al pie de un cartel" (Beggar at the Foot of a Placard) a crippled beggar and his newspaper (onto which coins fall) both speak.

In *Metropolitano* Barral demonstrates his interest in language as an element of experimentation as well as a source of ambiguity. Meanings are based on etymology as well as definition. Barral told interviewer Gracia Rodríguez in 1985 that when he wrote he modified the past of each word. Because words are polysemantic, poetic texts induce several possible readings, a condition Barral constantly strove to achieve: "Muchas veces me doy por bueno un verso cuando me doy cuenta de que tiene un número de lecturas que a mí me parece suficiente" (I consider a poem to be good when I realize that it contains a number of readings that seem sufficient to me). The poems of *Metropolitano* abound with archaisms, *cultismos* (erudite words), juristic terminology, and slang. The linguistic difficulties presented by such poetry may cause Barral's readers to make ample use of dictionaries. In light of *Metropolitano,* many viewed Barral's poetry as intellectual and baroque. The imagery also appeals to the senses. Barral identified this collection as a general prologue to his entire poetic production.

The publication of *Diecinueve figuras de mi historia civil* (Nineteen Figures of My Civil History, 1961), the overall scheme of which recalls Luis de Góngora's *Soledades* (Solitudes, 1613), not only signals a shift toward Barral's writing "social poetry" but also serves as a poetic antecedent of his three completed memoirs. Even though the collection includes themes common to socially engaged literature, such as the Spanish Civil War and the situation of postwar Spain, the poems concentrate on the personal history of the speaker and on the configuration of his identity. In the interview with Rodríguez, Barral described the collection as "una confesión autobiográfica desde el punto de vista del personaje social e histórico" (an autobiographical confession from the point of view of a social and historical character). This series of vignettes, which take place during the Spanish Civil War and the postwar period, document certain moments of the speaker's infancy and adolescence. The point of departure is often an anecdote that the speaker then develops in detail. He is characterized by his guilty social conscience, eroticism that borders on the voyeuristic, and his affinity for the sea. Given Barral's intent and the particular historical, temporal trajectory of the collection, the poems are more like short narratives than poetry. Thus language becomes more conversational and colloquial, and Barral shows a preference for similes over metaphors. Readers found *Diecinueve figuras de mi historia civil* to be more accessible than *Metropolitano,* and it was favorably received by the critics. Barral, however,

*The reading committee at Seix Barral publishing house in 1960: (from left to right) José María Valverde, José María Castellet, Joan Petit, Barral, and Victor Seix*

saw the collection as a continuation of *Metropolitano* in that the thematic content of both refers to the relation between the poet/speaker and the external world rather than the internal one.

In *Usuras* (Usuries, 1965), which consists of six poems, and *Figuración y fuga* (Figuration and Fugue, 1966), Barral's poetry is once again hermetic because of its linguistic experimentation and baroque style and sensibilities. The poet writes for those who have been initiated, for readers who have an interest in poems filled with sensuality and intelligence. Barral's propensity for semantically charged words resurfaces in the title *Usuras*: the word may refer to profiteering, but it also points to the meaning it retains in other romance languages – that of deterioration through use. Thus the underlying themes of the collection concern the erosion caused by time. These themes, along with the recurring ones of the horror of dying, the horror of decadence, and the passing of time, also permeate the other books of poetry he published between 1965 and 1970.

*Informe personal sobre el alba y acerca de algunas auroras particulares* (Personal Report on Daybreak and Concerning Some Particular Dawns, 1970) comprises fourteen poems. The speaker enumerates some calamities heralded by dawn, which returns him to the crude reality of the day, and he also describes dawn's arrival. He depicts dawn as if it were

an animal or a form of vegetation. The poems include sordid images, as the speaker is forced to confront himself and his daily responsibilities. Poems such as "Clave del insomne" (Key of the Insomniac) and "Clave del desvelado" (Key of the Wakeful) – the second of which is a liberal translation of two poems from Fernando Pessoa's *Cancioneiro* (Songbook) – focus on the physical degradation of the speaker. Like *Metropolitano,* the collection is set in an urban environment, but here the speaker finds himself in a personal crisis.

*Informe personal sobre el alba* is illustrated with photographs of nudes by César Malet. These pictures may be viewed as a companion pictorial text that visually captures the mood and intent of Barral's poems. Rafael Cordero, writing for *Cuadernos Hispanoamericanos* (1970), considers the photographs' poetic content to be latent, and he asserts that skin may be identified with dawn. Cordero feels that the play of light and dark in the photographs is basic for the presentation of day and for the interpretation of the poems. Malet's photographs effectively complement the speaker's erotic obsessions.

In 1973 Barral published *Usuras y figuraciones: Poesía 1952–1972,* which includes his complete works to that date as well as previously unpublished poems; 1975 and 1978 saw the publication of *Años de penetencia* (Years of Penitence) and *Los años sin excusa* (Years Without Excuse), two of Barral's memoirs. Oliart claims that, based on *Años de penetencia,* Barral was one of the best Spanish prose writers to surface in the last fifty years. Oliart commends Barral's ability to describe the ambiance of post-civil-war Barcelona. As proof of Barral's documentary skill, Oliart recounts a conversation with Raymond Carr, a Hispanist and historian, in which Carr claimed that the first of Barral's memoirs is one of the best depictions of the political and social climate of Francisco Franco's Spain from 1939 to 1950. The second memoir, *Los años sin excusa,* focuses on Barral's years as an editor: he writes of his travels, his friends, and his enemies. According to poet and critic José Manuel Caballero Bonald, in his memoirs Barral confuses facts at times, even distorts them, and mistakes names and dates. Caballero Bonald insists, however, that Barral never intended his memoirs to be reliable chronicles; rather they are selective, poetic searches influenced and shaped by the author's imagination.

*Catalunya des del mar* (Catalonia from the Sea, 1982) is one of several books Barral wrote in his native Catalan language. At a debate held during a colloquium at the University of Provence (4–6 December 1986), Barral described the volume as a book of travels, in which he writes of sailing in his boat, the *Capitan Argüello,* along the Catalonian coast. According to Barral, writing in Catalan required a great effort; the book's language is one used by fishermen and sailors and has little or no literary tradition. Despite Barral's modest assessment of the book, Oliart says that Barral reproduces the speech of the inhabitants of the Tarragonian coast with surprising accuracy, thereby preserving a dialect that has all but disappeared. The book is of extraordinary interest to scholars of Catalonian philology. The point is emphasized by the first part of the book's title, *Pel car de fora,* a phrase that cannot readily be translated. *Car,* an archaic Catalonian nautical term, refers to the lower part of a ship's lateen yard, from which a triangular sail is hung. Barral merely comments that he wrote the book in Catalan because of his "motivación de memorialista" (motivation of an amanuensis) – his need to transcribe the history and feelings of the Catalonian people.

In 1983 Barral published his only novel, *Penúltimos castigos* (Penultimate Punishments). He maintained (at the Provence colloquium) that the structure of the book is more like that of a poem and stated that it is a book about duality and the myth of Gemini and Janus. All the characters, including the protagonist, named Carlos Barral, have a double: one is real, the other imaginary. The novel offers a continual movement between fiction and reality. According to Oliart, "lo que de verdad es este libro-novela es un juego literario, un punto maligno, es una representación fabulada crítica y burlesca de la realidad" (the truth is that this book-novel is a literary game, a pernicious point, it is a fabulated critical and burlesque representation of reality). He concludes that the novel is too intelligent and strange to achieve the success it deserves.

After a decade of concentrating primarily on prose works, Barral published another poetry collection, *Diez poemas para el nieto Malcolm* (Ten Poems for Grandson Malcolm, 1984). This limited edition is illustrated with prints by Borja de Predo. *Lecciones de cosas: Veinte poemas para el nieto Malcolm* (Lessons of Things: Twenty Poems for Grandson Malcolm, 1986) includes some of the poems in *Diez poemas.* The title *Lecciones de cosas* refers to didactic illustrated books and encyclopedias that were familiar to children and adolescents of the post–Spanish Civil War generations. This cultural reference reveals one of Barral's intentions in *Lecciones de cosas:* he wanted to instruct a child about reality, offering "avisos para vivir" (advice about living) drawn from objects that surround the child. Through the familiar images of children's books, Barral also hoped to recuperate part of a world ruined by the passing of an age. He acknowledged that this "no es un libro para niños sino un libro que explica el sentimiento de decadencia, el miedo a la muerte, etc., que uno tiene a cierta edad, es decir, la experiencia: la más personal y la más actual" (is not a book for children but rather a book that explains the sense of decadence, the fear of death, etc., that one has at a certain age, that is, experience: the most personal and the most present).

In 1988, the year in which Barral lost his bid for a third term in the senate, his third memoir, *Cuando las horas veloces* (When Hours Pass Swiftly), was published. Oliart believes that this book is written in "una de las prosas más bellas que puedan leerse en estos tiempos" (the most beautiful prose that one can read in these times) but considers it to be a sad book, perhaps because it was destined to be Barral's last published work in his lifetime.

Before his death in December 1989 Barral had completed two chapters of his fourth memoir, "Memorias de infancia" (Childhood Memories). Barral planned to base the structure of this book on the dichotomy between a hostile urban world and a more primitive world: the marine environment of Calafell, where Barral's family spent many weekends and vacations. In Barral's writings, Calafell represents a mythical place which serves as a con-

*José Agustín Goytisolo, Jaime Gil de Biedma, Barral, Yvonne Hortet (whom he later married), Gabriel Celaya, and Celaya's wife, Amparitxu*

trast to bourgeois, urban Barcelona. The two chapters of "Memorias" were included in the 1990 edition of *Años de penetencia*.

At the time of his death Barral was also working on a new collection of poetry, "Extravíos" (Losses), some of whose poems Riera included in *Poesía* in 1991. In addition Barral was collecting his essays and articles for a book to be titled "Anotaciones a la mina de plomo" (Annotations to the Lead Mine). Barral was also preparing his "Cuadernos de trabajo" (Work Diaries) for eventual publication. In them Barral kept copious notes regarding the circumstances surrounding his creative efforts, including the composition of individual poems and collections. Luis García Montero edited and published *Diario de "Metropolitano"* (Diary for "Metropolitan," 1989), thereby providing Barral's readers with a valuable tool for understanding not only his first poetry collection but also his poetry in general.

According to novelist and critic Juan García Hortelano, Barral was a painstakingly slow writer, careful to the point of neurosis and, like his friend Gil de Biedma, very conscientious of the nature of his work. In a span of thirty-seven years (1952–1989) Barral published relatively few books of poetry; yet he was a prolific writer who left ample doc-

umentation of his times in his poetic and prose works. Barral produced a unified body of work which is shaped in part by his interest in the plastic arts and which presents the various permutations of his character and personality. Narrative, memoirs, and poetry are interrelated, and language and linguistic experimentation are of paramount importance. As his widow, Yvonne Hortet, states in a letter accompanying her translation of Barral's 1986 debate at Provence, without the poet Carlos Barral, Carlos Barral the writer of memoirs would not have existed, because almost everything about his life, including the titles of his three memoirs, can be found in his poetry. She describes her husband not as an autobiographical writer but rather as an "escritor . . . autográfico" (one who writes about the self ). In remarks made at Provence, Barral elaborated on this idea. He viewed his poetry as "una búsqueda de mí mismo y de la experiencia" (a search for myself and for experience) and stated that his primary intent in his memoirs was to explain his poetry. He wanted to place his verse within a context so that readers would understand the experience and the world in which it was produced. Barral believed that his life and works complemented each other: his life explained his creative works, and these works, in turn, created his life.

During his lifetime Carlos Barral's poetry did not receive the critical attention it deserved. However, in the years since his death critics have begun a serious evaluation of Barral's poems and a discussion of his contribution to Spanish letters. Special editions of *Insula* and *Revista de Occidente,* dedicated to Barral and Gil de Biedma, were published in 1990.

**Interview:**

Gracia Rodríguez, "Entrevista con Carlos Barral: A pesar de todo, poeta," *Quimera,* 43 (1985): 32–39.

**References:**

José Manuel Caballero Bonald, "Barral y el personaje de sus 'memorias,'" *Revista de Occidente,* 110–111 (July–August 1990): 73–78;

Rafael Cordero, "Carlos Barral y César Malet: *Informe personal sobre el alba," Cuadernos Hispanoamericanos,* 248–249 (August–September 1970): 657–661;

Juan García Hortelano, "Dos amigos," *Revista de Occidente,* 110–111 (July–August 1990): 5–10;

García Hortelano, "Prólogo a Carlos Barral," in Barral's *Antología poética,* edited by García Hortelano (Madrid: Alianza, 1989), pp. 7–18;

Luis García Montero, "Barral o los matices del conocimiento," *Insula,* 45 (July–August 1990): 25–27;

García Montero, "Presentación de un *Diario de trabajo,"* in Barral's *Diario de "Metropolitano,"* (Granada: Excma, 1988), pp. 11–33;

Jaime Gil de Biedma, "La visión poética de Carlos Barral," in his *El pie de la letra* (Barcelona: Crítica, 1980), pp. 40–47;

Juan Antonio Masoliver Ródenas, "Carlos Barral o las pasiones de la inteligencia," *Camp de l'Arpa,* 10 (March 1974): 8–13;

Alberto Oliart, "Carlos Barral: El hombre y el escritor (Recuerdos y consideraciones)," *Revista de Occidente,* 110–111 (July–August 1990): 21–50;

Carmen Riera, "Algunas notas sobre la poesía de Carlos Barral, en torno a los recursos lingüísticos," in *Homenaje al profesor Antonio Vilanova,* 2 volumes, edited by Marta Cristina Carbonell (Barcelona: Universidad de Barcelona, 1989), II: 541–555;

Riera, "Imágenes barcelonesas en dos poetas metropolitanos," *Revista de Occidente,* 110–111 (July–August 1990): 57–72;

Riera, Introduction to Barral's *Poesía,* edited by Riera (Madrid: Cátedra, 1990), pp. 9–70;

Riera, *La obra poética de Carlos Barral* (Barcelona: Península, 1990).

# Francisco Brines

## (22 January 1932 – )

### Susana Cavallo
*Loyola University of Chicago*

BOOKS: *Las brasas* (Madrid: Rialp, 1960; revised edition, Valencia: Formento de Cultura, 1971);

*El Santo Inocente* (Madrid: Poesía para Todos, 1965); republished as *Materia narrativa inexacta,* in *Poesía, 1960–1971: Ensayo de una despedida* (Barcelona & Madrid: Plaza & Janés, 1974);

*Palabras a la oscuridad* (Madrid: Insula, 1966);

*Aún no* (Barcelona: Llibres de Sindera, 1971);

*Poesía, 1960–1971: Ensayo de una despedida* (Barcelona: Plaza & Janés, 1974); enlarged as *Ensayo de una despedida, 1960–1977* (Madrid: Visor, 1984);

*Insistencias en Luzbel* (Madrid: Visor, 1977);

*Selección propia* (Madrid: Cátedra, 1984);

*Poemas excluidos* (Seville: Renacimiento, 1985);

*Francisco Brines: Antología poética,* selected by José Olivio Jiménez (Madrid: Alianza, 1986);

*Poemas a D. K.* (Seville: Mágico Intimo, 1986);

*El otoño de las rosas* (Seville: Renacimiento, 1987);

*El rumor del tiempo,* selected by Dionisio Cañas (Madrid: Mondadori, 1989);

*Antología poética,* selected by Harold Alvarado Tenorio (Bogotá: Tiempo Presente, 1990);

*Antología poética: Espejo ciego,* selected by Alejandro Duque Amusco (Valencia: Consell Valencià de Cultura, 1993);

Francisco Brines, along with Claudio Rodríguez, José Angel Valente, Angel González, Jaime Gil de Biedma, and others, belongs to the "Generation of the 1950s," or, according to critic Philip W. Silver, the "Rodríguez-Brines Generation," a term which underlines Brines's central role in the formation of this group. The poets of this generation differ from their immediate predecessors – Gabriel Celaya, Angela Figuera, Victoriano Crémer, Blas de Otero, and others – in several important ways. First, for the Rodríguez-Brines Generation, the poem is not an instrument of social change but an inquiry into the nature of reality and the mystery of human existence. This type of poetry is called the "poetry of discovery" by Andrew P. Debicki, or "la poesía del conocimiento" (the poetry of knowledge) by the poets themselves.

Second, the focus in the poems is not society but the individual engaged in a continuous struggle to achieve meaning in a meaningless world. This struggle is reflected in the verse in the cultivation of ambiguity and irony, in the use of dramatic speakers who offer an intensely personal vision of life, and in the imaginative reworking of universal themes: time and temporality, life and death, love, solitude, the problem of identity, and the enigma of being.

Third, the poem itself is seen as expression, not communication; it is the verbal embodiment of an untransferable human experience that is only accessible through the poetic word. The point of departure for the poem is not some abstract idea of society, but the poet's own lived experience. As a direct corollary of this more subjective view of the poem, Brines and his contemporaries show a renewed interest in aesthetic concerns generally associated with the Generation of 1927: a preoccupation with form; an awareness of the expressive power of everyday language; and an active cultivation of image, symbol, and metaphor.

Although many of these concerns were already present in the works of two of the best poets of the immediate postwar period, specifically in José Hierro's *Cuanto sé de mí* (All I Know of Myself, 1957) and *Libro de las alucinaciones* (Book of Hallucinations, 1964) and Carlos Bousoño's *Invasión de la realidad* (Invasion of Reality, 1962), it is perhaps in the works of Brines, more than those of any other poet of his generation, that this move toward a more intimate and meditative poetry crystallizes.

The known facts of Brines's life are few, and whoever wishes to reconstruct the poet's biography has to contend not only with this paucity of data, but with Brines's conscious silence, for it is his contention that the outer facts of his life are indistinguishable from those of any other individual. The

*Francisco Brines*

only life worthy of study, for Brines, is the inner life, and it can most properly be sought in a careful examination of his verse. However, there are several important sources for an accurate reconstruction of his biography: Brines's remarks to Rafael Alfaro and others, which appeared in a special issue of the Valencian journal *Cuervo* (November 1980) dedicated to Brines; and his own laconic autobiographical note in his *Selección propia* ([His] Own Selection, 1984).

Francisco Brines was born on 22 January 1932 in Oliva, a small town near the Mediterranean on the southernmost edge of the province of Valencia. His early years seem to have been idyllic. The prodigious landscape awakened in him a passionate attachment to the land; the emotional support of his family and childhood friends gifted him with a lifelong capacity for love; and a secure economic base enabled him to devote himself entirely to his studies and ultimately to the writing of poetry.

At the age of seven he was sent to the Jesuit boarding school in Valencia, where he gained experience of tremendous importance in the formation of his character and poetic persona. Brines wrote his first poems when he was fifteen, under the tutelage of one of the priests, Father Juan Bautista Bertrán, himself a poet. During this same time Brines experienced a profound religious crisis and an equally powerful awakening to his own sexuality. "Dios hecho verso" (God Made Verse), a still-unpublished book written when he was twenty years old, is the fruit of this period. Although he has chosen to suppress this work due to its confessional nature, he has occasionally discussed its significance. As the title indicates, Brines's conventional beliefs were supplanted by faith in the transcendent powers of verse and in the sacredness of the poetic act.

After finishing his secondary education, Brines studied law at the Universities of Deusto, Valencia, and Salamanca and earned his law degree

*Cover for Brines's second book: poems about a martyred child and Socrates,*
*later collected with a poem about Plato's* Republic *as* Materia
narrativa inexacta

from the last of these, although he never practiced law. During his stay in Salamanca, he befriended the Cuban critic José Olivio Jiménez, who was also studying at the university. From Salamanca, Brines moved to Madrid, where he enrolled in the School of Philosophy and Letters; he took courses in history and in romance philology with Bousoño. During this time Brines made other important literary contacts; he met Hierro and began to frequent the home of Vicente Aleixandre. These people were decisive in his career and personal life. Bousoño and Jiménez would later write what are arguably the best critical studies of Brines's verse; Hierro sponsored Brines's first public poetry reading in the Ateneo of Madrid; and Aleixandre aided him in the organization of his first published work, *Las brasas* (The Live Coals, 1960). In addition these and other

friends encouraged him to submit *Las brasas* to the prestigious Adonais Prize competition, which he won in 1959 and which led to the book's publication.

The remaining known facts of Brines's life are less dramatic and can be summed up in a few sentences. After winning the Adonais Prize, Brines traveled to England, where he taught for two years as a lecturer in Spanish at Oxford University. With the exception of extensive foreign travel, which is reflected in all his books from the publication of *Palabras a la oscuridad* (Words to the Dark, 1966) until the present, Brines has devoted himself exclusively to the writing of verse, dividing his time almost equally between Madrid and Valencia.

A study of Brines's works must begin with *Las brasas,* for critics have concurred in seeing it as a key to his entire oeuvre. First of all, despite its discreet size (there are only fourteen poems in the volume), *Las brasas* is the work of a mature poet. It shows both prosodic mastery and formal and thematic unity. Another salient feature of *Las brasas* is its prophetic quality: it anticipates Brines's later work. As Alejandro Duque Amusco observes in his prologue to Brines's *Antología poética (Espejo ciego)* (Poetry Anthology [Blind Mirror], 1993), Brines's poetry shows little evolution. The central themes, symbols, and techniques to which he has returned again and again throughout his career are delineated with clarity and precision in *Las brasas:* the bittersweet evocation of the landscape – the poet's personal Garden of Eden, an intemporal paradise where death has no dominion; the celebration of childhood with its passionate intensity and innocence; the spectral image of the family house – a repository of memories, of lost dreams and illusions, but also of unconditional love; the view of life as a solitary and arduous path; and the resigned meditation on time and temporality.

*Las brasas* was written during the summer of 1959 in Elca, a seaside town on the edge of Oliva, where Brines's family has long maintained a residence. In his prologue to *Selección propia* he reveals the real and symbolic value of Elca in his life and his verse: "Hay [en mi poesía] un lugar que aparece sin interrupción, aunque pocas veces viene señalado por su nombre: Elca. . . . Se trata de una casa, blanca y grande, situada en un ámbito celeste de purísimo azul, y rodeada de la perenne juventud de los naranjos. . . . En Elca transcurrió lo mejor de mi infancia, pues desde ese lugar me dispuse a contemplar con sosiego y temblor el mundo: el exterior, y el de mi cuerpo y mi espíritu. Para mí ha llegado a simbolizar el espacio del mundo" ([In my poetry] there is a place that appears constantly, although it is rarely identified by name: Elca. . . . It is a large white house, situated in a heavenly realm of the purest blue, and surrounded by the perennial youth of the orange trees. . . . The best part of my childhood took place in Elca, for it was from that place that I began to contemplate the world with tranquillity and trembling: the outer world, and the world of my body and spirit. Elca has come to symbolize for me the space of the world).

Elca is the predominant setting of *Las brasas:* the family house and the surrounding landscape with its orange groves, jasmine bushes, blue sea, and low garden walls. The time of day is sunset, and the season is autumn. The ample use of sensory images invites the reader into the setting.

The book is divided into three parts: "Poemas de la vida vieja" (Poems of the Old Life), which comprises eight poems; "El barranco de los pájaros" (The Birds' Ravine), which is composed of one long poem divided into seven parts; and "Otras vidas" (Other Lives), the shortest section, which has four poems. Each of the three sections focuses on a different set of experiences. In the first part the protagonist's childhood is evoked through the pessimistic gaze of the mature subject, who returns to his ancestral home and finds it in ruins. In the second section Brines symbolically presents human existence from childhood to old age. The third section treats the protagonist in relation to himself and to others, and it narrates his departure from the childhood landscape.

Unity is achieved through style, tone, point of view, meter, and form. *Las brasas* opens with a mysterious (unattributed) epigraph, "*Alguien ve siempre una muchedumbre de pequeñas brasas*" (Someone always sees a crowd of small live coals), and an even more puzzling introductory poem, which reinforces the association of human beings with smoldering fires (a Buddhist idea): "Su corazón será un cráter / apagado, que sin llanto, / que sin llanto" (His heart will be a burned-out crater / so empty of tears, / so empty of tears). Each section is introduced by an epigraph, and, unlike the three sections, none of the poems bears a title. The meter employed throughout is the unrhymed hendecasyllable. Stanzaic divisions are used sparingly, when at all, and the majority of the verses unfold in one unbroken strophe, with frequent enjambments and inner stops. This technique breaks up the regularity of the hendecasyllable and allows for a more discursive, freeflowing verse, which is more appropriate to the narrative tenor of these poems. Brines employs a thirdperson speaker whose distanced point of view and restrained, almost unemotional tone contrast sharply with the tragic figure of an unidentified old man, whom the speaker exhorts to silence in the first lines of the book: "Habrá que cerrar la boca / y el corazón olvidarlo" (One must remain silent / and the heart must forget it).

In his groundbreaking article on *Las brasas* (in *Cinco poetas del Tiempo* [Five Poets of Time], 1972) Jiménez remarks on the disparity between the relative youth of Brines (who was twenty-seven years old when he published *Las brasas*) and the advanced age of his protagonist, most certainly an alter ego of the writer. Bousoño, on the other hand, has explored Brines's use of symbols and temporal juxtaposition and superposition and has remarked on how the image of the old man, who in some poems

*Drawing of Brines by Antonio Quintana*

is already dead, dramatizes the transience of life and the devastating effects of time on human existence.

In "El barranco de los pájaros" an entire life is telescoped into one continuous experience: the speaker's daytime ascent to the mountain in the joyous company of his childhood friends, the unexplained struggle between the boys which ensues with the coming of night, the instantaneous aging of the participants, and the solitary descent of the protagonist, now an old man, against the harsh light of dawn. Like William Shakespeare's seven stages of man, the poem's seven sections make reference to different periods of life, including mentions of the freedom of childhood; the sensual awakening of the adolescent; the mature individual's confrontation with violence, and inevitably, separation and loss; and the old man's resigned acceptance of himself and his universe.

Brines's next work, *El Santo Inocente (The Holy Innocent,* 1965) approaches the same themes from

different perspectives: the lives of others. The book's two poems, "El Santo Inocente" and "La muerte de Sócrates," were later supplemented by a third, "En la República de Platón" (In Plato's Republic). The three poems were republished in the first (1974) and second (1984) editions of Brines's complete works but under a new title, *Materia narrativa inexacta* (Inexact Narrative Material).

The poem "El Santo Inocente" was inspired by Brines's visit to the reliquary of the Cathedral of Valencia. The speaker's contemplation of the remains of a child held in an urn is the point of departure for the poem. According to legend, the child is one of the infants who were murdered by King Herod (Matthew 2:16). The speaker, however, imagines several alternate biographies, which are more convincing and ultimately more moving. Perhaps the child died anonymously in the plague, like so many others, or he might have perished after having been abandoned by a mother who could not care for him. Brines's speculations not only humanize the grotesque image of the child; they paradoxically accord him proper posthumous respect. The child's sanctity, the speaker suggests, resides in his innocence and in the fact that he, like all creatures, carried within him the promise of life, which was prematurely aborted. On a symbolic level the mummified remains of the child represent both the hollowness of religious belief and the tragedy of human existence, an evanescent flame that rapidly turns to ash, leaving only "esta carne marchita y negra" (this withered and black flesh).

Brines uses the same mechanism in the other two poems: the portrayal of a historical subject, long dead, through the personal experience of the speaker. Both the form and structure of *Materia narrativa inexacta* prefigure the composition of *Palabras a la oscuridad*.

*Palabras a la oscuridad,* which received the Premio de la Crítica in 1967, is considered by many authorities to be Brines's finest work. What is immediately evident to the reader is its greater complexity on all levels. Sixty-three poems are arranged in seven sections. Inverting the format of *Las brasas,* Brines gives each poem a descriptive title but does not title the sections. Each section is introduced by a prose epigraph, which sets the tone for the poems and hints at their unifying theme.

The prosody of *Palabras* is complex. There are poems in free verse, blank verse, and a diversity of metric lines, such as the unrhymed hendecasyllable or heptasyllable, or a combination of these two and others. There is a conscious elaboration of stanzaic form: tercets; quatrains; poems with stanzas of contrasting length; and, in one case, a sonnet. Short lyrics alternate with long poems, and the historical-narrative form with autobiographical verse.

The most significant change, however, has to do with voice and persona. In contrast to the neutral observer of *Las brasas,* the protagonist of *Palabras* is a first-person speaker, who transmits his intuitions, perceptions, and feelings in an intimate, subjective tone. This lyrical "I" predominates throughout *Palabras,* heightening its confessional tenor. On some occasions the speaker uses the first- or second-person-plural forms of verbs to emphasize the universality of his plight or to implicate the reader directly in the poetic drama.

Jiménez's study of *Palabras* argues that each of the seven sections portrays a specific experience in Brines's life. In section 1 he returns to the site of his childhood. Although the tone is one of melancholy and nostalgia, the experiences evoked by the speaker are of a positive nature: love of the land, love of the self and others, and the solitary contemplation of nature's beauty. The only negative note is the speaker's acute consciousness of time, which appears like a shadow over the pristine landscape, reminding both himself and the reader that all life carries within it the seeds of its own destruction. As in *Las brasas* it is not necessarily physical death to which the speaker refers, but the death of the spirit.

Section 2 dramatizes the protagonist's journey into the surrounding world, with its attendant pain and pleasure. The epigraph signals his departure: "*Sus gestos, su mirada, eran extranjeros. Su corazón era de todos los lugares*" (His gestures, his glance, were foreign. His heart belonged to all places). This foreignness does not only stem from the speaker's experience of alien lands. As Amusco points out, the poetic subject of *Palabras* is the perpetual wanderer, estranged from himself and from the world. His estrangement is born of the painful realization that all that is precious in life is his only for an instant. Perhaps this fact is the reason that Brines initiates in this section an investigation into the nature of language, seeing the poetic act as a metaphysical necessity, a means of eternalizing the fleeting moment: "¿Y quién cantará el amor sino el poeta?" (And who will sing of love if not the poet?).

Section 3 comprises two historical poems, similar to the narrative verse of *Materia narrativa inexacta;* the fourth section treats in lyrical fashion Brines's residence in England. In one of his best poems, "La mano del poeta (Cernuda)" (The Poet's Hand [Cernuda]), he constructs an intimate identification between himself and Luis Cernuda, beginning with the biographical coincidences that both were lecturers at English universities and both suffered from loneliness in that hostile landscape. The speaker celebrates Cernuda's passionate and uncompromising approach to life and work, and ethical stance worthy of emulation.

"La mano del poeta" anticipates the subject matter and theme of section 5: love and the inevitability of its loss. In this section Brines's temporal preoccupation reaches the greatest intensity, for love is seen as the most contingent of all life's experiences. The human desire for permanence is never as acute as in love, yet in poem after poem, Brines reveals that love, too, like the youth and beauty of the beloved, is doomed to decay. The speaker accepts with gratitude the gift of love, ever conscious of its fragility, just as he accepts with painful serenity love's demise.

If section 5 represents the culminating moment of *Palabras,* sections 6 and 7 constitute respectively its denouement and conclusion. Section 6 is

*Cover for the first collected edition of Brines's poetry*

the long autobiographical poem "Relato super-viviente" (Surviving Tale), in which Brines evokes through the blurred lens of memory a series of disconnected past experiences. The fragmentary nature of the poem with its temporal and spatial dislocations mirrors the lack of meaning in the speaker's present existence. Section 7 is even more pessimistic. Not only does the speaker see his own life as over but everything around him is ruin, grief, and desolation. In one poem, "Solo de trompeta" (Trumpet Solo), the cause of despair is the inauthenticity of life, seen in the shadowy figures who frequent a nightclub with their hollow laughter and furtive encounters. Although this poem strikes a discordant note in the overall composition of *Palabras,* it provided a perfect transition to Brines's next work.

*Aún no* (Not Yet), published in 1971, surprised the critics. First there is a change of setting. The nat-

ural world is replaced by the urban landscape of Madrid, and the predominant time is late at night. Second, although the elegiac verse and intimate tone traditionally associated with Brines are present in sections 1 and 3 of *Aún no,* section 2, "Composiciones de lugar" (Compositions of Place), represents a new direction. It is composed of fourteen brief poems inspired, according to the epigraph, by the *Spiritual Exercises* of Saint Ignatius of Loyola. After founding the Society of Jesus in 1540, Loyola wrote the *Exercises* to provide his followers with a spiritual system based on the Gospels. Brines's satirical intent, however, is evident from the first, for, to the reader's amazement, far from tracing a path toward asceticism, "Composiciones de lugar" outlines an apprenticeship in hypocrisy, deceit, and adulation. In a series of devastating portraits of contemporary and past figures, the speaker unmasks

No sé lo que persigo al convocaros
en el largo camino hacia Corinto, en el repeso
freno de aquel mar.
testigos, o pretexto. Mira, ciego lector,
mi cuerpo entre las aguas,
entre las olas rotas el cuerpo derritado,
al pie de la alta roca de Escirón;
y mírame en la arena, bajo el azul,
aún joven, contemplador de mi sonrisa viva,
de mi existente luz, ahora que escribo verso
en la huérfana noche,
en el naufragio del amor.
No sé por qué os convoco,
testigos de mi dicha, falso pretexto
de un creador de palabras de sombra.
El día aquel lo destruyó el silencio,
y no ha quedado nada para nadie..

Mas acaso no habré llamado en vano.
Pretexto insuficiente, testimonio piadoso
ni sois fieles testigos de vuestra propia vida.

*Fair copy of "Entre las olas canas el oro adolescente," collected in* Aún no *(from* Peña Labra, *Spring 1986; by permission of Francisco Brines)*

FRANCISCO BRINES

# ANTOLOGÍA POÉTICA

ESPEJO CIEGO

Cierço, alias Septentrion.

Occidental, alias Poniente.

Leuante, alias Oriental.

Medio dia, alias Meridional.

COL·LECCIÓ
**ELS QUATRE VENTS**

CONSELL VALENCIÀ DE CULTURA

*Cover for a 1993 collection of Brines's poetry*

the falseness of the world of appearances and the futility of all human posturing. The tone of these poems is mordant, the language is laconic, and the speaker's perspective is cynical. César Simón has analyzed Brines's use of language and has shown the preponderance of rhetorical devices, such as understatement, wordplay, antithesis, paradox, and hyperbole. In the prologue to his anthology of Brines's verse, Amusco emphasizes the poet's debt to the Latin satire (Catullus) and to the Spanish baroque tradition (Francisco de Quevedo, Baltasar Gracián, and others). It is important to note, however, that *Aún no* represents a technical, not a thematic, evolution in Brines's poetic career. Its density of expression and pessimistic tenor respond to a gradual darkening of vision, which was already anticipated in certain poems of *Palabras*.

Brines's complete works were collected for the first time in 1974 under the title *Poesía, 1960–1971:*

*Ensayo de una despedida* (Poetry, 1960–1971: Exercise in Saying Goodbye) with an important prologue by Bousoño. Dionisio Cañas discusses the literal and symbolic meaning of the subtitle, "Ensayo de una despedida," relating the phrase to what he calls Brines's "mirada crepuscular" (crepuscular gaze). To say goodbye is to take leave, just as the afternoon sun disappears into the horizon, and life slowly ebbs into forgetfulness.

In 1977 Brines published his next book of verse, *Insistencias en Luzbel* (Insistencies in Lucifer), considered his most difficult work. As in *Aún no* there is a distinct division in the book's structure. Part 1, "Insistencias en Luzbel," consists of a rewriting of the biblical story alluded to in the title, and part 2, "Insistencias en el engaño" (Insistencies in Deception), includes an elaboration of Brines's personal myths. Yet both parts are intimately related. Because of Brines's lack of belief in a transcendent reality, which dates from his adolescence, he is impelled to construct his own meaning. Paradoxically, however, this attempt is also doomed to failure, for the true face of existence is a "negro Esplendor" (a black Splendor). Part 1 constitutes the arduous task of describing that mystery; part 2 unveils the essential nihilism of the speaker, for whom nothing – not love, beauty, or childhood illusion – has any lasting consistency or meaning. In "El porqué de las palabras" (The Why of Words) even the poetic word fails him. The writing of verse is seen as a futile defense against oblivion. Perhaps the most poignant line of *Insistencias en Luzbel* is this one: "¿Y qué es lo que quedó de aquel viejo verano / en las costas de Grecia?" (And what has remained of that far-off summer / on the coasts of Greece?). The reference is to the love affair that is the focus of section 5 in *Palabras*. It is the basis for all of *Poemas a D. K.* (Poems to D. K.), published in 1986.

*Poemas a D. K.* includes no new poems. As Brines explains in the prologue, it is a compilation of love poems that were written at different times and published in different places. Yet the poems have a striking unity, for they refer to the same person and the same experience, and they share a common tone. "D.K." is probably Detlef Klugkist, the person to whom one of the book's poems, "Causa del amor" (The Cause of Love), was dedicated. According to the poet, all of the verses reflect "una concreta experiencia amorosa" (a concrete love experience) which occurred during his youth, and was never repeated. Love is portrayed from a distance, as "vida ya vivida" (life already lived), for the true subject of *Poemas a D. K.* is the melancholy remembrance of love's plenitude. *Poemas excluidos* (Excluded Poems), published in 1985, achieves a similar unity. It is a miscellany comprising works that Brines had never intended to publish, for reasons he explains in the extensive notes that accompany each of the sixteen poems.

*El otoño de las rosas* (The Autumn of the Roses, 1987) represents the culmination of Brines's literary career. In 1987 Brines earned three prestigious awards: the Premio Pablo Iglesias de las Letras and the Premio de las Letras Valencianas for his complete works, and the Premio Nacional de Poesía for *El otoño de las rosas,* which comprises sixty-five poems, all of which bear expressive titles. Elca returns with its explosion of sensory impressions, detailed with the same care and precision as in *Las brasas,* as does the nocturnal landscape of Madrid. Voyages of discovery to northern Africa, from the Maghreb to Egypt, are described. There are poems which evoke the passionate intensity of Brines's trips to Greece and others which condemn merce-

nary love. For the first time in contemporary Spanish literature there are several erotic poems that openly exalt the beauty of homosexual love, including "Erótica secreta de los iguales" (Secret Erotics of Equals) and "El más hermoso territorio" (The Most Beautiful Territory). The nihilistic strains of *Insistencias en Luzbel* can still be heard in *El otoño de las rosas,* but the predominant lyrical voice is the elegiac one. The theme of this book, and of all of Brines's poetry, was already articulated in *Las brasas:* the passage of time – "Ay, se muere todo, / pasa la luz, la flor, los sentimientos / se marchitan." ("Ah, everything dies, / light passes, and flowers and feelings / they wither").

With the publication of *El otoño de las rosas* Francisco Brines achieved the status of a classic writer. Brines is to the current generation of Spanish poets what Cernuda was to the members of the Generation of the 1950s: an undisputed master.

**Interviews:**

Emilio Nuñez, "Encuentro con Francisco Brines," *Insula,* 22 (1967): 4;

Rafael Alfaro, "Experiencia de una despedida," *Cuervo: Cuadernos de Cultura,* special issue on Brines (November 1980): 11–17;

H. Alvarado Tenorio, "Con Francisco Brines," *Cuervo* (November 1980): 19–23;

Isabel Burdiel, "Entrevista a Francisco Brines," *Cuervo* (November 1980): 25–41;

Luis Antonio de Villena, "Entrevista: El gran año de Francisco Brines," *Insula,* 42 (August–September 1987): 18–19.

**References:**

Mark C. Aldrich, "Rereading Francisco Brines with the Help of Michael Riffaterre; Reading Riffaterre with the Help of Brines," in *Selected Proceedings of the Thirty-Ninth Annual Mountain Interstate Foreign Language Conference,* edited by Sixto E. Torres and S. Carl King (Clemson, S.C.: Clemson University Press, 1991), pp. 115–120;

Alejandro Duque Amusco, "Algunos aspectos de la obra poética de Francisco Brines," *Cuadernos Hispanoamericanos,* 346 (1979): 52–74;

Amusco, "Francisco Brines: Estética de la nada y del sufrimiento," *Insula,* 33 (March 1978): 1, 12;

Amusco, Prologue to Brines's *Antología poética (Espejo Ciego),* edited by Amusco (Valencia: Consell Valencia de Cultura, 1993);

Douglas K. Benson, "El amor contra la nada: Pedro Salinas, Francisco Brines y la tradición clásica

*Brines in 1992*

española," *Revista Canadiense de Estudios Hispánicos,* 15, no. 1 (1990): 1–18;

Benson, "Convenciones de lenguaje y alusiones literarias en la poesía de Francisco Brines: *Insistencias en Luzbel,*" *Hispania,* 69, no. 1 (1986): 1–11;

Benson, "Memory, Tradition and the Reader in the Poetry of Francisco Brines," *Modern Language Notes,* 99 (1984): 308–326;

Carlos Bousoño, "Prólogo: Situación y características de la poesía de Francisco Brines," in Brines's *Poesía, 1960–1971* (Barcelona: Plaza & Janés, 1974), pp. 9–94;

Carole A. Bradford, "The Dialectic of Nothingness in the Poetry of Francisco Brines," *Taller Literario,* 1 (Fall 1980): 1–12;

Bradford, "Francisco Brines and Claudio Rodríguez: Two Recent Approaches to Poetic Creation," *Crítica Hispánica* 2.1 (1980): 29–40;

Bradford, "El lenguaje como reflejo de la angustia del tiempo en la poesía de Francisco Brines," *Cuadernos Hispanoamericanos,* 381 (1982): 640–648;

Dionisio Cañas, "La mirada crepuscular: Francisco Brines," in his *Poesía y percepción (Francisco Brines, Claudio Rodríguez y José Angel Valente)* (Madrid: Hiperión, 1984), pp. 23–80;

José Luis Cano, "La poesía elegíaca de Francisco Brines: *Palabras a la oscuridad,*" in his *Poesía española contemporánea: Las generaciones de posguerra* (Madrid: Guadarrama, 1974), pp. 193–198;

Antonio Colinas, "Equilibrio de Francisco Brines," *Cuadernos Hispanoamericanos,* 302 (1975): 479–481;

Maria Cooks, "Francisco Brines and the Rebirth of Conceit in Spanish Contemporary Poetry," *Romance Languages Annual,* 1 (1989): 413–416;

Andrew P. Debicki, "The Generation of 1956–1971" and "Francisco Brines: Text and Reader," in his *Poetry of Discovery: The Spanish Generation of 1956–1971* (Lexington: University Press of Kentucky, 1982), pp. 1–19, 20–39;

Debicki, "El texto y el lector: La poesía de Francisco Brines," in *Homenaje a Antonio Sánchez Barbudo: Ensayos de literatura española moderna,* edited by Benito Brancaforte and others (Madison: University of Wisconsin Press, 1981), pp. 269–290;

Ricardo Defarges, "Francisco Brines, poeta esencial," *Cuadernos Hispanoamericanos,* 207 (March 1967): 514–523;

Bernado Delgado, "La obra completa de Francisco Brines," *Jugar con el Fuego: Poesía y Crítica,* 1 (1975): 35–39;

Vicente Gallego, "El tema del amor en la poesía de Francisco Brines," *Hora de Poesía,* 51–52 (1987): 55–66;

José Luis García-Martin, "La poesía completa de Francisco Brines," *Cuadernos Hispanoamericanos,* 420 (1985): 194–200;

José Olivio Jiménez, *Cinco poetas del tiempo,* revised edition (Madrid: Insula, 1972);

Jiménez, "Sobre *El Santo Inocente*" and "Realidad y misterio en *Palabras a la oscuridad* (1966), de Francisco Brines," in his *Diez años de poesía española, 1960–1970* (Madrid: Insula, 1972), pp. 175–204;

Jiménez, "Una poesía de la desposesión: *Ensayo de una despedida* de Francisco Brines," *Diálogo,* 75 (1977): 24–27;

W. Michael Mudrovic, "Ekphrasis, Intertextuality and the Role of the Reader in Poems by Francisco Brines and Claudio Rodríguez," *Studies in Twentieth-Century Literature,* 14 (1989–1990): 279–300;

Judith Nantell, "Francisco Brines' *Aún no:* Poetry as Knowledge," *Kentucky Romance Quarterly,* 31, no. 4 (1984): 413–424;

Nantell, "Retracing the Text: Francisco Brines' *Poemas excluidos,*" *Studies in Twentieth-Century Literature,* 13 (1989): 195–214;

Nantell, "Writing and Reading: Dialectical Correlatives in Francisco Brines' *Insistencias en Luzbel,*" in *After the War: Essays on Recent Spanish Poetry,* edited by Salvador Jiménez-Fajardo and John C. Wilcox (Boulder: University of Colorado Press, 1988), pp. 83–97;

Margaret H. Persin, "Francisco Brines' *Insistencias en Luzbel:* Toward the Limits of Language and Being," in her *Recent Spanish Poetry and the Role of the Reader* (Lewisburg, Pa.: Bucknell University Press, 1987), pp. 45–67; also published in Persin's *Poesía como proceso: Poesía española de los Años 50 y 60* (Madrid: Porrúa Turanzas, 1986), pp. 49–78;

Persin, "Sexual Politics: The Image of Self and Other in Three Poems by Francisco Brines," *Perspectives on Contemporary Literature,* 11 (1985): 87–92;

Alfonso Sanz Echeverría, "La insistencia de Francisco Brines," *Jugar con el Fuego: Poesía y crítica,* 3–4 (1977): 32–49;

Ricardo Senabre, "Un poema de Francisco Brines," *Letras de Deusto,* 19, no. 44 (1989): 299–309;

Philip W. Silver, "New Spanish Poetry: The Rodríguez-Brines Generation," *Books Abroad,* 42 (1968): 211–224; translated as "Nueva poesía española: La generación Rodríguez-Brines," *Insula,* 24 (May 1969): 14;

César Simón, "Algunos aspectos lingüísticos en la sátira de Francisco Brines," in *Cuadernos de Filología* (June 1971): 63–70;

Fidel Villar Ribot, "La mirada del tiempo (En torno a *El otoño de las rosas* de Francisco Brines)," *Hora de Poesía,* 51–52 (1987): 67–77;

Luis Antonio de Villena, "De luz, de tiempo, de palabras, de hombres: Sobre la poesía de Francisco Brines," *Insula,* 30 (January 1975): 4–5;

Villena, "Sobre *Insistencias en Luzbel* y la poesía de Francisco Brines," *Papeles de Son Armadans,* 89 (1978): 213–222.

# Eladio Cabañero
*(6 December 1930 –    )*

Susan Rivera
*University of Oklahoma*

BOOKS: *Desde el sol y la anchura* (Madrid: Sánchez, 1956);
*Una señal de amor* (Madrid: Rialp, 1958);
*Recordatorio* (Madrid: Taurus, 1961);
*Marisa Sabia y otros poemas* (Madrid, 1963);
*Poesía (1956–1970)* (Barcelona: Plaza & Janés, 1970);
*Señal de amor: Antología poética 1956–1991* (Madrid: Libertarias, 1992).

Eladio Cabañero is a prominent member of the "Generation of the 1950s," which created a turning point in the poetry written in post-civil-war Spain. Although his personal experience and background greatly differ from those of the other members of this same generation (he is of humble, peasant origins and self-educated, and most of the others were born into the middle or upper-middle class and received university educations), his poetry does share with theirs the same major characteristics. The effects of the war are overtly reflected in his work, but political protest loses force and yields to a stronger emphasis on poetic expression. Through his skillful and artistic use of colloquial language and the manipulation of images, Cabañero is able to give deeper meanings to everyday objects and events. He no longer sees poetry merely as communication but more as a vehicle for discovery: discovery of himself, the meaning of reality, and the power of language. While aesthetics plays a decisive role, his work has also been described as a poetry of experience – based on the desire to convert his personal experiences into profound moral reflections. What distinguishes him from most of the other poets of his group is his lack of intellectualism and the absence of irony in his work. Cabañero's originality stems from a sincere solidarity with the helpless, a love of humankind, and his particular religious view of the world. He participates in the poetic renewal brought about by the Generation of the 1950s, but his distinct voice is clearly discernible from the others.

Born in Tomelloso on 6 December 1930, Eladio Cabañero is the third and last son of Felix Cabañero Jareño and Justa López de Cabañero; his father, a teacher and lawyer, was the secretary of the Socialist party of his town and fought as a member of the Republican Army during the last months of the Spanish Civil War. After the war Felix Cabañero was imprisoned, sentenced to death, and executed in 1940. His wife was also incarcerated (for three years) simply for being a member of a Republican family. Eladio's maternal grandfather, an impoverished farmer and profoundly religious man, abandoned the Catholic church for the Protestant one, which he considered closer and more faithful to the words of Jesus Christ. From this grandfather, whom Eladio barely knew, the future poet inherited a volume of evangelical hymns that he memorized; the songs left a profound imprint in his imagination, and traces of them appear in his verses.

From the end of the war until his mother was freed from prison in 1942, Eladio Cabañero lived alternately with his grandparents and some of his maternal uncles. With them he worked in the fields. Then, from adolescence until the age of twenty-five, he worked as a mason. These situations and people appear in his poems. For example, in "La despedida" (The Goodbye, in *Una señal de amor* [A Sign of Love, 1958]) he evokes an image of his father as "fiado en la verdad, claro, indefenso" (trusting truth, candid, defenseless) and one of his mother as "atareada y fuerte entre nosotros" (busy and strong among us). In "Los trenes" (The Trains, in *Recordatorio* [Reminder, 1961]) he mentions his grandfather "Eladio López / el que volvía del campo sin camisa / y sin blusa por dar a los mendigos" (Eladio López / the one who returned from the fields without a shirt / and without a blouse for having given them to the beggars).

Cabañero had little schooling because of the upheavals of the war, which left his village without a teacher, and because of his family's difficult economic situation after the war. Nevertheless he quickly learned to read and write and soon proved to be a precocious, avid reader. In the public library of Tomelloso he found several volumes by the great authors of the Spanish Golden Age, such as Garcilaso de la Vega, Francisco Quevedo, and Miguel de Cervantes, whose books he read and reread incessantly. Novelist Francisco García Pavón and poet Felix Grande, both also from Tomelloso, strongly influenced Cabañero's choice of a literary vocation. At the age of twenty he began to write his first verses. In 1955, while still working as a mason, he received the Juventud Prize for his poem "El pan" (Bread), collected later in *Recordatorio*.

In 1956, after the death of his mother, Cabañero moved to Madrid, where he worked at the National Library for twelve years and then at Editorial Taurus for ten years. He entered the literary scene in Madrid and made friends with important writers, including Carlos Bousoño, Luis Rosales, Jorge Campos, Claudio Rodríguez, and Carlos Sahagún, who contributed to his literary education. After publishing his first collection, which established Cabañero as a poet, he became a member of the editorial staff of the literary journal *Estafeta Literaria,* of which he would later become editor in chief. Cabañero still resides in Madrid, where he works in the Publications Division of the Ministry of Culture. In 1992 he married fellow poet Eduarda Moro. Cabañero is a humble, unpretentious man. According to his friend Florencio Martínez Ruiz, "A pesar de sus éxitos – o precisamente por ellos – Eladio Cabañero ha seguido después el curso de una existencia sencilla" (In spite of his success – or precisely because of it – Eladio Cabañero later continued the course of a simple existence).

The topics and themes that prevail in his work are of a peasant nature: the people and landscape of La Mancha (his native region) obsessively capture his attention. Urban references are rare, although they are more frequent in the series of love poems dedicated to a childhood girlfriend, whom he calls Marisa Sabia (in his 1963 book). Except for his first poems, written while still in Tomelloso, Cabañero's work is defined by an evocative tone with elegiac nuances: he remembers his childhood and his native land from the perspective of another time (adulthood) and another place (Madrid).

His emphasis on humility, the pain of poverty, the injustice with which the peasants live, and the memory of the somber period of the civil war make his poetry an exponent of the "social" mode dominant in Spain when he was young. He often spoke of his adherence to this mode. In the anthology

*Eladio Cabañero and his wife, Eduarda. They were married in 1992.*

*Poesía ultima* (Latest Poetry, 1969), edited by Francisco Ribes, Cabañero states that "la poesía social es alta razón de eterna actualidad, no un tema de moda" (social poetry is an important account of eternal actuality, not a theme that is in vogue).

His obvious concerns for the helpless are determined by a profound religious sentiment that leads him to accept injustice and poverty with solidarity and resignation. According to him the poor will find redemption in the celestial sphere after suffering just as Christ did. In the poem "Jornalero" (Laborer, in *Desde el sol y la anchura*) he writes: "Tierras de promisión serán los astros, / ... y la muerte / por el borde de Dios irá cantando. / Mientras tanto a llevar la cruz a cuestas" (The promised lands will be the stars, / ... and death / beside God will go on singing. / Meanwhile one must bear one's cross). Cabañero believes charity and love are lacking in this world: "amamos poco al hombre" (we love man very little), he says in "La despedida." In "El pan" beggars are contemplated "con las manos extendidas a nuestra caridad, / que es lo mejor de ellos y de nosotros" (with their hands extended to our charity, / which is the best part of them and of us).

While Cabañero does not reject outbursts of accusation, protest, or rebellion, his resigned evangelical nature confers a distinctive and personal characteristic to his idea of social commitment, which is for him more emotional and sentimental than political. Although this stance does not disqualify him as a social poet, it places him in a singular position within the Generation of the 1950s, to which he belongs for chronological and aesthetic reasons.

For Cabañero, poetry is above all "cosa cordial" (a cordial thing), and in José Batlló's *Antología de la nueva poesía española* (New Spanish Poetry, 1968), he says that what interests him most about poetry is that it is "una forma de conocimiento, consuelo y protesta" (a form of discovery, comfort, and protest). He declares himself in favor of clarity, precision, and expressive simplicity. Among the poets he considers exemplary are Antonio Machado, César Vallejo, and Quevedo, all of whom obviously influenced his work.

The first of his books, *Desde el sol y la anchura* (From the Sun and the Open Space, 1956) reveals the strong influence of some Golden Age poets, especially Quevedo, Garcilaso, and Luis de Góngora; it also shows Cabañero's attentive reading of the works of Rubén Darío. Technical parallels to the poetry of the Renaissance and the baroque era suggest, as critic Andrew P. Debicki has pointed out, "the poet's conscious efforts to learn from and assimilate previous traditions, . . . recalling the process of learning by imitation of Miguel Hernández." The reference to Hernández is fitting: both he and Cabañero were autodidacts of humble origins who lived in close contact with nature and manifested a great talent for powerful verbal invention.

In the untitled poem that serves as a prologue to *Desde el sol y la anchura,* Cabañero states his decision to devote himself to La Mancha: "Me entrego a este paisaje enteramente / volcando mi raíz y mi simiente / sobre la tierra pobre, sobre el suelo" (I give myself completely to this landscape / spreading my roots and my seed / over the barren soil, over the earth). These lines define the major theme of the book, which is more narrative and descriptive than intimate and lyrical. Cabañero emphasizes the people and the land he contemplates rather than his own intimate feelings.

*Desde el sol y la anchura* is divided into three parts and is framed by the prologue and an epilogue. The first part, "Campesinos de La Mancha" (Peasants of La Mancha), describes some of the typical characters of his area; the second, "Otoño I" (Autumn I), presents typical aspects of the landscape of La Mancha, such as windmills and vineyards; and the third, "Otoño II" (Autumn II), is centered exclusively on wine, the most important source of income in the depressed economy of the region. The poems in the book refer to everyday tasks and ordinary people or things. Work defines human beings and is depicted as being as arduous and harsh as the landscape itself. Among Cabañero's rich lexical range, *huesos* (bones) and *piedras* (rocks) are the two most reiterated words, and thus they become emblems of the severity of the life-style and the geography.

Cabañero's metaphors often point to the similarity between nature and the inhabitants of La Mancha: the knees of the title character in "Campesino trágico" (Tragic Peasant) are "guijarros de dolor" (pebbles of pain); the lips described in "Campesina" (Peasant Woman) are "gruesa arcilla indócil" (thick indocile clay), and the woman's figure is "maciza como un árbol" (solid as a tree) — "algo de surco corre por sus brazos, / algo de tierra espesa por su sangre" (furrows run through her arms, / thick soil through her blood). The refined, metaphorical language, which brings to mind the rhetoric of the baroque period, transforms ordinary things into archetypes. Through the use of images the rain becomes a "minero de la dicha" (a miner of happiness); the vanes of the windmills turn into "encabritados miradores" (rearing bay windows); and, in a more abstract manner, "las viñas son las verdes / proporciones cuadradas del paisaje" (the vineyards are the green / square proportions of the landscape). Idealizing metaphors frequently multiply and take over entire stanzas. The influence of Quevedo and Góngora is evident throughout the book, but also present are traces of sensorial and aristocratic elements along with the love of luxury, jewels, and gems typical of the modernist movement. Everyday items undergo an aesthetic transformation and thus lose their natural quality and become artificial objects, as exemplified in "Soneto del racimo recién cortado" (Sonnet of the Newly Cut Cluster of Grapes), in which the branch is described as "Bien colmado y lujoso, reengarzado / en su collar de perlas" (overflowing and luxurious, mounted / on its pearl necklace).

These flashes of sensorial sumptuousness seem to contradict the harshness and elemental aspects of the life and landscape of La Mancha. But Cabañero's tendency toward idealization and abstraction is balanced by the frequent and powerful images that confer passion, life, and human or animal corporeity to inanimate objects: rocks are "vivas esponjas del silencio" (live sponges of silence) or compared to a "coágulo de Dios" (blood clot of God), and Cabañero hopes "que cada piedra tenga su hemorragia, cada raíz su erupto de ceniza" (that every rock will have its hemorrhage, every root its eruption of ash). By humanizing inert or vegetable matter, Cabañero transfers to all of nature the suffering of the people. Pain, not exclusive to human beings, also affects nature: "Les duele el sol caído a los trigales" (the fallen sun hurts the wheat fields).

In *Desde el sol y la anchura* Cabañero mostly relies on classical forms: hendecasyllabic verse and the sonnet. He demonstrates an exceptional mastery of form and linguistic creativity. Pain, poverty, ignorance, and the ability to work hard are some of the human traits that Cabañero describes, which has caused the book to be classified as social. But, according to Debicki, one should be careful not to attribute an overt social message to the book, "tempting though that may seem." As opposed to writing social protest poems, Cabañero almost always tends to justify or rationalize the situation of the peasants. Their lack of education, for example, is excused or compensated for by another type of wisdom, perhaps much more profound: a cart driver is "Un pobre analfabeto / que se sabe los nombres de la rosa" (A poor illiterate / who knows the names of the roses). In "Jornalero" the pain and misery of the workers are equal to the suffering of Christ and are in this way consecrated and accepted as the ultimate good: "Es bueno que Jesús sufriera tanto / en este mundo, es bueno el sudor rojo / para el jornal diario / y tener la garganta endurecida / y agotados los brazos" (It is good that Jesus suffered so much / in this world, red sweat is good / for everyday work / and having a hardened throat / and exhausted arms [is good]). Many of the scenes in this book are somewhat naive biblical illustrations: "eucarísticas rosas" (eucharistic roses) are seen in the heavens where "arcángeles vigilan" (archangels are on guard), and "las trompetas del ángel de la altura" (the trumpets of the angel on high) are heard. More than social poetry, *Desde el sol y la anchura* is an example of profoundly religious poetry, the result of a sincere and emotional sentiment, not of rebellion or protest but rather of pity and understanding.

In his second book, *Una señal de amor,* which won an honorable mention for the Adonais Poetry Prize, Cabañero shows his most personal voice, which also characterizes the rest of his work. His language is no longer modeled after classical rheto-

ric but after everyday, realistic forms of spoken language. The poetic meter is liberated from the rigidity of classical forms, and it tends toward a freer, more open form that gives Cabañero's diction an air of spontaneity. This structure reinforces the realism that, in contrast with his previous idealism, characterizes his writing from 1958 on. Because of his precise attention to detail and description, his interest in anecdotes and rural settings, and the inclusion of regional idioms and expressions, the realism of Cabañero sometimes borders on *costumbrismo* (art based on rural customs).

The first poem (untitled) of *Una señal de amor* explores and expresses his new sentimental state: "Como la hoz y el trigo estoy dispuesto; veo el amor que viene" (Like the sickle and the wheat I am ready; I see love coming). This intuition of imminent love inspired a series of five poems that, taken together, seem to be a brief narration of a frustrated love affair, a relationship that seems to have existed only in the desires and dreams of Cabañero. Although this love affair is not to be, he is left with a painful, indelible memory that he is unable to give up, because he knows that pain is the experience that most profoundly marks a human being. In "El olvido" (Oblivion) he observes that "Nada se olvida, dicen los que sufren" (Nothing is forgotten, say those who suffer).

To forget pain would be the same as erasing the purest aspect of existence, so Cabañero devotes himself to remembrance: "Mientras escribo ensancho la memoria" (While I write I expand my memory), he states in the poem "Carta" (Letter). The book becomes a desolate, moving elegy in which reality is defined by suffering; poverty and injustice are contemplated with pity and solidarity.

The most defining and personal aspects of Cabañero's poetry are present in *Una señal de amor:* his use of the first-person, intimist, lyrical narrative; and his autobiographical evocations that occasionally reveal the upheavals of history. In the first (untitled) poem, he remembers his experiences during the civil war: "había odio, / . . . duramos / puramente de limosna" (there was hate, / . . . we endured / solely out of charity); and he expresses his desire to write an affirmative poetry – "siempre diré que sí" (I will always say yes) – in defense of the persecuted. Metapoetic allusions are also present in the book. When Cabañero states, "vine a dejar palabras repartidas" (I came to distribute some words), he reveals his concept of poetry as communication, participation, and a giving of oneself.

In *Una señal de amor* the testimonial poetry, conceived as a surrendering of oneself to others; the concern for the persecuted; the recounting of the miseries of the civil war; and the profound solidarity with those who suffer are characteristics that point to the social aspect of Cabañero's writing. But, as in *Desde el sol y la anchura,* all these facets are imbued with a profound religiosity, which is the dominating sentiment in this book. Cabañero, who has little faith in ideas – "creo poco en las razones; canto, sólo" (I believe very little in reasons; I sing, only) – reiterates his firm, unambiguous faith in God: "Creo justamente en Dios" (I believe justly in God). God is presented as the determiner of the destinies of human beings: in "Acción de gracias por un hombre" (Thanksgiving for a Man) life is seen as predisposed so that "dependa de Dios todo" (everything depends on God). "Fotografía del pocero" (Picture of a Well Digger) also illustrates that resigned attitude. With his only hopes based on himself and God, the well digger, conscious of the fact that he "será pocero hasta morirse" (will be a well digger until his death), lives constantly postponing future plans "para después, cuando el Señor ayude" (until later, when the Lord will help), and he believes that "Ser pobre es lo de menos" (being poor is the least important of things).

The example of the well digger seems to indicate that people should limit themselves to their destinies regardless of how humble or painful they may be, without posing other, more-profound problems. In this respect the poem "El andamio" (The Scaffold), one of Cabañero's best, is significant. On a scaffold, a setting with which Cabañero is very familiar, some masons work and converse. Their attention is directed toward securing the scaffold "mucho mejor que aquel del accidente, / cuando murió el compadre de las barbas" (much better than the one of the accident, / when our bearded comrade died). They would prefer not to deal with problems unrelated to their immediate situation. The best idea is to "dejarse ya de guerras y políticas" (leave wars and politics aside): "No era aquel el momento / de censurar los tiempos tan difíciles. . . . / Allí no se trataba / de pasarse de listos . . . / sino de atar mejor aquel andamio / y comprender que el más sabio es el tiempo" (It was not the moment / to censure these very difficult times. . . . / There it was not a matter of / trying to be smarter . . . / but rather of better securing that scaffold / and understanding that time is the wisest of all). Without denying the possible realist reading of both poems, the images of the well digger and the masons – credible and real in all details – can also be considered, Debicki notes, as emblems or symbols of universal truths relative to the human condition. Cabañero seems to

be saying, much in keeping with his Christian vision, that the salvation of humans depends on themselves, although he never ceases to exalt the value of loving others and of having solidarity in misery or misfortune; when love and solidarity are lacking, the human condition is even more pathetic. Other alternatives, such as political action and social protest, are explicitly rejected in "El andamio."

In *Una señal de amor* Cabañero's religious conception of the universe has not changed. In other facets, though, the book reveals a different approach. Even when the thematic substance – the land and the people of La Mancha – is the same as in his previous book, the realistic presentation and descriptions confer a wholly new meaning on it. The settings, situations, and characters are no longer presented in archetypal or idealized versions. This book is an example of "poetry of experience," in which the retelling of what was experienced surpasses any sentimental evocation and results in a meditative evaluation – bitter but compassionate – of the meaning of human existence. In the poetry of Cabañero, as Miguel de Unamuno once said of ideal poetry (in "Arte poética," *Poesías,* 1907), "siente el pensamiento y piensa el sentimiento" (thought feels and feelings think).

To reinforce his realistic vision, in *Una señal de amor* Cabañero strips his poetic expression of the artificiality that characterized it before. He rejects the formal canon of the Golden Age and writes in free verse, although based on hendecasyllabic rhythm. Free from baroque rhetoric, the language is simple and direct, sparse in the use of adjectives, and modeled after colloquial speech. Metaphors are less numerous, and similes become more abundant. The imaginary plane of the comparisons is never pure rhetorical ornamentation or a gratuitous display of ingenuity but, rather, an effective means of intensifying the precariousness and helplessness of the human condition. Thus in a desolate landscape in "Carta," the sun dies "igual que las bombillas de los pobres" (the same as the light bulbs of the poor), and in "Compañera" (Companion) the speaker feels "más humano que un pájaro con frío" (more human than a bird that is cold). The positive influence of Vallejo is evident in both content and expression.

The third of Cabañero's books, *Recordatorio,* is considered his masterpiece by most critics. For Manuel Ríos Ruiz it is "un hito de la llamada poesía social" (a breakthrough in so-called social poetry), and Francisco Brines calls it "la meditación del corazón" (a meditation of the heart). The title of the book seems to indicate that it is a prolongation of the nostalgic attitude that characterized his previous poetry, and such is the case in the most intense, beautiful, and lucid parts of the book. Nevertheless, he does not limit himself to repetition: *Recordatorio* includes novelties that are the results of a change in perspective. What is remembered is further away, and the past is conceived as nebulous, wrapped in a light of unreality. "Qué fantasmal colmena es el recuerdo" (What a phantasmal beehive the memory is), he exclaims in "Primer recordatorio" (First Reminder). Time has elapsed, and the old, dear people, who before were so vivid in his memory, are no longer what they used to be, as he says in the same poem: "muertos míos, padres, / ahora que a veces ni os amo . . . os miro como a extraños, muy lejanos, / turbios, desconocidos" (my dearly departed, my parents, / now that I sometimes don't even love you . . . I see you like strangers, very far away, / blurry, unrecognizable). He is not even sure things were as he remembers them, and perplexity and doubt interrupt the course of his remembering. "¿Era aquél Tomelloso? / ¿Era yo aquél, aquél de por entonces?" (Was that Tomelloso? / Was I that person, that person way back then?), he asks in "Antes, cuando la infancia" (Before, During Childhood). Seen from a distance, the actualization of the past is more a result of dreams than of memory. In "Desde esta habitación" (From This Room) he declares, "Veo entre sueños – tiempo no recordable" (I see among dreams – time that cannot be remembered).

In the poem "Los trenes" (The Trains) the distance between present and past not only produces blurred memories – "el recuerdo llega turbio / como un documental retrospectivo" (memory arrives muddled / like a retrospective documentary) – but it also gives way to an interesting contrast of perspectives. The experience of the adult corrects the ingenious vision of the child who, from the desolate plain of La Mancha, saw the trains passing and thought they were going "hacia otro mundo de esperanza" (toward another world of hope). But Cabañero is now writing in a state of disillusionment, and although he does not state it explicitly, he insinuates that the beliefs of the child were merely a result of his poverty and unawareness of the world. They are the illusions typical of the poor "cuando son niños, siempre trabajando / y sin salir del pueblo para nada" (when they are children, always working / and never leaving the village for anything).

While tied to the past, Cabañero's perception of present moments, which in *Recordatorio* is much more vivid, produces unequivocal and perturbing temporal superpositions. In "Tú, la que yo amo" (You, the One I Love) the image of an old woman

serving wine in a tavern is confused in the memory of the speaker with the image of the young girl he loved when he was an adolescent. The result is a type of hallucination that cruelly illuminates the modifying effect of the passage of time: "Eres tú como eres y no eres: / joven cuando te vi con tu piel pálida / . . . tú, la vieja / que, como un animal, fuma y desparcha / este vino que bebo tristemente" (It is you as you are and as you are not: / young when I saw you with your pale skin / . . . you, the old woman / who, like an animal, smokes and serves / this wine that I sadly drink).

The consciousness of present time is perhaps the cause of the frequent bursts of protest and rebellion that surge forth in *Recordatorio*. Cabañero gives a new meaning to his evocations. In "Desde esta habitación," for example, he states that "saco a relucir vidas, materiales, historia, / de manera que nadie equivocado piense / que escribo algún poema misterioso / sino de alta protesta y de dolor" (I highlight lives, materials, history, / so that no one will mistakenly think / that I am writing some mysterious poem / but rather one of profound protest and pain).

Thus overt protest finally appears in the poetry of Cabañero. In an unequivocal and angry tone of moral reproof, he asks in "El salmo de los desconocidos" (Psalm of the Unknown): "¿Quién trajo el desamor, cómo anda el odio / en libertad y quién ha permitido / el hambre, ¡mala estrella!, el impasible / invierno que atraviesa a la pobreza / coronada de espinas?" (Who brought the lack of love, how can hate be / free and who has permitted / hunger, What misfortune!, the impasible / winter that crosses through poverty / crowned with thorns?). Behind this question lie those who are responsible, those whom Cabañero does not hesitate to denounce: the ones who exert power, "los que mandan" (the ones who rule) – "cocineros terribles" (terrible cooks) who "nos están guisando, malguisando" (are cooking for us, badly cooking for us) a dangerous destiny. In "Conversación con un amigo" (Conversation with a Friend) he states that "ya no basta vivir cobardemente" (it is no longer enough to live cowardly); rather, collective action is necessary because, as he says in "Sociedad limitada" (Limited Society), "Todos nosotros mal seremos nada / sin formar coro, sin pedir reunidos / los beneficios justos de los hombres" (it will be hard for us to be anything / without forming a chorus, without all of us together asking for / the just benefits of man).

Although religious allusions are not lacking in this book, Cabañero no longer reacts precisely with

Christian resignation in view of the injustices of this world. Thus Cabañero, in purpose and tone, comes closer to the social poets of his generation.

*Recordatorio* offers a few innovations in Cabañero's style. Images are used less frequently, and the language becomes more direct and colloquial, although always powerful and suggestive. The influence of Vallejo, as in *Una señal de amor,* enriches and intensifies the common idiom.

*Recordatorio* ends with two sections that are perhaps less important than the rest of the book: "Poemas varios" (Various Poems), in which Cabañero includes several previously unpublished poems from his early career; and "Doce poetas alrededor de una mesa" (Twelve Poets Around a Table), a series of eleven sonnets and a *silva* (a poem mixing iambic hendecasyllable and heptasyllable lines) written in homage to several different poets. These last poems show Cabañero's ingeniousness and mastery of classical forms.

*Marisa Sabia y otros poemas,* his next book, was awarded the 1963 Premio Nacional de Poesía. The most important part of this book centers on love. Although the topic is present in his previous writing, it is never as relevant as it is in *Marisa Sabia.* Love replaces all Cabañero's old obsessions, and he is engrossed in personal reactions toward his feelings and in the constant elaboration of the image of the beloved.

The series of fourteen poems dedicated to the girl he refers to as Marisa Sabia (not her real name) is divided into two distinct sections that are different in tone. Section 1 deals with Cabañero's initial joyous reaction to the amorous relationship. He records unforgettable days in minute chronological precision. In "Primeras vacaciones" (First Vacation) he enthusiastically proclaims, "¡Viva el día de ayer, día 2 de junio; / muera el olvido, el día de mañera!" (Long live yesterday, second day of June; / death to oblivion, tomorrow!). What is most important to him is his present happiness; what might occur in the future does not seem to worry him at this point. But tomorrow will arrive inevitably and oblivion – hinted at earlier – along with it. The second part of the book relates, in somber and pessimistic hues, the end of the relationship.

Various literary conventions converge in Cabañero's love poetry. The idealization of the loved one who is deified in the poem "La diosa" (The Goddess) reminds one of Renaissance love lyrics. Not unlike the troubadours, the speaker expresses his feelings chastely, and he believes that love will give him the power to realize impossible feats. In "Primeras vacaciones" he feels "capaz / de

desviar el lento caz del Duero, / . . . atarlo de un ramal, acarrearlo a la oficina o al café" (able / to divert the slow trench of the Duero [River], / . . . to tie it with a rope, to carry it to the office or the café). Later he accepts with complacency the suffering that love ultimately produces, as described in "En soledad" (In Solitude): "Soledad doloridamente hermosa" (Painfully beautiful solitude). His frequent introspective attitude and the violent expressions used to describe his feelings are reminiscent of certain aspects of Garcilaso's poetry, as in the following passage from Cabañero's "Primeras vacaciones": "giro desesperado; vengo y voy, / hago que olvido, finjo que no es cierto; / pongo el alma de punta, pongo en greña / mis venas tormentosas, / raspo rabiosamente con las uñas / la amaneada bestia gris del tiempo" (I turn desperately; I come and go, / I act like I forget, I pretend it is not true; / I get annoyed at my soul, I aggravate / my turbulent veins, / I rabidly scratch with my nails / the fettered gray beast of time). Cabañero shares with the Romantics the idea that love is an invention of the lover: "Amar es inventar, borrar un rostro / contra un espejo" (To love is to invent, to erase a face / against a mirror).

The literary conventions evident in the content are also reflected in the style: Cabañero returns to the sonnet form, and the language is, on occasion, more rhetorical than in his two previous books. Adjectives and metaphors that artificially idealize reality are more abundant, as in the following lines from "La noche me habla de ti" (The Night Talks to Me about You): "El arado romano, amante del silencio, / cortejea aún la mies y las cuidades" (The Roman plow, lover of silence, / still woos the fields and the cities).

But not everything is conventional in the poems dedicated to Marisa Sabia, nor does Cabañero exclusively explore his intimate feelings and reflect on the meaning of love. There are many references to the exterior world, allusions to a recognizable urban and rural geography – Madrid and Castile – and the poems reflect everyday episodes, thus leaving a sincere and truthful imprint on the writing. In many passages the book resembles a diary in which the author has recorded his experiences: certain events seem to have been registered right after they occurred.

In order to preserve his experiences with the girl, he records them cinematically as they happen. The reasoning behind this filmic approach is explained in the poem "La diosa" (The Goddess): "filmo en mi frente tu figura / y reúno las tardes y tu cara / en un fanal bellísimo, ya en sueños, / como en un cine mágico" (I film your image in my forehead / and I reunite the afternoons and your face / in a beautiful bell jar, already in my dreams, / as in a magical film). This strategy allows Cabañero to remember the beloved's image later, when he is alone, and rescue it forever from oblivion: "Ahora vivo contigo de memoria; / proyecto tu recuerdo, cine dulce, que morirá conmigo" (Now I live with you in my memory; / I project the memory of you, sweet film, / that will die with me).

But this "sweet film" will not always be an effective consolation when he feels definitively abandoned. The speaker, described as an "invitado de honor de los recuerdos" (guest of honor of memories), pathetically idealizes his pain: "ahora sufro la pena de elevarme / cerca ya de los techos del olvido, / muriéndome en silencio, en soledad" (now I suffer the grief of having to raise myself / close to the ceiling of oblivion, / dying in silence, in solitude). In his abandonment, he remembers the child he once was and, identifying with the youth, wants to return to the bright – although at times "oscuro" (dark) – landscape of his childhood. In "Esta tarde de lluvia" (This Rainy Afternoon) he explains: "Esta tarde aquel niño quiere irse . . . / de Madrid y su presente doloroso, / allí, a su Mancha" (This evening that child wants to go . . . / from Madrid and its painful present, / there, to his Mancha). With the communication of his desire to escape, Cabañero brings to an end the narration in verse of an unfortunate love affair.

The other poems, which complete the book, are an extension and a coherent ending to the Marisa Sabia series. They describe the return to childhood for which the abandoned lover had hoped. Cabañero uses the sonnet form and baroque or Renaissance rhetoric in order to idealize and sing the praises of the people and landscape of La Mancha, as in *Desde el sol y la anchura.* By returning, thematically and stylistically, to his point of departure, Cabañero has, in a sense, closed the circle of his lyrical evolution. Perhaps this closure explains his seemingly premature silence, his lack of much further writing, a quiescence that may be definitive: Cabañero has not written a book of new poems in thirty years. *Poesía,* winner of the Premio de la Crítica, and *Señal de amor: Antología poética 1956–1991* (published in 1992) are mostly collections of poems from his other books.

The scarcity of his work and his prolonged silence do not justify the relative indifference with which his poetry has been treated by critics in recent years. Within the Generation of the 1950s the voice of Eladio Cabañero is essential and should be remembered as one of the most intense and personal.

## References:

Laila Adib Abdul Wahed, "Eladio Cabañero: Poeta de la realidad," *Cuadernos Hispanoamericanos,* no. 381 (March 1982): 660–666;

José Batlló, ed., *Antología de la nueva poesía española* (Madrid: Bardo, 1968), pp. 334–336;

Francisco Brines, "Eladio Cabañero," *La Caña Gris,* 4–5 (Autumn 1961): 53–55;

Andrew P. Debicki, "Eladio Cabañero: Imagery, Style, and Effect," in his *Poetry of Discovery: The Spanish Generation of 1956–1971* (Lexington: University Press of Kentucky, 1982), pp. 165–182;

José Gerardo Manrique de Lara, "La voz personal y simplista de Eladio Cabañero," in his *Poetas sociales españoles* (Madrid: EPESA, 1974), pp. 147–152;

Manuel Mantero, *Poesía española contemporánea: Estudio y antología (1939–1965)* (Barcelona: Plaza & Janés, 1966), pp. 191–194;

Florencio Martínez Ruiz, Prologue to Cabañero's *Poesía (1956–1970)* (Barcelona: Plaza & Janés, 1970), pp. 9–23;

Francisco Ribes, "Notas para una conducta poética," in *Poesía última,* edited by Ribes (Madrid: Taurus, 1969), pp. 17–23;

Manuel Rico, Introduction to Cabañero's *Señal de amor: Antología poética 1956–1991* (Madrid: Libertarias, 1992), pp. 13–25;

Manuel Ríos Ruiz, "La poesía de Eladio Cabañero," *Cuadernos Hispanoamericanos,* no. 262 (April 1972): 151–167.

# Luis Cernuda

*(21 September 1902 – 5 November 1963)*

Salvador Jiménez-Fajardo
*State University of New York at Binghamton*

BOOKS: *Perfil del aire* (Málaga: Imprenta Sur, 1927);

*La invitación a la poesía* (Madrid: Altolaguirre, 1933);

*Donde habite el olvido* (Madrid: Signo, 1934);

*El joven marino* (Madrid: Héroe, 1936);

*La realidad y el deseo* (Madrid: Cruz & Raya/Arbol, 1936; revised and enlarged edition, Mexico City: Tezontle, 1958; enlarged again, 1965);

*Ocnos* (London: Dolphin, 1942; enlarged edition, Madrid: Insula, 1949; enlarged again, Jalapa, Mexico: Universidad Veracruzana, 1963);

*Las nubes* (Buenos Aires: Schapire/Rama de Oro, 1943);

*Como quien espera el alba* (Buenos Aires: Losada, 1947);

*Tres narraciones* (Buenos Aires: Imán, 1948);

*Variaciones sobre tema mexicano* (Mexico City: Porrúa & Obregón, 1950);

*Poemas para un cuerpo* (Málaga: Dardo, 1957);

*Estudios sobre poesía española contemporánea* (Madrid: Guadarrama, 1957);

*Pensamiento poético en la lírica inglesa: Siglo XIX* (Mexico City: Imprenta Universitaria, 1958);

*Poesía y literatura*, 2 volumes (Barcelona: Seix Barral, 1960, 1964);

*Desolación de la quimera* (Mexico City: Mortiz, 1962);

*Crítica, ensayos y evocaciones,* edited by Luis Maristany (Barcelona: Seix Barral, 1970);

*Egloga,* edited by Gregorio Prieto (Madrid: Arte & Bibliofilia, 1970);

*Antología poética,* edited by Rafael Santos Torroella (Barcelona: Plaza & Janés, 1970);

*Perfil del aire; Con otras obras olvidadas e inéditas, documentos y epistolario,* edited by Derek Harris (London: Tamesis, 1971);

*Poesía completa,* edited by Derek Harris (London: Tamesis, 1971);

*Poesía completa,* edited by Derek Harris and Luis Maristany (Barcelona: Barral, 1974; revised, 1977);

*Invitación a la poesía de Luis Cernuda,* edited by Carlos-Peregrín Otero (Barcelona: Seix Barral, 1975);

*Antología poética, Luis Cernuda,* edited by Philip Silver (Madrid: Alianza, 1975);

*Prosa completa,* edited by Harris and Maristany (Barcelona: Barral, 1975);

*Epistolario inédito,* edited by Fernando Ortiz (Seville: Ayuntamiento, 1981);

*La familia intererrumpida* [play], edited by Octavio Paz (Barcelona: Sirmio, 1988).

**Editions in English:** *The Poetry of Luis Cernuda,* edited and translated by Anthony Edkins & Derek Harris (New York: New York University Press, 1977).

TRANSLATIONS: Friedrich Hölderlin, *Poemas* (Mexico City: Séneca, 1942; revised edition, Madrid: Visor, 1974);

William Shakespeare, *Troilo & Cresida* (Madrid: Insula, 1953).

Luis Cernuda's relationship with the reading public was uneasy from the outset of his poetic career, that is, from the 1927 appearance of *Perfil del aire* (The Air's Profile), his first collection. Although some reviews of the book were encouraging, even enthusiastic, most were decidedly negative. Cernuda's reaction was bitter, though understandable in light of his already total commitment to his craft. Such an early and unflinching commitment also explains what was at times described as his fragile temperament and his unusual sensitivity to criticism. On the other hand, Cernuda was not only a most gifted poet but also a very acute reader of poetry — that of others as well as his own — perceptive enough to realize that his day would indeed come, as it undoubtedly did. José Angel Valente places him at the forefront of the Generation of 1927: "Two poets, the two greatest of their generation, already reside in their myth: Lorca and Cernuda." This is not an isolated judgment. In the 1962 issue of *La caña gris* dedicated to Cernuda, important critics are unstinting in their praise: Jacob Muñoz, editor of the issue, remarks on Cernuda's decisive im-

*Luis Cernuda*

pact on younger generations of poets; Juan Gil-Albert affirms that Cernuda "has become fully what he already was incipiently for many: the greatest Spanish poet of his time"; and Francisco Brines recalls his discovery of Cernuda's *Como quien espera el alba* (Like Someone Waiting for the Dawn, 1947), which he read "slowly and amazed."

One should approach Cernuda's poetry, his statements about poetry, and the available autobiographical material with a clear idea of the play of self-projection and withdrawal, evasion and assertiveness. He explicitly pointed in this direction himself when, for instance, writing on past criticism of Miguel de Cervantes, he says of nineteenth-century critics: "En este y otros sentidos son inferiores a los escritores precedentes del tiempo de la Restauración, los cuales no olvidan la máscara, tan necesaria siempre al artista" (In this and other senses they are inferior to the preceding writers of

the time of the Restoration, who do not forget the mask, always so necessary to the artist; *Poesía y literatura,* volume 1, 1960). Cernuda's rhetoric of evasion inevitably surfaces in his metaphoric statements, which in any case tend to be autobiographical.

For Cernuda, as he maintains in an article on Gérard de Nerval written in 1962, poetry *is* life: "Otra de las varias causas para el encanto ejercido por Nerval sobre algunos lectores, está en que en él no existe separación entre la persona y la obra; ésta es proyección de aquélla. No hay, claro, complacencia ni vanidad personal en dicha fusión" (Another of the various reasons for the charm worked by Nerval upon some readers resides in the fact that for him there exists no separation between the man and the work; the latter is the projection of the former. There is, of course, neither complacency nor personal vanity in such fusion; *Prosa completa,* 1975).

Luis Cernuda y Bidón was born in Seville on 21 September 1902, the youngest of three children – he had two sisters. His father, Bernardo Cernuda Mousa, a colonel in a regiment of engineers, had little acknowledged impact on the poet's life. For example, he appears only as an authoritative, distant figure in the acerbic poem "La familia" (The Family – from *Como quien espera el alba*). The poet's mother was Amparo Bidón de Cernuda.

After earning his *bachillerato,* Cernuda studied law at the University of Seville, where he also took some general literature classes with Pedro Salinas, his future friend and initial mentor. Salinas came to know Cernuda better during the latter's last year at the university (1924–1925), after reading some lines of Cernuda's in a student magazine. Salinas, only thirty-two himself, encouraged the younger man in his writing and suggested to him readings in the classics and in French literature.

Cernuda was not to practice law. His poetic vocation had been growing and became firm after he was introduced by Salinas to Juan Ramón Jiménez, in September 1925. Owing to the help of these two friends, he was able to have nine of his poems published in the *Revista de Occidente* (December 1925).

Cernuda had been vaguely drawn to poetry from an early age. He once mentioned his reading of the Spanish poet Gustavo Adolfo Bécquer's verse on the occasion of the transfer of the latter's remains to Seville (1911) and surmised that "algo debió quedar, depositado en la subconsciencia, para algún día, más tarde, salir a flor de ella" (something must have remained, entrusted to the subconscious, that would later, one day, surface) (*Prosa completa*). Cernuda's estimation of Bécquer would always remain high; Cernuda considered his Sevillian ancestor the only true romantic poet of Spain. He wrote his 1934 collection, *Donde habite el olvido* (Where Oblivion Dwells), in direct reminiscence of Bécquer. Not only did the spareness of Bécquer's poetry attract Cernuda but the vicissitudes of Bécquer's life, as well, to which Cernuda found parallels in his own – difficult economic circumstances, incomprehension of the public, and a hidden passion: "Tierno y sombrío, soñador y desengañado, retraído y excepcional, esta figura que así podemos componer, ¿es la verdadera imagen de Bécquer? Aquí chocamos con el escollo humano sempiterno. Nos desconocemos profundamente los unos a los otros" (Tender and somber, disillusioned and a dreamer, solitary and exceptional, this figure that we can thus compose, is it Bécquer's true image? Here we come against the eternal human obstacle.

We are profoundly ignorant of one another) (*Prosa completa*).

Cernuda first tried to compose poetry at about the age of fourteen. He emphasized the coincidence of his awakening to sex and his desire to write poetry. Later, he insisted on the erotic component of his creative drive and identified desire as the aesthetic root of his poetry. Another important moment in the early formation of the poet occurred during his military service with the cavalry, when he was about twenty-one. On a riding exercise "las cosas se me aparecieron como si las viera por vez primera, como si por primera vez entrara yo en comunicación con ellas, y esa visión inusitada, a la experiencia" (things appeared to me as if I was seeing them for the first time, as if for the first time I was entering in communication with them, and that unaccustomed vision, at the same time, roused within me the urgency of expression, the urgency to recount that experience) (*Prosa completa*). The possibility of such heightened awareness is linked to the erotic instinct, to desire, and it forms for Cernuda the essence of poetry. Although the poetry originating in that early experience has not survived, Cernuda's vocation had taken firm root. Soon he began to compose the poems that would be published as *Perfil del aire*.

Cernuda completed his law studies in 1925. It was necessary to earn a living, and with this in mind he traveled to Madrid. He met José Ortega y Gasset, Ramón del Valle-Inclán, and some other major literary figures. Through the intervention of Salinas, who introduced him to the poet and printer Manuel Altolaguirre, the latter published *Perfil del aire* as a supplement to the poetry magazine *Litoral,* which he and Emilio Prados had established in Málaga.

Cernuda awaited the volume's appearance with anguished impatience. Reviews of the book were mixed at best. In some cases Cernuda was immediately ranked as only a disciple of his friend the older poet Jorge Guillén and was practically dismissed as not yet mature. A smaller number of reviews were enthusiastic; they remarked on the purity of the poet's voice and its individuality. Guillén himself expressed dismay at the prevalent misreading of the collection and asserted those qualities as well as the young poet's already notable craftsmanship.

The reception of *Perfil del aire* hurt Cernuda deeply, leaving scars that would last until his death. He was very sensitive to any allusions to his "immaturity" at that time. His anger was never to abate. It surfaces still in "A sus paisanos" (To His

*Drawing of Cernuda by Gregorio Prieto (from Prieto's* Lorca y la generación
del '27, *1977)*

Countrymen), the last poem he wrote: "No me
queréis, lo sé, y que os molesta / Cuanto escribo.
¿Os molesta? Os ofende" (You don't like me, I
know, and all I write / Disturbs you. Disturbs you?
It offends you) – from *Desolación de la quimera* (The
Disconsolate Chimera, 1962; translation by Derek
Harris).

In his 1971 edition of study of *Perfil del aire*
Harris examines the problem of influences and
gives the best answer yet to the question. Doubtless
there was some influence of Guillén on Cernuda,
but it was neither sustained nor profound. More
important are the presences of Jiménez, Stéphane
Mallarmé, and Pierre Reverdy – the last being
identified by Cernuda himself when no one had
noticed it – that marked both his poetic vision
and his craft. Salinas also left his imprint, though
superficially.

The year 1927, in which *Perfil del aire* first appeared, has acquired watershed implications in contemporary Spanish poetry. It is used to identify a
generation that many critics and readers consider
the most important group of Spanish poets since the
Golden Age. Cernuda says, in *Estudios sobre poesía
española contemporánea* (Studies on Contemporary
Spanish Poetry, 1957), that he prefers the date 1925
as generation marker, because it is the midpoint
year in the publication of the major generation
members' first collections. The reason generally ad-
duced for using 1927 as a label is that it marks the
commemoration by the group of the tercentenary of
the death of the baroque poet Luis de Góngora. The
event signaled this generation's recovery of their
great ancestor from the near oblivion where traditional critics had relegated him under the accusation
of obscurity and artificiality. For the younger poets

he upheld the importance granted to imagery in great poetry – such as they wanted to write – a devotion to metaphor in particular and to language, per se, in general.

The poetic climate in which *Perfil del aire* arrived was one of enthusiasm, inventiveness, and ferment. Movements noisily broke into the scene, some to be quickly forgotten: futurism, cubism, vorticism, creationism, ultraism. . . . Only creationism, and to a lesser extent ultraism, had any lasting effect. Creationism's principal tenets, those that were adopted by the group as a whole, were the fundamental importance of the poetic image and the autonomy of the poem. Ortega y Gasset, in *La deshumanización del arte* (The Dehumanization of Art, 1925), also mentions the importance of the element of play and the contingency of the work of art. But the notion that was to have the most profound impact on the poets was that of "pure poetry." This notion was embodied in the work of Jiménez, who became the mentor of the younger generation, the admired master to them all. The aspiration toward pure poetry, which also relates to ludic and contingent aspects, probably originated in the theories of the French poet Paul Valéry, who sought to eliminate from the poem all anecdotal or ideological content in order to allow words full and untrammeled play.

At the time of *Perfil del aire* Cernuda was responsive to some vanguardist tendencies. The idea of pure poetry does play some role in those early poems. On the other hand, the ludic and aleatory aspect of the new poetry did not attract him. What influenced him most was Jiménez's total commitment to his art and his rejection of vulgarity, that is the idea inherited from Mallarmé (and Góngora) that difficult poetry creates its own public. Although Jiménez's influence on Cernuda was to diminish twenty years later, and admiration would become for Cernuda angry rejection, the older poet's presence is visible throughout Cernuda's early work.

*Perfil del aire* reveals the ambivalent feelings of a sensitive young man. It is a highly solipsistic collection, moderately precious *(conceptista)* in style. Moments of frustration or of narcissistic self-contemplation are interspersed with occasional light-hearted pieces. At this point Cernuda was struggling to define his erotic direction, while his language was still unequal to his poetic intuition. The results of such uncertainties are poems of some emotional imprecision and a shimmering, elusive picture of reality.

When Cernuda prepared the first edition of *La realidad y el deseo* (Reality and Desire, 1936), he left out some poems of *Perfil del aire* and reworded oth-

ers. His changes show that he was dissatisfied with the emotional ambiguity of some pieces. Although several of them were already remarkably precise and unadorned, he wanted to move toward even greater simplicity. The new title for that section of poems attests to this wish: "Primeras poesías" (First Poems). The modifications, in those pieces that he retained, involve generally a clearer syntactical articulation, the suppression of overingenious imagery, and an effort toward greater emotional precision.

In July 1928 Cernuda's mother died, and he felt free to move permanently to Madrid. There he worked at the bookstore of Sánchez Cuesta, where he read copiously from the surrealists: "el superrealismo, con sus propósitos y técnica, había ganado mi simpatía. Leyendo aquellos libros primeros de Aragon, de Breton, de Eluard, de Crevel, percibía cómo eran míos también el malestar y la osadía que en dichos libros hallaban voz. Un mozo solo, sin ninguno de los apoyos que, gracias a la fortuna y las relaciones, dispensa la sociedad a tantos, no podía menos de sentir hostilidad hacia esa sociedad en medio de la cual vivía como extraño. Otro motivo de desacuerdo, aún más hondo, existía en mí; pero ahí prefiero no entrar ahora" (Surrealism, with its aims and techniques, had won my sympathy. Reading those first books by Aragon, by Breton, and Eluard, by Crevel, I realized how the uneasiness and daring that found voice in these same books was also mine. A young man alone, with none of the supports that, thanks to fortune and connections society grants to so many, I could not but feel hostility toward that society in the midst of which I lived as a stranger. There existed in me another reason for discordance, even deeper, but I prefer not to enter into it now) (*Prosa completa*). This other reason was his homosexuality.

Through the intermediary of Salinas, Cernuda obtained a position in the fall of 1928 as lecturer at the University of Toulouse. He traveled to Paris during vacation. There is no record that he met any of the surrealist writers whose work he had read, but his visit to the French capital, where surrealism had originated, must have inspired him, for he wrote his first surrealist poems upon his return to Toulouse. They were to form part of the collection "Un río, un amor" (A River, a Love – in *La realidad y el deseo)*, which he finished in Madrid in 1929. In 1931 he completed his second surrealist selection: "Los placeres prohibidos" (Forbidden Pleasures – also in *La realidad y el deseo*).

Surrealism allowed Cernuda to delve deeper within himself, to assert freely and powerfully his

*Dámaso Alonso, Cernuda, Federico García Lorca, and Vicente Aleixandre*

discontent, and to introduce sociopolitical concerns into his poetry. Surrealism also answered the needs of his rebellious nature and sanctioned as legitimate certain poetic elements from the unconscious to which he had heretofore not given play.

In "Historial de un libro" (A Book's History, 1958) Cernuda describes the birth of his first surrealist poem: "al escribir el poema 'Remordimiento en traje de noche,' encontré de pronto camino y forma para expresar en poesía cierta parte de aquello que no había dicho hasta entonces ( . . . ) uno tras otro, surgieron los tres poemas primeros de la serie que luego llamaría *Un río, un amor*, dictados por un impulso similar al que animaba a los superrealistas" (As I wrote 'Remordimiento en traje de noche' [Remorse in Evening Dress] I found suddenly the way and form to express in poetry a certain part of that which I had not said until then. One after the other the first three poems of the series that I would call *Un río, un amor* surged forth, dictated by an impulse similar to that which animated the surrealists) (*Prosa completa*). Though this spurt of writing seems to suggest the well-known surrealist tenet of automatic writing, the underlying careful form of Cernuda's poems of this period contradict this assumption.

At any rate, Cernuda is careful to indicate that the impulse was *similar* to that of the surrealists.

With a few exceptions, the underlying theme of these surrealist-style poems is rejection. Love seems impossible, a vain yet devastating obsession. Social man is systematically indicted as either hypocritical, blind, or inconsequential. The poet's ability to see through the miasma of social habit is not a privilege but a burden — especially when escape is impossible. The mind is a rusted mechanism, consumed in some holocaust. When deprived of love, the poet is a ghostlike figure, the world gray and seamless.

However, the world of "Un río, un amor" and "Los placeres prohibidos" is not unabatedly negative. Several poems erect dreamlike landscapes where contraries merge and serenity is possible. "Nevada," for example (in "Un río, un amor"), offers scenery in which "Las noches transparentes / Abren luces soñadas / Sobre las aguas o tejados puros / Constelados de fiesta" (The transparent nights / Disclose dream lights on the waters, / Reflect the pure holiday-like / Constellated roof-tops — translation by Anthony Edkins). American names with exotic connotations of adventure, or the romance of the cinema, produce idealized horizons of the mind, as in "Durango" and "Daytona." In "Historial de un libro" Cernuda recalls: "Dado mi gusto por los aires de *jazz,* recorría catálogos de discos y, a veces, un título me sugería posibilidades poéticas, como este de 'I want to be alone in the South' . . . " (Given my taste for jazz tunes, I pored over record catalogs and, at times a title suggested poetic possibilities to me, such as that of *I want to be alone in the South* . . . ) Another such poem is "Sombras blancas en los mares del sur" (White Shadows in the South Seas), whose title was suggested by a movie.

His surrealist period liberated Cernuda both psychologically and poetically. Leaving behind the constraints of rhyme, he adopted free verse and also began to compose prose poetry. This component of Cernuda's work, which has only recently come under scrutiny – by James Valender in particular – would come to full fruition in *Ocnos* (1942), written in England. There are eight prose poems in "Los placeras prohibidos" as the collection now appears in *La realidad y el deseo.* Thematically speaking the prose pieces do not differ from those in verse; most often they refer to the failure of love.

In terms of form Cernuda's prose poems are the first of their kind in Spanish literature. Not to be confused with poetic prose, which had a significant history in Spain, the prose poem as Cernuda conceives it stems directly from the French tradition with which he had become familiar. Valender, who praises the unusual concentration achieved in the prose poems, considers them an autonomous cycle at the heart of "Los placeres prohibidos." They manifest the careful control of craft over the discontinuities of the self and the vision of an anchorless, empty world, and they confirm the selective use that the poet made of surrealist techniques.

Cernuda soon abandoned surrealism. At the end of his surrealist experiment, he wrote "Carta a Lafcadio Wluiki" (Letter to Lafcadio Wluiki, collected in *Poesía y literatura*), which may be considered an early version of Cernuda's poetics. The essay is particularly valuable because it captures an incipient stage of the poet's practice of self-diffraction. This mode was to evolve into his use of dramatic monologue in the 1940s (as in "Lázaro" and "Quetzalcóatl") and was to underpin the use of autodialogue – self-address as "tú" – that characterizes much of his poetry.

The "Carta" offers several ideas that will inform Cernuda's poetry henceforth: the fall from youth as the speaker's permanent condition, occasionally retrievable through poetry; the crucial importance of imagination; imagination as memory; memory as the repository of self-understanding; and the possibility of an individual ethics of "vitalism," though here the controlling world is "individual."

Cernuda wrote his next collection, *Donde habite el olvido,* to exorcise, or contain, an unhappy love affair. One of the fundamental ideas in *Donde habite el olvido* and the following collection, "Invocaciones" (Invocations, in *La realidad y el deseo*), is that of the fall. The fall from love in *Donde habite el olvido* actually expands, as it did in "Los placeres prohibidos," into the more broadly encompassing idea of a fall from grace, or a fall into time, as explored in "Invocaciones." Beyond this, however, it is from the aesthetic point of view that *Donde habite el olvido* is important. Cernuda had been rereading Bécquer at the time he wrote the collection (1932–1933); "Donde habite el olvido" is a line from the "Rima LXVI" (in *Rimas,* 1860–1861) by Bécquer. While Cernuda remembered the love experience at the source of the collection as sordid, he realized the book's importance as a key moment in the development of his craft.

*Donde habite el olvido* consists of sixteen numbered poems and a final, titled one, "Los fantasmas del deseo" (Ghosts of Desire). They represent an unremitting indictment of love. The opening poem presents the speaker's disillusionment and his implicit wish to escape from present suffering. *Donde habite el olvido* actually calls for the suppression of desire:

> Allá donde termine este afán que exige un dueño
>      a imagen suya,
> Sometiendo a otra vida su vida,
> Sin más horizonte que otros ojos frente a frente.
>
> (There where this longing – which requires a
>      master in its own image,
> Submitting its life to another life,
> No horizon except other eyes, face to face –
> There where this longing will end.)
>
> – translation by
> Anthony Edkins (in *The Poetry of Luis Cernuda,*
> edited by Anthony Edkins and Derek Harris, 1977)

The flaw at love's core appears to be its narcissistic nature. The suppression in the poem of any direct reference to the speaker's wishes results in a great concentration of effect. Cernuda's delineation of his "here and now" in terms of "there and never," shows that suffering is inescapable, since one can conceive of escape only in terms of one's imprisoning life. Death, or oblivion, offers a possible abstraction from the temporal. Childhood, although closer to nothingness – or liberation – is already limited

*Cernuda in 1932; drawing by Ramón Gaya*

by existence in *Donde habite el olvido.* However, childhood does appear at times as an inviolate Eden.

In 1931 Spain had become a republic, and two years later Cernuda had endorsed the leftist ideas of the revolutionary review *Octubre,* published by his friend and fellow poet Rafael Alberti. Cernuda's commitment to the Left would not be long, though he would continue to support the republic. His interest in politics was born of indignation, not deep-seated socialist conviction. Although liberal in his sympathies, he remained apolitical most of his life. Apart from the poem "Vientres sentados" (Settled Stomachs), which appeared in *Octubre* (April 1934), Cernuda wrote no specifically political pieces during the early 1930s. While participating in the ideological renewal brought about by the republic, he was wholly taken up with his craft.

In 1935 Cernuda began the poems of "Invocaciones a las gracias del mundo," whose later title was shortened to "Invocaciones." He began to study and translate Friedrich Hölderlin, with the

help of the German poet Hans Gebser. Their translations appeared in the review *Cruz y Raya* in 1936, the year when the first edition of *La realidad y el deseo* was also published.

The fall into time, which underlies the reminiscence of the fall into love in *Donde habite el olvido,* is also the theme that runs through "Invocaciones." But here Cernuda allows his imagination to generate fragments of stability. In this collection, he wanted to expand the limits of his lyricism, and he tried to compose longer poems, in reaction to the prevailing tendency toward the short, compact lyric. He was gaining confidence in his art and felt that it could express "everything" in contrast to the limitations of "pure" poetry. Cernuda was less interested in transmitting a vision – of the stable reality that the poet may at times fleetingly perceive – than in creating a vision through language. This broader horizon can only be grasped in contradistinction to the narrow one of actual existence. Therefore the contrast, or opposition, between society and a pagan ideal repeatedly issues forth. Social man is denounced as a fraud and an insubstantial copy.

In opposition, solitude can be fertile, and allow what is lasting and beautiful in nature to be revealed, as in "Soliloquio del farero." In this poem Cernuda uses for the first time the technique of personification to explore the effects of consciously sought solitude. Such solitude is an intrinsic part of the child's condition, as an inner radiance:

> De niño, entre las pobres guaridas de la tierra,
> Quieto en ángulo oscuro,
> Buscaba en ti, encendida guirnalda,
> Mis auroras futuras y furtivos nocturnos,
> Y en ti los vislumbraba,
> Naturales y exactos, también libres y fieles,
> A semejanza mía,
> A semejanza tuya, eterna soledad.
>
> (As a child, amid the poor dens of the earth,
> Quiet in a dark corner
> I sought you, inflamed garland,
> My future dawn and furtive evening stars,
> And I glimpsed them in you,
> Natural and exact, also free and faithful,
> In my likeness,
> In your likeness, eternal solitude.)

Humankind lost that early knowledge because they sought the company of their kind, misunderstanding the value of solitude; appearance veiled the shape of the world. Once regained, solitude makes possible cosmic awareness.

The somewhat hopeful cast of "Soliloquio" is also characteristic of all of "Invocaciones." With this collection Cernuda entered a period of slightly heightened expectations and growing confidence in his poetic craft. Such hope is relative and only perceptible because of the despairing nihilism of *Donde habite el olvido*. The most constant concern in "Invocaciones" continues to be temporality or topics related to it. In contrast to the preceding period, Cernuda indicates that some intuition of plentitude may at times be accessible to the poet.

The first period of Cernuda's development contains all the topics and formal characteristics of his later poetry. Society exhibits the most alienating aspects of reality, nature its most hopeful. The opposition also embodies a fundamental ambivalence in Cernuda's work: the poet *sees* insofar as he retains a pristine imagination that only closeness to nature can provide; but he can only speak if he is a skilled craftsman, a sophisticated artificer who can create form. His solution is that beauty and love can be expressions of an ideal reality and that the poem can express them: the artificial participates in the es-

sential. The solution, however, is not completely satisfactory. The tension remains a subtext in Cernuda's major compositions throughout and intensifies in the great poems on art and artists of *Desolación de la quimera*.

Another fundamental idea that emerges from the early poetry and Cernuda's theoretical comments is that the poetic text can be an instrument of self-knowledge. As he tries to plumb his inner truth the poet investigates projected figures of himself.

The Spanish Civil War broke out in July 1936. That same month, Cernuda was able to leave the country as secretary to the republic's ambassador to France, Don Alvaro de Albornoz, whose daughter, Concha de Albornoz, was the poet's good friend. Cernuda returned to Spain in September. In the winter of 1937 he went as a volunteer to the Guadarrama front, where he fought until the spring. In 1937 and 1938 he collaborated on the leftist magazines *Hora de España*, edited by Juan Gil-Albert, and Alberti's *El Mono Azul*. Cernuda left for England in 1938; his friend the English poet Stanley Richardson had obtained a visa for him as well as a post as assistant to the Spanish teacher in the Cranleigh School, Surrey. In January 1939 Cernuda became a lecturer at the University of Glasgow. He was never to return to Spain.

Cernuda wrote *Las nubes* (The Clouds, 1943) during this most turbulent period of his life. Having settled in England, he found that the climate and countryside did not suit him. World War II, hard on the heels of the Spanish Civil War, intensified his pessimism and misanthropy: the world seemed chaotic; history moved through bloodshed toward nothingness.

*Las nubes* shows Cernuda in control of his mature manner. He uses dramatic monologues to great effect, as well as, on occasion, the autodialogue. The poems tend to be long and tightly structured; the language is straightforward. Life with death, the equivalence of love and death, and the role of the poet are recurring themes. For the first time Spain makes its appearance as a subject of poetry. The title of the first poem in the book was to have been "Elegía a la luna de España" (Elegy to the Spanish Moon), according to Harris, and was later changed to "Noche de luna" (Lunar Night). No doubt the disaster of the civil war accounted for the bleak view of history that this poem expresses. The moon contemplates the violent follies of humankind and the barren future: "El silencio de un mundo que ha sido / y la pura belleza de la nada" (The silence of a world that has been / And the tranquil purity of nothingness). Yet, in the rush toward emptiness, the

*Guests at a dinner honoring Cernuda on the publication of his* La realidad y el deseo *(1936). Cernuda is seated at the head of the table.*

poet, a dreamer of eternities, also has his place. This initial meditation on death, history, and time anticipates topics treated in the rest of the collection.

While during the civil war Cernuda's sympathies were clearly on the side of the republic, the country's self-destruction elicited in him an appeal that transcended partisanship. In the poem "Elegía española (I)" Spain is the vital mother that overcomes all conflicts and will outlast this one, too: "Tú sola sobrevives" (You alone survive). The elegy incorporates a strategy of confrontation and resolution, through which the hackneyed metaphor homeland-equals-mother acquires new potency and concreteness. In *Las nubes* Cernuda develops further and with a surer hand the large-scale compositions that he had tried in "Invocaciones." During this time of turmoil Cernuda was particularly drawn to topics that would allow him to explore human relationships to God (or the gods). "Resaca en Sansueña" (The Surf in Sansueña), a dramatic meditation on the humans' distance from the pagan divine, turns on the lack of awareness of separation from the tutelary gods. "La adoración de los Magos" (The Adoration of the Magi), the most specifically Christian of these pieces, though more in its anecdote than its ultimate import, ends in disillusionment and also unawareness for the Magi. They

cannot recognize the god whose arrival they had come to salute. "Lázaro," another great dramatic monologue, examines the protagonist's unwilling return to life. For Lazarus, Christ's miracle is a summons to renewed penitence, but he sees in Christ's eyes the reflection of God's truth, if not God, and he seeks God's help through Jesus.

The last poem of *Las nubes,* "El ruiseñor sobre la piedra" (The Nightingale Above the Stone), is the first of Cernuda's compositions on Philip II though more specifically concerned with the Escorial than with its builder. The poem is a meditation on the palace-monastery, and on exile. In powerful strophes recalling the classical Spanish *lira* the poet sings of the building as the spirit of his country and of his confidence in the power of language to transcend his own ephemerality:

Y si tu imagen tiembla en las aguas tendidas,
Es tan sólo una imagen;
Y si el tiempo nos lleva, ahogando tanto afán insatisfecho,
Es sólo como un sueño;
Que ha de vivir tu voluntad de piedra,
Ha de vivir, y nosotros contigo.

(And if your image trembles in the extended
      waters,
It is merely an image;
And if time takes us, drowning so much unsatisfied

yearning,
It is only a dream;
For your will of stone is to live,
It is to live, and us with you.)

In this poem Cernuda achieves the spare power of his best work through a lyrical meditation that approximates the purity of song, which, he felt, is the attribute of all great poetry.

In the midst of World War II, the disasters of the Spanish Civil War still fresh in his mind, Cernuda needed constancy; his effort to stabilize memories became especially demanding. He composed the prose poems of *Ocnos* – whose first version was completed by 1941 – as "un rescate de mi vida, de la vida en general" (a salvaging of my life, of life in general) (as quoted by Valender). In *Ocnos* Cernuda re-creates for himself a mythical childhood. Albanio, the principal figure in these compositions, exists in an Edenic state of innocence, in touch with the divine core of his being, able to merge, at times, with the eternal present of creation. Later, as adolescence approaches, the state of innocence is threatened because it is conceptualized. The onset of sexual desire signals the youth's fall into the world. Possession now must remain always partial, unlike the total merging available to the child. At the same time, poetry offers the possibility of achieving some sort of transcendence. With *Ocnos* and his many other compositions in this style, Cernuda recovers the meditative tradition in poetry, which Spain had forgotten since the Golden Age.

*Como quien espera el alba,* Cernuda's next collection, opened a period of even more philosophical poetry. But even in his most contemplative pieces Cernuda never forgets the tenet of always keeping an "asidero plástico" (plastic hold – a grasp on reality) at the origin of his meditations. Perhaps the period when he composed the book (1941–1944), in the midst of World War II, led Cernuda to seek some distance from events, trying to consider values that would supersede the current madness.

Always present in Cernuda's poetry is the paradox of human mortality and the ability to create lasting beauty. Reflection on mortality leads him to question God's role, as in "Las ruinas" (The Ruins):

Oh Dios. Tú que nos has hecho
Para morir, ¿por qué nos infundiste
La sed de eternidad, que hace al poeta?
¿Puedes dejarás, siglo tras siglo,
Caer como vilanos que deshace un soplo
Los hijos de la luz en la tiniebla avara?

(Oh God. You who have made us to die,
Why did you fill us with the thirst
For eternity that creates the poet?
Can you allow the sons of light to fall,
Century after century, into the greedy shadow
Like thistle-down blown away on the wind?)
                                          – translation by Harris

The deity's power is set in doubt since humans are more frail than their own constructions. The poet learns that ephemeral beauty is beauty still and more worthy of his desire than "eternos dioses sordos" (deaf eternal gods). Yet, because the more individualized objects, beings, and events are, the more they are vulnerable to time; that is, potentiality is preferable to actuality, as childhood (or youth) is to maturity.

Traditionally students of Cernuda have followed his cues in reading his poetry, focusing on reality and desire, the wish for eternity within the flow of time, and the creation of beauty out of disjunction. To those themes should be added the changing configurations of the self that produce changing desire, which in turn produces a changing reality. The reality of death is also an important theme.

In an essay about Jorge Manrique, one of his favorite poets, Cernuda says: "La muerte no es algo distinto de la vida, es parte integrante de ella, cuya perfección misma se logra en la muerte, sin la cual la vida no tendría más sentido que un ocioso juego de luces y sombras" (Death is not something different from life, it is an integral part of it, whose very perfection is achieved in death, without which life would have no more sense than an idle play of lights and shadows) (*Prosa completa*). In *Como quien espera el alba* Cernuda reflects on death rather than reacting emotionally to it. The intellectual acquaintance with death's complexion is accompanied by a marked simplicity of language, an increasingly conversational tone, and the use of muted rhythms that follow the development of thought. In "Elegía anticipada" (Anticipated Elegy) death elicits acceptance. Because it joins love in affirmation, its anticipation no longer brings despair.

In the dramatic monologue "Quetzalcóatl," Cernuda confronts death from a different angle: his speaker is an older soldier (Bernal Díaz), a character totally unlike himself. The title refers to the god-king whose prophesied arrival, the Indians thought, was fulfilled by Hernán Cortés. The poem unites both aspects of Quetzalcóatl as god of life and death, but seen from the old soldier's point of view, on the brink of death and in terms of blood conquest. Like Quetzalcóatl, Cortés unites within him

*Cernuda, circa 1951 (photograph courtesy of the Mount Holyoke College Library)*

both life and death. Ultimately Cortés's fate is the same as that of Montezuma, his victim, and Quetzalcóatl is but another aspect of the sacrificial hero-king. From this perspective even art appears vulnerable to death, but the original darkness is also a source of light. Cernuda's consideration of death becomes a source of poetry. "Quetzalcóatl" is one of Cernuda's most successful dramatic monologues. He manages to re-create a thoroughly cogent point of view, alien from his own, allowing character to develop by means of a carefully paced narrative. At the same time, he succeeds in producing an infrastructure that interrelates constant concerns of his art: death in life; poetry; and myth.

From 1939 to 1943 Cernuda was lecturer in Spanish at the University of Glasgow, and from 1943 to 1945 at Cambridge, where he lived at Emmanuel College. These latter two years of his English residence are those he recalled with greatest

fondness. At this time Cernuda read the English classics and the King James Bible on a daily basis, as well as some philosophy, that of Søren Kierkegaard in particular. Cernuda also collaborated in the *Bulletin of Spanish Studies,* printed in Liverpool. From 1945 to 1947 Cernuda taught at the Spanish Institute in London. He did not enjoy the city and spent his vacations in Cornwall, near the coast. He did take advantage of the artistic scene in London and went frequently to concerts, especially of Wolfgang Amadeus Mozart's music.

In March 1947 Cernuda was offered a post at Mount Holyoke College, in South Hadley, Massachusetts. The position was facilitated by his friend Concha de Albornoz. On 10 September Cernuda left England for the United States. He looked forward to his new home with hope and much anticipation.

Cernuda began the poems in "Vivir sin estar viviendo" (Living Without Being Alive – in the

1958 edition of *La realidad y el deseo*) at Cambridge and completed the volume at Mount Holyoke. This collection elaborates his inner disjunction, already stated in the title. Though the first four pieces – "Cuatro poemas para una sombra" (Four Poems for a Ghost) – are love poems, many of the remaining compositions deal with humankind in history. The gaze backward that tries to situate past aspects of the self is the characteristic opening of several important compositions: "El poeta" (The Poet), "Las edades" (The Ages), "Ser de Sansueña" (Being of Sansueña), and "Viendo volver" (Seeing Return). Cernuda's expression continues to move toward straightforward, daily usage in muted rhythm. The autodialogue is used almost invariably. Again, many poems are meditations originating in some concrete experience.

During the last half of his residence in England, Cernuda wanted to look ahead undeluded. Although he hoped that the removal to the United States would bring with it a complete change and perhaps a new beginning, the loss of his past was like a loss of substance that creates a void. "Viendo volver" centers on this very problem, as a species of commentary on Heraclitus's famous dictum: "Upon those who step into the same rivers flow other and yet other waters."

> Irías, y verías
> Todo igual, cambiado todo,
> Así como tú eres
> El mismo y otro. ¿Un río
> A cada instante
> No es él y diferente?

> (You would go and you would see
> Everything the same, everything changed
> As you yourself are
> The same and another. Is not a river
> Each instant
> Itself and different?)

"Vivir sin estar viviendo" liquidated the past, as it were, as possible support of the identity that Cernuda sought. In "Con las horas contadas" (With Time Running Out – also in the 1958 *La realidad y el deseo*), the poems are imbued with the sense of pressing time implied by the title, a mood that continues into *Desolación de la quimera,* Cernuda's final book published in his lifetime. "Con las horas contadas" was written between 1950 and 1956, begun at Mount Holyoke, and finished in Mexico. The collection includes a series of poems on familiar topics – meditations on history, considerations by Cernuda of his own past as a man and as a poet, reflections on poetry, and also a separate group of love poems, *Poemas para un cuerpo* (Poems for a Body, separately published in 1957), which celebrates erotic fulfillment. In "Historial de un libro" Cernuda gives an overall view of the whole grouping. From the point of view of technique, he mentions that he was opting for shorter compositions with occasional assonant rhyme and the tendency toward song (*Prosa completa*).

The initial optimism that had buoyed Cernuda at Mount Holyoke was soon followed by the familiar sense of isolation that seemed to pursue him wherever he went. Relative economic comfort was not sufficient to allay such feelings. The winters of New England seemed interminable to him. In 1950 he applied unsuccessfully for a university post in Puerto Rico, and his efforts to obtain some summer teaching at the Colegio de México also failed.

While a resident of Massachusetts, Cernuda had been going to Mexico to spend his summer vacations. Though he found the states more pleasant than England, these interludes in a country where he could again speak his own language and where customs seemed in most respects more congenial to a son of Andalusia became quite important to him. The poet found it increasingly difficult to return to his Massachusetts home. After the summer of 1952 he decided to give up his teaching position, whose advantages could not be denied. Cernuda settled in Mexico in November 1952. He had entered into a love affair while in Mexico in 1951, one upon which he would look back with marked affection, as he would the poems that celebrated it, in *Poemas para un cuerpo*.

In spite of the earthiness the title leads one to expect, *Poemas para un cuerpo* deals with the interiorization of the love experience and attains at times levels of total, Platonic idealization. The body is the synecdoche of love, more than its object; it becomes simply the "loved one" and in the opening poem, "Salvador," is displaced at the very moment of its actualization as it becomes a poetic object. Out of a minute of love's existence eternities can be born. In these poems Cernuda is temporarily reconciled with reality, or with its image through a lover's eyes. Though the anguish of decay remains, it leads not to denial but to exaltation. For once, in the total subordination to the love experience as to an ethical imperative, desire and reality meet and coincide. Thus *Poemas para un cuerpo* is an effective answer to many of the queries of "Con las horas contadas."

Cernuda's reading interests were always wide-ranging. He was familiar, of course, with the Spanish mystics, but he was also acquainted with esoteric doctrine: for instance, he knew the writings of Abu-Bakr Muhammad Ibn-Arabi well and had probably read Louis Massignon's *La Passion d' Al-Hallaj* – Cernuda mentions the Muslim saint in "Historial de un libro." His contemplative turn of mind drew him also to philosophy. It was the philosophical bent of Hölderlin's poetry that had attracted him earlier, as well as the German poet's reflections on Greek myth. Cernuda's copious readings from the English poets, with special interest in the metaphysical tradition and in the Romantics, helped him produce *Pensamiento poético en la lírica inglesa: Siglo XIX* (Poetic Thought in English Lyricism: Nineteenth Century, 1958). During his stay at Mount Holyoke he had read Hermann Diels's *Fragmente der Vorsokratiker* (Fragments of the Pre-Socratics, 1903) and John Burnet's *Early Greek Philosophy* (1802). The results of such wide interests are apparent not only in Cernuda's poetry but also in his critical work, which encompasses Spanish, French, English, Russian, and Spanish-American literature, with occasional incursions into American literature. He dwelt with equal ease among the classics of the tradition and among minor figures, such as Ronald Firbank and Dashiell Hammett. In fact Cernuda's prose – which has not received sufficient attention – reveals a subtle essayist, who can be analytical and impressionistic at once and is always rewarding.

Cernuda's attitude toward Spain had grown ambivalent during his stay in England and the United States. The despair of seeing his country humiliated under Francisco Franco's yoke led him on occasion to feel the same humiliation in himself. Upon his moving to Mexico, Cernuda reexamined the burden of exile, feeling it more keenly because his new home seemed both closer to Spain and vastly different. The first poem of "Con las horas contadas" considers exile in a historical context: "Aguila y rosa" (Eagle and Rose) belongs to his Philip II trilogy (the other two poems in the set are "El ruiseñor sobre la piedra" [Nightingale upon the Stone] and "Silla del rey" [Throne of the King]). In "Aguila y rosa" Cernuda recalls Philip's stay in England, his marriage to Mary Tudor (the "rose"), and his return, alone, to Spain. The marriage proved a sterile failure that prompted Philip's departure, leaving Mary in England.

At times Cernuda seemed to feel that, though only the vaguest memories remained with him from his Andalusian youth, they were more substantial than much that was present. At other times, as in "Otra fecha" (Another Thing), he tries to convince himself that nothing is actually left of that past. Yet the rejection of nostalgia leaves one in an uncertain present. In "Limbo" the exilic condition is doubled: that of the poet among ordinary people and in a for-

eign land. Of the eight poems in "Con las horas contadas" that address exile in some manner, only one, "El viajero" (The Traveler), considers the new land, Mexico, another home. It is this poem, as well as some of Cernuda's comments in "Historial de un libro," that lends credence to the notion of Mexico's being a regained paradise for him.

Realizing that his past selves are to remain in essence irretrievable, Cernuda attends to his present condition with stark objectivity in "Nocturno yanqui" (Yankee Nocturne), one of his major meditations, which proceeds to a clear self-analysis in bare, laconic language. Irony and restraint help him to reassesss the ethical core of his being. His search for love remains paramount, part of the self-affirmation that always was the crucible of his integrity. The truth of the self lies in the present that contains and accepts all his past choices:

> Quien eres, tu vida era;
> Uno sin otro no sois,
> Tú lo sabes.
> Y es fuerza seguir, entonces,
> Aun el miraje perdido,
> Hasta el día
> Que la historia se termine,
> Para ti al menos.
>
> 　　　Y piensas
> Que así vuelves
> Donde establas al comienzo
> Del soliloquio: contigo
> Y sin nadie.
>
> Mata la luz, y a la cama.
>
> (You are now what your life was;
> You are not one without the other,
> You know that.
> And you must carry on then,
> Still after the lost mirage,
> Until the day
> When the story comes to an end,
> For you at least.
>
> 　　　And so you think
> That you are back
> Where you were at the start
> Of your soliloquy: alone
> With yourself.
>
> Put out the light and go to bed.)
> 　　　　　　　　　　　　– translation by Harris

Cernuda had begun his second volume of prose poems, *Variaciones sobre tema mexicano* (Variations on a Mexican Theme), in 1950, after returning from his first summer in Mexico, and it was pub-

La noche, el baile

Una queja burlona,
Una voz languorosa,
Voz que cantando habla
Íntimamente para un hombre,
Brilla con diamantes
Arrebatados a los ojos.

En un acento cuántas vidas.
La noche honda sobre un río,
Aguas abajo los amantes
Labio contra labio.

*Manuscript for a poem by Cernuda that was posthumously published in* Cuadernos Hispanoamericanos, *October 1976 (Collection of José María Capote Benot)*

Una mano sus pétalos abriendo
Sobre el andén que huye, ante los o
ojada luego
Lentamente se pliega a la tristeza

Un sol tras los cristales desmayado
Asan, asan, en la aventura

Ríe en las venas tan azules,
Ríe en las venas, en el cuerpo,
En el cuerpo de nuevo entre sus ala
a la luz del olvido.

Cernuda at Lake Arrowhead, California, in summer 1960, while he
was a visiting professor at UCLA

lished two years later. The theme of the book is the presence of Spain in Mexico. Cernuda felt that he was returning to his origins when he recovered his language and other aspects of his culture in this new country. He was equally fascinated by the turn that its people's traditions had given to those of Spain. But it is not Cernuda's intention in *Variaciones* to describe Mexican culture, but rather to reflect on it, to use it as another means of self-exploration. No doubt the fact that Cernuda fell in love while in Mexico, and that the affair seems to have been a positive experience, maintained in him the affection he felt for the country.

In Mexico, Cernuda stayed principally at the house of Concha Méndez and Manuel Altolaguirre, whose kindness and friendship he found most propitious for his work. *Estudios sobre poesía española contemporánea* was written during the early to mid 1950s; it first appeared in installments in the review *México en la cultura* (1953–1955). The unorthodox comments in the book caused some stir at first, es-

pecially because the nearly ceremonial gestures of praise, which had become de rigueur when speaking of certain major poets, were certainly absent from its pages. Nevertheless, the volume remains a penetrating analysis of its topic, original and informed, and still a most useful source. It was probably instrumental, for instance, in the reevaluation of the poetry of Miguel de Unamuno, whom Cernuda considered the greatest Spanish poet so far in the century.

From Mexico, Cernuda had traveled back to teach at UCLA during the summer of 1960 and at San Francisco State College for the 1961–1962 academic year. While at UCLA he met Carlos P. Otero, who was presenting a doctoral thesis on Cernuda's work; the friendship that ensued revitalized the poet, so that upon his return to Mexico he wrote the core of what was to be *Desolación de la quimera*. This collection would be completed while at San Francisco State College.

Although Cernuda's bitterness resurfaces in several poems of this collection, and certain *pièces de circonstance* express personal antagonisms still occasioned by the conviction that some critics had arbitrarily and obtusely misread him, recognition of his work was growing in Spain. In 1955 the review *Cántico* of Córdoba had published an homage to Cernuda. In 1962 the Valencian poetry review *La Caña Gris* devoted a double issue to another "Homenage a Luis Cernuda," in which the younger generation of poets asserted their indebtedness to him. In the meantime, an enlarged edition of *La realidad y el deseo* had appeared in Mexico (1958). A volume of his poetry (*Poesie*, 1962) was also published in Italy, in the prestigious collection "Poeti europei" by Lerici Editori in Milan. Such belated recognition only partially counteracted the echoes of his legend as a disdainful, oversensitive, somewhat dangerous, and unnecessarily complicated poet, echoes that still reached him from Spain.

In *Luis Cernuda: A Study of the Poetry* (1973) Harris describes *Desolación de la quimera* as "an attempt to summarize the lessons [Cernuda] has learnt from the long investigation of himself. This final collection of poems is his own conclusion to his life, produced under the shadow of a presentiment that he was soon to die, a presentiment that turns this book into a poetic last will and testament designed to leave behind him an accurate self-portrait and a duly notarized statement of his account with life." Besides the occasional pieces and personal reminiscences, the principal topics dealt with in the collection are still love, Spain, and exile, as well as a series of poems on artists and on aesthetic experience. Love and art had been the central facts of Cernuda's poet's existence. It was of fundamental importance at this late stage of his life for him to reassert them as the sufficient, powerful justifications of his being.

Cernuda wrote the first poem of the collection about his favorite composer, Mozart. The poem sets Mozart at the apex of all Europe's artistic achievement. According to Cernuda, one can learn liberation through such music should he open his mind to its nobility. Discontinuous reality is given form, and God's capricious creation is restructured by music. Music returns to humankind a parcel of divinity, the lasting essence that owes obeisance to no gods: "Si, el hombre pasa, pero su voz perdura, / Nocturno ruiseñor o alondra mañanera, / Sonando en las ruinas del cielo de los dioses" (Yes, man passes, but his voice lasts long, / Nocturnal nightingale or morning lark, / Ringing in the ruins of heaven and the gods).

For Cernuda, the artist does not reproduce reality, he recomposes it. Beauty exists in reality's artistic reincarnation, and the artist regenerates himself as his core of desire produces form. Cernuda's Titian, in "*Ninfa y pastor* por Tiziano" (*Nymph and Shepherd* by Titian), is as young and vibrant as the figures he paints, even though he is in the hundredth year of his life.

In "Luis de Baviera escucha *Lohengrin*" (Ludwig of Bavaria Listens to *Lohengrin*), the longest poem of *Desolación de la quimera*, Cernuda meditates on art and love together, as well as on the possible transcendence inherent in both and the achievement of a kind of permanence through music. Yet the disjunctions posited by the poem – those of inner and outer worlds, of self and image – do not in fact reach hypostasized unity. Ludwig's dream turns the legendary Lohengrin into his own mirror image, but self-love can find no consummation: "¿No le basta que exista, fuera de él, lo amado? / Contemplar a lo hermoso, ¿no es respuesta bastante?" (Is it not enough that what he loves exists outside him? / Is not the contemplation of beauty sufficient recompense?). The union, begun as spectacle on the stage and spectacle in his mind echoing one another, is completed in alienation: "Fundido con el mito al contemplarlo, forma ya de ese mito / De pureza rebelde que tierra apenas toca, / Del éter huésped desterrado. La melodía le ayuda a conocerse, / A enamorarse de lo que él mismo es. Y para siempre en la musica vive." (Fused with the myth he watches, / already part of that myth / Of rebel purity, hardly touching the earth, / The ether's exiled guest. The melody helps him to know himself, / To love his real self, and in the music he lives forever [translation by Harris]).

*Desolación de la quimera* contains Cernuda's harshest indictments of Spain and also his most poignant evocations of his homeland. In "Elegía española (I)" – from *Las nubes* – he appeals to the permanent essence of his country, beyond the fratricidal insanity of the civil war. He could still formulate an allegiance to the perennial values embodied in Spain's nurturing culture, his language, and his past. Soon, during the darkness of the Franco years, he was unable, even unwilling, to capture those values behind the prevalent obscurantism and the systematic vengefulness of the regime. The disjunction reaches its starkest expression in "Díptico español I & II" (Spanish Diptych I & II, in *Desolación de la quimera*) – where the ideal Spain of Benito Pérez Galdós, as an instance of what is valued, opposes the dismal present. These apparently irreconcilable extremes were to be temporarily resolved in his poem "1936" (from the same book), which acts as a kind of poetic therapy by allowing the poet to recapture the ideals that had been at stake in the civil war. After a poetry reading at San Francisco State College in 1961, a conversation with a former volunteer in the International Brigades brought back to Cernuda the noble, humanitarian values for which he himself had fought. The forgotten fire of the cause had been rekindled. The poem becomes an exemplum of how to keep the faith, and at the same time an instance of the exemplum's regenerative effect. Thus it becomes the gesture whereby the poet resolves his inner conflict regarding Spain.

Yet Cernuda's last poem in *Desolación de la quimera,* "A sus paisanos" (To His Countrymen), is a bitter invective against the incomprehension that, he feels, has greeted his work in Spain. Actually, Cernuda was wrong. By this time (1962), an entire generation of poets, and younger ones still to follow, were hailing him as their master. They saw Cernuda's work as the most congenial to their concerns – even more so than Lorca's. Some claimed that Cernuda was the greatest poet of the century. Lorca himself, in his own generous way, had saluted his fellow Andalusian as a "divine" poet (as quoted by Harris in 1973).

In 1960 Cernuda's two sisters had died. Cernuda had always felt that it was a family characteristic to die at about the age of sixty and truly began to feel that physically his time had run out. He returned to Mexico in June of 1962 and prepared to take up a year's appointment as visiting professor at UCLA, to June 1963. He returned again to Mexico after that. His next post was to be at the University of Southern California for the 1963–1964 school year. In the fall of 1963 Cernuda refused to undergo the necessary physical examination and gave up the position. He died of a heart attack in November of that year; he was sixty-one.

**References:**

André Breton, *Manifestes du surréalisme* (Paris: Gallimard, 1970);

*Cántico,* special issue on Cernuda, 9–10 (August–November 1955);

Derek Harris, *Luis Cernuda: A Study of the Poetry* (London: Tamesis, 1973);

Harris, ed., *Luis Cernuda* (Madrid: Taurus, 1977);

Harris, ed., *Perfil del aire. Con otras obras olvidadas e inéditas, documentos y epistolario* (London: Tamesis, 1971);

Harris & Anthony Edkins, trans. and eds., *The Poetry of Luis Cernuda* (New York: New York University Press, 1971);

Salvador Jiménez-Fajardo, *Luis Cernuda* (Boston: Twayne, 1978);

Jacobo Munoz, ed., *La caña gris,* special issue on Cernuda, 6–8 (1962);

Vicente Quirarte, *La poética del hombre dividido en la obra de Luis Cernuda* (Mexico City: Universitaria, 1985);

Pedro Salinas, *Ensayos de literatura hispánica* (Madrid: Gredos, 1958);

James Valender, *Cernuda y el poema en prosa* (London: Tamesis, 1984);

José Angel Valente, *Las palabras de la tribu* (Madrid: Siglo Veintiuno, 1971).

# Rosa Chacel

*(3 June 1898 – )*

Dona M. Kercher
*Assumption College*

BOOKS: *Estación. Ida y vuelta* (Madrid: Ulises, 1930; revised edition, Madrid: CVS, 1974);

*A la orilla de un pozo* (Madrid: Héroe, 1936; revised edition, Valencia: Pre-Textos, 1985);

*Teresa* (Buenos Aires: Nuevo Romance, 1941; revised edition, Madrid: Aguilar, 1963);

*Memorias de Leticia Valle* (Buenos Aires: Emecé, 1945; revised edition, Barcelona: Lumen, 1971);

*Sobre el piélago* (Buenos Aires: Imán, 1952); republished in *Icada, Nevda, Diada*;

*Poesía de la circunstancia. Cómo y por qué de la novela* (Bahía Blanca, Argentina: Universidad Nacional del Sur, 1958);

*La sinrazón* (Buenos Aires: Losada, 1960; revised edition, Bilbao: Albia, 1977; Barcelona: Bruguera, 1981);

*Ofrenda a una virgen loca* (Jalapa, Mexico: Universidad Veracruzana, 1961); republished in *Icada, Nevda, Diada*;

*Icada, Nevda, Diada* (Barcelona: Seix Barral, 1971);

*La confesión* (Barcelona: EDHASA, 1971);

*Saturnal* (Barcelona: Seix Barral, 1972);

*Desde el amanecer* (Madrid: Revista de Occidente, 1972; revised edition, Barcelona: Bruguera, 1981);

*Barrio de maravillas* (Barcelona: Seix Barral, 1976; revised edition, Barcelona: Bruguera, 1980);

*Versos prohibidos* (Madrid: Caballo Griego para la Poesía, 1978);

*Timoteo Pérez y sus retratos del jardín* (Madrid: Cátedra, 1980);

*Novelas antes de tiempo* (Barcelona: Bruguera, 1981);

*Los títulos* (Barcelona: EDHASA, 1981);

*Alcancía: Ida; Vuelta,* 2 volumes (Barcelona: Seix Barral, 1982);

*Acrópolis* (Barcelona: Seix Barral, 1984);

*Rebañaduras* (Salamanca: Junta de Castilla y León, Consejería de Educación y Cultura, 1986);

*Ciencias naturales* (Barcelona: Seix Barral, 1988);

*Balaam y otros cuentos* (Madrid: Montena, 1989);

*Obra completa,* 2 volumes, edited by Ana Rodríguez and Félix Pardo (Valladolid: Diputación Provincial de Valladolid & Centro de Creación y Estudios Jorge Guillén, 1989);

*Poesía (1931–1991),* edited by Antoni Marí (Barcelona: Tusquets, 1992).

MOTION PICTURE: *Memorias de Leticia Valle,* adapted from Chacel's novel and including dialogue by Chacel, Intimista, 1979.

OTHER: "Autopercepción intelectual de un proceso histórico," *Anthropos,* 85 (June 1988).

TRANSLATIONS: Renato Poggioli, *Teoría del arte vanguardia* (Madrid: Revista de Occidente, 1964);

Albert Camus, *La peste* (Barcelona: EDHASA, 1977);

Jean Racine, *Tragedias* (Madrid: Alfaguara, 1983);

Walmir Ayala, *Museo de Cámara* (Madrid: Xanela, 1986).

Rosa Chacel is a major Spanish intellectual. She was born Rosa Clotilde Cecilia María del Carmen Chacel in Valladolid on 3 June 1898. In the autobiography about her first ten years of life, *Desde el amanecer* (Since Dawn, 1972), she writes of her pride in having been born in the watershed year for a generation of important Spanish writers. Her own literary generation is primarily that of 1927, to whose members she has dedicated many poems.

Her poetry is a significant testimony to that generation's link to the forms and themes of Spanish Golden Age poetry and is an integral element of her multigeneric, often autobiographical literary output. All her books, written during a career that spans more than sixty years, also show her erotic aesthetics.

Though her novels have been grouped with other literature written in exile, Chacel's poetry is peninsular Spanish in origin and spirit. Her first

*Rosa Chacel, circa 1962*

book of poetry, *A la orilla de un pozo* (At the Edge of a Well), was published in Madrid in 1936. She has never published poetry outside Spain, by conscious choice, on which she elaborates in the foreword to her second book of verse, *Versos prohibidos* (Forbidden Poetry, 1978). A multiple self-censorship informs all her publications and includes a preference for prose, not verse, as the vehicle for her literary production; a strict adherence to a formal, classical style of poetry; and a vow to publish poetry only in Spain.

Although Chacel has achieved her greatest renown as a novelist, poetry is often important in her novels. For example, in *Memorias de Leticia Valle* (Memoirs of Leticia Valle, 1945) the young female protagonist recites a long poem by José de Espronceda, "La carrera" (The Race), at a town celebration for a teacher's silver anniversary with a local school. The performance of the poem is a public success but a private failure. As Leticia recites,

she realizes and comments to herself on the defects of the poem: poor rhymes, excessive onomatopoeia, and overbearing emotionality. Her failure is that her tutor, who later tries to molest her, walks out on the recital. Poetry in the novel is a catalyst for sexual and intellectual awakenings.

In all her autobiographical writing, including novels and memoirs, Chacel has placed particular importance on her early years and has focused on them in terms of an interior journey of the mind, which characterizes her recognition of what she calls "particular profunidad" (particular profundity). This secret life of thought, as she has referred to it, took the form of one particularly strong visual image, an oneiric apparition of a vertical glass thread, infinite and immobile, as described by Chacel in *Desde el amanecer:*

> Imposible recordar en qué tiempo logré tener una imagen clara de ello, pero cuando llegué a tenerla consistía,

simplemente en *un hilo.* Era un hilo de vidrio que estaba delante de mí, vertical: yo no veía su principio ni su fin, no veía dónde se apoyaba: era una columna de vidrio finísima que estaba inmóvil, pero yo sabía que fluía. No sé cómo lo sabía porque lo más atroz era su inmovilidad. Y nada más, no puedo añadir el más pequeño detalle porque todo consistía en eso, en que no había ningún detalle: era solamente la visión de aquel hilo, que permanecía delante de mí, indeciblemente próximo, tan próximo como si fuese yo misma. Y, esto es lo más importante: cuando a los cuatro o cinco años la visión era enteramente clara tenía siempre, en toda ocasión, el carácter de un recuerdo muy antiguo. Su aparición siempre me hacía decir: "Ya está aquí esto, lo de siempre!"

(Impossible to remember when I managed to have a clear image of it, but when I happened to have it, it consisted simply of a *thread.* It was a thread of glass which was before me, vertical: I could not see either its beginning or its end, I could not see where it was supported: it was a column of extremely fine glass, immobile, and yet I knew that it was flowing. I do not know how I knew it because the most atrocious part of it was its immobility. And nothing more, I cannot add even the smallest detail because everything consisted in that, in that there was no detail: it was only the vision of that thread, which remained in front of me, incredibly close, so close, as if it were I myself. And, this is the most important aspect: when at the age of four or five the vision was entirely clear it always had, on every occasion, the character of a very old memory. Its apparition always made me say: "There it is yet again, that same thing!")

Rosa Chacel was a frail, solitary child, though not lonely; she was educated by her mother, a teacher, at home in Valladolid. Chacel's early education was almost exclusively literary. With her father she used to exercise her prodigious memory by reciting verses, including those of the romantic poet José Zorrilla. Being a distant relative by way of marriage, Zorrilla was one of the family. The young Chacel visited his tomb and thought of it as that of an uncle. Because her health was poor and she was considered nervous, she visited doctors frequently. She has written (in *Desde el amanecer*) with special fascination of her visits to Dr. Luis Moreno, who prescribed that her bed be moved into a more open space and that she sleep under a blue light bulb. Another of his prescriptions was for Chacel and her family to spend time in the country; two months in Rodilana revitalized her health. She also encountered scenes in nature that reminded her of modernist drawings she had seen in the magazines *Blanco y Negro* and *Ilustración Iberoamericana.* Such natural imagery appears in her poetry.

Cinematic techniques are another aspect of her poems. Chacel's family was receptive to innovations such as the cinema. In *Desde el amanecer* she describes her first visit to the movies with her parents: "al fin se inauguró el Cine Pradera y fuimos los tres. Las luces se veían desde la calle de Santiago y se oía la música. Llegamos frente al órgano; los focos, los arcos voltaicos zumbando como insectos derramaban luz. Pero su derramar no era catarata, sino quietud resplandeciente que envolvía las figuras del órgano exaltando, sublimando los rosas, los azules, los oros de las tallas" (finally the Pradera Movie Theater was opened and the three of us went. The lights could be seen from Santiago Street and you could hear the music. We got up to right in front of the organ; the spotlights, their electric arcs buzzing like insects, were spilling out light. But their outpouring was not like a cloudburst, but rather a resplendent quietude that enveloped the figures on the organ, exalting, subliming the reds, the blues, the golds of the shapes). Cinema was to have a lasting impact on how Chacel saw and wrote. In *La confesión* (1971) she tells of how her questions about Luis Buñuel's movies motivated her to write and ask him to discuss them with her personally. Though much her senior, Buñuel granted the interview. Chacel confirms that her first book of poetry is a response to surrealist cinema. The comparison is hinted at in her prologue to *Versos prohibidos* when she favorably recalls Michelangelo Antonioni's characterization of himself as having "una mente infaliblemente activada por la visión" (a mind infallibly activated by sight).

All the arts have had an impact on Chacel and her poetry. Enthralled by a particular *zarzuela* (a traditional musical) performance she saw in her childhood, she observed the presence of poetry in time, to which she refers in the 1988 essay "Autopercepción intelectual de un proceso historico" (Intellectual Self-Perception of a Historical Process) as "una escala celeste" (a celestial scale): "las palabras y la melodía iban aumentando la presencia sugerida, manifestándola, apróximadola a fuerza de realidad" (the words and the melody together were augmenting the suggested presence, making it manifest, bringing it nearer through the force of reality). In *Desde el amanecer* Chacel marvels at manifestations of the poetic independence of signifiers in paired rhymes: "Eso es, con esa hermandad que sobrepasa su significado lógico como *paloma* y *carcoma,* como *beduino* y *molino,* que no se unen por su contenido racional, sino que se abrazan graciosamente, dejando al alejarse unidas una estela armónica" (That is, with that fraternity that exceeds their logical meaning as

*Chacel at work on a copy of a Greek bust at the Escuela Superior de Bellas Artes in San Fernando, where she studied from 1915 to 1918*

in *paloma* [dove] and *carcoma* [woodworm or anxiety], as in *beduino* [Bedouin] and *molino* [mill], that are not connected according to their rational content, but which graciously embrace, leaving behind a harmonic wake when they withdraw united). This belief in a harmonic copenetration of paired rhymes encourages special awareness of the effect of rhyme pairs in her book of sonnets, *A la orilla de un pozo*. A reading of the rhyme pairs does produce an incantation, an evocation of the person to whom the poem is dedicated.

In Valladolid, Chacel began to study drawing and sculpture. Her attitude and her admiration for Greek sculpture helped make her a child prodigy among students at least ten years older. There was a moment of recognition, of which she later wrote in *Desde el amanecer:* "El descubrimiento de la escultura griega significó para mí la vía de acceso a lo que *puede ser* – ya he repetido más de una vez esta frase y no será la última–, a lo que puedo penetrar y vivir, al mundo, tal como yo lo anhelaba y lo concebía" (The discovery of Greek sculpture meant for me the means of access to what *can be* – I have already repeated this phrase more than once and it

will not be the last time –, to what I can penetrate and live, in the world, such as I desired and conceived it). The statue of Apollo in the school's vestibule became the singular focus of her contemplations, "como la adquisición de todo el saber" (like the acquisition of all knowledge). Almost twenty years later she wrote the poem "Apolo" (in *Versos prohibidos*), in which the final lines – "Sobre mí, solo eterno / tu mandato de luz, Verdad y Forma" (Upon me, only eternal / your commandment of light, Truth and Form) – reflect the totalizing force of her experience. At the age of ten Chacel moved with her parents to Madrid, to the Barrio de Maravillas, the name of which would later be the title to one of her novels (1976), a portrait of herself as an adolescent artist.

In 1915 Chacel entered the Escuela Superior de Bellas Artes de San Fernando to study sculpture. Her time at San Fernando (1915–1918) was as important because of the friends she met as for her course of study. Among those who studied with Chacel were her future husband, the painter Timoteo Pérez Rubio, as well as Gregorio Prieto, Joaquín Valverde, Paz González, José Frau, Victoria Durán, and Margarita Villegas; Chacel dedicated sonnets to the first four of these (including Pérez Rubio) in *A la orilla de un pozo*. One of the teachers there was Ramón María del Valle-Inclán, one of the most brilliant innovators in the Spanish language. In the milieu of San Fernando Chacel began to consider a literary vocation. Putting aside her fine-arts studies in 1918, she began to frequent the intellectual gathering places of the time – the Ateneo, the Granja del Henar, and the Bolillería. During this period she read works by Friedrich Nietzsche and Plato, became part of the vanguard movement, and collaborated on the magazine *Ultra*. At the Ateneo she gave her first lecture; its topic was "la mujer" (woman), a subject on which she has written, spoken, and given interviews throughout her life. Nonetheless, she has never been comfortable with the label of "feminist." She even derided the idea of women's literature in her 1988 interview with M. Aguirre: "La literatura femenina es una estupidez" (Women's literature is nonsense). Her most cogent writing on the topic of woman is found in her essays, particularly in the huge book *Saturnal* (Saturnian, 1972) and in the collection *Los títulos* (The Titles, 1981), where she comments on Simone de Beauvoir's writing and on her own novels. Chacel's essay "La mujer en galeras" (The Woman in the Galleys, in *Los títulos*), on women not being marginalized but being enslaved, is archetypically instructive of her thoughts on the nature of woman, ideas posed intellectually in terms of the nature of man and always contextual, as the following passage illustrates: "La mujer, en este tiempo, sale de su mazmorra porque nuestra sociedad, nuestra cultura, nuestra economía, nuestra ciencia; el ser temporal que todos estos elementos componen, necesita estirar ese miembro entumecido, hacer que circule por él la sangre de la actualidad: necesita que ella actúe, no es ella quien más lo necesita. Si no sintiese la necesidad, si se resistiese a actuar, podemos asegurar que se la obligaría: me atrevo a decir que no se la obliga" (Woman, at this time, is coming out of her dungeon because our society, our culture, our economy, our science – the temporal being that all those elements compose – needs to stretch that numb member, to make the blood of the present circulate through it: it needs her to act; she is not the one who needs it the most. If she did not feel the need, if she resisted acting, we can be assured that it would force her: I dare say that it is not forcing her).

Ana Rodríguez, the coeditor of Chacel's *Obra completa* (Collected Work, 1989), has traced Chacel's "Cronología intelectual" (Intellectual Chronology) in an essay of that name in *Anthropos* (June 1988), detailing her literary "polos de atracción" (poles of attraction): on the one hand, Ramón Gómez de la Serna and Juan Ramón Jiménez; on the other, Miguel de Unamuno and José Ortega y Gasset. The divergent styles of these two groups influenced Chacel's prose. In August 1988 Chacel gave a major lecture on Gómez de la Serna at the Universidad Complutense de Madrid. Rodríguez has rightly noted the traces of *greguerías* (the type of aphorisms created by Gómez de la Serna) in Chacel's first novel, *Estación. Ida y vuelta* (Station. Round-trip, 1930). However, they are equally present in the humor of *A la orilla de un pozo*.

In the case of Jiménez, about whose *Platero y yo* (Platero and I, 1917) Chacel writes eloquently in *La confesión,* the admiration flows equally from the older master to the young Chacel. Jiménez was responsible for the publication in the magazine *Hora de España* of Chacel's poem "Narciso" (Narcissus) along with a line drawing of herself; both text and illustration are republished in *Versos prohibidos*.

Unamuno was an intellectual giant for Chacel's generation in its formative years in Madrid, but Chacel has faulted the slavish imitation of Unamuno by writers of that period. As Julián Marías notes in his prologue to the 1970 edition of Chacel's novel *La sinrazón* (The Unreason, 1960), she deals with many of the same concerns as Unamuno, in her "novela personal" (personal novel). This agonistic struggle between reason and faith surfaces in her 1941 poem "Encrucijada" (Crossroads), in *Versos prohibidos*.

The years from 1922 to 1927 represent an opening of European horizons for Chacel. After their marriage Chacel and Pérez Rubio left Spain for teaching positions at the Academia de España in Rome. They occasionally made excursions through Italy, Germany, Austria, and France. Her visit to Paris in the winter of 1924–1925 coincided with the fervor of the discussions of André Breton's *Manifeste du surréalisme* (1924), and surrealism heavily influenced Chacel's poetry.

In Rome, Chacel read other important works, including James Joyce's *Portrait of the Artist as a Young Man* (1916) and the first volume of Sigmund Freud's works to appear in Spanish translation. While in Rome she read Ortega y Gasset's articles in the *Revista de Occidente,* which he founded in 1923, and his book *Meditaciones del Quijote* (Meditations on the Quixote, 1914). Rodríguez has written eloquently of Ortega's effect on Chacel: "Además de un sistema y de unas ideas estéticas, Rosa Chacel admiró en Ortega la brillantez de su verbo. La niña

*Chacel posing for Gregorio Prieto, and the drawing that resulted (from Prieto's*
Lorca y la generación del '27, *1977)*

vallisoletana que había aprendido a hablar el castellano con un rigor que, sobrepasando lo gramatical, adquiría un profundo sentido ético, entendió y asumió la disciplina del lenguaje impuesta por Ortega: claridad, sencillez, exactitud . . . son valores que Rosa Chacel no olvidará en su modo de proceder con la palabra" (Besides a system and some aesthetic ideas, Rosa Chacel admired in Ortega the brilliancy of his style. The girl from Valladolid who had learned to speak Spanish with a rigor that, surpassing the grammatical, acquired a profoundly ethical sense, understood and assumed the discipline of the language imposed by Ortega: clarity, simplicity, precision . . . they are values that Rosa Chacel will not forget in her manner of proceeding with the word). In its careful definition of self-censorship and its ethical clarification of her circumstances in exile, Chacel's prologue to *Versos prohibidos* is one of many examples of Ortega's oblique, yet forceful, impact on Chacel's thought.

It was Ortega who gave Chacel her figurative passport back to Spain. She returned in 1927 to send him her first novel, whose protagonist lives out an idea, Ortega's concept of "razón vital" (vital reason). Because of changes in publishing houses, the novel did not appear until 1930, but Ortega befriended Chacel and invited her to collaborate on the *Revista de Occidente*. Her return to Madrid in 1927 coincided with the Gongoran tricentenary (the celebration of the three hundredth year since Luis de Góngora's death). In *A la orilla de un pozo* she reworks many lines of Gongoran syntax and echoes his metaphoric patterns.

In her foreword to the 1985 edition of *A la orilla de un pozo*, Chacel explains that the idea for the book originated as a kind of café game between her and Rafael Alberti in Berlin, where she spent about six months in 1933. Lamenting the abandonment of classical forms in the poetry of the day, they proceeded in jest to compose an erotic sonnet to a friend. Later, on her own, as a respite from the composition of *Teresa* (1941), Chacel's novelized version of the life of poet José de Espronceda's mistress, she wrote a total of thirty sonnets to friends. Whereas she called the collaboration with Alberti "politicoide y mezquinamente social" (satirically political and meanly social), her own sonnets included images of private confidences. Chacel labels the poems "extemporaneous" in her foreword, which is, entirely in character, ironically self-deprecatory.

*A la orilla de un pozo* holds a special significance because of its private link, through dedications, to other well-known authors and critics, such as Al-

berti, Pablo Neruda, María Zambrano, Luis Cernuda, Manuel Altolaguirre, Nikos Kazantzakis, and Angel Rosemblat. Moreover, because the reader is not privy to the intimate code of friendship, the sonnets' principal surrealistic effect, the "aura" of their time, to use Chacel's own word, is heightened. The sonnets emphasize the playful and oneiric aspects of language. What is most striking about the poems is that the reader, as was the designated recipient, may feel personally connected to these arbitrary, often bizarre, modern combinations. The sonnet to María Teresa León, Alberti's wife, who acted as scribe at Chacel and Alberti's first Berlin endeavor, is a verbal collage of Max Ernst's collages, which León and Chacel saw in Berlin. In its quatrains the poem recombines elements of Ernst's mechanical illustrations – a zinc plate, for example – and his anthropomorphic scenery – a woman's hair as nest, her veins that deep, bright blue so characteristic of Ernst's paintings:

Si el alcotán anida en tus cabellos
y el Nilo azul se esconde en tu garganta,
si ves crecer del zinc la humilde planta

no cierres el ocaso con los sellos
que el Occidente en su testuz aguanta:
tiembla ante el cierzo y el nublado espanta.
Si oyes jazmines corre a través de ellos.

(If the lanner makes a nest in your hair
and the blue Nile hides itself in your throat,
if you see the humble plant grow out of zinc

don't close off the sunset with the seals
that the West endures on its forehead:
tremble before the north wind and frighten away the
    cloud cover.
If you hear jasmines, run after them.)

The phrasing, the range of vocabulary – from Latinate echoes of Góngora to neologisms such as "bisiesta hora" (bisiesta hour) and "matronil regazo" (matronile lap) – and the mythological imagery all point to a strong classical underpinning in *A la orilla de un pozo*. Yet, while the title alludes to a fable of the goddess of fortune, a common tale in the Golden Age, fortune in Chacel's book often has the surrealist's meaning of "happy accident," a clash of objects and tone. The sonnet to Paz González begins, for example, in alliterative half-seriousness with the image of a girdle: "En un corsé de cálidas entrañas / duerme una estrella, pasionaria o rosa" (In a corset of warm entrails / sleeps a star, passionflower or rose).

*Cover for volume 1 of Chacel's published diaries (1982)*

No poem better illustrates the playful love of language with a classical sense than the ending of the sonnet to Rosemblat, the philologist:

La Afrodita Semántica, en su templo
de vivo enigma, te imbuirá cautivo,
filológo afán, tesón fecundo.

(The Semantic Aphrodite, in her temple
of live enigma, will imbue you with captivity,
philologistic zeal, fertile tenacity.)

The binary inversion – placing the adjective before, then after, the noun, a placement strongly marked by the final stress in the words *afán* (zeal) and *tesón* (tenacity) – recalls certain lines from Góngora's *Polifemo* (Polyphemus, 1613), such as the description of Acis as "el bello imán, el ídolo dormido" (the beautiful magnet, the sleepy idol).

Although conceived of in Fascist Berlin, with its police-state surveillance of foreigners, and pub-

lished in May 1936, shortly before the outbreak of the Spanish Civil War, *A la orilla de un pozo* is no more a political work than was *Polifemo*. As Chacel writes of *A la orilla de un pozo* in the prologue to *Versos prohibidos,* "el juego no era continuable: era un juego y yo, espontáneamente, derivo hacia la seriedad" (the game could not be continued: it was a game, and I am spontaneously inclined toward seriousness). During the 1930s and 1940s Chacel wrote, piecemeal, what may be termed her political poetry. Its seriousness lies in its form as well as in its content. Most of these poems were published for the first time in *Versos prohibidos,* which opens with her 1937 poem "Epístola moral a Sérpula de la verdad" (Moral Epistle to Serpula about Truth). As Chacel explains in her prologue, the poem is a gloss on Andrés Fernández de Andrada's "Epístola moral a Fabio" (Moral Epistle to Fabio, 1610), especially its concluding verses. Chacel's poem was inspired by her conversations in 1933 with her friend Concha Albornoz and their common pride, hopes, fears, and aspirations for Spain, for the republic. Together they found expressed in Fernández de Andrada's verses "todo el existencialismo español" (all Spanish existentialism). His "Epístola moral a Fabio" ends with a melancholy injunction: "Ya, dulce amigo, huyo y me retiro / de cuanto, simple, amé rompí los lazos. / Ven y verás el alto fin que aspiro / antes que el tiempo muera en nuestros brazos" (At last, sweet friend, I flee and withdraw / from everything which in my simplicity I love; I have broken the bonds: / come and you will see the great purpose to which I aspire, / before time dies away in our arms – translation by Elias Rivers). In Chacel's epistle this poetic sense of impending doom is heralded anaphorally by the phrase "antes que" (before): "Pero antes que la calma se ilumine, / antes que el tiempo su alentar regule, / un ritmo oculto o voluntad de norma / diseña trazos de la nueva escala. / ¡Antes que haya una luz limpia de sangre! / ¡Antes que el dolor sea rosa seca!" (But before the calm is illuminated, / before time regulates its breathing, / a hidden rhythm or a will to the norm / designs the traces of the new scale. / Before there is a light clean of blood! / Before the pain is a dried-up rose!).

Chacel wrote her epistle in Paris, where she had fled in early 1937 with her husband and young son, Carlos, and continued to pursue what she termed "mi actividad interior, meditativa" (my interior activity, meditative). Chacel's epistle ends with a call for self-affirmation, a keynote of all her epistolary poetry and all her poetry written outside of Spain: "Busca sólo en el centro de tu pecho / ese lugar o nido preparado / parece mecer al sueño de la vida / la dulce sien del hijo o del amante, / ese lugar o abismo en que está escrito / el sagrado secreto que escuchaste / dentro del seno donde amaneciste" (Seek alone in the center of your breast / that place or prepared nest / that seems to rock to the dream of life / the sweet temple of the son or lover, / that place or abyss in which it is written / the sacred secret you heard / inside the womb where you awoke). While asking some frightening questions – such as "¿Por qué temblar pensando en los que amamos, / qué amenaza o peligro los acecha?" (Why tremble thinking of those we love, / what threat or danger stalks them?) – the poem also shows elegant sensibility to both the history of the moment and the history of Spanish poetry. It is Chacel's poetic masterpiece.

"Epístola moral a Serpula" deals with the political atmosphere and was first published in *Hora de España* (June 1937), the Republican journal of Valencia, and Chacel also entered more directly the political scene. She was one of the early organizers of the Frente Popular (Popular Front). Along with those of many other intellectuals of the period, her name is found on numerous manifestos, including the 1936 writers' protest of the imprisonment of the poet Miguel Hernández. She worked as a nurse in a Red Cross hospital until she fled with her son to Barcelona during the siege of Madrid. In the eighth issue (15 October 1936) of the journal *Mono Azul,* a publication of the Alianza de Intelectuales Antifacistas, Chacel published her poem "Alarma!," about the bombing of Madrid by Francisco Franco's troops in October and November of 1936.

From Barcelona, Chacel followed many others to Valencia. She repeatedly published articles and poetry in *Hora de España* and also conceived a plan, along with Juan Gil-Albert, Neruda, Alberti, Cernuda, and others, to put poetry to work for the republic in exile. They were to write poems praising Valencian products, and the poems were to be published collectively. Although the gesture of solidarity failed, as the war intervened and the collection never materialized, Chacel finished her contribution. Her sonnets to the sardine, the bean, and the onion were eventually published in *Versos prohibidos,* in the section titled "Sonetos de circunstancias" (Sonnets of Circumstances). They mark a startling break from her previous sonnets to friends. Unlike Neruda's well-known product odes, Chacel's poems have not received their due attention.

Chacel has confirmed that her food sonnets were intended to be linked to the next poem in *Versos prohibidos* – "Oda al hambre" (Ode to Hunger) – from which they are separated in the book. Together they were to be part of the Valencian poets' project. Chacel's Valencian poems are interesting historical footnotes, and they reconfirm her place among the Generation of '27 poets. In contrast to later social-realist poetry, their complicated form and imagery make them virtually useless as marketing propaganda. What is most striking in Chacel's poems is the thread of military imagery that runs throughout. The food poems celebrate the defense of the home front. Beans fight in a "nutrido escuadrón" (well-fed squadron). The sardine is a "breve guerrera submarina" (compact submarine warrior).

In this wartime poetry peace is never mentioned. Chacel's food poems are presented as an integral part of the war effort and of its ideology. Today a few stalwarts refuse to forget Chacel's leftist wartime politics when judging her literary career. Nothing symbolizes the conservative undercurrent against her better than the 1988 refusal of three

*Painting of Chacel by her husband, Timoteo Pérez (Collection of Rosa Chacel)*

parish priests to ring their church bells during a city-wide tribute to Chacel in Valladolid. As reported in *El País* (9 June 1988), Felipe Galgo, one of the priests, was overheard to say, "Para esa señora roja no tocan estas campanas" (These bells will not ring for that red lady).

Like many other Republican intellectuals, Chacel left Spain for Paris in early 1937. In 1938, at the insistent invitation of her friend Máximo José Kahn, then the Republican ambassador to Greece, Chacel made an excursion to that country. Kahn, who was also a scholar who had studied the works of Judeo-Spanish poet Yehudá Haleví, gave her a black notebook inscribed "Posada de la sangre" (Resting place of the blood) in which she later wrote a diary of her years of exile in South America. The diaries – in two volumes, titled *Alcancía: Ida* (Memory Bank: Outward Journey) and *Vuelta* (Return) – were published in 1982.

The first entry, written in her port of departure, Bordeaux, on 18 April 1940, captures the tone and underscores one of the main themes of the first journal, "Me siento más amenazada que nunca, enteramente al borde del peligro, pero acaso sólo sea la fealdad lo que me amenaza, y ya es bastante. En este cuaderno estudiaré los progresos que hace en mí la idea del fracaso: cada día estoy más familiarizada con ella. ¿Por qué, de pronto, escribo esto? . . . No lo sé: a mí misma no me importa, ¿a quién puede importarle?" (I feel more threatened than ever, entirely on the brink of danger, but perhaps it is only ugliness that threatens me, and that suffices. In this notebook I will study the progress the idea of failure makes in me: every day I am more familiarized with it. Why, suddenly, am I writing this? . . . I don't know: I myself don't care, who can it matter to?). Feelings of inferiority and insignificance are so intimately tied to Chacel's ruminations on exile that she refuses to call her stay in South America an exile. Her point, which is particularly significant for women intellectuals of the post-civil-war era, is that the concept of exile is predicated on one's condition as a significant subject. For Chacel there are no easy definitions, certainly no facile self-definitions.

Because of her husband's art contacts in Brazil, the family set sail in 1940 for Rio de Janeiro; however, by the next year her friendship with Jorge Luis Borges's sister, Norah Borges, drew Chacel to Buenos Aires. (They had originally met in Paris.) In 1941 she celebrated her reencounter with Norah Borges with the poem "Epístola a Norah Borges del Arte" (Epistle to Norah Borges on Art), collected in *Versos prohibidos*. The poem recalls their shared times in Paris in the late 1930s after Norah had just given birth to a son. The initial lines of the poem refer to the drawing Norah made of Chacel as a mermaid: "Hacia ti, queridísima, mis brazos / como tú los pintaste, se dilatan, / como dos blancas ramas que, del tronco, / se alargan contra el viento del olvido" (Toward you, my dearest, my arms / as you painted them, extend / like two white branches which / stretch out from the trunk against the wind of forgetfulness).

Although Chacel had the satisfaction of finally publishing novels she had written earlier in Europe, *Teresa* and *Memorias de Leticia Valle,* her stay in South America was a highly uncertain time for her. She stopped writing novels; however, she still wrote stories and essays and continued to write poetry for her friends. In these poems, such as "A Elisabeth," a sonnet to Elisabeth Calipigia, a friend in Rio, Chacel discloses her existential distress. The Calipigia poem serves as the dedication for *Teresa.* The first tercet confronts a dark side of life: "No sabe qué hora es esta hora oscura / ni si la luz comienza o agoniza / ni por qué vino, pues no fue llamada" (She does not know which hour this dark hour is / nor if the light is beginning or agonizing / nor why she came, for she was not called). One senses that the psychological disorientation, and perhaps a momentary loss of direction, describes not only the state of mind of the character Teresa but Chacel's as well.

Despite such questioning, however, Chacel engaged in constant work and prolific writing. She wrote for the Buenos Aires daily *La Nación* (The Nation), as well as for the journals *Realidad* and *Anales de Buenos Aires,* and for the most important literary magazine of the time, *Sur.* Her regular contributions to *Sur* over a period of more than twenty years – short stories, articles, reviews, and poems – indicate

her involvement in the intellectual milieu of Buenos Aires. Some of her articles first published in *Sur* were reedited and collected in *Los títulos* along with her essays on other twentieth-century Spanish poets (Cernuda, Gil-Albert, and Alberti). As Jorge Luis Borges had done before her in *Fervor de Buenos Aires* (Fervor of Buenos Aires, 1923), Chacel wrote poetry about La Recoleta, the elegant Buenos Aires cemetery, which has a long history of being a favorite, fashionable strolling ground. For example, her poem "La ventana que da sobre la muerte" (The Window That Looks Out onto Death), published in *Sur* in 1942 and collected in *Versos prohibidos,* is similar to many of her other poems in its architectural metaphor. It underscores the idea that poetry for Chacel is "la túnica posada de la forma" (the posed tunic of form), as she suggests in her most metacritical poem, "Estudio" (Studio), in *Versos prohibidos.* Chacel presents poetry as a process, a silencing of conscious thought, that tries to approximate the sublime, the unspeakable. She enumerates a series of metaphors of nothingness. The line breaks, the pauses in the last line, and the repetition of the negating word *sin* (without) in the conclusion of the poem encompass her vision of poetry: "Vela sin viento en lago sin distancia / cáscara del adiós, piel del olvido, / vigía sin vigilia, la ventana / calla, sin aldabón, sobre la muerte" (Sail without wind in a lake without horizon / shell of good-bye, skin of forgetting / a reef without watchfulness, the window / is silent, without a handle, over death).

Dividing her time between Rio and Buenos Aires, Chacel also assiduously translated into Spanish a wide range of books in French, Italian, German, and English: poetry by T. S. Eliot, Rainer Maria Rilke, Stéphane Mallarmé, and Walmir Ayala; Renato Poggioli's seminal work *Teoria dell'arte d'avanguardia* (1962); Albert Camus's *La Peste* (The Plague, 1947); and Jean Racine's tragedies (1667–1677). In the symbolist Mallarmé's *Herodias* (1940) – a dialogue between a fierce, untamed virgin and her earthbound nurse – the translation of which closes Chacel's *Poesía (1931–1991)* (1992), she found both a kindred spirit in the tragic, innocent Herodias, "la niña en su corazón precioso exiliada / como un cisne que esconde en su pluma los ojos" (the child exiled in her precious heart / like a swan that hides its eyes in its plumage), and an enduring affirmation of her faith in poetry and beauty.

During this period Chacel also published two short-story collections, *Sobre el piélago* (On the High Seas, 1952) and *Ofrenda a una virgen loca* (Offering to a Crazed Virgin, 1961). Translating and writing provided a living, and as she notes in *Alcancía: Ida,*

*Chacel and Octavio Paz in Madrid, 1982 (photograph by Puerta)*

these were hard times financially for her and her family. Her poetry of this era, collected and published without dates in *Versos prohibidos,* testifies to how she was spiritually buoyed by friendships. She wrote occasional sonnets, similar in inspiration to those in her first collection. Chacel has confirmed that the "Sonetos de circunstancias," while different in tone, could be read as a continuation of *A la orilla de un pozo.* Each poem is both a gift to a friend and a formal exercise. The sonnet "A Vito" (To Vito), whose circumstances of composition in 1958 she describes in *Alcancía: Ida,* is an apt example of how these later sonnets both carry on the formal conception of the earlier poems and diverge from them through a stronger undertone of alienation. "A Vito" encapsulates several narratives: Vito, a close family friend in Rio, had dreamed of a red bird; after much scrimping and searching, Chacel had bought one for him, but it never sang until after Chacel left for Buenos Aires; Vito, a dying man in 1958, could no longer read; and Chacel recorded her sonnet on an audio disc and sent it through the mail. In this poem Chacel's image of herself moving

in the city is a baroque one full of complex neologisms, as in the second quatrain: "Corrí a la urbana selva, donde brama / el megaterio omníbuso y chirría / el freno astuto y va y viene a porfía / la hormiga menestral, que sufre y ama" (I ran to the urban jungle, where brawls / the extinct slothful bus creature and squealed / the astute break and comes and goes persistently / the manual worker ant, who suffers and loves). Furthermore, the city/country tensions, which echo classical topoi, are given modern, metropolitan expression in an Argentinean idiom, as seen in the combining of the words *omníbuso* and *megaterio* (a huge extinct sloth) to produce an image of a mechanical monster. Vito died without ever hearing Chacel's record, for the package was lost, then found and delayed in customs until it was too expensive to claim.

The incident is symptomatic of the frustrations in Chacel's life and writing in the 1950s. Where others may have given up, she looked inward. For ten years she worked on the novel *La sinrazón,* which became her masterwork in fiction. In this novel she returns to her philosophical and agonistic roots in the ideas of Unamuno and Ortega and confronts her psychic state of exile. Rodríguez summarizes the focus of the novel in her "Biografía comentada," saying that Chacel "concibe una novela en la que las ideas están inextricablemente mezcladas con las pasiones, un complejísimo universo dramático en el cual sentimientos y pasiones aparecen unidos a valores de la más alta categoría espiritual: ideas, principios morales, pensamiento religioso. Como Unamuno, frente al realismo de la escuela, Rosa Chacel postula una realidad íntima, esencial, cuyo eje es el problema de la existencia" (conceives a novel in which ideas are inextricably mixed with passions, an extremely complex dramatic universe in which feelings and passions appear united with the most highly esteemed spiritual values: ideas, moral principles, religious thought. Like Unamuno, opposed to a scholastic realism, Rosa Chacel postulates an intimate, essential reality whose structuring principle is the problem of existence). Although *La sinrazón* was published in Buenos Aires in 1960, its full critical impact did not occur until the 1970s, after it was reedited and published in Spain with a prologue by the Spanish philosopher and critic Julián Marías.

In 1959 Chacel was awarded a Guggenheim Fellowship to write on the problem of love. She went to New York City to write, travel, and lecture for two years. Her mood, as evident in *Alcancía: Ida*, was rather unhappy, though, and her writing was unfocused according to her earlier standards. The extended essay she wrote then was not published until revised much later as *Saturnal*. Chacel has always singled out the book as profoundly disturbing for herself as well as for her friends and critics. One cause of the unease toward the book may be traced to what Janet Pérez described in 1988 as Chacel's "attempt to isolate the essence of feminine psychology"; Chacel "concludes that on a deep, ancestral level, it is the fear of rape."

She did not write many poems in New York, but in her poem about the Hudson River, "Belleza en Nueva York" (Beauty in New York, in *Versos prohibidos*), she reflects on some of the same existential concerns, regarding the consciousness of time, with which she deals in *Saturnal*. As in much Spanish Golden Age river poetry, Chacel speaks directly to the river as she thinks of the passing of time. The phrase "hoy eres" (today you are) is repeated throughout. The poem ends with an impressive image of the river: "hoy eres ese agua que se llama / de luminarias que pasean, graves, / en círculo, a la altura de las torres" (today you are that water which is called to / from luminarias [sacred lights] that stroll, ceremoniously, / in a circle, at the height of the towers).

The Guggenheim also provided Chacel with enough money to take a trip to Europe and, most especially, to Spain. However, her two-year stay in Spain was a bitter disappointment. Her writing, so philosophically dense, was not in sync with the then-current vogue of social-realist novels. Her own novels were out of print. At sixty-five she was a member of another, older generation. She returned in May 1963 to Brazil and was at a critical crossroads. Heartened by the works of some new Spanish novelists, such as Martín Santos and Sánchez Ferlosio, she chose to look again at her past. Her next undertaking, the novel *Barrio de maravillas,* set in the Madrid neighborhood of her adolescence, interweaves the stories of two generations. This new autobiographical project became her passport back to Spain, this time in the form of a fellowship from the Fundación March. This return, begun when Chacel established a separate household in Spain in 1973 and made definitive after her husband's death in Rio in 1977, was a triumphant one. In 1976 *Barrio de maravillas* was published in Spain and garnered critical acclaim. She began to receive major literary prizes — twice receiving the Premio de la Crítica (1976, 1977) — and to become a cultural star of the new Spain; she was interviewed for print and television media and wrote for new literary magazines.

Chacel also marked her return to Spain with the composition and public reading (in November 1977 in Chamartín) of the last poem of *Versos prohibidos*, "Oda a la Alegría" (Ode to Joy). The epigraph from Friedrich Schiller — "Penetramos, / ¡oh divina alegría!, en tu santuario" (We enter, / Oh divine joy!, into your sanctuary) — sets the tone of mystical joy and release. Some of the imagery of ancient temples is reminiscent of other earlier Chacel poems, written when she studied sculpture and visited Greece. These classical elements are combined with meditations on time, love, and faith. The leitmotiv of the poem is a wave, a fluid overtaking itself: "Así, tú, de ti misma te encrespas y susurras / soberana recubres, transportas y atropellas . . . / tu glorioso esplendor centellea en las playas, / en las mentes y alientos, en latidos y gritos / Tu ímpetu te asemeja a la ola estruendosa" (Thus you crest up out of yourself and you murmur / you recover majestically, you transport and you push aside . . . / your glorious splendor sparkles on the beaches, / in minds and encouragements, in lashings and shouts. / Your impetus resembles the thunderous wave). While "Oda a la Alegría" is a mode of self-affirmation, of "self-recovery," Chacel's autobio-

*Chacel in her apartment in Madrid, August 1988 (photograph by Kesches)*

graphical thrust in her writing continues to be subsumed in intellectual questioning. The poem ends positing the horror of absence, of being forgotten: "Y tener, ¡oh terror!, que llegue al fin un día / en que, al oír tu nombre, pregunte: ¿De quién hablan?" (And to have, Oh terror!, at the end a day arrive / on which, upon hearing your name, someone asks: Who are they talking about?).

Since her return to Spain, Chacel has continued to write poetry sporadically. Of the major event, the publication of her collected poems in *Poesía,* Chacel remarked, "Soy inocente, completamente inocente de este libro" (I am innocent, completely innocent of this book). She has continued to disavow the significance of her poetry.

The title of the book-length section of new or newly published poems in *Obra completa* – "Homenajes" (Tributes) – indicates the status of much of her recent poetry as gestures of appreciation and literary attribution. With such works as "Paloma" (Dove), a long ballad composed for recital at the Fiestas de la Virgen de la Paloma in 1980, Chacel assumed the status of poet laureate of Madrid. Also by commission she wrote the sonnet "Pensamiento" (Thought) for a tribute to Antonio Machado in Turin in 1989. Both the aesthetic underpinning and the classical form of her earlier poetry are also constants of her latest work. She reiterates her commitment to traditional form in "Paloma": "yo me arrogué el privilegio / de innovar arcaizando, / de avanzar retrociendo" (I assumed the privilege / of innovating by imitating the archaic / of advancing by going back). Likewise the three sonnets of the section "Sonetos artesanales" (Artisanal Sonnets) in *Poesía* celebrate metacritically the work of the poet. The poem "Violante" plays on the title character's name, harkening back to Félix Lope de Vega's similar love sonnet. In the final tercet Chacel seems to observe how the poetic process works: "Radiante cría fue del inmortal / soneto, circulando por su nombre / la sangre excelsa que la idea engendra" (She was a radiant child of the immortal / sonnet, circulating through her name / the sublime blood that the idea engenders). The sonnet "Proverbio" (Proverb), which refers to and ends with the saying "El que hace un cesto, hace ciento" (He who makes a basket, makes a hundred), recalls the praise of workers in her Valencian product poems.

Reviewers have deemed the poem "Oda a Leónides" (Ode to Leonides), written to a playmate of hers during her youth in Tierra de Campos, the tour de force of her recent work. Chacel's mature voice is retrospective and, in her own words, "poeticofilosófica" (poetic-philosophical). She departs from vivid childhood memories – of running in cornfields and trying to catch an oriole – to recapture not just a shadow of her youth but another glimpse into the mystery of poetics. Remembering her early writing of verse and evoking the lamentational mood of Garcilaso de la Vega's eclogues, she meditates on Francisco de Quevedo's well-known metaphysical sonnet on the brevity of life: "'¡Ah de la vida!' . . . ¿Nadie me responde?'" ("Life ahoy!" . . . No one answers me?). She conflates inspiration, memories, and words into an image of light: "Se encendió refulgiendo en las tinieblas, / imponiendo el destello de su FUE, de su real HABER SIDO y no cediendo / a dejar de SER HOY, y ser mañana" (It flared up shining in the darkness, / imposing the flash of its WAS, of its real HAVING BEEN and not giving way / to stop BEING TODAY, and tomorrow). Chacel answers her metaphysical query – "¿Una palabra puede ser un hecho?" (Can a word be an act?) – affirmatively in the final stanza: "¿Por qué, despilfarrando teorías, / evoqué cosas vagas, cuando sólo / tu nombre es la verdad: es lo que fue / tan eterno, tan cierto y persistente / como lo que por sólo su virtud / perdura en la pureza de haber sido?" (Why, squandering theories, did I evoke vague things, when only / your name is the truth: it is what was / so eternal, so certain and persistent / as that which only due to its virtue / endures in the purity of having been?). These final lines of lament and affirmation, directed to both Leonides and God, culminate a metacritical exploration of poetic effects. They demonstrate the breadth of Chacel's poetry and, in particular, the ever-present link in her work between poetics and spirituality.

Inspired by the success of *Barrio de maravillas,* Chacel wrote two other autobiographical novels, *Acrópolis* (1984) and *Ciencias naturales* (Natural Sci-

ences, 1988), completing a remarkable trilogy. *Acrópolis* deals with the period of the 1920s until the beginning of the Spanish republic, the formative years for her intellectual generation. *Ciencias naturales* begins with a journey of exile. A professor and his young female companion, the latter being as yet without self-definition or a career, follow what was Chacel's own path to South America. The leitmotiv for the journey of exile is the total darkness of night on the open sea. As Marías says in his prologue to *La sinrazón,* referring both to Chacel's preference for the hermetic and to what was for much of her life the oppressive burden of unglorious exile, she "no era 'un emigrado que escribe,' sino una escritora en la emigración" (was not "an emigrant who writes," but a writer in [the state of] emigration). The Spanish government recognized the totality of Rosa Chacel's literary production and celebrated her worldwide reputation when in 1988 it awarded her the prestigious Premio Nacional de las Letras Españolas.

**Interviews:**

A. Nuñez, "Encuentro con Rosa Chacel," *Insula,* 25 (September–October 1970): 5;

E. Chamorro, "Rosa Chacel: 'Objetivismo no significa deshumanización,'" *Triunfo,* no. 473 (June 1971): 60–61;

M. Parajón, "Encuentro con Rosa Chancel," *Insula,* 27 (November 1972): 4;

F. G. Delgado, "Rosa Chacel y la necesidad del retorno," *Insula,* 30 (September 1975): 4;

R. M. Pereda, "Rosa Chacel: 'Soy consciente de mi inteligencia,'" *El País,* 6 May 1979, "Arte y Pensamiento," pp. iv–v;

G. Vidal and R. Zanner, "Rosa Chacel: La pasión de la perfección," *Camp de l'Arpa,* 74 (April 1980): 69–73;

M. Vincent, "Rosa Chacel en el Barrio de Maravillas," *El País,* 7 October 1981, pp. 11–12;

M. Sánchez Arnosi, "Conversación con Rosa Chacel en torno a *Alcancía,*" *Insula,* 38 (April 1983): 11;

Walmir Ayala, "A Memoria Imita a Eternidade," *MGSL,* 19 (14 January 1984): 8–9;

J. Guerrero Martín, "Sigo siendo una señorita de Valladolid," *Vanguardia,* 6 May 1984, pp. 6–11;

Eunice Meyers, "Interview with Rosa Chacel," *Hispania,* 67 (May 1984): 286–287;

R. Oliver, "Rosa Chacel: La pasión de la razón," *El País Semanal* (May 1984): 10–14;

M. Ciriza, "Rosa Chacel: 'La vejez es un fenómeno exacto e irrebatible,'" *Independiente,* 3 October 1987, p. 35;

Shirley Mangini, "Entrevista con Rosa Chacel," *Insula,* 42 (November 1987): 10–11;

M. Montero, "Escribo para explicarme y explicar lo que siento," *Comunidad Escolar,* 20 January 1988, p. 27;

M. Aguirre, "Entrevista a Rosa Chacel: 'La literatura femenina es una estupidez,'" *El País,* 30 January 1988, "Libros," p. 5;

Ana Rodríguez, "Rosa Chacel, un sistema que el amor presidía," *Quimera,* 84 (December 1988): 30–35;

Andrés Trapiello, "Vivimos un momento agónico," *El País,* 29 February 1992, "Babielia," pp. 11, 13.

## Bibliography:

Ana Rodríguez, "Biografía comentada," *Anthropos,* supplement 8 (May 1988).

## Biography:

Ana Rodríguez, "Cronología intelectual de Rosa Chacel," *Anthropos,* 85 (June 1988): 28–34.

## References:

Francisca Aguirre, "Rosa Chacel como en su playa propia," *Cuadernos Hispanoamericanos,* no. 296 (February 1975): 298–315;

Antonio de Albornoz, "Poesía de la España peregrina," in *El exilio español de 1939 (IV): Cultura y literatura,* edited by J. L. Abellán (Madrid: Taurus, 1977);

*Anthropos,* special issue on Chacel, 85 (June 1988);

Antonio Beneyto, "Rosa Chacel: Esencialmente, un ser libre," in his *Censura y política en los escritores españoles* (Barcelona: Plaza y Janés, 1977), pp. 235–239;

*Cartas a Rosa Chacel* (Madrid: Cátedra, 1992);

Rafael Conte, *Narraciones de la España desterrada* (Barcelona: EDHASA, 1970), pp. 137–143;

Conte, "Rosa Chacel: La inocencia en los infiernos; Leticia en el Barrio de Maravillas," *Revista de Occidente,* 10–11 (August–September 1976): 100–103;

Aurora Egido, "*Desde el amanecer:* La Memoria omnisciente de Rosa Chacel," *Cuadernos Hispanoamericanos,* no. 390 (December 1982): 645–661;

Egido, "Los espacios del tiempo en *Memorias de Leticia Valle,*" *Revista de Literatura,* 43 (1981): 107–131;

Clara Janés, "Diario de una escritora," *Nueva Estafeta,* 53 (1983): 90–92;

Janés, Prologue to Chacel's *Los títulos* (Barcelona: EDHASA, 1981), pp. i–ix;

Janés, "Quién es Rosa Chacel," *Nueva Estafeta,* 45–46 (1982): 49–53;

Shirley Mangini, "Women and Spanish Modernism: The Case of Rosa Chacel," *Anales de la Literatura Española Contemporanea,* 12, nos. 1–2 (1987): 17–28;

Julián Marías, "Azar, destino y carácter de Rosa Chacel," Prologue to Chacel's *La sinrazón* (Barcelona: Andorra, 1970), pp. 9–13;

Marías, "Camino hacia la novela," in his *Ensayos de convivencia hispánica* (Buenos Aires: Sudamericana, 1963), pp. 181–183;

Marías, "Las razones de *La sinrazón,*" *Insula,* 16 (September 1961): 5;

Marías, "Rosa Chacel: La memoria como invención," *Vanguardia,* 20 November 1987, p. 5;

José R. Marra López, "Rosa Chacel: La búsqueda intelectual del mundo," in his *Narrativa española fuera de España (1936–1961)* (Madrid: Guadarrama, 1963), pp. 133–147;

Ana María Moix, "La agonía de la razón," *Camp de l'Arpa,* 74 (April 1980): 74–76;

Moix, "Rosa Chacel," in her *24 x 24* (Barcelona: Península, 1972), pp. 141–146;

Eunice Myers, "Narcissism and the Quest for Identity in Rosa Chacel's *La sinrazón,*" *Perspectives on Contemporary Literature,* 8 (1982): 85–90;

Myers, "*Teresa:* Rosa Chacel's Novel of Exile and Alienation," *Monographic Review / Revista Monográfica,* 2 (1986): 151–158;

Wilma Newberry, "Rosa Chacel's *Barrio de maravillas:* The Role of the Arts and the Problem of Spain," *Hispanic Journal,* 9 (Spring 1988): 37–44;

Janet Pérez, "A Candidate for the Cervantes Prize," in her *Contemporary Women Writers of Spain* (Boston: Twayne, 1988), pp. 61–68;

Alberto Porlan, *La sinrazón de Rosa Chacel* (Madrid: Anjana, 1984);

Luis Suñén, "Rosa Chacel, memoria y estilo," *Quimera,* 84 (December 1988): 22–29.

# Antonio Colinas

## (30 January 1946 – )

### Stephen J. Summerhill
*Ohio State University*

BOOKS: *Poemas de la tierra y de la sangre* (León: Imprenta Provincial, 1969);

*Preludios a una noche total* (Madrid: Rialp, 1969);

*Truenos y flautas en un templo* (San Sebastián: Caja de Ahorros Provincial de Guipúzcoa, 1972);

*Leopardi* (Madrid: Júcar, 1974);

*Sepulcro en Tarquinia* (León: Institutión Fray Bernardino de Sahagún, 1975);

*Viaje a los monasterios de España* (Barcelona: Planeta, 1976);

*Conocer Vicente Aleixandre y su obra* (Barcelona: DOPESA, 1977);

*Astrolabio* (Madrid: Visor, 1979);

*Orillas del Orbigo* (León: Del Teleno, 1980);

*Poesía, 1967–1981* (Madrid: Visor, 1982);

*Aleixandre* (Barcelona: Barcanova, 1982);

*Noche más allá de la noche* (Madrid: Visor, 1982);

*La viña salvaje* (Córdoba: Antorcha de Paja, 1984);

*Un año en el sur ( para una educación estética)* (Madrid: Trieste, 1985);

*Larga carta a Francesca* (Barcelona: Seix Barral, 1986);

*Jardín de Orfeo* (Madrid: Visor, 1988);

*La llamada de los árboles* (Barcelona: Elfos, 1988);

*Hacia el infinito naufragio (Una biografía de Giacomo Leopardi)* (Barcelona: Tusquets, 1988);

*Libro de las noches abiertas* (Milan: Pfeiffer, 1989);

*El sentido primero de la palabra poética* (Madrid & Mexico City: Fondo de Cultura Económica, 1989);

*Pere Alemany y la música de los signos* (Barcelona: Ambit, 1989);

*Tratado de armonía* (Barcelona: Tusquets, 1991);

*Los silencios de fuego* (Barcelona: Tusquets, 1992).

OTHER: *Poetas italianos contemporáneos,* edited by Colinas (Madrid: Nacional, 1978);

Giacomo Leopardi, *Poesía y prosa,* edited by Colinas (Madrid: Alfaguara, 1979).

TRANSLATIONS: Eduardo Sanguineti, *Wirrwar,* translated, with a prologue, by Colinas (Madrid: Corazón, 1975);

Pier Paolo Pasolini, *Las cenizas de Gramsci,* translated, with a prologue, by Colinas (Madrid: Corazón, 1975);

Giacomo Leopardi, *Poesía y prosa; Diario del primer amor; Canti (bilingue); Diálogos,* edited and translated by Colinas (Madrid: Alfaguara, 1979);

Carlo Levi, *Cristo se paró en Eboli* (Madrid: Alfaguara, 1980);

Emilio Salgari, *Los tigres de Mompracen* (Madrid: Alianza, 1981);

Salgari, *La montaña de luz* (Madrid: Alianza, 1982);

Giuseppe T. Di Lampedusa, *Stendhal,* selected and translated by Colinas (Madrid: Trieste, 1989).

Antonio Colinas is usually identified with the *novísimo* (very new) poets of the late 1960s and 1970s – writers such as Pere Gimferrer, Guillermo Carnero, Antonio Carvajal, Luis Antonio de Villena, and Jaime Siles, among many others, who led a growing reaction against the social poetry that had dominated the postwar era in Spain; they introduced a more imaginative, self-conscious, and aesthetically achieved verse that was closer to mainstream European modernism. Over the years these poets have often been accused of culturalism, that is, of being aestheticists who burden their poetry with ornamentation and unnecessary artistic allusions. The reproach has some validity in terms of the early work of a few – Gimferrer or Villena, for example – but it cannot be applied to Colinas, who, though attracted to formal beauty and artistic allusion, seeks a meditative poetry oriented toward an exploration of the self and nature. This approach makes him stand apart from many of his contemporaries. His literary origins are romantic with strong influences from Giacomo Leopardi, Friedrich Hölderlin, and Novalis. He has also been deeply influenced by esoteric thought, including the mysticism of Saint John of the Cross; the *I Ching* and other Oriental writings; and the enigmatic works of the twentieth-century Spanish philosopher María Zambrano.

*Antonio Colinas*

Colinas was born in La Bañeza, in the province of León, on 30 January 1946. From 1961 to 1964 he attended secondary school in Córdoba; he later described the experience in his autobiographical novel *Un año en el sur (para una educación estética)* (A Year in the South [for an Aesthetic Education], 1985). He then spent six years in Madrid, first as an engineering student at the Complutense University and later as a budding writer and poet. During this latter period he developed a close relationship with the well-known "Generation of '27" poet Vicente Aleixandre, about whom he later wrote a critical study. After military service Colinas married María José Marcos in July 1970 and then moved with her to spend four years in Italy as a lecturer of Spanish at the Universities of Milan and Bergamo. Following three more years in Madrid, the couple moved permanently in 1977 to the island of Ibiza in the Balearics, where they live with their two children, Clara and Alejandro. Colinas earns his livelihood as a lecturer, contributor to newspapers and journals, and translator of Italian literature. As he has

become more recognized, he has traveled widely throughout Europe and the Americas. Consistent with some themes in his poetry, he has also become an amateur archaeologist and in recent years has taken an active role in the ecology movement.

Colinas describes himself as having evolved from an early phase in which he sought to exteriorize emotions in realistic poems, through a middle period when he centered his poetry on mystery and enigma, to a more recent stage in which he has returned to writing realistically. Whereas such a pattern can generally be found in his work, it cannot hide a deeper consistency that appears in all phases of his writing: his effort to recover a traditional or even classical understanding of poetry by articulating universal truths about love, time, death, and beauty that he believes have motivated Western art since antiquity but that have become lost amid the superficiality of present-day consumer society. Seeking to renew an appreciation of mystery and the sacred, he wants to rediscover the transcendent in nature, which he understands in typically romantic terms as a book whose contradictory signs he must decipher. As he does so, he recognizes that life is suspended over an opaque, cosmic emptiness that makes existence enigmatic and all things vulnerable to extinction. Although societies try to hide this fact, the role of the poet is to refuse such deception by reminding readers of the grandeur and fragility of the universe and human life.

Consistent with his romantic origins, Colinas cultivates a relatively unadorned style that is sometimes conversational and other times stately or majestic. He is attempting to express a visionary awareness of the sublime and the contradictory essence of the universe. This exploration leads him to cultivate paradox as a way of capturing the prerational truth of things, and it also produces in him a profound sensitivity to the musicality of verse. Colinas speaks repeatedly of the links among poetry, music, and breathing, as if the rhythm of inhaling and exhaling were a kind of song associated with poetic inspiration and nature. Stylistically such concerns often produce an incantatory diction in which obsessive repetitions evoke the sublime enigmas he seeks to uncover.

Colinas's first book, *Poemas de la tierra y de la sangre* (Poems of the Land and Blood, 1969) is a brief collection of six descriptive poems set in the natural environment of the province of León. Seeking refuge amid the pristine woods, mountains, and rivers of the region, the solitary poet feels the timeless beauty of nature as a counterweight against his growing sense that he is condemned to live in time and to die. He wants to share love with another but finds fulfillment in these austere, lonely places. The tone of the language is stately and meditative. Immersing himself in nature, the poet feels its force in his blood. Additionally readers see his fascination for something that will become constant in his later work: the ruins of the past, which echo with a mysterious music that speaks of humanity's struggle to overcome the passing of time. In spite of its brevity, the book shows a young poet instinctively gravitating toward the themes that mark his future work.

Nature remains central to Colinas's second book, *Preludios a una noche total* (Preludes to Total Night, 1969), which goes further toward creating a romantic vision of love and death. It centers on a love experience played out amid nature's passage from autumn to winter, which therefore functions as a symbol of the poet's feelings. The trees, birds, and changing natural light express the emotions of the lovers as they move from the Edenic happiness of the flowering of love to the harsh winter of its decline. As José Olivio Jiménez has said, love becomes

an experience of night lived as union with the cosmos. As love declines, the poet seeks a world of dreams in which winter brings the magic presence of the divine. At the end, he is left with a nostalgic longing for a childhood in which purity and joy counteract the absence of love.

Colinas believes that in these first two volumes he began to explore his personal voice as a poet and that in his next collection, *Truenos y flautas en un templo* (Thunderclaps and Flutes in a Temple, 1972), he turned to the voice of his generation. He means that *Truenos y flautas* is self-consciously aestheticist. It is his only book in this vein and shows him using new poetic forms: short lyrics, dramatic monologues, and apostrophic complaints about the decaying world. Written during a trip to England and France in 1970, the book describes a speaker who cultivates fantasy or imagination as both escape into pleasure and means of achieving insight. "¿Con qué alucinaciones construiré mis versos?" (With what hallucinations will I construct my verse?), he asks in the poem "Ocaso" (West). He answers by imagining himself a *duende* (enchanter) who brings the past alive by hearing the speech of ancient statues or voices in a temple. He sees fantastic animals such as a wounded deer drinking at a fountain, and he imagines himself as Ulysses tied to a boat and listening to the tempting songs of the sirens. The images portray one who is succumbing to the temptation of art, willingly drinking the "poison" of fantasy and reaching toward a kind of poetic folly. As he pursues this aestheticist vision, he scorns the vulgar masses, whom he describes as too cowardly to feel the divinity of the universe. The polemical tone and self-conscious aestheticism sustaining such attitudes contrast sharply with the contemplative calm of Colinas's earlier nature poetry and show a poet still uncertain about the directions of his work.

This uncertainty is resolved in the transitional volume *Sepulcro en Tarquinia* (Sepulchre in Tarquinia, 1975), which begins with the aestheticism of *Truenos* but shifts at midpoint to a new, visionary cosmology that is characteristic of Colinas's more mature second stage. The first part of the book is a product of his four-year stay in Italy from 1970 to 1974. There Colinas was drawn to both pagan and Christian ruins as expressions of humanity's search for permanence. His fascination for the Italian past culminated in one of his major achievements, the long elegy "Sepulcro en Tarquinia," in which the opening of an ancient Roman tomb becomes the point of reference for a haunting meditation on memory, love, and death. The final two sections of

*Drawing of Colinas by Ricardo Zamorano, circa 1983*

the book transport readers back to the region of León, where Colinas finds a new vision of nature based on a growing fascination for transcendent mystery. In the long poem "Castra Petavonium" (the Roman name for León) he describes a spiritual journey back in time toward the origin of nature. Withdrawing from the contemporary world, he says that "nuestro hambre es celeste" (our hunger is celestial), and he is led to meditate on the dark, empty spaces of the universe. As he does so, he becomes obscurely aware that death and mystery are the only constant experiences of humanity.

The direction taken in the last part of *Sepulcro en Tarquinia* appears connected to Colinas's decision to take up permanent residence on Ibiza in 1977. Withdrawing from modern society, he immersed himself in the starry skies, rocky terrain, and sundrenched sea. These elements form the basis of his next book, *Astrolabio* (Astrolabe, 1979), one of his major works. His goal in the poems is to recover an appreciation of the sacred quality of life by turning

his back on society and pursuing what he calls "el curso insondable del camino nocturno" (the unfathomable course of the nocturnal path). Meditating on the elementary natural forces of the environment, he feels imbued with "el orden y la locura de las estrellas" (the order and folly of the stars), that is, the power of an enigmatic being that has propelled the universe since the foundation of time. Colinas appears uncertain whether this being is a divine force on which all things depend or if it is an "eterno vacío astral" (eternal astral emptiness) devoid of ultimate purpose. He senses a kind of hidden music within nature that suggests the divine, but he also feels that it remains mysterious and unreachable, perhaps no more than a figment of the imagination. In the end, all he has are the lonely bonfires lit by island shepherds to protect themselves at night. They symbolize the vulnerability of humanity, clinging to life amid the abyss that surrounds it. The human species must forge its destiny in an empty universe, and, in this sense, a dominant

*Colinas, circa 1986*

theme of *Astrolabio* is the inevitable passing of all human experience into oblivion. In such a situation, love and beauty motivate the poet to listen to the music of nature and the ruins of the past surrounded by the emptiness of the world.

In 1982 Colinas won the prestigious National Poetry Prize of Spain for *Poesía, 1967–1981.* There followed another major volume, *Noche más allá de la noche* (Night Beyond Night, 1982). Composed entirely in alexandrines, *Noche* continues and enriches the visionary cosmology seen in *Astrolabio,* and at the same time it communicates a greater sense of the contradictory basis of nature. According to Colinas, the divine makes itself felt in the natural environment, but it is somehow both whole and empty. It is linked to contentment, grief, life, and death. Thus the sacred origin of all things is a kind of plenary nothingness, a contradictory quality of being and nonbeing. In turn, history and human events are a chaos of destruction that can only be countered by the achievement of love and beauty. In such a context music is even more prominent than ever, but instead of the flutes and violins mentioned in his earlier books, readers encounter the dark, somber tones of the oboe. The style of *Noche* is more formal and majestic than that of most of Colinas's earlier work. He expresses his sublime vision through a more openly paradoxical syntax and seeks to capture in words the inapprehensibility that constitutes the mystery of being.

*Astrolabio* and *Noche más allá de la noche* are the culmination of Colinas's second phase and stand as his most important works to date. As if drained by the effort to produce them, he began to publish different kinds of writing throughout the 1980s but always in a vein similar to his poetry. Notable among these other works are the first two parts of a projected trilogy of novels: *Un año en el sur* and *Larga carta a Francesca* (Long Letter to Francesca, 1986). Both are autobiographical bildungsromans that describe an artist's coming to consciousness through the experience of love, suffering, and death. Another group of his books includes collections of nature essays such as those in *Orillas del Orbigo* (Banks of the Orbigo River, 1980), a series of meditations on his native León; *La llamada de los árboles* (The Call of the Trees, 1988), a set of reflections on the symbolic meaning of trees; and *Libro de las noches abiertas* (Book of Open Nights, 1989), a group of meditations on his fascination for night. Colinas also published essays on his understanding of poetry, as in *El sentido primero de la palabra poética* (The Primary Sense of the Poetic Word, 1989) and *Tratado de armonía* (Treatise on Harmony, 1991). The former argues that poetry is a revelation of ultimate truths; the latter explores the celestial harmony of the universe and shows the increasing influence of mysticism on Colinas's thought. Another volume, *Pere Alemany y la música de los signos* (Pere Alemany and the Music of Signs, 1989), presents the painter Pere Alemany and his

*Cover for Colinas's 1979 book of poetry focusing on the elementary*
*forces of nature*

work in the context of the natural environment of Ibiza.

In 1984 Colinas published a brief, miscellaneous selection of previously unpublished verse, *La viña salvaje* (Wild Vineyard). Some poems in this collection were written in the early 1970s. The title poem is the most recent in the volume and deals with the absence of love. *Jardín de Orfeo* (Garden of Orpheus, 1988), like *La viña salvaje,* maintains many of Colinas's customary themes: humanity has lost its way; the gods have become dispersed; and the sacred is available only as a "música de sangre" (blood music) that the poet feels while contemplating such phenomena as the rock formations of his native León, a sunset, or the cathedral of Toledo. The title poem is one of his most complete attempts to capture the epiphanic moment when one fuses with "la nada plena" (plenary nothingness).

On the other hand, *Jardín de Orfeo* also reveals the first signs of a shift in perspective that Colinas believes is characteristic of his recent work. The vast cosmic spaces evident in his earlier volumes have been replaced by gardens and walls that appear emblematic of a restricted world he is trying to overcome in order to join a transcendent domain beyond. Ordinary experiences such as hearing an owl at night, seeing an almond tree covered by snow, or visiting the Mexican pyramids at Teotihuacán become points of departure for meditations on the search for mystical union. Colinas also alludes frequently to the poet as a marginal social being who grasps the secret of life and death but is never understood by those around him. Increasingly he is haunted by the gap separating him from the world.

This understanding is more intensely expressed in Colinas's *Los silencios de fuego* (The Silences of Fire, 1992). It begins as a somewhat miscellaneous collection that combines homages to favorite writers – Boris Pasternak, Antonio Machado, and Novalis, for example – with diverse reflections on daily life. Colinas describes the emptiness of listening to academic speeches while exploding oil wells – possibly those ignited during the Gulf War – contaminate the world. As the book progresses, however, familiar themes reappear. Colinas gradually withdraws into his beloved nature in search of "lo no escrito," "lo no hablado," and "lo no impuesto" (the unwritten, the unspoken, and the unimposed). He is haunted by visions of the otherwordly – angels of music and silent voices from beyond – and he pursues his mystic longing to fuse with the hidden source of the universe. This last tendency, the urge to become one with the silent fire of nature, is a prominent note of his recent verse and points to the increasing influence of mysticism on his writing.

Colinas has said that the two major trends of twentieth-century writing – avant-garde and social literature – have been exhausted. His explicit response is to urge a return to romantic poetry characteristic of the nineteenth century. Such a goal suggests that he is seeking a traditional poetry that would express the eternal verities represented over the centuries throughout European art. This tendency has made some critics ask if, by seeking to return to the past, Colinas is responding constructively to the problems of the present age or if he is merely anachronistic and escapist. However, a rediscovery of tradition is one of the major trends in the cultural phenomenon called postmodernism. Rejecting the tendency of contemporary society to subject all life to the manipulations of science and technology, conservative postmodernists have sought to resurrect ideas and beliefs of the past as a way of rediscovering meaning in an increasingly disoriented world. A new ecological sensitivity is part of this trend.

Antonio Colinas participates fully in such tendencies. His attempts to renew an appreciation for the sacredness of life and nature point to a future in which human beings would live in harmony with their natural environment. His admiration for love and beauty speaks of his desire to salvage that which is meaningful in the legacy of the past while at the same time offering something positive to readers. In this sense he stands as an important exponent of a tradition-oriented or conservative impulse within postmodern Spanish poetry, and he has provided a significant body of work.

**References:**

"Antonio Colinas: Armonía órfica, una poética de la fusión," *Anthropos,* special issue, 105 (February 1990);

Alonso Gutiérrez and Luis Miguel, *El corazón desmemoriado: Clares poéticas de Antonio Colinas* (Salamanca: Diputación Provincial de León, 1990);

José Olivio Jiménez, Prologue to Colinas's *Poesía, 1967–1981* (Madrid: Visor, 1982).

# Angel Crespo
## (18 July 1926 -   )

Alan S. Bruflat
*Wayne State College*

BOOKS: *Primera antología de mis versos (1942–48)* (Ciudad Real: Jabalón, 1949);

*Una lengua emerge* (Ciudad Real: Instituto de Estudios Manchegos, 1950);

*Quedan señales* (Madrid: Millán, 1952);

*La pintura* (Madrid: Agora, 1955);

*Todo está vivo* (Madrid: Agora, 1956);

*La cesta y el río (1954–1957)* (Madrid: Millán, 1957);

*Junio feliz* (Madrid: Rialp, 1959);

*Júpiter* (Madrid: Librería Abril, 1959);

*Oda a Nanda Papiri* (Cuenca: Piedra que Habla, 1959);

*Antología poética,* edited by Crespo and José Albí (Valencia: Verbo, 1960);

*Puerta clavada, 1958–1960* (Montevideo: Caballo del Mar, 1961);

*José María Iglesias* (Santander: Isla de los Ratones, 1962);

*Suma y sigue (1959–1961)* (Barcelona: Salinas, 1962);

*Situación de la poesía concreta,* by Crespo and Pilar Gómez Bedate (Madrid: Confección Gráfica de Francisco Nieva, 1963);

*Cartas desde un pozo, 1957–1963* (Santander: Isla de los Ratones, 1964);

*No sé cómo decirlo, 1962–1964* (Cuenca: Toro de Barro, 1965);

*Docena florentina* (Madrid: Poesía para Todos, 1966);

*En medio del camino (Poesía, 1949–1970)* (Barcelona: Seix Barral, 1971);

*Juan Ramón Jiménez y la pintura* (Río Piedras: Universidad de Puerto Rico, 1974);

*Claro: Oscuro (1971–1975)* (Zaragoza: Porvivir Independiente, 1978);

*Colección de climas (1975–1978)* (Seville: Aldebarán, 1978);

*Con el tiempo, contra el tiempo* (Cuenca: Toro de Barro, 1978);

*Conocer Dante y su obra* (Barcelona: DOPESA, 1979);

*La invisible luz* (Cuenca: Toro de Barro, 1981);

*Donde no corre el aire* (Seville: Barro, 1981);

*El aire es de los dioses (1978–1981)* (Zaragoza: Olifante, 1982);

*El bosque transparente (1971–1981)* (Barcelona: Seix Barral, 1983);

*Estudios sobre Pessoa* (Barcelona: Bruguera, 1984);

*Parnaso confidencial (1971–   )* (Jerez: Arenal, 1984);

*El ave en su aire (1975–1984)* (Barcelona: Plaza & Janés, 1985);

*El duque de Rivas* (Madrid: Júcar, 1986);

*Las cenizas de la flor* (Madrid: Júcar, 1987);

*La vida plural de Fernando Pessoa* (Barcelona: Seix Barral, 1988);

*Ocupación del fuego (1986–1989)* (Madrid: Hiperión, 1990).

OTHER: *Antología de la nueva poesía portuguesa,* edited by Crespo (Madrid: Rialp, 1961);

*Antología de la poesía brasileña; desde el Romanticismo a la Generación del Cuarenta y Cinco,* edited by Crespo (Barcelona: Seix Barral, 1973);

*Antología de la poesía modernista,* edited by Crespo (Tarragona: Tarraco, 1980);

"Mi experiencia postista," *Insula,* 44 (June 1989): 27–28.

TRANSLATIONS: Fernando Pessoa, *Poemas de Alberto Caeiro* (Madrid: Rialp, 1957);

Dante, *La divina comedia: Inferno* (Barcelona: Seix Barral, 1973);

Dante, *La divina comedia: Purgatorio* (Barcelona: Seix Barral, 1976);

Dante, *La divina comedia: Paradiso* (Barcelona: Seix Barral, 1977).

Poet, essayist, art critic, and teacher, Angel Crespo has distinguished himself as one of the most talented and productive members of the post–Spanish Civil War literary scene. His career, spanning half a century, has taken him across Europe, and to the United States and Latin America. Crespo is associated with a group of poets known as the "Generation of 1956," but such a link limits his importance, for he is a key figure in the wider context of Spanish poetry in the 1950s and beyond. Al-

*Angel Crespo (photograph by A. Lorente)*

though he has received somewhat less critical attention than such influential figures from the generation as Angel González or Francisco Brines, it is clear that, through his wide-ranging experiences and his contact with other literatures and cultures, particularly those of Portugal, Brazil, and Italy, Crespo has helped broaden the scope of Spanish poetry and has thus carved for himself a place in its history.

Angel Crespo y Pérez de Madrid was born on 18 July 1926 in Ciudad Real, a town approximately one hundred miles south of Madrid. His father, Angel Crespo y Crespo, was a telegrapher, was politically conservative, and was not well read; however, through the literary interests of his mother, María de Los Angeles Pérez de Crespo, and through an uncle's knowledge of the "Generation of 1927," the young Angel got his first taste of literature. The Crespos had a small farm near Alcolea

called the Cuesta del Jaral, and Angel's early rural experiences developed his love of nature, which was to be the defining element of the poetry he wrote during the early part of his career.

Crespo was ten at the outbreak of the civil war and, as a result, did not attend school regularly, but he still read widely at home. Among his favorite subjects were French (taught by a family friend), heroic verse, and mythology; these were to be influences throughout Crespo's poetic career. At the age of seventeen, discouraged by his family from pursuing a degree in arts and letters, Crespo went to Madrid to study law. During this period his love for poetry blossomed, and, despite the demands of the legal curriculum, he started frequenting salons and making the acquaintance of local poets.

Perhaps the most important influence on Crespo during the late 1940s was *postismo,* a poetic movement that sought innovation in metaphor and imagery and an opening up to European influences, at a time when realistic, socially oriented poetry dominated the Spanish literary scene because of the work of such poets as Blas de Otero and José Hierro. Crespo was introduced by friend and fellow poet Juan Alcaide to *postista* poet Carlos Edmundo de Ory in 1945 and subsequently to Eduardo Chicarro and Silvano Sernesi. He later collaborated with them to establish some short-lived journals, *Postismo* and the *Cerbatana*. After earning his law degree in 1948, Crespo ventured to Morocco, then returned to Alcolea to begin work on what was to become *Una lengua emerge* (A Language Emerges, 1950), his first major volume of poetry.

In the 1950s Crespo gradually integrated himself into Spanish literary life. In addition to publishing more books of poetry, he also coedited two important literary magazines, the *Pájaro de Paja* and *Deucalión*. Because these and other journals were often underfunded and because they attacked the conservative establishment, they usually lasted little more than a year. Nevertheless, they were an important outlet for new, avant-garde poets such as Crespo. While the principal postwar poets were writings works of social relevance in colloquial language, Crespo was exploring ways to transform everyday, natural scenes and images into a magical world of symbol, allegory, and allusion. Because of Crespo's departure from the realistic poetry of the day and his tendency to employ natural imagery in novel ways, critics José Albí and José María Balcells have called Crespo's early period "magic realism" (though not in the sense applied to fiction). This early period ended with *Suma y sigue* (Balance Forward, 1962). In this phase Crespo experimented with different techniques, many of them conventional (such as allegory), in search of a poetic voice. The strong presence of the poetic speaker in the first-person narration can be noted throughout *Una lengua emerge,* as in "La voz" (The Voice), in which Crespo attempts to portray the poetic voice as birds breaking into song:

> En todas partes una lengua emerge
> que entre los árboles canta, canta.
> Sube una voz. Ignoro cuántos pájaros
> tiene mi voz que en los árboles vive.
>
> (Everywhere there emerges a voice
> singing, singing in the trees.
> A word comes out of me. I do not know how many birds are
> in this voice of mine that dwells in the trees.)

One notes immediately the symbiotic relationship between the poet and his surroundings; external reality and internal creation are unified and spontaneous.

Crespo is noted for personifying animals and plants to illustrate human traits. This technique is especially evident in his early work. The poem "Las cosas" (Things) appears to describe a rural scene yet shifts perspective, through personification, to yield a new insight:

> Por los caminos encontramos bueyes.
> Vamos contando testas de animales cornudos.
> En los caminos encontramos árboles.
> Vamos contando ramas de vegetales altos.
> Vamos por los caminos contando hierbas.
> Pero también los bueyes cuentan presencias de hombres.
> Y los árboles cuentan nervudos brazos de hombre.
> Y las hierbas nos cuentan las pestañas.
>
> (Along the way we see oxen.
> We count the heads of the horned animals.
> Along the way we see trees.
> We count the branches of the tall green plants.
> We count the grasses along the way.
> But the oxen also count the presence of humans.
> And the trees count the sinewy human arms.
> And the grasses count our eyelashes.)

Critics of this poem generally agree that its change in perspective, from the speaker's contemplation of reality to his realization that he himself is being watched by nature, shocks the reader and forces him to work to discover broad themes. Several ideas emerge, all in keeping with Crespo's poetics: the speaker, representative of humankind, becomes insignificant in a larger context; the natural world retains its dominion; and the simplicity of the everyday world contains transcendent values that people must seek lest they lose a sense of unity with the natural world and end up fragmented and useless. A social message is apparent as well, for the structure of the poem recalls medieval didactic verse and fits in well with the view of humankind in a social context that predominated in the 1950s.

Another theme that emerges in Crespo's early work is that of the poet as creator. The poet must use words to combat the destructive forces of time, since artistic creations are eternal in their beauty. Although this idea is not new and echoes earlier works in Spanish poetry, such as Federico García Lorca's *Llanto por Ignacio Sánchez Mejías* (1935; translated as *Lament for the Death of a Bullfighter,* 1937), its expression in Crespo's work reveals his affinity for the visual arts, especially painting. In *La pintura* (Painting, 1955) the poet becomes his own god, cre-

## El ciervo

Sobre el atardecer camina un ciervo,
mientras al sol la noche desposee.
El hocico del ciervo, malherido,
sangre derrama encima de las nubes.

Tiemblan las casas, crujen levemente,
mientras inquietos van sus habitantes
del espejo al balcón y, una vez más,
contemplan su mirada en los espejos.

Un ciervo a tales horas
corre el camino que ante el hombre pende,
devorando las hierbas luminosas
que alimentan los ojos.

Un ciervo abre sus fauces,
ciervo feroz de boca cotidiana,
que con los dientes rompe las cortinas
de la diaria luz, mientras derrama
sangre herida de sol en mi camino.

*Fair copy of "El ciervo," which was included in* Todo está vivo *(from Peña Labra, Winter 1977–1978; by permission of Angel Crespo)*

ating his work as would an artist on canvas. This long, elaborate poem ends with an admonition:

> Antes que nos pise
> esa sombra que avanza por los campos,
> huyamos por la luz de los pinceles
> dejando nuestra sangre en las cortinas.
>
> (Before we are trampled
> by the shadow advancing across the meadows,
> let us flee by the light of the artist's brush
> leaving behind our blood on the curtains.)

By the skillful use of such traditional poetic devices as allegory, symbol, and personification, Crespo in his early poems uses nature and art to contemplate humankind's place in the universe, seemingly insignificant but capable of transcending the ordinary through works of beauty. Moreover, his interest in the visual arts was to blossom into a career that encompasses art criticism, comparative literature, and poetry.

Although Crespo spent the 1950s involved in the literary world of Madrid, he maintained his legal career as well. In 1953 he went to work as a lawyer for an insurance company, where he eventually rose to department head. In 1956 he married María Luisa Madrilley (whom he later divorced), and a year later a son, Angel, was born. As Crespo worked to balance his daily life with his literary ambitions, he also entered the art world of Madrid, taking charge of the art gallery of the Librería Abril in 1959. The following year the first comprehensive collection of his work was published, with an excellent critical introduction by José Albí. By the 1960s Crespo was beginning to receive more critical attention for his poetry.

One aid to studying the evolution of Crespo's poetry has been the publication of collected works. To date, the two most important books of this type are *En medio del camino* (In the Middle of the Road, 1971), comprising poems written between 1949 and 1970, and *El bosque transparente* (The Transparent Forest, 1983), made up of poems written between 1971 and 1981. The poet's own grouping of his work helps scholars to identify his periods and note changes within a period. Thus while Crespo's earliest poems employ allegory and natural imagery, his works composed in the latter 1950s, such as *La cesta y el río* (The Basket and the River, 1957) and *Junio feliz* (Happy June, 1959), are more varied, with the magic realism and unusual imagery more intense as the poet becomes more philosophical and transcendent. In *Junio feliz* "La tarde: el pájaro" (Afternoon: Bird) shows the diminishing importance to Crespo

of the concrete. The bird is not described except in terms of its activity; visual images in general (especially colors) are lacking. The preponderance of verbs lends the bird a fleeting quality and intensifies the folly of human attempts to control it:

> He perseguido al pájaro oculto de la tarde
> buscándole en la sombra
> del olivar, tocando sólo su sombra al pie del derruido
> muro, llegando tarde.
> . . . . . . . . . . . . . . . . .
> perseguir este pájaro es difícil,
> incluso hallar la pluma
> que perdió en el esfuerzo de la huida:
> solitario trofeo de la tarde.
>
> (I have pursued the hidden bird of the afternoon
> seeking it in the shadows
> of the olive tree, touching only its shadow at the foot of
>     the crumbling wall, too late.
> . . . . . . . . . . . . . . . . . . . . . . .
> It is difficult to chase this bird,
> even to find the feather
> that it lost in its efforts to flee:
> the lone trophy of the afternoon.)

The poet has achieved a poem of great detail and effect without resorting to traditional descriptions of color and form. In this progressive abstract quality of Crespo's work one finds that the sense of mystery and philosophical questioning is heightened. Crespo's work embodies the increasingly open-ended poetry popular in the late 1950s and early 1960s.

Another important current of Crespo's poetry emerges during this period: the use of specific writers and artists as thematic material. From *Oda a Nanda Papiri* (Ode to Nanda Papiri, 1959), based on drawings of Papiri, the wife of Crespo's friend and fellow poet Eduardo Chicarro, to such poems as "Carta al siglo XII" (Letter to the Twelfth Century) and "A Joan Miró," both in *Suma y sigue,* Crespo demonstrates his interest in communicating, through poetry, with the art and artists of his earlier ages in order to show that the artist is the only true spokesperson for an era, since he alone is able to capture its essence.

Crespo's poetry of the early 1960s also reveals his increasing contact with Portuguese and Brazilian literature and art, an interest which was to form an integral part of his career. Crespo first met one of Brazil's most influential poets, Joao Cabral de Melo Neto, when the latter was secretary of the Brazilian embassy in Madrid. Through this association Crespo founded the *Revista de Cultura Brasileña,* which he edited from 1962 to 1970. Not only did

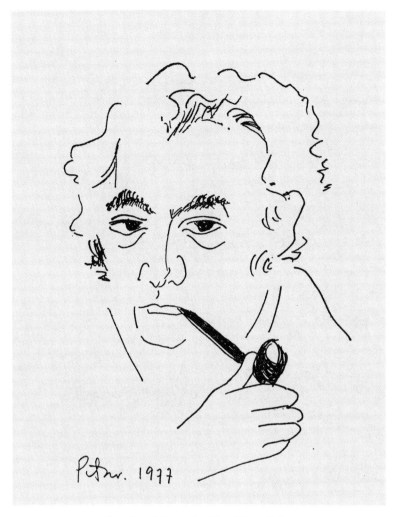

*Drawing of Crespo by Pilar Gómez Bedate*

this involvement expand Crespo's knowledge of and appreciation for Brazilian arts and letters, but it also provided a complement for his increasing interest in Portuguese literature, in particular the work of Pessoa, some of whose poetry Crespo translated and interpreted. The 1960s also saw Crespo travel to Italy, Brazil, and the United States and decide to devote himself full-time to poetry, translation, and criticism. At the same time he abandoned his legal career, he began another, as a student and teacher. After marrying Pilar Gómez Bedate in 1967, he went with her to the University of Puerto Rico in Mayagüez, where both taught (she, literature; he, art). Crespo earned an M.A. in art there in 1970, after studying the relationship between painting and poetry in works by Juan Ramón Jiménez; Crespo then received his Ph.D. from the University of Uppsala (Sweden) in 1973, having written his thesis on El Duque de Rivas, a romantic poet and playwright.

Between studies came trips to Europe, including Spain, where Crespo began translating Dante's *Divine Comedy*.

Critics generally agree that Crespo's first major period ended with *Suma y sigue* and that the second ran from 1962 to 1978. Works from this second period demonstrate a further broadening of Crespo's poetry toward a cultural humanism centered on art. This tendency should not be surprising, given Crespo's forays into the art world throughout the 1960s and his travels to Italy and Brazil. Whereas in his earlier poetry he seeks to express the human condition in an environment that is typically Spanish – that is, he is borrowing from the tradition of Antonio Machado and García Lorca in using local color and everyday details as thematic material – in the newer works he often shows his inspiration being based on other lands and cultures. This multicultural vision reflects both the transfor-

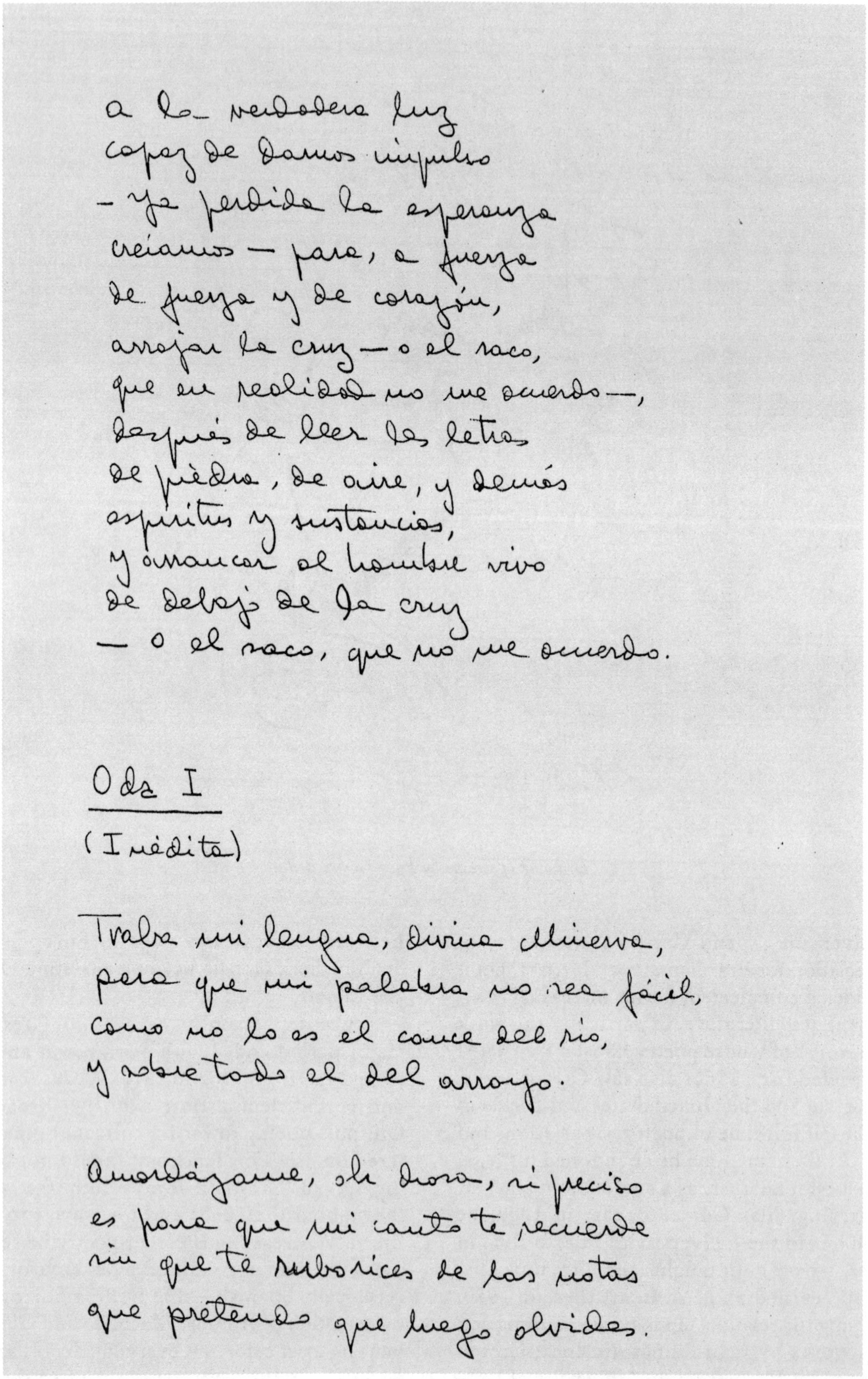

a la verdadera luz
capaz de darnos impulso
—ya perdida la esperanza
creíamos— para, a fuerza
de fuerza y de corazón,
arrojar la cruz —o el saco,
que en realidad no me acuerdo—,
después de leer las letras
de piedra, de aire, y demás
espíritus y sustancias,
y arrancar al hombre vivo
de debajo de la cruz
—o el saco, que no me acuerdo.

## Oda I

(Inédita)

Traba mi lengua, divina Minerva,
para que mi palabra no sea fácil,
como no lo es el cauce del río,
y sobre todo el del arroyo.

Amordázame, oh diosa, si preciso
es para que mi canto te recuerde
sin que te ruborices de las notas
que pretendo que luego olvides.

*Fair copy of an unpublished poem, "Oda I," preceded by the concluding lines of "Cruzo saco," which appeared in* La cesta y el río *(from* Peña Labra, *Winter 1977–1978; by permission of Angel Crespo)*

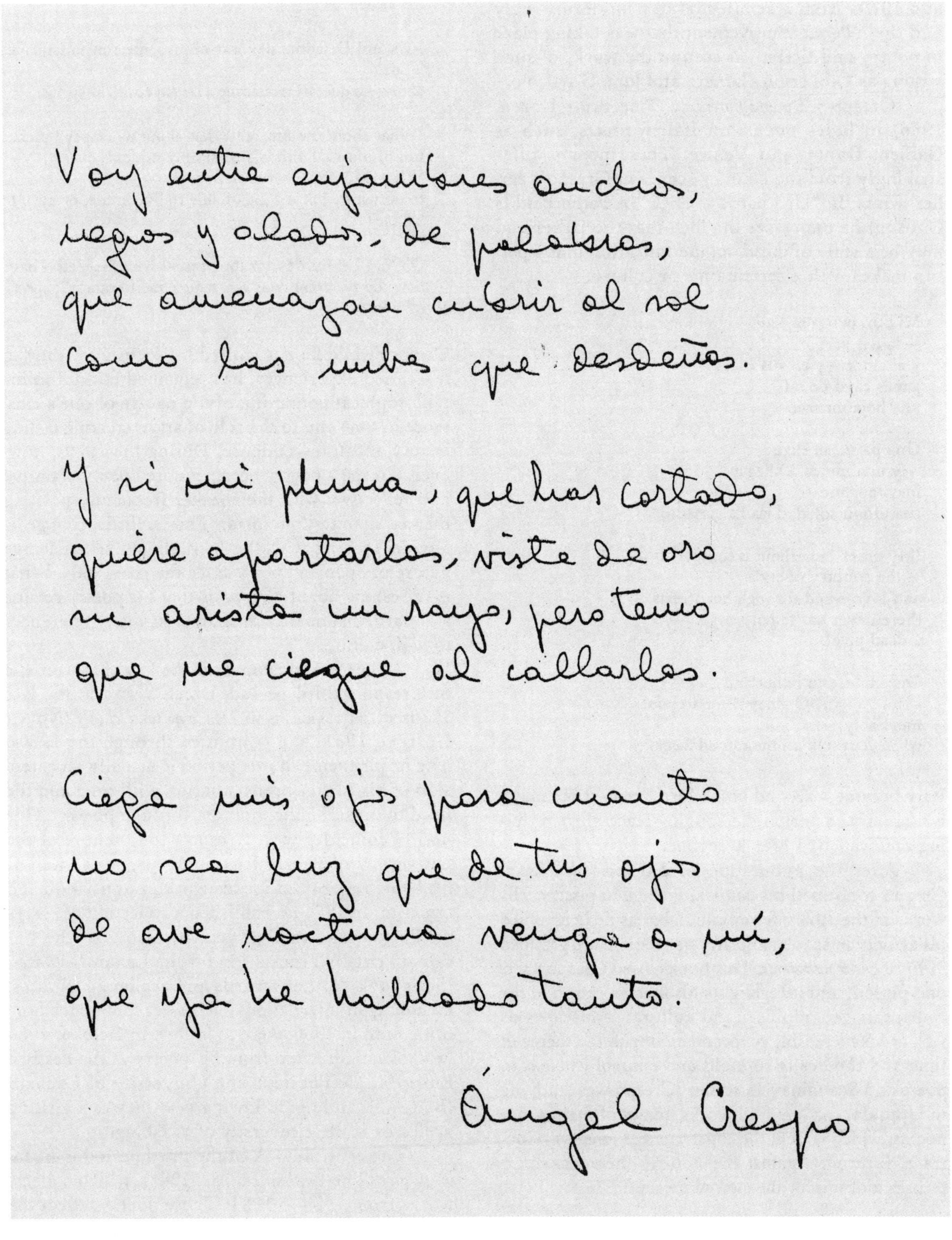

Voy entre enjambres anchos,
negros y alados, de palabras,
que amenazan cubrir el sol
como las nubes que desdeñas.

Y si mi pluma, que has cortado,
quiere apartarlos, viste de oro
su arista un rayo, pero temo
que me ciegue al callarlos.

Ciega mis ojos para cuanto
no sea luz que de tus ojos
de ave nocturna venga a mí,
que ya he hablado tanto.

                          Ángel Crespo

mation that Spain was undergoing during the 1960s and 1970s from a semifeudal to a modern society and the *culturalista* movement that was taking place in poetry and fiction, as seen in the works of such writers as Guillermo Carnero and Juan Goytisolo.

Crespo's *Docena florentina* (Florentine Dozen, 1966) includes poems on Italian topics, such as Galileo, Dante, and Venice. These poems differ strikingly from the country scenes of Crespo's earlier works. In "Una patria se elige" (A Fatherland Is Chosen) he expresses the idea that the fatherland may be a state of mind, an identification that a person makes with a certain time or culture:

> Mi otra patria es Italia
> – la del verbo
> y el amor – y en sus calles
> jamás cayó de mí
> una hoja muerta.
> . . . . . . . . . . . . . .
> Una patria se elige
> – y una mujer. O llegan,
> inevitablemente,
> cuando tu soledad las ha ganado.
>
> (My other fatherland is Italy
> – the country of style
> and love – and through her streets
> there never has fallen
> a dead petal.
> . . . . . . . . . .
> One chooses a fatherland
> – and a wife. Or they come to you,
> inevitably,
> when your solitude has earned them.)

Italy became a second home for Crespo. Like many writers of the period, he sought solace abroad during the Francisco Franco regime.

After the publication of *En medio del camino* Crespo continued his cultural voyage in poetry. His works of the 1970s, fewer in number as he heightened his activity in scholarship and translation, are grouped in *El bosque transparente*. This book closed Crespo's second period, and it highlights his incorporation of the European geographical and cultural landscapes as well as his increasing preoccupation with the theme of time and the desire to mold and control it. Next to poems on Scandinavian scenes (Crespo was studying in Uppsala) readers find works, many of them prose poems, which lament the constraints of time. In "Contra el futuro" (Against the Future) the speaker expresses a desire for the eternal present:

> ¿Qué del futuro? ¿Qué de sus playas vacías llenas de
> animales insólitos o simplemente inexistidos? ¿Qué
> tengo

> yo que ver con lo que no podrá vivirme, ni siquiera
> matarme? . . .
>
> ¡Oh, no! Dejadme devorar el presente con mis dientes
> de
> ahora; no queráis reducirme a las expectativas ajenas.
>
> (What about the future? What about its empty beaches
> full of unusual animals or simply nonexistent?
> What do I have
> to do with what will be unable to live in me, or even to
> kill me? . . .
>
> Oh, no! Let me devour the present with the teeth I have
> now; do not think you can reduce me to others' expectations.)

Crespo, while he has shifted his focus according to his varied experiences, has remained faithful to his philosophical pondering of the nature of one's existence in time and to the role of art in creating lasting beauty and transcendence. During the 1970s, however, Crespo's poetry became more openly plaintive and reflective, with the speaker frequently positing themes in question form. This stylistic change is also in keeping with the increasingly self-reflexive nature of Spanish poetry since the late 1960s. What is refreshing about Crespo is that his poetry retains a nonartificial quality in spite of its many references to high culture.

A sense of spirituality is the key characteristic of Crespo's third period, which began in the late 1970s with the poems in *Donde no corre el aire* (No Air Current, 1981) and continued through the 1980s. The major theme of this period is actually an extension of his earlier preoccupation with time and the need to preserve the moment through poetry. This period coincides with Crespo's long tenure at the University of Puerto Rico in Mayagüez as well as his being recognized for his work in translation and criticism. In 1984 he published a collection of essays on Pessoa, and in that year he also won the National Prize in Translation for the Italian *Canzionere* (Songbook). Other awards and academic tributes, including an international *homenaje* (conference honoring him) in 1986, were to follow. In October 1986 he spoke and recited from his poetry at the Festival Européan de Poesie at the University of Louvain (Belgium), and the following year he was a visiting professor at the University of Washington.

The central book of the third period is *El ave en su aire* (The Bird in Its Air, 1985), which collects works from 1975 to 1984. These poems reflect the yearning for an ideal, and the speakers look heavenward rather than to the far corners of the earth. References abound to Greek mythology and to the gods with whom the poet feels kinship as fellow creators. In *El aire es de los dioses* (The Air Belongs to the Gods, 1982) the speaker states categorically: "Soló quien cree en los dioses / . . . / puede decirse hermano suyo / y espejo ser de un dios" (Only he who believes in the gods / . . . / can call himself their brother / and be the mirror image of a god). Along with the attempt to assert the poet's importance as creator of lasting works, Crespo continues his process of self-discovery, asserting that the poet can achieve self-awareness only through critical examination of his work and his place in the universe. As the title of *Parnaso confidencial* (A Confidential Parnassus, 1984) suggests, this theme is connected not only to the Hellenic but to the symbolist mode. In this regard Crespo is prefiguring the neosymbolist poetry of the late 1980s in Spain. In the title of his collected works from this period (*El ave en su aire*) Crespo has returned to one of his favorite images, the bird; just as it is central to his poetry of the late 1950s and early 1960s, it is also a key symbol within the context of his poetic creation in the 1980s.

The critical attention focused on Angel Crespo in recent years is fitting, for his lifetime of poetic activity, teaching, travel, and support for the arts has made him one of the most accomplished figures of the generations of poets that began writing in the 1950s. The fact that he is difficult to place in any one generation is also pertinent, as his poetry combines the social realism of the 1950s with the cultural movement of the 1960s and the returning spirituality of the 1970s and 1980s. Crespo will perhaps be remembered best as a latter-day Renaissance man who did as much as anyone in Spanish letters to promote the study of literature and the arts throughout the world. His poetry reflects this thematic variety but never departs from his central concerns: the relationship of the self to the universe and the transcendence of artistic creation.

In 1988, after some twenty years of teaching at the University of Puerto Rico in Mayagüez and in various visiting professorships at universities in the United States, Angel Crespo returned to Spain with his wife, Pilar. They currently reside in Barcelona.

**Bibliography:**
*Suplementos Anthropos,* special issue on Crespo, 15 (June 1989).

**References:**
José Albí, "Introducción a la poesía de Angel Crespo," in *Antología poética,* edited by Crespo and Albí (Valencia: Verbo, 1960), pp. 9–83;
*Anthropos,* special issue on Crespo, 97 (June 1989);
José María Balcells, *Poesía y poética de Angel Crespo* (Palma de Mallorca: Prensa Universitaria, 1990);
María Teresa Bertelloni, "Angel Crespo: *Parnaso confidencial,*" *Cuadernos Hispanoamericanos,* 131 (February 1985): 183–188;
Bertelloni, *El mundo poético de Angel Crespo* (Madrid: Toro del Barro, 1983);
Bertelloni, "El sentido del tiempo en la poesía de Angel Crespo," *Nueva Estafeta,* 11 (October 1979): 59–64;
Andrew P. Debicki, *Poetry of Discovery: The Spanish Generation of 1956–1971* (Lexington: University Press of Kentucky, 1982), pp. 183–192;
Carlos de la Rica, "Vanguardia de los años cincuenta," *Papeles de Son Armadans,* 37 (April 1965): i–xvi; (May 1965): xxv–xlvii; (July 1965): iii–xv;
Pilar Gómez Bedate, "La contestación de la realidad en la poesía de Angel Crespo," *Revista de Letras,* 1 (December 1969): 605–645;
Linda D. Metzler, "The Poetry of Angel Crespo," Ph.D. dissertation, University of Kansas, 1978.

# Álvaro Cunqueiro

(22 December 1911 – 27 February 1981)

Xoan González-Millán
*Hunter College of the City University of New York*

BOOKS: *Mar ao norde* (Santiago de Compostela: Nós, 1932);

*Cantiga nova que se chama riveira* (Santiago de Compostela: Resol, 1933; enlarged edition, Vigo: Monterrey, 1957);

*Poemas do sí e non* (Lugo: Un, 1933);

*Poemas: Antología de inéditos* (Lisbon: Descobrimento, 1934);

*Elegías y canciones* (Barcelona: Apolo, 1940);

*Balada de las damas del tiempo pasado* (Madrid: Alhambra, 1945);

*San Gonzalo,* as Álvaro Labrado (Madrid: Nacional, 1945);

*Dona do corpo delgado* (Pontevedra: Soto, 1950);

*Crónica de la derrota de las naciones* (Coruña: Atlántida, 1954);

*Merlín e familia, i outras historias* (Vigo: Galaxia, 1955); translated [from Galician into Castilian] by Cunqueiro as *Merlín y familia* (Barcelona: AHR, 1957);

*As crónicas do sochantre* (Vigo: Galaxia, 1956); translated by Cunqueiro as *Las crónicas del sochantre* (Barcelona: AHR, 1959);

*El caballero, La muerte y El diablo, y otras dos o tres historias* (Madrid: Grifón, 1956);

*Teatro venatorio y coquinario gallego,* by Cunqueiro and José María Castroviejo Blanco Cicerón (Vigo: Monterrey, 1958); republished as *Viaje por los montes y chimeneas de Galicia: Caza y cocinas* (Madrid: Espasa-Calpe, 1962; revised and enlarged, 1978);

*O incerto señor Don Hamlet, príncipe de Dinamarca* (Vigo: Galaxia, 1958 [i.e., 1959]);

*Escola de menciñeiros* (Vigo: Galaxia, 1960);

*Las mocedades de Ulises* (Barcelona: Argos, 1960);

*Si o vello Sinbad volvese ás illas* (Vigo: Galaxia, 1961); translated by Cunqueiro as *Cuando el viejo Sinbad vuelva a las islas* (Barcelona: Argos, 1962);

*Rutas de España: El camino de Santiago* (Madrid: Españolas, 1962);

*Itinerarios turístico-gastronómicos por la provincia de Pontevedra* (Vigo: Faro de Vigo, 1964);

*Tesouros novos e vellos* (Vigo: Galaxia, 1964);

*El camino de Santiago* (Vigo: Faro de Vigo, 1965);

*Lugo, La Coruña, Pontevedra, Orense* (Madrid: Españolas, 1967);

*Lugo* (León: Everest, 1968);

*Flores del año mil y pico de ave* (Barcelona: Taber, 1968);

*El envés* (Barcelona: Taber, 1969);

*Un hombre que se parecía a Orestes* (Barcelona: Destino, 1969);

*La cocina cristiana de occidente* (Barcelona: Taber, 1969);

*Pontevedra – Rías Bajas* (León: Everest, 1969);

*Laberinto y cía* (Barcelona: Taber, 1970);

*El descanso del camellero* (Barcelona: Taber, 1970);

*Vigo y su ría* (León: Everest, 1971);

*Xente de aquí e de acolá* (Vigo: Galaxia, 1971);

*Vida y fugas de Fanto Fantini* (Barcelona: Destino, 1972);

*A cociña galega* (Vigo: Galaxia, 1973); translated by Cunqueiro as *Cocina gallega* (Madrid: Everest, 1981);

*Don Hamlet e tres pezas mais* (Vigo: Galaxia, 1974);

*El año del cometa con la batalla de los cuatro reyes* (Barcelona: Destino, 1974);

*La otra gente* (Barcelona: Destino, 1975);

*Rías Bajas gallegas,* trilingual edition [Spanish, English, and French] (Madrid: Everest, 1975);

*Tertulia de boticas prodigiosas y Escuela de curanderos* (Barcelona: Destino, 1976);

*Os outros feirantes* (Vigo: Galaxia, 1979);

*Obra en Galego completa,* 4 volumes: *Poesía, teatro; Narrativa; Semblanzas; Ensaios* (Vigo: Galaxia, 1980–1991);

*Vigo en su historia* (Vigo: Caja de Ahorros Municipal de Vigo, 1980);

*Las Historias gallegas* (Madrid: Banco de Crédito e Inversiones, 1981);

*Ver Galicia* (Barcelona: Destino, 1981);

*Fábulas y leyendas de la mar* (Barcelona: Tusquets, 1982);

*Antología poética,* bilingual edition [Galician and Castilian], translated by César A. Molina (Barcelona: Plaza & Janés, 1983);

*Tesoros y otras magias* (Barcelona: Tusquets, 1984);

*Viajes imaginarios y reales* (Barcelona: Tusquets, 1986);

*Herba aquí ou acolá / Hierba aquí o allá,* bilingual edition [Galician and Castilian], translated by Molina (Madrid: Visor, 1988);

*Escritos recuperados,* edited by Anxo Tarrió Varela (Santiago de Compostela: Universidade de Santiago de Compostela, 1991).

Poetry always played a constant and privileged role within Álvaro Cunqueiro's diverse literary output. From *Mar ao norde* (Sea to the North, 1932), his first book of poems, to his last poems – published as *Herba aquí ou acolá* (Grass Here or There) in volume one of his *Obra en Galego completa* (Complete Galician Works, 1980–1991), then separately published in 1988 – Cunqueiro cherished the genre, and he mostly wrote poems in Galician. However, his narrative and journalistic work, quantitatively greater, especially after the Spanish Civil War, is written largely in Castilian. Despite the language difference there are thematic and formal parallels between his fiction and poetry. The roots of this generic transcodification should be seen in the context of Galician literature which, after Francisco Franco's triumph, showed a disenchantment with "pure poetry" and found the only valid determinant of literary worth in the engagement of the poetic voice with historical circumstances. The civil war stunted artistic production in Galicia, suppressed Galician publishing (causing Cunqueiro to resort to writing poems in Castilian), and ended his development of surrealist and neotroubadour styles, the latter based on the fin de siècle rediscovery of medieval Galician troubadours' verses, as he elaborated it in his early books of poetry. In the postwar period Cunqueiro did not accept the aesthetic principles of the winning ideology, and neither did he accept the rigidity of the new socially conscious literature that emerged as a formulaic response to the young Fascist regime. Deprived of the readers who in the prewar years had hailed him as one of the most original avant-garde voices, Cunqueiro began to channel his creative energy into narrative discourse, where his lyric voice triumphs. His fiction always includes a fantastic element touched by nostalgic irony, which transcends the linguistic code, intimately linking it to his verse.

Álvaro Cunqueiro Mora was born in Mondoñedo, near Lugo, on 22 December 1911 and died in Vigo on 27 February 1981. His parents, Joaquín Cunqueiro, a pharmacist, and Josefa Mora de Cunqueiro, an imaginative and sensitive woman, both descended from a long line of established Galician families. Among Álvaro Cunqueiro's ancestors were Benito Vicetto, Father Benito Feijoo, and Ramón María del Valle-Inclán, all illustrious Galician writers. The young Cunqueiro was fascinated by Charles Dickens, and Cunqueiro's innate curiosity and prodigious memory made him an exceptional reader. At the age of eleven he was sent to the city of Lugo to attend secondary school. There he first began to consider Galicia a specific cultural entity.

After finishing his secondary studies Cunqueiro enrolled at the University of Santiago de Compostela in the Department of Philosophy and Letters and majored in history. The experience proved disillusioning to him, but the intellectual atmosphere of the city did not. The *tertulias* (literary circles) at the Café Español, the new friends, and the avid readings and discussions of the latest literary trends opened a vast cultural horizon that was to inform all his work.

It was the historical moment of the avant-garde. In Galicia the proliferation of magazines devoted to the new aesthetic included *Alfar* (1920–1927), *Ronsel* (1924), *Yunque* (1932), *Nós* (1920–

1935), and *A Nosa Terra* (1916–1936; revived in the 1980s), and in several of these Cunqueiro published poems and translations. He also created and edited two short-lived periodicals, *Galiza* (1920) and *Papel de Color* (1932). The first of these was a monthly broadside presenting the "new poetry," and many distinguished Galician poets collaborated on it. There, too, Cunqueiro published several poems that were never republished. He dedicated two elegies to poet Manoel Antonio, for whom Cunqueiro felt a special admiration and whose *De catro a catro* (From Camp to Camp, 1928) is the most important book of poetry of the Galician avant-garde. During these early decades of the twentieth century Cunqueiro read medieval songbooks and poetry by the *modernistas,* the Generation of 1927, the French surrealists, and many others.

In this period Cunqueiro published his first books of verse: *Mar ao norde, Cantiga nova que se chama riveira* (New Song Called Shore, 1933), and *Poemas do sí e non* (Yes-and-No Poems, 1933). With a clearly discernible literary calling, Cunqueiro left his university studies and embarked on the career he pursued for the rest of his life: he was a professional writer, an exceptional circumstance among Galician authors at the time. He worked as a journalist for the dailies *Pueblo Gallego* in Vigo (1937–1939) and *Noche* and *A.B.C.* in Madrid (1939–1949) and then, most important, for the *Faro de Vigo,* of which he was editor for several years. He also collaborated on various literary journals, among them *Vértice* in San Sebastian, from 1937 to 1946, and *Escorial* in Madrid, from 1940 to 1950.

As the youngest member of a generation represented by, among others, Antonio, Armado Carballo, and Blanco Amor, Cunqueiro initiated his poetic career at the age of twenty with the slim volume of avant-garde verse titled *Mar ao norde.* During the next year *Poemas do sí e non,* the first surrealist book in Galician literature, was published, and *Cantiga nova* marked a culminating point in the neotroubadour school of poetry. His ability to write in such diverse styles showed great promise for the future. Following the civil war and the repression of the 1940s, Cunqueiro resumed publishing his poetry in Galician (after having written three books in Castilian), but only his poems in the neotroubadour style had an apparent immunity – perhaps because of their medieval inspiration – to the still-rigorous censorship of the Franco regime, which was dedicated to combating every influence of foreign modernity. Cunqueiro's *Dona do corpo delgado* (Girl with the Delicate Body, 1950) and a new edition (1957) of *Cantiga nova,* which includes six previously unpublished poems, showed that he was still able to take Galician poetry to new heights within the restrictions imposed on it. In order to define the early-twentieth-century intellectual and aesthetic climate of Galicia, in which Cunqueiro played a prominent role, one must understand that the region's sociopolitical and historical situation was subject to the rhythm of European cultural life and at the same time was mediated by circumstances in Spain. Galician writers appropriated certain of these influences while making their own contributions. The group connected to the magazine *Nós* (in the 1920s and 1930s) passed to on the poets of the avant-garde – among them, Cunqueiro – this awareness of the latest trends in art and literature.

The *novecentistas* (authors born at approximately the turn of the century) directed the artistic movement that established boundaries between nineteenth-century and modern Galician verse and brought about a change in the way art and its function in society were perceived. The new approach affirmed for Galician writers, once and for all, the right to one's personal voice in poetry, the right to express one's preoccupations, and a new way to view and speak of the world from the vantage point of a marginal language.

The particular character and individuality of the Galician avant-garde can be traced to three specific influences: the nationalist spirit inherited from the *Irmandades da Fala* (Civic Discussion Societies, 1916–1936) and the *Grupo Nós* (1920–1936); Galician relations with Portugal, and, specifically with the writer Teixeira de Pascoais, who greatly influenced young poets of the region; and, finally, the discovery of the Galaico-Portuguese medieval songbooks (*cancioneiros medievais*), which had a great impact in heightening the prestige of the Galician language. Writers who had felt the burden of using a language considered for centuries only a medium for peasant tales and rural traditions now saw European scholars studying Galician as the fountainhead of lyric poetry at the courts of the later Middle Ages and Renaissance.

The characteristics of the new Galician literature, born of the synthesis of the European avant-garde with the nationalist atmosphere, are the acceptance of the three great poets of the nineteenth-century Galician renaissance – Rosalia de Castro, Eduardo Pondal, and Curros Enríquez, writers whose authority was acknowledged in the context of Galicia's recovering its historical and cultural memory; the young writers' participation in a national vindication of Galician culture; the exclusive use of Galician as a linguistic medium; and, finally,

the assimilation of the new modes of the avant-garde, principally cubism, creationism, and ultraism.

In 1954 the journal *Atlántida,* of Coruña, devoted a separate issue to Cunqueiro and his work; for this issue he wrote the following "Poética":

> No he pretendido nunca ser un poeta inspirado y luminoso. Con mis propios poemas he intentado explicarme a mi mismo qué cosa es la poesía. Una larga y esperanzada impaciencia es mi actitud ante la creación poética.
>
> No concibo un poema que no dependa, en última instancia, de la boca humana que lo dice. Reconozco, pues, a la poesía una esencial e insoslayable impureza. Con [Arthur] Rimbaud creo que el poeta roba fuego: "si lo que trae de abajo tiene forma, da forma; si informe, da lo informe."
>
> Creo en el encantamiento por las palabras como la serpiente cree en la flauta, y este juego de aprendiz de brujo es, quizás, aparte una violenta nostalgia y una confortadora melancolía, la razón por la cual mis poemas fueron escritos y publicados.

> (I have never tried to be an inspired and luminous poet. With my poems I have tried to explain to myself what poetry is. I approach poetic creation with a long and hopeful impatience.
>
> I cannot conceive of a poem that does not depend, ultimately, on the human mouth that utters it. As such, I recognize poetry as an essential and ineludible impurity. Like Rimbaud, I think that the poet steals fire: "if what he brings from below has form, he gives form; if unformed, he gives what is formless."
>
> I believe in the power of words to enchant as a serpent believes in the flute and this playing at sorcerer's apprentice is, perhaps, aside from violent nostalgia and comforting melancholy, the reason my poems were written and published.)

This manifesto, of a more reflective than programmatic nature, offers invaluable insight for the comprehension of Cunqueiro's poetry.

*Mar ao norde* is a work of youth and should be read as such, including as it does an unconditional adherence to the current avant-garde, a lack of maturity, and the evidence of influences from a spectrum of Cunqueiro's early readings. It is marked by an implicit reaction against its Galician literary context and against the entire Galician lyric tradition.

The book comprises four sections: "Porto" (Port), made up of three poems; "Mar outa" (Other Sea), which has nine poems; and "Illa" (Island) and "Terra adentro" (Inland), both composed of extremely brief, concise, schematic pieces. The central reference is the sea, which represents a theme that

*Cunqueiro when he was a young man living and writing in
Santiago de Compostela*

was emblematic to the Galician avant-garde. Although a product of the Galician literary climate of the time, the book also has links with two other literary traditions: the Castilian and the French. The first of these is represented by the members of the Generation of 1927, in particular Rafael Alberti, Jorge Guillén, Pedro Salinas, and Gerardo Diego. The work of the first two of these poets visibly influences Cunqueiro's book. Guillén's *Cántico* (Canticle, 1928) is of fundamental importance in this respect, as is Paul Valéry's *Le cimitière marin* (The Graveyard by the Sea, 1920).

In *Mar ao norde* Cunqueiro identifies himself more with creationism and cubism than with any other avant-garde movement. The way the lines are placed on the page reflects a fragmentation of reality. *Mar ao norde* presents a youthful perspective on land- and seascapes. The forms and compositional elements are derivative, but their elaboration is purely autochthonous. Cunqueiro begins to create his own literary space.

*Cantiga nova,* Cunqueiro's first successful book, initiated the neotroubadouresque strain in his work. This inclination was born in the context of the fascination with the discovery and dissemination of the medieval Galician songbooks, a fascination which became especially widespread after the appearance of two collections of them edited by J. J. Nunes, *Cantigas de amigo* (Songs of the Lover, 1928) and *Cantigas de amor* (Songs of the Beloved, 1932). Cunqueiro had a poetic grace not found in other neotroubadouresque poets, such as Fermín Bouza-Brey, the first one. The fluidity of Cunqueiro's verse stems from his neopopularism, put into vogue by the members of the Generation of 1927, particularly Alberti and Federico García Lorca. These poets' enthusiasm for folklore and for the poetry of Gil Vicente, Juan del Encina, and Lope de Vega was the root of the movement. The basic combination of avant-garde imagery with traditional, popular meter is frequent in *Cantiga nova,* as it is in Lorca and Alberti's principal contributions to Castilian poetry in this mode. Bouza-Brey was above all a scholar who sporadically used neotroubadourism in writing poetry, while Cunqueiro was a poet with the ability to learn new and old forms and infuse them with new life.

The primary theme of *Cantiga nova* is love, and the book shows various convergent influences: Nunes's editions; Bouza-Brey's first book, *Nao senlleira* (Singular Roundship, 1933); and Alberti's early works, especially *La amante, canciones* (The Beloved, Songs, 1926), for which Cunqueiro felt great admiration. The second edition of *Cantiga nova,* published in 1957 at the height of postwar neotroubadourism, presents six new *cantigas* that, according to Cunqueiro, had been written before 1936. This statement seems to suggest that he only wrote neotroubadouresque poetry before the war, but the six new poems are different from previous ones, much less neopopularist, and more directly rooted in the medieval Galaico-Portuguese tradition, as seen in these lines:

> Amanecéu bico ou onda do mar,
> ai a cantiga do dondo amor!
> Cantouna meu amigo!
> Cantouna meu amigo!
>
> (It dawned as a kiss or a wave of the sea,
> the song of gentle loving!
> How my love sang it!
> How my love sang it!)[.]

The poems have a texture of scholastic pastiche and avant-garde ideation and represent the sector of Cunqueiro's work most readily accepted till now by conservative critics and by readers less predisposed to the difficulties of decoding.

*Poemas do sí e non,* a more difficult work, is an exercise in symmetry. It is a book of love poetry that includes a prologue, three sections equal in length and homogenous in content, and an epilogue consisting of three poems. In total there are twenty-four poems, conceived from an avant-garde perspective with the free play of ideas, language, and meter that characterizes such an approach. The book is written in a free-verse style reminiscent of Alberti's *Sobre los ángeles* (1929; translated as *Concerning the Angels,* 1967). One can also detect the influence of Charles Vildra, Jean Cocteau, and Paul Eluard. Of the three, Eluard's influence is particularly prominent, especially his book *Capitale de la douleur* (Capital of Sorrow, 1926).

Like *Mar ao norde, Poema do sí e non* is an abstract work, poetry constructed on shadows of significance that mutually nullify their meanings in the linguistic chain and lead readers to absolute opacity. It is a constant upheaval of objects in hallucinatory relation to one another. Associations are arbitrary and do not constitute semantic chains of perceptible symbolic significance. *Poema do sí e non* is the chief work of Cunqueiro's purely avant-garde production, and it is the most difficult to summarize. The presence of Eluard's free-verse style is felt, although there is very little in *Poema de sí e non* that is strictly surrealist. The avant-garde impulse Cunqueiro follows is simply one of total liberty, taking elements from all philosophies and literatures with which he was familiar. One could say that this book of verse introduced surrealism to Galician literature, but the movement was to have no truly outstanding followers. Written only a year after *Mar ao norde,* the collection does not mark any great advance in the maturational process of Cunqueiro, but it does reveal the novelty and the appropriateness of his having chosen one firm direction – surrealism – within the wide spectrum offered by the avant-garde. The elegiac tone in some of the poems seems dominated by an almost naive innocence that permeates the entire work. *Poemas do sí e non* is a desperate book. The solitary lover does not seek the loved one in order to lose his anguish in her presence; rather the encounter with the loved one represents the union of two solitudes that, having merged, experience an intensification of their pain.

*Dona do corpo delgado* includes poems probably written at very different times. There are three sections: "Dona do corpo delgado," "Duas elexías" (Two Elegies), and "Cantigas de amor cortés" (Songs of Courtly Love). In the first section there are three poems, written in, respectively, alexandrines, hendecasyllables, and heptasyllables. This metrical imperative, unusual in the work of Cunqueiro, links him to the classicism of postwar poetry and the Castilian traditionalism represented by the journal *Garcilaso* (1943–1946). Cunqueiro follows the path of some contemporary Galician poets who took refuge in this style as a result of the ideological censorship of the Franco regime.

*Dona do corpo delgado* is a product of Cunqueiro's maturity, with the exception of the last section, written before 1936. "Recomendación do alma e do corpo" (Recommendation of the Soul and the Body) opens the book and serves as a prologue. Next come the three classicist poems, on the theme of love. This section is prefaced by the opening quatrain of Shakespeare's Sonnet 36:

> Ainda que o amor faga de nós dous un soio,
> déxame confesar que temos de vivir arredados:

tódalas luxas, pois, que sober min pesan
eu soio as levaréi, sin a tua auxda.

(Let me confess that we two must be twain,
Although our undivided loves are one:
So shall those blots that do with me remain,
Without thy help, by me be borne alone.)

Following this are two elegies for Feliciano Rolán and Manoel Antonio. The book closes with "Cantigas do amor cortés" – ten compositions, each different in its design though similar to the others in archaic style. In these Cunqueiro returns to the neotroubadouresque mode, following the same impulse as in *Cantiga nova*. The heterogeneity of the book does not detract from its quality but does seem to foreshadow his incipient and progressive abandonment of poetry.

"Cantigas do amor cortés" is close to the medieval Galaico-Portuguese tradition, though there are echoes of neopopularism. Special mention should be made of two loose rondeaux, with refrains by François Villon and the medieval Galician troubadour Arias Nunes. These songs deal with two medieval noblewomen's tombs located in Vilar de Donas and San Xoán de Badón. Villon held a particular fascination for Cunqueiro, whose short story *Balada de las damas del tiempo pasado* (Ballad of Ladies from the Past, 1945) transposes a poem by Villon and is an early example of the thematic coherence between verse and prose that develops through Cunqueiro's work up to *Herba aquí ou acolá*. In *Dona corpo delgado* Villon is not the only French influence; the bitter melancholy of Pierre de Ronsard is also perceptible in the rondeaux. Cunqueiro highlights his favorite medieval texts in masterful Galician neotroubadour poetry combining nostalgia for his youthful fervor and the discoveries of maturing and aging.

*Herba aquí ou acolá* is the most extensive and most intense of Cunqueiro's verse collections. He began writing the book in the 1960s, and in 1979 Manuel González Garcés arranged its thirty compositions for him. The work is divided into two sections: the first, "As historias" (The Stories), consists of fourteen poems; the second, "Vellas sombras e novos cantos" (Old Shadows and New Songs), comprises sixteen. In this book there are groups of poems that initially belonged to other planned books: "Eu son," "Retorno de Ulises," and *Crónica de la derrota de las naciones* (I Am, Return of Ulysses, and Chronicle of the Defeat of Nations – the last one published in 1954).

The publication of *Herba aquí ou acola* in 1980 marked a peak in the career of a poet who had always been on the cutting edge of modernity in each one of his books, offering superior interpretation of trends and polished, creative originality. The majority of the poems in *Herba* had appeared, with some variations, in different literary journals.

*Herba* includes Cunqueiro's most valuable work and probably the finest Galician poetry of the twentieth century. Through contrast he expresses thoughts on literary, historical, and fictional texts and characters, as in "Eu son Edipo" (I Am Oedipus):

Aquela baluguiña de manteiga
aquel peliño mouro, aquelas mancinas inquedas
era eu, regresado a nái como varón,
e á coroa de Tebas como asesino.

(That little spot of grease
that patch of black hair, tiny unquiet hands
was I, come home to mother as a man,
and to the crown of Thebes as assassin.)

Cunqueiro uses literary or historical-legendary pretexts to create absolute inventions. The neotroubadouresque and classic hendecasyllabic styles appear in the poems, although there are three general characteristics that separate this work from the rest: meditation on human problems, literary re-creation, and thematic interrelation with his prose works. Re-creations of historical and cultural characters abound in Cunqueiro's narrative works. In fact, many of the poems were written parallel to his novels. Another underlying current in *Herba* is lyrical, a mode in which Cunqueiro manifests his existential anxiety. Echoes of T. S. Eliot, Ezra Pound, and W. B. Yeats are heard.

Burdensome melancholy, sadness, and the premonition of death in the form of a black shadow are dominant in the section "Vellas sombras e novos cantos." Although in all Cunqueiro's previous works, both in Castilian and Galician, the themes of the passage of time and the ephemeral quality of life are present, *Herba* presents a direct confrontation with death and the fear of it. However, Cunqueiro seems to have trust in the permanence of earth and in the resurrection of the flesh. While a form of permanence is seen in the survival of the literary work, much as if it were a soul freed from his body, Cunqueiro sees resurrection from a pantheistic and cyclic perspective, a sort of eternal return. This preoccupation with time's passage grows rich and intense in his elegiac poems. Long, solemn verses, with a calm, deliberate rhythm – not wholly free from irony – show a pensive, crepuscular vision: "Sin descatarse da resurreción da carne de Álvaro Cunqueiro, / un novo corpo limpio que

*Cunqueiro, circa 1981 (photograph by Ramón Dimas)*

soñaba co vento" (Without even noticing a resurrection of the flesh of Álvaro Cunqueiro, / a new, clean body which he dreamed in the wind).

The existential uneasiness already seen in *Dona do corpo delgado* is more intense. A common note, that of profound melancholy sung in long, serene lines with unrestrained musicality supported by classical cadences, unifies *Herba* rhythmically and conceptually.

Perhaps *Herba* will eventually be seen as a turning point in the development of Galician poetry in the twentieth century. With this work Cunqueiro indicates the paths back to the poetry of the past, centered on the melancholy meditation on death, the nostalgia for a lost love, and the bitterness of old age. Friedrich Hölderlin and the great Romantics always seem present in the background. In terms of form as well as content *Dona do corpo delgado* had revealed in some of its poems the seeds of *Herba*: the predilection for

long, undulating, blank-verse lines suited to the free expression discovered in the years Cunqueiro devoted, in the early 1930s, to the practice of surrealism.

Cunqueiro's Castilian poetry constitutes an uneven corpus that can be grouped into five divisions: those poems in the journal *Mensajes de poesía,* which Eduardo Moreiras edited in Vigo from 1951 to 1952; the poems collected in *Crónica de la derrota de las naciones;* poems published in the *Faro;* miscellaneous pieces; and *Elegías y canciones* (1940), which includes Cunqueiro's first verses in Castilian, written during 1934, 1935, and 1936. Systematically suppressed by Cunqueiro, *Elegías y canciones* was never republished. The book has three sections: "Elegías," "Canciones," and "Favorable prision de sueño" (The Pleasant Prison of Sleep). In this last section there are four compositions written originally in Galician. The book reveals an attempt to break from Cunqueiro's previous work and seek new routes by using the (then) only officially recognized language. Stylistically this poetry is different, and it is also different in terms of intention, although it does not follow the general tendencies of the postwar poets, except in a few religious overtones. There is a broad metaphysical preoccupation in *Elegías y canciones*. The presence of death, the passing of time, and the permanence of love as ephemeral consolation all give clues that lead to Cunqueiro's work of the period following *Dona do corpo delgado*. There is a certain romantic cast in *Elegías y canciones*, much in line with Novalis, Heinrich Heine, and, of course, Hölderlin, of whose work Cunqueiro was one of the first translators into Spanish. The youthful speaker in *Elegías y canciones* has many doubts. He trusts in natural forces, in a primeval state, and in a cosmos that, like Rainer Maria Rilke did, Cunqueiro turns into a vital and poetic land of origin.

Under the apparent diversity of tones in Cunqueiro's poetry there are three particular poetic stages that exist without one necessarily taking precedence: the surrealist experimentation of his first, avant-garde books, comparable to the best Castilian poetry of those years; the neotroubadouresque mode, which affected a large part of the Galician avant-garde and which implies an attempt to take hold of tradition from an avant-garde standpoint; and, finally, the elegiac and ironic style in which the constant cultural references serve to hide or obfuscate the poetic persona and to place his resigned knowledge of death in a far-off setting, in an erudition that often seems divinatory guesswork.

## Bibliographies:

César Antonio Molina, "La obra poética completa de Álvaro Cunqueiro," *Sábado Literario* (17 January 1981);

Antonio Odriozola, "Lembranza de Álvaro Cunqueiro e unha bibliografía mais da sua obra," *Grial,* 72 (1981): 235–260.

## Biographies:

Xosé Francisco Armesto Faginas, *Cunqueiro: Unha biografia* (Vigo: Xerais de Galicia, 1987);

Francisco Fernandez del Riego, *Álvaro Cunqueiro e o seu mundo (vivencias e fabulacións)* (Ferrol: Ir Indo, 1991).

## References:

*Atlántida,* special issue on Cunqueiro, 1 (January–February 1954);

Ricardo Carballo Calero, *Aportaciones a la literatura gallega contemporánea* (Madrid: Gredos, 1955);

Xosé Filgueira Valverde, *Álvaro Cunqueiro* (Coruna: Real Academia Galega, 1991);

Xosé L. Franco Grande, "Introducción a Alvaro Cunqueiro," *Grial,* 42 (1973): 403–416;

Xoan González-Millán, *Álvaro Cunqueiro: Os artificios da fabulación* (Vigo: Galaxia, 1991);

*Homenaxe a Álvaro Cunqueiro* (Santiago de Compostela: Universidade de Santiago de Compostela, 1982);

Basilio Losada, "Poeta sobre todo," *A Nosa Terra,* 2 (1984): 23;

César Antonio Molina, "La poesia de Álvaro Cunqueiro," *Nueva Estafeta,* 38 (1982);

Pilar Pallarés, "Sobre *Herba aquí e acolá:* A arte como salvazon," *A Nosa Terra,* 2 (1984): 37–40;

Giancarlo Ricci, "Álvaro Cunqueiro, poeta," in his *Miscellanea* (Pisa, Italy: Pacino, 1974);

Claudio Rodríguez Fer, "A poesía galega de Álvaro Cunqueiro," *Grial,* 72 (1981): 171–182;

Francisco Salinas Portugal, "Formulas neo-trovadorescas e vanguarda," *A Nosa Terra,* 2 (1984): 25–30.

# Gerardo Diego

*(3 October 1896 – 8 July 1987)*

Ana María Alfaro-Alexander
*Castleton State College*

SELECTED BOOKS: *El romancero de la novia* (Santander, 1920; revised edition, Madrid: Hispánica, 1944);

*Imagen* (Madrid: Ambos Mundos, 1922);

*Soria* (Valladolid: Libros para Amigos, 1923; enlarged edition, Santander: Zuñiga, 1948); enlarged again as *Soria sucedida* (Esplugas de Llobregat: Plaza & Janés, 1977);

*Manual de espumas* (Madrid: Ciudad Lineal, 1924);

*Versos humanos* (Madrid: Sáenz, 1925);

*Viacrucis* (Santander, 1931);

*Fábula de Equis y Zeda* (Mexico City: Alcancía, 1932);

*Poemas adrede* (Mexico City: Alcancía, 1932; revised edition, Madrid: Adonais, 1943);

*Angeles de Compostela* (Barcelona: Patria, 1940; enlarged edition, Madrid: Gráficas Valera, 1961); edited by Francisco Javier Díez de Revenga and republished with *Alondra de verdad* (Madrid: Castalia, 1985);

*Alondra de verdad* (Madrid: Escorial, 1941); edited by Díez de Revenga and republished with *Angeles de Compostela* (1985);

*La sorpresa, cancionero de Sentaraille* (Madrid: CSIC, 1944);

*Hasta siempre* (Madrid: Mensajes, 1949);

*La luna en el desierto y otros poemas* (Santander: Fons, 1949);

*Limbo* (Las Palmas: Arca, 1951);

*La navidad en la poesía española* (Madrid: Ateneo, 1952);

*Variación* (Madrid: Millán, 1952);

*Biografía incompleta* (Madrid: Cultura Hispánica, 1953; enlarged, 1967);

*Amazona* (Madrid: Agora, 1955);

*Paisaje con figuras* (Madrid: Papeles de Son Armadans, 1956);

*Evasión* (Caracas: Lirica Hispana, 1958);

*Amor solo* (Madrid: Espasa-Calpe, 1958);

*Canciones a Violante* (Madrid: Punta Europa, 1959);

*Glosas a Villamediana* (Madrid: Palabra & Tiempo, 1961);

*Mi Santander, mi cuna, mi palabra* (Santander: Diputación Santander, 1961);

*Nuevo escorzo de Góngora* (Santander: Universidad Internacional Menéndez Pelayo, 1961);

*La rama* (Santander: Isla de los Ratones, 1961);

*Sonetos a Violante* (Seville: Muestra, 1962);

*La suerte o la muerte* (Madrid: Taurus, 1963);

*Nocturnos de Chopin* (Madrid: Bullón, 1963);

*El jándalo* (Madrid: Palabra & Tiempo, 1964);

*El cerezo y la palmera* (Madrid: Alfil, 1964);

*El Cordobés dilucidado y Vuelta del peregrino* (Madrid: Revista de Occidente, 1966);

*Odas morales* (Málaga: Librería Anticuaria de Guadalhorce, 1966);

*Variación 2* (Santander: Clásicos de Todos los Años, 1966);

*Preludio, aria y coda a Gabriel Fauré* (Santander: Bedia, 1967);

*La fundación del querer* (Santander: Isla de los Ratones, 1970);

*Versos divinos* (Madrid: Fundación Conrado Blanco, 1971);

*Cementerio civil* (Barcelona: Plaza & Janés, 1972);

*Manuel Machado, poeta* (Madrid: Nacional, 1974);

*Carmen Jubilar* (Salamanca: Alamo, 1975);

*28 pintores españoles contemporáneos vistos por un poeta* (Madrid: Ibérico Europea de Ediciones, 1975);

*Crítica y poesía* (Madrid: Júcar, 1984).

**Collections:** *Romances* (Madrid: Patria, 1941);

*Primera antología de sus versos* (Buenos Aires & Mexico City: Espasa-Calpe, 1941);

*Poemas,* edited by Manuel Altolaguirre (Mexico City: Secretaria de Educación Pública, 1948);

*Antología* (Salamanca: Anaya, 1958);

*Poesía amorosa* (Barcelona: Plaza & Janés, 1965, enlarged, 1970);

*Segunda antología de sus versos* (Madrid: Espasa-Calpe, 1967);

*Antología poética* (Madrid: Dirección General de Enseñanza Media & Profesional, 1969);

*Versos escogidos* (Madrid: Gredos, 1970);

*Poesía de creación* (Barcelona: Seix Barral, 1974);

*Gerardo Diego*

*Poemas mayores* (Madrid: Alianza, 1980);

*Poemas menores* (Madrid: Alianza, 1980);

*Cometa errante: Obras completas* (Barcelona: Plaza & Janés, 1985).

OTHER: "Posibilidades creacionistas," *Cervantes: Revista Hispanoamericana* (October 1919): 23–28;

*Antología poética en honor de Góngora, desde Lope de Vega a Rubén Darío,* compiled, with an introduction, by Diego (Madrid: Revista de Occidente, 1927);

*Tántalo: Versiones poéticas,* translated by Diego (Madrid: Agora, 1960).

Gerardo Diego's reputation in contemporary Spanish poetry derives from his multifaceted and fertile poetic talent. He was a rebellious poet who embraced the disjointed, avant-garde maxims of *ultraísmo* (the ultraist movement), the main tenets of which were to admit the modern urban world into lyric poetry and to make the unusual metaphor the cornerstone of the poem, and *creacionismo* (the creationist movement), which emphasized free imagery as opposed to realism.

Diego belongs to the renowned "Generation of 1927," who incorporated aspects of French symbolism into the "pure poetry" of ultraism and creationism while retaining the traditional metric constructions of Spanish poetry. The generation was inspired by popular traditions and by the great masters of Spanish poetry. The most important poet for this generation was Luis de Góngora (1561–1627). Several young poets paid homage to him during the tercentenary of his death, after which they named themselves the Generation of 1927. Góngora's refined style and delicate images, along with his vast vocabulary, were alternatives to the chaotic visions in works by the young poets' immediate predecessors.

Diego's poetry is distinguished from that of his contemporaries because it more fully shows the accomplishments made possible by use of the ultraist-

*Diego on the day of his first Communion, 1906*

style metaphor. His *Imagen* (Image, 1922) and *Manual de espumas* (Manual of Seafoam, 1924) are two of the most remarkable works of ultraist poetry. The raw talent of Diego, however, surpassed the constraints of ultraism. From the beginning of his career he was able to venture into the avant-garde as well as to explore the more traditional themes and manners of poetry. These qualities best characterize Diego's poetry: traditional themes cast in nontraditional structures. This marriage of styles has confused many critics who accuse Diego of not having a controlling or unifying theme in his poetry.

Gerardo Diego Cendoya, the youngest child of Manuel Diego Barquín and Angela Cendoya Uría, was born in Santander on 3 October 1896. He had six siblings: Manuel, Marcelino, José, Angela, Flora, and María. Gerardo was promptly baptized in the parish of the Santísimo Cristo de la Catedral, and his godfather was his oldest brother, Manuel, who died at the age of twenty-one. Gerardo later remembered his brother/godfather in the poem "Lección de inglés" (English Lesson), collected in

*Mi Santander, mi cuna, mi palabra* (My Santander, My Cradle, My Word, 1961):

> Llega Manolo; su mirada ardiente
> de un brillo singular. Los tres hermanos
> balbucimos inglés y él sonriente
> nos bendice en secreto con sus manos.

> (Manolo arrives; his gaze on fire
> with a peculiar light. The three brothers
> babble in English and smiling he
> blesses us secretly with his hands.)

The house in which Gerardo Diego was born and reared became an unforgettable place for him. The building was a typical nineteenth-century structure. The first floor was a store, and the fourth housed the family. The store, which sold fabrics, umbrellas, skirts, and buttons, along with other dry goods, was founded in 1871 and run by Diego's father until he died. In 1941 the building burned in the fire which virtually destroyed Santander.

Diego's childhood was deeply affected by the paradise and playpen represented by his father's store. Diego recalls it in his poem "La novela de una tienda" (The Novel of a Store), in *Mi Santander, mi cuna, mi palabra:*

De una tienda que existía
quiero narrar la novela.
Pieza en cascada vertía,
nueve o diez varas de tela.
"Géneros del Reino" a fe
. . . . . . . . . . . . . . . . . . . . .
Ay viejas letras del título.
Y un mostrador con barniz para jugar al desliz.
Y este es el primer capítulo.


(Of a store that once existed
I wish to narrate the novel.
Bolts in cascades it poured,
nine or ten links of fabric.
"Fabrics of the Kingdom" in truth
. . . . . . . . . . . . . . . . . . . . . . . . .
Oh old letters of the title.
And a stained counter to use as a slide.
And this is the first chapter.)

The young Diego studied under the tutelage of private instructors until 1906, when he became a student at the Instituto General y Técnico de Santander. Under the mentorship of Narciso Alonso Cortés, Diego first encountered and studied the modernist poetry of Rubén Darío, who was not yet popular with the people of Santander. Diego's education at the institute coincided with the inauguration of the municipal library, where, according to his biographer Antonio Gallego Morell, he read works by José María de Pereda, Marcelino Menéndez y Pelayo, Concha Espina, Luis Coloma, José de Espronceda, and José Zorrilla. Diego's years as a youngster were characterized by intense readings of the classics and constant attempts at writing poetry.

Diego began his university education in 1912 at the Jesuit University of Deusto in Bilbao. In 1916 he graduated and went on to study for his doctorate at the Universities of Salamanca and Madrid. During his years as a doctoral student Diego started to articulate his aesthetic ideas and poetic tenets. The best-known example of this articulation took place at the Ateneo de Santander on 16 November 1919, when at a conference Diego elaborated and expanded on his views of poetry. His presentation prompted a lively debate, during which Diego explained that "poesía nueva" (new poetry) had discovered the "cuadratura del circulo" (squareness of the circle) and that the only limitation of new poetry "es no hacer lo que ya se ha hecho, ni de la manera que se ha hecho y en especial en estos últimos años" (is not to do what has already been done, in the manner in which it has been done and especially in the last years) (as reported in the newspaper *Atalaya,* 24 November 1919).

In April 1920 Diego paid for the publication of *El romancero de la novia* (The Romance of the Bride). He had started it five years earlier when he first fell in love with a woman who, without any explanation, soon broke his heart. In his prologue Diego says that poetry is like another woman, one capable of soothing his broken heart.

In the introduction to *Versos escogidos* (Chosen Verses, 1970) Diego states that he did not write poetry systematically until February 1918. Before that he had written mostly to express his feelings or to experiment with different metric techniques. But by 1920, to his surprise, Diego had published his fledgling poetry in well-known literary avant-garde periodicals such as *Grecia, Cervantes, Reflector,* and *Ultra.* At the same time, he continued to theorize on the new aesthetic trends he favored. Editor and critic Francisco Javier Díez de Revenga points out that Diego created conceptual poetry, such as that in *Imagen.* As Diego described such poetry (in his October 1919 essay in *Cervantes*), "No explica nada; es intraducible a la prosa. Es la Poesía, en el más puro sentido de la palabra" (It explains nothing; it is untranslatable to prose. It is Poetry, in the purest sense of the word).

After earning his doctorate in 1920 at the University of Madrid, Diego reaffirmed his friendship with the poet Juan Larrea, whom he had previously met in Bilbao. Diego introduced Larrea to the works of Chilean author Vicente Huidobro, and in 1926, when Larrea published with Peruvian Cesar Vallejo the only two issues of the *Favorables Paris Poema* magazine, Diego was one of its selected contributors. Huidobro, whose poetry enthralled Diego, had arrived in Madrid in May 1919 to lead a conference at the Ateneo; Diego and Huidobro began a long-term friendship. A few years later, during summer 1922, when Diego went to Paris, he was invited to stay at the Huidobro residence for a fortnight; he returned there in 1924. Huidobro was the founder of literary creationism, and Larrea was to become the best-known practitioner of it. Diego admired both poets and soon followed in their footsteps by beginning to write books of vanguard poetry, *Imagen* and *Manual de espumas.* During these early years of experimentation Diego also wrote *Evasión,* his first book, published separately in 1958. It was written during 1918 and 1919 and included in *Imagen.* To Diego the connotation of the title

*Diego and Juan Larrea*

*Evasión* meant his rebellion against poetic conventions, his evasion of literary "prisons," of strophic "cages." For him it also meant the love of risk and the exploration of the unknown. The book captures the essence of a poetic voice groping to find its adequate tone, its creationistic intent.

Diego wrote prolifically during the 1920s. He was living in Soria, where he was the youngest and one of the brightest professors at the Instituto de Soria. His circle of friends included Blás Taracena; Gervasio Manrique; Pepe Tudela, a librarian; Antonio Machado; Mariano Granados, the only one of them who owned a car; and Mariano Iñíguez. Diego wrote of the last three in *Soria* (1923).

While living there, Diego continued to write *Imagen,* which was published on Easter 1922. Diego signed and dedicated the book to many of his friends, including Ramón del Valle Inclán. But Diego's greatest personal moment took place during the same week, when Machado honored him by going to his apartment to pick up a copy of Diego's

book and to excuse his absence at Diego's recent reading from *Imagen* at the Ateneo in Madrid.

An astonishing avant-garde collection, *Imagen* is divided into three parts: "Evasión" (1918–1919), "Imagen múltiple" (1919–1921), and "Estribillo" (Refrain, 1919–1921). The book follows the tenets of Huidobro and the practices of Larrea. In the section "Imagen múltiple," the poem "Gesta" is a portion of Diego's autobiography transposed into irrational images. In the section "Estribillo" the poem "Estetica" (Aesthetic), dedicated to the musician Manuel de Falla, appropriately includes musical images, as well as architectural metrics which show Diego's playfulness:

Estribillo        Estribillo        Estribillo
    El canto más perfecto es el canto del grillo
Paso a paso
        se asciende hasta el Parnaso
Yo no quiero las alas de Pegaso


(Refrain        Refrain        Refrain
    The most perfect song is the song of the cricket

Danzar
      Cautivos del bar.
La vida es una torre
Y el sol un palomar.
Lancemos las camisas tendidas a volar.

(To dance
      Prisoners of the bar.
Life is a tower
And the sun is a pigeon coop.
Let us throw the hanging shirts to the wind.)

The landscape and setting of Soria had a special, enriching influence on Diego and inspired him to go beyond the limitations of creationism. Thus he wrote some more-traditional poems that he later included in *Versos humanos* (Human Verses, 1925). Soria continued to be a place of inspiration for Diego, so it is not surprising that throughout the years he continued to return there. In 1924, at the monastery of Silos, Diego got his inspiration for the sonnet "El ciprés de Silos" (The Cypress of Silos), in *Versos humanos*. Again in Soria in 1949, Diego wrote his "Epístola a mis amigos de Soria" (Epistle to My Friends of Soria), published in *Paisaje con figuras* (Landscape with Figures, 1956). The epistle includes inside information, understandable only in Diego's circle of friends:

Pacen unos corderos, muere la última rosa
y un francés que se llama, como Alejandro, Dumas
se bebe, sorbo a sorbo, Castilla sin espumas.
Castilla, y la que Antonio llamaba barbacana,
gloriosa de domingo, diáfana, cristiana.

(Some sheep graze, the last rose dies
and a Frenchman who is called, like Alexandre, Dumas
drinks, sip by sip, Castilla without foam.
Castilla, and the one Antonio used to call barbican,
gloriously from Sunday, diaphanous, Christian.)

*Versos humanos* shared with Rafael Alberti's *Marinero en tierra* (Sailor on Land) the 1925 National Prize of Literature. The jury was made up of renowned, demanding artists such as Antonio Machado, Menéndez Pidal, Moreno Villa, and Gabriel Miró. In *Versos humanos* one finds a coalescence of creationistic images and traditional themes.

Diego's multifaceted voice and thematic variations also come to life in *Viacrucis* (Way of the Cross, 1931). At first the religious overtones and the intention of praying in verse perplexed Diego. He thought the book would be old-fashioned. He was also afraid of what the general reaction would be to such a book. However, he found that with the *décima* (decameter) form he could achieve the humble tone of a prayer and a comfortable fusion

Drawing of Diego's wife, Germaine, by José Escassi (published in Diego's La sorpresa, cancionero de Sentaraille, 1944)

Step by step
      one ascends the Parnassus
I do not want the wings of Pegasus)[.]

*Imagen* and *Manual de espumas* are Diego's creationistic signature books. *Manual de espumas* was written in Gijón in 1922, while Diego was teaching there, and in it he paints a delightful, worriless metaphysical optimism, which permeates the thirty poems of the collection. This existential pleasure is best seen in the initial stanza of the poem "Paraíso" (Paradise):

*Drawing of Diego by Gregorio Prieto (from Prieto's* Lorca y la
generación del '27, *1977)*

of refined and popular voices, along with absolute
sincerity. *Viacrucis* is the opposite of the paganistic
*Versos humanos;* it seems to be the devout religious
chant of one of God's creatures, a chant that Diego
later strove to perfect in *Versos divinos* (Divine
Verses, 1971).

In 1925 Diego became obsessed with creating
a magazine. In 1927, as a professor at the Real Instituto Jovellanos in Gijón, he was able to publish a
poetry magazine, *Carmen.* It was printed in Santander so that Diego could benefit from the printing
knowledge and help of his friend Rafael Calleja,
who lived and worked there and printed the magazine for Diego. Luis Alvarez Piñer, a former student
of Diego, and Manuel de la Escalera were Diego's
assistants on the production of *Carmen,* which survived for only seven issues. In 1928, in the last
issue, Diego published a verse and prose supplement titled "Lola, amiga y suplemento de Carmen"
(Lola, Friend and Supplement of Carmen), which
includes these lines:

Sin temor a los líos que la armen,
desenvuelta, resuelta y española
aquí tenéis a Lola,
que dirá lo que debe callar Carmen.

(Without fear of the troubles that might bother her,
confident, determined and Spanish
here you have Lola,
who will say what Carmen has to keep silent.)

Thus Diego introduced *Lola,* the magazine that
succeeded *Carmen* later in 1928. Like that of *Carmen,*
the purpose of *Lola* was to promote the vanguard currents of creationism and ultraism. *Lola* was published
in Sigüenza under the supervision of Bernabé
Herrero, and in its first issue is a chronicle of the tercentenary of Góngora's death; the report was a defiant answer to the anti-Góngora posture of the Royal
Spanish Academy.

Diego's pro-Góngora position thus became well
known in 1927. By then Diego had already met Alberti, Federico García Lorca, Pedro Salinas, Jorge

*Gathering of writers in Madrid to honor the publication of Vicente Aleixandre's* La destrucción o el amor *(1935). Diego is seated on the ground. Also included in the photograph are Miguel Hernández, J. Panero, Luis Rosales, L. F. Vivanco, J. F. Montesinos, A. Serrano Plaja, L. Panero, Pedro Salinas, María Zambrano, E. Díez Canedo, Vincente Aleixandre, and J. Bergamín.*

Guillén, Dámaso Alonso, and Vicente Aleixandre. The young poets decided to commemorate Góngora and his work with a series of editions in which Góngora's works would be republished. Diego compiled an anthology in honor of Góngora, and others arranged similar publications. These planned books, by the "nietos de Góngora" (grandchildren of Góngora), as they chose to call themselves, were announced in the first issue of *Lola*. The poets also celebrated a funeral in memory of the great poet of Córdoba, the one whose hermetic poetry was favored by those interested in cultivating the ultraist-style metaphor. Diego was one of the few to keep his word, and in 1927 he published his *Antología poética en honor de Góngora, desde Lope de Vega a Rubén Darío.* (Poetic Anthology in Honor of Góngora, from Lope de Vega to Rubén Darío). The year finished with the well-known excursion to Seville, on which almost all the group went. During this trip the poetic identity of most of the group was established as the Generation of 1927.

*Fábula de Equis y Zeda* (Fable of X and Z, 1932) and *Poemas adrede* (Poems on Purpose, 1932) consti-

tute a predictable deviation in Diego's career. They are permeated by the classical, baroque ideas and forms that he admired in Góngora's work, and they attest to Diego's technical and thematic versatility. For *Fábula* Diego chose the *sextina real* (royal sestina), a stanzaic form favored by Góngora, but the content is modern in its irrationality and arbitrary imagery. The style of the mythological fable allows for a thematic resemblance to Góngora's *Fábula de Polifemo* (1613). The tone of Diego's *Fábula* is serious, and at times the tale can be almost tragic in spite of its illogical overtones. The creationistic facet is as alive in *Fábula* as it is in *Poemas adrede,* which is of the same vein: classic meters with imagistic and arbitrary images, the result being modern poetry encased in traditional wrappings.

At Santander, during August 1929, in the garden of the Instituto de Burgos, Diego met a young Frenchwoman, Germaine Berthe Louise Marin, who was a student at the institute. In 1930 Diego returned to Santander to visit her, thus beginning a long relationship. On 11 June 1934 in Toulouse, France, the thirty-seven-year-old Diego married the twenty-five-year-old Marin. Three days later a religious ceremony took place at the church of Sentaraille, France. *La sorpresa, cancionero de Sentaraille* (The Surprise, Songbook of Sentaraille, 1944) tells of the first ten years of Diego's marriage. The book details the wedding, the honeymoon, and the happiness provided by the couple's children, even as World War II began. The title *La sorpresa* was chosen because Diego kept the book a secret from his wife until its publication. The couple had six children: Elena, Javier, Isabel, Luis, Julián, and Carlos.

From 1934 through 1936 Diego wrote *Alondra de verdad* (Lark of Truth, 1941) and the first version of *Angeles de Compostela* (Angels of Compostela, 1940). In July 1936, when the Spanish Civil War broke out, Diego was with his family in Sentaraille and remained there. The Diego family did not return to Spain until the end of the next summer. In 1939 Diego was appointed to a permanent professorial post at the Instituto de Beatriz Galindo in Madrid, where he taught until he retired in 1966. Diego spent the postwar years working on his new books, and though the times were difficult, he managed to immerse himself in his work. Diego's technical mastery of creating poetic images culminated in his best poetry, ironically not in an avant-garde book but in two of his most traditional and classical collections: *Alondra de verdad,* an intimate diary written in forty-two sonnets, and *Angeles de Compostela,* an architectural-style poem in which each composition plays a crucial role in the whole. The fusion of modernity and classicism and the structural harmony of the collections make these two related books perhaps Diego's best. The link that establishes a clear relation between the books is in the sonnet "Ante las torres de Compostela" (Facing the Towers of Compostela, in *Alondra de verdad*), a poem which in turn inspired the sonnet "Aquella noche" (That Distant Night) in *Angeles de Compostela.* Díez de Revenga states that a desire to subjectivize reality (in landscapes, places, and real situations) unites these two books; he also says that readers ascend from the pantheism of *Alondra de verdad* to the mystical yearnings of *Angeles de Compostela.*

In 1948 Diego was named to a seat in the Royal Spanish Academy. His productive life of poetry writing and publishing continued almost at a breakneck pace, with *Hasta siempre* (Forever, 1949), *La luna en el desierto y otros poemas* (The Moon in the Desert and Other Poems, 1949), and *Limbo* (1951). However, Diego did not feel that he had completed an accomplished work of poetry until his *Biografía incompleta* (Incomplete Biography) was published in 1953. The work is dedicated to Huidobro. Thirty-four years had passed since Diego first met Huidobro; nonetheless, the remarkable influence and friendship still continued. *Biografía incompleta* is a creationistic work written in blank verse. These are poems in which Diego tries to fuse outer reality with the inner reality created by his imagination.

*Amazona* (Amazon), though published in 1955, was largely written in 1949, and some poems were added in 1952. Diego calls *Amazona* a book of love poetry in which love becomes a feeling brought about by remembrances and his imagination, which abolished time to actualize his intense emotions. Love became an imperative theme for Diego. He wrote four other books on variations of the same topic: *Amor solo* (Love Alone, 1958), *Canciones a Violante* (Songs to Violante, 1959), *Glosas a Villamediana* (Glosses to Villamediana, 1961), and *Sonetos a Violante* (Sonnets to Violante, 1962). Diego depicted the contrasts between love as a subjective feeling and as a reflection of the world that surrounded him. *Amazona* was the best expression of those feelings, and it was awarded the 1955 Larragoiti Prize of the Cervantine Society.

Diego's next book, *Paisaje con figuras,* was recognized with the National Prize of Literature in 1956. *Paisaje con figuras* was born when Camilo José Cela asked Diego for an original text with which he could inaugurate his Collección Juan Ruiz series to be published by Papeles de Son Armadans in Madrid. *Paisaje con figuras* brings to attention the fact that landscapes without figures are the creations of modern painters. Diego claimed that up to the nineteenth century human figures were found in all paintings. In Diego's book there are human figures in the poems. In "Visitación de Gabriel Miró" (Visitation of Gabriel Miró) Miró is centered in a landscape that seems to strengthen Miró's character. However, this is not the case for all the poems: in the "Epístola a Mis Amigos de Soria" (Epistle to My Friends in Soria) the background of Soria has a much more prominent stature than that of the several figures that appear in the poem.

*Paisaje con figuras,* moreover, is also indicative of one of the most recurrent motifs in Diego's poetry: landscapes. His poetry is permeated with places, landscapes, and figures of Spain and other parts of the world. In 1928 he led conferences and gave poetry readings in Argentina, Uruguay, and the Andalusian region of Spain; in 1929 he visited Galicia and Santiago de Compostela, which inspired the collection *Angeles de Compostela.* In 1931 he returned to his birthplace, Santander, and in 1934 he visited the Philippines. As his popularity grew, so did the demands for poetry readings and conferences inside and outside Spain.

*Diego in 1963*

Diego's later years were spent writing new poetry, augmenting editions of his earlier work, giving conferences and recitals, and attending tributes to himself. He traveled extensively in Belgium, Latin America, Morocco, and Spain, and he was ensconced as a master of Spanish lyric poetry. In 1968 he received the Spanish Gold Medal of Work and the prize of the Societé des Poétes Françaises, which firmly established him as a recognized international figure. In 1979 one of his final honors was sharing the Cervantes Prize with Jorge Luis Borges.

Diego continued to write poetry in which he experimented with difficult techniques. He constantly tried to better his skills as a poet. *Tántalo: Versiones poéticas* (Tantalus: Poetic Versions, 1960) was conceived based on the premise that translating works by others will improve one's own work. The book comprises his translations of poems by various authors.

*La rama* (The Branch, 1961) was written after novelist and poet Manolo Arce, a friend of Diego's,

requested that he send him a new book to be included in the Colección Poetas de Hoy (Poets of Today Collection) being published in Santander. In this book Diego included poems written as far back as 1943 and as recently as 1960. Unfortunately he thus took to an extreme the lack of thematic and stylistic cohesion that had troubled his critics.

*La suerte o la muerte* (Luck or Death, 1963) is a collection which makes clear Diego's lifelong passion of bullfighting. Diego addresses the bullfight in its entirety, from the preliminary moments – the testing of the spirits of the bull, the penning, and the challenge – to the final traditional rites. The book is a poetic history of bullfighting as seen by Diego. He evokes some of the best-known characters of bullfighting in such poems as "Oda a Belmonte," "Elegia a Joselito," and "Egloga de Antonio Bienvenida."

One year later Diego published *El jándalo* (The Andalusian, 1964). The book is about a northerner who has gone south to Andalusia and returns to his native area, speaking with the accent and intonation of an Andalusian and loving all which is typical of this region. Diego composed the book after spending time in Seville and Cádiz. Machado had already spoken of Diego as a *jándalo* in a poem Machado wrote after reading Diego's *La suerte o la muerte*. Machado's poem, "A Gerardo por su poema taurino" (To Gerardo for His Taurine Poem), prefaces *El jándalo*.

The themes of bullfighting and of the *jándalo* reappear in *El Cordobés dilucidado* (El Cordobés Made Clear), which was published in 1966 with *Vuelta del peregrino* (The Return of the Pilgrim). The book, however, does not function as a unity. *El Cordobés dilucidado* is a continuation of the taurine motifs of *La suerte o la muerte,* and it was born out of Diego's desire to portray a bullfighter known as El Cordobés, who intrigued the poet because to him El Cordobés was the opposite of what a bullfighter should be. The book also sings of lesser-known figures, such as a horse that suffers tragedy in "No me ven" (They Do Not See Me); a novillero; and a banderillero.

*Vuelta del peregrino,* the other half of the book, does not follow the same vein of *El Cordobés dilucidado.* The collections were conceived as separate entities that were married by fate upon publication. In *Vuelta del peregrino* the traveler or pilgrim is Diego, who, after his pilgrimage to Compostela, embarks on an extensive trip throughout Spain. Diego sings of his many friends, adventures, and experiences and of the landscapes which frame such figures as de Falla and more intimately known persons such as Diego's mother and grandmother.

An editor and friend, Angel Caffarena, approached Diego in 1966 and asked him to write an original book for the series Cuadernos de José María (Notebooks of José María), published in Málaga. Diego titled his creation *Odas morales* (Moral Odes, 1966). With this book Diego obviously ventured beyond the then-popular social poetry by condemning violence and writing of freedom and the suffering of those who fought and died for it.

*Variación 2* (1966) is the third book that Diego published in the span of one year. Structural variety and thematic versatility characterize this book, which comprises seventeen poems with their corresponding counterparts or variations. In a way Diego was practicing his skills at reproducing or translating poetry as he did in *Tántalo*. The difference this time was that he translated and transformed his own poetry.

For years Diego had been thinking about a poem which would later become *Preludio, aria y coda a Gabriel Fauré* (Prelude, Aria, and Coda to Gabriel Fauré, 1967). In this book Diego strives to echo the music of Fauré – with its internal rhythms and heightened feelings – and to create a fervent meditation on its meaning. The poem is in three parts. The prelude and coda are lyrical poems, and with them Diego attempts, as he once said, to move the soul of the reader just as the music of Fauré moved Diego's. The central aria reveals the extent to which music inspired Diego.

Two years before his death, in "Cometa errante" (Wandering Comet), the collection of poetry that begins his *Obras completas* (Complete Works, 1985), Diego asked a fundamental question: "¿Qué es nacer, ser poeta?" (What is it to be born, to be a poet?). In Diego's case being a poet meant also being a creator of music.

Gerardo Diego died peacefully on 8 July 1987 in Madrid. Although he had already established himself as one of the best Spanish poets, his critical reputation has continued to grow. He is still acclaimed as a poet with an intense dedication to his art. For him, writing poetry was synonymous with existing.

**Bibliography:**

Antonio Gallego Morell, *Vida y poesía de Gerardo Diego* (Barcelona: Aedos, 1956), pp. 221–265.

**Biography:**

Antonio Gallego Morell, *Vida y poesía de Gerardo Diego* (Barcelona: Aedos, 1956).

**References:**

José Luis Cano, *La poesía de la generación del 27* (Madrid: Ediciones Guadarrama, 1970), pp. 92–101;

Carl W. Cobb, *Contemporary Spanish Poetry (1898–1963)* (Boston: Twayne, 1976);

Francisco Javier Díez de Revenga, "Introducción, biografía y crítica," in Diego's *Angeles de Compostela; Alondra de verdad,* edited by Díez de Revenga (Madrid: Castalia, 1985), pp. 9–66;

Angel González, Prologue to *El grupo poético de 1927,* edited by González (Madrid: Taurus, 1976), pp. 7–39;

Luis Felipe Vivanco, "La palabra artística y en peligro de Gerardo Diego," in his *Introducción a la poesía española contemporánea* (Madrid: Guadarrama, 1957), pp. 177–220.

# Salvador Espriu

## *(10 July 1913 – 22 February 1985)*

### Peter Cocozzella
#### *State University of New York at Binghamton*

BOOKS: *Israel: Esbozos bíblicos* (Barcelona: Oliva de Vilanova, 1929);

*El Dr. Rip* (Barcelona: Llibreria Catalònia, 1931); enlarged as *El Dr. Rip i altres relats* (Barcelona: Edicions 62, 1979);

*Laia* (Barcelona: Llibreria Catalònia, 1932);

*Aspectes* (Barcelona: Llibreria Catalònia, 1934);

*Miratge a Citerea* (Barcelona: Quaderns Literaris, 1935);

*Ariadna a laberint grotesc* (Barcelona: Quaderns Literaris, 1935);

*Letízia i altres proses* (Barcelona: Janés, 1937);

*Cementiri de Sinera* (Barcelona: Palau-Fabre & Triadu, 1946);

*Primera història d'Esther* (Barcelona: Aymà, 1948); translated by Philip Polack (Oxford: Dolphin, 1989);

*Les cançons d'Ariadna* (Barcelona: Ossa Menor, 1949; enlarged edition, Barcelona: Proa, 1973);

*Obra lírica: Cementiri de Sinera; Les hores; Mrs. Death* (Barcelona: Ossa Menor, 1952);

*Anys d'aprenentatage: Laia; Aspectes; Miratge a Citerea; La pluja* (Barcelona: Selecta, 1952);

*El caminant i el mur* (Barcelona: Ossa Menor, 1954);

*Final del laberint* (Barcelona: Atzavara, 1955);

*Antígona; Fedra* (Palma de Mallorca: Moll, 1955); *Antígona,* revised and published separately (Barcelona: Edicions 62, 1969);

*Evocació de Rosselló-Pòrcel i altres notes* (Barcelona: Horta, 1957);

*La pell de brau* (Barcelona: Salve, 1960); translated by Raffel Burton as *The Bull-Hide* (Calcutta: Writers Workshop / Thompson, Conn.: Inter Culture Associates, 1977);

*Obra poètica* (Barcelona: Alberti, 1963);

*Narracions* (Barcelona: Edicions 62, 1965);

*Ronda de Mort a Sinera,* by Espriu and Ricard Salvat (Barcelona: Barrigòtic, 1966); translated by Peter Cocozzella as *Death around Sinera,* in *Modern International Drama,* 14, no. 1 (1980): 3–60;

*Obres completes,* 5 volumes (Barcelona: Edicions 62, 1968–1990);

*Tarot per a algun titella del teatre d'Alfaranja* (Barcelona: Tarot, 1969);

*Setmana Santa* (Barcelona: Polígrafa, 1971);

*Formes i paraules: Aproximació a l'art d'Apel·les Fenosa, en homenatge* (Barcelona: Edicions 62, 1975); translated by J. L. Gili as *Forms and Words* (Oxford: Dolphin, 1980);

*Dibuixos (amb algun mot) sobre temes clàssics,* by Espriu and César Estrany (Barcelona: Estrany, 1976);

*Una altra Fedra, si us plau* (Barcelona: Edicions 62, 1978);

*D'una vella i encerclada terra* (Barcelona: Excursionista de Catalunya, 1980);

*Fem pinya!* (Barcelona: Diàfora, 1981);

*Vox diccionari manual de sinònims amb antònims i exemplés* (Barcelona: Biblograf, 1981);

*Les roques i el mar, el blau* (Barcelona: Edicions del Mall, 1981);

*Sobre Xavier Nogués i la seva circumstància* (Barcelona: Edicions 62, 1982);

*Aproximació a Santa Coloma de Farners* (Barcelona: Edicions del Mall, 1983);

*Llibre de Sinera* (Barcelona: Edicions 62, 1983);

*Poemes i dibuixos* (Barcelona: Taller de Picasso, 1984);

*Petites proses blanques, la pluja i altres relacions* (Barcelona: Gaya Ciència, 1984);

*Per a la bona gent* (Barcelona: Edicions del Mall, 1985);

*Fragments; Versots; Intencions; Matisos* (Barcelona: Edicions 62, 1987).

**Editions in English:** *Lord of the Shadow: Poems by Salvador Espriu,* translated by Kenneth Lyons (Oxford: Dolphin, 1975);

*Selected Poems of Salvador Espriu,* translated by Magda Bogin (New York: Norton, 1989).

*Salvador Espriu ( photograph by Serra d'Or)*

OTHER: "Mariàngela l'herbolària" and "Tres soro-
res," in *Antologia de contistes catalans,* edited by
Joan Triadú (Barcelona: Selecta, 1950);
"Sota la fredor parada d'aquests ulls," in *Els 7 pecats
capitals vistos per 21 contistes* (Barcelona: Selecta,
1960);
*Pla Narbona, dibuixos, dibujos, drawings,* edited by Espriu (Barcelona: Llibres de Sinera, 1968).

The Catalan domain stretches southward
from Roussillon in the French Pyrenees, through
the eastern edge of the Iberian Peninsula, down to
the city of Alicante, and extends beyond the main-
land to encompass the Balearic Islands and the
Sardinian town of Alghero. The Catalan-speaking
people boast an illustrious cultural tradition that
began in the early Middle Ages, and the versatile

Salvador Espriu is an outstanding representative of
that tradition. The second of five children, he was
born 10 July 1913 to Francesc Espriu i Torres and
Escolàstica Castelló i Molas de Espriu, in Santa Coloma de Farners, a town in the Catalan hinterlands
northeast of Barcelona. Though fond of his birthplace, he associated the happy memories of his
childhood with the coastal village of Arenys de
Mar, which lies straight south of Santa Coloma.
Arenys, where the Espriu family used to vacation
regularly during the summer, eventually was given
a prominent role in Espriu's writing. He called it
Sinera, and it is the hub of his fictional world, popu-
lated mainly by characters based on the townspeo-
ple he came to know during his formative years. Except for those summers and some other short intervals, Espriu resided in Barcelona, beginning in 1915

when his father found permanent employment there as a *notari* (estate lawyer). Espriu transformed that city into the fictionalized Lavínia.

Showing a penchant for introspection, Espriu once provided a profile of himself: "Sóc un home solitari. Sóc un home aïllat. Per raons de salut i també per temperament" (I am a solitary man. I am an isolated man. On account of my [frail] health and temperament, too). He also said, "La guerra civil va trencar el curs de la meva vida" (The [Spanish] civil war interrupted the course of my life). After earning, at the age of twenty-one, both a degree in law and a licentiate in ancient history from the Universitat Autònoma de Barcelona, Espriu watched the conflict of 1936–1939 thwart his youthful ambition of pursuing an academic career as a teacher and scholar. He had to settle for a job he found particularly dull: after his father died in 1940, he took over the flourishing law practice. For twenty years his drab daily routine was punctuated by the same walk or subway ride, back and forth, from apartment to office. Things did not change much after he became director of a small insurance firm founded by his brother, Josep Espriu, M.D.

Salvador Espriu wrote in his spare time. Because of the confinement caused by his humdrum life-style, his frail health, and his melancholic spirit (exacerbated by the death of his close companion Bartomeu Rosselló-Pòrcel in 1938 at the age of twenty-four), a mood of pessimism pervades his oeuvre. In the refuge of his personal world, Espriu came to terms with his bitterness during the aftermath of the civil war. In his civic sensitivity and social awareness Espriu equaled any coeval Spanish author. In this respect he could be considered the leading Catalan representative of the war-torn generation of 1936, which includes such poets as Miguel Hernández, Luis Rosales, Leopoldo and Juan Panero, Luis Felipe Vivanco, Idelfonso-Manuel Gil, Germán Bleiberg, Gabriel Celaya, Dionisio Ridruejo, José Luis Cano, and a Catalan contingent: Agustí Bartra, Joan Teixidor, and Joan Vinyoli, among others. Espriu did not miss the opportunity to support, in a visible way, a worthy political ideology. For example, together with the venerable Jordi Rubió and other noted scholars, he took part in the sit-in organized in the spring of 1966 by some university students at the Franciscan monastery in Barcelona's suburb of Sarrià – an incident which drew the international community's sympathy for the demonstrators and reprobation for the violent intervention by the Spanish police.

Counterbalancing his staunch loyalty to Catalonia, Espriu cherished the ideal of a harmonious coexistence of all the peoples of the Iberian peninsula. He envisioned a supernational sociopolitical organism, which he usually called Sepharad in appreciation of Spain's Hebraic heritage. Throughout Espriu's meditation on the fate of Catalonia in particular and of Spain in general led him to formulate distinctive dialectics between the microcosm of Sinera and the macrocosm of Sepharad and between the individual poet and society at large. The basic coordinates in Espriu's works have striking antecedents in the discourse of another group of Spanish authors – Miguel de Unamuno, Ramón del Valle-Inclán, Pío Baroja, Azorín, and Antonio Machado – who foreshadow the writers of 1936 in that they also bore the brunt of a fateful event attended by disastrous consequences: the Spanish-American War of 1898. Espriu acknowledged the influence of the Generation of 1898. In a 1965 interview with Román Gubern, he stated, "pienso dejar sentada mi admiración y respeto por toda la generación del 98. . . . Es mi vinculación literaria que reconozco como más auténtica" (I want to declare my admiration and respect toward all the members of the Generation of 98. . . . This is my literary filiation I recognize as most valid).

In emulation of these revered masters, he developed a technique of interior duplication by projecting himself into a favorite alter ego. Thus, just as Valle-Inclán, Baroja, and Machado portrayed themselves suitably in their respective personas, Espriu created in his own image the taciturn intellectual named Salom de Sinera. Salom is a Hebraic name that can be anglicized as "Shalom" (the Hebrew word for peace that is used as both a greeting and a farewell). The character is introduced in the brief story "La llàstima" (Pity), published in 1934 in *Aspectes* (Aspects), a collection of short narratives. Specifically, with Unamuno and Azorín, Espriu shared the perspective of the observing subject and the observed object. Espriu capitalized on the potential of the dialogue that the persona sustains with the "other" he discovers at the core of his selfhood. At the same time, Espriu experimented with the type of perspectivism Valle-Inclán developed into an aesthetic of distortion – the art of the grotesque, which Valle-Inclán based on the optics of the concave mirror and called *esperpento*. Valle-Inclán probably also inspired Espriu with the evocation of the awesome demiurge, a formidable figure that Espriu identifies as a *sotjador,* one who waits in ambush.

In fashioning the Sinera and Sepharad myths, Espriu often captured a kind of Nietzschean circularity with the orchestration of recurrent motifs. Introduced at one phase of Espriu's career and taken up again at a later stage, these motifs confer to his creativity a cyclical configuration, a pattern of reiterative amplification, which in the minds of some perceptive readers evokes the windings of a spiral. Paramount in Espriu's theme-and-variation arrangement is the leitmotif associated with the occasional manifestation of the prophet or the Messiah. These intimations of the presence of the Savior may be another inspiration from Unamuno.

In order to do justice to the breadth and depth of Espriu's worldview, critics often focus on the cyclical orientation of his writing. They also call attention to the overall syncretism (the fusing of different forms) and to some distinctive synchronic features, which J. M. Castellet, relying on Northrop Frye's seminal theories, explains as evidence of an "encyclopaedic form." By this term Castellet refers to Espriu's ability to integrate elements derived from diverse sources, such as the Bible, Greek and Egyptian mythologies, baroque literature, gnostic thought, and *philosophia perennis* (the perception of traces of the divine throughout history).

A spate of relatively short prose compositions makes up the earliest cycle of Espriu's production. Published in 1929, *Israel,* a collection of sketches adapted from the Bible, is the first of his books and the only one he wrote in Castilian. By 1931, with *El Dr. Rip,* Espriu had reached the sophistication of a full-fledged narrator. In a protracted dramatic monologue, the protagonist – a physician fated to witness his own inexorable deterioration from cancer – combines a valiant attempt at dispassionate self-diagnosis with compulsive reflections on mortality. In *Laia* (1932) the title character is the embodiment of the demiurge as a femme fatale. After evolving into a sinister *sotjador,* she casts an irresistible spell of tragedy and death on an unsuspecting victim, her infatuated lover, Anton.

*Aspectes* and *Ariadna al laberint grotesc* (Ariadne in the Grotesque Labyrinth, 1935) further attest to Espriu's inventiveness. The compositions in these diverse collections exhibit some affinities with traditional genres, such as the ballad of the street-corner singer, the picaresque anecdote, the episode of a diary or a memoir, and the character sketch. However, in their resolutions they are unconventional and unusual. They demonstrate Espriu's conviction that his writings cannot be subjected to a hard-and-fast categorization: "jo no crec gaire en els gèneres literaris" (I am not a firm believer in literary genres).

*Miratge a Citerea* (Mirage at Citerea), another publication of 1935, consists of a diary supposedly written by a teenager, Carlota, during her residence at an exclusive prep school. Two years later, in "Fedra" (Phaedra), in *Letízia i altres proses* (Letízia and Other Stories), Carlota returns as a first-person narrator in Espriu's intriguing modernization of Jean Racine's, Seneca's, and Euripides' classic. In her function, which resembles that of the Greek chorus, Carlota invests the narrative with the momentum of a theatrical performance. Espriu's textual strategies show that dramaturgy is important to his entire aesthetic enterprise.

"Letízia" is a first-person account of the funeral of the title character. In the narrator's morbid evocations and gloomy reveries, there are traces of Edgar Allan Poe's influence. The narrator's rakish disposition and unusual mixture of the macabre and the erotic also call to mind the fanciful confessions of the effete Marqués de Bradomín in Valle-Inclán's *Sonatas* (4 volumes, 1902–1905). To this mood of fin de siècle decadence, Espriu adds an experimentation with the stream-of-consciousness technique.

In the same book with "Letízia" and "Fedra" is a collection titled "Petites proses blanques" (Minuscule White Compositions), in which Espriu hones his artistry and achieves an eloquent terseness, which critic Joaquim Molas links to the lyricism of those writers of the Spanish Generation of 1927. Whatever their antecedents, these delicate vignettes, together with four kindred prose poems written between 1936 and 1938 and published in 1952 under the general title "La pluja" (Rain) in *Anys d'aprenentatage* (Years of Apprenticeship), harbinger, both in style and complex exposition, Espriu's books of poems.

*Cementiri de Sinera* (Sinera's Cemetery, 1946), his first published poetry collection, ties in with "Petites proses blanques" and "La pluja" because of the frequent intimations of the primordial forces of nature that come to bear on the eternal conflict between death and life. Thus Espriu lays down the principles of his minimalist art and existentialist orientation. At the same time, *Cementiri de Sinera* evinces a typical Mediterranean ambiance drenched in sunlight – "olors de mar vetllada / per clars estius" (smells of sea guarded / by bright summers); conveys inklings of a myth about Osiris through the use of nautical and arboreal imagery; and presents a distinctive elegiac mode – the elegy of the self – reverberating with strains as haunting as those one finds in the verses of Antonio Machado and Juan Ramón Jiménez.

The title itself provides the key for the temporality at issue in "Les hores" (The Hours), in *Obra lírica* (Lyrical Work, 1952). The poet combines references to the linearity of clock time with subtle hints of the circularity implicit in the natural day/night cycle and in the daily and seasonal recurrence of the canonical hours. Espriu's imagination brings into effect a paradoxical harmonizing of extremes: dark and light, nightfall and daybreak, and deterioration and regeneration – a transcendental treatment of the central motif. The painful subject of the Spanish Civil War is acknowledged, if vaguely, throughout the book in such statements as "en clos de nit bornaven / guerrers" (in the enclosure of the night, warriors / battled) and "sang que no he versat / m'ha destruït el món" (the blood that I have not shed / has destroyed my world). The "solitari / crit sense cant" (solitary / cry without song) is an emblem of inner exile. Also of interest are enigmatic mentions of the "arbre Déu en la nit" (tree God in the night), "la barca del déu" (the ship of the god), and "sacerdots remadors" (rowing priests), which Castellet relates to the lore of the ancient god Osiris.

The poems of "Mrs. Death" (in *Obra lírica*) focus on death as individual and communal. Espriu assembles a gallery of portraits: marionettes, ragamuffins, a funambulist, a pipe smoker, and a blind musician. In the first poem, "Mentre representem" (While We Perform), the third-person narration – "Titelles / prou espatllats supliquen / bon repòs . . ." (Puppets, quite dilapidated, beg for a good rest) – mutates into first person: "esperem només jeure, / mesclats, dintre la capsa / ben closa" (we simply hope to lie down, tossed at random, within the box closed tight).

Espriu circumscribes a tragic space within which he occasionally spotlights a character of epic stature. Such is the case of a star-crossed lover conjured from Dante's *Inferno,* canto 5. In a spin-off of the story of Paolo and Francesca, Espriu keeps the woman silent and has only the man speak. The resulting dramatic monologue is appropriately titled "Paolo." The protagonist's muffled cry betokens a desperate search for communication with his elusive companion.

Castellet explains that in "Mrs. Death" Espriu brings together for the first time the major facets of his art: the civic, satiric, ethical, and elegiac. Espriu shows the fourth facet by resuming, in the last ten poems, the elegy of the self.

In terms of metaphysical acumen and purity of form, Espriu's lyricism reaches its high point in *El caminant i el mur* (The Wayfarer and the Wall, 1954), which has a tripartite structure. In the first poem, "No t'he de donar accés al meu secret" (I Must Not Grant You Access to My Secret), the expression "crit avall" (a yell on the way down) evinces a

sound reverberating with interiority. There are other determinants – "m'allunyava endins" (I got further and further inside), "cor endins" (deep within the heart) – which likewise convey the sense of a cavernous inner self. The second poem, "Petit eco en el Styx" (Small Echo in the Styx), yields additional glimpses of the psychic space of the poet. His consciousness is at first in "presó" (prison) and then in an ambiance of eeriness: "el clos / on tinc només amb mi els laments de Gadara" (the enclosure / in which I can only keep to myself the laments of Gadara), a reference to the biblical passage in Matthew 8.28–34 which describes some demoniacs coming out of tombs. He then says that a serpent, wrapped around his body, is dragging him on a spiraling fall into the bottomless pit.

The serpent imagery is reminiscent of a passage from Dante's *Inferno* (5.1–12), which describes how Minos encircles the damned with his tail and determines in each case the degree of culpability by the number of windings. There is also a special connection between "Petit eco en el Styx" and Pedro Calderón de la Barca's crystallization of the tragic in one passage of his *La vida es sueño* (Life Is a Dream, 1635) – Segismundo's soliloquy, with which Espriu's lines vibrate in unison not only in the mood of despondency but also in the use of exactly the same stanza, the *espinela clásica* (octosyllabic lines rhyming *a b b a a c c d d c*). There are some expressions of Espriu's – "Presoner de mancament" (Prisoner of deficiency), for instance – which bear considering in the light of Segismundo's desolate cry of abandonment: "el delito mayor del hombre es haber nacido" (man's greatest crime is to have been born).

Part 2 of *El caminant i el mur,* "Cançons de la roda del temps" (Songs of the Wheel of Time), describes a "sortida al dia" (exit into the day), inspired, as Castellet notes, by the ancient Egyptian myths related to the *Book of the Dead* and the worship of Ra. Also worthy of mention is the Dantean pilgrim, who, after reaching the bottom of hell, is ready to come out "a riveder le stelle" (to see the stars anew). Thus, Satanic time, symbolized by the serpent or Minos's tail, makes way for the divine transcendence manifested in the solar cycle. Set to music and popularized by Raimon, the Valencian folk singer, the *cançons* contain some of Espriu's most stirring expressions, as in this passage:

El sol ha anat daurant
el llarg somni de l'aigua.
Aquests ulls tan cansats
del qui arriba a la calma
han mirat, han comprès,
oblidaven.

*Drawing of Espriu by J. M. Subirachs*

(The sun has tinged in gold
the lasting dream of the water.
These tired weary eyes
of one who attains calm
have looked, have understood,
have usually forgotten.)

Part 3 bears the title "El Minotaure i Teseu" (The Minotaur and Theseus), and the epigraph is "Crida lo sol plorant ab cabells negres" (The sun cries and weeps with his hair turned black), a verse by Roís de Corella, a Renaissance poet from Valencia. The image is especially jarring when compared to the previous *cançons* refulgent with sunlit air. Paradoxical though it may seem, the obscure and labyrinthine setting is attendant on an attempt by the poet to clarify the orientation and sharpen the definition of his metaphysics. In the very opening lines

of the first poem one sees assertiveness of the speaker: "Hem pujat el nostre crit a tu / i ens posàvem de puntetes per semblar més alts" (We have raised our mournful cries to you / and we used to stand on tiptoe so as to appear a bit taller).

In "Assaig de càntic en el temple" (Rehearsing a Canticle in the Temple) the persona has not only the stateliness of a prophet worthy of conversing with God but also the solidarity of a patriot in his dealings with the fellow citizens of Sepharad. The poem begins with a declaration of aversion toward the motherland — "Oh, que cansat estic de la meva / covarda, vella, tan salvatge terra" (Oh, how tired I am of my / cowardly, old, quite savage land) — but it ends with an assertion of kinship and deep affection:

Car sóc també molt covard i salvatge
i estimo a més amb un

desesperat dolor
aquesta meva pobra,
bruta, trista, dissortada pàtria.


(Besides I too can be cowardly and just as savage
and after all I love
out of despair and grief
this piteous land of mine,
this brutish, sad, woebegone country.)


Espriu underscores the symbiosis between the poet and his people by erasing, at least in this poem, the distinction between poetic language and the speech of common folk.

For all the usage of ordinary language, the striving for a clarification of principles, and the search for secure bearings, the enigma remains. Occasionally, Espriu's protagonist tantalizes the reader with a straightforward explication. In "Noves paraules d'augur" (New Words of Prognostication), "caminant" and "mur" are listed as epithets of death, as are "jo que parlo" (I who speak) and "tu que escoltes" (you who hear). Espriu thus consummates a drastic reductive process: wayfarer, wall, speaker, and listener are all related to the moment of death, perceived through the consciousness of an individual who is a resident of a community. As well as the coordinates of *endins* (within), Espriu postulates those of *enllà* (beyond). While the former refers to the venturesome journey into the "galerías del alma" (galleries of the soul) or the "noche oscura del alma" (dark night of the soul) — in the respective terminology of Machado and Saint John of the Cross — the latter points to the steadfast endurance of the spirit. Espriu envisions a wistful alternative to the fall into death's black hole.

In *Final del laberint* (End of the Labyrinth, 1955) he broaches the potential of a refurbished notion of *no-res* (no-thing) in line with the ideologies of medieval mystic Meister Eckehart and Renaissance thinker Nicholas Cusanus, both of whom Espriu quotes in the epigraphs. Inspired, as Castellet reveals, by Eckehart's negative theology, by Cusanus's *docta ignorantia* (ignorance doctrine), and probably by the reflections on incomprehensibility of Azriel, the cabalist from Girona, Espriu leaps beyond indeterminate guilt, fateful damnation, and the grandeur of tragedy by focusing on such bucolic topics as a shepherd and his flock (in poems 3, 4, and 5), a hunter pursuing a stag (poems 6, 7, and 11), a mysterious centaur (poems 27 and 28), springtime, and limpid waters, as in these lines:

Diré dels meus ulls i de l'aigua.
Si tot ho mira el llac,
jo tinc les nines blanques.

(I will speak of my eyes and the water.
As the lake looks at all things,
my pupils will be all white.)

The idyll is redolent of the "Song of Solomon" and the sublime "Cántico" (Canticle, 1584) by Saint John of the Cross.

In the last poem, after a stark statement of primordial contraposition — "De la llum a la fosca, / de la nit a la neu" (from the light to the dark, from the night to the snow) — Espriu writes, "Enllà de contraris / veig identitat" (beyond contraries / I see identity). Castellet considers *Final del laberint* a compendium of "aventura espiritual, que té per model la mística" (spiritual adventure, modeled after the mystical experience).

*Les cançons d'Ariadna* (The Songs of Ariadna, 1949) is a showcase of variations. The enlarged edition of 1985 (in *Obres completes*) includes poems written as late as 1980 and is sufficiently ample and diverse to represent the salient trends in Espriu's entire oeuvre. Readers find the primordial tension which conditions Espriu's "encyclopaedic form" and determines the dialectic between two concentric spheres, one of microcosmic concentration and the other of macrocosmic projection. With his centripetal drive of introspection he defines the inner core of the microcosm and the consciousness of being a victim of fate and circumstance:

Uns tristos mots qui sap si portaran
vestigis d'alegria a la tristesa:
davallades cisternes del temps,
esglaons del meu fred fins als ulls del no-res.

(Some sad words will bring perhaps
vestiges from happiness to sadness:
descended cisterns of time,
a stairway of my coldness to the eyes of no-thing.)

But by using his talent for the sudden shift, Espriu can make readers sense the recoiling of that victim from the limitations of the grotesque and the tragic. Out of the labyrinth of isolation, out of the pit of anguish, suffering, and damnation, originates the instinct for an expansive movement, the centrifugal flight of liberation, as in the poem "Mishnà": "Enllà del temps de nit, veus de prínceps imposen / els preceptes eterns de les llavors, de les festes" (beyond the time of night, voices of princes impose / the eternal precepts of the seeds, of the feasts). Assuming a prophetic role, the character Salom is such a prince, and during an ephemeral respite from his many disenchantments and frustrations, he is ready to rise to the contemplation of a new dawn (in "Cançó d'Enone"): "Jadesdetrencd'alba/ s'arboren cav-alls" (now from daybreak / horses turn into trees).

Amid the myriad functions and aspects of what Ricard Salvat called in 1966 "l'univers creacional d'Espriu" (the universe of Espriu's creativity), of special interest is the emergence of a persona with a distinctive voice, in poems such as "Vietnam" and "Veient Rosie a la finestra" (Seeing Rosie Leaning Out the Window). In the language of the ordinary man or woman of the street, a Catalan speaker voices concerns in reaction to contemporary events. The extraordinary poem "Petites cobles d'entenebrats" (Tiny Strophes for Silhouettes) is emblematic of the method by which Espriu brings to the fore the centrality of one poetic consciousness surrounded by various characters who remain hidden in a shadowy limbo. In the final stanza Espriu affixes his memorable signature on a self-proclaimed identity and speaks out in a clear but quiet manner:

> Em dic Salom, fill de Sinera,
> Contemplo el buit, mirant enrera.
> I, temps enllà, tan sols m'espera
> desert, tristor d'hora darrera.

> (My name is Salom, son of Sinera,
> I face a vacuum, when I look backward.
> A desert awaits me, in years ahead,
> and the sadness of the final hour.)

Espriu's accomplishments in two other spheres of creativity, drama and literary criticism, provide a natural frame of reference for his poetry. A decade before *Cementiri de Sinera* was published, he began to show a fascination for the stage. In November 1936, after the Spanish Civil War had begun, Espriu, seeking some distraction from the horrific circumstances, wrote "Fedra" (his version of *Fedra* by the Majorcan writer Llorenç Villalonga). Then he wrote *Antígona* (1955), completed in 1939, the last year of the civil war. Espriu's re-creation of the plight of the Sophoclean heroine established him as a writer with a mature civil conscience that transcended partisan biases and sectarian agendas.

Espriu's unquestionable masterpiece in drama is *Primera història d'Esther* (The First Story of Esther, 1948), written between May 1947 and February 1948. Thanks to the magic of Espriu's staging, the episodes in the ancient kingdom of Susa are transported across the millennia so that they also become events in modern Sinera. Thus biblical events function as the foci of a play within a play. In the judgment of such critics as Salvat and Ricardo Domé-

nech, with *Primera història d'Esther* Espriu vies in originality and innovation with Valle-Inclán, Lorca, and Rafael Alberti.

The coalescence of the past with the present, among other dramatic strategies and effects, are the crucial issues Espriu analyzes, from a critic's perspective, in a series of essays published between 1948 and 1953 and collected in 1957 under the title *Evocació de Rosselló-Pòrcel i altres notes* (Evocation of [Bartomeu] Rosselló Pòrcel and Other Notes). By the end of the 1950s Espriu's civic conscience called him more urgently than ever and drove him out of the labyrinth of his solitude in order to set him, as openly as circumstances would allow, upon what Castellet calls "el camí del compromís del poeta amb el món" (the road of the poet's engagement with the world). By that time the political silence in Catalonia had become just as deafening as the reverberations of the anguished cry within the psyche of the poet. In response to that need, Espriu wrote between 1957 and 1958 the fifty-four poems to be published in 1960 under the title of *La pell de brau* (translated as *The Bull-Hide,* 1977).

*La pell de brau* conveys the effect of a remarkable widening of horizons. In his verbal medium, Espriu created the Catalan answer to Pablo Picasso's *Guernica* (1939). *La pell de brau* is a collage in which the poetry reaches plenitude and fulfillment in a harmonious blend of the artist's expression and that of the citizens:

> Nosaltres volem
> només,
> amb esperança
> humil,
> la plenitud eterna
> de la rosa,
> una suprema eternitat
> de flor.

> (We wish
> simply,
> in humble
> hope,
> the eternal plenitude
> of the rose,
> a supreme eternity
> of a flower.)

In his analysis of *La pell de brau* Arthur Terry dwells on a central parable (in poems 15–20), in which Espriu introduces the symbol of "l'ocell del sol" (the sunbird) and brings back to the limelight the figure of Jehudi, who also appears in *Primera història d'Esther.* Terry sketches a profile of these enigmatic entities, seeing them, respectively, as "a life-force, a source of hope and order," and "the tailor of Sepharad, who witnesses the martyrdom of the bird and hangs himself in sympathy." Fraught with unsettling ambiguities, this most complex of Espriu's books recalls Unamuno's description of the Iberian countryside as a metaphor for the unchanging history of human suffering. Espriu's persona, a spokesman of the community, concludes the book with these words:

> i anem escrivint
> en aquesta pell estesa,
> en un cor amagat i immortal,
> a poc a poc el nom
> de Sepharad.

> (and we go on writing
> upon this outstretched hide,
> with a hidden and immortal heart,
> little by little the name
> of Sepharad.)

In his later books Espriu shows he can reiterate his themes without being repetitious and recycle his imagery without losing the freshness of his inspiration. What distinguishes *Llibre de Sinera* (Book of Sinera, in *Obra poètica,* 1963; separately published in 1983) is a pervasive aura of nostalgia stemming from vague "retalls de records" (cutouts of memories) concerning childhood scenes and places associated with the early years of the poet's life – such as, to name but one example, the "jardí dels cinc arbres" (garden of five trees). In this evocation of the actual yard in the family house at Arenys and in similar references or allusions, Espriu not only renews his aspirations for a romanticized place of pristine bliss but also employs the matrix of his most revealing symbols. Some of these pertain to the moment of death; others relate to a point of recognition, which in a Greek tragedy would be known as *anagnorisis:* "Ah, jutge, jutge de mi mateix, i alhora / apassionat acusador davant aquest jutge!" (Alas, judge, judge of myself, and all the while / impassioned accuser in front of this judge!).

Among distant reminiscences of life in his hometown, Espriu's imagination educes scenes of public religiosity. Easter services in particular spawn myriad reveries and reflections, out of which Espriu elaborated another book, *Setmana Santa* (Holy Week), written between 1962 and 1970 and published in 1971. The phantasmagoria and multifarious details of the paschal season are recast within the ambiance of Sinera, in terms of Espriu's fixations on the banquet, the Logos, the apocalypse, and the suffering. Thus the Christian Liturgy, in

unison with the constant recurrence of winter and spring, gives rise, in Espriu's mind as it did in medieval times, to visions of lugubrious processions adumbrating events of cosmic proportions. Through the mechanism of the sudden shift, the visionary is often complemented by the grotesque.

Espriu's next significant collection of previously uncollected poems, *Per a la bona gent* (For the Good People, 1985), begins with a section – "D'una vella i encerclada terra" (About an Old and Besieged Land) – suffused with patriotic sentiments, couched in one composition, "M'han demanat que parli de la meva Europa" (They Have Asked Me to Talk about My Europe), in a type of poetic prose. This preamble of sorts comprises, in the main, poems commissioned by or dedicated to friends or relatives. Part 2, "Intencions" (Intentions), consists of short pieces in an exquisite satirical vein, reminiscent of Machado's mordant witticisms. The next section, "Aproximació a l'obra d'alguns artistes" (Approach to the Works of Some Artists), employs a method of homage and depiction with which Espriu had become comfortable and effective. No less striking as signs of Espriu's imagination are the verses published posthumously in 1987 under the general heading of *Fragments; Versots; Intencions; Matisos* (Fragments; Versifications; Intentions; Shades of Meaning). The self-deprecating terms are Espriu's own.

Theater never lost its allure for Espriu. He collaborated with his good friend Salvat, the prominent Catalan director, on some projects designed to transform into dramatic representations assorted works originally conceived as lyrical and narrative. The experiment began in 1960 with *La pell de brau,* a theatrical adaptation of the book. In 1963 *Gent de Sinera* (People of Sinera) was produced as a dramatization of selections by Espriu in verse as well as in prose. *Ronda de mort a Sinera* (produced, 1965; published, 1966; translated as *Death around Sinera,* 1980) was a resounding success, spectacular in more ways than one. Its showing received unreserved acclaim not only in Barcelona but also, subsequently, in Madrid, Paris, Reggio Emilia, and Venice. Thanks to its comprehensive scope, syncretic exposition of salient themes, and incisive focus on fundamental concerns, this unusual dramatized anthology may prove to be the most effective compendium of Espriu's works.

Outside the partnership with Salvat, Espriu continued his own playwriting. *Una altra Fedra, si us plau* (Another Phaedra, If You Please) premiered and was published in 1978. The terseness and brevity of the play created problems for the production team and left the audience somewhat perplexed.

*Espriu, circa 1954*

In February 1985 Espriu became very ill; on the twenty-second day of that month he died of myocardial infarction. Many Catalans then came to pay their respect to the poet, whose body was lying in state in the Palau de la Generalitat in Barcelona. He was buried in Arenys, in the cemetery he had celebrated in his 1946 book.

Espriu had received many honors during his lifetime. In 1980 he received two honorary doctorates, one from the University of Barcelona and the other from the University of Toulouse. His awards included the Montaigne Prize from the University of Tübingen (1970); the Premi d'Honor de las Lletres Catalanes (1971), the most illustrious title to be conferred on a Catalan intellectual; the Premi de la Crítica (1972); the Premi Ciutat de Barcelona (1981); and two gold medals, one from Barcelona and one from Catalonia (both in 1982). In 1984 he was inducted into the Acadèmia de Bones Lletres, one of the oldest and most renowned institutions on the Iberian peninsula. In 1982 the Madrid government had offered him the Cruz de Alsonso X, which he politely declined for political reasons.

In the early 1970s and 1980s a group of Catalanists, led by Castellet, presented, time and again with no success, Espriu's candidacy for the Nobel Prize, and he was officially nominated in 1970 and 1980 but never won. In some wry comments, Espriu himself assessed the insurmountable odds he had to face: "No crec gens, en absolut, que em donin el premi Nobel . . . no crec que cap règim des de Madrid recolzi mai la meva obra per al premi Nobel" (I do not believe in the least that I will be given the Nobel Prize . . . I do not believe that any regime from Madrid will ever sponsor my work for the Nobel Prize). These words express the disdain of a leading representative of Catalonia whose lifetime ambition was to establish an existential dialogue between the self and the outside world, represented by the Catalan nation and the Spanish state.

**Interviews:**
Román Gubern, Interview with Espriu, *Primer Acto*, 60 (1965): 13–17;
Baltasar Porcel, "Salvador Espriu, foc i cendra," *Serra d'Or*, 8 (1966): 387–395.

**Bibliography:**

Maria Isabel Pijoan Picas, "Selección bibliográfica de Salvador Espriu," *Nuevo Hispanismo,* 2 (1982): 233–249.

**Biographies:**

Maria Aurèlia Capmany, *Salvador Espriu* (Barcelona: DOPESA, 1972);

Antoni Batista, *Salvador Espriu: Intinerari personal* (Barcelona: Empúries, 1985).

**References:**

Pedro Altares, "Un nombre para el Nobel: Salvador Espriu," afterword to Espriu's *Primera història de Esther,* translated by Santos Hernández (Barcelona: Aymá, 1968), pp. 119–121;

Alfred Badia, *"Antígona" i "Fedra," de Salvador Espriu* (Barcelona: Empúries, 1985);

Lluís Busquets i Grabulosa, "Salvador Espriu i la seva obra," introduction to Espriu's *Petites proses blanques, la pluja i altres relacions* (Barcelona: Gaya Ciència, 1984), pp. 7–43;

Rodolfo Cardona and Anthony N. Zahareas, *Visión del esperpento: Teoría y práctica en los esperpentos de Valle-Inclán* (Madrid: Castalia, 1970);

J. M. Castellet, *Iniciació a la poesia de Salvador Espriu* (Barcelona: Edicions 62, 1971);

Peter Cocozzella, "Recollection and Introspection in Salvador Espriu's *Cementiri de Sinera,*" in *Catalan Studies,* edited by Joseph Gulsoy and Josep M. Solà-Solé (Barcelona: Hispam, 1977), pp. 259–265;

Cocozzella, "*Ronda de Mort a Sinera:* An Approach to Salvador Espriu's Aesthetics," in *Actes del Segon Col·loqui d'Estudis Catalans a Nord-Amèrica (Yale, 1979),* edited by Manuel Durán and others (Montserrat: Publicacions de l'Abadia de Montserrat, 1982), pp. 307–330;

Cocozzella, "Salvador Espriu's Idea of a Theater: The *Sotjador* versus the Demiurge," *Modern Drama,* 29 (1985): 472–489;

Cocozzella, "Salvador Espriu's Prophetic Mode: The Voice of a Historicist Persona," *Revista Canadiense de Estudios Hispánicos,* 14 (1990): 209–234;

Cocozzella, "La visió tràgica a la poesia de Salvador Espriu: Assaig d'una definició," *Catalan Review,* 1, no. 2 (1986): 9–21;

Rosa Maria Delor i Muns, "L'estructura del laberint a 'El caminant i el mur' de Salvador Espriu," in *Actes del Sisè col·loqui internacional de llengua i literatura catalanes (Roma, 28 setembre – 2 octubre 1982),* edited by Giuseppe Tavani and Jordi

Pinell (Montserrat, West Indies: Abadia de Montserrat, 1983), pp. 461–485;

Delor i Muns, *Salvador Espriu o "El cercle obsessiu de les coses"* (Barcelona: Abadia de Montserrat, 1989);

Ricardo Doménech, "Introducción al teatro de Salvador Espriu" in Espriu's *Primera historia de Esther,* translated by Hernández, pp. 9–27;

Maria Escala, *L'obra d'Espriu en el teatre català contemporani* (Barcelona: Pòrtic, 1978);

Agustí Espriu i Malagelada and others, *Aproximació històrica al mite de Sinera* (Barcelona: Curial, 1983);

Joan Fuster, Introduction to Espriu's *Obra poètica* (Barcelona: Albertí, 1963), pp. xiii–lxxii;

Giulia Lanciani, "Salvador Espriu: Da *Les cançons d'Ariadna* a *Setmana Santa,*" *Estudis Universitaris Catalans,* 23 (1979): 361–372;

Carles Miralles, "Salvador Espriu," in *Història de la literatura catalana,* volume 10, edited by Joaquim Molas (Barcelona: Ariel, 1988), pp. 389–446;

Joaquim Molas, "La poesia de Salvador Espriu," *Serra d'Or,* 6 (1964): 227–230;

Lluís Pasqual, Introduction to Espriu's *Una altra Fedra, si us plau* (Barcelona: Edicions 62, 1978), pp. 5–16;

Maria Isabel Pijoan Picas, *Salvador Espriu o els itineraris de la poesía: Estudi d'hermenèutica simbòlica de Cementiri de Sinera* (Barcelona: Abadia de Montserrat, 1991);

*Primer Acto,* (section on Espriu); 60 (1965): 4–42;

*Primer Acto,* special issue on Espriu, 78 (1966);

Ricard Salvat, *Els meus muntatges teatrals* (Barcelona: Edicions 62, 1971), pp. 49–63;

Salvat, "*La piel de toro* de Salvador Espriu: Notas sobre un montaje épico," *Primer Acto,* 60 (1965): 22–26;

Salvat, *El teatre és una arma?,* volume 1 of *El teatre contemporani* (Barcelona: Edicions 62, 1966), pp. 266–275;

Kurt Süss, *Untersuchungen zum Gedichtwerk Salvador Esprius* (Nuremberg: Carl, 1978);

Arthur Terry, *Modern Catalan Poetry: A European Perspective* (London: University of London, Department of Hispanic Studies, 1991);

Terry, "The Public Poetry of Espriu: A Reading of *La pell de brau,*" *Iberoromania,* 9 (1979): 76–97;

Antoni Vilanova, "El símbol del mur a la poesia de Salvador Espriu," in *Homenatge a Antoni Comas* (Barcelona: Facultat de Filologia, Universitat de Barcelona, 1985), pp. 569–587.

# Ana María Fagundo

## (13 March 1938 –   )

### Candelas Newton
*Wake Forest University*

BOOKS: *Brotes* (La Laguna, Tenerife: Maype, 1965);

*Isla adentro* (Santa Cruz de Tenerife: Gaceta Semanal de las Artes, 1969);

*Diario de una muerte* (Madrid: Alfaguara, 1970);

*Vida y obra de Emily Dickinson* (Madrid: Alfaguara, 1972);

*Configurado tiempo* (Madrid: Oriens, 1974);

*Invención de la luz* (Barcelona: Vosgos, 1978);

*Desde Chanatel, el canto* (Seville: Angaro, 1982);

*Como quien no dice voz alguna al viento* (Santa Cruz de Tenerife: Confederación de Cajas de Ahorros, 1984);

*Retornos sobre la siempre ausencia* (Riverside, Cal.: Alaluz, 1989);

*Obra poética, 1965–1990* (Madrid: Endymión, 1990);

*Isla en sí, 1965–1989* (Madrid: Rialp, 1992).

OTHER: "El tablero de Ajedrez," *Tagoror Literario* , 28 December 1969, p. 21;

*Alaluz: Revista de Poesía, Narración y Ensayo,* edited by Fagundo, 1969–  ;

"Mi literatura es mía en mí," in *La Chispa '85: Selected Proceedings* (New Orleans: Tulane University Press, 1985), pp. 83–92;

*Antología bilingüe de la poesía norteamericana contemporánea: 1950–1980* (Madrid: Porrúa Turanzas, 1988).

The intrinsic cohesiveness of Ana María Fagundo's body of work demonstrates a profound commitment to poetry that has established her mark in twentieth-century Spanish verse. Fagundo has also played a substantial role in the promotion of Spanish and Latin-American literatures through *Alaluz,* a journal of poetry, narratives, and essays, which she founded in 1969 and has directed and edited since. This journal has published the work of well-known authors, as well as more-experimental writers, from Spain and Latin America, including Vicente Aleixandre, Jorge Guillén, Nicanor Parra, and Ernesto Cardenal. *Alaluz* also gave women authors a voice long before feminism became popular. Moreover,

Fagundo has written several articles and books on American and Spanish poets.

As Fagundo writes in the 1985 essay "Mi literatura es mía en mí" (My Literature Is Mine in Me), "La poesía parece haber estado siempre en mí; tan connatural a mí misma como mi propia respiración . . . es una realidad consanguínea a mí misma" (Poetry seems to have been always with me; as connatural as my own breathing . . . it is a consanguineous reality with my own self ). In Fagundo's poems the poetic process seems to originate from the physical being of the speaker, leading to a view of the poems as the "hijos de mi espíritu" (children of my spirit), as Fagundo refers to them. She has indicated how the period of artistic gestation varies, some poems taking four or five years, others longer. For Fagundo, the word is the means to inquire into the mystery of being, and the poem, like a sudden illumination into a never fully disclosed mystery, becomes a vehicle with which to pursue ontological knowledge.

Fagundo often writes about the island of Tenerife, where she was born on 13 March 1938. Fagundo, the daughter of Ramón Fagundo Hernández (an elementary-school teacher) and Candelaria Guerra de Fagundo, spent her childhood and adolescence in Tenerife, and, following her father's advice to study for a practical career, in 1950 she registered in the Escuela Profesional de Comercio; she graduated in 1957. The only female in a class of some forty students, Fagundo was one of only six or seven who successfully completed the curriculum. After a year of studying English she applied for and won the Anne Simpson Scholarship, offered to a European student by the University of Redlands in California. In 1958 she traveled to Los Angeles via New York. Although Fagundo's original goal was to advance her business studies, she soon abandoned them in favor of a literary vocation.

The four years at Redlands were fundamental to Fagundo's development as a writer. Financially unable to return to Tenerife, Fagundo wrote long, detailed letters home concerning her daily life and state of

*Ana María Fagundo, January 1993 (photograph by Ilsa Garza)*

mind. This exercise proved to be invaluable for her literary work. She also read extensively the works of Spanish, English, and American writers and received a B.A. in English and Spanish literatures in 1963.

During the 1962–1963 academic year Fagundo studied at the University of Illinois. From her experiences in the summer of 1963 came her first short story, "El tablero de Ajedrez" (Chessboard). That summer she participated as a "native informant" in the National Defense Education Act (NDEA) Summer Institute for High School Teachers at the University of Southern California. She also performed this task the following summer at the University of New Hampshire and in California again in 1965. Dissatisfied with the academic program at Illinois, Fagundo enrolled in the graduate program at the University of Washington in Seattle in fall 1963 and earned her M.A. in Spanish literature and her Ph.D. in comparative literature in 1964 and 1967 respectively. Since then Fagundo has been teaching Spanish literature and creative writing at the University of California, Riverside, with the exception of spending two years (1976 and 1977) in Barcelona, where she directed the Education Abroad program, and one semester as a visiting professor at Stanford University.

At the University of Washington Fagundo began to consider her writing as a public project. Her first published poem appeared in *Gánigo,* a Tenerife journal directed by her father's friend Emeterio Gutierrez Albelo, who also encouraged her to publish her poems in book form. When her *Brotes* (Buds, 1965) was being prepared, Gutierrez Albelo wrote the prologue for it.

The image of the *brote* in the title of Fagundo's first book points to her commitment to poetry as a never-ending process of gradually seeking to capture being in the texture of words. *Brotes* echoes the works of Juan Ramón Jiménez, whose poetry Fagundo read while at Illinois and later chose as the topic for her master's thesis. Through Jiménez, Fagundo discovered the poetry of Emily Dickinson, the subject of one of her scholarly works (originally her dissertation). The four sections of *Brotes* – "Búsqueda" (Search), "Caos" (Chaos), "Remanso" (Haven), and "Camino abierto" (Open Path) – delineate the poetic journey the speaker is beginning. The poems "Mi poesía" (My Poetry), "Poeta" (Poet), "La página en blanco" (Blank Page), and "Parto o poema" (Childbirth or Poem) are reflections on the poetic process as well as the problems of poetic language and its link with the world. As a process of giving birth, writing a poem is an attempt

*Fagundo in 1954, when she was a student at the Escuela Profesional de Comercio*
*in Tenerife*

to re-create the ontological fullness the poet feels in her innermost being. However, no single poem can achieve that goal, hence in "Caos" the birthing of the word is confronted with its emptiness or distance from the world it purports to configure. The inadequacy of the word reflects Fagundo's frustration about her self-identity and the futility of her desire to articulate being.

Loss of direction is resolved in "Remanso" by a return to the inner self or its counterpart, the naked word. All verbal adornment or trapping is discarded in favor of what is "lo mío inextinguible" (the inextinguishably mine), the essential word that the speaker contextualizes in the landscape of Tenerife. Time is a contrary force whose movement dispels all attempts to make the word coincide with the fullness it pretends to represent. Thus all remains "en ciernes" (in blossom). As the title of the book indicates, the search for po-

etic and ontological fulfillment is never achieved, and what remains is the constant process to which the epigraph refers: "Poesía es lo que no puede ser / y está siempre siendo" (Poetry is what cannot be / and is always being).

*Isla adentro* (Island Inside, 1969) further attests to the importance of Fagundo's native landscape in her poetry. She usually returns to spend summers and Christmas vacations in Tenerife. Every third year she takes a one-year sabbatical from her teaching position in order to return to Spain and immerse herself in her native language and culture. *Isla adentro*, like *Brotes*, has four sections, which point to concerns in Fagundo's writing: "Isla-poesía" (Island-poetry), "Isla-hombre" (Island-man), "Isla-amor" (Island-love), and "Isla-muerte" (Island-death). The geography of Tenerife is for Fagundo a recurring symbol of the existential question surrounding the human condition. The tenacious presence of the island in the midst of an ocean that threatens to engulf it is a powerful image for the drive toward self-affirmation and expression. Like the island, her word wants to affirm its presence vis-à-vis the ocean of reality with which it never fully coincides and which threatens to efface it.

The word/island, constantly trying to inscribe itself, coincides with the individual's impulse toward self-affirmation in spite of time and death. Time is a spiral, an image representing the unresolved and endless process of Fagundo's speaker, caught between her desire to inscribe her being and the frustration of that desire. The sense of poetic and existential incompleteness is counterbalanced by an equally strong thirst to persist with her poetic project. Her frequent use of gerunds; her reference to March as the month of rebirth; and her mentions of the wind, birds, and ocean are hopeful signs of the existential movement of desire and love in search of plenitude.

*Diario de una muerte* (Journal of a Death, 1970), which was inspired by the death of her father at the age of fifty-seven, chronicles her bitter experience of this tragic loss. Two lines by Dylan Thomas are quoted as the epigraph: "Do not go gentle into that good night. / Rage, rage against the dying of the light." Fagundo received her early education from her father, and *Isla adentro* is dedicated to him as her best friend and teacher. He always encouraged his daughter to write. While Fagundo was away from home he would read portions of her letters aloud to her mother and sister, Nina, and delight in the beauty of her descriptions. *Diario de una muerte* is divided into four sections corresponding to the four seasons, with the associations of autumn with agony, winter with death, spring with rebirth, and summer with vitality. Agony is the slow inscription of silence, whose progress the speaker's word is attempting to block. Although writing emerges as the only means to counteract death, in Fagundo's poems its power is confronted by the stone manuscript of the grave against which words are petrified. She does not deprive death of its ugliness, and she has expressed her discomfort with the common practice of making cemeteries look like beautiful parks and of covering the dead person's face with cosmetics.

Her three following collections, *Configurado tiempo* (Time Configured, 1974), *Invención de la luz* (Invention of the Light, 1978), and *Desde Chanatel, el canto* (From Chanatel, the Song, 1982), also focus on the process of writing as the means to counteract the destructiveness of time. "Tiempo-recuerdo" (Time-

remembrance), the first section of *Configurado tiempo*, is an attempt to make the word articulate the jubilant Tenerife landscape, for Fagundo the origin where word and world were naturally linked before time separated them. The enumeration of elements from that landscape (palm trees, brooms, grapevines, and medlars) is an attempt to conjure up the landscape through the material sound and presence of words. This attention to nature stems from Fagundo's childhood: with her parents and sister she traveled to different villages in the Canary Islands in whose schools her father taught. According to Fagundo, her memory is aided by the sensation of the hand touching the page while imprinting the words on it, recovering her youthful being in the weaving of those words. In this process of recovery and rediscovery that is writing, everything becomes a "presente comprobado" (confirmed present). In "Tiempo-amor" (Time-love) and "Tiempo-vida" (Time-life), although the speaker is aware of the invention implicit in the creative process, she persists in it as the only means to counteract the erasure of time.

The necessity of invention is reaffirmed in a quotation from André Malraux that serves as the epigraph for *Invención de la luz*, a book which won the Carabela de Oro Prize in 1977. For Malraux the mystery of human existence is not its spatial and temporal nature but that "in this prison we can fashion images of ourselves sufficiently powerful to deny our nothingness." The book is divided into three parts – "Invención de la luz," "Tinieblas" (Darkness), and "Reinvención de la luz" (Reinvention of the Light) – and Fagundo locates the nucleus of the artistic project in the invention of the word, which, like the original light, will bring forth the order of creation.

In part 1 the word (personified) admits its power to create the world: "existís porque yo os creo / . . . / y pongo nombre a vuestros perfiles de niebla" (you exist because I create you / . . . / and because I place a name upon your foggy profiles). As with the biblical command "Let there be light," the universe is created in the act of naming, in the words the speaker weaves in the poem, as if she were making a pattern or forming a mold. But words cannot be expected to elucidate the mystery of being when so much of the world is incomprehensible. For Fagundo it is not that the word is perceived as inadequate but that its power lies in what it suggests rather than in what it explicitly expresses.

In "Tinieblas" poetry is an enterprise of hope and love. It allows the creation of worlds of light thus filling "el hueco del vacío sin voz" (the hollow and voiceless emptiness) created by time and distance. Naming is a means of leaving imprints of being: "No sé tener más cuerpo que este

*Fagundo with her father, Ramón Fagundo Hernández, in Tenerife, 1962*

que moldea / tu voz en son de tacto en este instante / de espacio conseguido, / de concreción a
voluntad" (I do not know how to have more body
than this one molding / your voice in sound of
touch in this instant / of achieved space / of con-
cretion at will). The book ends by proclaiming
that the justification for life is committing oneself to the writing of the poem as an enterprise
forever "en ciernes" (in blossom). The artistic
and existential project is presented as a never-
fulfilled becoming of constant re-creation.

Writing, as inventing or shaping being, is associated by Fagundo with the concept of "Chanatel," which refers to an imaginary place in *Desde
Chanatel, el canto,* a finalist (before publication) for
the 1981 Angaro Poetry Prize. Chanatel is a poetic
re-creation of Fagundo's childhood in Tenerife.

The concrete shape of words corresponds to the
shape and form she gives to her imaginary Chanatel
on the paper. The book represents a willed desire to
create life, reflecting her native island standing erect
in the ocean.

In opposition to this poetic universe created
by the word, the speaker is located in the specific
context of California: "en esta llanura que no
tiene isla" (in this plain that has no island). The
stasis of that context is opposed to the fluidity of
the universe of the book. Fagundo insists on the
pliable nature of the word, which does not conform to an exact referent but which is open to a
multiplicity of possibilities.

Chanatel is articulated as an inner context of
vital resources from which to generate the word. It is
associated with the *regazo* (womb), with the island, and

*Fagundo addressing a 1976 gathering in honor of Carmen Conde. Seated at the table are José María de Lera, Carmen Conde, Carlos Bousoño, Angelina Gatell, and Salustiano Maso.*

with the word as a concentrated desire to affirm being. Chanatel is thus the genesis of a song "de ser que no quiere dejar de ser" (of being that does not want to stop from being). Fagundo strongly affirms the willful character of her writing, which is not "inspired" but rather is a task during which she is fully aware of the problems and possibilities of the word. Chanatel exemplifies the existential movement of a return to the past through memory and of an advance to the future through anticipation. It equally describes the poetic project, in which the word represents a constant movement back and forth from its formal system of signs to that of the world. Poems and life emerge from the space of Chanatel, where past, present, creation, and reality meet.

The harmony and plenitude of that imaginary space is disturbed by the presence of the "Duendes" (Elves) – the title of the second part of the book. Those *duendes* are the malefic spirits of modern civilization and its attempts to curtail and control life. In major urban centers such as London, Istanbul, New Delhi, and Chicago, the speaker witnesses the constant effacing of life – babies who are senselessly aborted, abandoned in

the streets, or whose lives are preprogrammed in test tubes.

Fagundo's counterbalance is always found in returning to the word, her "amante no entregada nunca" (her never-surrendered lover). But in "Vértigo" (Vertigo), the third and final section of the book, the enthusiasm found in Chanatel is superseded by the realization that it was an invention that never existed. All that remains is the mere persistence in the affirmation of being. The book concludes with the knowledge that life is "ir / yéndonos / y quedándonos" (going / by leaving / and remaining), that nothing "tiene punto de comienzo ni final" (has a beginning or end), and that all is reduced to the song, to Chanatel, the "isla erguida pugnando por serse eternamente" (erected island fighting to be itself forever).

Fagundo's dedication in *Como quien no dice voz alguna al viento* (As One Who Does Not Say Anything to the Wind, 1984) refers to the book as her seventh attempt to inscribe light in the existential path. As if it were a religious rite, the first section, "Introito" (the first part of the traditional Catholic mass), initiates an investigation into the nature of the word and is followed by sections titled "Palabra" (Word), "Materia"

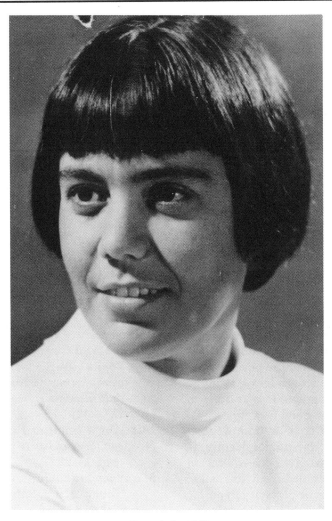

*Fagundo in 1969*

(Matter), "Visión," and "Finale." "Introito" is highly metapoetic in its appeal to and comment on the power of the word to achieve enlightenment. But the word is elusive. Moving between presence and absence and between desire and fulfillment, the word names reality but cannot capture it. Fagundo's speaker struggles between her complete dedication to the life-affirming process of writing and the increasing awareness of its absurdity.

That struggle explains Fagundo's attention to matter as the evidence of physical being. Several poems refer to archaeological remains as matter that has persisted in spite of time. Fagundo has often declared her love for archaeology and antiquity and her fondness for television programs devoted to those subjects. Her poetic speaker proclaims with jubilation that matter "dice que somos / y deja huellas de que hemos sido" (says that we are / and leaves marks that we have been). Matter is the concrete evidence of being, but matter is also chaos when it disintegrates. In

a tone reminiscent of Plotinus and his meditation on the phantasmagoric nature of matter, Fagundo's speaker realizes that beings and things may take form in matter but do not remain in it. Matter reflects being but cannot constitute its essence.

Bud, island, poem, body, and matter are images that articulate the dynamic between desire and frustration. The will to self-affirmation that they connote never culminates in fulfillment: "No eras ni arena, ni estrella, ni mar, / ni espuma. / No eras" (You were neither sand, nor star, nor sea, / nor foam. / You were not). However, in the last poem, "Trinos" (Trills), with March announcing the coming of spring outside the window, the speaker surrenders once again to proclaiming life through writing.

*Retornos sobre la siempre ausencia* (Returns to the Ever-Present Absence, 1989) is, as the title indicates, a repeated return through memory to Fagundo's childhood in Tenerife. The opening poem is "Oración de la palabra" (Word's Prayer), in which the metapoetic meditation returns to the word as a physical body whose touch, voice, and breadth, like the lava and sand of Tenerife, come from time immemorial to take concrete shape in the speaker's lips and touch while she re-creates it on the page in the process of writing.

As the book's title further implies, the artistic project is aimed at conjuring up the return of a past of plenitude to counteract the constant presence of its absence. In this context it is relevant to comment on the poem "Daguerrotipo propio" (My Own Daguerreotype). Through an old picture of the speaker as a child, the past is recaptured. The child that so intently looked at the camera as if it were the distant horizon is the woman looking at the picture in the present. The word emanates from the here and now, refracting itself toward the past and recapturing it, and toward the future, thus configuring the "ser en ciernes" (being in blossom). The horizon penetrates the child's gaze and represents the future, which today is the present turned already into past. This realization reinforces Fagundo's belief that the present is "el único siempre posible" (the only possible always). Only here and now, as in the instant frozen by the photograph, is it possible to capture being in all its eternity and fugacity.

The epigraph for the book is from Seneca: "Nadie restituirá los años. / Nadie te los devolverá" (No one will restore the years. / No one will return them to you). The book is dedicated to family, friends, and the landscape as the necessary frame for the "devenir" (becoming) that life is. The closing poem, "Canción sin despedida" (Song without Farewell), expresses the speaker's desire to be left in her island at the time of her death. The insular geography is again identified with the speaker's inner self, from which her voice will continue to emerge forever singing.

Fagundo's poetry is a constant meditation on the word and on time as a process in which life – which to her is mostly love and writing – is marked by an absence or hollow emptiness that impedes the bud from blossoming fully. What remains is the word, which, like "manos de amor" (hands of love), persists in lovingly shaping and modeling life. The word conjures up presence in the same stroke as it flees away from it. The more it gives the world a concrete name and definition, the more the world escapes from the boundaries of its verbal system. This fusion of presence and absence makes the word synonymous with being and life. The word is "volcado volcán sobre sí mismo" (a volcano overturned upon itself) – that is, a world whose passion is not directed toward the outside but reverts upon itself, a self-reflected phenomenon echoing its own nature. In its never-fulfilled plenitude Fagundo's word leaves the imprint of the incompleteness or otherness that is a mark of the existential condition. Each of her poetry books is a landmark in an existential and poetic project among the best in contemporary Spanish poetry.

**Interviews:**

Victoria Urbano, "Entrevista a Ana María Fagundo," *Letras Femeninas,* 10 (Fall 1984): 74–81;

María Victoria Reyzabal, "Ana María Fagundo, mensajera de nuestra cultura en USA," *Comunidad Escolar* (Madrid), 14 October 1987;

Diana Battaglia and Diana Salem, "Entrevista con Ana María Fagundo," *Alga de América,* 1 (July 1991): 387–394;

Rafael Alcalá, "Entrevista a Ana María Fagundo," *Parnaso,* 7, no. 34 (1992): 19–26.

**References:**

Héctor Mario Cavallari, "El límite de las palabras: Poesía y tragicidad en *Como quien no dice voz alguna al viento* de Ana María Fagundo," *Anales de la literatura española contemporánea,* 12 (1987): 227–242;

Luz María Jiménez Faro, *Panorama antológico de poetisas españolas (siglos XV–XX)* (Madrid: Torremozas, 1987), pp. 235–242;

Mercedes Junquera, "Ana María Fagundo: Is-Is Not an Island," *Mid-American Review,* 8, no. 2 (1988): 155–167;

Antonio Martínez, "La continuidad del ser en la palabra: *Retornos sobre la siempre ausencia* de Ana María Fagundo," *Monographic Review,* 6 (1990): 145–157;

Candelas Newton, "La poesía de Ana María Fagundo (Poniéndole hechura al ser por la palabra)," introduction to Fagundo's *Obra poética, 1965–1990* (Madrid: Endymión, 1990), pp. 21–65;

Newton, "Signos poéticos en la obra de Ana María Fagundo," in *De Scripta Hispanica: Estudios en homenaje a Enrique Ruiz-Fornells,* edited by Juan Fernández Jiménez and others (Erie, Pa.: ALDEEU, 1990): 453–459;

Enrique Ruiz-Fornells, "El mar como símbolo en la poesía de Ana María Fagundo," in *Studies in Modern and Classical Languages and Literatures* (Madrid: Orígenes, 1989), pp. 173–184;

Teresa Valdivieso, "La poesía última de Ana María Fagundo: Voces de un texto," in *Studies in Modern and Classical Languages and Literatures,* pp. 149–157.

# J. V. Foix

*(28 January 1893 – 29 January 1987)*

Patricia J. Boehne
*Eastern College*

BOOKS: *Gertrudis* (Barcelona: L'Amic de les Arts, 1927);

*KRTU* (Barcelona: L'Amic de les Arts, 1932);

*Sol, i de dol* (Barcelona: L'Amic de les Arts, 1936);

*Les Irreals Omegues* (Barcelona: L'Amic de les Arts, 1949);

*Còpia d'una lletra tramesa a na Madrona Puignau, de Palau Ça Verdera* (Barcelona: Dau al Set, 1951);

*On He Deixat les Claus . . .* (Barcelona: L'Amic de les Arts, 1953);

*Del "Diari 1918"* (Barcelona: Horta, 1956);

*Onze Nadals i un Cap d'Any* (Barcelona: L'Amic de les Arts, 1960);

*Antología lírica,* edited by Enrique Badosa (Madrid: Rialp, 1963);

*L'Estrella d'en Perris* (Barcelona: Fontanella, 1963);

*Obres poètiques de J. V. Foix* (Barcelona: Nauta, 1964);

*Catalans de 1918* (Barcelona: Edicions 62, 1964);

*Escenificació de cinc poemes* (Barcelona: Rocas, 1965);

*Els lloms transparents* (Barcelona: Edicions 62, 1969);

*Antología de J. V. Foix,* bilingual edition [Catalan and Castilian], edited by Badosa (Barcelona: Plaza & Janés, 1969);

*Darrer comunicat* (Barcelona: Edicions 62, 1970);

*Allò que no diu La Vanguardia* (Barcelona: Proa, 1970);

*Mots i maons; o, A cascú el seu* (Barcelona: L'Amic de les Arts, 1971);

*Tocant a mà* (Barcelona: Edicions 62, 1972);

*Desa aquests llibres al calaix de baix* (Barcelona: Nauta, 1972);

*Antología poètica* (Barcelona: Proa, 1973);

*J. V. Foix en els seus millors escrits,* edited by Maurici Serrahima (Barcelona: Arimany, 1973);

*El Pell de la Pell,* by Foix and Joan Ponç (Barcelona: Polígrafa, 1974);

*97 notes sobre ficciones poncianes* (Barcelona: Polígrafa, 1974);

*Obres completes,* 3 volumes (Barcelona: Edicions 62, 1974, 1979, 1985);

*Una Lleu sorra* (Barcelona: Edicions 62, 1975);

*Set sonets* (Barcelona: Ferrer, 1984);

*Poemes i dibuixos* (Barcelona: Taller de Picasso, 1984);

*Narcis Comadira* (Barcelona: Laia, 1985);

*Cròniques de l'ultrason; L'estació* (Barcelona: Quaderns Crema, 1985);

*XL sonets* (Barcelona: Asociacion de Bibliofilos de Barcelona, 1986);

*Album Foix* (Barcelona: Quaderns Crema, 1990).

**Editions in English:** *As for Love,* translated by M. L. Rosenthal (New York: Oxford University Press, 1987);

*When I Sleep, Then I See Clearly* (New York: Persea, 1988).

Catalan poetry has remained alive and well throughout the turbulent twentieth century due to the inspiration and courage of a mere handful of writers. Preeminent among those who wrote in Catalan and encouraged study of the Catalan language, literature, and culture was Josep Arseni Vicenç Foix, who wrote as J. V. Foix.

Foix's preeminence is due to several factors: his sheer longevity; his linkage of Catalonia's great medieval and Renaissance literary past to the late twentieth century; his ability to maintain the heritage of the nineteenth century and yet evolve through and beyond visual poetry and surrealism to achieve his own universal view of reality; his breadth of scholarship and literary activity, ranging from the *trobar clus* (troubadour poetry) to modern art and crusading journalism; his linguistic and stylistic gifts to renew and enrich the Catalan language as it is written and spoken today; and the variety, duration, and remarkable quality of his literary contributions. Catalan writing began to reappear in the late 1960s and 1970s, and young poets in Catalonia began to emulate Foix and pay homage to his style and themes in their poems.

This study will focus primarily on Foix the poet, as he is best known, rather than on his roles in

*J. V. Foix*

language and journalism. The latter was principally during the early 1930s as an editor on literary, art, and cultural topics for the *Publicitat,* a Barcelona newspaper. He has received the most prestigious literary awards of Spain: in 1964 the Premi Nacional de Literatura Catalana; in 1966 the Premio Nacional de Literatura; and in 1984 the Premio Nacional de las Letras Españolas. He was twice nominated for the Nobel Prize in literature.

Foix was born on 28 January 1893 in Barcelona to Josep Foix i Ribera and Paulina Mas i Rubinat de Foix, who ran two bakery shops in Sarrià, a small suburb. The young Foix attended elementary school in Sarrià and then went to high school at the Colegi Ibéric in Barcelona. After studying law for about a year at the University of Barcelona, Foix dropped out to help with the family business and to write, his first poems being published in the journal *Revista* in 1916 and 1917. How-

ever, he kept his writing a secret from his conservative parents, who died never knowing that he had published anything.

Chronologically Foix fits into the generation who began writing about sixty years after the nineteenth-century revival of Catalan letters. He was preceded by Mossèn Jacint Verdaguer, Joan Maragall, and the *noucentistes* (those seeking an updated, French approach). The setting in which young Foix initiated his literary career in the 1920s began with the *Renaixença* (Rebirth), a revived sense of Catalan patriotism, language, and culture with intellectual overtones. Poetry was a major factor in the intellectual and social aspects of the *Renaixença,* and poetry was, and still is, a great nourisher of the language and culture. Verdaguer's tender lyric poems are still popular. His Franciscan attitude toward nature and his evocations of Catalonia were formative for Foix and other poets.

Maragall was also well known to Foix. Maragall was interested in aesthetics and the act of creating poetry. The moment of inspiration was his touchstone. He admired German and Greek literature but wrote of his own inner feelings on love, death, resurrection, and Catalonia.

A third major Catalan poet during Foix's youth was Miguel Costa i Llobera, a Majorcan priest and student of Horace. Costa i Llobera combined the beauty and serenity of the Mediterranean with controlled but deeply felt Christian fervor and use of classical meters.

Catalan poets of the early twentieth century had studied the classics and were well versed in French poetry and the latest literary fads in Paris. They were also acquainted with the *modernismo* of Rubén Darío and Castilian poetry. Among the young writers with whom Foix associated and collaborated were Josep Carner, Joaquim Folguera, Joan Salvat-Papasseit, Bartolomé Rosselló-Porcel, Gabriel Ferrater, and Carles Riba. Foix greatly admired this group, especially Ferrater and Riba. Folguera was Foix's earliest encourager in experimentation and the search for an authentic voice; he wrote the introduction to Foix's first poems in the *Revista*.

Foix's highly individual voice and his unusual style of prose poems with titles and "glosses" have been difficult for critics to classify. He refused to be labeled as a follower of any school or poet. On occasion he did follow the language and ideas of the great medieval scholar and poet Ramon Llull and the dense, brilliant poetic style of Ausiàs March. The difficulty in classifying Foix stems from his use of the entire Catalan literary tradition combined with symbolic imagery. He was not a surrealist, not a symbolist, and not a follower of any of the nineteenth- or twentieth-century Catalan or European poets, yet he was intensely Catalan in his language, style, and ideas. It is more accurate to call him a Mediterranean man, a student of the classics. He insisted that he was an "investigador en poesía." This title indeed offers clues to his style and content. Foix constantly investigated the act of poetic creation. Poems, he said, would come to him in dreams at early dawn. He would rise, go to the typewriter, and let the poem reach paper, refining as it flowed. Sights, memories, and ideas were fodder for poetic investigations.

The point at which Foix's investigations become transformations is the epiphany of each poem. Enrique Badosa, who was a poet and friend of Foix, in "Un investigador en poesía" (1993) has pointed to Ovid, whose work is the quintessence of images

transformed. Ovid, Badosa says, provided Foix with the concept of "dreaming awake" in metareality.

Foix's technique for achieving an oneiric transformation was not something he hid. In fact, because he had been called by some critics (who had not understood his aims and process) an obscurantist and an elitist, he felt compelled to describe his poetic process in numerous articles and poems.

Foix's choice of models – particularly Llull, March, and Roiç de Corella – his Catalan consciousness; the linguistic adroitness with which he explored, stretched, and enriched the language; and his transforming perspectivism are hallmarks of his style. These characteristics run throughout his work, both in prose and poetry. His writing of blank verse and long works referred to as prose poems dates from his first volume, *Gertrudis* (1927). These styles comprise the major part of his oeuvre. Among his major prose-poem volumes, consisting of brief and long works, are *Darrer comunicat* (Last Communiqué, 1970), which he believed at that time would be his final volume and poetic statement; *Tocant a mà* (Within Reach, 1972); and *Allò que no diu La Vanguardia* (What the *Vanguardia* Does Not Say, 1970). (The *Vanguardia* is a leading Barcelona newspaper.) Foix's transformation of journalism in this last volume consists of surreal newspaper headlines or poem titles, followed, as is his custom, by the article, or gloss, which is presented as a prose poem. Indeed, the original idea of the titles in many of his works is at once medieval and journalistic.

Although he never stopped writing until his death, Foix did not publish much during the 1940s. Those were difficult times for speakers and writers of Catalan, and Foix had family, marital, and business concerns as well. He and his wife had separated early in their marriage. They never reconciled. He continued to spend part of the summer on the Costa Brava, a renewing source of inspiration for him, and to write and think there, in Port de la Selva, as well as in his flat in Sarrià.

Foix's close association with Joan Miró, Salvador Dalí, and other artists helped to classify him initially as avant-garde. While he did not particularly object to this labeling, he generally rejected classification during his entire career. He participated in experiments in visual poetry along with his colleague Josep Junoy in the journal *Trossos*. Paul Eluard was a friend of Foix's, and he knew many other French poets, especially during the first half of the twentieth century. Foix was a part of the most radical artistic thinking of the time. However, all his life he eschewed the label of avant-garde as well as

*Writers and artists of Barcelona, circa 1927: Manuel Font, Foix, Sebastià Gasch, Lluís Muntanyà, Josep Carbonell, Federico García Lorca, Salvador Dalí, and M. A. Cassanyes (Estate of García Lorca)*

all others, preferring the title "investigator in poetry." In fact, through his collaborations in literary journals and circles, and his newspaper critiques of new artists, he was a major force in introducing new ideas and styles into Catalan culture. His poems have been immortalized in paintings by Dalí, Miró, Joan Ponç, A. Tàpies, and others. They recognized in Foix's writings and attitudes a guiding spirit of surrealism and abstraction permeated with a new way of seeing, an intellectual perspectivism which could be made visible. Foix and Dalí became alienated in later years, but Foix always remained in contact with Miró, whom he mentioned in his poems more than once. He collaborated with Ponç in a book of drawings and aphorisms, *El Pell de la Pell* (The Skin of the Skin, 1974).

Foix's poems have been referred to as word paintings. For Foix, "poetic investigator" was a broad term, avoiding all schools and movements. It is a concept that allowed him to conjure modern words in an ancient language and syntax, or vice versa. The medieval tonalities in vocabulary, meter, and rhyme are coupled with the anguish and alienation of twentieth-century culture. The laments of Llull and March are interpreted by Foix in words which could describe the paintings of Giorgio De Chirico and his close friends Dalí and Miró.

This dichotomy/duality of time and style was conscious on Foix's part. In a poem from *Sol, i de dol*

(Alone, and in Mourning), his 1936 volume of classical sonnets, he writes of his love for the very old and for the exploration of the new:

> Em plau, d'atzar, d'errar per les muralles
> Del temps antic, i a l'acost de la fosca,
> Sota un llorer i al peu de la font tosca,
> De remembrar, cellut, setge i batalles.
> . . . . . . . . . . . . . . . . . . . . . . . . . . . . . . . .
> L'antic museu, les madones borroses,
> I el pintar extrem d'avui! Càndid rampell:
> M'exalta el nou i m'enamora el vell.
>
> (It pleases me randomly, to wander amid walls
> Of ancient time, and at approach of darkness,
> Beneath a laurel and at the base of the crude font,
> To recall, eyes closed, siege and battles.
> . . . . . . . . . . . . . . . . . . . . . . . . . . . . . . . .
> The ancient museum, the blurred madonnas,
> And the extreme painting of today! Candid whim:
> The new exalts me and the old enamors me.)

The processes of creation and transformation for Foix go hand in hand. Another sonnet from *Sol, i de dol* expresses his art:

> És per la ment que se m'obre Natura
> A l'ull golós; per ella em sé immortal
> Puix que l'ordén, i ençà i enllà del mal,
> El temps és u i pel meu ordre dura.
> . . . . . . . . . . . . . . . . . . . . . . . . . . . . . .

Del bell concret faig el meu càlid joc
A cada instant, i en els segles em moc
Lent, com el roc davant la mar obscura.

(It is through my mind that Nature opens herself
To my hungry eyes; through her I know myself to be
   immortal
Since I decree it and, on either side of evil,
Time is one and by my order endures.
. . . . . . . . . . . . . . . . . . . . . . . . . . . . . . . . .
From the concrete I create my heated game
At each instant, and through centuries I move
Slowly, as does the rock by the darkened sea.)

The mind, reason, and inspiration are Foix's paths to creation and transformation. Time is halted, and only the brief moment exists. It is an instant of reality, and it is concrete, not a dream, unreality, or the ideal. The closing tercet expresses a concept Foix repeated many times: that his poetic transformations, his investigations into poetry, were initiated in real objects, people, emotions, and events. Concrete reality was the basis for his new, transformed interpretation of reality. For a Catalan poet living through the Spanish Civil War and Franco years, such altered reality might well have been a survival technique.

From *Les Irreals Omegues* (The Unreal Omegas, 1949) comes this title, below, of a long poem. Such titles serve as the initial metamorphoses of reality. They are followed by extended and elaborated metaphors, which take the form of more-traditional poems. Pere Gimferrer, poet and friend of Foix, writing in *ABC Cultural* (29 January 1993), describes the long poems of this group as basically combinations of alexandrines and hendecasyllables, both Catalan and Italian, similar to those of Roiç de Corella, Salvatore Quasimodo, and Federico García Lorca. One must also recognize the titles as prose poems, the "heads," and the much longer, extended sections which follow as the developed "bodies" of the work. Here is a title, for example:

BAIXAVA DE COLL FORMIC AL BRULL, I EN ÉSSER PROP DE LA MORERA EM VAN ATURAR ELS CÍCLOPS. VOLIA FUGIR, PERÒ, BURXANC EN MÀ, EM VAN FORÇAR A MIRAR COM ENSACAVEN LLIBRES I MÉS LLIBRES MEUS, IMPRESOS I INÈDITS, PERGAMINS DELS AVANTPASSATS SOSTRETS AL RECTOR DELS TORRENTS DE LLADURS I MANIFESTS EVERSIUS. EL MEU COS FULLAVA COM UN FAIG, I UN ULL DESCLÒS ALS BRULLS DEL FRONT EM VA FER VEURE, AIGUOSA I TRANSPARENT, LA MEVA PRÒPIA IRREALITAT.

(I DESCENDED FORMIC GORGE TO THE FIELDS, AND AS I NEARED THE MULBERRY TREE THE CYCLOPS HALTED ME. I WANTED TO FLEE, BUT, STAVE IN HAND, HE FORCED ME TO WATCH WHILE BOOKS AND MORE BOOKS OF MINE, PRINTED AND UNPUBLISHED, ANCESTRAL PARCHMENTS TAKEN FROM THE RECTOR OF TORRENTS DE LLADURS AND MANIFESTOS TURNED INSIDE OUT WERE STUFFED IN BAGS. MY BODY RUSTLED LIKE A BEECH, AND AN EYE VISIBLE BENEATH HIS MATTED BROW MADE ME SEE, WATERY AND TRANSPARENT, MY OWN UNREALITY.)

The sense of unreality and alienation which runs through Foix's works was an asset in his transformation process. While all the poems begin in concrete reality, it is perhaps easier for readers to connect with the small group of poems he composed just prior to the civil war; they present ominous metaphors of the days and months preceding the conflict. The following is a title, or "heading poem," written in September 1936 and published in his 1953 volume, *On He Deixat les Claus . . .* (Where Have I Left the Keys . . . ):

A L'ENTRADA D'UNA ESTACIÓ, SUBTERRANIA, LLIGAT DE MANS I PEUS PER DUANERS BARBOSOS, VAIG VEURE COM LA MARTA SE N'ANAVA EN UN TREN FRONTERER. LI VOLIA SOMRIURE, PERÒ UNA MILICIÀ POLICÈFAL SE'M VA ENDUR AMB ELS SEUS, I VA CALAR FOC AL BOSC

(AT THE ENTRANCE TO A SUBTERRANEAN STATION, TIED HAND AND FOOT BY BEARDED CUSTOMS OFFICIALS, I SAW THAT MARTA WAS LEAVING ON A TRAIN FOR THE FRONTIER. I WANTED TO SMILE AT HER, BUT A POLICING MILITIAMAN TOOK ME AWAY WITH HIS GROUP AND SET FIRE TO THE FOREST.)

After the 1960 publication of some of his Christmas and New Year's poems in *Onze Nadals i un Cap d'Any* (Eleven Christmases and One Year End), Foix increased his output of prose poems, which comprise two volumes of his *Obres completes* (Complete Works, 1974, 1979, 1985). The 1960s were an extremely fertile, energetic period of writing for him. Foix maintained his poetic voice, mature and reflective, which was initiated in *Gertrudis*. His prose poems of the 1960s are even more intentionally in a style and language especially for readers of Catalan and signal a new standard for Catalan usage.

*J. V. Foix, circa 1985*

Foix's literary contributions and his linguistic contributions are both extremely significant. The latter held a special place in his Catalan consciousness. All his life he was a student and scholar of Catalan phonology, etymology, usage, and style. As a journalist and cultural editor in the early 1930s, he was an arbiter and model of usage. For his lifelong crusade for the Catalan language he was appointed to the philological section of the Institut d'Estudis Catalans.

His prose poems are generally untitled – that is, without the initial headings found in his other poetry. The exception is *Allò que no diu La Vanguardia*. This title might appear to indicate a protest volume; the implication is that the newspaper does not tell the whole truth. In fact, Foix's prose poems, almost haikulike at times, are brief "headlined" news items, or simply headlines to be glanced at in his own transformed world, the poet's universe of imagination. An example is the journey of a wounded rose, from the section called "noves de darrera hora" (latest news):

### UNA ROSA AMB UN GANIVET AL PIT SALTA, SAGNANT, PER LA FINESTRA

Acoltellada per una mà càlida, realista i experta, una autèntica rosa, gràcies a la seva remarcable valor física, va resistir l'hemorràgia. Pètals batent, va salvar plans,

selves, rius, munts, illes i ports, i pertot va deixar caure la molsa vermella de la nafra. Es va aturar a contemplar, dels dalts estant, pàl.idament ombrosos, els antàrtics deserts glacials, el bosc petrificat i els peixos fòssils d'ara fa tres milions d'anys. Va aterrar a Nova Zelanda on va morir sota les rodes d'un vergonyós tricicle. La magistratura n'ha disposat l'autòpsia per a establir la causa de tan irreparable esfullament.

### (A ROSE WITH A KNIFE IN ITS BOSOM JUMPS, BLEEDING, OUT THE WINDOW

Knifed by a warm hand, realistic and expert, an authentic rose, thanks to its remarkable physical strength, resisted a hemorrhage. Petals beating, it went over fields, forests, rivers, mountains, islands, and ports, letting its vermilion essence fall everywhere. It stopped awhile to contemplate, on pallidly shaded heights, the fossilized fish of three million years ago. It landed in New Zealand, where it died beneath the wheels of a shameful tricycle. The authorities have arranged for an autopsy to establish the cause of such an irreparable defoliation.)

Contemporaneous with these whimsical poems are those in *Darrer comunicat* and *Tocant a mà*, both prose-poem volumes similar in style, based on narrative incidents and memories. As often, some of the works deal with the mysteries of Foix's creative process. Each poem can stand alone as a word painting, a dreamlike metaphor of transformed reality.

Just as Foix was a poet of interior landscapes, he was a poet who consciously wrote of exterior landscapes, particularly those of the Costa Brava. He spent many of his happiest and most productive hours in his fishing boat along the northern coast of Catalonia and tramping over the hills nearby to ancient monasteries and ruins. Many of his most evocative works reflect this coastal seascape and landscape.

Various critics have endeavored to label Foix, commenting on his singularity, his plurality, his symbolism, his sense of both concrete and fragmented reality, the musicality of his words, and his archaic vocabulary and syntax. He was a Christian poet as well, articulating his faith as clearly as he articulated his culture. Not a poet of any generational group, he preserved the great traditions of classical Latin and Greek poetry, those of his own linguistic forebears, with an unexpected futurism. He was the twentieth century's Catalonian poetic investigator.

## Letters:

*Salvador Dalí correspondal de J. V. Foix, 1932–1936* (Barcelona: Mediterrània, 1936).

## Biography:

Pere Gimferrer, "J. V. Foix en su centenario: Semblanza de J. V. Foix," *ABC Cultural,* 65 (29 January 1993): 15–19.

## References:

Enrique Badosa, Introduction to Foix's *Antología lírica,* edited by Badosa (Madrid: Rialp, 1963);
Badosa, "Un investigador en poesía," *ABC Cultural,* 65 (29 January 1993): 19+;
Patricia J. Boehne, *J. V. Foix* (Boston: Twayne, 1980);
*Catalan Review,* special issue on Foix, 1, no. 1 (1986);
Joan Fuster, *Literatura Catalana Contemporànea* (Barcelona: Curial, 1972);
Pere Gimferrer, *La poesía de J. V. Foix* (Barcelona: Edicions 62, 1974);
Josep Roca-Pons, *Introduction to Catalan Literature* (Bloomington: Indiana University Press, 1977);
Giuseppe Sansone, "J. V. Foix, trovatore e surrealista," in his *Studi di Filologia Catalana* (Bari, Italy: Adriatica, 1963), pp. 268–285;
Arthur Terry, "Sobre les Obres Poètiques de J. V. Foix," *Serra D'Or* (March 1968): 47–52;
Joan Triadú, ed., *Anthology of Catalan Lyric Poetry* (Berkeley: University of California Press, 1953).

# Vicente Gaos

*(21 March 1919 – 17 October 1980)*

Patricia E. Mason
*University of South Carolina*

BOOKS: *Arcángel de mi noche: Sonetos apasionados* (Madrid: Hispánica, 1944);

*Sobre la tierra* (Madrid: Revista de Occidente, 1945);

*Luz desde el sueño* (Valladolid: Santarén, 1947);

*La poética de Campoamor* (Madrid: Gredos, 1955; revised and enlarged, 1969);

*Poesía y técnica poética* (Madrid: Ateneo, 1955);

*Profecía del recuerdo* (Torrelavega: Cantalapiedra, 1956);

*Temas y problemas de literatura española* (Madrid: Guadarrama, 1959);

*Poesías completas (1937–1957)* (Madrid: Giner, 1959);

*Mitos para tiempo de incrédulos* (Madrid: Ágora, 1963);

*Concierto en mí y en vosotros* (Río Piedras: Universidad de Puerto Rico, 1965);

*Claves de la literatura española* (Madrid: Guadarrama, 1971);

*Un montón de sombra* (Valencia: Fomento de Cultura Ediciones, 1972);

*Poesías completas II (1958–1973)* (León: Provincia, 1974);

*Cervantes: Novelista, dramaturgo, poeta* (Barcelona: Planeta, 1979);

*Última Thule* (León: Provincia, 1980);

*Obra poética completa,* 2 volumes (Valencia: Institution Alfonso el Magnánimo, 1982).

OTHER: *Itinerario poético de Dámaso Alonso,* 2 volumes, edited by Gaos (Madrid: Escelicer, 1956);

Ramón de Campoamor, *Poesía,* edited by Gaos (Zaragoza: Ebro, 1962);

*Antología del grupo poético de 1927,* selected, with an introduction and notes, by Gaos (Salamanca: Anaya, 1965); revised by Carlos Sahagún (Madrid: Cátedra, 1975);

Juan Ramón Jiménez, *Antología poética,* edited by Gaos (Salamanca: Anaya, 1965);

Miguel de Cervantes, *Don Quijote de la Mancha,* edited by Gaos (Madrid: Giner, 1967);

Cervantes, *Viaje del Parnaso,* edited, with an introduction and notes, by Gaos (Madrid: Castalia, 1973);

Pedro de Alarcón, *El sombrero de tres picos,* edited, with an introduction and notes, by Gaos (Madrid: Espasa-Calpe, 1975);

*Diez siglos de poesía castellana,* edited by Gaos (Madrid: Alianza, 1975);

Cervantes, *El ingenioso hidalgo Don Quijote de la Mancha,* 3 volumes, edited by Gaos (Madrid: Gredos, 1987).

TRANSLATIONS: *Charles Péguy: Poesías* (Madrid: Adonais, 1943);

Arthur Rimbaud, *Poesías* (Madrid: Adonais, 1946);

Percy Bysshe Shelley, *Adonais* (Madrid: Adonais, 1947);

T. S. Eliot, *Cuatro Cuartetos* (Madrid: Rialp, 1951);

Shelley, *Adonais y otros poemas breves* (Buenos Aires: Espasa-Calpe, 1954);

*Especulaciones: Ensayos sobre humanismo y filosofía del arte* (Mexico City: UNAM, 1979);

*Traducciones poéticas completas,* 2 volumes (Valencia: Institución Alfonso el Magnánimo, 1986).

Vicente Gaos belonged to the first generation of post–Spanish Civil War poets. Although his collections of poetry were published to critical acclaim, in his later years he often appeared to be forgotten or overlooked in his native Spain. It was ironic, therefore, that he should posthumously win the National Poetry Prize in 1981, with his last collection, *Última Thule* (Farthest Point, 1980), published shortly after his death. An early demonstration of his contemporaries' high regard for his poetry was the inclusion of some of his work in the *Antología consultada de la joven poesía española* (Selected Anthology of New Spanish Poetry, 1952), which included poems by the nine best living poets of the postwar period. In 1960 the poet and critic Carlos Bousoño, reviewing the first volume of Gaos's collected poetry (1959), wrote: "No creo que pasen de tres o

*Vicente Gaos, circa 1961*

cuatro los nombres de poetas de su generación que puedan dignamente colocarse a su lado . . . uno de los pocos poetas primerísimos de nuestra poesía de posguerra" (I do not believe that there are more than three or four names of poets of his generation who can fittingly stand alongside him . . . one of the few first-rate poets of our postwar poetry).

In addition to writing poetry, Gaos was also a prolific literary critic and a translator of French and English poetry, all testimony to his creativity and erudition. Yet in some ways he was out of the mainstream: he was never given a professorship at a Spanish university; he lived and taught outside Spain for several years; and new collections of his poetry were perhaps published too sporadically to sustain the interest of the public. After his return to Spain in 1955, he lived mostly in the provinces and did not participate in the literary life of the capital. During the vogue of social poetry, Gaos rejected the trend, and, following in the footsteps of Miguel de Unamuno, he wrote poetry that examines existential issues: human an-

guish and solitude; the existence of God; death; and *la nada* (the void) – "la nada que ha cortejado como pocos poetas" (the void that he has courted as few poets [have]), according to critic Manuel Mantero.

Vicente Gaos González-Pola was born on 21 March 1919 in Valencia into a cultivated, middle-class family that became remarkable for the intellectual and artistic achievements of the children. Vicente's oldest brother, José, was an important philosopher and a disciple of José Ortega y Gasset. Angel, a communist activist and intellectual, was condemned to death at the end of the civil war but was ultimately pardoned and imprisoned. Another brother, Alejandro, was, like Vicente, a poet and professor, and their sister Lola was a popular stage and screen actress. The family had Republican sympathies; as a result of the civil war some relatives went into exile (José lived in Mexico until his death in 1969), and others were imprisoned. Vicente went into exile after the war.

His writing career began when he was a high-school student in Valencia, where he wrote for the student newspaper *Frente Universitario.* He wrote his first poems during the civil war and read them to Antonio Machado, then living in Rocafort, a small town near Valencia. In 1940 Gaos left Valencia for Madrid. There his passionate interest in poetry led to a friendship with Vicente Aleixandre and Dámaso Alonso. In *Los encuentros* (The Encounters, 1958) Aleixandre recalls the twenty-one-year-old Gaos, whom he likens to a young eagle: "Enjuta la cara, el ojo penetrante, implantada como un pico corvo la nariz avizor, todo aquel rostro decía vigilancia y tensión (the face lean, the eye penetrating, the vigilant nose implanted like a curved beak, that whole face bespoke vigilance and tension).

Alonso introduced Gaos to the public in late 1941 or early 1942, when Gaos gave a reading of the sonnets that were later published in his first book, *Arcángel de mi noche: Sonetos apasionados* (Archangel of My Night: Passionate Sonnets, 1944). He had just completed his licentiate in classics at the University of Madrid when *Arcángel de mi noche* was a joint winner of the first Adonais poetry prize in 1943; the following year it was published by Hispánica in the Collección Adonais series. The book includes an introduction by Alonso. Commenting on the appropriateness of the subtitle, *Sonetos apasionados,* Alonso writes, "Es poesía de vena profunda, atormentada, espoleada y poderosa. Es poesía de hirviente pasion" (It is poetry in a profound vein, tormented, stirred up, and powerful. It is poetry of boiling passion).

The poems of *Arcángel de mi noche* were written between 1939 and 1943. Although the majority are neoromantic love poems, there is also a series that constitutes a rebellious, tormented dialogue with God. In many of the poems there is a seemingly paradoxical identification of passion with serenity, and the many references to frenzy and passion are juxtaposed with their opposites: calm and peace. The poet longs for that heightened state in which everything is light, ecstasy, and serenity. (The need for *luz* [light] is a constant theme in Gaos's first three books.) When this ideal state is reached, he experiences perfect contentment, as in "Armonía del Mundo" (Harmony of the World): "Dejadme, porque ya no aspiro a nada. / El mundo rueda fiel, gira seguro. / Arrebato de amor, hora exaltada. / ... No, para mí este mundo no es oscuro" (Leave me, because I no longer aspire to anything. / The world turns faithfully, it spins secure. / Ecstasy of love, exalted hour. / ... No, for me this world is not dark).

But this state of exaltation is difficult to achieve and impossible to sustain. Disillusioned in the knowledge that he cannot remain in that state in "Con-

denados" (The Condemned), Gaos rebels against God, who has condemned him to ignorance and death:

Libre ya, vuelo hacia la luz creciente.
Nadie oscurecerá este mediodía.

Un arcángel mortal ahora me guía.
En sus alas amparo yo mi frente.
Sombrío Dios de mi niñez poniente,
no volverás a ser la a estrella mía.

(Free now, I fly toward the growing light.
No one will darken this midday.

A mortal archangel now guides me.
In his wings I shelter my forehead.
Gloomy God of my setting childhood,
you will not be my star again.)

Critics have noted the influence of Fray Luis de León in these poems, in the many references to cosmic harmony, the serenity of the celestial bodies, the music of the spheres, and the night sky filled with stars.

In the introductory poem, "La forma" (Form), Gaos explains his own rationale for using the sonnet form, much in vogue in the early 1940s. Far from imposing limitations on him, he sees the strict formal requirements as allowing him to structure and impose order on the passionate content of the poems: "Más, no, soneto, tú no me encadenas, / conduces mi pasión, riges mi anhelo, / ... / No me encadenas, me desencadenas" (But, no, sonnet, you do not shackle me, / you lead my passion, you rule my longing, / ... / You do not shackle me, you set me free).

In *Sobre la tierra* (On the Earth, 1945) the exaltation achieved through passion in *Arcángel de mi noche* is replaced by disillusionment and despair, as Gaos realizes that the moments of passionate ecstasy to which he aspired are only fleeting. Mantero sees these poems as an expression of anguish: "Angustia de ser vivo y tener que morir, angustia de no conocer, angustia amasada con dolor por la conciencia de un yacer en las tinieblas" (Anguish of being alive and having to die, anguish of not knowing, anguish mixed with pain by the awareness of lying in darkness). The questioning of God becomes more intense, and the pessimism is evident in the titles of such poems as "La vida, engaño" (Life, Deception); "Tribulación"; and "La vida no es hermosa ... " (Life Is Not Beautiful ... ), in which one reads these lines: "La vida, / su cósmico dolor, sobre mi pesa. / La vida es una inmensa sombra espesa / que envuelve el alma, en carne ya dormida" (Life, / with its cosmic pain, weighs upon me. / Life is an immense heavy shadow / that envelops the soul, in flesh already asleep). The "mano sabia de Dios" (wise

*Gaos speaking on poetry. The audience includes (from left) José Hierro, Dámaso Alonso, José García Nieto, and Carlos Bousoño (Foto Archivo José Luis Cano)*

hand of God) of *Arcángel de mi noche* is replaced by the "mano vengativa" or "tiránica" (vengeful or tyrannical hand); the star-filled sky is seen as "un hondo hueco negro, un Dios ausente" (a deep black hole, an absent God). Inanimate objects and vegetable life are to be envied for being closer to the longed-for state of immutability and serenity than are human beings. Yet there are still moments of hope and consolation in nature, as in "Hermosa presencia" (Beautiful Presence), and through love.

Gaos's third book, *Luz desde el sueño* (Light from Sleep, 1947), has less unity than his other collections, and the tone is less passionate and urgent. As in his earlier works, the themes of death and the absence of God remain prominent, but love continues to be a way of achieving transcendence and realizing fleeting happiness.

The year 1947 is generally regarded as marking the end of the first stage of Gaos's writing career. That was the year he left Spain to go first to France and then to Mexico and the United States. It was eight years before he returned to Spain, and during his absence no new books of his poetry were published. He went first to study in Paris, where he had been awarded a scholarship by the French government. The following year he went to Mexico, and in 1949

(when he was teaching in the United States) he completed his doctorate at the Universidad Nacional de México. In 1948 he was named visiting professor of Spanish at Smith College, where he taught for two years. In 1950 he moved to the West Coast to take up a teaching position at the University of Southern California in Los Angeles. He returned to the East two years later to teach at Fordham University. In addition to these appointments, he also taught a summer-school course at Berkeley. Soon after his return to Spain, he told an anonymous interviewer from *Insula* (15 March 1955) that he had had no personal contact with American writers while in the United States. He did, however, contribute to several American literary magazines, and, in addition to his teaching responsibilities, he worked on literary criticism and his poetry. The interviewer found him changed: "Más calvo, más afilado, más intelectual que nunca, pero también más humano e irónico . . . más fatalista" (Balder, sharper, more intellectual than ever, but also more human and ironic . . . more fatalistic).

Back in Spain, among other teaching responsibilities, he taught in the study-abroad program in Valencia, sponsored by the San Francisco College for Women, and later taught English in high schools in Segovia and Valencia. He seems to have lived a very private life.

*Profecía del recuerdo* (Prophecy of Memory, 1956) is usually regarded as initiating a new stage in Gaos's poetry. He states in the introduction to his *Poesías completas (1937–1957),* published in 1959, that *Profecía del recuerdo* is "algo distinto" (somewhat different) from his previous work. Although there are some changes (new verse forms; a more meditative mood, which replaces the passion of the earlier works; and much less emphasis on the love theme), there are also many similarities. Most of the important themes of his previous work persist: the existential anguish and the tension between hope and pessimism and between God and death/*nada*. But death is not to be feared, as he writes in "Madre muerte" (Mother Death): "Tranquila y buena tú, madre piadosa / de todos. Madre nuestra. Madre muerte. / Deja que duerma en tu regazo inerte. / Méceme en tu ternura poderosa" (Peaceful and good thou, pious mother / of all. Our mother. Mother death. / Let me sleep in your still lap. / Rock me in your powerful tenderness). Although maturity has shown him that the serenity and ecstasy to which he aspired in his youth are illusory, the realization, though painful, does not lead to despair. He can still find joy in the beauty of nature and comfort with the woman he loves. This acceptance of life with its attendant sorrows and a reaching out to his fellow human beings are expressed in the often-cited poem "No, corazón, no te hundas" (No, Heart, Do Not Sink):

Te quejas. Dices que sufres.
Dices que no puedes mas.
Aún volverás a sufrir, y a amar, y a sufrir de nuevo,
. . . . . . . . . . . . . . . . . . . . . . . . . . . . . . . . . . . . . . . .
Habla, habla, pero no contigo.
Déjate de soliloquios y silogismos y sentimentales
　monólogos.
Habla con el cartero, con el conductor del tranvía (aun-
　que esté prohibido);
habla con el niño que está jugando en la acera,
vete a beber unas copas con el primer borracho de la
　esquina.
¿Creías que el mundo termina donde tú acabas?
Tú eres ya no fin, ni siquiera comienzo de ninguna
　cosa.
. . . . . . . . . . . . . . . . . . . . . . . . . . . . . . . . . . . . . . . .
No tengas ninguna prisa en morirte.
No te esfuerces en buscar lo único que posees seguro.


(You complain. You say that you suffer.
You say you cannot go on.
You will suffer again, and love, and suffer again,
. . . . . . . . . . . . . . . . . . . . . . . . . . . . . . . . . . . . . . . .
Speak, speak, but not to yourself.

Stop the soliloquies and syllogisms and sentimental
　monologues.
Speak to the mailman, to the tram driver [although it is
　forbidden];
speak to the child playing on the sidewalk,
go and have a few drinks with the first drunk on the
　corner.
Did you think the world ends where you stop?
You are not the end, nor even the beginning of any-
　thing.
. . . . . . . . . . . . . . . . . . . . . . . . . . . . . . . . . . . . . . . .
Do not be in a hurry to die.
Do not strive to seek the only thing you possess for sure.)

The less idealized tone and more autobiographical themes of *Profecía del recuerdo* are expressed in freer verse forms than the carefully crafted stanzas of Gaos's early poetry (though only in *Arcángel de mi noche* does he use the sonnet exclusively). *Profecía del recuerdo* includes poems written in long, loosely structured lines that have the rhythms of natural speech and use a colloquial language, very different from that of his early sonnets.

*Poesías completas (1937–1957)* begins with "Primeras poesías 1937–1939" (First Poems). These earliest poems show the young Gaos's religious faith. The tone is jubilant and optimistic as he discovers love and the wonders of life and nature. Even death is viewed as a serene and unavoidable experience. This initial section is followed by the poems of his four previously published collections. The book ends with three poems under the title "Primeros cantos solemnes (1957)" (First Solemn Songs) and five "Poemas sueltas" (Separate Poems).

Gaos won the Agora Prize in 1963 (the only time it was awarded) with *Mitos para tiempo de incrédulos* (Myths for a Time of Unbelievers), ten new poems which were republished in *Concierto en mí y en vosotros* (Concert in Me and You, 1965), interspersed among the other poems. Mantero recalls his first reaction on reading *Mitos:* "Nunca olvidaré la inicial sensación de reventón espiritual al leer aquellos versos. Era un mundo interior en ruinas" (I will never forget the initial sensation of a spiritual explosion on reading those poems. It was an interior world in ruins).

*Concierto en mí y en vosotros* was published in Puerto Rico, and, perhaps as a result of being published outside Spain, it did not achieve the recognition that some critics felt it deserved. For Mantero "es un libro nervioso, con la emoción mas seca" (it is a nervous book, with the driest emotion). The thirty-two poems (only four of them sonnets) are far removed in their content, style, and tone (reflective, often skeptical and pessimistic) from Gaos's early work. In the long opening poem "Preludio" (Prelude) he declares his intention to reach out beyond himself to establish a dialogue with the "vosotros" (plural *you*) of the title: "No quiero hablar / conmigo. . . . / No quiero hablar de mí. Entendámonos: / de mí sin vosotros" (I do not want to talk / to myself . . . . / I do not want to talk about myself. Let us understand each other: / about myself without all of you). The one absolute certainty is that "todos, todos: tú, y tú, y tú, y yo, / todos hemos de morir" (everyone, everyone: you, and you, and you, and I, / everyone has to die). The last lines, characteristically, express his hopes and doubts, his need to believe and the impossibility of total faith: "Silenciosamente, / confiadamente esperemos / que Dios nos tenga de su mano, / si tiene manos y existe Dios" (Silently, / confidently let us hope / that God will take us by his hand, / if he has hands and if God exists). "Preludio" is followed by five sections: "Cantos solemnes," with themes drawn from history, myth, and literature; "Tema y variaciones de la Nada" (Theme and Variations on the Void); "Canción de la niebla" (Song of the Mist); "Suposiciones" (Suppositions); and "El caminante" (The Traveler), in which he comes to an understanding of life as an integration of all experience, both positive and negative:

> Y la vida se le presentó
> como una tela entretejida
> de deseo y espera, de olvido
> y de ilusión, de soledad
> y companía. . . . Como una tela
> extraña, vaga, no del todo
> indescifrable. . . .
> Como una tela
> no acabada. Al llegar al fin
> todo estaba por empezar.
>
> (And life presented itself to him
> like a cloth interwoven
> with desire and hope, with oblivion
> and with illusion, with solitude
> and company. . . . Like a cloth
> strange, vague, not completely
> indecipherable. . . .
> Like a cloth
> unfinished. Upon arriving at the end
> everything was about to begin.)

In the introduction that accompanies his poems in Leopoldo de Luis's anthology *Poesía religiosa: Antología (1939–1964)* (1969), Gaos writes: "Me considero poeta religioso y buena parte de mi poesía es religiosa. . . . Para que la poesía sea religiosa no es necesario que hable de Dios. Hable de lo que quiera, de Dios está hablando, sin mencionarlo, o, a veces, mencionándolo para negarlo" (I consider myself to be a religious poet and a good part of my poetry is religious. . . . For

poetry to be religious, it does not have to talk about God. No matter what it talks about, it is talking about God, without mentioning him, or, sometimes, mentioning him to deny him). Emilio Miró, in a review in *Cuadernos Hispanoamericanos* (January 1968), summed up *Concierto en mí y en vosotros* as a "libro radicalmente religioso, pero de una religiosidad desesperada, con rabia, en agonía" (radically religious book, but a desperate religiosity, with rage, in agony). There is skepticism in the book: "No hubo, ni hay, ni habrá paraíso / en la tierra ni en el cielo. Eso / son historias, cuentos de niños" (There was not, there is not, nor will there be paradise / on earth or in heaven. Those / are stories, children's tales). And the poems "Padre nuestro" (Our Father) and "El sermón de la niebla" (The Sermon of the Mist) parody and mock the words of the Lord's Prayer and the Sermon on the Mount. (Among the unpublished poems Gaos left at his death was "Abjuración" [Abjuration], written at the end of his life, in which he asks God's forgiveness for the mockery of these poems. Despite the doubts and vehement denials expressed in much of Gaos's poetry, Dámaso Alonso and Enrique Molina Campos claim that he never totally abandoned his religious beliefs.)

In *Concierto en mí y en vosotros,* and indeed in all of Gaos's work, there are themes, allusions, and quotations drawn from many sources, not all of them acknowledged. In *La poética de Campoamor* (Poetics of [Ramón de] Campoamor, 1955) Gaos says originality lies not in the ideas themselves but in the way they are expressed: "la originalidad del autor – o mejor dicho, de la obra artística – es la de su forma, la de su estructura. Las ideas – originales o no – son algo *previo* a la obra, no forman parte de ella, porque la poesía no se hace *con* ideas" (the originality of the author – or, rather, of the artistic work – is its form, its structure. The ideas – whether original or not – are something *prior* to the work; they do not form part of it, because poetry is not made *with* ideas).

Gaos's *Poesías completas II (1958–1973),* published in 1974, comprises *Concierto en mí y en vosotros, Un montón de sombra* (A Mass of Shade, 1972), and the previously unpublished "Las señales y la sabiduría" (Signs of Wisdom). In a review in *Insula* (November 1974) Miró characterized the poems as "amasados con la experiencia de la edad y la pasión de la vida, con la inutilidad de la esperanza y con su imposible renuncia. Con Dios y con la nada, aunque más con la segunda, con el vacío, con la ausencia, con la desolación" (mixed with the experience of life and the passion for life, with the futility of hope and with the impossibility of renouncing it. With God and the void,

*Vicente Gaos (Foto Archivo José Luis Cano)*

though more with the latter, with emptiness, with absence, with desolation). "Testamento" (Testament), from "Las señales y la sabiduría," may be taken as a summation of Gaos's state of mind at this point in his life:

> Yo, natural de la nada,
> habitante de la nada,
> destino a la nada, anónimo,
> me acerco ya al encuentro del supremo Notario
> ...........................................
> Y éste es el testamento ilusorio que otorgo en plena
>     posesión de mis facultades mentales,
> posesión de quien sólo posee dolor, ignorancia,
>     muerte,
> y un corazón cuyo único deseo es el de cesar ya en su
>     tremendo pálpito, en su amoroso latido.

> (I, native of the void,
> inhabitant of the void,
> destined for the void, anonymous,

> I now approach my encounter with the supreme Notary
> ...........................................
> And this is the empty testament that I give in full
>     possession of my mental faculties,
> possession of one who only possesses pain, ignorance,
>     death,
> and a heart whose only desire is to cease in its terrible
>     throbbing, in its tender beating.)

This book was the last collection of Gaos's poems to be published during his lifetime. On 17 October 1980 he died of a heart attack in Valencia. Shortly after his death *Última Thule* was published and was awarded the Antonio González de Lama Prize and the National Poetry Prize. Since it by no means includes Gaos's best work, these posthumous awards may have been attempts to make amends for past oversights.

There is little concern with style in the twenty-three, mostly short poems, only one of them a sonnet. The familiar juxtapositions of life/love and life/death are found in the first section, "Tiempo intemporal" (Atemporal Time). As in his earlier works, love can save him from death and the void, and, despite the inexorable passing of time, it is still possible to find pleasure in love and the beauty of nature. There is an abrupt change of tone in the second section, "Tiempo presente" (Present Time), which addresses then-contemporary issues. Love is absent in a world that has produced destruction, greed, inequality, and hate. The ironic poems "Sociedad de consumo" (Consumer Society) and "Christmas" are a late appearance in Gaos's work of the social poetry he had earlier denounced. In the final section, "Tiempo y muerte" (Time and Death), Gaos returns to a basic theme of his poetry: the inevitability of death and the void. Even love is futile when "La muerte nos acecha tras el hueso" (Death lies in wait for us behind the bone). In the last poem, "De Senectute" (On Senectitude), possibly written in anticipation of his own death, Gaos reiterates the idea that people are condemned to death from birth, "cuando el niño aun no puede / caminar, cuando en la matriz, en la celda / del penal materno . . . no puede protestar ni apelar a nadie por su inaudita condena" (when the child still cannot / walk, when in the womb, in the cell / of the maternal prison . . . he cannot protest nor appeal his outrageous sentence). At the end of life there is neither hope nor even the consolation of memories:

Desmemoriado y sin esperanza
contémplate sentado entre los cipreses
setos en flor y carcomidas estatuas,
el pájaro en la rama, la paloma en la piedra. Mira toca
en el marmol
tu muerte ayer, tu diaria ceniza. Advierte la fuente,
el agua que corre. . . . Y quédate solo
con la ilusoria renta de tus manos
luces borradas, palabras caídas.


(Forgetful and hopeless
contemplate yourself sitting among the cypresses
hedges in flower and decayed statues,
the bird on the branch, the dove on the stone. Look
touch the marble
your death yesterday, your daily ashes. Observe the
fountain,
the water that flows. . . . And remain alone
with the empty return of your hands
lights effaced, fallen words.)

Although Gaos's poetry is usually viewed as falling into two periods, divided by his absence from Spain (1947–1955), the same themes recur throughout the forty years of his poetic output: the search for transcendence, his strained relationship with God, human anguish and solitude, the passing of time, the appreciation of beauty, and the juxtaposition of opposites: life/love and death; God and the void; faith and despair; and light and darkness. When Gaos died, his friend and editor Vicente Giner wrote of him, "Su vida ha sido ejemplar. Vicente sufrió mucho, pero amó más" (His life was exemplary. Vicente suffered a lot, but he loved more). The anguish, but also the consoling power of love, is evident in his poetry.

**Interview:**
"Charlas en *Insula:* Vicente Gaos," *Insula,* 10 (15 March 1955): 9.

**References:**
Vicente Aleixandre, *Los encuentros* (Madrid: Guadarrama, 1958), pp. 233–238;
Dámaso Alonso, "Permanencia del soneto," in his *Poetas españoles contemporáneos* (Madrid: Gredos, 1958), pp. 390–396;
Carlos Bousoño, "La poesía de Vicente Gaos," *Papeles de Son Armandans,* 19 (October–December 1960): 75–100;
José Luis Cano, "En la muerte de Vicente Gaos," *Insula,* 35 (November 1980): 4;
Elaine Marie De Costa, "The Poetry of Vicente Gaos: Intimate and Transcendent Reality," Ph.D. dissertation, University of Wisconsin, 1976;
Ana María Fagundo, "Trayectoria poética de Vicente Gaos: De lo ideal a lo real," *Cuadernos Americanos,* 34 (March–April 1975): 189–199;
Luis Jiménez Martos, "Vicente Gaos, a la luz de la muerte," *Nueva Estafeta,* 25 (December 1980): 67–71;
Nancy Mandlove, "Patterns of Unity in the Poetry of Vicente Gaos," Ph.D. dissertation, University of New Mexico, 1973;
Manuel Mantero, *Poetas españoles de posguerra* (Madrid: Espasa-Calpe, 1986), pp. 89–115;
Enrique Molina Campos, "Hacia una interpretación de la poesía de Vicente Gaos," *Nueva Estafeta,* 48–49 (November–December 1982): 75–82;
Jaime Siles, "Vicente Gaos" (1919–1980), *Insula,* 35 (November 1980): 4, 7.

# Juan Gil-Albert

## (1 April 1906 – )

### Salvador Jiménez-Fajardo
#### State University of New York at Binghamton

*La fascinación de lo irreal* (Valencia: Gutenberg, 1927);

*Vibración de estío* (Valencia: Gutenberg, 1928);

*Cómo pudieron ser* (Valencia: Gutenberg, 1929);

*Gabriel Miró (El escritor y el hombre)* (Valencia: Vich, 1931); revised and enlarged as *Gabriel Miró, remembranza* (Madrid: Torre, 1980);

*Cómo pudieron ser* (Valencia: Vich, 1931);

*Crónicas para servir al estudio de nuestro tiempo* (Valencia: Levante de España, 1932);

*Elegía a los sombreros de mi madre* (Cádiz: Isla, 1934);

*Misteriosa presencia* (Madrid: Héroe, 1936);

*Candente horror* (Valencia: Nueva Cultura, 1936);

*7 romances de guerra* (Valencia: Nueva Cultura, 1937);

*Las ilusiones, con los poemas de El convaleciente* (Buenos Aires: Imán, 1944);

*Poemas (El existir medita su corriente)* (Madrid: Librería Clan, 1949);

*Concertar es amor* (Madrid: Rialp, 1951);

*Intento de una catalogación valenciana* (Valencia: Mis Cosechas, 1955);

*Contra el cine* (Valencia: Mis Cosechas, 1955);

*Poesía (Carmina manu trementi ducere)* (Valencia: Caña Gris, 1961);

*Concierto en "Mi" menor* (Valencia: Caña Gris, 1964);

*La trama inextricable* (Valencia: Esteve & Arnau, 1968);

*Fuentes de la constancia* (Barcelona: Llibres de Sinera, 1972);

*Los días están contados* (Barcelona: Tusquets, 1974);

*Crónica general* (Barcelona: Barral, 1974);

*Mesa revuelta* (Valencia: Torres, 1974);

*Valentín: Homenaje a William Shakespeare* (Barcelona: Gaya Ciencia, 1974);

*La meta-física* (Barcelona: Barral, 1974);

*Memorabilia* (Barcelona: Tusquets, 1975);

*Heraclés, sobre una manera de ser* (Madrid: Betancor, 1975);

*Cantos rodados* (Barcelona: Linosa, 1976);

*A los pre-socráticos seguido de Migajas del pan nuestro* (Madrid: Difusora de Cultura, 1976);

*Homenajes e in promptus* (León: Institución Fray Bernardino de Sahagún, 1976);

*Drama patrio* (Barcelona: Tusquets, 1977);

*El retrato oval* (Madrid: Cupsa, 1977);

*Un mundo: Prosa; Poesía; Crítica* (Valencia: Artes Gráficas Soler, 1978);

*El ocioso y las profesiones* (Seville: Salesianas, 1978);

*Razonamiento inagotable* (Madrid: Caballo Griego para la Poesía, 1979);

*Breviarium vitae* (Alicante: Caja de Ahorros de Alicante y Murcia, 1979);

*Mi voz comprometida (1936–1939),* edited by Manuel Aznar Soler (Barcelona: Laia, 1980);

*Los arcángeles* (Barcelona: Laia, 1981);

*Variaciones sobre un tema inextinguible* (Seville: Viguera, 1981); translated as *Variations on an Unextinguishable Theme,* bilingual edition (Barcelona: Instituto de Estudios Norteamericanos, 1982);

*Obra poética completa,* 3 volumes (Valencia: Institución Alfonso el Magnánimo, 1981);

*El ocio y sus mitos* (Málaga: Begar/Sur, 1982);

*Taurina* (Valencia: Quites entre Sol y Sombra, 1982);

*Obra completa en prosa,* 12 volumes (Valencia: Institución Alfonso el Magnánimo, 1982–1989);

*España: Empeño de una ficción* (Madrid: Júcar, 1984);

*Azorín o la intravagancia* (Alicante: Anales Azorinianos, 1985);

*Monólogo en la Alhambra* (Granada: Aula de la Poesía, 1985);

*Tobeyo, o del amor: Homenaje a México* (Valencia: Pre-Textos, 1990).

Juan Gil-Albert, though attracted to Mediterranean antiquity and landscapes, is not a simple emulator of the ancients. His imagination does not seek merely to retrace and relive the myths of antiquity. As he writes of the shifting permanence of human relationships to reality, he uncovers the present relevance of the classical writers' under-

*Juan Gil-Albert*

standing of those relationships. As he says in *Concierto en "Mi" menor* (Concerto in E Minor, 1964), "Los mitos lo son porque se acoplan expresivamente a nuestras realidades. . . . Los mitos son verdad porque se están encarnando permanentemente" (Myths are such because through their expression they match our reality. . . . Myths are true because they are being permanently incarnated).

Beauty, for Gil-Albert, is the highest expression of life, and to perceive it is the human means of self-affirmation. Only solitude will afford the poet the means of fully realizing the fleeting beauty of reality and of achieving the fruitful meditation that will lead to complete self-awareness. Yet, intimately connected to the necessary affirmation of beauty, there is also a moral imperative at the root of Gil-Albert's writing. He has remained committed to the principle that gives his work — prose and poetry alike — a peculiar ethical and aesthetic weight: the celebration of life as such and of its incessant renovation. This principle is the fulcrum of Gil-Albert's poetry and provides the guidelines to its evolution: from the early love sonnets of *Misteriosa presencia* (Mysterious Presence, 1936), which

sing of the discovery of clandestine, homoerotic love; through his socially committed poetry of the 1930s, including *Candente horror* (Candescent Horror, 1936), *7 romances de guerra* (Seven War Ballads, 1937), and *Son nombres ignorados* (Their Names Are Unknown, 1938), which show anger at those who seek to reduce and imprison all that is vital; to his mature dialectic explorations of the contradictory nature of our human condition, death-bound but with a spirit unvanquished by death.

Gil-Albert is never openly didactic, but he realizes that he is not merely a writer; he is a type of legislator. In *Los días están contados* (The Days Are Rare, 1974) he writes: "Uno se ha dicho: soy poeta; y el tiempo pasa, nuestras intenciones se nos van aclarando y un buen día, hecha la plena luz, corregimos; legislador: ésa ha sido la verdadera apetencia de mi alma: legislar. Nuestro desconcierto repentino se palía con aquello de que: ¿Anhela otra cosa el poeta que poner orden, que ordenar el caos, que organizar auténticamente la vida, que establecer una ordenación consistente y hermosa, medida, rítmica — que ande ordenadamente — y musical?" (One has told oneself: I am a poet; and time passes, our intentions grow clearer and one day, in full light, we make the correction; legislator; that has been the true craving of my soul: to legislate. Our sudden discomposure is palliated with that notion: what can the poet desire but to make order, to order chaos, to organize life authentically, to establish a consistent and beautiful organization, measured, rhythmical – proceeding in an orderly manner – and musical?). Gil-Albert writes not only because he needs to understand but also because he wants to communicate. He has cultivated his solitude both by desire and necessity, and the bulk of his poetry may be described as a prolonged soliloquy. Like Luis Cernuda, he knew that his public would have to come to him gradually. And gradually Spaniards did realize that they had in their midst a truly great writer who had continued his work patiently, stubbornly, and in interior exile. Gil-Albert had returned from political exile in Mexico in 1947, and in 1974 – which has been labeled Gil-Albert's *anno mirabilis* (greatest year) – *Los días están contados, La meta-física* (The Metaphysics), *Valentín, Mesa revuelta* (Mixed Table), and *Crónica general* (General Chronicle) were published. Leopoldo Azancot, one of the many enthusiastic reviewers of his work, declared in *Estafeta Literaria* (June 1974): "Gil-Albert es un autor que no dudo en calificar de uno de los mayores en lengua castellana de nuestro siglo" (Gil-Albert is an author whom I do not hesitate to characterize as one of the greatest to write in Castilian in our century).

Juan Gil-Albert was born on 1 April 1906 in Alcoy, an industrial town north of the Mediterranean city of Alicante. His father, Ricardo Gil, owned a prosperous hardware concern, and his mother came from a landowning family of the region. Juan was the oldest child and only son; he had two sisters, Cristina (Tina) and Elena. During his childhood in Alcoy he went to a nuns' school and also had a private tutor. In 1912 the family moved to Valencia, where Juan attended the school taught by the Piarist fathers.

In 1915 Gil-Albert began secondary school at the Instituto de Enseñanza Luis Vives. Despite being an uneven student, he remembers his school days with some fondness. He recalls excelling in grammar, philosophy, and hygiene, although his sharpest memory concerns his qualities as a reciter: on the occasion of his rendering a passage from *Don Quixote,* one of the fathers told him that he was an artist. For Gil-Albert, who was much impressed, this event was a revelation. He had friends and was a relatively popular boy but he never particularly sought the company of others; he always felt different from his classmates – not superior, as he recalls, but somehow marked for a differ-

ent destiny. These pacific years are remembered by Gil-Albert in *Crónica general* and *Concierto en "Mi" menor.* In the latter book he recalls with special pleasure the family's summer residence at Mont-Sant, near Játiva, at the country home of Gil-Albert's maternal grandfather.

On the whole, Gil-Albert's contemplative memoirs, which make up more than half the twelve volumes in his complete prose works (1982–1989), describe the happy, privileged youth of a gifted young man whose artistic promise was soon recognized. The events that left their mark are those that seemed to threaten the child's or adolescent's investment of faith in the secure unfolding of reality and custom – such events as the death of the Piarist provincial or that of a young woman of the family's acquaintance in Játiva. This latter, inexplicable tragedy revealed to Gil-Albert the fissures in a world he had thought reasonable and where, as he says in *Concierto en "Mi" menor,* "Las cosas ocupaban, como entidades mágicas, su puesto definitivo y los seres cumplían, misteriosamente claros, sin prevaricación, unos fines que parecían consustanciales con la especie de eternidad de la que era un trasunto cada persona" (Things, like magical entities, occupied their definitive place, and human beings, mysteriously clear, without prevarication, achieved ends that seemed consubstantial with the kind of eternity of which each person was a faithful instance). At the time of the family's move to Valencia, Gil-Albert's father built El Salt, a country house outside Alcoy. There Gil-Albert was later to do much of his writing, before and after his exile.

In 1920 he earned his *bachillerato* (high-school certificate) and registered as a law student at the University of Valencia. He became actively interested in the city's intellectual life and discussed literature and art with a group of friends who met at the Ideal Room, an elegant café catering to the middle class. He read works by Ramón del Valle-Inclán, Oscar Wilde, Ricardo León, and Gabriel Miró. In 1922 Gil-Albert traveled to Tours, France, where he enrolled in French classes and visited nearby châteaus. He discovered Michel de Montaigne's work and that of the Pléiade poets (Pierre de Ronsard and Joachim Du Bellay in particular).

After his return to Valencia, Gil-Albert abandoned his law studies and, to the disappointment of his father, decided to devote his energies to writing. He traveled to Madrid, where he paid his respects to Miró and visited the Prado museum. Both events later figured in Gil-Albert's work, in a long essay on Miró (1931) and a book devoted to several paintings in the museum – *Cómo pudieron ser* (How They Might Have Been, also 1931). In 1927 he published

*La fascinación de lo irreal* (The Fascination of the Unreal) at his own expense. This collection of prose pieces, notably influenced by Wilde and Miró, proved to be one of his most successful early books. It was warmly reviewed in regional newspapers such as the *Provincias* and *Noticiero Regional* and was also noted by the prestigious critic José Francés of Madrid. In 1928 Gil-Albert published *Vibración de estío* (Vibration of Summer), also at his own expense. He was then reading the works of José Ortega y Gasset, Miguel de Unamuno, Ramón Pérez de Ayala, and Antonio Machado. Meanwhile the political climate had become turbulent and had led to Gen. Miguel Primo de Rivera's dictatorship. Although he would never belong to any party, Gil-Albert's liberal humanism gradually drew him toward left-wing politics. His relationship with his father, who had grown more conservative as time went on, became difficult.

In 1931, the year Spain became a republic, Gil-Albert's *Gabriel Miró (El escritor y el hombre)* (Gabriel Miró [The Writer and the Man]) was published, as was *Cómo pudieron ser.* The latter work is a series of historical interpretations of various portraits Gil-Albert had seen at the Prado. Although certain influences are quite obvious, notably those of Valle-Inclán and Wilde, the ironic tone, a deliberate attention to detail, and the free play of imagination clearly prepare one for Gil-Albert's mature works.

*Crónicas para servir al estudio de nuestro tiempo* (Chronicles for the Study of Our Time, 1932) is a series of essays on celebrities of the day, such as Isadora Duncan; Mary, Queen of Romania; and the Romanov family. The Romanov essay he later expanded and rewrote as *El retrato oval* (The Oval Portrait, 1977).

Gil-Albert was contributing regularly to the literary section of such regional newspapers as the *Mercantil Valenciano* and *Noticiero Regional* and to Ernesto Giménez Caballero's influential *Gaceta Literaria* (Madrid). From 1934 to 1936 Gil-Albert made the acquaintance of many poets who were to be among the most important of the century: Luis Cernuda, Federico García Lorca, Juan Ramón Jiménez, Vicente Aleixandre, León Felipe, José Moreno Villa, Miguel Hernández, Pablo Neruda, Octavio Paz, and Rafael Alberti. He met many of them again toward the end of the Spanish Civil War as the Republican government retreated to Valencia and Gil-Albert's house became a meeting center for Republican intellectuals. In Valencia, under the guidance of Antonio Sánchez Barbudo, Rafael Dieste, the painter Ramón Gaya, and Gil-Albert, and with the financial support of the Republican government, the review *Hora de España* was founded. Together with *Nueva Cultura,* to which Gil-Albert also con-

tributed, it was one of the most important literary and artistic publications to appear during the war.

In 1936 Gil-Albert published his first two collections of poetry, *Misteriosa presencia* and *Candente horror. Misteriosa presencia* is a collection of thirty-four sonnets – thirty on love, plus four dedicated to the Valencia region – in the *gongorista* (baroque) style (based on that of Luis de Góngora), set in a classical landscape, with occasional surrealistic touches. While the sonnets demonstrate an exceptional mastery of form, some emotional imprecision at times weakens their impact. In spite of its unevenness, the collection demonstrates Gil-Albert's poetic gifts and introduces some of his most cherished themes: the search for permanence in mutability; the paramount importance of the Mediterranean landscape, particularly Valencia; and the presence of the classical world of myth. The tone and intent are radically different in *Candente horror,* written between 1934 and 1935. The collection comprises eighteen poems in generally long lines of a Whitmanesque cast and with a clearly surrealistic inspiration, which GilAlbert ascribes to the impact of Neruda's *Residencia en la tierra* (Residence on Earth, 1933). In Gil-Albert's introduction to his *Fuentes de la constancia* (Sources of Constancy, 1972) he says, "*Misteriosa presencia* y *Candente horror,* libros de fecha coincidente, se me aparecen como la inocente manifestación de lo que podríamos llamar un destino contradictorio. El *ego* y el *populus;* el intimismo y lo social" (*Misteriosa presencia* and *Candente horror,* books that coincide in their date of publication, appear to me as the innocent manifestation of what could be termed a contradictory destiny. The *ego* and the *populus;* the intimate and the social). *Candente horror* is Gil-Albert's first politically committed collection of poetry. In the poem "Cultura estallante" (Exploding Culture) he writes:

> Se hace imposible ya no morir con un asco de rabia,
> con un furioso vendaval que se desata,
> golpeando con la feroz saliva del instinto
> las caras rasuradas de estos monstruos.

> (It now becomes impossible not to die with raging disgust,
> with a furious unbound windstorm,
> striking with the ferocious saliva of instinct
> the close-shaved faces of these monsters.)

With his most forceful language Gil-Albert rejects and accuses as messengers of death all those who embrace the new European regimes of violence. According to him, such people would deny the vital bonds that nourish humanity and would tap those dark recesses of the soul that breed fanaticism. Gil-Albert opts for life and human dignity and enjoins people to hold back the vertiginous powers of emptiness:

"Ha llegado el momento de sujetar las piezas con las manos. / Si es el mundo residuo, abolido tesoro lentamente, / salvaremos el foco donde nace la vida" (The moment of holding the parts together with our hands has arrived. / If the world is a residue, a slowly abolished treasure, / we shall save the core where life is born).

The impact of these poems is all the greater when contrasted with those of *Misteriosa presencia,* which, regardless of their quality as examples of "pure" poetry, might have led one to believe that Gil-Albert was opting for vanguardist, aesthetic escapism. On the contrary, the compositions of *Candente horror* attest to his moral commitment as well as to his emotional and intellectual generosity. In fact the tone, imagery, and prosody of these poems, unlike anything Gil-Albert later wrote, perfectly capture the turmoil, sorrow, and fury provoked by the threatening shadow that right-wing totalitarianism was casting over Europe.

In 1937 Gil-Albert published *7 romances de guerra,* in which he tried to echo the voice of the people engaged in a heroic, defensive struggle. Years later, in his preface to *Homenajes e in promptus* (Homages and Impromptus, 1976), he describes such moments of poetic creation as "delirantes" (delirious), for in them "el poeta se confunde con [el pueblo] como un hombre más y palpita al unísono. Porque siente, y sabe, que ese momento es puro, es verdadero, es sagrado. Es coincidente" (the poet merges with [the people] as one more man and throbs in unison. Because he feels, and knows, that that moment is pure, is true, is sacred. It is coincident). The ballads describe individuals and circumstances of the civil war – for example the communist student Juan Marco Martín, in the "3 romances de Juan Marco" (Three Ballads on Juan Marco); the anarchist Buenaventura Durruti, in "El romance de la niña Durruti" (Ballad of the Little Durruti Girl); and the cavalry-officers' corps, in the "Romance valenciano del Cuartel de Caballería" (The Valencian Ballad of the Cavalry Barracks). This cavalry ballad became the most popular in the region of Valencia, and the Republican ministry of propaganda had five thousand copies printed and distributed. The ballads never become merely propagandistic, and they maintain a high poetic quality unusual for the genre at that time.

*Son nombres ignorados* is the last collection of committed poetry that Gil-Albert published, although he continued to write occasional poems of social protest throughout his career. The intrusion of the brutality of the war and the overwhelming pervasiveness of death into his interior landscape

give the poems of this collection a generally elegiac, sorrowful tone. Critic Juan Lechner, in his *El compromiso en la poesía española del siglo xx* (Compromise in Spanish Poetry of the Twentieth Century, 1968), comments that *Son nombres ignorados* is "poesía elegíaca si se quiere entender por el término 'elegíaco' . . . 'dolorida reflexión sobre el destino humano' y aun así no delimitamos bien el concepto, ya que hay dolor en la poesía de Juan Gil-Albert, pero se manifiesta como melancolía, en tono menor" (elegiac poetry if one understands by the term "elegiac" . . . "sorrowful reflection on human destiny" and even thus we are not defining the concept well, since there is sorrow in the poetry of Juan Gil-Albert, but it manifests itself as melancholy, in a minor tone).

The reality that Gil-Albert confronts in these poems is unpredictable and violent, a manifestation of the forces of society and history, forces of movement and change that are destructive and blind. Yet the poet's own deepest impulses seek underlying permanence, repetition in transformation. Thus the event or situation that elicits the poem is often a mere excuse for a meditation on deeper currents or on the reactions that events provoke as perennial components of humanity. In "Elegía a una casa de campo" (Elegy to a Country Home) Gil-Albert reflects on his intimate reaction to the requisition of his cherished country retreat by a group of young Republican militiamen. He cannot condemn the actions of the soldiers who fight for a cause he endorses, yet the "invasion" is painful:

¡Oh desgarradura que ni se oye ni se ve!
¿Sobre qué cataclismos
y en qué frágiles andas navegaba la vida,
si las ineptas carabinas de esos muchachos
han disipado como el humo un palpitante juego?

(Oh torn wound that is neither heard nor seen!
Upon what cataclysms
and on how fragile a platform did life navigate,
if the inept carbines of those young men
have dissipated like smoke a palpitating game?)

The event itself is of little importance, but it symbolizes, as a heedless invasion of intimacy, the very situation of the poet, who was solicited by the unavoidable moral demands of the conflict and who felt himself trapped and torn from his soliloquy by a cause that was just, but unrelenting.

"Lamentación," the poem immediately following "Elegía a una casa del campo," has been justly praised as one of the most moving in the book because, while dealing with an ominous aspect of the

*Gil-Albert (right) with poet Jaime Gil de Biedma, circa 1975*

war – the presence of Arab soldiers on Iberian soil – the poem is motivated by compassion rather than anger or adversarial politics:

> ¡Oh víctimas terribles de la sangre,
> incautos cervatillos del desierto!
> Los hoyos que os han dado como tumbas
> son la sola verdad de vuestras vidas.
>
> (Oh terrible victims of blood,
> unwary fawns of the desert!
> The holes they have given you as tombs
> are the only truth of your lives.)

Gil-Albert's committed poetry transcends the circumstances of its writing because it rises above any political cause and registers the war as a replay not only of historical and social forces but also of the perennial human conflicts described in myth and by the deep structures of human relationships to reality.

In the spring of 1939 Gil-Albert was among the thousands of refugees who crossed the border into France. In May he traveled to Mexico, the country that opened its doors to the largest number of Spanish exiles. He settled in Mexico City and shared an apartment with the Valencian painter Enrique Climent and the architect Mariano Orgaz. Octavio Paz, whom he had met in Valencia, offered him work as secretary of the review *Taller,* which Paz directed. Gil-Albert also contributed to various other reviews. The meager earnings from these activities, together with a small stipend provided by the JARE (Junta de Ayuda a los Republicanos Españoles) committee, allowed him to survive. Besides Paz and his wife, and the exiled Spanish intellectuals residing in Mexico, Gil-Albert befriended the Mexican poets Carlos Pellicer and Xavier Villaurrutia. He read works by Dante, Friedrich Nietzsche, and T. S. Eliot, and he collaborated on *Laurel,* an anthology of Spanish-American poetry (1941), with Paz, Villaurrutia, and fellow poet and exile Emilio Prados.

Gil-Albert had begun to compose the poems of *Las ilusiones, con los poemas de El convaleciente* (The Illusions, with the Poems of The Convalescent, 1944). In 1942, with his friend Máximo José Kahn, he set sail on a circuitous trip to Río de Janeiro, where he remained for six months. There he met the poets Cecilia Meireles and Gabriela Mistral. In early 1944 Kahn and Gil-Albert left for Buenos Aires, where Gil-Albert would remain for almost a year. In Buenos Aires he met Mariquiña del Valle-Inclán – the daughter of don Ramón – whose husband's editorial house, Imán, published *Las ilusiones.* The book is divided into three parts – "Las ilusiones," "El Convaleciente," and "Oráculos" (Oracles) – with a total of sixty-eight compositions of varied length, tending to be long and principally in hendecasyllables, henceforth Gil-Albert's preferred line style.

*Las ilusiones* is his first fully mature work of poetry and, together with his next collection, *Poemas (El existir medita su corriente)* (Poems [Existence Meditates Its Flow], 1949) – also written in exile, though published soon after his return to Spain – represents an anchor for all his poetry. Given its nature as an "exile" book, one would expect *Las ilusiones* to have backward glances to the homeland and considerations of the war or of the break between his present state and his immediate past. Such concerns, however, are quite infrequent, although Gil-Albert is by nature a poet of exile, his condition is linked to those moments of his childhood when he intuited a rupture between his pristine sense of a continuous, predictable reality and reality's arbitrariness, as seen in the instances of inexplicable death. Gil-Albert feels disconnected from his childhood, not as a period of innocence but of plenitude. The poet seeks to retain his "illusions," to reconstruct nurturing links to the past, not necessarily the historical past (although he does so on occasion). These illusions are intuitions of a former landscape, the classic shores of the Mediterranean. He insistently returns to myth as the fundamental signifying underlay of nature, as in the poem "Los viñedos" (The vineyards):

> Los poderes ocultos,
> los genios infatigables de la oscuridad
> turban el reposo sagrado
> de las divinidades que aman en el hombre
> su gracia pasajera.
> (The hidden powers,
> the indefatigable spirits of darkness
> disturb the sacred repose
> of the divinities who love in man
> his passing grace.)

It should not surprise us that Gil-Albert makes so few references to the North or South American landscape. Despite his expressions of deep gratitude for being made welcome – notably seen in *Tobeyo, o*

*del amor: Homenaje a México* (Tobeyo, or Love: Homage to Mexico, 1990) – he considered the vast tropical extensions outside his ken. Away from the Valencian coast, he felt disconnected, not only because he left but also because he seemed to have lost his past, in particular his childhood. Nostalgia for his youth and his native landscape tinges with disenchantment and melancholy the majority of the compositions in *Las ilusiones,* as seen in "A un carretero que cantaba" (To a Singing Cart Driver):

> ¿Dónde estarás ¡oh dulce somnolencia!
> ¡oh triste sino!, ¡astilla en noble pecho!
> aquella voz sonando hacia los montes
> por el hondo camino de la muerte?
>
> (Where may you be, oh sweet somnolence!
> Oh sad destiny!, shard in a noble breast!
> that voice sounding toward the hills
> along the deep road to death?)

As before, in *Las ilusiones,* Gil-Albert's strongest commitment is to life. This commitment drives his search for life's profoundest sources in renovated myths and gives his poetry its peculiar nonreligious moral force. In "Fuentes de la constancia" (republished in the 1972 book of that name) he celebrates the primal source of life:

> estar soñando
> con un rumor confuso y delicioso,
> como al borde de un agua inesperada,
> que no es más que la vida, allí fluyendo,
> su tiempo inapresable y su grandeza.
>
> (to be dreaming
> with a confused and delicious rumor,
> as on the brink of unexpected water,
> that is nothing but life, there flowing,
> its ungraspable time and its greatness.)

*Poemas,* written between 1945 and 1947, during Gil-Albert's trip through South America and after his return to Mexico, comprises fifteen poems and is divided into four parts. Of it Gil-Albert says, "Es significativo que, en esa última producción mía de América, el libro venga a resultar, a todas luces, un homenaje al Mediterráneo, expresión geográfica patente de mi vida emotiva y cultural" (It is significant that, in that last of my productions in America, the book should turn out to be, in all evidence, a homage to the Mediterranean, the clear geographic expression of my emotional and cultural life). The collection opens with "El Mediterráneo," where the sea is celebrated by the poet as the source of his being and of his song:

Padre de dioses, hijo de clementes
fuerzas y gracias, mar de los cimientos,
ligeros pies de arcilla que sostienen
la flor impetuosa de los mundos

(Father of gods, son of peaceful
forces and graces, sea of the foundations,
light feet of clay sustaining
the impetuous flower of the worlds)[.]

The first group, with six poems, is titled "Hijo póstumo" (Posthumous Son), affirming the poet's sense of belonging to the Mediterranean tradition and his responsibility as one of its modern-day poets. Gil-Albert constantly engages the classical — mainly Greek — world but not merely to reproduce it. He wants to meditate on the values and impulses, the love of life and thought, that underpin his own existence and similarly subtended that of his favorite Greek ancestors, Pindar, Anacreon, and the pre-Socratics. This effort was essential to his sense of continuity for he was writing in an alien climate. In this sense the poetry had a therapeutic value, allowing Gil-Albert to overcome frustration and anguish, if not melancholy. In the last poem of the book, "A mi madre como Deméter" (To My Mother as Demeter), the poet uses myth as a means of finding consolation by integrating the death of his sister to the forces of renewal in nature.

The sixty-seven sonnets of *Concertar es amor* (To Harmonize Is Love, 1951) are further examples of Gil-Albert's classicist vein, although they deal with a great variety of topics. Sober and elegant in their tone, masterful in their form, these sonnets are free of the baroque imprint that marked those of *Misteriosa presencia.* The poet is in full control of his means, able to produce a perfect poem on a bumblebee ("El abejorro"), on Frédéric Chopin ("Chopin"), or on a soldier in dress uniform (sonnet 45).

In 1947 Gil-Albert returned to Spain. After the death of his brother-in-law who was married to his older sister, he assumed responsibility for his five nephews and nieces. In 1950 his father's death left him in charge of the family hardware business. He found little success in this venture, being unaccustomed to the world of commerce. As a writer Gil-Albert remained marginalized and virtually unknown, but he still wrote indefatigably. The family's financial situation underwent serious reversals, and Gil-Albert was reduced to selling the country home. Gradually his literary fame began to grow. In 1968 critic Juan Lechner, in *El compromiso en la poesía española del siglo xx* praised Gil-Albert's poetry quite highly, and in 1972 Jiménez Martos included works by him in the anthology *La generación poética de 1936* (The Poetic Generation of 1936). This inclusion does not altogether agree with Gil-Albert's views, since he believes he has more in common with the poets of the 1927 group. The year 1972 also saw the publication of his highly praised poetry collection *Fuentes de la constancia.*

Between 1947 and 1961 Gil-Albert wrote *Poesía (Carmina manu tremendi ducere)* (1961) and *Migajas del pan nuestro* (Crumbs from Our Bread); this latter group of poems was published together with *A los presocráticos* (to the Pre-Socratics) in 1963 in *Cuadernos Hispanoamericanos,* then later as a book in 1976. In all these collections, the poet follows his reflexive bent, engaging "final questions" although without offering solutions — merely asking. His interest in the pre-Socratics, for instance, arises not from their being philosophers but from their being philosopher/poets: "Desde el primer contacto, en mi juventud, con el pensamiento estético, que esto es la filosofía, una ambición y un anhelo de dar forma coherente y seductora al pensar, los pre-socráticos me atrajeron muy especialmente. Lo que había en ellos, en su pensamiento, de 'físico,' me cautivaba" (From the first contact, in my youth, with aesthetic thought, which is what philosophy is, an ambition and a yearning to give thought a coherent and seductive form, the pre-Socratics especially attracted me. I was captivated by the "physical" element in them, in their thought). As usual, it is human nature that most interests Gil-Albert — how these early thinkers meditated on nature, rather than their actual conceptions of nature.

In Gil-Albert's *La meta-física* his style of expression is more compact, though never enigmatic. In a principally declarative tone, using prosodic variety (with lines that range from four to thirteen syllables), and in a syntax tightly and economically bound to the thought it conveys, he pursues his introspective interrogation of emotional and material reality, as in "La apelación última del ser" (The Ultimate Beckoning of Being):

Hay una breve pausa material
repleta de silencio.
De un silencio más fértil que la idea,
o tal vez el silencio en que se gesta
la idea misma
la idea redentora
de que estamos viviendo.

(There is a brief immaterial pause
replete with silence.
With a silence more fertile than the thought,
or perhaps the silence in which is generated
the thought itself
the redemptive thought
that we are living.)

Gil-Albert has an undeterred vitalism that not only pervades his poetry but his prose writing as well. He pursues a patient, insistent, detailed exploration of his circumstances.

*Homenajes e in promptus* is generally considered Gil-Albert's *opera summa* (best work) in poetry. Pedro de la Peña says it is a book in which "hasta lo melódico se vuelve mental, creando un tipo de pensamiento plástico que nos entra por el asombro, por la participación o por la adhesión intelectual, pero que se transforma dentro de nosotros en imagen cuajada de una finura táctil, de un refinamiento sonoro o visual" (even what is melodic becomes mental, creating a type of material thought that enters us through wonder, through intellectual participation or attachment, but that turns within us into an image imbued with tactile fineness, of sonorous or visual refinement). *Homenajes* principally celebrates various important figures in intellectual tradition by emphasizing certain notions or ideals that, for Gil-Albert, hold the key to their achievement. These poems are both soliloquies and dialogues in the sense that the poet proffers his personal views in implicit dialogue with the voice of the individual to whom the homage is dedicated. The preferred line continues to be the hendecasyllable, and the language remains largely unadorned and straightforward, acquiring its strength from compact articulation.

The first homage, "El presentimiento" (Presentiment), dedicated to Antonio Machado, is a meditation on solitude and the anticipation of death:

> A veces pienso el mundo se ha acabado:
> desciendo por la senda de la vida
> y dejo atrás el orbe luminoso
> que me encontré al llegar.

> (Sometimes I think the world has ended:
> I go down the path of life
> and leave behind the luminous orb
> that I found upon arriving.)

A subtle gradation of contrasts between darkness and light accompanies reflections on the reciprocal valuations of life and death and on the variations in intensity of life's moments, as in the poem "La infelicidad" (Unhappiness), to Benjamin Constant:

> Qué otro prodigio
> habrá de acontecernos que no sea
> ver la luz extendida y murmurante
> como una proyección
> de vida nueva de vida retadora, horrible, clara,
> plena de oscuridades, sugestiva
> repelente

> (What other prodigy
> can overtake us if not
> to see extended and murmuring light
> like a projection of new life
> of challenging, horrible, clear life,
> filled with darknesses, suggestive
> grim)[.]

Contrastive pairs extend from a central, generative darkness/light (life/death) antithesis to include other oxymoronic pairs, such as anguish and hope or matter and mind in "El genio – Doctor Faustus – (Homenaje a Oppenheimer)" (The Genius – Doctor Faustus – [Homage to Oppenheimer]); self and others in "El prójimo – a Pablo de Tarsis" (Our Fellow Creatures – To Paul of Tarsis); and solitude and companionship in "A Bernard de Clairvaux." In such instances the poem becomes an epistemological instrument, a means of discovery. The collection shows how Gil-Albert's meditations take the next step toward the poetry of investigation practiced by the best Spanish poets of the 1960s and 1970s. Such an approach is one reason his work has finally been given an enthusiastic reception by such important writers as Francisco Brines and Jaime Gil de Biedma, themselves engaged in comparable tasks. It becomes particularly clear with *Homenajes* that the site of significance of Gil-Albert's poetry is the poetic tradition, from Pindar through the Pléiade and the Golden Age to the current times.

The third volume in Gil-Albert's *Obra poética completa* (1981) comprises three works: *El ocioso y las profesiones* (The Idler and the Professions, 1978), "Varios" (Various), and "La siesta" (The Afternoon Nap). These collections, especially *El ocioso*, pursue the philosophical thrust that is a characteristic of Gil-Albert's work, as in the poems "La costurera" (The Seamstress), "El ceramista" (The Ceramist), and "Los metalúrgicos" (The Metalworkers). The collection opens with "El ocioso." Idleness has been a cherished gift for Gil-Albert, for it is generative, the necessary interval between moments of creativity: "De tanto no hacer nada / se me fueron los ojos tras el hombre / que se mueve afanoso" (From so much doing nothing / my eyes were drawn by the man / who moves in toil). The toil of others is a seed for the poet's future toil.

The key to *El ocioso* is the implicit circularity of the first and last poems of the cycle of poems about crafts: "El pintor" (The Painter) and "El psicopompos" (The "Psycho-pomp" – as represented by Hermes, the transporter of the dead). There is thus a connection between creation (art) and death, but death remains in communication with life, as suggested by the conclusion to "El psico-pompos":

*Gil-Albert in the late 1980s*

    ¿Quién diría
que la renovación de la existencia,
que los agrestes goces terrenales,
van en el corazón, sobre aquel solio,
conduciendo a la muerte?

    (Who would say
that the renovation of existence,
that the rustic earthly joys,
ride in the heart, on that throne,
leading to death?)

    Such a cosmogony is again pursued in "La siesta," a very long poem mostly in hendecasyllables. The poem is also circular in structure; it traces the dream's circuit between sleep and waking, and its ambitious program is to attempt to trace Western cultural history. Peña describes it as a "catedral que va de los ciminetos a la cima" (cathedral that rises from the foundations to the summit). One of the poem's most interesting elements is its confirmation of Gil-Albert's pagan syncretism, as he shows how at ease he feels in the pre-Christian world, and how essential he considers those values to have remained, behind the veneer of Christianity, for himself and for humankind. The poem retraces and asserts the cultural inheritance that the poet has always avowed.

    In the preface to his interview of Gil-Albert, *El razonamiento inagotable de Juan Gil-Albert* (The Inexhaustible Reasoning of Juan Gil-Albert, 1984), Luis Antonio de Villena remarks, "Marginado moral, sexual, literariamente, Juan Gil-Albert nos ha dado un ejemplo excelente de *libertad,* de la gloria y del sacrificio también que en ocasiones puede significar ese *ser libre*" (Morally, sexually, literarily marginalized, Juan Gil-Albert has given us an excellent example of *freedom,* of the glory and also the sacrifice that *being free* can occasionally signify).

153

Finally Gil-Albert enjoys the renown that is his due. Beginning in 1976 he has received various literary prizes, including the Pablo de Olavide Prize for testimonial literature, 1976; the Juan Ramón Jiménez Prize, 1975; the 1979 Aldebarán Prize, for *El ocioso y las profesiones*; and the Prize for Valencian Letters in 1982. The city of Alcoy named a street after him in 1978; five years later it named him its favorite son and gave him the city's gold medal. Such belated fame is not without its irony for Juan Gil-Albert, who said in 1974, "Me llega unido mi júbilo con mi jubilación" (My jubilation arrives together with my retirement).

**Letters:**

*Cartas a un amigo* (Valencia: Pre-Textos, 1987).

**Interview:**

Luis Antonio de Villena, *El razonamiento inagotable de Juan Gil-Albert* (Madrid: Anjana, 1984).

**Biography:**

César Simón, *Juan Gil-Albert: De su vida y obra* (Alicante: Instituto de Estudios Alicantinos, 1984).

**References:**

Manuel Aznar Soler, "Estudio preliminar," in Gil-Albert's *Mi voz comprometida (1936–1939),* edited by Aznar Soler (Barcelona: Laia, 1980);

Carole Bradford, "The Personal and the Universal Visions in *Homenajes e in promptus* of Juan Gil-Albert," *Hispanic Journal,* 6 (Fall 1984): 101–109;

*Calle del Aire,* special issue on Gil-Albert, 1 (1977);

Joaquín Calomarde, *Juan Gil-Albert, imagen de un gesto* (Barcelona: Anthropos, 1988);

Pedro de la Peña, *Juan Gil-Albert: Estudio y antología* (Madrid: Júcar, 1982);

Luis Antonio de Villena, "Heracles invoca a Hylas," *Papeles de Son Armadans,* 243 (June 1976): 311–323.

# Pere (Pedro) Gimferrer

*(22 June 1945 – )*

## Glenn Morocco
### *La Salle University*

BOOKS: *Mensaje del Tetrarca* (Barcelona: Trimer, 1963);

*Arde el mar* (Barcelona: Bardo, 1966);

*3 poemas* (Málaga: Librería Anticuaria el Guadalhorce, 1967);

*La muerte en Beverly Hills* (Madrid: Ciencia Nueva, 1968);

*Poemas, 1963–1969* (Barcelona: Llibres de Sinera, 1969); enlarged as *Poemas, 1962–1969* (Madrid: Visor, 1988);

*Els miralls* (Barcelona: Edicions 62, 1970);

*30 años de literatura,* by Gimferrer and Salvador Clotas (Barcelona: Kairós, 1971);

*Hora foscant* (Barcelona: Edicions 62, 1972);

*Foc cec* (Barcelona: Edicions 62, 1973);

*La poesía de J. V. Foix* (Barcelona: Edicions 62, 1974);

*Antoni Tàpies i l'esperit català* (Barcelona: Polígrafa, 1974); translated by Kenneth Lyons as *Tàpies and the Catalan Spirit* (New York: Rizzoli, 1975);

*L'espai desert* (Barcelona: Edicions 62, 1977);

*Miró, colpir sense nafrar* (Barcelona: Polígrafa, 1978);

*Poesía, 1970–1977* (Madrid: Visor, 1978);

*Radicalidades* (Barcelona: Bosch, 1978);

*Lecturas de Octavio Paz* (Barcelona: Anagrama, 1980);

*Dietari, 1979–1980* (Barcelona: Edicions 62, 1981);

*Mirall, espai, aparicions: Poesía, 1970–1980* (Barcelona: Edicions 62, 1981); republished as *Espejo, espacio, apariciones: Poesía 1970–1980,* bilingual edition [Catalan and Spanish] (Madrid: Visor, 1988);

*Segon dietari, 1980–1982* (Barcelona: Edicions 62, 1982);

*Max Ernst* (Barcelona: Polígrafa, 1983); translated by Norman Coe (New York: Rizzoli, 1984);

*Fortuny* (Barcelona: Planeta, 1983);

*Los raros* (Barcelona: Planeta, 1985);

*Cine y literatura* (Barcelona: Planeta, 1985);

*Giorgio de Chirico* (Barcelona: Polígrafa, 1988); translated by Anthony Curran (New York: Rizzoli, 1989);

*El vendaval* (Barcelona: Edicions 62, 1988; bilingual edition [Catalan and Spanish], 1989);

*Toulouse-Lautrec* (Barcelona: Polígrafa, 1990); translated by Angela Patricia Hall (New York: Rizzoli, 1990);

*La llum* (Barcelona: Edicions 62 / Península, 1991); republished as *La llum / La luz,* bilingual edition [Catalan and Spanish] (Barcelona: Edicions 62 / Península, 1992).

OTHER: Statement on poetics, in *Antología de la nueva poesía española,* edited by José Batlló (Madrid: Bardo, 1968), pp. 340–341;

"Poética," in *Nueve novísimos poetas españoles,* edited by J. M. Castellet (Barcelona: Barral, 1970), pp. 154–158;

*Juan Goytisolo: Voces,* volume 1, edited by Gimferrer (Barcelona: Montesinos, 1981);

"Perfil de Vicente Aleixandre," *Vuelta,* 112 (March 1986): 7–12;

"Itinerario de un escritor," *Anthropos,* 140 (January 1993); 19–23.

In 1966 Pere (Pedro) Gimferrer won the Premio Nacional de Poesía of Spain for *Arde el mar* (The Sea Is Burning), published that year. The book became the principal model for poetic revolution in Spain during the late 1960s. As one of the leaders among the poets born after the Spanish Civil War, Gimferrer adopted a confrontational attitude and represented himself and his work as "una ruptura" (a breaking away) from the then-prevalent social poetry which had held sway since the 1950s and whose practitioners based aesthetic judgments on the social content of poetry rather than its structure.

The impact of *Arde el mar* was based on Gimferrer's claim that poetry should not be a realistic likeness of society, a biographical account, or a political diatribe as it had been for the social poets. At the beginning of his career Gimferrer wrote more poetry than theory, but through his statements in anthologies his position on the generational climate

*Pere (Pedro) Gimferrer in the late 1970s*

can be discerned. In José Batllo's *Antología de la nueva poesía española* (Anthology of the New Spanish Poetry, 1968), Gimferrer gives indications that a new movement was underway, and he points out the shift in perspective: "quizá mi generación vuelva los ojos nuevamente a temas y procedimientos que preocupaciones éticas más urgentes hicieron desoír a algunos en un pasado no muy lejano" (perhaps my generation will turn its glance toward themes and procedures which more-urgent ethical concerns caused some to disregard in a not-so-distant past). He also says that he has barely begun and views his poetry as experimental, "un intento de renovar en lo posible el inerte lenguaje poético español" (an attempt to renovate as much as possible the inert Spanish poetic language).

The change manifested by members of Gimferrer's generation was attacked because their reaction implied a rejection of the realistic aesthetic of social poetry as well as its political underpinnings. Controversy ensued in 1970 with the publication of J. M. (Josep María) Castellet's anthology *Nueve novísimos poetas españoles* (Nine Very New Spanish Poets). This influential book, considered by many to have been largely inspired by Gimferrer, named the generation *novísimos*. The polemic esca-

lated because Castellet's introduction to his anthology is in essence a poetic manifesto which affirms the supremacy of those young poets whose primary concern was the exploration of the imaginative possibilities of language. The controversy was intense because ten years earlier Castellet had defended social realism and, for the anthology of 1970, selected only nine poets who all lived in Barcelona, excluding other considerable young talents.

In a 1989 interview with Víctor García de la Concha, Gimferrer tried to affirm that both the selection of poets and the introduction are Castellet's work despite the special mention he receives in Castellet's dedication to the anthology. Yet he also stated that Castellet, setting a rare example, met with the younger poets to read his introduction to them and to listen to their observations. In *Anthropos* (January 1993) Julia Barella recalls that Castellet approached an already-extant Barcelona literary circle. Gimferrer, keenly aware of the aesthetic changes that were occurring in Spain during the late 1960s, informed Castellet of those innovations. The young Gimferrer corresponded with Vicente Aleixandre for eighteen years, as well as with Octavio Paz, and received the support of the publisher Carlos Barral. At age twenty-two he was one of the "consejo asesor" (advisory board) of the Batlló anthology. Among his contemporaries in Barcelona, Gimferrer was considered the leader of the new generation: Leopoldo María Panero said in *Poesía* ( June 1979), "mi generación se llama Pedro Gimferrer: fue él que la construyó como lo que las generaciones son, un grupo teórico. Y Pedro Gimferrer creó nuestra ideología, y fue el verdadero autor de los novísimos y, por qué no decirlo, de mí" (my generation is named Pedro Gimferrer: he was the one who made it what generations are, a theoretical group. And Pedro Gimferrer created our ideology, and was the true author of the *novísimos* and, why not say it, mine too).

"Poética" (Poetics), the short statement that Gimferrer wrote for the Castellet collection, discloses important biographical information. Born in Barcelona on 22 June 1945, he first learned to speak in Catalan. His parents were Pere Gimferrer and Carmen Torreni de Gimferrer. As a result of childhood illness, he developed a predilection for reading and began to write poetry at about the age of thirteen. He describes himself as timid, isolated, and totally devoted to art. By the age of eighteen he had written several books of poetry, published one – *Mensaje del Tetrarca* (Message of the Tetrarch, 1963) – and discovered jazz and the movies, especially American films of the 1940s and 1950s. As he reached his nineteenth year, he became so interested in the movies that he set his poems aside and did not think of publishing them for a while.

His literary tastes at that time were already marked by a lack of interest in the reigning current literature of Spain; he preferred the poetry of the modernists, the Spanish "Generation of 1927," and of seventeenth-century Spanish writers. In his writing he also drew on foreign sources such as Marcel Proust, Henry James, William Faulkner, St. John Perse, and the surrealists.

However, the major literary associations in his life were with Aleixandre and Paz, whom Gimferrer calls his teachers. His initial impulse to publish poetry came from Aleixandre, who read it and gave advice until he was no longer able to read. They remained friends until Aleixandre died in 1985. At age nineteen Gimferrer discovered Paz, who influenced the younger man in his attitude toward art.

Gimferrer also explains in "Poética" that he liked to compose with music – jazz on the radio – playing in the background. He describes his style of writing as distinguished by his concern for "la palabra bella" (the elegant word), musicality, and fragmentation. Additionally, a principal method of his style was to suppress the connectives of conven-

tional logic in favor of an elliptical style reminiscent of modern writers such as T. S. Eliot.

Gimferrer's approach to the art of poetry in *Arde el mar* can be traced to a substratum of poets who did not ascribe to the majority views and who gave greater importance to the tenets of the Generation of 1927. The dominant social poets had rejected those ideas, assuming the absolute instrumental value of thematic and realistic expression through the use of the worldly and direct "I." What distinguishes the minority groups is the investigation of poetry as a creative act as well as a reflection on the poetic task. Barral, Jaime Gil de Biedma, Claudio Rodríguez, and others had made efforts to replace the ideological compromise of social poetry with a conception of poetry as a means of knowledge.

In *30 años de literatura* (Thirty Years of Literature, 1971) Gimferrer accuses the poetry of postcivil-war Spain of putrefaction, fossilization, and linguistic inertia, and he advocates the fundamental importance of innovation. Seven years later, however, in *Radicalidades* (Radicalities, 1978), Gimferrer reveals some reserved acknowledgment of his predecessors' merits: the social poets had used diction that was free of the late-Romantic emphasis and rhetoric favored in modernism and *garcilasismo* (a type of Neoplatonism based on the poetry of Garcilaso de la Vega). However, they had not attained the tense and conflictive language of the Rimbaudian model of contemporary poetry, which in Gimferrer's vision is based on a more spiritual and aesthetic outlook.

*Arde el mar* presents a young man whose actual life is interwoven with a remote poetic life. His artistic side allows him to contemplate the other life, as expressed in "Primera visión de marzo" (First Vision of March):

Veo
con otros ojos, no los míos, esta plaza
soñada en otros tiempos, hoy vivida,
con un susurro de algas al oído
viniendo de muy lejos

(I see
with other eyes, not mine, this square
dreamed in other times, present today,
with a whisper of algae in my ear
coming from afar).

As the two forms of life are contradictory, the young poet questions the visions: "¿No me mentís?" (You are not lying to me?). Poetry is thus the experience of another existence rooted in the totality of the poet's cultural background and felt in terms of his present emotions. It is important to recognize that the poet is not the same as the historical person. The poet is an "other" who communicates his inner lights in a language that does not submit to logic or biography. The vision that emerges in his poetic existence is made of imaginative evocations that become beautiful, sometimes melancholy, events.

The poem "Band of Angels" exemplifies the artistic procedure of *Arde el mar* with an explicitness that is rare in Gimferrer's work. The speaker envisions the childhood he never had and reveals "un perfil desconocido, el mío, y en sus ojos / otra luz de leyenda, un mundo" (an unknown profile, mine, and in his eyes / another light of legend, a world). That world includes the speaker's own "tumba abierta / de un niño, tumba oscura, aún mi pelo / rizado estaba" (open tomb / of a child, dark tomb, my hair still / was curly). Having opened the past by imagining the child he once was, the poet, now a young man, anticipates and speaks of love:

Ven hasta mí, belleza silenciosa,
. . . . . . . . . . . . . . . . . . . . . . . . .
ven hasta mí y tus labios y tus ojos
y tus manos me salven de morir

(Come to me, silent beauty,
. . . . . . . . . . . . . . . . . . . . . . .
come to me and let your lips and your eyes
and your hands save me from dying).

To a greater degree than Gimferrer's theoretical writings, *Arde el mar* and *La muerte en Beverly Hills* (Death in Beverly Hills, 1968) set the guidelines for the "new" generation of poetry. In *Arde el mar* readers find poems on many topics, including classical culture, the medieval world, romantic visions, European travels to Venice and Geneva, historical and literary figures from the world over, adolescent ambivalence as an attempt to forget pain, the nature of poetry, the doubting of identity, and the hope for self-recognition. *Arde el mar* seems disorganized, as Gimferrer is preoccupied with irrationally juxtaposed memories that unsettle commonplace notions of reality.

In his introduction to *Poemas, 1963–1969* (1969) Gimferrer points out that he wrote *Arde el mar* in the least deliberate and most nonchalant way because of his aversion to social poetry. He also states that these poems come from his experiencing movies, comic books, novels, literature, historical writings and the plastic arts. He attempts to make sense of the world and himself as he states in the poem "Primera visión de marzo": "Ordenar estos datos es tal vez poesía" (to order these facts is perhaps poetry).

Remembrance of a literary, artistic, or historical past is one of the common characteristics in *Arde el mar* and in all the poetry Gimferrer wrote in Castilian before 1970. (His later work is in Catalan.) This characteristic is a key element in the aesthetic breakthrough that Gimferrer and the *novísimos* achieved in moving away from the poetry that had preceded them. In such retrospection there is an implicit structure that critic and poet Guillermo Carnero identifies as based on an "analogous historical person" and an objectifying device of other artwork as well as poetry. Often the device is self-conscious and metapoetic, as seen in "Primera visión de marzo":

Visión, sueño yo mismo,
contemplaba la estatua en un silencio
hecho sólo de memoria, cristal o piedra tallada
pero frío en las yemas, ascendiendo
como un lento amarillo sobre el aire en tensión.
Hacia otro, hacia otra
vida, desde mi vida, en el común
artificio o rutina con que se hace un poema,
un largo poema y su gruesa artillería,
sin misterio, ni apenas
este sordo conjuro que organiza palabras o fluctúa
de una a otra, vivo en su contradicción

(Vision, myself a dream,
I contemplated the statue in a silence
made only of memory, glass or chiseled stone,
but cold on the fingertips, ascending
like a slow jaundice on the air in tension.
Toward the other, toward another
life, starting with my life, in the common
artifice or routine with which a poem is made,
a long poem and its heavy artillery,
without mystery, not even
this noiseless conjuration that organizes words or fluctuates
from one to another, vivid in its contradiction).

In *La muerte en Beverly Hills* Gimferrer seeks to reach the reader by writing about the American cinema. His introduction to *Poemas, 1963–1969* states that he meant to free himself from the nonchalant ordering he gave to his previous book by composing an integral poem which tells an intimate story. His reconstruction of the golden years of Hollywood movies is sad, and the themes of the book are nostalgia and young love. Allusions to Jean Harlow, Charlie Chan, and Ava Gardner touch on the complexities of persons, personas, roles, and an era of the cinema that has become a myth and an obsession. Gimferrer thus replaces the personal experi-

Conjur

Els guerrers més augusts ja són ombres
sota l'ombra del vell alzinar.
Mondaca, la nit espetega.
Cops de trall, lladrucs, llamps llunyans.
Al poc morts les cornelles grinyolen.
Esvaren el corser mans de glaç.
La tempesta. El sol verd d'aiguii negres.
No em conec. Mort, el pit és un glaç.
   Vaixell d'or, ceàdal foses el dia.
El meu cos, com la corda d'un arc.
Da feineja l'hivern, quan esquinça
les cortines, teatre del mar.
S'emmascara ens les boires feixugues.
Aoques negres deturen el fru pas.
S'encercara l'argent d'atzar sega.
La rageta coreix el vial.
Pam a pam morrem la fossana.
   Fang i fulles ens feien el jas.
El saint d'or del bargues crema i crema
la llacuna, de neu i safrà.
No pensàreu que fos tota blanca.
Ara vénen les hosts del enllà,
les hosts vénen. Verdor de l'alzina
als ulls morts, als ulls buits, plens de calç.

*Fair copy of a poem published in* Foc cec *(from* Peña Labra, *Summer 1987; by permission of Pere Gimferrer)*

ence in poetry with a fabricated, cultural, and literary one. He approaches the world on an aesthetic level and suppresses the concept of self held by previous generations – that is, the biographical identity.

The poems collected in the section "De extraña fruta y otros poemas" (Of Strange Fruit and Other Poems) in *Poemas, 1963–1969* are the last poems Gimferrer wrote in Castilian. His introductory observations indicate that in "De extraña fruta" he produces a book of sad and skeptical reflections on the value of poetic language as in "Recuento" (Recount), a typically disjointed poem that mentions not only Ernesto (Che) Guevara, collaborator in the 1959 Cuban revolution, but also an Italian reformist priest and a well-known Italian painter, both of whom lived in the fifteenth century:

> cuánto quise decir que mis versos no dicen
> cuánto mis versos dicen que yo no sabía decir
> . . . . . . . . . . . . . . . . . . . . . . . . . . . . . . . . . . . .
> mis ojos han visto la hoguera de Savanarola
> la muerte de Ernesto Guevara
> y como Sandro Botticelli la fría luz de una plaza
>     desnuda
> edificios vacíos como un esbozo de arquitecto
> *Los milagros de san Zenobio* pintado hacia 1500
> ya no tenía fe
>
> (all that I meant to say that my verses do not say
> all that my verses say that I did not know how to say
> . . . . . . . . . . . . . . . . . . . . . . . . . . . . . . . . . . . .
> my eyes have seen the pyre of [Girolamo] Savanarola
> the death of Ernesto Guevara
> and like Sandro Botticelli the cold light of a naked
>     square
> empty buildings like an architect's sketch
> *The Miracles of Saint Zenobius* painted about 1500
> no longer had faith).

The historical characters of "Recuento" allow the poet to speak of himself by analogy as he contemplates his loss of faith. In keeping with Gimferrer's breaking away from the direct and personal discourse of social poetry, "Recuento" is a lyric poem which depicts the poet's emotion through historical figures, whose circumstances reflect what he feels. While the element of faith is manifest, the choice of characters and the unusual syntax require participation on the reader's part in order to understand the poem.

With "Farewell," another poem in "De extraña fruta," Gimferrer uses the American cowboy movie *Shane* (1953) to give another form to his faltering confidence in poetry. The poem is a long, incomplete simile which begins with these lines:

> Como Shane, el hombre de los valles perdidos,
> que tenía los ojos azules y cantaba viejas baladas del
>     Oeste,
> como Shane, que tenía dos pistolas nacaradas
> y la alegría de la inmortalidad en sus pupilas,
> como Shane, que hablaba de lejanas praderas y
>     bosques
>
> (Like Shane, the man of lost valleys,
> who had blue eyes and sang old ballads of the West,
> like Shane, who had two pearl-handled pistols
> and the joy of immortality in his pupils,
> like Shane, who spoke of distant prairies and forests).

Shane is the only explicit component of the comparison. The nostalgic tone is expressed through the accumulation of attributes, and Shane's absence is underscored by verbal paradigms such as *lost*. Shane is a symbol of Gimferrer's skepticism about poetry and also, by implication, provides the poet with several roles through which he may represent his doubts: a disappointed boy, as in the film, who watches his hero ride away, and the other missing part of the simile, who, like Shane, once spoke of distant places and has also gone away.

In "Canción para Billie Holiday" (Song for Billie Holiday) the speaker has a dialogue with the well-known American jazz singer whose 1939 rendition of the song "Strange Fruit" inspired Gimferrer's title. The speaker tells of situations which express the futility, frustration, and negativity central to the poems in this collection: "Lady Day / Con dos vueltas de llave cerraron la cocina / No nos dan mermelada ni pastel de cereza / ni el amor ni la muerte extraña fruta que deja un sabor ácido" (Lady Day / They have locked up the kitchen / they will not give us jam or cherry pie / or love or death strange fruit that leaves a bitter taste).

"De extraña fruta y otros poemas" is the culmination of Gimferrer's cycle of poetry composed in Castilian. In a 1971 interview with Federico Campbell, Gimferrer stated that his first book in Catalan, *Els miralls* (The Mirrors, 1970), represents a deeper "rupture" than mere change of language: "*Els miralls* es un libro de replanteo; es casi un ensayo o discusión teórica sobre la poesía; se trata al mismo tiempo de un libro de poemas y de una indagación sobre el sentido de la poesía" (*Els miralls* is a book about a new ground plan; it is almost an essay or theoretical discussion on poetry; it is a question of a book of poems and at the same time an inquiry on the meaning of poetry). Carnero's 1978 article in *Insula* points out that Gimferrer's work in his native language stems from his desire to resolve two problems. On one hand there is the moral issue of elevating Catalan to the level of a literary language, after the prohibition of its use in Catalonia during the Franco regime. Additionally, Catalan allows Gimferrer new possibilities of expression in the language he had not previously used in his poetry.

Although it would seem that the adoption of his native language marks a break from his previous works, the new direction he takes is a continuance of the literary journey undertaken by romantic, symbolist, and surrealist writers. Their concept of language as the means of searching a reality that goes beyond social realism has always been a fundamental part of Gimferrer's poetry.

*Els miralls* marks another transition in the development of Gimferrer's work. In "De extraña fruta," the self-critical artist has supplanted the nostalgic adolescent who had relied on the resources of art and the rhetoric of allusion. *Els miralls* is a search carried out by a self-conscious poet who integrates meditations on reality with the process of converting them to poetry, as expressed in "Segona visió de març" (Second Vision of March): "així el poema alhora pateix de la imperiosa necessitat de designar el real / i no el pot designar: li calen les paràfrasis / per al·ludir al tránsit d'un núvol, a l'estiu" (thus the poem suffers both from the imperious necessity to designate reality / and its inability to designate: it needs paraphrases / in order to allude to the passing of a cloud in summer). The themes of the collection are crystallized in the poem "Paranys" (Snares), which bears epigraphs from Joan Brossa, "Un joc de miralls permet veure l'altra banda del poema" (A play of mirrors allows us to see the other side of the poem), and from Wallace Stevens, "Poetry is the subject of the poem." The poems "Paranys" and "Sistems" (Systems) posit poetry as an operation founded on a precarious system of mirrors which produce partial reflections of reality. Gimferrer ends *Els miralls* with "Op. 98," a tribute to Johannes Brahms that questions all art:

"Quan l'art s'anul·la, quan es fa transparència
i és allò que està dient, i només diu el que és,
quan s'ha fet evident i alhora, expositiu – la llum
que en té prou essent la llum – ¿per què, un cop més,
     ens sobta,
ens fereix, ens demana, torna a ser art? ¿El gir
s'ha acomplert en sentit invers, i així la música,
restableix el silenci i la pintura el buit – il la paraula
l'espai en blanc?

(When art is nullified, when it is made transparency
and is what it is saying and says only what it is,
when it has become evidence and exposition as well –
     from it the light

takes satisfaction in being light – why once again, does
     it surprise us,
injure us, make claims on us, go back to being art? Has
     the circle been completed in reverse, so that music
     reestablishes silence and painting the void – and the
     word the blank space?).

In 1970 Gimferrer began working in the literary department at the Seix Barral publishing company in Barcelona. He married the pianist María Rosa Caminals the following year.

*Hora foscant* (Dark Hour, 1972), as Arthur Terry suggests in *Anthropos* (January 1993), has certain baroque tendencies, because Gimferrer perceives the world as the inexorable passage of time and the tension between body and spirit. In this work Gimferrer continues to speculate on an idea formulated in *Els miralls:* that a dark void is both the origin and the end of life, though he writes in "Juny" (June), "L'obscuritat promesa als meus ulls és més tendra" (The obscurity promised to my eyes is sweeter).

For the most part Gimferrer has abandoned the technique of expressing his lyricism with historical and cultural analogies and develops other aspects of his poetry. Through free associations, changes in expressive levels, and the use of unusual, often broken syntax, he utters aesthetic and moral truths in an idiom of his own making. As such, the investigation on the meaning of poetry and reality, linked with Brossa's image of the mirror as the other side of the poem, results in a dark and tragic vision. The inquiry becomes a search that is destined to failure and produces a sense of helplessness in the poet's work. Visible objects become metaphors of the unnameable other side of reality, as in the title poem "Hora foscant": "Camps de destral, al cel. De bosc. Falgueres, / amb tanta pell de llop, de teixó, l'eina / nocturna, l'ullal fosc, metall o marbre, / palpebra closa" (Hatchet fields, in the sky. Forest. Ferns, / with so much wolf fur, badger, the tool / of night, the dark fang, metal or marble, / closed eyelid).

The perception in "Llum de tardor" (Autumn Light) is frustration: "tot és capvespre i or i subterfugi, roba negra als sentits!" (all is dusk and gold and subterfuge, black cloth on the senses!). And with a deep sense of frailty he faces the subsequent question: "¿I hi ha res a comprendre?" (Is there something to understand?).

In *Hora foscant* and *Foc cec* (Blind Fire, 1973), the theme of love, portrayed earlier in the late-adolescent relationships of *La muerte en Beverly Hills,* is now part of the poet's inner vision of reality and will deepen with the poet's ontological concerns in

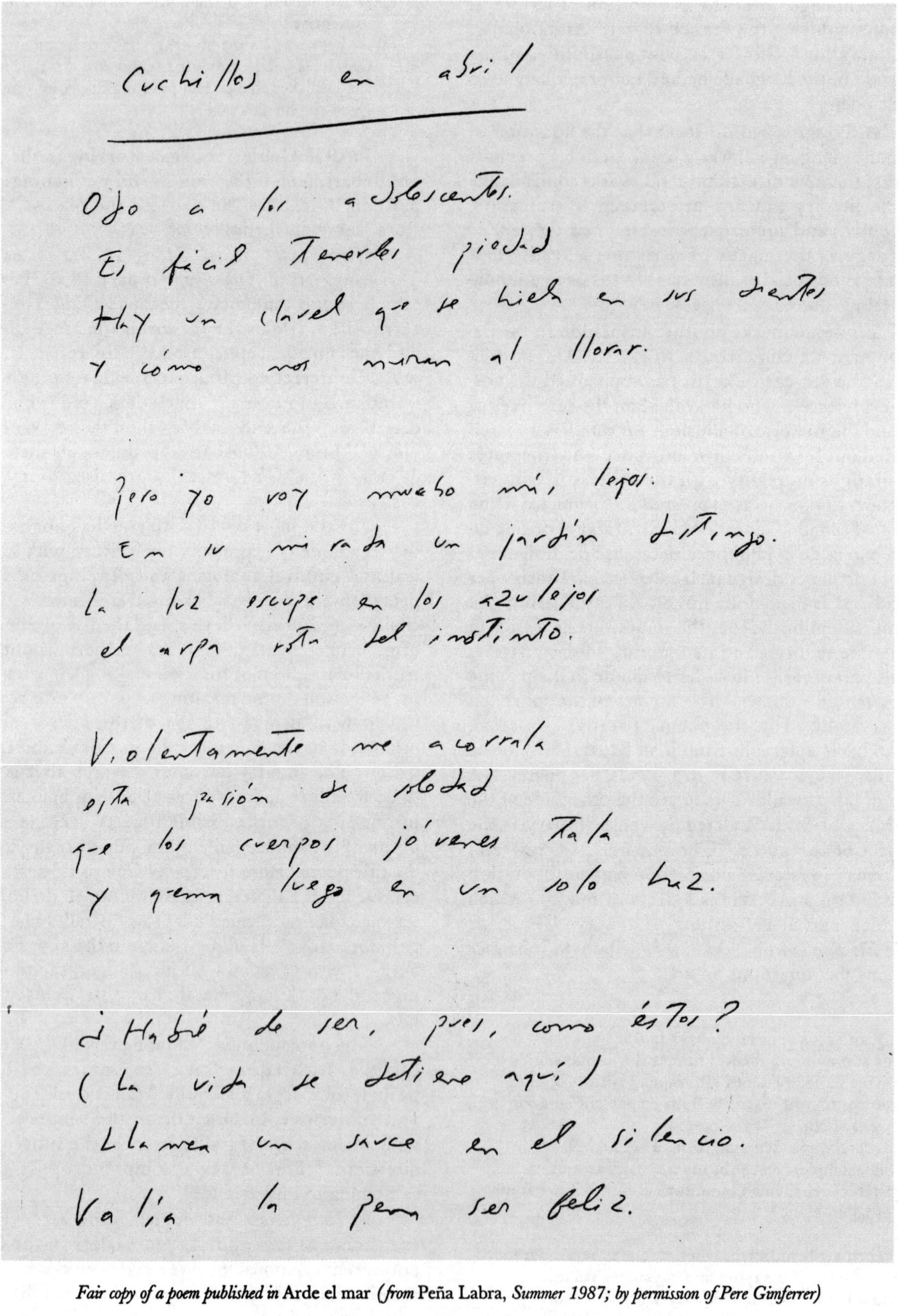

Cuchillos en abril

Ojo a los adolescentes.
Es fácil tenerles piedad
Hay un clavel que se hiela en sus dientes
y cómo nos miran al llorar.


Pero yo voy mucho más lejos.
En su mirada un jardín distingo.
La luz escupe en los azulejos
el arpa rota del instinto.


Violentamente me acorrala
esta pasión de soledad
que los cuerpos jóvenes tala
y quema luego en un solo haz.


¿Habré de ser, pues, como éstos?
(La vida se detiene aquí.)
Llamea un sauce en el silencio.
Valía la pena ser feliz.

*Fair copy of a poem published in* Arde el mar *(from Peña Labra, Summer 1987; by permission of Pere Gimferrer)*

later works. A continuation of the meditation on poetry initiated in *Els miralls,* the love theme in *Foc cec* signals the tensions and preoccupations shared by lover and writer, as exemplified in "Solstici": "Els mots / celen un clos pregon, i l'escriptura / llatzera el cos del tigre. / Escrit amb foc / i escrit amb llum, a la lunar contrada, / pasturatge dels morts. L'amant albira, / enllà dels membres contorçats, l'obscur" (Words / hide a profound enclosure and writing / lacerates the tiger's body. / Written with fire / and written with light, in the lunar district, / pasture of the dead. The lover glimpses, / beyond the entwined limbs, the obscure). Gimferrer has not written love poetry in the strict sense. Rather, he has made it part of his poetic inquiry which reveals the limits of human existence.

*L'espai desert* (Desert Space, 1977) is considered Gimferrer's best work to date and one of the most significant published in Spain in the 1970s. It is a long poem in ten sections in which he contemplates animal and botanical worlds, adolescence, oppression, the family, and his fascination with the night.

Eroticism acquires a special importance in the book, and the culmination of the meditation on this theme is reached in section 4. Love, in terms of the sexual act, is a profound experience that becomes a metaphor of cognizance:

> el de la fusió que atueix el sentit i obre el coneixement,
> i'annul·lant l'ésser, fa retrobar l'ésser,
> perquè som l'altre cos, l'altra percepció,
> en un temps blanc i buit, en un espai desert,
> som el revers, som aquell que ens veurà
> des de l'altre costat del mirall on veiem
> els gestos de l'amor

> (one of the fusion that knocks down sense and opens cognizance,
> and annulling the being, has the being recovered,
> because we are the other body, the other perception,
> in a time white and empty, in a desert space,
> we are the reverse, we are that one who will see us
> from the other side of the mirror where we see
> the likeness of love).

Physical love discloses a space for transcendence toward contact "amb el soterrat ritme planetari" (with the hidden planetary rhythm) in a desert space, a "white time." Love is a dramatic paradox, physical and spiritual, and represents the possibility to bring about the marriage of opposites. Such a union is one concern of Gimferrer. Terry has suggested that *L'espai desert* demonstrates how language can make sense of the world by means of a vision of reality whose implications go beyond the words themselves.

*L'espai desert* ends with Gimferrer's view of the external world as seen from the desert space:

> sento el batec, sóc el batec, el cel
> que batega, la llum que ha retingut l'alè
> per deixar una claror despullada a l'espai,
> per despullar l'espai fins i tot de claror,
> perquè vegem el fons del sot de l'esser,
> perquè vegem l'espai sense claror ni fosca,
> perquè vegem l'espai on no hi ha espai,
> perquè vegem l'espai que és tot l'espai

> (I feel the beat, I am the beat, the sky
> which beats, the light which has retained breath
> in order to leave a clarity stripped in space,
> in order to strip space down to total clarity,
> so that we see the depths of the pit of being,
> so that we see space without clarity or darkness,
> so that we see space where there is no space,
> so that we see space that is all space).

The complex vision of reality continues in later poetry, some of which appeared in reviews and then was republished in the collection *Mirall, espai, aparicions* (1981): "Dos homenatges" (Two Homages, 1978), in honor of Aleixandre and Antoni Tàpies; "Aparicions" (Apparitions, 1980); and "Com un epileg" (Like an Epilogue, 1981).

In "Aparicions" Gimferrer writes of dreams: "El somni no té sempre color ni moviment: / sovint és un estat" (The dream does not always have color or movement: it is often a state). That state is a search for the instant before existence — "abans de ser-hi jo, abans d'aquell instant / en què diré 'Sóc jo,' i encara serà un somni" (before I exist, before that instant / when I say 'I am' and it will still be a dream) — and for identity: "Perquè el tema del somni / és la idea del jo" (Because the theme of the dream / is the idea of the "I"). Identity is the center of individual consciousness: "¿Podríem viure / si no sentíssim que tenim un centre? / Es aquest el regal del somni" (Could we live / if we did not feel that we have a center? / This is the gift of the dream).

Gimferrer's next collection of poetry, *El vendaval* (Windstorm), was published in 1988 and won him his second Premio Nacional de Poesía. In the interim he was appointed the director of the literary department at the Seix Barral publishing company in 1981. Among the notable books he then published are the collections of essays *Dietari* (Journal, 1981) and *Segon dietari* (Second Journal, 1982) and the novel *Fortuny* (1983). *El vendaval* brings a new perspective to his doubts about the viability of poetry. The collection is composed of four sections: 1

and 3 present longer poems typical of Gimferrer; 2 and 4 are innovative in that they include prose poems and sonnets. The first poem, "Paraules per a un lapidari" (Words for a Lapidary), contains transformations and correspondences: "al fons de l'armari dels núvols lluu només una pedra: un present de la fosca i la llum que acaba de collir Joan Miró" (in the depths of the armoire of clouds shines only one rock: a gift of the dark and the light that Joan Miró just captured). In the poem Miró touches, looks at, and listens to the stone: the stone becomes art. The poet, an implied presence, uses this transformation to set the stage for the visual play of dark and light to follow.

Startling correspondences are produced by juxtaposing vague, one-word titles against abstruse imagery. For example, the love theme in "Epitalami" (Epithalamium), a nuptial song, takes form in stark oppositions of the sexual experience with which Gimferrer hopes to reveal and reconcile love's conflicting aspects. The woman in the poem is "Ampolla de vinagre, ampolla negra d'ambre a la bescambra" (Cruet of vinegar, black cruet of bathroom amber).

In part 3 of this book, "Himne d'hivern" (Hymn of Winter), Gimferrer goes back to gloomy motifs established in his earlier poetry. The title poem of this section announces "el matí de la mort" (the dawn of death) with negative images of snow, ice, bright light, and winter storms, causing a sensation of a cosmic void: "Arrecerats, veurem el bosc de la temença / i el cant dels ocells morts dirà el nostre destí" (Sheltered, we will see the forest of fear / and the song of dead birds will tell our destiny).

The unspoken void is expressed through the insistence on the white of winter mist, snow, and ice, which in turn are teamed with a blinding sky and flashes of light. White is thus the color of absence, the partner of black. In "Exili" (Exile) the world is tarnished by the shadow of words. An insurmountable frontier persists between words and the objects they try to designate: "la desafecció del mot i el món visible: / diem mots, però no diem el món" (dislike for the word and the visible world: / we say words, but we do not say the world).

In the fourth section, "El belvedere" (The Belvedere), Gimferrer invokes the Catalan Renaissance and the tradition of the sonnet. His sonnets represent a strict meter and include symbolism taken to the limits, acting as a window on his poetic obsessions, as in "Paisatge" (Landscape): "El món en el claror s'escriu / com la llum en la pedra dura. / El mot a la plana s'atura / a l'arquitectura que viu"

(The world is written in splendor / like the light on hard rock. / The word is obstructed on the page, / in the architecture that lives).

In *La llum* (The Light, 1991) Gimferrer again uses the sonnet and other classical forms as if in tribute to Stéphane Mallarmé and other symbolists. The first of these thirty-five poems, "Himne" (Hymn), sums up the concept and the poetic procedures of this collection. The accumulation of word associations — "com un timbal de fosca, el capvespre granat" (like a drum of obscurity, the scarlet dusk), followed by "el mar color de sang colpeja les drassanes" (the sea of blood color beats the shipyards) — creates the atmosphere for a melding of vision and myth. As the sky of this sonnet fills with noises of bursting and uproar, a drumbeat signals war, and the lance of morning tears the "túnica teixida" (woven tunic) of night and day. In the final stanza, "Un rapte de centaures flameja en la nit púnica / als enderrocs que miren les armes del passat" (An abduction of centaurs flames in the Punic night / amid the spoils that weapons of the past watch). As in his earlier poetry, Gimferrer fuses and deepens his themes with myth and history: centaurs are the "light" of a constellation as well as creatures in the treacherous and historic night. This complex mingling also appears in "Faula" (Fable), when the speaker says that "vivents per esdevenir mite / en la claror d'un temple escita / la mort ens deixa un sangtraït" (living to become myth / in the resplendence of a Scythian temple / death leaves us bruised).

The play between darkness and light is revealed as the fight between truth and falsity in "Crespuscular": "El sol borni i tèrbol de la nit encalça / la claror del vespre com moneda falsa" (The one-eyed and turbid sun of night pursues / the counterfeit money of the resplendent afternoon). In "El mot de la llum" (The Word of the Light), a sonnet of images of brilliance and uproar, the light speaks, "tota aquesta gatzara — diu la llum — és un frau — / i tanta de claror viu i mor per dir: — Sí" (all this din — says the light — is a fraud — / and so much brilliance lives and dies to say: — yes). The poet examines the reality of life in "Medalló" (Medallion) and comes to recognize that all is fake, even death, "com una mascareta de vellut, / com una mascareta es fa mascara" (like a mask of velvet, like a mask that becomes a smudge).

In the last poem, "Final," the speaker, under the constellation Leo, laments: "i la mort, en la llum, tanta / que a l'extermini clar del papel llis / fútilment he vassat el paradís" (and death, in the light so much / that in the clear extermination of the

*Gimferrer in the late 1980s*

smooth paper / futilely I have spilled paradise). Gimferrer's choice of such classic forms as the sonnet is not a surprise, for, ever since his work in *El vendaval,* such forms have furnished a scheme for the tension and debate of his poetic obsessions. "Final" illustrates that those obsessions are moving away from the metapoetic toward the ontological: "Fútil despatx, porpra i lli / fútil llum color de vi, / tan de debò que ens espanta:" (Futile dispatch, purple and flaxen / futile light of wine color, / how it truly frightens us).

While *La llum* shows the evolution of a poet who is attentively writing toward the limits of modernity, it is not appropriate to regard Pere Gimferrer as only a poet. His books of essays and criticism bear witness to a wide range of interest and talent. Beyond the anthologies, introductions, and prologues he has prepared on poetry, he has written various articles of literary criticism and has authored books on such artists as Miró, Antoni Tàpies, Max Ernst, and Henri de Toulouse-Lau-

trec. His fondness for the movies led him to write *Cine y literatura* (Cinema and Literature, 1985). After receiving many literary prizes and awards, in 1985, as further proof of the importance of his accomplishments, he was elected to the Spanish Royal Academy of Language. The induction ceremony took place in Madrid on 15 December of that year, when Gimferrer delivered his inaugural speech, "Perfil de Vicente Aleixandre" (Profile of Vicente Aleixandre), before taking the chair that his mentor had previously occupied at the Royal Academy.

Enric Bou's 1989 article on Gimferrer as a public figure states that the poet has been portrayed as an eccentric man of letters who strolls along the Rambla de Catalunya, one of Barcelona's main avenues, dressed in a raincoat and armed with an umbrella even in the sultry month of August. Gimferrer lives in the Eixemple, an eminent district of Barcelona near his favorite repertory cinema and the publishing companies for which he works, such as Edicions 62, where he is an adviser for poetry collections and literary translations to Catalan. In his home on the Rambla de Catalunya he utilizes a small room filled with books and a television set and has said that, like Proust, he reads and writes in bed. Bou infers that the rapid communications of contemporary culture have allowed Gimferrer to create several images of himself. The poet has made good use of the media at his disposal in order to assume very distinct attitudes because of his status of famous writer, his bilingualism, and the variety of his interests and talents.

Gimferrer spoke of his career as a writer with a more historical approach in a speech he delivered to the Ateneu Barcelonès in 1989, from which selections have been published as "Itinerario de un escritor" (Itinerary of a Writer) in the January 1993 edition of *Anthropos*. After talking about his earliest recollections of the literary vocation, Gimferrer states that at age thirteen he found himself at the crossroads because of the circumstances in which he grew up. As one of those born soon after the Spanish Civil War, he asserts that he belongs to a special generation because it is the only one of twentieth-century Europe that lived under fascism from infancy. As seen through his young eyes the Barcelona of 1958 left him with the sensation of existing in an atmosphere of imposture, homogeneity, and enforced monolinguism, all of which produced mediocre art and literature.

In 1963, while he was in law school, he was so impressed by a poetry reading that he was inspired to produce a type of literature that would be as different as possible from the imposture that surrounded him. His attempt was not meant to be a rebellion against the social and political climate but rather a protest on the aesthetic level, one that embraced the literary tradition of Europe. This is linked to his conception of poetry as an operation of language which characteristically has a lasting effect in time. As a model of the literature he believes in, Gimferrer cites Arthur Rimbaud as one who attempted to take language toward new forms and new knowledge. For Gimferrer the history of any literary itinerary is the way in which the artist comes to feel the special desire to create another reality with language.

## Interviews:

Federico Campbell, "Pere Gimferrer o la ruptura," in his *Infame turbia* (Barcelona: Lumen, 1971), pp. 72–75;

Sergio Vila-San Juan, "Entrevista con Pere Gimferrer. Una poesía ensimismada," *Quimera*, 7 (May 1981): 12–15;

Víctor García de la Concha, "Entrevista a Pere Gimferrer," *Insula*, 44 (January 1989): 27–28.

## References:

*Anthropos,* special issue on Gimferrer, 140 (January 1993):

Julia Barella, "Poesía en la década de los setenta: En torno a los novísimos," *Insula,* 36 (January 1981): 4–5;

Enric Bou, "Un 'Novísimo en la Academia: Imágenes de/en Pedro/Pere Gimferrer," *Ojáncano,* 2 (April 1989): 29–40;

Guillermo Carnero, "Culturism and the 'New Poetry.' A Poem by Pedro Gimferrer: 'Cascabeles' from *Arde el mar,*" *Studies in Twentieth Century Literature,* 16 (Winter 1992): 93–107;

Carnero, "La etapa catalana en la poesía de Pedro Gimferrer," *Insula,* 33 (September 1978): 1, 5;

J. M. Castellet, *Nueve novísimos poetas españoles* (Barcelona: Barral, 1970), pp. 11–47;

Andrew P. Debicki, "Una poesía española de la postmodernidad: Los novísimos," *Anales de la Literatura Española Contemporánea,* 14 (1989): 33–50;

Víctor García de la Concha, "Primera etapa de un novísimo: Pedro Gimferrer, *Arde el mar,*" *Papeles de Son Armadans,* 17 (January 1972): 45–61;

Leopoldo María Panero, "Ultima poesía no española," *Poesía,* 4 (June 1979): 110–111;

Margaret Persin, "Snares: Pere Gimferrer's *Los espejos / Els miralls,*" *Studies in Twentieth Century Literature,* 16 (Winter 1992): 109–126;

Timothy J. Rogers, "Verbal Collage in Pere Gimferrer's *Poemas, 1963–1969,*" *Hispania,* 67 (May 1984): 207–213;

Fanny Rubio, "Gimferrer y su arte," *Olvidos de Granada,* 7–8 (May–June 1985): 6–8;

Arthur Terry, "Pròleg: La poesía de Pere Gimferrer," in Gimferrer's *Mirall, espai, aparicions: Poesía, 1970–1980* (Barcelona: Edicions 62, 1981), pp. 7–92;

Manuel Vilas, "Pere Gimferrer, *Extraña fruta:* El misterio de una disolución poética," *Cuadernos de Investigación Filológica,* 11 (May–December 1985): 123–140.

# José Agustín Goytisolo

*(13 April 1928 –  )*

Niza Fabre
*Ramapo College of New Jersey*

BOOKS: *El retorno* (Madrid: Rialp, 1955);

*Salmos al viento* (Barcelona: Instituto de Estudios Hispánicos, 1958);

*Claridad* (Valencia: Diputación Provincial de Valencia, 1961; Mexico City: Nuevas Generaciones, 1961);

*Años decisivos: Poesía 1954–1960* (Barcelona: Literaturasa, 1961);

*Hacia una formalización de la ciudad en el espacio* (Barcelona: Blume, 1968);

*Algo sucede* (Madrid: Ciencia Nueva, 1968);

*Pierre le maquis,* translated into Italian by Ubaldo Bardi (Florence: Collettivo R, 1972);

*Bajo tolerancia* (Barcelona: Llibres de Sinera, 1973);

*Taller de arquitectura* (Barcelona: Lumen, 1977);

*Del tiempo y del olvido* (Barcelona: Lumen, 1977);

*Palabras para Julia y otras canciones* (Barcelona: Laia, 1980);

*Los pasos del cazador* (Barcelona: Lumen, 1980);

*A veces gran amor* (Barcelona: Laia, 1981);

*Sobre las circunstancias* (Barcelona: Laia, 1983);

*El lobito bueno,* by Goytisolo and Juan Ballesta (Barcelona: Laia, 1983);

*El príncipe malo,* by Goytisolo and Ballesta (Barcelona: Laia, 1983);

*La bruja hermosa,* by Goytisolo and Ballesta (Barcelona: Laia, 1984);

*El pirata honrado,* by Goytisolo and Ballesta (Barcelona: Laia, 1984);

*Final de un adiós* (Barcelona: Lumen, 1984);

*El rey mendigo* (Barcelona: Lumen, 1988);

*La noche le es propicia* (Barcelona: Lumen, 1992).

OTHER: Darío Puccini, *Romancero de la resistencia española, 1936–1965,* translated by Goytisolo and others (Mexico City: Era, 1967);

*Posible imagen de José Lezama Lima,* edited by Goytisolo (Barcelona: Llibres de Sinera Ocnos, 1969);

*Nueva poesía cubana: Antología poética,* compiled by Goytisolo (Barcelona: Península, 1969);

*Jorge Luis Borges: Poemas escogidos,* edited by Goytisolo (Barcelona: Llibres de Sinera Ocnos, 1972);

*Joan Salvat Papasseit: Cincuenta poemas,* edited by Goytisolo (Barcelona: Seix Barral, 1975);

*Lezama Lima: Esferaimagen,* edited by Goytisolo (Barcelona: Tusquets, 1979).

TRANSLATIONS: *Cesare Pavese: Antología poética* (Santander: Isla de los Ratones, 1962);

*Salvador Espriu: La piel de toro* (Paris: Ruedo Ibérico, 1963; Barcelona: Lumen, 1983);

Salvatore Quasimodo, *25 poemas,* selected and translated, with a prologue, by Goytisolo (Santander: Isla de los Ratones, 1963);

*Pier Paolo Pasolini: Mamma Roma* (Barcelona: Seix Barral, 1965);

*Poemas de Sergio Esenin* (Santander: Isla de los Ratones, 1967);

*Poetas catalanes contemporáneos,* compiled and translated, with an introduction, by Goytisolo (Barcelona: Seix Barral, 1968);

*Gabriel Ferrater: Mujeres y días,* translated by Goytisolo, José María Valverde, and Pere Gimferrer (Barcelona: Seix Barral, 1979);

*Agostinho Neto: La lucha continúa,* translated by Goytisolo and X. L. García (Barcelona: Laia, 1980);

*Joan Vinyoli: Cuarenta poemas,* selected and translated, with an introduction, by Goytisolo (Barcelona: Lumen, 1980);

*José M. de Sagarra y Casterllanau: Vida privada,* translated, with a prologue and notes, by Goytisolo (Barcelona: Plaza & Janés, 1984);

Carles Riba, *Elegías de Bierville* (Barcelona: Mall, 1985);

J. V. Foix, *Crónicas de ultrasueño* (Barcelona: Anagrama, 1986);

María Manent, *Las acacias salvajes* (Barcelona: Mall, 1986);

*Joan Vinyoli: Alguien me ha llamado* (Barcelona: Marca Hispánica, 1986);

*José Agustín Goytisolo in Barcelona, 1985*

*Joseph Carner: Nabí* (Barcelona: Marca Hispánica, 1987);

*Toda la poesía de Bartomeu Rosselló Pòrcel* (Barcelona: Ediciones del Mall, 1987).

SELECTED PERIODICAL PUBLICATIONS –
UNCOLLECTED: "Sobre el rastro poético de Vicente Huidobro," *Laye,* 24 (1954);

"En la isla," *Papeles de Son Armadas,* 57 (December 1960);

"Homenaje a Carlos Riba," *Papeles de Son Armadas,* 58 (November 1961);

"Unamuno, hoy: 25 aniversario de la muerte de Unamuno," *Insula,* 16 (December 1961): 4;

"Foix de Sarria," *Quimera,* 41 (September 1984): 49.

José Agustín Goytisolo is a prolific and prominent writer who belongs to a very important poetic movement that includes Carlos Barral, Jaime Ferrán, Jaime Gil de Biedma, and Alfonso Costafreda. The literary life of Goytisolo, like the literary life of his peer group, flourished in the 1950s under Francisco Franco's regime. Early in his life Goytisolo started to write poems but did not try to publish them. He first became known to the public through his successful participation in two of the most important Spanish literary contests, the Adonais Prize of Madrid and the Boscán Prize of Barcelona. He has received several awards for his work, which is characterized by his solidarity and concern for the state of mind and social situation of his fellowman. Goytisolo's lifelong interest in confronting existential preoccupations has led him to create poetry dealing with basic spiritual needs, such as love, happiness, and fulfillment; he is also interested in studying the place of humankind in the world and its role in society. Goytisolo has distinguished himself not only as a creative writer but also as an anthologist of contemporary Catalonian and Cuban poetry.

José Agustín Goytisolo-Gay was born on 13 April 1928 in Barcelona. His great-grandfather Agustín Goytisolo, a Basque, had immigrated to Cuba when very young. There he made a fortune rapidly. In 1918 in Barcelona, José Agustín's father, José María Goytisolo, married Julia Gay, the eldest of the two daughters of Ricardo Gay and Marta Vives,

*Goytisolo and Blas de Otero on a balcony in Reus, 1956*

both Catalonians. José María and Julia had five children: Antonio, José Agustín, Juan, Marta, and Luis. Antonio died in 1927 at age seven.

José Agustín Goytisolo lived the first years of his life in the Bonanova and Sarriá neighborhoods of Barcelona. He, Juan, and Marta attended a Catholic school, the Colegio de las Teresas, in Barcelona. His childhood was drastically changed by the Spanish Civil War. During the war his family was forced to leave Barcelona and take refuge in Viladrau, a small town in Catalonia, until the war was over. However, on 17 March 1938 his mother, on a visit to her parents in Barcelona, was killed, a victim of a raid by Benito Mussolini's airplanes during a Nationalist bombardment. After two days of waiting, the Goytisolo family was notified of her death.

During the civil war food was scarce, and Goytisolo and his siblings used to steal watercress, pumpkin stems, potatoes, and chestnuts from the neighbors' vegetable gardens. After the war ended, José Agustín and Juan would stand in line for hours, in front of the local social service office, for bites of

bread or omelet. During the time he could not attend school he filled the empty hours playing with spent bullets, leftovers of the war, and he and Juan explored vacant houses until their father discovered their activities and reprimanded them.

During the summer of 1939 Goytisolo left Viladrau and went to Barcelona to prepare for his high-school entrance examination. He attended the Colegio de Jesuitas de Sarriá but was expelled in the fall of 1943; then his father transferred him and his younger brothers, Juan and Luis, to a much more liberal school, the Colegio de los Hermanos de la Doctrina Cristiana. (Juan was to become a well-known novelist.) José Augustín's early basic education was followed by specialized courses in mercantile-related subjects, intended to prepare him for a teaching career. In 1944 he started university studies in Barcelona and in Madrid, and he obtained a law degree in 1950 from the Universidad Central in Madrid. While finishing his law degree, he stayed in the Colegio Mayor Universitario Nuestra Señora de Guadalupe. This residence, located then in the Argüelles neighborhood, was first created for Latin-American young men who took courses in Spain, but Spaniards who had been awarded a scholarship could also stay there.

Drafted by the army in 1952, Goytisolo did his military service in Mahón. After that he began working on his first book, *El retorno* (The Return, 1955), and competed for the Adonais Prize. He won an *accésit* (honorable mention) in 1954 for the manuscript of *El retorno*. Later he went to work as an administrative adviser in a private water company which dispensed water to the city. Although Goytisolo was working on a full-time basis for the company, he never lost contact with his friends, the intellectuals and writers of *Laye* magazine. As he said in an unpublished interview in 1992, "Aunque la revista *Laye* fue cerrada por la censura mi amistad con Carlos Barral, Jaime Gil de Biedma, Gabriel Ferrater, Juan Ferrater y José María Castellet nunca se interrumpió. Vivíamos cerca, en la misma ciudad y asistíamos a la misma universidad. Los conocí desde siempre. Ellos han sido mis amigos de toda la vida" (Although the *Laye* magazine was discontinued by censorship, my friendship with Carlos Barral, Jaime Gil de Biedma, Gabriel and Juan Ferrater, and José María Castellet was never disrupted. We lived nearby, in the same city, and attended the same university. They were my lifetime friends).

Between 1944 and 1950 Goytisolo and his friends frequently participated in the university's literary conversational groups or in the ones at the bar called by the students the "Bar de Juanito." In 1950 and 1951 Goytisolo formed part of the literary group that met at the Turia bar; also, between 1951 and 1955, Goytisolo and his friends frequently met at the Boliche bar. In 1953 and 1960 he frequented the Cristal City bar and participated in all literary conversational groups that met there. In all these groups the participants spoke of poetry and expressed their thoughts through lively conversations. These meetings helped the poets to maintain their intellectual capabilities and to enliven the hours of their daily routines.

The tragic events during the civil war affected Goytisolo for life and influenced his writings. *El retorno* includes lyric poetry in a mournful tone. The book is an elegy dedicated to his late mother. In the poems he voices nostalgia for those days when his mother was still alive, and he urges her return:

> Vuelva el día
> vivido a transportarse, lejano,
> entre los chopos.
> Allí te esperaré
> . . . . . . . . . . . . .
> De nuevo en pie, siguiendo tu estatura,
> regresaré a la casa, lentamente,
> cuando todo suceda.

> (Return again [on] the day
> that lived by transporting itself, far away,
> among the poplar trees.
> Right there I will wait for you
> . . . . . . . . . . . . . . . . . . . . . . . .
> On my feet again, following your stature,
> I will return home, slowly,
> when everything is taking place.)

*Salmos al viento* (Psalms to the Wind, 1958), awarded the Boscán Prize of 1957, stresses social themes already dealt with in *El retorno* but this time focusing on human loneliness of existential origin. Irony and sarcasm blend as Goytisolo remembers his youth, when he used to walk around the neighborhoods of Madrid and Barcelona. He also describes, in a bittersweet tone, what he sees in the society in which he lives. He criticizes the bourgeoisie and its Francoist values. In general *Salmos al viento* is a denunciation of the social situation in 1950s Spain.

*Claridad* (Clarity, 1961) won the 1959 Ausìas March Prize in Castilian poetry, sponsored by the town councils of Gandía and Beniarjó in commemoration of the quincentenary of the death of Catalan writer Ausìas March. In *Claridad* Goytisolo insists on a poetry dealing with political issues and criticizing the political and social situation of Spain. At the same time, he challenges the rigid historical view of Spanish sociopolitical problems during the past two centuries and re-creates social reality through verses expressing disappointment and hope. The poet directly addresses political themes hoping for political changes.

*Años decisivos* (Decisive Years, 1961) is a compilation of Goytisolo's first three books: *El retorno, Salmos al viento,* and *Claridad*. When *Años decisivos* was published, Goytisolo caught the attention of those who were aware of the most recent tendencies of Spanish poetry. María Payeras Grau notes that the book was published by Literaturasa Publishing House as part of a promotional series aiming to help young writers who had difficulties in publishing their works.

*Algo sucede* (Something Happens, 1968) reflects a society in crisis because of the slow agony of the political system which followed the civil war. Goytisolo expresses in his poems a clear, precise exposition of valuable documentary facts.

*Bajo tolerancia* (Below Tolerance, 1973), like most of Goytisolo's books, is in essence a manifesto of rebelliousness against an unjust social system. The poet is concerned not only with the Spanish social system but also with Spanish-American reality, including that of Cuba and Peru. Goytisolo is also interested in the literary creations of Latin-American writers such as José Lezama Lima, among others. Besides irony, sarcasm, and criticism of society in general, the

*Cover for Goytisolo's 1981 collection of poetry, in which he praises love as a weapon against aging*

book also deals with the injustices a poet has to endure in society. Goytisolo points out that a poet receives credit for his work after his death, and Goytisolo draws a parallel between a poet and a prostitute: "Así son los poetas / las viejas prostitutas de la historia" (Thus are the poets / the old prostitutes of history). *Bajo tolerancia* is one of Goytisolo's most important books. It includes some of the most enriching, original poems of late-twentieth-century Spanish poetry. In this book Goytisolo has blended the lyricism of *El retorno* and the sarcasm of *Salmos al viento*. The long poems reach a momentum of maximum lyricism, and the verbal economy and carefully created imagery reflect not only Goytisolo's personal world but the world of his time.

*Taller de arquitectura* (Architecture Shop, 1977) offers an investigation of the human emotional condition, both by using historic and literary examples of known facts and by using Goytisolo's experiences. History, life, and literature, although different from one another, merge in this work. The city as a theme is presented in a positive way. Goytisolo thinks that architectural works should be linked to the necessities and comfort of the city residents. He has said that he is interested in architecture as a subject because he has a tendency to create, in his imagination, gloomy rooms, labyrinthine castles, streets in constant festivals, and mutant cities in which people behave in a bizarre way, as one can see in the following lines: "Ahora ya es tarde para lamentarse

*Writers Gabriel Celaya, Otero, Goytisolo, and Jaime Gil de Biedma*

y ahí quedan / escaleras absurdas parterres en los áticos pasillos increíbles / chimeneas pintadas de colores" (Now it is too late to complain and right there are left / absurd stairs boulevard gardens in the attic incredible corridors / colorful chimneys). Goytisolo believes that the architect and the poet have the same mission, to create for posterity.

In *Del tiempo y del olvido* (Of Time and Oblivion, 1977) Goytisolo considers the possibility of a reunion with the past. But finally he accepts the fact that bygone days will never return. He realizes that, in spite of his efforts to hold onto the past, life, like a river renewing its water, constantly changes its path. And one day the time to say farewell to memories will come, enabling him to start a new life. But his intentions of saying goodbye to memories of his mother are hindered because he cannot forget the day she left, never to return. His eagerness to detach himself from the past has been instrumental in the creation of a rich poetic language enhanced by a firm tone characteristic of all great nostalgic poetry.

*Palabras para Julia y otras canciones* (Words for Julia and Other Songs, 1980) presents a poetry of human solidarity and hope. In the following lines of the poem "Palabras para Julia" the poet looks toward the future and tells his daughter of the good things awaiting her: "Tu destino está en los demás / Tu futuro en tu propia vida / Tu dignidad es la de todos" (Your destiny is in everyone / Your future is in your own life / Your dignity is the dignity of everyone). Goytisolo teaches his daughter the goodness of life in spite of his own disappointments: "Tendrás amor / tendrás amigos" (You shall have love / you shall have friends). While looking toward the future through his daughter, he returns to his past, as if he wants to remind his readers that his present and his future are rooted in his past, primarily represented by his mother. For example, he named his daughter Julia, after his mother, whom he remembers in these lines: "Como la piel de un fruto suave / a la amenaza de los dientes / iluminada casi alegre / ibas camino de la muerte" (Tender as a soft-skin fruit / before threatening teeth / glowing gingerly / you went toward the pathway of death).

*Los pasos del cazador* (The Steps of the Hunter, 1980) is set in a rural environment. An urban man disenchanted by the city gives up his habitat and escapes to the country, where he regains his individuality, which he had lost among the thousands of city dwellers. A rifle on his shoulders and a woman's love are

*Goytisolo, circa 1986*

the sole companions of the man when he goes on hunting trips. In *Los pasos del cazador* Goytisolo shares with the reader his most rewarding experiences: hunting and love. Hunting partially fills the emptiness of his life since he lost his mother. Writing about hunting helps him bring back to life his earlier hunting experiences.

*A veces gran amor* (At Times Great Love, 1981) is a book made mainly of poems from other books. Reusing the same protagonists is Goytisolo's way of keeping contact with his characters: he introduces them again in new books without changing their identities. The young protagonists help him establish a dialogue with the past. *A veces gran amor* is a hymn to the capability to experience love. For Goytisolo love is a weapon against aging. As Arcipreste de Hita said in a well-known poem, "ove de las mujeres a veces gran amor" (I had for women at times great love).

*Sobre las circunstancias* (About the Circumstances, 1983) presents an urban man detached from himself. Even surrounded by luxury, he is impoverished by his human condition, which is determined by his basic daily needs:

Entonces yo me afeito con cuidado.
Pongo una de mis caras más miserables

guardo un par de alkaseltzers en el bolsillo
e inauguro mi vida social.

(Then I shave carefully.
I put on one of my saddest faces
pop a couple of Alka Seltzers in my pocket
and start my social life.)

Goytisolo opens the book with a list of circumstances linked to an individual's life, circumstances that help shape one's destiny in society. The protagonist, in bourgeois society, faces all the limitations and frustrations of those who expect to attain the impossible from life.

In collaboration with Juan Ballesta, Goytisolo wrote four books for children: *El lobito bueno* (1983), *El príncipe malo* (1983), *La bruja hermosa* (1984), and *El pirata honrado* (1984). These books present the contradictions in certain aspects of life.

In *Final de un adiós* (End of a Goodbye, 1984) the longing for maternal love reappears as alien to death. Painful memories make life difficult. According to Goytisolo, life is not hard, but memories and evocations are difficult to endure. In *Final de un adiós* his infancy seems farther away and definitely lost. A man who remembers is an adult experiencing life in all its crudity. He faces the awful truth that childhood is gone and that it is impossible to become a child again. Goytisolo cannot keep alive the child within him. The elegy is tainted with rage and refusal to be passive: "era el dolor el duelo no deseado / que me empujaba al odio" (it was pain the unwelcome grief / that put me on the verge of hate). Rage and guilt wipe away a smile from the child's face and defeat the man, snatching him away from peace and happiness.

In *El rey mendigo* (The Beggar King, 1988) Goytisolo again tries to analyze the human condition by examining the mental and emotional states of some people in the most crucial moments of their lives. He bases his work on his own experiences or on facts known to him. Referring to the book, he once said: "History, life, and literature, although distinct from each other ... are always blended in my sensibility." In *El rey mendigo* the presence of Goytisolo's father replaces the presence of his mother. The image of a young woman walking to her death is replaced by the frail figure of an ill, elderly man.

Goytisolo belongs to an energetic group of writers of international importance. He aims to reproduce reality as he sees it, transformed by his imagination; while one aspect of his writing focuses on daily life, portraying social, political, and economic situations of contemporary society, another aspect of Goytisolo's poetry aims to explore man's state of mind and his role in society. Goytisolo blends irony, sarcasm, tenderness, and sadness in his creations. Individuality and collectivity interact in his poems, because he writes for everyone who, like himself, lives in a disgusting society.

In 1990 Carmen Riera gave the name "Escuela de Barcelona" (School of Barcelona) to a group formed by Goytisolo and his friends, also sometimes known as the "Grupo del 1950s" (Group of the 1950s). According to Goytisolo the word *group* (not *generation*) should be used to classify his circle of Spanish poets in Barcelona.

Goytisolo is preparing a new book, titled "Novísima oda a Barcelona" (Very New Ode to Barcelona), to be published soon. His *La noche le es propicia* (The Night is Favorable) was published in September 1992 and was awarded the 1993 Premio de la Crítica de Poesía en Lengua Castellana. Goytisolo frequently travels in Spain, Europe, the United States, and Hispanic America. He was named a member of the Hispanic Society of America in December 1991. José Agustín Goytisolo lives in Barcelona with his wife, María Asunción Carandell de Goytisolo; they were married on 24 September 1955.

**References:**

José García Nieto, " 'Poesía eres tú' y una feliz parodia escrita en nuestros días," *Boletín de la Real Academia Española*, 240 ( January–April 1987): 21–28;

Juan Goytisolo, *Coto vedado* (Barcelona: Seix Barral, 1985);

Goytisolo, *En los reinos de taifa* (Barcelona: Seix Barral, 1986);

Antonio Jiménez Millán, " *Bajo tolerancia:* Del sarcasmo a la utopía," *Insula*, 45 ( July–August 1990): 67–69;

Manuel López de Aviada, "La ironía como rasgo generacional definidor en los comienzos del grupo del 50: Apostillas a tres poemas representativos de José Agustín Goytisolo, Jaime Gil de Biedma y Angel González," *Diálogos Hispánicos de Amsterdam*, 9 (1990): 45–46;

Juan José Mandu and Pere Peña, "El amor y la identidad poética del personaje en la obra de José Agustín Goytisolo," *Insula*, 45 ( July–August 1990): 62–63;

Emilio Miró, "José Agustín Goytisolo," *Insula*, 36 (March 1981);

Miró, "Los 'años decisivos' de José Agustín Goytisolo: *Retorno y Claridad*," *Insula*, 45 ( July–August 1990): 63–65;

María Payeras Grau, "Literatura Sociedad Anónima," *Insula*, 45 ( July–August 1990): 8–11;

Kay Pritchett, " 'Becquer en Veruela, julio de 1864' by José Agustín Goytisolo: A New Style and Voice," *Anales de la Literatura Española Contemporánea*, 3 (1988): 249–259;

Carmen Riera, "Amistad a lo largo," *Quimera*, 74 (February 1988): 48–55;

Riera, "De *El retorno* a *Final de un adiós*: Algunas notas sobre la elegía en José Agustín Goytisolo," *Cuadernos Hispanoamericanos*, 429 (March 1986): 155–167;

Riera, *La escuela de Barcelona: Barral, Gil de Biedma, Goytisolo: El núcleo poético de la generación de los 50* (Barcelona: Anagrama, 1988);

Riera, *Hay veneno y jazmín en tu tinta: Aproximaciones a la poesía de José Agustín Goytisolo* (Barcelona: Anthropos, 1991);

Riera, "El núcleo poético de la 'Escuela de Barcelona': Vocación de modernidad," *Insula*, 45 ( July–August 1990): 7–8;

Josep María Sala Valldaura, "El lenguaje de *Salmos al viento*," *Insula*, 45 ( July–August 1990): 60–61;

Jordi Villaronga, "De un abrir y cerrar los ojos: Una aproximación a la obra poética de José Agustín Goytisolo," *Insula*, 45 ( July–August 1990): 60–61.

# Miguel Hernández
## (30 October 1910 – 28 March 1942)

### J. Eric Diehl
#### *Collège Montmorency*

BOOKS: *Perito en lunas* (Murcia: Sudeste, 1933);

*Quién te ha visto y quién te ve y sombra de lo que eras* (Madrid: Cruz & Raya, 1934);

*El rayo que no cesa* (Madrid: Héroe, 1936); translated by Michael Smith as *Unceasing Lightning* (Dublin: Dedalus, 1986); enlarged as *El rayo que no cesa y otros poemas,* edited by Rafael Alberti (Buenos Aires: Ferreiro, 1942); enlarged again as *El rayo que no cesa; El silbo vulnerado; Poesías publicadas en El Gallo Crisis,* edited by José María de Cossío (Madrid & Buenos Aires: Espasa-Calpe, 1949);

*Viento del pueblo* (Valencia: Socorro Rojo, 1937);

*El labrador de más aire* (Valencia: Nuestro Pueblo, 1937);

*Teatro en la guerra* (Valencia: Nuestro Pueblo, 1937);

*El hombre acecha* (Valencia: Subsecretaría de Propaganda, 1939);

*Sino sangriento y otros poemas* (Havana: Verónica/ Altolaguirre, 1939);

*Seis poemas inéditos y nueve más,* edited by Vicente Ramos and Manuel Molina (Alicante: Ifach, 1951);

*Antología poética de Miguel Hernández,* edited by Francisco Martínez Marín (Orihuela: Aura, 1951);

*Obra escogida,* edited by Arturo del Hoyo (Madrid: Aguilar, 1952);

*Dentro de luz y otras prosas,* edited by María de Gracia Ifach (Madrid: Arión, 1957);

*Cancionero y romancero de ausencias,* edited by Elvio Romero (Buenos Aires: Lautaro, 1958);

*Los mejores versos de Miguel Hernández,* edited by Molina (Buenos Aires: Nuestra América, 1958);

*Los hijos de la piedra* (Buenos Aires: Quetzal, 1959);

*Obras completas,* edited by Romero and Andrés Ramón Vázquez (Buenos Aires: Losada, 1960);

*Antología,* edited by Ifach (Buenos Aires: Losada, 1961);

*Canto de independencia* (Havana: Tertulia, 1962);

*Poemas de adolescencia; Perito en lunas; Otros poemas* (Buenos Aires: Losada, 1963);

*El hombre acecha; Cancionero y romancero de ausencias; Últimos poemas* (Buenos Aires: Losada, 1963);

*Imagen de tu huella; El rayo que no cesa; Viento del pueblo; El silbo vulnerado; Otros poemas* (Buenos Aires: Losada, 1963);

*Poemas,* edited by José Luis Cano and Josefina Manresa (Barcelona: Plaza & Janés, 1964);

*Poesía* (Havana: Consejo Nacional de Cultura, 1964);

*Poesías,* edited by Jacinto Luis Guereña (Paris: Seghers, 1964; Madrid: Taurus, 1967; enlarged edition, Madrid: Narcea, 1973);

*Dieci sonetti inediti di Miguel Hernández,* edited by Dario Puccini (Rome: Società Filologica Romana, 1966);

*Unos poemas olvidados de Miguel Hernández,* selected by A. Fernández Molina (Caracas: Universal, 1967);

*La prosa poética de Miguel Hernández (Tres obras desconocidas; Valoración),* edited by Juan Cano Ballesta (Palma de Mallorca: Papeles de Son Armadans, 1968);

*Cinco sonetos inéditos,* compiled by Dario Puccini (Caracas: Revista Nacional de Cultura, 1968);

*Poemas de amor,* edited by Leopoldo de Luis (Madrid: Alfaguara, 1969);

*El hombre y su poesía,* edited by Cano Ballesta (Madrid: Cátedra, 1974);

*Obra poética completa,* edited by Luis and Jorge Urrutia (Bilbao: Zero, 1976);

*Reformatorio para adultos 1942* (N.p., 1976);

*Teatro* (Havana: Arte y Literatura, 1976 [i.e., 1977]);

*Poesía y prosa de guerra y otros textos olvidados,* edited by Cano Ballesta and Robert Marrast (Pamplona: Peralta, 1977);

*Poemas sociales de guerra y de muerte,* edited by Luis (Madrid: Alianza, 1977);

*Teatro completo,* edited by Vicente Pastor Ibáñez, Manuel Rodríguez Maciá, and José Oliva (Madrid: Ayuso, 1978);

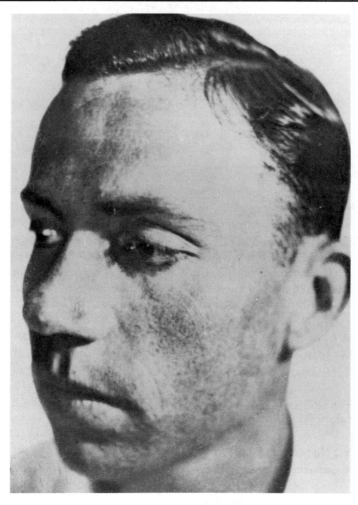

*Miguel Hernández in Madrid, 1938*

*Poesías completas,* edited by Sánchez Vidal (Madrid: Aguilar, 1979);

*Veinticuatro sonetos inéditos,* edited by José Carlos Rovira (Alicante: Instituto de Estudios Juan Gil-Albert, 1986);

*Prosas líricas y aforismos,* edited by Ifach (Madrid: Torre, 1986);

*El torero más valiente,* edited by Agustín Sánchez Vidal (Madrid: Alianza, 1987);

*Dos cuentos para Manolillo (para cuando sepa leer),* edited by Rovira (Madrid: Palas Atenea, 1988);

*Ultimas ausencias para un niño,* edited by Rovira (Madrid: Palas Atenea, 1988);

*Obra completa,* 2 volumes, edited by Sánchez Vidal, Rovira, and Alemany Bay (Madrid: Espasa-Calpe, 1992).

**Editions in English:** *Songbook of Absences: Selected Poems of Miguel Hernández,* translated by Thomas C. Jones, Jr. (Washington, D.C.: Charioteer, 1972);

*Miguel Hernández and Blas de Otero: Selected Poems,* edited by Timothy Baland and Hardie St. Martin, includes translations by Baland, St. Martin, Robert Bly, and James Wright (Boston: Beacon, 1972);

*The Unending Lightning: Selected Poems of Miguel Hernández,* translated by Edwin Honig (Riverdale-on-Hudson, New York: Sheep Meadow, 1990).

PLAY PRODUCTIONS: *El refugiado,* Alicante, Teatro Principal, 27 April 1938;

*Los hijos de la piedra,* Buenos Aires, Teatro del Pueblo, 11 April 1946;

*El labrador de más aire,* Madrid, Teatro Muñoz Seca, 17 October 1972;

*Quién te ha visto y quién te ve y sombra de lo que eras (auto sacramental),* Orihuela, Teatro Circo de Orihuela, 13 February 1977.

OTHER: "Poemas de Miguel Hernández (1930–1932) no recogidos hasta la fecha," in *Literatura alicantina,* edited by Vicente Ramos (Madrid & Barcelona: Alfaguara, 1965);

"Miguel Hernández," in *Modern European Poetry,* edited by Willis Barnstone (New York: Bantam, 1966).

When Concepción Gilabert Giner de Hernández gave birth to her second son, Miguel, both she and her husband, Miguel Hernández Sánchez, a poor herdsman and dealer in sheep and goats, took for granted that their son would soon be hard at work helping with the family business, eventually taking it over with his older brother, Vicente. From a very early age the young Miguel was expected to perform tedious and menial tasks around the house and stable. A lengthy, enriched education was out of the question, both for economic and sociocultural reasons; so, instead of starting school at the usual age, he was forced for years to shepherd his father's flock and to sell the milk he had drawn with his own hands. This grueling, solitary experience had a profound impact on the sensitive youth. His work on the farm led him to establish a special bond with nature, and he later drew on that experience in his poetry.

At first Hernández's father had no inkling of the boy's predilection for literature, but when his passion for reading and writing became evident, his dour, cantankerous father tried hard to discourage such impractical pursuits and frivolous daydreams. However, the determined young goatherd had made a conscious decision to become a poet. Gifted with an ability to versify and a phenomenal memory, he survived a difficult apprenticeship during which, with the help and advice of close friends and mentors, he managed to learn Hispanic literature and culture, particularly the poetry and theater, at the same time mastering a wide variety of styles of poetry from earlier decades and other cultures. Against enormous odds, he broke loose from the severe limitations of his humble beginnings to emerge as one of the greatest and best-loved Spanish poets.

Miguel Hernández Gilabert was born on 30 October 1910 in the town of Orihuela, near Murcia, in southeastern Spain. Orihuela is in a valley watered by the Segura River and shaded by the peaks of the Sierra de la Muela. This rich agricultural land, with palm trees, orange groves, and lush flower and vegetable gardens, supported a community bound by proudly maintained traditions and by allegiance to the ubiquitous and ultraconservative Catholic church, which had not changed much since Orihuela was reclaimed from its Muslim inhabitants in the thirteenth century.

Hernández was one of seven children, including his brother Vicente, two younger sisters – Elvira and Encarnación – and three other siblings who died at early ages. When he was three years old the family moved to a rather poor district on La Calle de Arriba, inhabited for the most part by herdsmen, shoemakers, bricklayers, and their families. The Hernándezes' property, however, did provide them with certain amenities: a stable, a well, a large garden, and an orchard that eventually included mulberry, lemon, and fig trees – some planted by the poet himself. It is impossible to overemphasize the importance to Hernández of this garden and orchard – "huerto mío" (my orchard), as he referred to it affectionately – a small, quasi-Arcadian oasis of beauty and calm where he wrote several of his earliest poems.

Hernández's mother, known as Concheta, was submissive, timid, quiet, and long-suffering but also ready to protect her son as best she could from the unjust criticism and often harsh treatment he received at the hands of his father, Miguel, who was obstinate, harsh, authoritarian, and choleric to the point of being violent. Throughout his lifetime, in fact, the poet suffered from painful headaches which (as he wrote his wife, Josefina Manresa de Hernández, from prison on 29 January 1940) he suspected might have been caused in part by the frequent blows to the head that he had received from his father.

Almost until the age of nine, Hernández had as his "school" the garden and orchard around his house, the hills of the Sierra de la Muela, and the nearby waters of the Segura River. Throughout his poetry are images assimilated during that often difficult, yet pastoral, youth.

Much has been made of Hernández's spectacular rise from obscure shepherd to literary giant, and many a myth has arisen around his self-education: as Yolanda Guerrero wrote in *El País* (13 April 1992): "Su formación escolar fue corta, apenas un año. El hambre pudo más. Abandonó los libros por las cabras, pero la fidelidad del 'niño' . . . hacia la literatura le regresaron al primer amor" (He spent a short time in school, hardly a year. Hunger was a stronger calling. He left his schoolbooks for his goats, but his loyalty . . . toward literature made him return to his first love). The facts are that he was in school from age nine to age fifteen; he was then unceremoniously forced to withdraw by his father. However, during his early preschool years Hernández was not entirely cut off from school; his

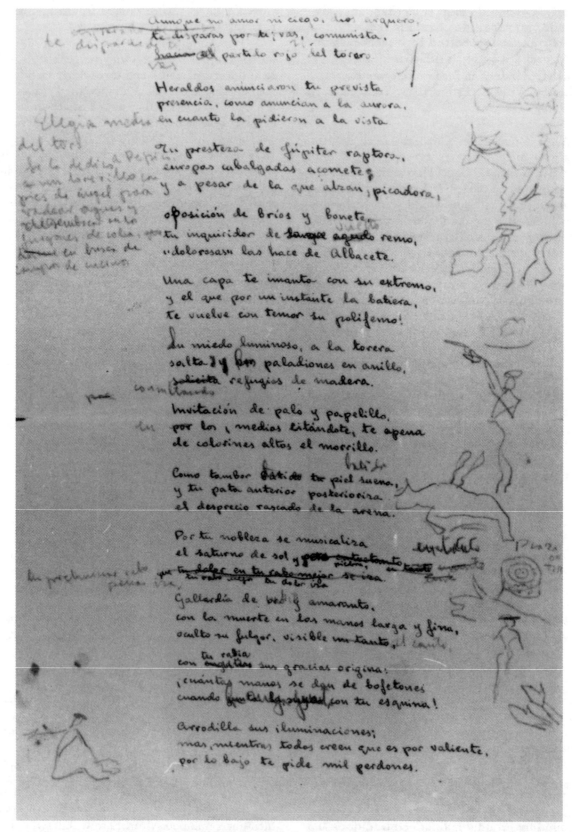

*Page 1 of the manuscript for Hernández's "Elegía media del toro," written circa 1933 and collected in Obra poética completa, 1976 (by permission of the Heirs of Miguel Hernández)*

older brother, Vicente, was enrolled in school, and Hernández would often help him with his homework, learning practically as much in the process. When he was almost nine years old, Hernández began his formal schooling at Escuela del Ave María, a school annex for poor children located in the shadows of another school, the Colegio de Santo Domingo de Orihuela, a Jesuit-run, upper-middle-class private college that had been attended by, among others, the novelist Gabriel Miró, also a native of Orihuela. In 1923, at age thirteen, Hernández, an excellent student and already far better educated than the vast majority of his social class, was honored by an invitation to study at the college and was the only disadvantaged student in the group, an "alumno de bolsillo pobre" (empty-pocketed student), as one friend called him.

There he became enthralled by Spanish literature, especially drama and poetry, and he was soon reciting poems to large audiences and playing important roles in school plays. His Jesuit teachers had suggested to his parents that he consider a vocation in the priesthood, though Hernández felt no such inclination himself, and the teachers had offered to pay his way through school.

However, he had no choice in the matter, for in March 1935, when he was fifteen — and rated first in his class — his father obliged him to leave the college because he was needed to help tend his father's growing herd and to sell the milk. Hernández was devastated by his father's decision and longed to be back with his Jesuit "fathers" and his classmates. One common thread in the lives of so many of Hernández's contemporaries is their education, erudition, and worldliness; unlike them, he was rigidly forbidden to indulge in such interests by his uneducated and overly practical father, who saw no use for formal education or for what his son wrote and recited. Throughout most of his youth Hernández was in conflict with his father over his desire to read and study, and later over his ambition to become a poet.

Fortunately Hernández had spent enough time at the Colegio de Santo Domingo to enable him to continue nurturing his desire for knowledge and love of literature. There were, of course, neither books at home nor money with which to buy them, but his single-minded determination to read led him to borrow them from many sources. While a college student, Hernández had been influenced and aided by don Luis Almarcha, the local vicar and founder of the Federation of Catholic Farmers' Unions — and later bishop of León — who was amazed by the young student's thirst for knowledge and tireless energy in pursuing an education. Almarcha became

one of the poet's greatest benefactors, referring to him affectionately as "Miguel . . . y mártir" (Miguel . . . and martyr). The vicar loaned him books and helped him in every possible way.

Among Hernández's other favorite sources of books were the local libraries, especially those of the Casino, a sociopolitical club, and the Círculo de Bellas Artes de Orihuela, whose employees happily encouraged his literary pursuits. Among his college classmates were two in particular who regularly provided him with books and literary discussion: Augusto Pescador Sarget, who became a well-known professor of philosophy and dean of several Hispano-American universities; and José Marín Gutierrez, who wrote under and became known by the nom de plume Ramón Sijé.

Hernández read everything he could get his hands on: works by classical writers such as Garcilaso de la Vega, San Juan de la Cruz, Luis de León, Miguel de Cervantes, Tirso de Molina, Lope de Vega, Luis de Góngora, and Francisco Quevedo; by more-modern writers such as Juan Ramón Jiménez, Rubén Darío, Gustavo Adolfo Bécquer, Antonio Machado, Jorge Guillén, Rafael Alberti, and Federico García Lorca; by popular writers such as José Marí Gabriel y Galán, Pérez Escrich, and Luis de Val; and by foreign writers such as Paul Verlaine and Paul Valéry. But Hernández especially loved the works of his fellow *oriolano* Miró, for the richness of his language and the splendor of his imagery. Miró was perhaps the first writer to have shaken the complacent, orthodox Catholic establishment of Orihuela, and Hernández adopted both Miró's fascination with words and images and his critical stance toward the local conservative religious hierarchy. They also shared a love of Orihuela and its lush surroundings, a love that can be seen throughout their works, which exude pantheistic sensuality.

Whenever Hernández was not tending herd or doing chores, he was reading or discussing literature with friends. For example, he and his friend Carlos Fenoll, whose father was a baker, often carried on such discussions in the streets as they delivered their milk and bread. One of his habitual reading places was the bedroom he shared with Vicente. Another of Hernández's reading places, perhaps his favorite, was out on the Orihuelan plains and hillsides where he took his herd to graze. He read relentlessly day after day, so bent on his task that he occasionally lost track of his flock.

Soon the zealous reader began trying his hand at writing poems of his own, using as often as not a goat's back for a desk. These poems were shaped and inspired as much by the numbing routine of his

*A 1936 photograph of Hernández that he inscribed to Josefina
Manresa, whom he married the following year*

pastoral chores as by the poets whose works he
read. At eighteen he started writing poems in classical *arte mayor* (major art) and *arte menor* (minor art)
meters — mostly simple, bucolic poems, quintes-
sentially Virgilian, reworking the archaic forms and
grand vocabulary he learned from the great poets.

His day-to-day chores provided a common
motif in many early poems, such as "En cuclillas,
ordeño una cabrita y un sueño" (Squatting on My
Heels, I Milk My Goat and My Dream, in *Obra completa,* 1992), a short poem which illustrates his
early predilection for creating visual and auditory
metaphors out of the down-to-earth scenes of everyday life. In "Aprendiz de Chivo" (The Appren-

tice Kid, also in *Obra completa*) Hernández depicts
the miracle of birth, the awkward yet splendid
first moments of a newborn goat as it slowly
awakens to the pleasures of its mother's milk and
the sheer joy of being alive. In "Leyendo" (Reading, also in *Obra completa*) a sequence of visual images captures the highlights of the young Hernández's
daily ritual, savored down to the last precious
rays of dusky sunlight:

Me pongo sentado. Leo.
(La muriente luz se enjambia
fingiendo una gran Alhambra
de mármol cristaloideo.)

(Trunca el ave su gorgeo.
Por el oriente descuella
la noche.
                    ¿Nace una estrella?)
No quedan luces.... No leo.

(I now sit straight up. I read.
[The swarming rays of dying day
trace a grand Alhambra
of crystallized marble.]

[The bird cuts short its cheery tune.
From the east the night
descends.
                    Is that a star I do not know?]
There's no more light.... I cannot read.)

Although many of Hernández's early poems probably have not survived, about forty of them were
published for the first time in *Obra completa,* which
includes over one hundred previously unpublished
works.

In the years immediately after Hernández left
school, probably the greatest influence on the
young poet was the circle of friends that grew out of
poetry meetings held at the bakery run by the
Fenoll family on Calle de Arriba near his house.
Señor Fenoll had a considerable reputation in the
neighborhood for his *coplas* (popular verses), and he
passed on his passion to his children, most notably
Carlos, who was an inseparable part of Hernández's
social and intellectual life. Sijé (Marín Gutierrez)
was drawn to Hernández for the latter's poetry and
intellect. For years this trio regularly held court
within the warm, welcoming confines of the bakery,
where, while waiting for the dough to rise or surrounded by the heady aroma of freshly baked
bread, they recited poems or dramatic works to
each other or tried out their own verse on friends.
They eventually managed to draw into their *tertulia*
(literary circle) several of those who lived in the vi-
cinity, such as Jesús Poveda and Manuel Molino,
who would sit in ever-increasing numbers listening
to or reciting poetry and participating in dramatic
recitals. Miró and Orihuela were the two forces that
joined and held the group together, and the main attraction, as he had been while a student at college,
was Hernández, in Carlos Fenoll's words "un genial
actor, tan bueno como poeta" (a genius actor, as
well as a good poet). Always drawn to the theater,
Hernández helped the tertulia form a theater group,
which they called the *Farsa,* after the drama publication of the same name.

Sijé became Hernández's mentor and guru,
suggesting that he study in great depth the six-
teenth- and seventeenth-century Spanish poets and
dramatists and teaching him to fashion his verse
with particular care for allegory, semantics, and
symbols. Finally, one of his poems, "Pastoril,"
which he had written in his beloved orchard, was
published in the *Pueblo de Orihuela* on 13 January
1930; his career as a published poet had begun. Obviously the work of a neophyte, this poem shows
the unmistakable influence of de la Cruz, Garcilaso,
and Darío, as well as the counterinfluences of Romantic poetry and popular verse.

Sijé got Hernández invitations to recite his poetry both at the Casino and at the Círculo Católico,
but reading his poetry to listeners at the Casino was
no match for doing so for his friends, among whom
he could give full vent to his emotions and his penchant for dramatic expression. Not loath to use
coarse language among friends, in 1936 Hernández
wrote Fenoll from Madrid: "Vale más un 'me cago
en ...' entre ellos, que un elegio de ninguno de
éstos" (Better an "I don't give a shit for ..." from
them [his friends] than heaps of praise from those
others [big-city literati]).

On 1 May 1930 his old friend Almarcha, writing from Madrid, asked Hernández to write a poem
in honor of human labor; the result was "Al
trabajo" (To Work, in *Obra completa*), clearly influenced by the poet's readings of Darío – especially
his "Marcha triunfal" (Triumphal March, in *Cantos
de vida y esperanza* [Songs of Life and Experience,
1905]). Read aloud by a laborer, Hernández's poem
was very well received, encouraging his long-held
dream of traveling to Madrid, the cultural and intellectual center of the country and the logical place to
go – as it had been for Bécquer and countless others
before him. But it was at least a year before
Hernández could finally make that first trip. On one
occasion he tried to join the army by registering for
the draft, but his number was never called, much to
his disappointment.

He became involved with Juventudes So-
cialistas de Orihuela, serving as its president, alongside directors Pescador Sarget, José Bellod, and José
María Ballesteros. In the spring of 1931 Hernández
won first prize with his poem "Canto a Valencia"
(Song to Valencia, in *Obra completa*) in a regional poetry competition in Elche sponsored by Orfeón
Ilicitano (a cultural association). Disappointed that
the prize turned out to be only an ornamental ink-
stand, an unfortunate choice for a poet who wrote
exclusively in pencil, Hernández nevertheless felt
more encouraged than ever to make his long-post-
poned journey to Madrid. Chief among those nudg-
ing him in that direction was Sijé's friend don José
Martínez Arenas, who gave Hernández a letter of

*Hernández reading a eulogy for writer Ramón Sijé, at the dedication of*
*a plaza named for Sijé in their hometown, Orihuela, 14 April 1936*
*(Collection of the Heirs of Miguel Hernández)*

introduction to Concha de Albornoz, daughter of the minister of justice. Hernández's father said that, when his son ran out of food (which his father felt would surely be soon), he could always come home.

Hernández had hardly arrived in Madrid on 30 November 1931 when his boundless enthusiasm was dispelled by the cool reception he met with in the cold, unfriendly Spanish metropolis, which might just as well have been a foreign city. The tension caused in Hernández by the differences between big-city and country life was to affect him and pervade his poetry at every stage of his life.

When his long-anticipated visit to Concha de Albornoz did not open the doors he had hoped, Hernández visited literary critic Ernesto Giménez Caballero in December 1931, but there, too, any hopes for a quick solution to his problems were dashed when the critic wrote a mildly ironic article about him in the *Gaceta Literaria* (14 January 1932). Another article, written by Francisco Martínez

Corbalán for *Estampa* (22 February), was much more positive: "Este es el hombre. Tiene lo que no se compra; le falta lo que se puede adquirir" (This is the man. He has that which cannot be bought; he lacks that which can be learned). Neither article, however, had much impact in Madrid circles. Nevertheless, Hernández managed to survive through the winter until 15 May, thanks to old school friends Pescador Sarget and Bellod, who were attending the university in Madrid; they lent him food, money, and books and continued to encourage his writing.

Just before Hernández returned to Orihuela, Giménez Caballero published one of Hernández's poems, "Reloj rústico" (Rustic Clock, now in *Obra completa*), in the *Gaceta Literaria* (1 May 1932), but this attention was too little and too late to keep the disillusioned poet in Madrid any longer. Desperate for the money for a ticket home, he decided to use a friend's unused railway ticket, but, not having the proper travel documents with him when he was stopped by the Guardia Civil, he was promptly arrested and imprisoned – the first of two such arrests that left indelible impressions on Hernández. He was obliged to contact his family and friends for funds to get him out of jail, where he remained for several days. He felt that his six months in Madrid had been a disaster; help from the cultural powers had not been forthcoming, nor would it be for years to come.

Back in Orihuela, Hernández at first worked as a bookkeeper for the Globo, a fabric company, but later he found a better (though still low-paying) job as a clerk in a notary's office. While out celebrating at a carnival with his friends on a hot August day in 1932, he saw Josefina Manresa among a crowd of girls and began flirting with her. The daughter of an officer of the Guardia Civil, and a seamstress by trade, she was beautiful, shy, and easily embarrassed. She ignored Hernández completely, retreated to the safety of her circle of friends, and promptly forgot him, unaware that she had changed the course of his life and her own and would inspire some of his greatest poetry. He, on the other hand, was totally smitten from the moment he saw her and would remain so throughout their lengthy courtship and eventual marriage.

Sijé's influence on Hernández became especially strong following his return in seeming disgrace from Madrid, at that time a hotbed of political and cultural ferment, awash in philosophies to suit every taste. One in particular, neo-Góngorism, propelled by traditionalist fervor, had coalesced around celebrations in 1927 honoring the three hundredth anniversary of the death of Góngora, the poet of verbal enigma. The movement had proven irresistible to both Sijé and Hernández. Among the many books that Sijé suggested his friend read and reread were Góngora's *Fábula de Polifemo* (Fable of Polyphemus, 1613) and *Soledades* (Solitudes, also 1613), as well as books by modern imitators, such as Gerardo Diego's *Fábula de Equis y Zeda* (1932) and Rafael Alberti's *Cal y canto* (Stone and Mortar, 1929).

Under Sijé's tutelage, and entranced by neo-Góngorism's hermetic imagery, labyrinthine metaphors, and classical forms such as the *octava de arte mayor,* Hernández was hard at work composing his first book, "Poliedros" – published as *Perito en lunas* (Lunar Expert, 1933) on the advice of his publisher, Raimundo de los Reyes. Hernández was unaware that in literary circles interest in that style had already peaked and was rapidly waning. He would never have been able to publish the book had Al-

marcha not loaned him the money, later refusing to take back the loan. Almarcha did not like the style of the book, telling Hernández: "Mis gustos literarios no van por ahí" (my literary tastes do not include such as this). The book did not get the attention for which Hernández had hoped from the critics, probably because his hermetic style was beyond the scope of most uninitiated readers, though it was fully intentional, as he explained in "Mi concepto del poema" (My Concept of the Poem, in *Obra completa*):

El poema no puede presentársenos Venus o desnudo. Los poemas desnudos son la anatomía de los poemas. ¿Y habrá algo más horrible que un esqueleto? Guardad, poetas, el secreto del poema: esfinge. Que sepan arrancárselo como una corteza. ¡Oh, la naranja: qué delicioso secreto bajo un ámbito a lo mundo!

(Poems should not appear nude or Venuslike. Nude poems are poetic anatomy. Could there be anything more horrible than a skeleton? Poets, guard well the secrets of your poems: sphinx. Make the reader grasp the peel of meaning. Oh, orange: what delicious secrets lie hidden within your tiny world!)

Although Hernández had absorbed through his reading the styles and techniques of baroque pastoral poetry, his "lunar" Arcadia was as far removed from its aristocratic source as Hernández's "huerta-vergel" (orchard-garden) was from the gardens of Aranjuez (near Madrid). Beneath the artifice of his *culteranismo* (art for the sake of art) conceits, the quality of the poetry shines through the regional themes, rustic flavors, and popular images intimately linked with the common elements of life on the land: wells and irrigation systems; trees and vegetation; bulls and roosters; and palms and snakes – proof of Hernández's deep attachment to the natural world around him, the wellspring of his pantheism.

Dismayed by the critics' lack of enthusiasm for his work, on 10 April 1933 Hernández wrote Lorca a letter denouncing them passionately, saying that his book had "más personalidad, más valentía, más cojones . . . que el que casi todos los poetas consagrados a los que, si se les quitara la firma, se les confundiría la voz" (more personality, more valor, more balls . . . than all the works of most well-known poets, who all sound alike, except for their signatures). Lorca replied: "Tu libro es fuerte, tiene muchas cosas de interés y revela a los buenos ojos pasión de hombre, pero no tienes más c. . ., como tú dices" (Your book is powerful, has much that is interesting, and reveals the soul of a man of passion, but

*Hernández (kneeling) in Madrid with fellow members of the Fifth Regiment of the Republican Army, shortly after the start of the Spanish Civil War (Collection of the Heirs of Miguel Hernández)*

you do not have more b. . . , as you say). Lorca refers to "c . . ." rather than "cojones," managing to put some distance between himself and the more plebeian Hernández. Yet Lorca encouraged Hernández, telling him to be patient and trust in his innate ability. Though with different backgrounds and educations, both poets admired each other's work.

Everyone who knew Hernández well has testified to his probity and genuine goodness, yet at least on one occasion he employed his verbal skills against one particular individual. In fall 1932 the writers Carmen Conde and Antonio Oliver, in conjunction with the Universidad Popular de Cartagena, organized a special ceremony and meeting in Orihuela in honor of Miró. The conference was opened by Sijé, followed by Hernández's reading from his works. The keynote speaker, Giménez Caballero, who had written so patronizingly about Hernández earlier in 1932 and had just come back

from a trip to Italy, disrupted the conference by attacking Miró's aesthetic principles; his speech drew the ire of many in attendance and caused an uproar, resulting in the arrest and brief detention of Hernández and several others, including Conde and Oliver, who soon became Hernández's close friends and admirers. Perhaps in response to this provocation, Hernández dedicated the twelfth poem of *Perito en lunas* to Giménez Caballero. Titled "Lo abominable," the poem uses complicated metaphors to laud the utilitarian marvels of the common toilet, showing that Hernández may indeed have gotten the last word where Giménez Caballero was concerned.

With the publication of *Perito en lunas* Hernández had finally proved himself a full-fledged poet with uncanny ability. His career took off rapidly from that point, evolving from the hermetic baroque style of *Perito en lunas* through the sensual love poems and quasi-religious themes of early versions of *El silbo vulnerado* (The Injured Whistle, post-humously published in 1949), to the crystal clarity and sexual candor of the sonnets in later versions of *El silbo vulnerado* and *Imagen de tu huella* (Image of Your Footprint, published in 1963), which were reworked in Hernández's first major work, *El rayo que no cesa* (1936; translated as *Unceasing Lightning*, 1986).

In order to hold Hernández's wavering interest in traditional forms, Sijé repeatedly urged his friend to write poetry and criticism for *Destellos* and *Voluntad,* two journals that he edited. In 1933, unsatisfied with those journals, Sijé conceived a new journal, the *Gallo Crisis: Libertad y Tiranía,* a neo-Catholic publication inspired by and dedicated to activist Catholic principles, along the same lines as *Cruz y Raya,* the journal edited by José Bergamín.

Still under Sijé's aegis, Hernández started working on an *auto sacramental* (miracle play), which he first called "La danzarina bíblica" (The Biblical Dancer). Eventually published as *Quién te ha visto y quién te ve y sombra de lo que eras* (He Who Has Seen You and He Who Sees You and the Shadow of What You Were, 1934; performed, 1977), it is written in *verso clásico popular* (popular classical verse) and combines bucolic, allegorical, and religious elements in the style and spirit of Pedro Calderón de la Barca. However, though Hernández had always been fascinated with drama, he had little technical and practical experience and was also at a disadvantage with respect to the techniques needed to craft a dramatic work, relying instead to a great extent on his intuition as an artist and a poet, which had a negative effect on the work's dramatic structure and characterization.

In late 1933 Hernández had three main preoccupations. First, his clerical job paid so little that he could not afford to buy new clothes or shoes. Second, he was still at odds with his father over his choice of profession, though this was countered by the help and encouragement that his mother and his sister Elvira provided him and by the growing critical acclaim for his work. Finally, toward the end of 1933, Hernández was becoming obsessed with Josefina, and the resulting sexual tension began to be reflected in his increasingly erotic and sensual love poetry.

On 28 February 1934 there was a benefit performance at the Círculo de Bellas Artes de Orihuela to collect money for Hernández's next trip to Madrid. The local town council provided him with a monthly subsidy of fifty pesetas, which he used to settle into modest quarters on Calle de la Aduana in Madrid in March 1934. The city was in cultural and political turmoil. He was no longer unknown, and

he had friends to see and acquaintances to renew, among them Lorca, Alberti, Guillén, Manuel Altolaguirre, Luis Cernuda, Carlos Salinas, María Zambrano, Delia del Carril, and others who warmly welcomed and accepted him. Many of these were politically active on the Left and published their work in journals such as Emilio Prados's *Litoral.* Two such poets, Pablo Neruda and Vicente Aleixandre, were to play important roles in Hernández's life and work.

That summer Hernández again ran out of money, a common occurrence in his life, and had to return to Orihuela to find the peace and tranquility needed to finish his play (*Quien*). The final act was composed in the Sierra de la Muela and published in *Cruz y Raya* (July–September 1934). Hernández's love affair with Josefina was blooming. Her seamstress shop was on the way to his notary office, so he was able to flirt with her on occasion. His poetry at this time, though still conceptual, was increasingly sexual and down-to-earth, befitting a twenty-three-year-old poet in love. Josefina became more and more the muse behind his love poems in the various early versions of *El silbo vulnerado* – poems with titles such as "Cántico corporal" (Corporeal Canticle) and "Primera lamentación de la carne" (First Lament of the Flesh), reflecting Hernández's youthful vigor and sexual energy. The final version of *El silbo vulnerado* followed not long afterward, together with four more sonnets, to which he gave the name *Imagen de tu huella.* These love poems show the poet caught between two conflicting tendencies: on the one hand, lusty and blatant sexuality is reflected in the sensual, fertile images of acacia and orange blossoms and ripe figs, and succulent oranges; on the other hand, themes of anxious virtue and love show Hernández's emotional attachment to the baroque aesthetic ideal, to pure poetry, to Sijé and his Christian principles, and to the lofty ideals of social justice. Though already present in *Perito en lunas,* this tension between the spirit and the flesh had become fully developed in Hernández's poetry by this period.

One of the images most often found in his works is that of the bull, a symbol of sexuality, virility, and love. The poet is portrayed as bullfighter, for example, in poem 3 of *Perito en lunas,* "¡A la gloria, a la gloria toreadores!" (Onward to Glory, Onward to Glory, Toreadors!), and the bull symbolizes death. As Lorca had before him, Hernández honored the fallen bullfighter Ignacio Sánchez Mejías with his own poem, "Citación final" (Final Citation), which includes one of the major themes found throughout Hernández's works, his defiant

*Hernández reading his poetry on the radio in Madrid, 4 December 1936 (Collection of the Heirs of Miguel Hernandez)*

fear of death: "Estoy queriendo, y temo la cornada de tu momento, muerte" (I long for and fear the moment of your horn's thrust, death).

For someone so passionately involved with life, Hernández was notably shy in his dealings with Josefina to the point that, on one occasion, when he hand-delivered a sonnet he had written expressly for her, biographer María de Gracia Ifach says that Hernández felt too awkward to do anything but smile and walk away almost immediately. They finally started seeing each other formally on 27 September 1934, and his poetry began to reach new depths of feeling and humanity.

In October 1934 Hernández put the finishing touches on his next play, *El torero más valiente* (The Bravest Bullfighter), dedicating it to Bergamín. Sijé published scenes 4 and 5 of act 3 in the *Gallo Crisis* (Autumn 1934), but the play was never published in its entirety in Hernández's lifetime and was thought lost until his wife found the complete manuscript

in 1961. (It was published, as edited by Agustín Sánchez Vidal, in 1987.) On 30 November 1934 Hernández set out for Madrid with his cousin Antonio Gilabert and wrote the first of his many long letters to Josefina on the following day, from his room on Calle de los Caños. Full of great expectations, he was once again forced to concede defeat and returned home empty-handed in late December to face expectant friends and family — and also frustration and isolation.

Hernández was back in Madrid by mid February 1935 and found that, finally, his luck had changed. His friend Enrique Azcoaga immediately offered him a job with the "misiones pedagógicas" (pedagogical missions) traveling throughout the countryside bringing books and culture directly to the inhabitants — reminiscent of Lorca's Barraca theater company — which brought Hernández closer to the lives of the people but kept him from his literary work in Madrid. He soon found some employment better suited to his talents and more favorable to the creation of poetry when José María de Cossío offered him a job as a staff writer to work on an encyclopedia of bullfighting titled *Los toros* (The Bulls, 3 volumes 1943–1947). That work, which Hernández found boring and soon tired of, involved sifting through anecdotal information and historical documents and writing biographies of famous personalities such as Reverte, Espartero, and Tragabuches.

In Madrid, Hernández was being drawn deeper and deeper into the circle of poets that favored the Republican government and its socialist views, removing him further and further from Sijé's influence. When Sijé paid him a visit in Madrid, it was clear that, though they remained close friends, irreconcilable changes had drawn a permanent intellectual barrier between them. Hernández remained torn between two worlds, between the artificial, decadent city and the pure, Arcadian countryside: Madrid, with its dirty streets overflowing with too many people, trams, and cars – and too much garbage and smoke – and Orihuela, with the Segura, Sierra de la Muela, and traditions. To add to Hernández's frustrations, relations between him and Josefina became decidedly cool during the spring and summer of 1935. At first he wrote her more long letters from Madrid, writing less frequently later during his affair with Maruja Mallo, a Galician artist well known in literary circles. He was never completely dishonest with Josefina about his activities but did not shed full light on them until they were long over.

Hernández's decision in 1933 to write a play in the *auto sacramental* tradition had been made due in great part to Sijé's influence, but by 1935 Hernández realized that his real interests and talents lay elsewhere than in the realm of mystical-aesthetic and neo-Catholic poetry, toward which Sijé had been trying to lead him. Neruda, an established literary figure in Madrid, where he was Chilean consul, had shown increasing interest in Hernández's work. Both poets had a natural affinity for each other and enjoyed each other's company, often at Neruda's home on Casa de la Flores, which was open to his friends at any time. A lasting friendship developed between Neruda and Hernández, who was helping to proofread Neruda's *Residencia en la tierra* (Home on the Land, 1935).

When Aleixandre published his *La destrucción o el amor* (Destruction or Love) in 1935 and Hernández could not afford to buy it, he wrote Aleixandre asking for a free copy and went to Aleixandre's estate, Velingtonia, to pick it up. Aleixandre, like Neruda, became a lifelong friend and mentor to the younger poet. In Ifach's view Aleixandre probably helped fill the void created by Hernández's loss of Sijé's friendship. Leopoldo de Luis, discussing Aleixandre's friends in *Poesía española contemporánea* (Contemporary Spanish Poetry, 1965), wrote that if friendship could be reduced to one name, if solidarity and companionship had one voice, that name would be "Miguel" [Hernández]. That he ever felt comfortable and secure in Madrid can only be attributed to the influence and affection of Neruda and Aleixandre, two giants among poets who eventually became Nobel laureates and whose homes became Hernández's favorite haunts prior to the outbreak of the Spanish Civil War.

In June 1935 Hernández collaborated on an homage to Neruda which included a warm dedication (collected in *Obra completa*) and three then-unpublished *cantos materiales* (material songs) from *Residencia en la tierra*. Hernández sent copies to Juan Guerrero Ruiz and to Sijé, along with a letter to the former in which he spoke effusively of his warm feelings for Neruda and his poetry. Sijé, with whom Hernández had not corresponded for some time, wrote back offended at Hernández's choice of friends, admonishing him for his poor taste in poets, and urging him to return to Orihuela for an obviously well-needed rest.

Hernández did return, but not until August, at which time he had been away in Madrid for almost seven months. Notwithstanding the warm welcome from family and friends, including Sijé, the meeting between Hernández and Sijé highlighted how much they had drifted apart. Furthermore, relations with Josefina were still unsettled: she was disdainful and cool toward him, and it seemed as though their relationship was over. The return to Orihuela, in fact, did nothing to appease Hernández's anguish over wanting to be both with his friends in Madrid and with those in Orihuela. As he often did at such times, Hernández turned to his writing, working tirelessly on his next dramatic work, *Los hijos de la piedra* (The Sons of the Stone, performed 1946; published, 1959), inspired by the Asturian miners' strike of 1934. Events in Asturias and Catalonia had raised the political stakes in the country, and writers and intellectuals such as Hernández were actively being recruited to take up the political challenge.

While in Orihuela, Hernández received a letter from Neruda urging him to return to Madrid to help with the new poetry journal *Caballo Verde para la Poesía*, which he and Altolaguirre were preparing for publication. Regarding Sijé, Neruda wrote: "Tú eres demasiado sano para soportar ese tufo sotánico-satánico" (You are too sane to be associated with that

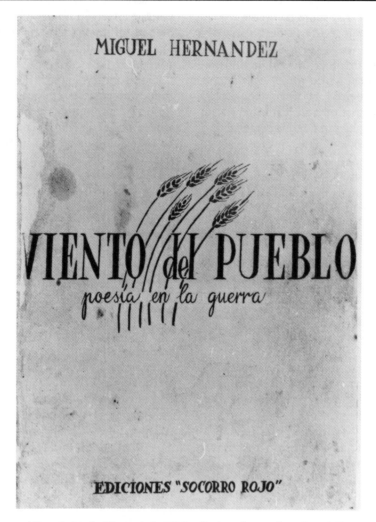

*Dust jacket for Hernandez's 1937 collection of romantic and patriotic
poems, which was popular with Republican forces*

soutanic-satanic fanatic). Earlier, in January 1935, Neruda had written Hernández: "Le hallo demasiado olor a iglesia, ahogado en incienso. . . . Ya haremos revista aquí, querido pastor, y grandes cosas" (It [the *Gallo Crisis*] smacks too much of church and incense. . . . We will soon put together our own journal here, dear shepherd, and do great things). Hernández had tried without success to bridge the gaps between the rival groups and their different visions: that of Aleixandre, Altolaguirre, and above all Neruda; and that of Sijé. The conflict between the two groups gradually played itself out in various issues of both journals, with each side taking indirect shots at the other through poems and articles.

Hernández returned to Madrid in August 1935 with mixed feelings. He had left Orihuela on far better terms than before, there having been a certain rapprochement between him and his family.

However, his differences with Josefina had not been mended, and the end of their relationship seemed imminent. Furthermore, his fading friendship with Sijé left him emotionally drained. And, while bathing in the Segura just before his departure, Hernández dove from a cliff into unfamiliar waters and cut his forehead, requiring several stitches and bandages. That shedding of blood, a powerful recurring image throughout Hernández's work, gave rise to one of his most remarkable poems from this period, "Sino sangriento" (Bloody Fate, now in *Obra completa*), published in the journal *Revista de Occidente*.

Upon his return to Madrid, Hernández resumed his work on *Los toros* and, along with Conde, Oliver, and Altolaguirre, was spending much of his spare time working with Neruda on *Caballo Verde para la Poesía*. Altolaguirre offered him a copy of the first issue, in which his poems "Vecino de la muerte" (Neighbor of Death) and "Mi sangre es un camino" (My Blood Is a Road) appeared. Two of his best works at this time were an ode he dedicated to Aleixandre – "Oda entre arena y piedra" (Ode between Sand and Stone) – and an ode to Neruda, "Oda entre sangre y vino" (Ode between Blood and Wine). (All these poems are in *Obra completa*.)

Hernández wrote Sijé during autumn to ask for his forgiveness and understanding, but an answer was long in coming. Eventually Sijé wrote Hernández on 29 November 1935, complaining that Hernández had not sent him a copy of the first issue of *Caballo Verde* and wondering what had happened to his old friend Miguel. His letter was full of recriminations against Neruda, Aleixandre, and Alberti and everything they represented. Yet, in the last issue of the *Gallo Crisis* (Spring–Summer 1935), Sijé, despite his earlier criticism of Hernández, included one of Hernández's poems, "El silbo de afirmación en la aldea" (The Whistle of Affirmation in the Village, now in *Obra completa*), in which the poet reflects on his unhappiness and sense of alienation in Madrid in tones similar to those of Lorca's *Poeta en Nueva York* (1940; translated as *The Poet in New York,* 1940). By publishing this particular poem, Sijé clearly hoped to gain something in his struggle against Neruda for Hernández's loyalty, but his plans may well have backfired, for the poem had in fact been written long before it was published, and the emotions and feelings expressed, though still present, no longer dominated Hernández's heart.

One of the contacts Hernández made through Neruda was Raúl González Tuñón, an Argentine journalist whose complex views on the social role of poetry in times of crisis and revolution made a deep impression on Hernández, pushing him even further in Neruda's direction. The poem "Sonreídme" (Rejoice with Me, in *Obra completa*), written by Hernández at about this time, shows how completely his ideas had evolved. At about the same time Hernández was writing "Sonreídme," Sijé was stricken with pneumonia and septicemia in late December 1935 and died on Christmas Eve. Much to his chagrin, Hernández only found out about it sometime later.

Devastated by the news and beset by terrible feelings of guilt, Hernández turned inward to concentrate and distill his sorrow, composing an elegy to Sijé that many critics consider to be one of the finest elegies in the Spanish language, sufficient to have ensured the poet's fame had he never written another word. First published in *Revista de Occidente* on 10 January 1936 (and collected in *El rayo que no cesa*), the elegy is an earthy evocation of his friendship and love for Sijé and of Sijé's long-standing influence on Hernández:

> Yo quiero ser llorando el hortelano
> de la tierra que ocupas y estercolas,
> compañero del alma, tan temprano.
>
> Alimentando lluvias, caracolas
> y órganos mi dolor sin instrumento,
> a las desalentadas amapolas
>
> daré tu corazón por alimento.
> Tanto dolor se agupa en mi costado
> que por doler me duele hasta el aliento.
> . . . . . . . . . . . . . . . . . . . . . . . . . . . . . . .
> Tu corazón, ya terciopelo ajado
> llama a un campo de almendras espumosas
> mi avariciosa voz de enamorado.
>
> A las aladas almas de las rosas
> del almendro de nata te requiero,
> que tenemos que hablar de muchas cosas,
> compañero del alma, compañero.

> (I want to be the grieving gardener
> of the earth you fill and fertilize,
> my dearest friend, so soon.
>
> With rain and snails my stifled sorrow
> nourishes the organs of your body
> and I would feed your heart
>
> the drooping poppies. Pain bunches up
> between my ribs till every breath I draw
> becomes an aching stitch.
> . . . . . . . . . . . . . . . . . . . . .
> My greedy lover's voice cries out to you,
> summoning your crumpled velvet heart;
> come to the drifting almond sprays;
>
> come to the winged roses blooming
> in the almond tree so creamy white;
> we've so many things to talk about,
> my friend, my dearest friend.)

> – translation by Edwin Honig (from *The Unending Lightning,* 1990)

In this poem Hernández rages against death and the return to nothingness, immortalizing in the elegy not only his loss but all such losses. In one sense Sijé would not have been flattered by Hernández's natural, concrete imagery and avoidance of conceits in this poem, where the pristine purity of Sijé's style of verse ("pure-white almond blossoms") are contrasted with Hernández's sensual and earthy vitality ("blood-red poppies"). Hernández was later to show his mastery of the elegy on many other occasions, such as in "Epitafio desmesurado a un poeta" (Epitaph Without End to

AL SOLDADO INTERNACIONAL
CAIDO EN ESPAÑA

Si hay hombres que contienen un alma sin fronteras,
una esparcida frente de mundiales cabellos,
cubierta de horizontes, barcos y cordilleras,
con arena y con nieve, tú eres uno de ellos.

Las patrias te llamaron con todas sus banderas,
que tu aliento llenara de movimientos bellos.
Quisiste apaciguar la sed de las panteras,
y flameaste henchido contra sus atropellos.

Con un sabor a todos los soles y los mares,
España te recoge porque en ella realices
tu majestad de árbol que abarca un continente.

A través de tus huesos irán los olivares
desplegando en la tierra sus más férreas raíces,
abrazando a los hombres universal, fielmente.

MIGUEL HERNÁNDEZ

*Postcard publication of a poem from* Viento del pueblo

a Poet), dedicated to Julio Herrera y Reissig, and "El ahogado del Tajo" (The Drowned Poet of the Tagus), inspired by Bécquer, both of which are in *Obra completa*.

Another irony in the Hernández-Sijé relationship can be seen in Hernández's review of Neruda's *Residencia en la tierra,* written prior to Sijé's death though not published until 2 January 1936 in the *Sol,* in which Hernández eloquently defends Neruda's full-blooded poetry:

> Estoy harto de tanto arte menor y puro. Me emociona la confusión desordenada y caótica de la Biblia, donde veo espectáculos grandes, cataclismos, desventuras, mundos revueltos, y oigo alaridos y derrumbamientos de sangre. Me revienta la vocecilla mínima que se extasía ante un chopo, le dispara cuatro versitos y cree que ya está hecho todo en poesía.

> (I have had enough of minor and pure art. Give me the disorganized and chaotic confusion of the Bible, where one can read about spectacular events, cataclysms, misadventures, and world-shaking events and hear shouts and sniff the smell of gushing blood. Not for me the dainty voice that swoons ecstatically at the glimpse of a poplar and then dashes off four lines of verse which supposedly contain all there is to be said about poetry.)

Hernández's enthusiasm for Neruda's brand of poetry was not surprising: both poets were impassioned and impelled by the same forces. Moreover, Neruda had often predicted that Hernández's break with Sijé would surely come in time.

Thus, though up to 1934 Hernández had been for the most part a partisan of neo-Góngorism, from 1935 to his death in 1942 he evolved from a tendency toward servile traditionalism to greater and greater independence of form and imagery. His early preference for the *octava* and the sonnet and his penchant for *la tropología culterana* (culturalist tropology) eventually gave way to the simpler textures and more direct language of the *canción* (song) and the *romance* (ballad), revealing his kinship with Machado and Lorca. This coexistence of popular and sophisticated art, common throughout most of Spanish history, was also typical of Spanish literature in the 1930s.

The culmination of Hernández's enthusiasm for traditional forms can be found in *El rayo que no cesa.* These poems were composed over a crucial two-year period in Hernández's career: 1934, when he was writing poems for Sijé and the *Gallo Crisis* and preparing his play *Quién,* and 1935, when he was publishing poems in *Caballo Verde* and working on his proletarian-inspired play *Los hijos de la piedra.* As such, *El rayo que no cesa* is a pivotal work

in Hernández's development as a poet. His discovery of love, in the person of Josefina, caused him to search out a richer, yet more restricted, vocabulary, less excessively decorative and more functional.

In these sonnets Hernández still exhibits a love of wordplay, conceits, and occasional verbal and rhetorical excess, but much less so than in his neo-Góngorist works. More often than not in *El rayo que no cesa* his poetic fireworks produce gems, such as the elegy to Sijé, which Hernández included in the book at the last minute in his honor. The influence of the religious eroticism latent in the Song of Songs and de la Cruz's *Cántico Espiritual* (Spiritual Canticle, 1584) can be felt throughout, as well as echoes of Neruda's *Residencia en la tierra* and Aleixandre's *La destrucción o el amor.*

Of thirty poems in *El rayo que no cesa,* twenty-seven are sonnets. There is also a long opening poem, a long fifteenth poem that divides twenty-six of the sonnets into two groups of thirteen, and the elegy of Sijé (poem 29), which is followed by the final sonnet. Some critics, particularly Dario Puccini, have analyzed how this collection reflects Hernández's poetic growth and maturity from the earlier *El silbo vulnerado* and *Imagen de tu huella.*

Although Josefina is nowhere mentioned by name in the poems — only as "you" — the clues to her influence on them are everywhere; all the poems in *El rayo que no cesa,* with the exception of the elegy, were inspired by her. However, on closer inspection one realizes that the real focus of the poems is the poet and his love, rather than the beloved. This love is definitely carnal and frankly desired but unfulfilled; the anguished lover is both Hernández and Everyman, and his eros and agape are the same forces that rage within all humans. The central images are the knife, blood, the ever-present bull, and a relatively new one, *el barro* (clay), developed in the central poem (number 15):

> Me llamo barro aunque Miguel me llame.
> Barro es mi profesión y mi destino
> que mancha con su lengua cuanto lame

> (My name is clay although I am called Miguel.
> Clay is my profession and my destiny
> and stains everything that it touches with its tongue)[.]

The publication of *El rayo que no cesa* effectively concluded the first chapter of Hernández's poetic career. At about the time Hernández published *El rayo que no cesa,* José Ortega y Gasset was urging him to write more material for *Revista de Occidente.*

*Hernández and his wife, Josefina, in Jaén in April 1937, the month following their wedding (Collection of the Heirs of Miguel Hernández)*

In January 1936 Hernández took a fateful trip to San Fernando del Jarama. Poorly dressed as usual on a cold, rainy day, and having forgotten to bring the proper identification papers with him, Hernández was stopped by the Guardia Civil and imprisoned, only managing to secure his freedom on the strength of a phone call to Neruda in Madrid. This second arrest by the Guardia Civil made such an impression on the young poet that he wrote Josefina, saying: "Tengo odio a la Guardia Civil, menos a tu padre, Josefina" (I abhor all civil guardsmen, with the exception of your father, Josefina). Hernández carried such distrust and hatred with him to the grave.

Hernández was determined to end the stalemate between himself and Josefina, with whom he had not been in touch for quite some time. In a desperate attempt to set things right between them and find out whether she still loved him, Hernández wrote her father, Manuel Manresa, for information, asking him to intercede on his behalf. Manresa wrote back immediately, offering his support and saying that his

daughter had been waiting for Hernández's letters and his return, hoping for their reconciliation, and suffering alone in silence.

On 10 April, Hernández returned to Orihuela with mixed feelings. His reunion with Josefina was passionate and joyful, and the welcome he received from his friends was very warm. But his happiness was tempered by sadness when he visited Sijé's parents and Josefina Fenoll, Sijé's former fiancée. The city of Orihuela unveiled a plaque in honor of Sijé on 14 April in a ceremony attended by many people, including Hernández, who read the eulogy.

He and Josefina Manresa planned to marry within two weeks, but Manuel Manresa was transferred to the town of Elda, in another jurisdiction, so they had to postpone their wedding plans indefinitely, and Hernández was once again forced to return to Madrid without her. With Josefina and her family in Elda, Hernández felt isolated in Madrid, in spite of his ever-expanding circle of friends. Josefina had become associated with nature (its quietness, peace, and solitude), one of the two poles of his creative energy. Neruda, Aleixandre, and other urban intellectuals represented the city, the other side of Hernández's nature (bustle, people, ideas, and movement).

On 18 July 1936 a Spanish military uprising led by Generalissimo Francisco Franco in the North African province of Melilla caused vital Spanish services, such as mail and trains, to come to a stop. Sometime during the next day, Lorca, who ironically had left Madrid to seek the comparative peace and safety of his beloved Andalusia, was captured by the military and killed with some other prisoners near Granada. Such mass executions and other chaotic events threw the country into turmoil and exemplified the wanton death and destruction of the next three years. The Spanish Civil War was to have a disastrous effect on all aspects of life in the country, particularly those involving culture. Many of the greatest intellectuals and finest artists eventually left the country to live in exile; others, like Lorca, Miguel de Unamuno, and Machado, died at the onset or during the war; and a few others, such as Hernández, died not long afterward as a direct result of that brutal conflict and the subsequent savage reprisals and executions.

Yet many in Spain seemed oblivious, including the citizens of Orihuela, where summer festivities were in full swing when Hernández returned there for a visit on 29 July. But tragedy soon struck again; on 13 August, Manuel Manresa and three other civil guards were killed in an armed attack while Josefina and Hernández were spending the day together in Cox.

The Madrid to which Hernández returned on 18 September showed signs everywhere of the effect that the war was having on Spain. On 27 September Hernández enrolled in the well-known Fifth Regiment, part of the Republican forces fighting Franco and the Nationalists. They built barricades and dug ditches in the town of Cubas, which was overflown daily by enemy bombers heading toward Toledo. Taken ill, Hernández returned to Madrid to recuperate and begin working on a play titled *Pastor de la muerte* (Shepherd of Death, in *Obra completa*). He soon joined the First Calvary Company of the Peasants' Battalion as a cultural-affairs officer, reading his poetry daily on the radio. He also traveled extensively throughout the area, organizing cultural events and doing poetry readings for soldiers on the front lines, or even pitching in where necessary to dig a ditch or defend a position. As more and more war poems flowed from his pen, and as his name and poems could be heard increasingly on the lips of his com-

patriots, he slowly approached the status of prime poet of the nation during the war years.

Together with Pablo de la Torriente Brau, a Cuban and fellow officer, Hernández organized a cultural evening in Alcalá de Henares on 27 November, attended by several well-known figures including Prados and Alberti. Three weeks later Brau was shot dead, his leather vest (a gift from Hernández) riddled with bullet holes. His death was yet another blow to the poet and inspired the second elegy in the soon-to-be-published *Viento del pueblo* (Wind of the People, 1937).

With the war opening up and more and more people dying or getting injured, Hernández, worried by a lack of news from Josefina (due to irregular mail service) and plagued by loneliness, thought incessantly about their postponed marriage plans. He wanted to get married as soon as possible, perhaps by January, but she refused to get married under those circumstances, due to her father's murder and also because her wedding dress was not ready. Consequently Hernández involved himself increasingly in the war effort in an attempt to take his mind off his personal problems.

At about this time Machado moved to Valencia, and Neruda accepted a posting to the Chilean embassy in Paris. Ortega had also left Spain, and Unamuno died on 31 December under house arrest, causing shock waves throughout the country. While in Valencia in January, Hernández wrote the poem "Recoged esta voz" (Take Up This Cry), which he eventually read to the forces at the front and which is collected in *Viento del pueblo*. He was surprised at how peaceful Valencia was compared to Madrid, a fact that perhaps explained why the Republican government had already started moving to Valencia. From the town of Jaén he wrote Josefina in early March that in four days he would be coming to marry her.

Hernández and Josefina were finally married in Orihuela on 9 March 1937 in a no-frills civil ceremony attended by close friends Carlos Fenoll and Jesús Poveda. The atmosphere at the wedding was not entirely happy, for Manual Manresa had only been dead for seven months, but Hernández's postmarital poetry soon took on new tones and colors, full of sensuality and sexuality seemingly fulfilled. Unfortunately, after only forty days with his bride, Hernández had to return to his regiment on 18 April. Four days later tragedy struck once again when Josefina's mother died. In order to take his mind off the almost constant stream of tragic events, Hernández kept busy working on his poetry, correcting proofs of *Viento del pueblo* and pre-

*Hernández reciting his poetry to Republican troops, circa 1937*
*(Collection of the Heirs of Miguel Hernández)*

paring speeches. When his propaganda unit was shifted to Castuera in Estremadura province, he took time off from his exhausting pace to see Josefina and came down with a severe case of anemia. Hugh Thomas, noted Spanish Civil War historian, mentions the accelerating pace of Hernández's literary activities during the war years, a pace that inevitably took a heavy toll on the poet's health and required him to rest and recuperate on several occasions.

Back with his unit after his recovery, he devoted himself to finishing *Teatro en la guerra* (Theater in the War, 1937), a group of short propaganda plays of a kind one would have expected from an officer with the government propaganda unit, and certainly not among the best of his dramatic works that have survived. However, Hernández had undergone an important change since the beginning of the war. In the prologue to the book he wrote that since 18 July 1936 "entiendo que todo teatro, toda poesía,

todo arte, ha de ser, hoy más que nunca, un arma de guerra" (I know that all theater, all poetry, all art must be, today more than ever, a weapon of war). This prologue, stating clearly his involvement with and commitment to the Republican side, was one of the main documents used against him after the war.

In July 1937 well-known writers from all over the world converged on Madrid for the first of two sessions of the International Writers' Congress; the second session was held in Valencia. Hernández was reunited with Neruda and made or renewed acquaintance with such important figures as André Malraux, Octavio Paz, Cesar Vallejo, Stephen Spender, Claude Aveline, and Jean Cassou. During this congress Hernández had the opportunity to get much closer to Machado, who made a very moving closing address. Hernández and Neruda saw each other whenever they could, touring the area where Neruda had lived and visiting his bombed-out flat in Casa de las Flores, where little was left save some scattered manuscripts, which the Chilean poet chose to leave where they lay among the rubble.

After the congress, and with *Viento del pueblo* and *Teatro en la guerra* set for publication, Hernández managed to spend some time with Josefina in Cox, where he put the finishing touches on *Pastor de la muerte*. On 21 August, Vicente Ramos and Manuel Molina organized a ceremony to honor Hernández at the Alianza de Intelectuales in Alicante, and the poet took the audience by storm with readings of both prose and poetry, including several of his new poems from *Viento del pueblo*.

In August, Hernández was invited by the Republican government to be part of a group of Spanish intellectuals attending the Fifth Festival of Soviet Theater in Moscow. After a two-day stopover in Paris, where he met with Paz, Hernández flew to Moscow, then Leningrad and Kiev in September for an action-packed month of plays, concerts, ballets, and banquets, as well as interviews with journalists. He was impressed with Russian culture, especially the theater, and took copious notes he intended to use in writing new dramatic works.

Back in Spain in early October, he spent time at home with Josefina, who was pregnant. *Viento del pueblo* had finally been published to generally favorable reviews. Although some had criticized its plebeian or vulgar aspects, most praised its earthy appeal to the heart rather than the mind, which may explain why it had such a strong effect on the Republican forces at war; it raised the morale of most who heard or read it. The first poem, "Primera elegía" (First Elegy), dedicated to the memory of Lorca, is reminiscent of Jorge Manrique's fifteenth-century couplets on the death of his father. Lorca had been almost like a god for Hernández; his death meant not only the loss of a friend but also that of a colleague, mentor, and helpful critic of Hernández's dramatic works. In his prologue to the book, Hernández wrote: "Los poetas somos viento del pueblo: nacemos para pasar soplados a través de sus poros y conducir sus ojos y sus sentimientos hacia las cumbres más hermosas" (The poets are like the winds of the people: we are born to blow through their pores and to raise their eyes and feelings to the most beautiful peaks).

In *Viento del pueblo* Hernández does not use many traditional poetic molds. He practically abandons the sonnet, whose formal constraints tended to imprison his spontaneity; instead he employs the blank verse and free forms that Neruda had suggested he use. He made extensive use of the *romance*, a form more appropriate to much of his subject matter. For the most part the tone is passionately belli-cose and virile, as in "Recoged esta voz" and "El sudor" (Sweat), and full of optimism, in poems such as "Canción del esposo soldado" (Song of the Married Soldier). There are also denunciations of enemy atrocities and statements of concern for the wounded, the sick, the hungry, and the dead, as in "Sentado sobre los muertos" (Seated atop the Dead).

Already working on his next collection, *El hombre acecha* (The Man Watches, 1939), Hernández continued writing other poems in the same vein as *Viento del pueblo,* such as "Canción de la ametralladora" (Song of the Machine Gun). In early November he joined the front at Teruel, where the trenches were snowed in and the smell of death was everywhere, inspiring his poem "Teruel":

Teruel como un cadáver sobre un río.
La efusión de las piedras y las ramas,
la vida derramando un vino rudo
cerca de aquel cadáver con escamas.
. . . . . . . . . . . . . . . . . . . . . . . . . . . . . . . .
En su sangre se envuelve la victoria.

(Teruel, like a corpse overlooking a river.
The shedding of rocks and limbs,
life spilling its crude wine
near that scaly corpse.
. . . . . . . . . . . . . . . . . .
Victory is wrapped up in its blood.)

Hernández's first son, Manuel Ramón Hernández, was born on 19 December 1937, while Hernández was in Aragon. He saw his son for the first time on 24 December, the second anniversary of Sijé's death. His play *El labrador de más aire* (The Most Elegant Farmer, performed in 1972) was finally published in Valencia at about this time (December 1937), although it had been ready for publication for about a year. Whereas Hernández had been very active in 1937, the next year saw him spending more time in Cox and traveling less. In the spring of 1938 he joined the coastal patrol and transferred to the Valencia area, where his poems from *Viento del pueblo* were frequently aired on the radio.

Emotionally and physically drained, and aware that the Republican cause was showing signs of faltering, he continued writing *El hombre acecha,* which, compared to *Viento del pueblo,* was better structured and conceived and denser both in form and in meaning, though less brilliant, exhortative, and polemical, reflecting Hernández's growing pessimism about life, humankind, the course of the war in general, and about his own immediate circumstances in particular. The opprobrium and associ-

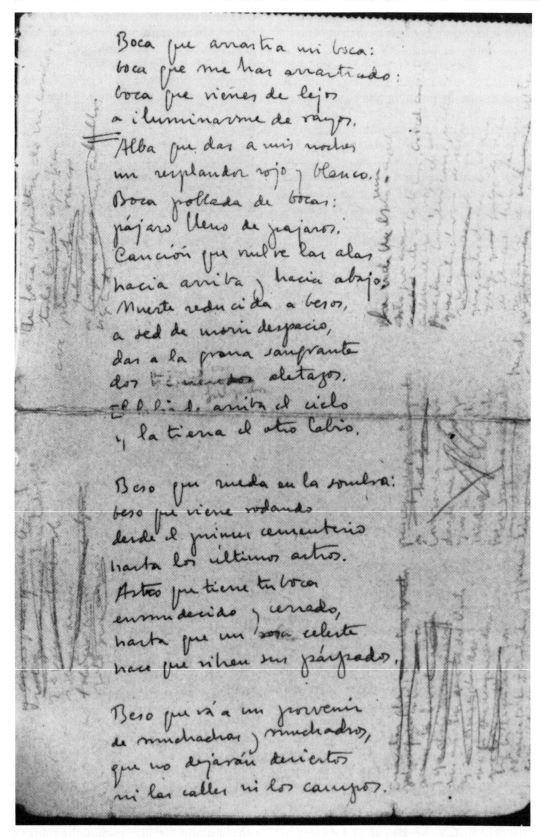

*Page 1 from the manuscript for a poem Hernández wrote in 1938. It was published as "La boca" in* Cancionero y romancero de ausencias *in 1958 (by permission of the Heirs of Miguel Hernández).*

ated images vented on the enemy in *Viento del pueblo* are generalized and applied to all humankind in *El hombre acecha*. Nevertheless, these poems, whose main images are of *sangre, herido,* and *cuchillo,* (blood, pain, and knife), evolve naturally from *Viento del pueblo*. For example, the image of hands, constructive and caring in *Viento del pueblo,* has given way to the image of hands that claw and club victims. In *Viento del pueblo* nature seems to be on the side of righteousness. All of Spain is the poet's orchard to be defended. The titular image of the poet as the saving wind of the people gives way in *El hombre acecha* to nature – the countryside – in horrified retreat from humankind in "Canción primera" (First Song). Humankind, which had risen up to defend itself, had at the same time revived the basest of human instincts: hatred, the desire for revenge, and the urge to kill. *El hombre acecha* closes, however, on a note of hope in the redeeming power of love, expressed in the "Canción última" (Final Song). Hernández was already working on his next work, *Cancionero y romancero de ausencias* (Songbook and Romance of Absences, 1958), a work that many feel reflects the influence of Machado's *Juan de Mairena* (1936).

The Hernándezes' first son died on 19 October 1938, exactly ten months after his birth. Hernández reacted with a flurry of activity, composing some of his most memorable poems, such as "A mi hijo" (To My Son, in *Cancionero y romancero*). He fell sick and had to convalesce in Benicasim, where he met the writer Antonio Buero Vallejo for the first time. Hernández's second son, Manuel Miguel, was born on 4 January 1939, when the exodus of people fleeing the doomed republic was growing day by day. Machado, together with his elderly mother, immigrated to France on 22 January, only to die of pneumonia a month later; three days afterward his mother also died. His death was an enormous blow to Hernández. The exodus swelled as 28 March approached, the day that signaled the end of the war. In mid March Hernández picked up the printed but unbound copies of *El hombre acecha;* however, with the war rapidly coming to an end, the book was never bound and thus never marketed in that form. It first became widely available in *Obras completas* (1960).

Hernández sought help from the Chilean embassy, but Carlos Morla Lynch, then in charge of business matters, was not encouraging. Hernández remained in the Cox-Orihuela area until late April, trying to decide whether to leave Spain or not. He could not bring himself to believe that he would be in any danger, but on 22 April he eventually decided to make his escape via Andalusia. He crossed the border into Portugal at Rosal de la Frontera, not far from Huelva, but was spotted by a Portuguese police patrol, arrested, and returned on 4 May to Rosal de la Frontera, where police interrogated him for a week in an attempt to incriminate him. On 6 May, after being allowed to communicate with Josefina, he was first moved via Huelva to Seville, his first place of detention, and subsequently to Torrijos Prison in Madrid, where he was held from 18 May to 17 September. Between the time of his arrest and his death he was moved some twelve times.

Through his sister Elvira, Hernández maintained contact with Aleixandre, who gave him as much support as possible, lending him whatever books he needed. Cossío visited him, bringing him food on occasion, as did Elvira and her husband. Hernández wrote frequent long letters to Josefina, who had been forced to sell many of their possessions, including their goat, in order to make ends meet and still have something left over for her husband. In his letters to Josefina at this time, he gave vent to his constant preoccupations about his son, fearing that they might lose their second and last child. Hernández was composing what would prove to be his purest, deepest, and most refined poetry (later published in *Cancionero y romancero*), whose main themes are love (of spouse, children, and family), loss of freedom, absence (of those loved), and deprivation, with only a secondary role given to war, poverty, and hatred.

Matters were made worse when the Franco government refused to pay Josefina her mother's widow's pension because Manuel Manresa, a Guardia Civil officer, had remained loyal to the republic. In Paris, Neruda was trying to help in every way possible, contacting Cardinal Baudrillart, the archbishop of Paris, whose possible influence in getting Hernández released many consider apocryphal. As if by magic, he was freed on 17 September, most probably through some administrative error, although some critics do not discount the possible involvement of Hernández's many influential friends. Before leaving for Cox Hernández used his unexpected freedom in Madrid to visit Cossío, Aleixandre, and another close friend, Antonio Aparicio, who had sought asylum in the Chilean embassy and who wrote years later that Hernández had told him he had made friends with Spain's best at Torrijos.

Hernández and Josefina spent twelve days of freedom together in Cox, but already Hernández's enemies in Orihuela had heard of his release and were plotting against him. Conservative Orihuela

*Drawing of Hernández by Antonio Buero Vallejo that was printed on posters circulating while he was in prison (from* Como fue Miguel Hernández *by Manuel Muñoz Hidalgo, 1975)*

sympathized with Franco, shunning and persecuting Republican sympathizers such as Hernández. When he let it be known that he wanted to visit his family, his old friends Carlos Fenoll and Manuel Molina went to Cox to try to dissuade him, suggesting instead that he leave the country. Hernández, however, seemed to feel that, having been released, he was safe and no longer seen as a threat. Molina wrote that Hernández "did not, could not believe in people's gratuitous maliciousness, and that was his downfall."

Hernández did visit his family in Orihuela and was visiting the Sijé family on 29 September 1939 when he was arrested, handcuffed, and – to his utter amazement and embarrassment – walked across the city to Orihuela Prison, formerly the Seminario de Orihuela, which had played such a role in the lives of so many *oriolanos*. He was incarcerated incommunicado in a basement room for several days without light or fresh air, unable to believe the treachery and cruelty of his fellow citizens;

hence he later wrote the sonnet "Sigo en la sombra" (Return to Darkness, in *Cancionero y romancero*).

During his two awful, debilitating months in Orihuela Prison, Hernández could receive no mail. He was desperate for contact with his family and friends, knowing that Josefina, who had begun working again as a seamstress to make ends meet, was hard-pressed to provide for their son, her two sisters, and her imprisoned husband. However, there were a few people during the coming years who smuggled letters from him out of prison. His frequent letters to Josefina describe the dismal conditions in which he lived. Although Neruda and other friends managed to send financial help through Germán Vergara, a Chilean embassy official, even this help was often unreliable and insufficient.

On 3 December, Hernández was transferred to the Conde de Toreno Prison in Madrid; he never again returned to Orihuela. Fortunately, better facilities and food at the Madrid prison improved both his health and his vigor. He renewed his friendship with fellow inmate Buero Vallejo, with whom he carried on lengthy discussions on poetry, life, death, love, and the nature of the deity. Though Hernández had little access to paper, he used his excellent memory, his best archive, to record and keep track of his poems. Vallejo described Hernández's poetic process in prison as one of composing, reciting, rethinking, retouching, and reciting the corrected versions from one day to the next in an extended poetic trance; Hernández often worked overnight to transpose his verses onto his cell walls with the help of whatever writing implements were available.

One such poem was "Sepultura de la imaginación" (Tomb of the Imagination, in *Cancionero y romancero*), in which the poet sees himself as a mason building the walls of the future only to find "aquel hombre labraba su cárcel. Y en su obra / fueron precipitados él y el viento" (that man was building his own cell. And through his work / both he and his wind were lost). Vallejo remained one of his closest friends and admirers; for him, Hernández was "un poeta necesario" (a necessary poet), a status that few poets achieve, a status reserved for "Manrique, o San Juan de la Cruz, o Fray Luis, o Machado." Hernández gave more life and reality to everyday things – such as brooms, sweat, light, shadows, kisses, and onions – than most poets do. When Vallejo was elected a member of the Real Academia Española years later, he said, "Me gustaría que estuviera Miguel Hernández que, además debería estar dentro, sentado en los sillones, claro" (I wish Miguel Hernández were here; in fact, he clearly deserves to be, seated here among us, in one of these chairs). Notwithstanding such praise, Hernández himself shunned such privileges, a view he expressed eloquently in the poem "Llamo a los poetas" (A Call to Poets), in *El hombre acecha*.

As Christmas 1939 approached, his first in prison, Hernández received food and mended clothes from family and friends, who were permitted to visit on Mondays. Josefina turned twenty-four on 2 January 1940, and Manuel Miguel's first birthday was 4 January. Across the first page of Hernández's birthday letter to his son, the prison censors, with incredible spite, wrote in big blue letters that he should keep it short or that his letters would be torn up. The last page of this letter is missing. Yet he kept on writing long letters anyway, and many got to their destinations.

For urging that art and literature be dedicated to and employed in the war against fascism, for his activities as cultural-affairs officer in the Republican army, for writing *Teatro en la guerra,* and for his direct involvement in some military operations, Hernández was tried, convicted, and sentenced to death by a military court in mid January 1940, but the sentence was eventually commuted to thirty years in prison – probably through the intercession of friends such as Neruda, Aleixandre, and Cossío. More indefatigable than most in seeking to save the life of his friend and former employee, Cossío enlisted the help of some highly placed Falangists, among them the poet José María Alfaro and the writer and minister Rafael Sánchez Mazas, to try to get Hernández's sentence commuted. Hernández would doubtless have abhorred the notion that he be considered a prisoner "more equal than others," though that was the argument Cossío used in insisting that the government could not afford another scandal such as the one that had resulted from Lorca's assassination. Hernández could have gotten off scot-free with a full pardon had he resigned from the Republican army, signed on with the new regime, and agreed to write articles and poetry for Falangist journals such as *Redención,* which had been specially created to publish work by recanting Republicans, but he steadfastly refused to do those things.

The most difficult aspect of prison life was being separated from his family and friends. His letters to Josefina show tenderness for and interest in her welfare, that of their son, Manuel, and that of his two sisters-in-law; he often included drawings for them or for his son. Among his best poems from the first year of his imprisonment are those inspired by his anguished concern for the welfare of his son; in Ifach's opinion they are some of the most brilliant examples of poetry written by a poet for his child. For example, "Nana de la cebolla" (Lullaby of the Onion, in *Cancionero y romancero*) is a poem Hernández wrote for Manuel after Josefina had lamented in a 1939 letter that she had nothing to feed him but onions.

While Josefina was forced to sell their son's crib and many other possessions to buy food, Hernández was struggling against boredom, hunger, and isolation from his family. At times in his letters he adds a touch of wry humor, as when he wrote on 12 September 1939, "También paso mis buenos ratos espulgándome, que familia menuda no me falta nunca, y a veces la crío robusta y grande como el garbanzo. Todo se acabará a fuerza de uña y paciencia, o ellos, los piojos, acabarán conmigo" (I also spend some of my best moments delousing myself, for I am always surrounded by my large family, and I grow them as big and healthy as beans. I need a lot of nails and patience, or they, the bugs, will surely finish me off).

Madrid. 5 de febrero 1940

Mi queridísima hija Gertrudis:
Muy bien. Así me gusta. Ya era hora de que me
escribieras. Tú dices que no me escribes porque vas a
la sierra, pero eso es una excusa. Algún rato tendrás
que no sea para ir a la sierra por leña. Quiero
que me sigas escribiendo. Me gusta que me hayas
mandado pelo del niño. Que te compre Josefina
una miloja. Te la mereces. Pronto nos veremos y
os traeré a Madrid. Dime quién es la que se lava
la cara todos los días antes y se peina más veces. Debes ser tú, que eres la más limpia. Dime
si es verdad que te acuerdas de mí. Pronto iré y en
un rato llegue, por la noche te contaré un cuento.
Te abraza y besa tu padre    Miguel

Madrid. 5 de febrero 1940

Mi queridísima Conchipotita, hija mía, la
más pequeña y la más traviesa de Cox: Estoy
muy bien y no olvidaré llevarte una caja o una
ja,a de milojas para Manolillo y para ti. También olvidaré las galletas y la muñeca, aunque
me dice Gertrudis que no haces nada. Yo creo
que exagera un poquito ella y que algo harás,
aunque no será mucho. Di a Josefina de mi parte que te compre por lo pronto una miloja en
donde las haya, que yo se la pagaré. Desde
luego eres la que mejor escribe de las tres. Di
a Carmen que me escriba, que quiero aprender
solfa. Dime quién es la que se pelea y grita más.
Dime si estás gorda. Toma un abrazo y muchos
besos de tu padre el más joven    Miguel

*Two letters Hernández wrote to his wife's sisters while he was in prison (by permission of the Heirs of Miguel Hernández)*

By March 1940 the couple had been married for three years but had hardly lived together for much of that time. Hernández felt less and less inclination to read and write poetry, occupied as he was by prison work and preoccupied by family and friends. He wrote Josefina letters filled with love, including one in which he repeated the word *quiéreme* (love me) twenty-seven times in a row. Hernández never seems to have given up hope of once more being recognized as a Spanish citizen and an important poet, yet he often fell victim to doubt and frustration about his fate. Some of his last poems included in the *Cancionero y romancero de ausencias* bear out this idea, including the sonnet "Sonreír con la alegre tristeza del olivo" (To Smile with the Joyful Sadness of the Olive Tree). Hernández had for the most part abandoned the sonnet after publishing *El rayo que no cesa,* yet he chose the sonnet form for this and four other poems in *Cancionero y romancero de ausencias,* in which he distilled the pain and anguish from his years of incarceration. Another of those sonnets, "Sigo en la sombra, lleno de luz: ¿Existe el día?" (I Go on in the Dark, Lit from Within: Does Day Exist?), is filled with ironic observations on the turbulent relationship between life (light/day) and death (dark/night). Hernández, who had taken solitary walks in the countryside whenever he had returned to Orihuela, must have suffered immeasurably from the confinement of his last three years.

On 22 September 1940 he was transferred to the provincial prison in Palencia, where he remained until 26 November. In a moment of levity on 23 September, he wrote to Josefina that he felt as though he were a tourist on holiday touring prison after prison. He suggested that Josefina and Manuel come to live in Palencia, where he could see them regularly even if it were only ten minutes a week, but Josefina preferred to remain in Cox. Hernández really suffered from the cold in Palencia, a debilitating and damp cold that lowered his resistance and gave him a bout of pneumonia, probably setting the stage for the downward spiral of disease that finally claimed him. He was never quite fully well again.

However, he left the Palencia cold on 26 November for the Adult Reformatory in Ocaña, near Toledo, where he remained until 23 June 1941. From 1 December until Christmas he was in solitary confinement, allowed neither to send nor receive any messages. In honor of his having survived that ordeal, several fellow inmates, including friends from other places and better times, organized a special feast in Hernández's honor, complete with program, guest list, illustrations, dedications, and a menu with items such as "cuarto once sopa"

(Room Eleven Soup) — eleven being the number of his cell.

Finally, on 3 February 1941, Josefina agreed to move to Madrid (about fifty miles from Ocaña), but the plans were thwarted, so Hernández was forced to make do with a recent photo of Josefina and Manuel. Hernández was transferred to the Adult Reformatory in Alicante in June; he was destined never to leave alive. Once again he was kept incommunicado for almost a month, as in Ocaña. Ifach imputes this rough treatment to Hernández's activities as a revolutionary poet and Republican cultural officer during the war. One of the few poems that Hernández managed to write during this difficult period was "Eterna sombra" (Eternal Sleep), included in *Obra completa.* The density of conceit and wordplay so prevalent in his earlier works gives way in these later poems to feeling and emotion, including despair. Yet even in his most devitalized and exhausted moments, Hernández remained true to his essential optimism.

After his period of solitary confinement, Hernández met and made many new friends at the Alicante reformatory, as he had earlier in Ocaña. According to one of them, Luis Fabregat Terrés, when Hernández had first made his appearance among them, he had seemed extremely weak and emaciated, as can be witnessed in two drawings made of him a month or two later by fellow inmate Ricardo Fuente. Too weak to write in a chair, Hernández did most of his writing — mostly letters — lying down. The authorities finally granted Josefina and Manuel permission to visit on 26 July, but the officials showed unbelievable callousness when they allowed Hernández to embrace the boy but not his wife, because they did not consider the couple to have been legally married in the Catholic church. Yet she and Manuel were allowed to visit every week (having moved in with Hernández's sister's family in Alicante), and Manuel soon began to recognize his father from among the other prisoners, an enormous source of pleasure and satisfaction for someone who had been denied so much. The families of prisoners were in large part responsible for what the prisoners managed to eat, yet Hernández on many occasions asked Josefina to keep for herself and Manuel what food she was able to bring him.

One of the main sources of Hernández's frustration was the fact that although his mother and sister Elvira had kept in touch with him, neither his father nor his brother Vicente or sister Encarnación had been to see him. The poet was sadly lacking in clothes at this time, referring to his sense of shame

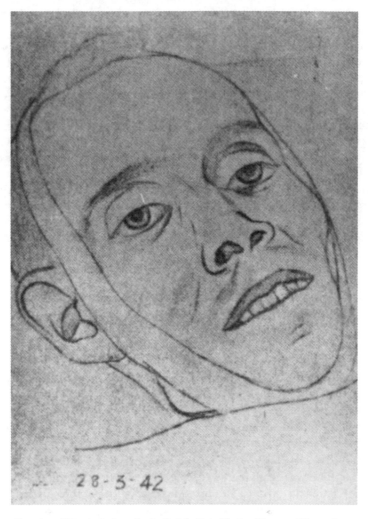

*Drawing of Hernández just after he died, by Luis Giménez Esteve, a fellow prisoner*
(*from* Como fue Miguel Hernández)

at being seen by visitors in the rags which were his only clothes. Yet none of Hernández's family or friends on the outside had much money with which to help him. Eventually this situation of poverty and tension caused relations between Elvira and Josefina to become strained, prompting Josefina to move into an aunt's house nearby and then back to Cox, where she could obtain some peace of mind. Josefina continued to visit Hernández every Friday but had to get up much earlier to catch the morning train from Cox to Alicante. The last visit of this type took place on Friday, 28 November 1941. The next Friday, weak from his lingering bronchial pneumonia and incipient tuberculosis, Hernández suffered a bout of typhus fever, which caused the authorities to withdraw visiting privileges temporarily. Although Hernández wrote his wife and family that he would soon be healthy again, he never recovered

from the effects of typhus; he continued to weaken, which was not surprising considering the dilapidated state of the infirmary and the paucity of medical supplies.

When his condition worsened and he contracted a full case of tuberculosis, the staff doctors attempted to get Hernández transferred to a sanatorium where he could receive the kind of attention his case required. By early February 1942 his condition was far worse than expected. Yet, in spite of his discomfort, Hernández continued to write, putting the finishing touches on a short booklet, complete with illustrations, that comprised two stories for children. He had translated and adapted the tales from English versions. *Dos cuentos para Manolillo (para cuando sepa leer)* (Two Stories for Manolillo [For When He can Read]) was eventually published in 1988. Hernández was no longer writing letters as such but mere notes scribbled on pieces of scrap paper and even toilet paper; often they did not reach their destination.

The authorities continued their unusual cruelty in refusing Josefina permission to be near her dying husband, always on the grounds that they were not legally married. Prison officials had badgered Hernández for years to rejoin the church and had promised to allow Josefina permission to enter the cell with her husband if they agreed to be married within the church. Although long reluctant to do so, Hernández eventually realized that this route was the only way they would ever again be together, and also the only way to legalize Josefina's status as a married woman in the event of his death. Their subsequent marriage on 4 March in the infirmary resembled more a wake than a celebration, in spite of the spring that was blooming outside the prison walls.

The official permit to transfer Hernández to a sanatorium arrived on 21 March at a time when his tuberculosis was so advanced that moving him would have been more dangerous to his health than keeping him in Alicante. Yet, on his deathbed, determined not to give up without a last word, Hernández managed to scribble the following verses onto the wall next to his cot:

Adiós hermanos, camaradas, amigos,
despedidme del sol y de los trigos.

(Farewell, brothers, comrades, friends,
Give my goodbyes to the sun and the wheat fields.)

Josefina saw him alive for the last time on 27 March. She had come alone, much to Hernández's consternation, for he felt his life ebbing away quickly and wanted his son to be there also. Hernández died at 5:30 the next morning, 28 March 1942 – exactly three years to the day after the end of the Spanish Civil War. His death portrait, drawn by Luis Giménez Esteve, a fellow prisoner, shows Hernández's eyes wide open; they would not close due to hyperthyroidism. He was buried in the Cementerio de Nuestra Señora del Remedio in Alicante.

Chronologically, Hernández's work can be separated into three periods: 1) Youth (1930–1936); 2) War Years (1936–1939); and 3) Last Years (1939–1942). His poetry can also be divided into four phases according to the predominant style used: 1) neo-Góngorist *octavas de arte mayor* in *Perito en lunas;* 2) Petrachan sonnets in *El rayo que no cesa;* 3) ballads of the soldier/poet in *Viento del pueblo;* and 4) songs and ballads of the prisoner in *Cancionero y romancero de ausencias.* In Hernández's early poetry the experience that engendered the poem was less

important than the poetry itself. However, in his last works, poem and experience converge and are transformed and renewed. Hernández's poetry written while in prison can be viewed from a variety of perspectives relating to one or another form of human suffering, whether caused by natural disasters or by human beings. In this later poetry there is a sense both of the brevity of life and of the cosmic, timeless permanence of human experience.

Most critics, while including him in the "Generation of 1936," treat him as though he were not really a part of it and suggest that in a country of individualistic people strangely prone to one philosophy or another, he remained unbeholden to and unclaimed by any movement. Certainly the question of his influence on the succeeding generation of postwar poets is difficult to assess, due to strong censorship of his works and to the fact that much of his work was not collected and published until some time after – in some cases, long after – his untimely death. Conde wrote of Hernández that he was destined to establish his own school. Many question whether he led a school; had he lived, he surely would have, but in the opinion of many he stands alone, or on a pinnacle alongside Machado, Jiménez, and Lorca, as Juan Guerrero Ruiz aptly suggests in his last letter to Hernández.

Hernández was, in many ways, probably closest to his early idol Lorca. A common thread linked them in death, for they both returned to their hometowns to what eventually turned out to be a painful death. The Franco regime was as guilty of Hernández's death in prison, the result of harsh treatment, hunger, and neglect, as they would have been had they stood him up immediately before a firing squad. Also, Hernández shared many of the same concerns as Lorca. They were doubtless troubled, each in his own way, by the fate of the destitute, ignorant, and downtrodden masses – with, however, one significant difference: Hernández had himself grown up within and broken away from those masses and that milieu, and his interest in them was more realistic and far less romantic than that of Lorca, whose upper-middle-class background and education were quite dissimilar. In terms of background, Hernández had much more in common with the self-taught Leonese poet Victoriano Crémer, whose *poesía social* clamored for social and economic justice for the wretched and disenfranchised of the earth.

Letters:

*Las cartas a José María de Cossío* (Santander: Casona de Tudanca, 1985);

*Epistolario,* edited by Agustín Sánchez Vidal (Madrid: Alianza, 1986);

*Cartas a Josefina,* edited by Concha Zardoya (Madrid: Alianza, 1988).

**Bibliography:**

Agustín Sánchez Vidal, José Carlos Rovira, and Carmen Alemany Bay, eds., *Obra completa,* 2 volumes (Madrid: Espasa-Calpe, 1992), II: 2763-2793.

**Biographies:**

Concha Zardoya, *Miguel Hernández Vida y obra; Bibliografía; Antología* (New York: Hispanic Institute, 1955);

María de Gracia Ifach, *Miguel Hernández, rayo que no cesa* (Barcelona: Plaza & Janés, 1975);

Ifach, *Vida de Miguel Hernández* (Barcelona: Plaza & Janés, 1982).

**References:**

F. Bravo Morata, *Miguel Hernández* (Madrid: Fenicia, 1979);

Juan Cano Ballesta, *La poesía de Miguel Hernández* (Madrid: Gredos, 1962; revised, 1971);

Marie Chevalier, *L'homme, ses oeuvres et son destin dans la poésie de Miguel Hernández* (Paris: Institut d'Etudes Hispaniques, 1974); Spanish translation, two volumes: *La escritura poética de Miguel Hernández* (Madrid & Mexico City: Siglo XXI, 1977); *Los temas poéticas de Miguel Hernández* (Madrid & Mexico City: Siglo XXI, 1978);

Claude Couffon, *Orihuela et Miguel Hernández* (Paris: Institut d'Etudes Hispaniques, 1963);

Juan Guerrero Zamora, *Miguel Hernández, poeta* (Madrid: Grifón, 1955);

*Hermanamiento: Miguel Hernández–Federico García Lorca,* special issue (1990);

María de Gracia Ifach, ed., *Miguel Hernández* (Madrid: Taurus, 1975);

*Insula,* special issue on Hernández, 15 (November 1960);

Charles D. Ley, "Miguel Hernández," in his *Spanish Poetry since 1939* (Washington, D.C.: Catholic University of America Press, 1962);

*Litoral,* special triple issue on Hernández, 73–75 (1978);

Marcela López Hernández, *Vocabulario de la obra poética de Miguel Hernández* (Cáceres: Universidad de Extremadura, 1992);

Josefina Manresa, *Recuerdos de la viuda de Miguel Hernández* (Madrid: Torre, 1980);

Manuel Molina, *Miguel Hernández y sus amigos de Orihuela* (Málaga: Guadalhorce, 1969);

Manuel Muñoz Hidalgo, *Como fue Miguel Hernández* (Barcelona: Planeta, 1975);

Geraldine Cleary Nichols, *Miguel Hernández* (Boston: Twayne, 1978);

Jesús Poveda, *Vida, pasión y muerte de un poeta: Miguel Hernández* (Mexico City: Oasis, 1975);

Dario Puccini, *Miguel Hernández: Vida y Poesía* (Buenos Aires: Losada, 1970); revised and enlarged as *Miguel Hernández: Vida y poesía y otros estudios hernandianos* (Alicante: Instituto de Estudios Juan Gil-Albert, 1987);

Vicente Ramos, *Miguel Hernández* (Madrid: Gredos, 1973);

*Revista de Occidente,* special issue on Hernández, 139 (October 1974);

William Rose, *El pastor de la muerte: La dialéctica pastoril en la obra de Miguel Hernández* (Barcelona: Puvill, 1983);

Agustín Sánchez Vidal, *Miguel Hernández, desamordazado y regresado* (Barcelona: Planeta, 1992);

Sánchez Vidal, *Miguel Hernández, en la encrucijada* (Madrid: Edicusa, 1976);

Andrés Sorel, *Miguel Hernández, escritor y poeta de la revolución* (Madrid: Zero, 1976);

*Symposium,* special issue on Hernández, 22 (Summer 1968).

# Clara Janés
## (1940 – )

Janet Pérez
*Texas Tech University*

BOOKS: *Las estrellas vencidas* (Madrid: Agora, 1964);

*La noche de Abel Micheli* (Madrid: Novela Popular, 1965);

*Desintegración* (Madrid: Júcar, 1969);

*Límite humano* (Madrid: Oriens, 1973);

*En busca de Cordelia y Poemas rumanos* (Salamanca: Alamo, 1975);

*La vida callada de Federico Mompou* (Barcelona: Ariel, 1975);

*Cartas a Adriana* (Madrid: SARPE, 1976);

*Antología personal (1959–1979)* (Madrid: Rialp, 1979);

*Libro de alienaciones* (Madrid: Ayuso, 1980);

*Eros* (Madrid: Hiperión, 1981);

*Sendas de Rumania* (Barcelona: Plaza & Janés, 1981);

*Vivir* (Madrid: Hiperión, 1983);

*Kampa* (Madrid: Hiperión, 1986);

*Federico Mompou: Vida, textos y documentos* (Madrid: Fundación Banco Exterior, 1987);

*Lapidario* (Madrid: Hiperión, 1988);

*Los caballos del sueño* (Barcelona: Anagrama, 1989);

*Creciente fértil* (Madrid: Hiperión, 1989);

*Jardín y laberinto* (Madrid: Debate, 1990);

*El hombre de Adén* (Barcelona: Anagrama, 1991).

OTHER: *Las primeras poetisas en lengua castellana,* edited, with an introduction, by Janés (Madrid: Ayuso, 1986).

TRANSLATIONS: Vladimir Holan, *Avanzando* (Madrid, 1982);

Holan, *Antología* (Barcelona, 1984);

Jaroslav Seifert, *Breve antología* (Madrid: Hiperión, 1984);

Holan, *Dolor* (Madrid: Hiperión, 1986).

Though her first books date from a decade before Francisco Franco's death, Clara Janés is classed with the post-Franco writers; she was little known before 1975, and most of her work, including her most significant, was published after that year, during the reign of Juan Carlos and the transition to democracy. She is also more akin to post-Franco generations in "liberated" critical spirit.

Janés, the daughter of publisher Josep Janés Olive, was born in Barcelona in 1940, when Spain was still wracked by the enmity, rancor, and violence resulting from the Spanish Civil War and postwar purges. Reconstruction was delayed for many years because of the magnitude of destruction and the ongoing hostilities of World War II, which diverted attention from Spain and rendered foreign assistance unavailable. Barcelona, with its recent history of short-lived Catalan independence, suffered additional repression by the Franco regime. Having been the last capital of the republic, the city was hard hit in bombardments. Those who spoke and wrote in Catalan found their language outlawed (although they continued to speak it in their homes, and Clara Janés learned it as a child). The Franco regime ridiculed regional cultures, especially the Catalan and Galician ones, and many who had been heroes of Catalan nationalism were executed or imprisoned. Although young enough not to have a political record, Janés's father was a fervent partisan of Catalan culture and had achieved a modest reputation as a poet writing in Catalan.

As the eldest of the three daughters of Janés Olive, who owned an independent Catalan publishing firm, Clara Janés benefited from growing up in an atmosphere of exceptional culture, surrounded by books – written by established and aspiring authors – and a family ambience in which intellectual and artistic achievement were the norm. Her parents had met when applying for scholarships to further their artistic aspirations, her father as a writer and her mother as a concert pianist and harpsichordist. These careers were put in abeyance after their marriage, but the love of art remained, and the home was constantly filled with music and musicians, among them their close friend the great Catalan composer Federico Mompou (the subject of two books by Clara Janés).

*Clara Janés in 1989*

Her memoir of childhood and adolescence, *Jardín y laberinto* (Garden and Labyrinth, 1990), provides a wealth of information about her family and frequent visitors, as well as her parents' regular attendance at the opera, ballet, concerts, and theater; frequent entertaining; daily readings aloud; translation almost as a game; and impromptu recitals. She reconstructs conversations verbatim (her first published writing in Catalan) and recalls titles of works read, snatches of songs, and lines of poetry. In their childhood Clara and her sister Nona began learning to translate German, and Nona eventually became a university teacher of German. (Their much younger sister, Elisenda, is now a doctor.) Clara's reading of classics of world literature dates from when she was about seven, but she did not soon develop a literary vocation.

Memories of the family's large home in Pedralbes — then a luxurious suburb, now the site of Barcelona's University City — suggest an almost opulent life-style, with servants including a chauffeur and a gardener. The title *Jardín y laberinto* alludes to the girls' time spent in the family's walled garden, where they were physically isolated but intellectually free, and the title implicitly contrasts the ease of life behind the wall with the complexity on the other side. Janés's most vivid recollections are of the music room, with its harpsichord, harmonium,

and piano; the various walls lined with original artworks, including a large portrait of her mother; her father's extensive library; and flowers everywhere. The future poet refers repeatedly to her mother and guests in formal attire and to the dining room filled with mirrors and candelabras and crystal chandeliers. Janés often recalls her mother's playing instruments (including at public concerts that Clara could not attend, due to childhood diseases, but heard on the radio), as well as informal performances in their home by musical greats including Mompou and the flamenco guitarist Narciso Yepes. Various writers would often come to read from their work in progress.

But this intellectually stimulating world rested on shaky economic foundations, with long periods in which the major asset was her father's skill in fending off creditors. It ended with shocking suddenness one day in March 1959 when Janés's father, one of his brothers, and a cousin (associates in the publishing house) were killed in an automobile accident in another town. Clara and her mother had to identify the bodies — a nightmarish experience recreated several times in her poems. Janés affirms that it is because of her father's death that she turned to poetry. (Actually she had written a few things earlier but had destroyed them.) Her mother changed overnight and, dressed severely in black, began taking a briefcase daily to the publishing office; she also became almost obsessive in her religious observances. Not long afterward she began liquidating the objects of luxury, sold the mansion in Pedralbes, and moved back to the modest quarters where they had lived when Clara was born. The enclosed garden and magical world of Pedralbes had Edenic qualities (although she does not use that term), and expulsion from that paradisiacal setting definitively marked the end of an idealized existence and the end of her childhood. Janés and her mother became estranged.

These events almost coincided with Janés's departure for college. She studied for a time in Pamplona but eventually graduated from the University of Barcelona. During the late 1940s and the 1950s Janés had attended a private girls' school, run by nuns (the norm for girls of her class in these years). The late 1950s and 1960s included periods of unrest in Spain, and although strikes and student attempts at liberalizing conditions in the universities were harshly repressed by the regime, Janés, as a university student, became quite politicized, associating with young liberal intellectuals and protest movements. After she earned her degree in history at the University of Barcelona, she reportedly later received the equivalent of a master's degree in comparative literature from the Sorbonne; she also apparently studied literature at the Universities of Perugia, Grenoble, and Oxford. Janés suspends her autobiography in *Jardín y laberinto* essentially at the point when the family moved from Pedralbes, taking it up again some twenty years later when she finally became reconciled in some measure with her father's death. Nonetheless, it seems clear that she spent several years of study abroad, learned several languages, and specialized in literature at the graduate level. There are indications that she worked extensively in English literature and also explored a long-standing interest in Oriental poetry and in Greek classics. Although she has not to date depicted Perugia, Grenoble, or Oxford in her published works, travels in Germany and studies at the University of Barcelona appear in her novel *Desintegración* (Falling Apart, 1969); Pamplona and the Sorbonne are depicted in the novel *Los caballos del sueño* (Dream Steeds, 1989). Pamplona, a provincial capital in the north of Spain, had been a center of Falangist activity before the civil war, and the oppressive presence of political, religious, and moral intolerance there must have contrasted sharply with the comparative intellectual freedom in which Janés was raised. The differences between the Pamplona atmosphere – and, indeed, of most of Spain under

Franco – and that of 1960s Paris under the sway of existentialism, Parisian student radicalism, and French permissiveness (which Janés subsequently encountered at the Sorbonne) can hardly be overstated.

Janés entered a phase of idealized political leftism. The Franco regime defined all opposition as communist, and many anti-Franco intellectuals did, in fact, join the Communist party, the only well-organized and well-disciplined group among the necessarily covert and clandestine opponents of the dictatorship. There is no evidence that Janés became a card-carrying party member, but her growing anti-Franco sympathies led to significant stays in the Soviet Union, one at the invitation of the Communist government of Romania.

In the 1970s Janés traveled extensively, especially in south central Europe (Czechoslovakia, Romania, Yugoslavia, and Italy). Something of an expatriate, she spent enough time in Prague that she mastered Czech to an extent permitting her to translate poetry from that language for publication in Spain, including her rendering of Jaroslav Seifert's *Breve antología* (1984) and Vladimir Holan's *Avanzando* (1982), *Antología* (1984), and *Dolor* (1986). She developed relationships with some Czech poets whose works she later translated, including an intensely romantic attachment to the much older Holan. Many of her poems have epigraphs from Holan's poetry or allude to him or one of his poems, and the four poetic cycles in her *Kampa* (Camp, 1986; written between 1975 and 1978) are an outcry of pain at losing him. Holan apparently withdrew into himself to die. Her poetry is neither anecdotal nor confessional, and while it communicates emotion, very seldom does the reader find biographical details.

*Las estrellas vencidas* (Conquered Stars, 1964), Janés's first collection of poems, suffused with existential themes, expresses the poet's special feeling for the night as a time of liberation and of self-encounter, of being in touch with her own depths in a way that was not possible in the light of day. In the poems she explores Barcelona, as she wanders along the port area and past the fish market, through narrow, winding streets of the *barrio gótico* (Gothic quarter, the medieval part of the city), by taverns, beggars, and workingmen's quarters. With new awareness of her self and her body, she takes cognizance of her being and of temporality. Seeking expression yet never quite voiced are her solitude, disorientation, despair, and suffering at her father's death. The shock was so great that she had been unable to cry.

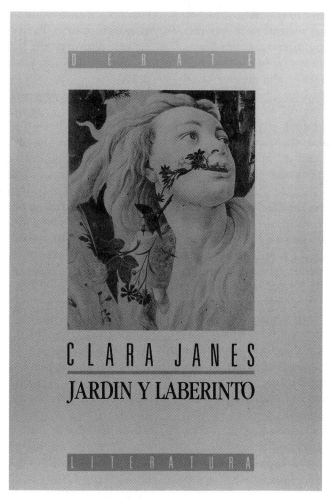

*Cover for Janés's memoir of her childhood and adolescence*

Her next work, *La noche de Abel Micheli* (Abel Micheli's Night, 1965), has been variously identified as a novella, a long short story published separately, and a novel. Apparently published in a limited edition, it is long out of print and difficult to find.

Several years passed after these initial publications – nearly a decade before the next collection of poetry and almost five years until the appearance of *Desintegración*. This novel re-creates what was, at the time of writing, the recent past, life in Barcelona in the early 1960s as seen from the perspective of a female Spanish university student. The action spans the time from the first year of the narrator/protagonist's study there until the winter of her final year, with the first three years narrated retrospectively from the vantage point of late summer prior to beginning the final year. The novel is structured in two unequal parts, the longer, initial one covering her first three years at the university, in flashbacks recalled during her visit to a friend who

has immigrated to a factory town in northern Germany. The shorter, second part covers the time between her return to Spain in October and the December holidays of that same year. The beginning and ending of the novel correspond to her relationship with the Jordán family, her failed engagement to Martín Jordán (a classmate, aspiring Don Juan, and precocious alcoholic), her friendships with his siblings, and her eventual emotional attachment to his brother David. Existential elements appear in the abortive attempts at communication, the lack of existential authenticity of most characters, the absurdity of certain situations, and the radical solitude or alienation of the major figures. The absence or nonexistence of ultimate truths, the limitations of human reason and the human situation, and the inability to cope with freedom are likewise significant, and such elements also appear in Janés's poetry, especially in *Límite humano* (Human Limits, 1973) and *Libro de alienaciones* (Book of Alienations, 1980).

Feminist attitudes appear in the novel in the subversion of traditional, patriarchal arguments buttressing the relegation of women to secondary, "object" status; doubts expressed concerning idealized romance; and the protagonist's final rejection of marriage or commitment in favor of an uncertain future – alone but independent. While the novel was written with some caution (censorship still being a reality), a clear undercurrent of rebellion can be detected. *Desintegración* was a finalist for the 1969 Nadal Prize, then among the most prestigious Spanish literary awards.

With *Límite humano* Janés began to make poetry her primary preoccupation, publishing future collections with more regularity. Two decades elapsed before her next novel, *Los caballos del sueño.* In *Límite humano* she attempts to decipher the enigma of human existence, to understand the nature of man as a being who aspires to the absolute yet is constantly bound by his own (human) limitations, seeking, questioning, and reflecting. Motifs of light and darkness, seeing and blindness, recur along with images of mist, fog, twilight, futility, and fear. The ancient literary topos of life as a road appears, but the road is dusty, lonely, and leads nowhere, without the traveler's realizing it. In contrast with *Las estrellas vencidas, Límite humano* portrays spaces that are not urban but predominantly rural. Solitude, anguish, the existential sense of "being-toward-death," and a quest for ontological meaning combine to lead the poet toward love. Although solitude endures even in love relationships and the poetic persona violently rejects love's limitations and failures, love begins to emerge as the one thing that endows existence with meaning.

Janés indicates in the prologue to her *Antología personal (1959–1979)* (1979) that she continued to experience that unceasing search for meaning, always frustrated by her limitations, and that it was reading Holan's poetry that caused her to return to poetry, writing *En busca de Cordelia y Poemas rumanos* (In Search of Cordelia and Romanian Poems, 1975), "Isla del suicidio" (Suicide Island), and *Libro de alienaciones. Antología personal* includes some previously unpublished works, including parts of *Kampa* and several poems from "Isla del suicidio" (which subsequently became the first part of *Libro de alienaciones*). "Isla del suicidio" repeats some of the themes and motifs of *Las estrellas vencidas* and *Límite humano,* including rebellion, temporality, death, and questioning. Skepticism and irony are more in evidence, as are – occasionally – pain and indignation, as the poetic persona continues to seek and to encounter limits impossible to transcend. In "Poemas

rumanos" Janés writes of other poets, the dead, silence, infinity, desire, and the unknown or imponderable, while "Isla del suicidio" exudes a mythological air, intensified by an unidentified poetic space – perhaps Ibiza (seaside, waves, wind, sand, and sea) – including statuesque figures, ancient fig and olive trees, cemeteries, images of pagan gods, and volcanic outcroppings. Nudity, insanity, anguish, blindness, terrible remorse, and silence are major motifs.

In the rest of *Libro de alienaciones* death is linked to eroticism and lasciviousness – sexuality divorced from procreation, and prostitution of both sexes. The speaker continues her quest for meaning, momentarily lured by the siren songs of ephemeral love, then overcome by anguish, solitude, silence, and deceptive appearances. Some of Janés's most surrealistic descriptions appear in *Libro de alienaciones,* occasionally evoking the atmosphere of Federico García Lorca's *Poeta en Nueva York* (1940; translated as *The Poet in New York,* 1940), particularly in her poems "Asesinato" (Murder) and "Pregón" (Proclamation). Notes of suffering and despair are more intense, and the speaker distrusts those who have never contemplated suicide. Violence, irreparable loss, emptiness, and nothingness alternate with the search for a friend, sister, kindred spirit, or lover and the wish to respect another's liberty with a sense of separation. Desperately alone, the main persona imagines being able to hold herself in her arms and provide needed warmth and comfort; life is escaping, and the abyss of nothingness terrifies her.

*Eros* (1981) develops the theme of love as the primary contact with meaning, even though reality eventually proves disappointing and the poet's ontological search is frustrated again. Less than perfect communication and incomplete sharing or surrender of oneself doom the quest for oneness with "the other," and the limits of the human condition are such that love remains a yearning, providing fleeting glimpses of the absolute yet allowing ontological plenitude to elude the seeker's grasp. Love and physical passion are major thematic nuclei for Janés, and she has been identified as one of Spain's great feminine love poets by Rosa Chacel, one of the senior Spanish women novelists. (Janés has dedicated several poems to Chacel.) In her poetry of the 1970s onward, Janés is more concerned with language per se, and her style evolves in the direction of a finely chiseled form, moving away from the free-verse style of earlier collections but without returning to any traditional metrics.

Janés preferentially employs brief and deceptively prosaic forms, some of her poems being as short as three or four lines, and a significant proportion being seven to eleven lines. Some lines consist of a single word; the longest run to sixteen or eighteen syllables. Avoiding both rhyme and assonance, Janés constructs most of her poems without recourse to traditional prosody or recognizable patterns. Some of her briefest compositions resemble the haiku. Discussing her modus operandi in *Jardín y laberinto,* Janés indicates that many of her poems were composed while walking and that sometimes their cadence echoes the rhythm of her aimless steps, stopping, turning, heading back, lingering, or moving forward.

Avoidance of traditional metrics does not indicate lack of interest in form; on the contrary, Janés frequently makes specific reference in her poems to questions of form, the concern for formal perfection, and the formal superiority of "naked poetry" (a probable echo of Juan Ramón Jiménez). Her predominant metrics may be described as structured free verse, paradoxical as the term might seem. The result approaches blank verse, technically nonexistent in Spanish, as is iambic pentameter. Janés at times comes close, with her predilection for unrhymed hendecasyllabic lines. Her second most frequently used metric length is the heptasyllable, which together with the hendecasyllable accounts for two-thirds to three-fourths of her metric patterns. Despite the occurrence of lines varying from three to fifteen or sixteen syllables, the predominance of seven- and eleven-syllable lines creates a disciplined and rather uniform impression, notwithstanding the almost studied absence of either assonance or rhyme.

Janés's poetry abounds in intertextual allusions, citations, and references. Several poems in *Vivir* (To Live, 1983) are dedicated to other authors, ancient and modern, especially women writers, including Chacel, María Victoria Atencia, and María Zambrano. Some poems constitute a sort of homage to the writer named in the dedication, an imitation of some aspect of that person's style, a recollection of times together, and a tribute to shared preoccupations; at other times the motives for Janés's dedications remain inscrutable.

Poetic devices preferred by Janés include subtle cadences, condensation, repetition, ellipsis, parallel constructions, occasional (rare) internal rhyme, prosopopoeia, enumeration, and allusion. She relies also on the reiteration of concepts – a kind of idea rhyme – in which existential topoi are most significant: solitude and the impossibility of real communication, combined with a longing for full and complete exchange; anguish or nausea and absurdity;

being-toward-death and concern for time; a nearly visceral rejection of a rapidly changing, increasingly depersonalized and technological world; and the perennial search for meaning, friendship, eroticism, love, and the peace in nature. Over time the existential motifs become somewhat less insistent, giving ground to nature itself, while the overall tone becomes increasingly affirmative.

Janés employs appellative symbology with some consistency, and names of protagonists or titles of works may provide clues to interpretation. Existential preoccupations are evinced by the titles of *Límite humano, Libro de alienaciones,* and *Vivir,* while the titles of *Eros* and *Lapidario* (Stonecutter, 1988) aptly denote their primary emphases. (*Lapidario* focuses on gems and their history and symbolism.) Another major interest of Janés revealed through titles is her fascination with Romania, seen also in her many references to Romanian poets. The title of *Desintegración* provides a hermeneutic key: in this novel things fall apart, ideals unravel, groups and families disintegrate, and friends and lovers separate. The artistically inclined, university-educated young women who function as protagonists of Janés's two major novels (*Desintegración* and *Los caballos del sueño*) are modern embodiments of Psyche, sharing enough traits with Janés to allow viewing them as masks or personae of her, although neither novel is fully autobiographical. Aspiring writers who move in paraliterary circles, both protagonists are erotically vulnerable (true to the Psyche archetype) and experience obsessive, overpowering needs to know more about their lovers.

Perhaps because of her studies of English, Janés experiments with secondary accentuation or stress, which (as Miguel de Unamuno observed) are largely ignored in Spanish poetry. Like most of the *novísimos* ("very new" poets of the late 1960s or early 1970s who rejected the neorealist "social poetry" of the 1950s and 1960s), Janés writes for a cultured audience, avoiding the colloquial register of the social poets. Her poetry exemplifies postmodernism insofar as the abundant intertextuality establishes dialogues with other poets' works and thereby endows her poems with multivocal passages. Quotes from Johann Wolfgang von Goethe, John Keats, Plato, William Shakespeare, Greek and Roman mythology, and scientific and sacred texts all form part of her intertextual mosaic. Erudite, archaic, and foreign words are not uncommon in her poetic lexicon, but neither are they so frequent as to make her discourse hermetic.

No single practice emerges in her titling of poems. Janés usually establishes a normative practice within a given volume (most or all poems being titled, for example, or nearly all untitled); however, sometimes she uses numbers or Roman numerals, or she combines the latter with a title without this necessarily indicating the existence of other poems with the same title. For instance, *Vivir* includes compositions identified as "Porcelana VII," "Lurra IV," and "Lurra XVI," but no poems titled simply "Porcelana" or "Lurra" appear. If some meaningful relationship exists between these numerals and the poet's creative activity, it might involve the number of drafts; lacking such information, the reader may consider the numerals arbitrary or expendable. Some titles approach the ironic (their relationship to the content of the composition possibly a negative or seemingly nonexistent one), while others provide reliable clues to understanding the poem or the poet's sentiment.

*Kampa* contains four cycles of which one is musical. Janés was accustomed to musical performance and composition from early childhood and has turned to the musical plaint in moments of great emotional intensity: in *Jardín y laberinto* she recounts her attempt to compose a kind of memorial elegy on the twentieth anniversary of her father's death and how it eventually became a wordless, yet voiced, melodious lament. Another cycle in *Kampa* is composed mostly of sounds, syllables not connected by a sequence of meaning or causality but which constitute a kind of meditation on morphology or etymology, which are poetic in their alliteration and onomatopoeia and which employ the lyric device of repetition. The remaining two cycles comprise poems of enormous passion and frankness on the love of Janés for Holan, her desperation and depression at the termination of the relationship, her despairing desire to infuse the dying, aged poet with her own will for him to live, and her slow coming-to-terms with his retreat from life. Although the relationship may have been platonic (and nothing in Janés's poems proves the presence of anything more erotic than desire), the poems are in the vein of Pedro Salinas's erotic lyrics that aspire to complete and total possession and penetration of the soul of the beloved. Significantly there is a reference in *Jardín y laberinto* to Janés's discovery of Salinas's works.

Over the course of her career Janés's initial existential sentiment, concern for time, and rebellious rejection of a rapidly changing world have given way to a more complex thematics including affirmation of life, love, friendship, and nature (including animals, objects, and landscapes). *Lapidario* displays thematic unity with its focus on precious stones and

light – elements present in Janés's early poetry but which now assume more-important roles. Each poem in *Lapidario* describes a different gem and constitutes a recapitulation of earlier beliefs or practices concerning it.

In addition to her 1975 biography of Mompou and her 1987 biobibliographical study of his works, Janés has published other nonfiction works, including a travel book, *Sendas de Rumania* (Paths of Romania, 1981), and several short stories. Though fiction, her novel *Los caballos del sueño* has been hailed as the definitive history of her generation. Although part of the novel is an adolescent love story, it also offers a mosaic of characters and motifs set into the overall fabric of Spain's evolution from the 1960s to the 1980s, with a progressive loss of ideals and undermining of values as consumerism develops. A novel almost two decades in the writing, it is a complex work that incorporates various genres: epistle, drama, philosophical essay, diary, poetry, and narrative. Striking thematic and structural similarities between this novel and *Desintegración* may belie the two decades separating them, but the later novel is clearly more mature, approaches rhetorical perfection, and displays a marked increase in lyricism, with baroque elements not present in its predecessor. Both novels involve romantic triangles comprising the female narrator and two closely related male rivals, representing physical and spiritual alternatives; in each case a third male is briefly introduced near the end. Both novels make extensive use of the voyage topos, in both literal and figurative terms (life as a journey), noted also in some of her poetry, and both novels are similarly imbued with existential motifs. *Los caballos del sueño* begins in Pamplona and follows its characters into midlife, studying the long-term, crippling emotional effects upon the three major personages of their religious and ideological indoctrination. Because it spans some twenty years, the narrative incorporates the decisive transition from young adulthood through incipient decline, communicating a deep sense of disillusionment and despair. The protagonist reaches an important existential turning point near the end of *Los caballos del sueño,* leaving her husband after years of psychological misery and physical abuse (an emotional self-liberation that echoes the decision to go it alone made by the protagonist/narrator of *Desintegración*).

*Creciente fértil* (Fertile Crescent, 1989) is a book of poetry that not only alludes to the ancient epithet for Mesopotamia but points to the Muslim world as exuding refined sensuality, erotic variety and expertise, and linkages of sexuality and paradise. Incorporating into her book Persian mythology, allusions to astrology, Arabic architecture and art, Janés weaves together a collection of considerable unity, with all three dozen poems having to do with amorous encounters (or the anticipation or recollection thereof) set in stylized Islamic ambience with a great deal of fleshly emphasis; images of sexual arousal, lovemaking, and penetration; and powerfully lyrical, transparent metaphors of copulation and fecundation. Sexuality is much more explicit than in *Kampa* and *Libro de alienaciones,* the most erotic of Janés's prior poetry collections. Structurally the poems of *Creciente fértil* often recall the parallelisms and repetition of biblical verse.

*El hombre de Adén* (The Man of Aden, 1991) echoes the Arabic motifs of *Creciente fértil* and is the most openly sensual and erotic of Janés's prose works to date. Difficult to classify, it has characteristics of the novel, the memoir, and the travel book. Janés uses a first-person perspective and narrative, and the voyage topos reappears, but she leaves the reader to decide whether this book is a true piece of autobiography or a fictionalized memoir, whether the narrative *I* speaks for Janés or corresponds to a fictional entity, and even whether Janés has been a tourist in the Arab emirates along the Gulf of Aden (as content insinuates) or if the journey and corresponding amorous adventures are fantasy. A significant difference between this prose narrative and *Creciente fértil* is the appearance of distinctly feminist notes and explicit criticism of a sociocultural context in which women have no control over their bodies, their lives, and their destinies. At the same time that Janés's works become progressively more explicit concerning female sexuality, she clearly affirms woman's right to choose as a subject and not as an object.

Janés possesses a distinct and personal lyric voice, a poetic persona conditioned by her being Catalan, even though she has published no poetry in that language. Enormously frank and yet rarely anecdotal or confessional, she presents the distilled emotional essence of experiences, most often abstract and detached from concrete, specific details. The exception is *Kampa,* but even this outpouring of personal passion is far from exhibitionistic or autobiographical, for the poet's sense of privacy – her own and that of the beloved – prevails. Unlike Ana Rosetti, in whose works eroticism can be frankly ludic, Janés infuses the erotic with seriousness; her existential quest for ontological meaning has yet to produce anything other than love.

**References:**

Janet Pérez, "Clara Janés," in *Continental Women Writers,* edited by Katharina M. Wilson (New York: Garland, 1991), pp. 2–3;

Pérez, "The Novels of a Poet: Clara Janés," in *Critical Essays on the Literature of Spain and Spanish America,* edited by Luis González de Valle and Julio Baena (Boulder, Colo.: Society of Spanish & American Studies, 1992), pp. 197–207.

# Juan Ramón Jiménez

## (24 December 1881 – 29 May 1958)

### Howard T. Young
#### Pomona College

SELECTED BOOKS: *Almas de violeta* (Madrid: Moderna, 1900);

*Ninfeas* (Madrid: Moderna, 1900);

*Rimas* (Madrid: Fernando Fe, 1902);

*Arias tristes* (Madrid: Fernando Fe, 1903);

*Jardines lejanos* (Madrid: Fernando Fe, 1904);

*Elegías puras* (Madrid, 1908);

*Elegías intermedias* (Madrid, 1909);

*Olvidanzas I: Las hojas verdes* (Madrid: Revista de Archivos, 1909); enlarged as *Olvidanzas* (Madrid: Revista de Archivos, 1909);

*Eligías lamentables* (Madrid, 1910);

*Baladas de primavera* (Madrid: Revista de Archivos, 1910);

*Poemas mágicos y dolientes* (Madrid: Revista de Archivos, 1911);

*La soledad sonora* (Madrid: Revista de Archivos, 1911);

*Pastorales* (Madrid: Renacimiento, 1911);

*Melancolía* (Madrid: Revista de Archivos, 1912);

*Laberinto* (Madrid: Renacimiento, 1913);

*Platero y yo* (Madrid: Biblioteca de Juventud, 1914; enlarged edition, Madrid: Calleja, 1917); translated by William and Mary Roberts as *Platero and I: An Andalusian Elegy* (Oxford: Dolphin, 1956; New York: Duschnes, 1956); translated by Eloïse Roach as *Platero and I* (Austin: University of Texas Press, 1957; London: Nelson, 1958);

*Estío* (Madrid: Calleja, 1916);

*Sonetos espirituales* (Madrid: Calleja, 1917);

*Diario de un poeta recién casado* (Madrid: Calleja, 1917); republished as *Diario de poeta y mar* (Buenos Aires: Losada, 1948);

*Poesías escojidas (1899–1917)* (New York: Hispanic Society of America, 1917);

*Eternidades* (Madrid: Angel de Alcoy, 1918);

*Piedra y cielo* (Madrid: Fortanet, 1919);

*Antolojía poetica* (Buenos Aires: Losada, 1922);

*Segunda antolojía poética, 1898–1918* (Madrid: Espasa-Calpe, 1922);

*Poesía* (Madrid: Talleres Poligráficos, 1923);

*Belleza* (Madrid: Talleres Poligráficos, 1923);

*Presente* (Madrid: Aguirre, 1933);

*Canción* (Madrid: Signo, 1936);

*Política poética* (Madrid: Instituto del Libro Español, 1936);

*Ciego ante ciegos* (Havana: Secretaría de Educación, 1938);

*Españoles de tres mundos* (Buenos Aires: Losada, 1942);

*Voces de mi copla* (Mexico City: Stylo, 1945);

*El zaratán* (Mexico City: Antigua Libraría Robredo, 1946);

*La estación total con las Canciones de la nueva luz* (Buenos Aires: Losada, 1946);

*Romances de Coral Gables* (Mexico City: Stylo, 1948);

*Animal de fondo* (Buenos Aires: Pleamar, 1949);

*Antología para niños y adolescentes,* selected by Norah Borges and Guillermo de Torres (Buenos Aires: Losada, 1951);

*Tercera antolojía poética (1898–1953)* (Madrid: Biblioteca Nueva, 1957);

*Libros de poesía,* edited by Agustín Caballero (Madrid: Aguilar, 1957);

*Moguer* (Madrid: Dirección General de Archivos & Bibliotecas, 1958);

*Primeros libros de poesía,* edited by Francisco Garfias (Madrid: Aguilar, 1959);

*El romance* (San Juan: University of Puerto Rico, 1959);

*Olvidos de Granada* (Río Piedras: University of Puerto Rico, 1960);

*Cuadernos,* edited by Garfias (Madrid: Taurus, 1960);

*La corriente infinita,* edited by Garfias (Madrid: Aguilar, 1961);

*Por el cristal amarillo,* edited by Garfias (Madrid: Aguilar, 1961);

*El trabajo gustoso,* edited by Garfias (Mexico City & Madrid: Aguilar, 1961);

*Primeras prosas,* edited by Garfias (Madrid: Aguilar, 1962);

*Juan Ramón Jiménez*

*La colina de los chopos* (Barcelona: Círculo de Lectores, 1963);

*Sevilla,* edited by Garfias (Seville: Ixbiliah, 1963);

*Poemas revividos del tiempo de Moguer* (Barcelona: Chapultepec, 1963);

*Dios deseado y deseante,* edited by Antonio Sánchez-Barbudo (Madrid: Aguilar, 1964); translated as *God Desired and Desiring* (New York: Paragon House, 1987);

*Libros inéditos de poesia,* 2 volumes, edited by Garfias (Madrid: Aguilar, 1964, 1967);

*Retratos líricos* (Madrid: Díaz-Casariego, 1965);

*Estética y ética estética,* edited by Garfias (Madrid: Aguilar, 1967);

*Con el carbón del sol,* edited by Garfias (Madrid: EMESA, 1973);

*El andarín de su órbita,* edited by Garfias (Madrid: EMESA, 1974);

*En el otro costado,* edited by Aurora de Albornoz (Madrid: Júcar, 1974);

*Crítica paralela,* edited by Arturo del Villar (Madrid: Nárcea, 1975);

*La obra desnuda,* edited by Villar (Seville: Aldebarán, 1976);

*Leyenda, 1896–1956,* edited by Antonio Sánchez Romeralo (Madrid: Cupsa, 1978);

*Historias y cuentos,* edited by Villar (Barcelona: Bruguera, 1979);

*Espacio,* edited by Albornoz (Madrid: Nacionale, 1982).

**Editions in English:** *Fifty Spanish Poems,* translated by J. B. Trend (Oxford: Dolphin, 1950; Berkeley: University of California Press, 1951);

*Selected Writings,* translated by H. R. Hays, edited by Eugenio Florit (New York: Farrar, Straus & Cudahy, 1957);

*Three Hundred Poems, 1903–1953,* translated by Roach (Austin: University of Texas Press, 1962);

*Forty Poems,* translated by Robert Bly (Madison, Wis.: Sixties, 1967);

*Still Waters of the Air,* bilingual edition, edited by Richard Lewis (New York: Dial, 1970);

*Selected Works,* edited by Bly (Boston: Beacon, 1973);

*Selected Poems* (Harmondsworth, U.K. & Baltimore: Penguin, 1974).

PLAY PRODUCTION: *Jinetes hacia el mar,* translated by Jiménez and Zenobia Camprubí Aymar from John Millington Synge's *Riders to the Sea,* Madrid, Teatro Ritz, 1920.

SELECTED TRANSLATIONS: Romain Rolland, *Vida de Beethoven* (Madrid: Residencia de Estudiantes, 1915);

John Millington Synge, *Jinetes hacia el mar,* translated by Jiménez and Zenobia Camprubí Aymar (Madrid: Fortanet, 1920);

Rabindranath Tagore, *Obra escojida,* translated by Jiménez and Camprubí Aymar (Madrid: Aguilar, 1955).

SELECTED PERIODICAL PUBLICATION – UNCOLLECTED: "Espacio," *Poesía Española,* 28 (April 1954): 1–11.

Juan Ramón Jiménez, known simply as Juan Ramón in the Hispanic world, dominated Spanish poetry for the first three decades of the twentieth century, and at the outbreak of the Spanish Civil War in 1936 he was still a figure of influence and importance. Later, in exile in the United States and Puerto Rico, he expanded his already considerable influence, made the acquaintance of Robert Frost and Ezra Pound, and was greeted with a frenzy of enthusiasm on a trip to Buenos Aires in 1948. The unabashed and imperfectly assimilated modernism of Jiménez's first books yielded in *Rimas* (Rhymes, 1902) and *Arias tristes* (Sad Airs, 1903) to a delicate, sensitive, and sentimental tone that drew much from Spanish romanticism. After 1916 he entered a new phase, for which he is justly well known. Stripping anecdote and obvious sentiment from his lines, he made heavy use of symbols in a self-referential poetry surprising for its sheerness and its difficulty. Its major themes are the relation of the poet to poetry; of poetry to the world; and love, memory, and death. This phase gradually gave way just before the civil war and afterward to a period in which moments of epiphany become longer and deeper and the poet experiences a serene union with nature. His final works apotheosize the creative spirit and carry forward the romantic, symbolist tradition of the poet as a divine seer. *Platero y yo* (1914; translated as *Platero and I,* 1956), a series of vignettes of small-town life and rural scenes in and around his birthplace, Moguer, has been translated into fifteen languages. The combination of Platero and Moguer may be, after that of Don Quixote and La Mancha, one of the most universally known in literature. Jiménez's Andalusian roots were, like William Butler Yeats's Irishness, a source of inspiration and pride. As the Spaniard's fame grew, he never ceased to remind his public of his Andalusian heritage. No idle boast underlies the sobriquet he provided for himself: "El andaluz universal" (The Universal Andalusian).

The Jiménez family operated a comfortable business as wine and tobacco merchants with their own warehouses, ships, and vineyards, and their products were well known in Gibraltar and throughout southern Spain. Such commerce enabled the young Juan Ramón Jiménez Mantecón, the third child of the family, to enjoy the upbringing of a typical Andalusian *señorito* (well-to-do young gentleman). He remembered pleasant visits to his father's (Victor Jiménez's) ships and warehouses and rides in the country astride his colt "Almirante." But Juan Ramón was also an introspective, solitary boy who spent long hours letting his imagination run riot with a kaleidoscope. In October 1893, after finishing primary school in Huelva, he and his brother Eustaquio entered the Jesuit Colegio de San Luis Gonzaga in Puerto de Santa María near Jerez de la Frontera. Except for the view from his dormitory window that looked out on the ocean with Cádiz in the distance, Juan Ramón found school gloomy and disturbing. A delicate and docile nature made him the easy butt of his classmates' pranks. At the onset of puberty his natural sensitivity grew more marked, and his character began to show a strong narcissistic trend, a development that was abetted by his mother's love and indulgence.

At the *colegio* Jiménez filled the margins and blank pages of his textbooks with drawings. His favorite subject was French, and selections that he read in this school by the sea made an indelible impression on his mind, for one finds references to them among the hundreds of notes that he left as an adult poet. He also enjoyed texts on rhetoric, as well as an 1882 edition of Thomas à Kempis's *The Imitation of Christ,* in which Jiménez underlined passages that confirmed his penchant for reticence and solitude; one such passage is "Show not thy heart to every man." In 1896 he concluded his studies for the *bachillerato* (high-school diploma).

Two aspects of Jiménez's life between the ages of thirteen and sixteen are especially revealing for a deeper understanding of the man and his poetry. The adolescent boy had, he admitted, a tyrannical nature; he argued endlessly with his uncles and insisted on having the last word on all matters pertaining to literature and art; he verbally attacked one of his cousins whenever she came to dinner, because of a nervous tic she had. The *señorito* would go storming to his room after these scenes, refusing to apologize and leaving his mother in tears, a reaction on her part that increased his guilt and consequently his fury. The young boy's tendency toward

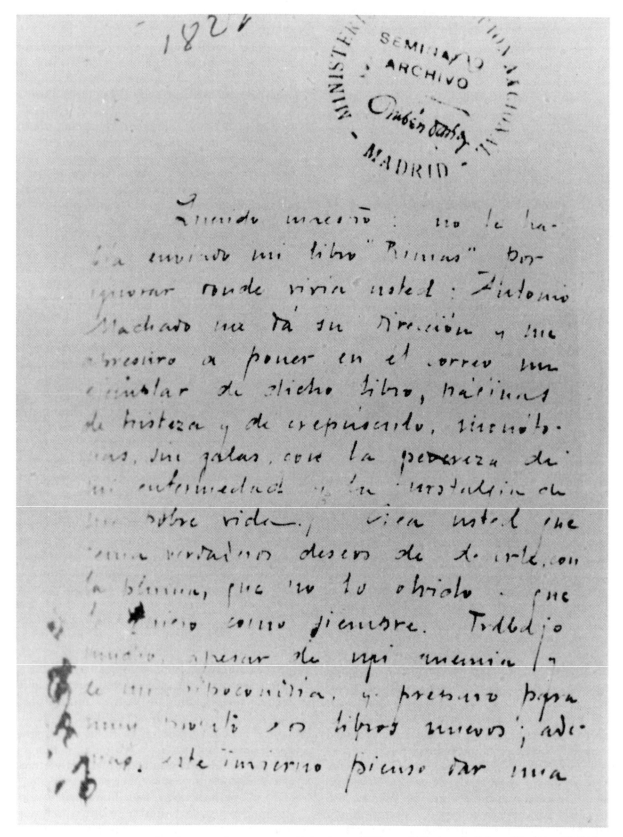

*First page of a 1902 letter from Jiménez to Nicaraguan poet Rubén Darío (Biblioteca del Instituto de Cultura Hispanica, Madrid)*

violence took an especially disturbing tack. Guns fascinated him, he recalls in *Por el cristal amarillo* (Through the Yellow Glass, 1961), a collection of prose pieces about Moguer, and he hunted everything that was fair game and much that was not, including his turtle and his cousin's pet eaglet. He shot all kinds of birds by the score. The adult Jiménez's fondness for birds, symbols for him of the natural divine music that poetry should emulate, stands in startling contrast to the image of this youth, in critic Donald F. Fogelquist's phrase, "cannonading the countryside." Although this aspect of Jiménez's character might come as a surprise, assiduous readers have long recognized his darker side, the sinister alter ego mentioned in a few of his poems – the individual dressed in black peering at him through his bedroom window; it is Jiménez brushed by what Charles Baudelaire called "the wings of madness." Such instability of character was to plague Jiménez throughout his life. Furthermore, in the adult Jiménez, the doyen who brooked no deviations from the course he had set, one sees the boy at the dinner table who insisted on having the last word in matters of arts and letters.

The tyrannous adolescent Jiménez fell in love with Blanca Hernández-Pinzón, the daughter of Moguer's judge; she was descended from a family who had befriended Christopher Columbus. Blanca and Juan Ramón met through her brother José, who was courting Juan Ramón's sister Victoria. Blanca and Juan Ramón's relationship included stolen kisses while her mother dozed over rosary beads. Blanca's family, rightfully fearful of such an impetuous Moguer marksman, discouraged the association. Graciela Palau de Nemes, the poet's principal biographer to date, believes that this young and unrequited love planted in Jiménez's mind the ideal of the white, chaste, beautiful, and unattainable woman, one of the guiding symbols for his verse. Blanca's name could not have been more appropriate. She was the first of his many sweethearts, real and fanciful. Like Percy Bysshe Shelley, he was in love with love.

Victor Jiménez wanted his son Juan Ramón to be a lawyer, but the young man believed he had talent as an artist and cherished the thought of becoming a painter. It was finally decided that he would begin the course of studies for prelaw at the University of Seville and at the same time take instruction in studio art. In autumn 1896 he enrolled in the university and began his art apprenticeship in the studio of Salvador Clemente, a genre painter from Cádiz, whose many scenes of vineyards and flamenco dancers sold well to tourists. Under the tutelage of the capricious Clemente, Jiménez drew the obligatory still lifes and landscapes and showed himself an apt pupil in the impressionist style. His paintings reveal a more-than-ordinary talent and a preference for a blend of subdued blues, grays, whites, and greens that coincides exactly with the hues in his poetry. While his chromatic sense was exceptional and became especially notable in his verse, the craftsmanship of his drawings betrays an eye still struggling with perspective. He continued to paint busily until 1900. In the exhibition of his paintings and drawings arranged in Moguer on the occasion of the centennial of his birth, the gentle impressionistic landscapes and the portraits of gypsy girls were the best indication of the plastic skills that yielded to the art of painting with words. Jiménez once remarked that of the three great loves of his life – painting, poetry, and music – painting beckoned first when he was fifteen and then gave way a year or two later to poetry. (His devotion to music began when he was twenty.) The reasons for his decision not to continue as a painter are unclear. Certainly the bohemian life-style of Clemente and his friends did not appeal to the correct young man, who was compulsive about neatness and order. Ruminating on the situation afterward, Jiménez said that if he had had a different master, he might have gone on to become a painter of note.

His year at the University of Seville saw the crystalization of his ambition to be a poet. He immersed himself in lyrical verse, read through the night, and composed his own lines as he walked along the banks of the Guadalquivir, which glides through Seville out into the Atlantic. In the city that much of Europe viewed as the quintessence of romance, Jiménez spent his money and most of the energy and time he was not devoting to art lessons to reading and declaiming the poetry of Alphonse Lamartine, Lord Byron, and Heinrich Heine. These initial encounters installed in his temperament a need for the insistent expression of personal feelings and confirmed his tendency toward sentimentality and melancholy. He did not, however, neglect the poets of his native language. Poetry by José de Espronceda, the "Spanish Byron," made an impression, as did, most notably, Gustavo Adolfo Bécquer, whose *Rimas* (1860, 1861), published two decades before Jiménez's birth, resembled works by Heine and Shelley and foreshadowed the suggestive musicality of the French symbolists. (It was no accident that Jiménez's first important book is also titled *Rimas*.) At this early stage he also became acquainted with the delicate poetry of Rosalía de Castro, a Galician poetess who, like Bécquer, signaled

*Cover for an issue of the literary magazine founded by Jiménez and other young writers in Madrid. Only eleven issues were published, but the magazine exerted a powerful influence on the modernist movement in Spain.*

the way to a more finely tuned expression of self-consciousness, lower in pitch than the romantic megaphone of Espronceda, and who also, like Emily Dickinson, made of her solitude and subjective eye for nature a topic for poetry.

Early in 1897 the *Programa,* a Seville newspaper, accepted one of Jiménez's poems, and, thus encouraged, he joined a literary group in Seville called the Ateneo and began to send more poems to provincial magazines and newspapers. Soon he enjoyed a good reputation in the city and started work on a book of poetry to be called "Nubes" (Clouds). The demands of poetry and painting left him no time for studies, and, upon failing Spanish history, he withdrew from the university at the end of the spring term to devote himself full-time, with the blessing of

an indulgent family, to painting and writing. He collaborated on the reviews *Hojas Sueltas* and *Quincena,* the latter under the guidance of the novelist and playwright Timoteo Orbe. Orbe was a product of *krausismo,* a form of German idealism introduced into Spain by Julián Sanz del Río that had a decided effect on an intellectual minority with liberal tendencies. At a time when an air of pessimism hung heavy over Europe, this small cadre believed that in the powers of art and the highly selective spirit of the artist lay a way of lifting from humankind the weight imposed by the ideas of Friedrich Nietzsche and Charles Darwin.

In the small library maintained by the *Quincena,* Jiménez ran across the verses of Rubén Darío, the great poet from Nicaragua. Blending

French romanticism, Parnassianism, and symbolism, Darío had managed to inject new life into Hispanic poetry at the turn of the century. Jiménez long remembered the exhilaration produced by this first contact with Darío's works.

*Vida Nueva,* a Madrid review, accepted a poem by Jiménez that was inspired by a humanitarian concern for the lower classes. "Las amantes del miserable" (The Beggar's Lovers) has some compassionate, if overwrought, lines about a beggar on a cold winter night in Madrid; his only friends are the prostitutes Loneliness and Death. *Vida Nueva* published this piece on 3 December 1899 with a photo of the broodingly handsome young author and sent him, on the basis of his apparent concern with social problems, five pieces by Ibsen, already translated into Spanish, which Jiménez polished into poetic prose. Thus began a lifelong interest in the art of translation. *Vida Nueva* published his Ibsen translations on 7 January 1900, and the stage was set for Jiménez to go to Madrid.

A postcard signed by Darío and Francisco Villaespesa, a young poet who was an avid reader of *Vida Nueva,* invited Jiménez to come to Madrid and assist in the task of revitalizing Spanish poetry. Needing no urging, he packed his bags and arrived in Madrid on Good Friday of 1900, to be swept up into the bohemian life of the *modernistas.*

Darío, fresh from the triumph in 1896 of his *Prosas profanas* (Profane Prose), was sent by *La Nación* of Buenos Aires to report on conditions in Spain after its devastating defeat at the hands of the United States in 1898. He arrived in early 1899 at the age of thirty-two, preceded by the reputation gained from the success of his *Azul* (Blue, 1888) and *Prosas profanas,* and he found what he thought was an old, tired country, with a middle class indifferent to the disaster of 1898 and most of the writers past their prime. Baudelaire, Paul Verlaine, the decadents, and the Parnassians were not unknown in Spain when Darío arrived (Jiménez having read works by Verlaine before meeting Darío), but Darío's masterful synthesis of these currents, plus traces of the influence of such classic Spanish writers as Saint Teresa and Luis de Góngora, pointed the way toward a successful renovation of poetic language. Darío's themes were limited, but his skill was unquestionable, and his lines have an elegance and sensuality about them that stand in vivid contrast to the lyrics of Ramón de Campoamor, Gaspar Núñez de Arce, and Juan Zorrilla, the reigning poets at that time. Thus Darío, a mestizo from Central America, who had the face of an Indian, the hands of a marquis, and a deep love for bohemian

life, became the leader of the reform movement in Spanish poetry.

Spanish political stagnation was on a par with that of its poetry. The restoration of the Bourbon monarchy in 1874 and the suppression of Carlist opposition in 1876 had established a solidly reactionary basis of government, and during the last decades of the nineteenth century the political system seemed to be devised to keep anyone from rocking the boat: liberals and conservatives rotated in power, and debates in the *Cortes* (parliament) were either vapid or baroque. No one tackled the large social problems.

Nevertheless, while Darío's assessment of poetry may have been accurate, Spanish literature was far from moribund. Miguel de Unamuno's trenchant style and erudition, after a flirtation with Marxism, took the lead in the development of a multifaceted body of essays, novels, and philosophical works that, if only for its lack of frivolity and suppression of sensuality, contrasted sharply with the *modernistas.* Azorín (José Martínez Ruiz), moving away from his early anarchistic sympathies, was, along with Pío Baroja, about to reinvigorate the Spanish novel, and Ramón del Valle-Inclán, who intellectually absorbed the decadent trends from France and England more thoroughly than some of his cohorts, was soon to introduce to readers his infamous alter ego, the Marqués de Bradomín, an old, ugly, sentimental, and Catholic Don Juan (in the *Sonata* novels, 1902–1905).

This was the atmosphere into which the idealistic, somewhat affected, and very proper Andalusian poet Jiménez appeared in the middle of April 1900. He formed a lasting friendship with Darío, saw a lot of Valle-Inclán, met Azorín and the playwright Jacinto Benavente (who, like Jiménez, went on to win a Nobel Prize), and became good friends with Gregorio Martínez Sierra, a dramatist later to be of some influence on him. His companions saw that the large amount of material he had tentatively titled "Nubes" could easily be divided into two books, and he set about to follow their advice. The disorderliness, to say nothing of the debauchery, of bohemian life did not suit Jiménez, and six weeks after his arrival in Madrid he was back in Moguer, busy separating and regrouping the poetry of "Nubes."

*Almas de violeta* (Violet Souls) and *Ninfeas* (Water Lilies), printed respectively in violet and green ink, were published in September 1900. *Almas de violeta,* whose title was suggested by Darío, includes a passionate prologue by Francisco Villaespesa; Valle-Inclán introduced *Ninfeas;* and Darío

*Self-portrait of Jiménez as a young man (Collection of the Heirs of Juan Ramón Jiménez)*

wrote from Paris to bless Jiménez and welcome him into the ranks of the guardians of beauty. The older Jiménez took a violent dislike to these early effusive books of his poetry and destroyed every copy he could get his hands on, thus assuring their rarity. The critical reception was almost equally negative and violent, but, like most juvenilia, these poems are of interest for the glimpses they provide of a nascent talent, and they are valuable historical records of the tastes, themes, and spasms of early Spanish modernism. Although Jiménez eventually remedied most of the faults, some of the themes were too imbedded in his life ever to disappear.

Villaespesa's combative prologue to *Almas de violeta* underscores the schism between the modern, cosmopolitan, generous young writers and their critics, whom he characterizes as eunuchs. He emphasizes that his cohorts are immoral and pagan by

nature and that "Art for Art's Sake" is inscribed on their banner.

But Jiménez was not by nature very immoral and certainly not pagan: he drank with moderation and intensely disliked brothels. His inability to live up to decadent standards of conduct may, along with the callowness of his years, account for the sense of contrivance and superficiality that many readers have found in his first two books. He once remarked that the sadness that encrusted his work was attributable in large part to a sense of not belonging, of being apart from the crowd. The encounter with the *modernistas,* invigorating and beneficial as it was, did little to alleviate this underlying notion of apartness, probably connected with Jiménez's narcissism, which, in conjunction with other aspects of his character, clouds his poetry with such heavy melancholy.

*Almas de violeta* shows this sentimental sadness. The loss of a young and tender loved one seems to lie behind such sorrow: "¡Ya murió la virgen que me consolaba!" (The virgin who consoled me is now dead!) is repeatedly announced in various ways throughout both *Almas de violeta* and *Ninfeas*. Edgar Allan Poe postulated that the death of a beautiful woman is the quintessential subject for poetry, and Dante Gabriel Rossetti, whom Jiménez came to admire, exploited the same theme.

One side of Jiménez's abiding neurosis was his abnormal fear of death. In *Almas de violeta* he sublimates this necrophobia by dwelling on innocent faces in white coffins. At times he leans dangerously toward an unhealthy attraction to a dead little body: "Elegíaca" (Elegiac) focuses on the work of worms as they eat away the small white face and burrow into the heart once inflamed by passion.

One or two poems give glimpses into Jiménez's sense of himself. In "Negra" (Black) he manages to achieve a certain ironic distance from his gloomy nature: his pains, he writes, are so fatigued at the end of the day from fighting him that they fall asleep exhausted, only to awake next day, refreshed and ready to do battle once again.

A natural and delicate voice occasionally breaks through in the book, as in the rendition of Andalusian popular songs. "Remembranzas" (Remembrances) is a poem so good that Jiménez incorporated it without change in his next book and eventually rewrote it toward the close of his life in a masterful summary of the prolongation of childhood and its memories. "Remembranzas" tells in sincere and simple verse of how the magical dimensions that childhood bestows on time and place disappear with age. Coming from a poet not yet twenty-one, it is nonetheless an elegiac poem.

The unfortunate aspects of *Almas de violeta* are continued and exacerbated in the longer *Ninfeas*. The highly mannered vocabulary (one does not "kiss"; one "osculates") carries the same themes, with less morbidity perhaps, but certainly not lacking in overwrought passion. There is still the claim, rooted in romanticism, that the poet will never encounter the pure innocence he so ardently seeks, and there are moments of what would become the mature Jiménez voice, such as in "Recuerdos" (Memories), with its suggestion of Verlaine's style. Obverse to the topic of unrequited love is a scene that is repeated often in Jiménez's later books: the poet tenderly takes leave of a beautiful young girl, presumably in search of the ideal. *Ninfeas,* in terms of metrics, registers seven attempts by Jiménez to re-create the remarkable rhythm of the Colombian poet José Asunción Silva's *Nocturnos,* which had been published in Spain in 1900.

Juan Ramón had been back in Moguer six weeks when, on 3 July 1900, his father died suddenly. The shock aggravated the morbidity noticeable in his first books and further activated in him the abnormal fear of death, the symptoms of which he never completely overcame. He believed that he, too, would die suddenly like his father, and, in order to prevent this occurrence, he insisted on always being near a doctor, or knowing where one was immediately available. This compelling need ordered all living arrangements for the rest of his life. Although examinations continually proved the contrary, he was convinced that he had a defective heart. During periods when his neurosis worsened, he required a doctor at his side. The most dreaded aspect of his illness, and the one that made life difficult for his associates, came in the recurring bouts of heavy despondency that eventually led to depression. Long fallow stretches appeared in his creative life; in his last years in the United States he often entered a hospital for treatment of this emotional state. Between these bouts Jiménez could be active, cheerful, assiduously warm, elaborately courteous, full of Andalusian wit, and remarkably fecund. He was truly, as he himself noted, a man whose life was presided over by fierce Manichaean contrasts, such as light and darkness, sanity and madness.

During the year following his father's death, Jiménez's symptoms mounted, and his family, via contacts in southern France through their wine business, sent him to the sanatorium of Castel d'Andorte, near Bordeaux, to be placed under the care of Jean Gaston Lalanne, a noted authority on persecution complexes. The dark, withdrawn, and handsome poet arrived at the sanatorium in the first part of May 1901. An investigation by the late Ignacio Prat has shed much light on this period. In between fits of despondency Jiménez was reasonably active, making short trips into the Pyrenees and delighting in the company of Dr. Lalanne's children. In a letter of 18 July 1901 to the poet's mother, Lalanne described what was to become the common pattern of Jiménez's life: he would begin to feel a bit better and give himself up to poetry, his ruling passion; then the intellectual effort would reawaken the neurasthenia, causing a kind of vicious circle. Jiménez had other passions besides poetry. Internal evidence in the poems he wrote at the sanatorium and the studies of Prat indicate that he proved irresistible to the women he encountered in France, including Lalanne's wife and the children's governess. By the end of August, Jiménez was gone from France, and

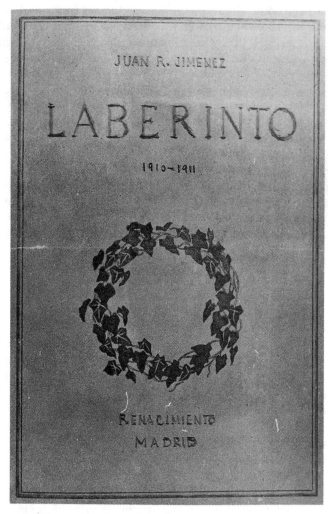

*Jiménez's design for the title page of his 1913 book, in which he collected poems written near the end of his self-imposed "exile" in Moguer, 1905–1912 (from Juan Guerrero Ruiz, Juan Ramón Jiménez de viva voz, 1961)*

soon he settled down in a rest home in Madrid and formed a lasting friendship with the neurologist Luis Simarro.

In later life Jiménez said that it was during his stay at Castel d'Andorte that he first read Baudelaire and made the acquaintance of such French poets as Albert-Victor Samain, Jean Moréas, Jules Laforgue, Stéphane Mallarmé, Henri Frédéric Amiel, and Verlaine. However, Jiménez's poetry written during that time, under the tentative title "Rimas de sombra" (Shadow Rhymes), published as *Rimas,* registers no significant traces of these authors. Instead *Rimas* reflects the continuing influences of the *modernistas* he had met at the beginning of 1900, notably that of Villaespesa, plus touches of Darío, and surprising notes from the sonorous Spanish romantic Zorrilla. Bécquer's is, however, the presiding spirit, from the title to many of the images, as well as some of the metrical combinations.

*Rimas* met with critical success and is an improvement over Jiménez's first two books, for he has toned down the excesses of modernism and allowed more latitude to the lyrical voice buried under the earlier sentimentality and melancholy.

Although an epigraph from Augusto Ferrán, Bécquer's contemporary, stresses that death is possible every day, there is much that is not morbid in *Rimas.* The scenario of lovers taking leave of each other is deftly handled, and the first of many hauntingly beautiful gardenscapes makes an appearance in Jiménez's poetry. Children's voices, which echo in much of European poetry in the late nineteenth and early twentieth century (in that of Verlaine, T. S. Eliot, and Antonio Machado, for example), sound among these early Jiménez gardens, and there is also a vision of a delicate white-robed virgin. Eventually she is changed into a rose so that the values attached to her may have a wider symbolic radius. One poem records an early instance of Jiménez's urge to transcend, an urge that dominates his late poetry: by running to the horizon he hopes to lose himself in the stars. In *Rimas*, as Angel González notes, Jiménez introduces the poet as narrator and subject of much of the poetry for the first time. The discovery of this persona enabled Jiménez to channel his subjectivity into an alter ego that would help him control his emotions and advance toward what would eventually be a major topic: the relation of poetry and the poet to the world.

The Sanatorio del Rosario, located in what was then a semirural part of Madrid, provided Jiménez with two of the happiest years of his life (1902 and 1903). Close to doctors and ministered to by the sisters of the Sanatorio, he felt suitably protected and cared for and was able to give full vent to his creative interests. The individuals who trooped in and out of his rooms turned them into a kind of literary salon: Valle-Inclán, Benavente, Manuel Reina, Salvador Rueda, Martínez Sierra, Pérez de Ayala, and the Machado brothers. With the exception of Unamuno, the key writers of the time came to the Sanatorio to talk literature. *Modernismo,* still vilified by older authors and bourgeois critics, had nevertheless taken hold in Spain. In Jiménez's room these literati hatched the plans for a *modernista* review to be called *Helios*. One of the most coherent and successful platforms for Spanish modernism, *Helios* (April 1903–May 1904) was carefully edited by Jiménez, who contributed translations of Verlaine as well as many unsigned pieces. Notably international in outlook and hospitable not only to French but to Anglo-American literature, *Helios* was impressive also for its idealistic and restrained tone. The absence of decadent frissons may be partially charged to the changing times, but the influence of Jiménez, who had come to see the errors of *Almas de violeta* and *Ninfeas,* cannot be denied.

*Arias tristes,* published in 1903, includes the poetry he wrote at the Sanatorio. It is Jiménez's first well-balanced and cohesive book, one in which his natural lyric voice, expressed in the traditional ballad meter of eight syllables to the line, receives full range. Critics from José Ortega y Gasset to Darío praised it, and its success established Jiménez as a poet of undeniable talent.

The structure of *Arias tristes* reveals his deep love of music. Each of the three sections is preceded by the score of a lied by Franz Schubert. This striking conjunction of notes and words suggests the profound relationship between poetry and music that informed Jiménez's life. (In America, Arturo Toscanini was his great cultural hero.) The senti-

mental beauty of Schubert's songs finds its counterpart in the poetry. In a small introduction to the nocturnes of part 2, Jiménez acclaims Heine, Bécquer, Verlaine, and Alfred de Musset as the poets in whom he encounters like sentiments. The emotional inspiration, then, of *Arias tristes* is essentially a throwback to romanticism. Between these two camps – romanticism and *modernismo* – Jiménez was to write, with varying effect but increasing frustration, until 1913, when he began to sense a new pathway.

Fogelquist aptly describes the many landscapes of *Arias tristes* with their subdued light, mist-shrouded valleys, quiet rivers, and a lonely star. Jiménez resorts frequently to a device first labeled by the romantics: the pathetic fallacy. Alongside nature and the poet, one finds the nearly continuous presence of a woman, represented only by the pronoun *ella* (her), for which the referents are both specific and general. Soon Jiménez was to expand the pronoun to include the concepts of beauty, music, and poetry, all nouns of feminine gender in the Spanish language.

The neurologist Dr. Simarro, whom Jiménez had first met in Madrid on the way to Bordeaux, proposed to offset the loneliness that ensued after the death of Simarro's wife in 1903 by inviting Jiménez and a young biologist, Nicolás Achúcarro, to take rooms in his house. Simarro, who practiced medicine and taught at the University of Madrid, introduced Jiménez to some of the scientific ideas of the period. In Simarro's well-stocked library Jiménez first encountered works by Nietzsche, whose aphoristic prose impressed him mightily, and he also read books by William Shakespeare, Johann Wolfgang von Goethe, and Shelley.

Through Simarro, Jiménez came to know the work of the Institución Libre de Enseñanza. An offspring of the idealism of the *krausistas,* the Institución believed that the reform of Spain must begin in its educational institutions. Founded in 1876 by Francisco Giner de los Ríos as a lay school at a time when all education was under the aegis of the Catholic church, the Institución deeply affected the life of a liberal intellectual minority. Jiménez accompanied Simarro to its lectures and noted that they always came away with many new ideas. The Institución's religiosity, unattached to dogma and the church, provided Jiménez with a broad and liberal religious impulse that he, too, pointedly kept free of entanglement with any specific form of Christianity. Jiménez's friendship with Ortega y Gasset also dates from this period. Through these

*Jiménez in 1916*

contacts the sensitive and talented author of *Arias tristes* gradually broadened his outlook and increased his intellectual concerns.

*Jardines lejanos* (Faraway Gardens), published in February 1904, is the last part of a trilogy that begins with *Rimas* and includes *Arias tristes*. *Jardines lejanos* continues the practice of introducing each section with a musical score: this time the composers honored are Christoph Willibald Gluck, Robert Schumann, and Felix Mendelssohn-Bartholdy. Dedicated to "Divine memory of Enrique Heine," *Jardines lejanos* essentially continues the themes of *Arias tristes*. A more pronounced sensuality, an occasional flash of humor, and persistent memories of Francina – the Lalanne children's governess, with whom Jiménez had a brief affair – set *Jardines lejanos* apart from its predecessors. The gardenscapes in particular pulsate with underlying sexuality. In one poem, as he peers into a fountain in expectation of seeing a rosebush reflected, the speaker instead is startled by the image of a naked woman (which is likely the first appearance of this key Jiménez icon); he senses a stirring of unsaintly feelings and, in a masterful synesthesia, says "Todo era aroma de senos" (All was the odor of breasts).

One of the most compelling poems begins with a question: "¿Soy yo quien anda esta noche / por mi cuarto, o el mendigo / que rondaba mi jardín / al caer la tarde?" (Is it I who wanders / about my room tonight, or is it the beggar / who patrolled my garden / at dusk?). Jiménez has allowed his apprehension of a dual personality within himself to enter into his poetry, and from this point on it appears intermittently in his work, always pointing to important questions about identity.

Giner de los Ríos was an avid nature lover, and he persuaded Jiménez to accompany him on excursions to the Guadarrama Mountains, which border Madrid to the north. These hikes accounted for the poetry of *Pastorales* (written in 1904 but not pub-

224

lished until 1911). After writing these pleasant and gentle songs of nature, Jiménez temporarily retired the ballad meter he had introduced in *Rimas* and began to experiment with longer lines and different stanza forms that clothe a troubled and monotonous content.

In view of the illness of Dr. Simarro and the absence of several close friends (among them, Martínez Sierra, who had gone to Brussels, and Achúcarro, who was studying in Germany), Jiménez in the fall of 1905 decided to return to Moguer. There he stayed until 29 December 1912, when he left to go back for good to Madrid. Thus for nearly seven years the poet lived with his family in the semiseclusion of their Andalusian village. He renewed his idyll with Hernández-Pinzón and became infatuated with María Almonte, the wife of the local doctor. Jiménez's struggle with his morbid obsession drained a good deal of his psychic energy, and, to add to his woes, the family's financial plight, economic problems that in 1911 resulted in bankruptcy, began to be apparent. On the whole, however, little is known about his life during this period, which he later referred to as a time of "soledad literaria" (literary solitude).

Seven years of provincial exile in Moguer, interrupted by an occasional trip, turned out to be, save for bouts of depression, incredibly productive. Jiménez wrote enough to fill several collections of poetry and one book of prose that were published beginning in 1908, and sufficient material remained to fill seven posthumous volumes.

Aside from the obvious technical virtuosity of this poetry, its main interest lies in offering an example of how a hypersensitive and repressed poet handled the fin de siècle decadent themes in a provincial environment. Recurring topics are anecdotal love scenes (real or imaginary) disguised in flower symbolism; pervasive and at times seemingly self-indulgent sadness bordering on despair and ennui; sensitivity to nature and music; and predominant gardens. Good individual poems tend to be blanketed by the surrounding repetition. The persona of the poet, introduced in *Rimas,* fades into the background. Eroticism in itself was insufficient to meet the needs of Jiménez's psyche. Yearning for the ideal woman (also the dream of Shelley, Espronceda, and Bécquer) nourishes his spiritual life and proves once more how firmly rooted he was in this aspect of the romantic tradition.

*Olvidanzas I: Las hojas verdes* (Forgettings I; Green Leaves), written in 1906 and published in 1909, and *Baladas de primavera* (Spring Ballads), composed in 1907 and published in 1910, represent a transition from *Pastorales* into the more lugubrious work that follows. Memories of the sanatorium at Castel d'Andorte and readings of French poetry (by Verlaine, Samain, and Laforgue) crowd the sorrowful pages of *Las hojas verdes.* On the other hand, *Baladas de primavera* celebrates nature in a lighter tone: the perfection of the day finds expression in a phrase, apt for the Andalusian sky and resonant of works by Victor Hugo and Mallarmé: "Dios está azul" (God is blue). Three volumes of *Elegías* (Elegies, written in 1908 and 1909 and published respectively in 1908, 1909, and 1910) crowd out any sense of buoyancy and introduce low spirits and mournfulness: "Días sin emoción, sin novia y sin correo / desesperanza en tiempo de fríos y de niebla" (Days without feelings, women or mail / desperation in weather of chill and fog).

Another sheaf of poems, written in 1908, was printed three years later under the title *La soledad sonora* (Sonorous Silence), a phrase from San Juan de la Cruz. Descriptions of abandoned palaces and old towns relieve the usual panorama of dulcet gardens and amorous longings. Jiménez, nearing thirty years of age, dedicated this book to Luisa Grimm de Muriedas, an American woman he had met in 1905. Estranged from her Spanish husband, Luisa, a native of Philadelphia, left Spain to live in England, Switzerland, and France, but she kept in touch with Jiménez. In their lengthy correspondence, which began in 1907, Luisa sets herself up as his guide to the pleasures of English verse, urges him to read Yeats and Francis Thompson, and constantly quotes her beloved Byron. Echoes of these writers can be found throughout Jiménez's subsequent writings. The rapport between him and Luisa strengthened his growing conviction about the high value of Anglo-American poetry.

In the mostly lusterless Moguer period of Jiménez's writing, *Platero y yo,* his most universally acclaimed book, sparkles like Venus in the evening sky. Nothing he wrote before or after gained such a wide readership. Read with pleasure by both schoolchildren and adults, the descriptions of life in a small Andalusian town, as seen through the sensitive eyes of the poet/narrator and his inseparable companion, the woolly white donkey Platero, have reached, after *Don Quixote,* perhaps the widest audience of any work in Spanish literature.

Jiménez began to write *Platero y yo* in 1906, shortly after he returned to Moguer, and in tone and style it resembles *Baladas de primavera,* of which it was originally intended to be a part. He took the manuscript when he went back to Madrid. There he met his future wife, Zenobia Camprubí Aymar, who

*Jiménez's wife, Zenobia Camprubí, circa 1917*

had a strong interest in children's literature, knew Charles Lamb's *Tales from Shakespeare* (1807), and was translating into Spanish Rabindranath Tagore's vignettes about children in *The Crescent Moon* (1913). The first edition of *Platero y yo* was published in 1914, followed by a considerably enlarged final edition in 1917. Assigned reading for schoolchildren in many countries, *Platero y yo* has been associated with children's literature but does not exclusively belong to that category any more than does Mark Twain's *Tom Sawyer* (1876). In a prologue that has too often been omitted from the hundreds of editions of *Platero y yo,* Jiménez took pains to point out that he had never written directly for children because he believed, with certain obvious exceptions, that adults and children could read with profit the same books.

The 138 vignettes of *Platero y yo,* written in poetic prose, register a Franciscan love of animals and nature; an idealism not far removed from the Institución Libre de Enseñanza and its founder, Giner de los Ríos; and an almost biblical acceptance of solitude and apartness as a means of achieving the good life. The poet/narrator, wearing a long Nazarene beard and a wide-brimmed black hat, is taunted by the village ragamuffins as he rides off into the countryside astride his little burro to contemplate the spectacle of a sunset, while the rest of the town, redolent with cigars and brandy, heads for a bullfight. In a benevolent monologue the poet/narrator comments gently and sometimes sadly on the passing scene. The use of the burro as an alter ego, perhaps suggested by certain poems by Francis Jammes, provided Jiménez with the foil that he needed to keep free of the philosophical labyrinths of his *Elegías.*

*Platero y yo* presents a gallery of village portraits, ranging from dirty, unkempt gypsy children to the kindly village doctor, and shows a decided sympathy for the downtrodden and unfortunate.

The book consists of equal doses of Blakean innocence and experience and of happiness and grief, emotions paired, says Jiménez, like Platero's ears. Against the backdrop of cobalt blue skies, bougainvillea, bees, butterflies, and bird songs, there are rabid dogs, cockfights, fear, superstition, idiocy, and poverty. The ingredients of life in a poor Mediterranean village in the second decade of the twentieth century combine with a delicate and balanced poetic tone to account for the accomplishment of *Platero y yo.*

In 1911 the Banco de España had impounded the vineyards of the Jiménez family. Such economic restraints had joined forces with Jiménez's growing sense of frustration to enable him to take a step that he had long been considering: a return to Madrid. He had arrived there near the end of 1912, and although the people of Moguer saw him in the summers and as an occasional visitor, he had finally broken the firm ties to his birthplace. He struck up a friendship at once with the avant-garde writer Ramón Gómez de la Serna and entered into the literary and intellectual life of the capital.

Given his innate liberalism and his contact with Dr. Simarro and the Institución in 1903, Jiménez found himself quickly attracted to an offshoot of the Institución – the Residencia de Estudiantes, a dormitory set up in 1910 along the lines of a university college at Oxford or Cambridge. By 1912 it had been enlarged by three new buildings and was well on its way to becoming an important intellectual center in Spain and, to a certain extent, a cultural haven in Europe during World War I. All the great Spanish writers of the 1920s and 1930s (such as Jiménez, Unamuno, Ortega y Gasset, and Machado) were associated with it in some way; Federico García Lorca, Luis Buñuel, and Salvador Dalí lived there as students; and its doors were open to such distinguished foreigners as John Maynard Keynes, Albert Einstein, and Paul Valéry.

At a lecture given at the Residencia in July 1913 on Columbus, Jiménez met Zenobia, a pert, blonde woman, twenty-six years old, who spoke Spanish with a slight English accent because, although born in Barcelona, she had been educated in the United States. Zenobia was descended on her mother's side from Benjamín Aymar, a highly successful New York merchant; her father was a Catalan engineer who met and married Isabel Aymar in Puerto Rico. Jiménez fell in love at once with Zenobia, and a long and volatile courtship ensued. They were married in New York City on 2 March 1916. It would be difficult to exaggerate her impact on his life. Vivacious, optimistic, and outgoing, her temperament was a perfect foil for his moody, withdrawn, and doleful nature. Bilingual in Spanish and English, she was a cultivated woman (like Luisa) who further acquainted him with the world of Anglo-American poetry. After 1916 such poems replaced the French ones as the chief influences on his verse. His deep and abiding love for Zenobia played a large part in reordering his poetry, leading him partially out of his narcissistic snare and allowing him the rare privilege of encountering in his private life a situation in which for considerable periods of time the ideal and reality were contiguous.

Much of what Jiménez had written in Moguer held little appeal for Zenobia (she particularly disliked *Laberinto,* published the year they met), but she was sensitive to his stature as a poet. Her own interest in writing was fully developed, and by 1912 she had contributed articles to *Vogue, St. Nicholas,* and the *Craftsman.* Juan Ramón exploited their common love of literature and used it as a bond to hold them together during their difficult courtship. He helped Zenobia prepare her translation of Tagore's *The Crescent Moon* in the summer of 1914. It was published as *La luna nueva* (1915), and its immediate success led them to continue their collaboration; eventually they translated and published twenty books by the prolific Tagore, all of which sold well in Spain and Latin America. During their courtship, they began a translation of Lamb's *Tales from Shakespeare* and some poems by Shelley. After their marriage they translated John Millington Synge's 1903 play *Riders to the Sea* as *Jinetes hacia el mar* (1920) and saw it produced in Madrid the same year it was published in Spanish. Scenes from this translation influenced Lorca's *Bodas de sangre* (performed, 1933; published, 1936; translated as *Blood Wedding,* 1939). Translation continually played an essential role in the Jiménezes' life together. They had begun work on a selection of Yeats's poetry as well as his plays *The Countess Cathleen* (1892) and *The Land of Heart's Desire* (1894), but, when an argument over royalties could not be resolved, Yeats refused publication permission. With the help of Zenobia, Jiménez prepared and published translations of works by Dickinson, Frost, William Blake, Francis Thompson, and Eliot.

The period from 1913 to 1916 was a time of transition from Jiménez's early sentimental and mournful stage to the hermetic symbolism; transcendent sense of nature; and clear, *desnudo* (naked) style of his second epoch. Glimpses of the new manner and tone first appear in the *Sonetos espirituales* (Spiritual Sonnets), which he began writing in 1914 and published in 1917. His use of the Italian sonnet form produced a successful book. From background readings of Shakespeare and Garcilaso de la Vega, he derived a series of love sonnets loosely modeled on the Renaissance tradition and directed to Zenobia. Other themes take on importance as well, for in this book he begins to demonstrate that identification of his mind with nature can provide an escape from the labyrinth of the self. Perhaps the most significant event in the *Sonetos espirituales* is the rediscovery of the poet persona. Sonnet 40, "A mi alma" (To My Soul), foreshadows one of the great themes of Jiménez's mature period: the relationship between the creative intelligence and its ambience (the poet and the world). By 1914 he was beginning to see that poetic intelligence could place an indelible signature on reality, that through his sensitivity he could re-create the world, and that uppermost among his responsibilities was the need to be alert and prepared for this task.

Even more significant in these months of transition is *Estío* (Summer), written in the summer of 1915 and published at the end of the following year. Shelley's "Mutability," which the Jiménezes were translating into Spanish, is the epigraph for *Estío*. Zenobia's changing moods, her indecision about their future together, and her whims and caprices could be summed up by the title of Shelley's poem. How to describe the mingling in the encounter of love is a problem Jiménez solves with a delicate touch: the lovers are portrayed as blending together unwittingly as do the sea and the sky. Sentient variations find more meaningful metaphors than in his past poetry: "Yo no sé cómo saltar / desde la orilla de hoy" (I know not how to leap / from the edge of today).

When Zenobia stipulated that their marriage take place in New York City, she unwittingly supplied the context for one of the most unusual books in modern Spanish poetry. *Diario de un poeta recién casado* (Diary of a Newly Wed Poet, 1917) is a record in poetry of Jiménez's feelings and thoughts about his journey from Cádiz to New York and his stay in the United States. He describes his first encounter with the sea and goes on to register experiences of bewilderment, frustration, and amazement in the milieu of New York City, as well as a reaction to American poetry. *Diario* was to have considerable influence on the poetry written in Spain during the next decade.

In terms of form, *Diario* introduces what Jiménez christened "poesía desnuda" (naked poetry), or "verso desnudo" (naked verse). After writing *Sonetos espirituales* he began to experiment with free verse in *Estío* and for *Diario* perfected a short stanza, usually of no greater length than a dozen lines, in which rhyme is excluded and the measure of the lines themselves varies, according to no set pattern, from three to eleven syllables. Internal rhyme, delicate diction, and a conscious but restrained use of repetition provide the musical substance for "verso desnudo." The form pleased Jiménez and suited the temperament of his new style. (It was used to varying degrees in the early poetry of, among others, Pedro Salinas and Lorca.) The sections of *Diario* dealing with New York City, Boston, and American poetry societies are written in prose poetry. Using phrases from advertisements and brochures, snatches of newspaper headlines, translations of Dickinson, quotations from Thompson and Amy Lowell, and the sensitivity of observation typical of *Platero y yo*, Jiménez created a noteworthy experiment along the lines of a collage.

In its subject matter *Diario* is self-referential, but the anecdotal quality diminishes; emotions, instead of being baldly stated, begin to be implied; and the symbolic value of words comes to be realized. Emotions are set out in pellucid verse, and the continuity of experience is fragmented into intensely idealized moments. Fourteen poems directly concerning his love for Zenobia are less effective than the ones that speak of wonderment in the face of the ocean. When the book was published in 1948, Jiménez appropriately retitled it *Diario de poeta y mar* (Diary of Poet and Sea). It is a dramatic encounter between the creative mind and a vast imposing presence that seems as if it should have a consciousness worthy of its size but is also a slate-gray *nada* (nothingness). In a key metaphor Jiménez compares the movement of the waves and their relation to each other to his own thoughts: an eternal series of meetings and partings, of knowing and not knowing. Groundwork is thus laid for the fusion of subject and object that he was to carry out in the coming years. In this attractively varied book he presents several Saussurian musings on the linguistic experience inherent in being plunged forcibly into a foreign-language environment. Struck by the arbitrary relationship between the signifier and the signified, he wondered, for example, at the gap of feeling, and perhaps meaning, between the English word *sky* and the Spanish word *cielo*, which can also mean "heavens" or "canopy."

With a new direction for his poetry firmly in mind and a steamer trunk full of volumes of Anglo-American verse to be read and translated, Jiménez returned to Spain in July 1916 to begin the most significant period of his life. Several books and chap-

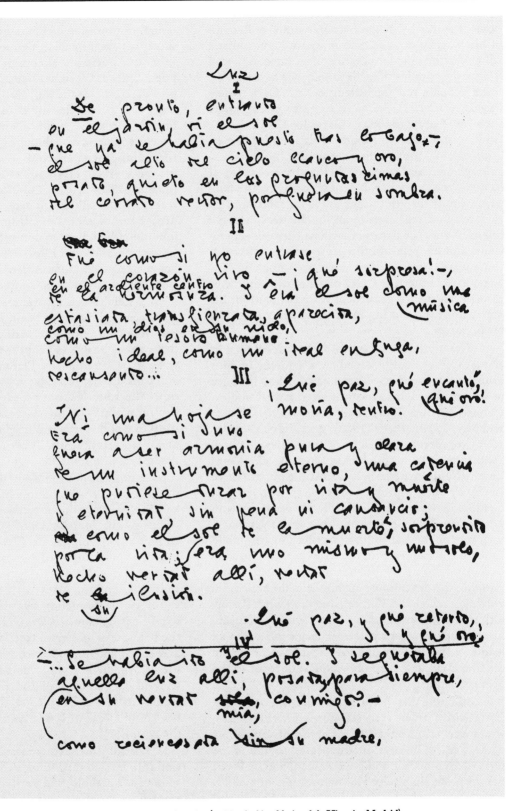

Draft for "De pronto, entrando," collected in Poesía (1923; Archivo Nacional de Historia, Madrid)

books of his new poetry, seventeen of his translations of works by Tagore, an influential collection of his lengthy oeuvre, and numerous journalistic collaborations made these the most important and fruitful years of his life. His dominance of the poetic scene in Spain was unchallenged. In *Indice,* a review he edited in 1921, he gave space to young poets such as Lorca, Salinas, Gerardo Diego, Jorge Guillén, and Dámaso Alonso. This so-called Generation of 1927 took its first steps with Jiménez's encouragement and support. As the group developed its own tone and voice, Jiménez, displaying the temperament of the adolescent boy who refused to be gainsaid in discussions of arts and letters, became offended with the natural reactions between generations, and his relationship grew acrimonious with the constellation of new poets to whom he had been, at the outset, the soul of generosity and who, in turn, learned a great deal from his diction, his high standards, and his unwavering devotion to the art of poetry.

The style hinted at in *Estío* and developed in *Diario* becomes fully joined with content in four books that stand as examples of what Jiménez now considered his constant goal: naked poetry. *Eternidades* (Eternities, 1918), *Piedra y cielo* (Stone and Sky, 1919), *Poesía* (1923), and *Belleza* (Beauty, 1923) represent the height of his achievement in Spanish poetry and put him in the ranks of Valéry, Yeats, and Rainer Maria Rilke. At the outset one of Jiménez's chief topics, as with the three poets just mentioned, was poetry itself. *Eternidades* opens with a statement that his ultimate word is not yet made, and, in a poem that follows, he pleads with intelligence itself to give him the exact word, knowing that inspiration must be controlled by intellect and also that the exact name for him is multileveled, involving intelligence, himself, and the world. Recognition that words operate with a plurality of meaning and that language possesses magic qualities that lead to a special way of knowing makes this poem the first clear statement of symbolist doctrine in the Spanish language.

Pursuing his favorite symbol, he writes in *Eternidades* a celebrated statement of his poetics, which can also be read as a capsule history of his verse. Poetry, he says, first appeared to him in the form of an innocent and pure woman, and he loved her with the simplicity and naturalness of a child. Unfortunately she began to dress ostentatiously and to hide her purity. Gradually, however, the pompous gowns slipped off, and the lovely lady appeared in her original tunic, which in the last stanza she removes to stand before him as the passion of his life.

Both Yeats and Tagore wrote about the necessity of stripping adornment from their songs, and for Yeats there was great value in figuratively walking naked. Jiménez's poem is a sketch of various stages in his poetry: the early romanticism, the modernist paraphernalia, the erotic labyrinths of Moguer, and finally the "poesía desnuda" of 1916. Naked poetry implies sheerness, lucidity, and pellucidness. However, its generic vocabulary as used by Jiménez — rose, stone, woman, and so on — ranges through various levels of meaning that, coupled with its self-referential base, makes "poesía desnuda" not as simple or as accessible as it seems at first glance. The dedication of many of his books to "La inmensa minoría" (the immense minority), with its echoes of Ortega y Gasset and Eliot, implies that his hermetic verse, like much modernist writing, demands a special effort in order to be appreciated.

A heightened awareness of his methods and goals caused Jiménez to begin speaking of "la Obra" (the Work). The capital *O* adds dignity and force to the word as he muses about the nature of what he is writing; it also implies a Platonic ideal of which the work on the written page may be, at times, only a dim reflection. He longs for his *Obra* to be like the sky on a starry night: a sense of the presence of truth free of history (as in *Piedra y cielo*). He wonders about the relationship of his *Obra* to the future, to readers, and to himself.

A nascent need in *Rimas* and *Pastorales* to identify affectively with nature has attained full force and foreshadows the unusual mysticism of his final writings. His four books of 1918, 1919, and 1923 contain many epiphanies. Elements of nature meld together under his gaze — does the light sustain the leaf, or the leaf the light? (*Poesía*) — and eventually the contemplator fuses with the object: it is not sweet russet branches swaying in the afternoon wind, it is his soul (*Belleza*). He feels himself to be the trunk of a universal tree, enmeshed with birds and stars, and should a woodsman swing his axe, the firmament will come crashing down (*Eternidades*). Each day the poetic consciousness (soul) carries out the role first discovered in the sonnet "A mi alma" of *Sonetos espirituales:* it will remake the world.

One of Jiménez's greatest triumphs in this period is to broach the ultimate theme of death and, in spite of his pathological morbidity, present it in humanistic and noble terms. In an existentialist insight he saw that life cannot be meaningfully lived without the persistent awareness of death. The cord, he says in *Poesía,* that links one's life to life in general should, when need be, bind one to death. Death depends on life, Jiménez avers in one of his most moving poems, and, therefore, one should have no fear, for one's life guides blind death and obligates it to one's presence (*Poesía*).

Also during this period, perhaps influenced by George Bernard Shaw, Jiménez decided to simplify Spanish spelling and make it more phonetic. Accordingly, with the publication of *Eternidades,* he introduced some orthographic variations from standard Spanish. These are slight – including the substitution of *j* for *ge* and *gi,* and *s* for *x* before certain consonants – and represent, at best, a quixotic endeavor, for Spanish orthography was already highly phonetic. In any event, the concern and care he brought to all aspects of his books became legendary. His insistence on the use of Elzevir type, set on quality paper with wide margins, produced volumes that in appearance contrast sharply with much of the shoddy publishing efforts in Spain at that time.

After the publication of *Belleza* many years passed before Jiménez published another book of original verse. He participated heavily in newspapers and journals; undertook the task of editing his "complete" works, a project that involved an enormous amount of revision, for he, like Yeats, developed an antagonism toward his juvenilia; and continued sporadically his translations of works by Anglo-American poets such as Blake, Frost, and Eliot.

Political events soon forced a radical change in his life. His lecture *Política poética* (Poetic Politics), prepared in May 1936 for the annual Spanish book fair, struck what seemed to many an impossibly idealistic note in view of the turbulence of the Spanish scene. Ascribing to poetry, as did Shelley, a moral force and an inclination toward social justice, Jiménez proposed that poets should become legislators. The admonition must have fallen on unbelieving ears, yet sometime later in the United States, when he met Henry A. Wallace, he saw that a creative and sensitive person could also be a politician.

Jiménez and his wife had often talked of returning to America. The outbreak of the Spanish Civil War gave them the motive to do so, and on 26 August 1936, carrying the title of honorary cultural attaché of the Spanish Republican government, Jiménez sailed with Zenobia from Cherbourg to New York. It was the last they would see of Europe. In New York and Washington, D.C., he tried with limited success to drum up support for the Republican cause. He visited the editorial offices of the *New Republic* and talked with Malcolm Cowley. Jiménez toured Puerto Rico and Cuba amid the adulation of poets young and old, and he returned to

settle down in Coral Gables, Florida, where the climate and lowlands reminded him of his beloved Moguer. In his new environment his reticence and aloofness became less marked, and, for a time, he was a more outgoing figure who could be occasionally persuaded to give special lectures. At the University of Miami, where he and Zenobia taught, he presented two lectures in 1940 that are keys to understanding his ideas about poetry and society. "Poesía y literatura" (Poetry and Literature) begins with the distinction made by Verlaine between the two and goes on to develop it in more explicitly Platonic terms: the poet is a medium possessed by a god, and what he writes is original; literature is merely a translation of these divine seizures. "Aristocracia y democracia" (Aristocracy and Democracy), influenced by Giner de los Ríos and the idealism of the Institución, says that true aristocracy resides in a cultivated and naturally sincere individual and that there are many examples among the Spanish common people. *Política poética* underwent a title change to become "El trabajo gustoso" (Pleasant Work) and was presented in Puerto Rico, Cuba, and Miami. These and other lectures were collected in 1961 under the title *El trabajo gustoso.*

Ten days after Pearl Harbor was attacked by the Japanese, Jiménez wrote to Richard Pattee in the State Department to offer whatever services a fifty-nine-year-old poet could provide to the country that had treated him with such hospitality. The response was slow, but in July 1943 the Office of the Coordinator of Inter-American Affairs requested him to prepare ninety fifteen-minute programs to be broadcast to Latin America. The lectures were to treat two topics: modernism in Spain and Latin America, and contemporary U.S. poetry. Jiménez prepared more than a dozen of these lectures and had notes for several others, but in October he withdrew from the project for reasons partially involved with the question of censorship. The lectures already written were subsequently published in Colombia, Argentina, and Puerto Rico. Jiménez continued to be an important antifascist Hispanic voice for the State Department, and on 21 June 1944 he was invited to Savannah, Georgia, to participate in the launching of the liberty ship *Rubén Darío.*

Restlessness marked the lives of Jiménez and his wife during the 1940s in the United States as they sought work teaching and writing and battled his sieges of depression. After teaching at Duke University in 1942, they moved to Washington, D.C. The year 1944 began their association with the University of Maryland, where today the Juan Ramón Jiménez Hall of Languages commemorates that rela-

*When the editor of a periodical called* La Isla de los Ratones *wrote Jiménez requesting material, the poet sent this inscribed photograph and a manuscript for a poem. The inscription reads "A mis amigos de 'La Isla de los Ratones,' con cariño. Juan Ramón /49" (To my friends at 'The Island of Mice,' with fondness; from* La Isla de los Ratones, *no. 9, 1950).*

tionship. In 1946 he was hospitalized for eight months in Takoma Park, Maryland. Two years later he accepted an invitation to give a series of lectures in Buenos Aires. The press trumpeted his arrival, crowds pressed to see the author of *Platero y yo,* and in Montevideo the senate went into special session to hear him speak.

After *Platero y yo* Jiménez's greatest prose work is *Españoles de tres mundos* (Spaniards of Three Worlds, 1942), a series of lyrical caricatures written between 1914 and 1940. The Spaniards of three worlds (Europe, America, and the "other world") range from close friends, to well-known acquaintances, to dead authors whose works had special meaning for Jiménez. The caricatures balance skillfully the mordant and the lyrical. Nowhere in his many works are the baroque exuberance and the nervous tension that exist as the obverse of his controlled pure style better displayed than in these flashing portraits.

Many of the poems in *La estación total con las Canciones de la nueva luz* (The Total Season with the

Songs of New Light, 1946), which contains material composed between 1932 and 1936, describe transcendent experiences. Evidently the moments of epiphany limned in *Eternidades* and *Belleza* have expanded and deepened. Nature closes in and envelops the speaker with a feeling of unity so that his spirit identifies with a sublime sense of the landscape. Woman, poetry, love, music, and roses – all these symbols are drawn into the center of a divine circle. Harbingers of this transcendence are often birds, and two poems, "Criatura afortunada" (Fortunate Creature) and "Mirlo fiel" (Faithful Blackbird), are moving evocations of the pantheistic effect of bird song; these poems are comparable with the best of Blake and William Wordsworth. The poems that open and close *La estación total* show the importance of the perceiver: the poet's senses provide infinite resources. That glory arises from within is Jiménez's Blakean message, tinged with the idealism of the *institucionalistas.*

As the title announces, *Romances de Coral Gables* (Ballads of Coral Gables, 1948) signals a return to the eight-syllable line of the traditional Spanish ballad, and the delightful lyrics, composed in the Miami suburb that reminded Jiménez of Andalusia, recall the delicate musical voice in his early poetry and his "poesía desnuda." Once again, the sea represents a sense of infinity. Childhood is evoked as the common state from which people never truly exit – "el niño soy yo de viejo" (the boy I am as an old man).

Contact with the sea inevitably freed Jiménez's spirit. The voyage on the steamship *Río Juramento* that preceded his glorious welcome to Buenos Aires in 1948 was no exception. Twenty-nine poems in free verse, all with sustained inspiration, were published in 1949 as *Animal de fondo* (Animal of Depth). Despite the vocabulary common to the classical Spanish mystics (fire, flame, torch, love), Jiménez's poetry does not accord in a doctrinaire manner with this tradition. The initial poem points out that the god to be celebrated is not a redeemer, brother, son, or father – in other words, not the Christian God – and the poet insists also that, unlike the mystics, he has nothing to purge. *Animal de fondo*, in clarion tones, extols the discovery of a "dios deseado y deseante" (a desired and desiring god). This dynamic god, identified explicitly as "conciencia" (consciousness), is desired by the poet as an expanded creative existence that at the same time is desirous of the poet, a relationship best described metaphorically as that of air and flame: mutual need in rapidly shifting contours. All former symbols were seen by Jiménez as mere surrogates for this final divinity.

Ezra Pound, whom the Jiménezes had been visiting at Saint Elizabeth's Hospital in the first half of 1948, wrote in a note to Jiménez that "Basic Animal" was a fine book, much needed in the "post-Hegelian squalor." The collection is the culmination of the romantic-symbolist tradition of the poet as a divine seer who through the use of words can unlock universal secrets, and, like Blake, whom Jiménez read and translated, *Animal de fondo* praises the divinity that resides within the human being.

Spurred on by the opinion of Octavio Paz, recent critics and poets have acclaimed Jiménez's long prose poem "Espacio" (Space, 1954). For a writer who had maintained since 1918 that good poetry is inevitably brief and that inspiration must always be subject to the control of intelligence, "Espacio" seems revolutionary, for its length is inordinate and its content the result of a pell-mell association of ideas that, in places, bears a resemblance to automatic writing.

In "Espacio" Jiménez ruminates on all his usual themes and employs all the tried-and-true symbols to recap his career. The large, flat, lowland space of the Everglades is no more infinite than the space in his mind, and the homesick poet allows images of the past to blend into the present. The sound of a barking dog is the same in Madrid, New York City, or Miami. Again the creative mind becomes the locus for meaning; identification and memory, out of the past, take shape only in the present. External space is internalized and expressed in the flow of time. The lines relentlessly move onward, impelled by the technique of association: the poet is not only the present but also a torrent of flight, an eternal succession of impressions and memories.

If there is a link between the first two fragments of "Espacio," it is the theme of love, which is the single constant. The third fragment, concluded in Puerto Rico in 1954, well after *Animal de fondo*, opens with a series of recondite personal allusions, goes on to equate destiny with life and death, recounts how the poet demolished a crab on the beach, and concludes with a humanistic cry asking how a soul can leave a body that has loved it. Repeating the opening line of the first fragment, he proclaims once more the insight of *Animal de fondo*: "The gods had no more substance than I."

The Jiménezes moved to Puerto Rico in 1951 and remained there until their deaths. Its benign climate, associations with Zenobia's past, and above all the return to a Spanish-speaking environment influenced the poet in the last few active years of his life. He donated his papers and books to the University of Puerto Rico at Río Piedras, taught a course on modernism there in 1953, and continued to write and publish poetry along the lines of *Animal de fondo*. The latter he intended to incorporate into a larger book to be called *Dios deseado y deseante* (published posthumously in 1964). Unfortunately he was about to lose his loyal and devoted helpmate. Zenobia, who had undergone an operation for cancer in 1951, worsened after a period of remission. On 28 October 1956, just three days after the Swedish Academy voted to award Jiménez the Nobel Prize for literature, she died. With her death, he more or less ceased to write. He occasionally visited the room at the university that housed his papers, stared at her photos, and awaited his own death. It came finally, that "great knowledge of the shadow" (*Poesía*), at 5 A.M. on 29 May 1958.

Letters:

*Monumento de amor: Cartas de Zenobia Camprubí y Juan Ramón Jiménez* (San Juan, P.R.: La Torre, 1959);

*Cartas, primera selección,* edited by Francisco Garfias (Madrid: Aguilar, 1962);

*Selección de cartas* (Barcelona: Picazo, 1973);

*Cartas literarias,* edited by Garfias (Barcelona: Bruguera, 1977).

**Interviews:**

Ricardo Gullón, *Conversaciones con Juan Ramón Jiménez* (Madrid: Taurus, 1958).

**Bibliography:**

Antonio Campoamor González, *Bibliografía general de Juan Ramón Jiménez* (Madrid: Taurus, 1982).

**Biographies:**

Francisco Garfias, *Juan Ramón Jiménez* (Madrid: Taurus, 1958);

Ricardo Gullón, *El último Juan Ramón* (Madrid: Alfaguara, 1968);

Howard T. Young, "Luisa and Juan Ramón," *Revista de Letras,* 6 (1974): 469–486;

Graciela Palau de Nemes, *Vida y obra de Juan Ramón Jiménez: La poesía desnuda,* 2 volumes (Madrid: Gredos, 1975);

Antonio González Campoamor, *Vida y poesía de Juan Ramón Jiménez* (Madrid: Sedmay, 1976);

Paulau de Nemes, *Inicios de Zenobia y Juan Ramón Jiménez en América* (Madrid: Fundación Universitaria Española, 1982);

Ignacio Prat, *El muchacho despatriado: Juan Ramón Jiménez en Francia (1901)* (Madrid: Taurus, 1986).

**References:**

Aurora de Albornoz, ed., *Juan Ramón Jiménez* (Madrid: Taurus, 1980);

Richard A. Cardwell, *Juan R. Jiménez: The Modernist Apprenticeship, 1895–1900* (Berlin: Colloquium, 1977);

Melvyn Coke-Enguídanos, *Word and Work in the Poetry of Juan Ramón Jiménez* (London: Tamesis, 1982);

Leo R. Cole, *The Religious Instinct in the Poetry of Juan Ramón Jiménez* (Oxford: Dolphin, 1967);

Angel Crespo, *Juan Ramón Jiménez y la pintura* (Río Piedras: University of Puerto Rico, 1974);

*Estudios sobre Juan Ramón Jiménez* (Mayagüez: University of Puerto Rico, 1981);

Donald F. Fogelquist, *Juan Ramón Jiménez* (Boston: Twayne, 1976);

María Teresa Font, *"Espacio," Autobiografía lírica de Juan Ramón Jiménez* (Madrid: Insula, 1972);

Bernardo Gicovate, *La poesía de Juan Ramón Jiménez: Obra en marcha* (Barcelona: Ariel, 1973);

Angel González, *Juan Ramón Jiménez* (Madrid: Júcar, 1974);

Juan Guerrero Ruiz, *Juan Ramón Jiménez de viva voz* (Madrid: Insula, 1961);

Ricardo Gullón, *Estudios sobre Juan Ramón Jiménez* (Buenos Aires: Losada, 1960);

Paul R. Olson, *Circle of Paradox: Time and Essence in the Poetry of Juan Ramón Jiménez* (Baltimore: Johns Hopkins University Press, 1967);

Michael P. Predmore, *La obra en prosa de Juan Ramón Jiménez* (Madrid: Gredos, 1966);

Predmore, *La poesía hermética de Juan Ramón Jiménez: El "Diario" como centro de su mundo poético* (Madrid: Gredos, 1973);

Antonio Sánchez-Barbudo, *La segunda época de Juan Ramón Jiménez (1916–1953)* (Madrid: Gredos, 1962);

Ceferino Santos-Escudero, *Símbolos y dios en el último Juan Ramón Jiménez: El influjo oriental en "Dios deseado y deseante"* (Madrid: Gredos, 1975);

Carlos del Saz-Orozco, *Dios en Juan Ramón* (Madrid: Razón & Fe, 1966);

John C. Wilcox, *Self and Image in Juan Ramón Jiménez* (Urbana: University of Illinois Press, 1987);

Howard T. Young, *Juan Ramón Jiménez* (New York: Columbia University Press, 1967);

Young, *The Line in the Margin: Juan Ramón Jiménez and His Readings in Blake, Shelley, and Yeats* (Madison: University of Wisconsin Press, 1980).

**Papers:**

Jiménez's manuscripts, letters, memorabilia, and personal library are held in three separate collections: the Archivo Histórico Nacional of Madrid; the Casa Municipal de Cultura "Zenobia y Juan Ramón Jiménez" in Moguer; and the "Sala Zenobia y Juan Ramón Jiménez" in the Biblioteca General, Río Piedras, University of Puerto Rico.

# Ana María Moix

## (12 April 1947 –    )

### Martha LaFollette Miller
*University of North Carolina at Charlotte*

BOOKS: *Call me Stone* (Barcelona: Esplugues de Llobregat, 1969);

*Baladas del Dulce Jim* (Barcelona: Saturno, 1969);

*Julia* (Barcelona: Seix Barral, 1970);

*Ese chico pelirrojo a quien veo cada día* (Barcelona: Lumen, 1971);

*No time for flowers y otras historias* (Barcelona: Lumen, 1971);

*24 x 24: Entrevistas* (Barcelona: Península, 1972);

*Walter ¿por qué te fuiste?* (Barcelona: Barral, 1973);

*La maravillosa colina de las edades primitivas* (Barcelona: Lumen, 1976);

*María Girona: Una pintura en llibertat,* by Moix and Josep María Castellet (Barcelona: Edicions 62, 1977);

*A imagen y semejanza: Poesía 1969–1972* (Barcelona: Lumen, 1983);

*Cantar de Mío Cid* (Barcelona: Lumen, 1984);

*Mi libro de . . . Los Robots* (Barcelona: Bruguera, 1985);

*Las virtudes peligrosas* (Barcelona: Plaza & Janés, 1985);

*Miguelón* (Madrid: Anaya, 1986);

*La niebla y otros relatos* (Madrid: Alfaguara, 1988).

OTHER: "Poética," in *Nueve novísimos poetas españoles,* edited by José María Castellet (Barcelona: Barral, 1970), pp. 221–222;

*Litoral femenino: Literatura escrita por mujeres en la España contemporánea,* edited by Lorenzo Saval and J. García Gallego, includes two previously unpublished sonnets by Moix (Málaga: Litoral, 1986), p. 321.

TRANSLATIONS: Mary Wollstonecraft Shelley, *Frankenstein* (Barcelona: Lumen, 1987);

Samuel Beckett, *Esperando a Godot* (Barcelona: Tusquets, 1990);

Alexandre Dumas *fils, La dama de las camelias* (Barcelona: Ediciones B, 1991).

One year after publishing her first two books of poetry, Ana María Moix acquired instant notoriety as the only woman to be included in José María Castellet's epoch-making 1970 anthology, *Nueve novísimos poetas españoles* (Nine Very New Spanish Poets). Her first two volumes, the slim *Baladas del Dulce Jim* (Ballads of Sweet Jim, 1969) and the even briefer *Call me Stone* (also 1969), have been followed by only one more book of poetry, *No time for flowers y otras historias* (No Time for Flowers and Other Stories), published in 1971. All three collections were revised and republished together in 1983 under the title *A imagen y semejanza* (In the Image and Likeness). Though scant, Moix's poetry is significant for placing her within the group of poets that Castellet dubbed "la coqueluche" (the whooping cough) for their youthful peskiness. Born after the Spanish Civil War and raised under Francisco Franco, these writers largely rejected the premises of the social poets that had preceded them, and they sought their inspiration more in the mass media than in the literary canon. Moix's poetry, however, represents only part of her literary production. In a precocious and intense burst of creativity that started in her early twenties and lasted four years, she wrote not only her poems but her innovative novels *Julia* (1970) and *Walter ¿por qué te fuiste?* (Walter, Why Did You Go Away?, 1973), as well as the stories in *Ese chico pelirrojo a quien veo cada día* (That Red-Headed Boy I See Every Day, 1971). Moix subsequently slowed her pace. Her only significant literary publication after *Walter* was published has been a collection of five narratives, *Las virtudes peligrosas* (Dangerous Virtues, 1985).

As her sometimes-autobiographical works suggest, Moix experienced with her contemporaries the social upheavals of the late 1960s. Born Ana María Moix Meseguer on 12 April 1947 to a bourgeois, conservative Barcelona family, she has described her childhood as unhappy, declaring in an unpublished interview with Margaret E. W. Jones that

*Ana María Moix*

"Es un asco la niñez. No se sabe nada. Sólo se mueve en un mundo de sombras e intuiciones y misterios" (Childhood is disgusting. You do not know anything. You live only in a world of shadows and intuitions and mysteries). Ana María was the youngest of the three children in her family, and she indicates that each of them began writing at an early age. In her "Poética" (a statement on poetics) in Castellet's anthology she states that her brother Miguel, who died at age seventeen, wrote poems to the Virgin and "aventuras interplanetarias" (interplanetary adventures). Her other brother, Ramón Terencio, later known as Terenci, was to become one of the leading Catalan writers of his generation. Ana María wrote her first book at age twelve. Titled "Todos eran unos marranos" (They Were All Swine), the unpublished work expressed "la vaga sensación de que alguien me había estafado" (the vague sensation that someone had cheated me).

The influence of Terenci Moix on his sister was a decisive one. Not only did he offer advice on what she should read (despairing at one point over her indifference to political engagement à la Jean-Paul Sartre), but he also brought her into contact, while still a teenager, with such young writers

as Pere Gimferrer, Vincente Molina-Foix, and Guillermo Carnero, poets whose works would appear alongside hers in *Nueve novísimos poetas españoles.* Through contact with this group she assimilated international cultural currents and developed a fascination with the mass media, especially movies and popular songs. But only sometimes did she follow her friends' abundant advice on what to read, and she gave advice as well as getting it. After reading her first published story, Gimferrer was sufficiently impressed to ask her opinion of his poetry. As to her affinities with Terenci, Moix points to her sensitive nature and her tendency for paranoia and depression. Apparently less-decisive influences on her literary development were her studies in humanities at the University of Barcelona in the same period during which she became acquainted with Terenci's circle of friends.

Moix has come to be known more for her prose works than for her poetry and is more apt to be categorized as a novelist than as a poet. Nevertheless her prose and poetry show considerable overlapping in themes, characters, and settings, and her writings tend to transcend traditional genre distinctions. Her shortest book of poems, *Call me Stone,* was first published in a limited edition and later re-printed in *No time for flowers y otras historias.* Consisting of six sections of one to three short verse paragraphs each, *Call me Stone* eschews rhyme, as do *Baladas del Dulce Jim* and *No time for flowers,* for the most part. Like those books, *Call me Stone* includes different narrative voices and wisps of narrative threads that defy exact interpretation. Unlike the longer collections, this brief book is not laden with references to icons from literary and popular culture, but it does begin to establish the intertextual webbing that runs through Moix's works as a whole. The enigmatic character Walter Stone, she explained in her interview with Federico Campbell, is actually *Dulce* Jim, "pero más cansado de la vida" (but more weary of life). Jim, she stated, came into being when Gimferrer invented him as an imaginary companion for Moix. A later incarnation of Walter Stone is the fictional boyfriend the character Lea creates in *Walter ¿por qué te fuiste?* Further evidence of intertextual linkage among her works includes the lines from *Call me Stone* that are duplicated in *Baladas del Dulce Jim,* such as the statement "Desde siempre presentí que las sombras tienen reacciones insospechadas" (I always suspected that ghosts have unexpected reactions) or the observation that "Te ves más viejo desde la última vez" (You look older than last time; directed to Adolf Hitler in the original *Baladas del Dulce Jim* but to God in the slightly revised version published in *A imagen y semejanza*). Thus, though Moix creates individual works, she gives them permeable borders. Further signs of intertextual permeability in her works are the allusions to and imitation of other authors, works, and styles, often from popular culture. Significantly Moix says in "Poética" that there is little difference between *la vida* (life) and such vehicles of culture as "libros, tebeos, películas y canciones" (books, comics, films and songs). By using clichés and borrowed cultural references, as well as by quoting her own work verbatim, she emphasizes the primacy of verbal culture over the mimetic communication of unrepeatable, individual experience.

*Baladas del Dulce Jim* can be divided into three main parts: the "Baladas del Dulce Jim" per se, "Una novela," and Epilogues I and II. The first of these starts out as a disconcerting mixture of prose and verse that tells the story of the speaker's encounter with a stranger (Jim) who is sweet but sinister. Jim's sordid past includes a love triangle involving his brother Johnny and a Broadway dancer, Nancy Flor, that ended melodramatically when Jim killed Johnny. This part of the poem continues with twenty-nine short, disconnected prose paragraphs

evoking madness, repression, dreams, and death. A few of these paragraphs are parodic versions of the autobiographical world Moix depicts in her novels; most, however, are surrealistic fantasies that arise from an amalgam of the clichés and patterns of popular songs and movies, with references to and fragments from Federico García Lorca's *Poeta en Nueva York* (1940; translated as *The Poet in New York,* 1940) and resonances of works by Gustavo Adolfo Bécquer. The intrusive second part (listed separately from *Baladas del Dulce Jim* in the index of *A imagen y semejanza*) calls attention to the violation of distinctions between literary genres, as well as to the rupture of the traditional integrity of books of poems. Titled "Una novela," it consists of ten chapters, each just a brief, disconnected sentence. The two epilogues consist of the incongruous description of the beefsteak cure for black eyes and a final word on the fate of Rossy Brown, a character who appears early on in the book in a story-within-the-story. Thus, the structure of *Baladas del Dulce Jim* is as confusing and disconnected as some of its imagery. Although "Una novela" seems separate from *Baladas del Dulce Jim,* nevertheless the second epilogue picks up threads from both preceding parts. The sometimes unnatural syntax of the book alludes to and evokes the cross-cultural nature of cinematic influences and underlines Moix's consciousness of the problematic relationship between language and reality.

*No time for flowers* illustrates more clearly than *Baladas del Dulce Jim* the essential oneness of Moix's creative world. More unified than the earlier book, the work's five sections paint a melancholy portrait of Aquella Chica (That Girl), a young woman whose unconventional manners earn her the reputation of a whore. She wanders the bars and parks of Barcelona; an unrequited love eventually leads to her suicide and to the surprising discovery in her autopsy that she is still a virgin. As in *Baladas del Dulce Jim,* Moix largely rejects conventional verse forms, differentiating her language from prose only through the frequent insertion of spaces to indicate pauses and the occasional use of rhyme. Like her novels, *No time for flowers* has doubled characters and multiple narrative voices. Moix's language at times seems to imitate the clichés of the movies and of the popular songs that played such an important role in the cultural background of her generation. She presents unnamed characters through dialogue and gestures: "he esperado años, y luego, tras una pausa y mordiéndose los labios, creí que no iba a llegar nunca" (I've waited years, and then, after a pause and biting his lips, I thought it would never arrive),

*Clockwise from left: Ana María Matute, Moix, Gil de Biedma, unidentified woman, Carlos Barral, Juan Marsé, Yvonne Barral, and an unidentified woman, mid 1970s*

and incorporates song fragments: "gotas de agua que el sol resecó" (drops of water that the sun dried up); "Solamente una vez" (Only once); "Cuando calienta el sol" (When the sun is warm). Thus she emphasizes the fact that her vision is mediated by film techniques and popular song. Literary references are also frequent. In the first section of the book the line "Federico, cuánto tiempo, la ventana abierta sobre una noche, un tejado, y aquel gato, maullando" (Federico, how long, the window open onto a night, a roof, and that cat, meowing) combines one of Moix's many references to Lorca with an allusion to Tennessee Williams's *Cat on a Hot Tin Roof* (1955).

In the first section of *No time for flowers* – set in a bar at three o'clock in the morning – Aquella Chica is seen through the eyes of a male drinker. In the presence of a younger man companion and a young woman, the drinker feels suddenly old, and overtones of jealousy and hostility appear. In part 2 a friend recounts the tragedy of Aquella Chica – her transformation from innocent schoolgirl into apparent tramp, her abandonment by her lover the

day before her death, and her vow at that time to return home. Aquella Chica's self-destructive drunkenness in part 3 foreshadows her demise, and hints of homicide as well as suicide appear. In part 4 Christina Georgina Rossetti's line "When I am dead, my dearest, sing no sad songs for me" introduces Aquella Chica's somewhat maudlin portrait of herself in death. In keeping with Moix's tendency toward doubling and transforming characters and with Aquella Chica's dual nature as worldly and innocent, her unfaithful lover is both a man and her doll Pinocchio. In the final section a return to the bar of part 1 is accompanied by images of destruction, explosion, death, and disintegration.

*No time for flowers* received the Premio Vizcaya del Ateneo de Bilbao in 1970. Despite that fact and the inclusion of works by Moix in *Nueve novísimos poetas españoles* the same year, critical interest in Moix has centered largely on her prose works, all of which – except the 1985 collection *Las virtudes peligrosas* – date from roughly the same period as her books of poetry. The worlds created in the two novels *Julia* and *Walter* overlap in characters, themes, and setting. The first tells the story of the isolation, pain, and sense of rejection felt by Julia, a shy young misfit who ultimately attempts suicide, and the second centers primarily on her cousin Ismael. His return as an adult to the summer home of their childhood unleashes a flow of words. From this verbiage emerge the stories of several members of his extended family as they come of age and rebel in various ways against their repressive upbringing. In *Julia* and *Walter*, Moix's sensitivity to the viewpoints of children and adolescents is apparent. In both works, as in some of her poetry, sexuality is sometimes associated with violence. The two novels subtly portray lesbian attachments. In this regard it is significant that Moix at one time announced her intention to collaborate with the feminist Carmen Alcalde on a book on lesbianism, to be titled "La otra opción amorosa" (The Other Love Option).

*Walter,* considered Moix's most outstanding achievement, presents a complex portrait of the Catalan bourgeoisie at a moment of intense social change, especially for youth. The rich elaboration of different points of view and the combination of first-, second-, and third-person narration give access to the struggles of several young people to come to terms with their sexuality and their politics amid the repressive atmosphere of the Franco regime. Moix skillfully portrays the ideological narrowness of certain family members and of an educational system that could be vicious and sadistic. Treatment of sexual issues comes across as bold for the times, despite the forty-five cuts by censors. Some characters from *Julia* reappear, including Julia herself. But her death in an institution belies the possible regeneration and hope that her confrontation with her five-year-old self in the earlier novel seemed to signify. And, instead of completing or complementing Julia's story, *Walter* presents a rewriting of her life and an alternative version of the keys to her character. The women she adored in *Julia* – her mother, her aunt, her professor – are replaced in *Walter* by her cousin Lea, presented as her almost lifelong obsession. Thus Julia exemplifies the psychic doubling and the alternative realities that undermine mimesis in some of Moix's other works. *Walter* also includes a surprising admixture of fantasy in the form of the love between the character Ismael, supposedly a circus cowboy, and Albina, half woman, half horse. A metafictional element emerges from the characters' inner monologues, which suggest imagination as memory's companion in the process of creation. The short stories of *Ese chico pelirrojo* give further evidence of Moix's range

and quality as a writer. Fantastic elements appear, along with references to madness, repression, and cruelty. Moix's tender sensitivity to children can again be noted at times, along with her interest in animals.

The intense creative effort that allowed Moix to complete *Julia* in twenty-five days and *Walter* in one and a half months also resulted, during the same period, in substantial journalistic accomplishments. In 1972 Moix published *24 x 24: Entrevistas* (Twenty-Four by Twenty-Four: Interviews), her lively record of encounters with twenty-four cultural figures ranging from Salvador Dalí to her brother Terenci; the interviews were originally published in the newspaper *TeleXprés*. For about two years in the late 1970s, Moix was cultural director of the radical women's magazine *Vindicación Feminista,* founded by Lidia Falcón. In addition to criticism on literature, film, and drama, Moix contributed to the journal a monthly satirical column on the life of a young woman from an uppermiddle-class milieu: "Diario de una hija de familia" (Diary of a Daughter of the Family). Other outlets for Moix's creativity have been her books for children and the translations she has spoken of as a source of income. Her children's books are *La maravillosa colina de las edades primitivas* (The Marvelous Hill of Ancient Times, 1976), *Cantar de Mío Cid* (a version of the early Spanish epic, the Poem of the Cid, 1984), *Mi libro de . . . Los Robots* (My Book of Robots, 1985), *Miguelón* (Michael, 1986), and *La niebla y otros relatos* (Fog and Other Stories, 1988). Her translations include Mary Wollstonecraft's *Frankenstein* (1987), Samuel Beckett's *En attendant Godot* (*Esperando a Godot* [Waiting for Godot], 1990), and *La dame aux camélias* by Alexandre Dumas *fils* (*La dama de las camelias* [The Lady of the Camelias], 1991). She has also collaborated on a work in Catalan, *María Girona: Una pintura en llibertat* (María Girona: Painting in Liberty, 1977).

The publication of *Las virtudes peligrosas* in 1985 renewed critical interest in Moix's fiction. The five narratives in the book have been compared to those of Virginia Woolf and Katherine Mansfield. In them Moix develops further the ambivalence toward language and narration expressed in *Walter,* but in a more abstract, conceptual manner than in the earlier work. An example of this abstraction is the narrative "El problema," whose protagonist, instead of a person, is a sexual problem.

Ana María Moix's literary reputation rests almost exclusively on the works she first published between the ages of twenty-one and twenty-six. Critical attention to her writings has probably been

*Ana María Moix, circa 1976*

limited by her failure to publish major works of fiction or poetry between 1973 and the mid 1980s, when *Las virtudes peligrosas* and the two sonnets included in *Litoral femenino* appeared. Further fictional or poetic works by Moix would be greeted with interest by critics, but even without such publications, she is entitled to a secure place within Spanish letters for the qualities she has already displayed as a writer: technical innovativeness and skill, a fertile imagination, and the ability to portray inner psychological states and social milieus.

**Interview:**

Federico Campbell, "Ana María Moix o la sobrevivencia," in his *Infame turba* (Barcelona: Lumen, 1971), pp. 26–41.

**References:**

Catherine G. Bellver, "Division, Duplication, and Doubling in the Novels of Ana María Moix," in *Nuevos y novísimos: Algunas perspectivas críticas sobre la narrativa española desde la década de los 60,* edited by Ricardo Landeira and Luis T. González-del-Valle (Boulder, Colo.: Society of Spanish and Spanish-American Studies, 1987), pp. 29–41;

Andrew Bush, "Ana María Moix's Silent Calling," in *Women Writers of Contemporary Spain: Exiles in the Homeland,* edited by Joan L. Brown (Newark: University of Delaware Press / London & Toronto: Associated University Presses, 1991), pp. 136–158;

Luis F. Costa, "Hipocresía y cine en la obra de Ana María Moix," *Letras Femeninas,* 4 (Fall 1978): 12–22;

Margaret E. W. Jones, "Ana María Moix: Literary Structures and the Enigmatic Nature of Reality," *Journal of Spanish Studies: Twentieth Century,* 4 (Fall 1976): 105–116;

Lucy Lee-Bonanno, *The Quest for Authentic Personhood: An Expression of the Female Tradition in Nov-*

els by Moix, *Tusquets, Matute* and *Alós* (Ann Arbor, Mich.: University Microfilms, 1985);

Linda Gould Levine, "Behind the 'Enemy Lines': Strategies for Interpreting *Las virtudes peligrosas* of Ana María Moix," in *Nuevos y novísimos: Algunas perspectivas críticas sobre la narrativa española desde la década de los 60*, pp. 97–111;

Levine, "The Censored Sex: Woman as Author and Character in Franco's Spain," in *Women in Hispanic Literature: Icons and Fallen Idols*, edited by Beth Miller (Berkeley & Los Angeles: University of California Press, 1983), pp. 289–315;

Ellen Engelson Marson, "Mae West, Superman and the Spanish Poets of the Seventies," in *Literature and Popular Culture in the Hispanic World: A Symposium* (Upper Montclair, N. J. & Gaithersburg, Md.: Montclair State College Hispámerica, 1981), pp. 191–198;

Juan Antonio Masoliver Rodenas, "La base sexta contra Ana María Moix," *Camp de L'Arpa,* 9 (January 1974): 9–12;

Geraldine Cleary Nichols, "*Julia*: 'This Is the Way the World Ends . . . ,'" in *Novelistas femeninas de la postguerra española,* edited by Janet W. Pérez (Madrid: Porrúa Turanzas, 1983), pp. 113–124;

Sara E. Schyfter, "Rites Without Passages," in *The Analysis of Literary Texts: Current Trends in Methodology. Third and Fourth York College Colloquia,* edited by Randolph D. Pope (Ypsilanti, Mich.: Bilingual Press, 1980), pp. 41–50;

C. Christopher Soufas, Jr., "Ana María Moix and the 'Generation of 1968': *Julia* as (Anti-)Generational (Anti-)Manifesto," in *Nuevos y novísimos: Algunas perspectivas críticas sobre la narrativa española desde la década de los 60*, pp. 217–228;

Michael D. Thomas, "El desdoblamiento psíquico como factor dinámico en *Julia,* de Ana María Moix," in *Novelistas femeninas de la postguerra española,* pp. 103–111;

Noel M. Valis, "Reality and Language in Ana María Moix's *Walter ¿por qué te fuiste?*," *Ojáncano: Revista de Literatura Española,* 4 (October 1990): 48–58.

# Eugenio de Nora

*(13 November 1923 –   )*

## Eleanor Wright

BOOKS: *Cantos al destino (1941–1945)* (Madrid: Hispánica, 1945);

*Amor prometido* (Valladolid: Halcón, 1946);

*Pueblo cautivo,* anonymous (Madrid: FUE, 1946; facsimile edition, Madrid: Poesía Hiperión, 1978);

*Contemplación del tiempo* (Madrid: Adonais, 1948);

*Siempre (1948–1951)* (Madrid: Insula, 1953);

*España, pasión de vida (1945–1950)* (Barcelona: Instituto de Estudios Hispánicos, 1953 [i.e., 1954]);

*La novela española contemporánea,* 2 volumes (Madrid: Gredos, 1958, 1962; revised and enlarged, 3 volumes, 1968–1970);

*Poesía (1939–1964)* (León: Institución Fray Bernardino de Sahagún, 1975).

OTHER: "Respuestas muy incompletas," in *Antología consultada de la joven poesía española,* edited by Francisco Ribes (Santander: Hermanos Bedia, 1952), pp. 149–157;

"Espadaña, 30 años después," *Espadaña. Revista de poesía y crítica* (León: Espadaña, 1978), pp. ix-xvii.

SELECTED PERIODICAL PUBLICATIONS – UNCOLLECTED: "Antonio Machado ante el futuro de la poesía lírica," *Cuadernos Hispanoamericanos,* 11–12 (1949): 583–592;

"Poesía y verdad: Carta abierta a Victoriano Crémer," as Juan Martínez, *Espadaña,* 46 (1950);

"Sobre la poesía en crisis, la humanización y otras interesantes vulgaridades," *Insula,* no. 124 (15 March 1957): 5;

"Sobre la llamada poesía social (Respuesta a Leopoldo de Luis, para su *Antología de la poesía social española contemporánea,* de próxima aparición)," *Realidad,* 2 (May 1965): 96–98.

Eugenio García González de Nora made his most lasting contribution to the development of postwar Spanish poetry by reviving and adapting the practices of social realism from the 1930s to the situation of the Francisco Franco dictatorship.

Despite harsh censorship of communication Nora found ways to publish poems of political protest by utilizing magazines with small circulations and, in the case of *Pueblo cautivo* (Captive People, 1946), with anonymous and clandestine publication. Committed to making others aware of the injustice and oppression of dictatorship, Nora championed the view that literature and historical reality are inextricably related and therefore that the course of events may be influenced by literary creation.

Assiduous readers of Spanish poetry became acquainted with these ideas in Nora's work as early as 1945 with the publication of *Cantos al destino (1941–1945)* (Songs to Destiny). Other readers encountered his work in the widely discussed *Antología consultada* (Consulted Anthology, 1952), edited by Francisco Ribes. Nora may be considered most aptly as the figure that links such poets as Rafael Alberti, Pablo Neruda, and César Vallejo – who were actively protesting in the 1930s – to those poets who rose to prominence in the 1950s and 1960s after the appearance of Nora's sociopolitical poems.

Nora was born on 13 November 1923 in the Leonese village of Zacos, situated in a region of great natural beauty. His parents were Ricardo García González and Jesusa de Nora de García. He was the only surviving child of their union. At an early age Nora exhibited mature intellectual qualities. In 1933 his parents decided to better their son's educational opportunities by leaving Zacos for the provincial capital. To do so, they gave up their small carpentry business and, in León, established a repair garage. They enrolled their son in the Instituto de Enseñanza Media. At the outbreak of the Spanish Civil War three years later, the Nationalists requisitioned the repair garage. Nora's education was interrupted by the flight of many teachers from the *instituto*.

In October 1942 Nora entered the University of Madrid. There he specialized in romance philology and graduated in June 1947. He received his doctorate from the same university in 1960 with a dissertation discussing the transition in Spanish literature from *deshumanización* (aestheticism) to real-

*Eugenio de Nora (Fotos Lagos, Madrid)*

ism. Nora prepared his dissertation under Dámaso Alonso. During Nora's year of obligatory military service, spent in Huesca beginning in 1947, he met Carmina Pac Baldellou. They married in October 1950 and the following year became parents of twins. In 1949 Nora began his long teaching career at the University of Bern (Switzerland). He was a full professor by 1970 and now chairs the Department of Spanish.

At the intellectually impressionable age of sixteen, Nora had met Antonio González de Lama, a priest well versed in philosophy and literature who was the director of the library in León. De Lama guided Nora in the formation of his literary tastes by exposing him to diverse authors. Nora also attended weekly meetings over which De Lama presided. Several young people at those sessions became the nucleus of the writers for the journal *Espadaña*. De Lama was particularly attentive to deceased and exiled poets whose popularity had be-

come eclipsed by the Nationalist victory. As a result of De Lama's guidance, Nora acquired a solid grounding in Spanish literature and was on his way to finding a personal poetic voice.

While Nora pursued studies at the University of Madrid, he found sufficient time to cultivate his literary interests. Most of the poems for which he has become noted were written during this period. They form the whole or significant portions of all his collections except *Siempre, (1948–1951)* (Forever, 1953) and "Angulares" (Angulars, in *Poesía, (1939–1964)* 1975). He also became acquainted with various writers of his own generation, such as Carlos Bousoño, José María Valverde, and Blas de Otero; and he met those of the previous generation who had remained in Spain, including Alonso, Vicente Aleixandre, and Gerardo Diego. These associations were useful to Nora as he sought publication for his poems in the poetry magazines extant in the postwar era. With De Lama and Victoriano

*Nora, Victoriano Crémer, and Luis López Anglada in the early 1940s. They were members of the group associated with the journal* Espadaña.

Crémer, who were in León, he founded *Espadaña*. The three of them published forty-eight issues between 1944 and 1950 despite economic hardship which made acquisition of paper difficult and despite the surveillance of censors.

Under the title *Cantos al destino* Nora collected poems written during his first three years at the university. The unifying device is his reference to *destino* as a sign of life and death simultaneously. Most of the poems rely on familiar romantic images, but "Otra voz" (Another Voice) elaborates on Neruda's dictum to humanize poetry, and "España mía" (My Spain), a group of three poems, heralds the path of Nora's patriotic poetry.

*Amor prometido* (Promised Love, 1946) includes the best of Nora's juvenile poems, which show the influences of Antonio Machado, Federico García Lorca, and Jorge Guillén in the profound sentiment from which they arise as well as in the lyrical brevity of

their expression. Other poems, on a variety of related themes, demonstrate an experimental quality in their variations in verse and stanza length.

In 1945 Nora became associated with the Federación Universitaria Escolar (FUE), an illegal student organization which united student opposition to the dictatorship. Nora then wrote the ten poems of *Pueblo cautivo*. With the assistance of others in the FUE, Nora published the work secretly near the end of 1946. *Pueblo cautivo* was known to few people until it was republished in 1978, still as an anonymous work. Not until 1980, in a published interview, did Nora acknowledge his authorship; he did so on condition that the work be viewed as a document of a particular period of history. In theme and style the poems of *Pueblo cautivo* resemble many of those in his *España, pasión de vida, (1945–1950)* (Spain, Life's Passion, 1954). In fact, Nora has stated that they all arose from the same source, differing only in that some were publishable once corrected for the censors while others were not, and thus did not appear until much later.

*Contemplación del tiempo* (Contemplation of Time, 1948), dedicated to Alonso, deals with the fleetness of time, the transitoriness of life, and the transcendence of these through the contemplation of nature, the giving of love, and the commitment to justice. Among poems illustrating this last theme is "Lo que yo pienso sobre ello" (What I Think about It), which at the time of its appearance awoke considerable controversy over its audacious treatment of political repression. With this poem Nora used a practice he employed earlier in *Cantos al destino* with the poems of "España mía" and later in *Siempre* with "Cantico final" (Final Canticle); that is, he placed poems of protest at the end of otherwise unobjectionable collections, thus obviating the censoring that a homogenous work of protest certainly would have received.

Nora's longest lyrical work, *Siempre,* consists of forty-four poems on the transforming power of romantic love. The poems were written during Nora's courtship of Carmina and the first year of their marriage. The book, dedicated to his wife, is technically accomplished, has much musicality and purity of expression, and offers profound insights into the eternal nature of love. The titles of more than half of the poems begin with "Carmen de" (Verse of), a linguistic play on the name of the person who inspired these poems. Quite different from the works usually associated with Nora, *Siempre* has been overshadowed and consequently undervalued.

Between 1945 and 1950 Nora wrote the poems of *España, pasión de vida.* He published most of them singly, but several times, when he tried to publish the group as a whole, he ran into difficulties because of censorship. Not until he entered the work in contention for the Premio Boscán and received the unqualified backing of two judges on the panel, José María Castellet and Alfonso Costafreda, was he able to secure publication by winning the prize. Even so, Nora was required to make corrections and change certain expressions to satisfy censors. Within these limitations Nora carried out his long-standing intention to compose a book of poems to Spain which would reflect the past, future, and truncated present through the conscience of a young Spaniard. The work is notable for having incorporated the frustration, discouragement, and resurgent hope Nora experienced while composing the poems during one of Spain's most difficult and repressive periods.

During the late 1940s, in his contributions to *Espadaña,* Nora expressed his political views more and more explicitly. He had become known for his preference for sociopolitical literature. What was new was that he extended his critical attitude to encompass the moral behavior of others, whom he challenged to take a stand instead of aimlessly drifting. The trend of these contributions culminated in an incriminatory open letter to Crémer which appeared in *Espadaña* in 1950. The letter was headed "Poesía y verdad" (Poetry and Truth). Not entirely coincidentally, *Espadaña* suspended publication shortly thereafter amid difficulties with censors.

After 1951 Nora's writing of poetry diminished. He attributed this relative silence to a dislike of repeating himself, reasoning that to reiterate the protest of *Pueblo cautivo* or the patriotic sentiment of *España, pasión de vida* was unnecessary. Then too, cultural repression had decreased once economic prosperity made its appearance. Perhaps the overriding reason, however, was that Nora had become absorbed in the preparation of a study of the Spanish novel, the largest and most authoritative of its kind. *La novela española contemporánea* (The Contemporary Spanish Novel, two volumes, 1958, 1962) is an appraisal which covers the work of writers living in Spain as well as those who lived in exile; thus it demonstrates that even under censorship and expatriation the Spanish novel continued and even flourished.

In 1975 Nora published *Poesía (1939-1964).* This volume collects most, but not all, of Nora's poetry. For example, the poems of *Pueblo cautivo* have been omitted. Included, though, are nine new poems, grouped under the title "Angulares," which approach familiar themes from a more contemplative and mature perspective but with characteristic passion, reminding readers of a voice and persona which played a singular role in the development of social realism in Spanish poetry.

**References:**

José Manuel López de Abiada, "Observaciones en torno a la poesía de posguerra. Conversacion con Eugenio de Nora," *Insula,* no. 407 (15 October 1980): 3-4;

López de Abiada, ed., *Entre la cruz y la espada: En torno a la España de posguerra* (Madrid: Gredos, 1984), pp. 9-18, 345-360;

Amaro Soladana Carro, *La poesía de Eugenio de Nora* (León: Institución Fray Bernardino de Sahagún, 1987);

Eleanor Wright, *The Poetry of Protest under Franco* (London: Tamesis, 1986), pp. 57-72.

# Carlos Edmundo de Ory

## (27 April 1923 –    )

### Linda D. Metzler
#### Kenyon College

BOOKS: *Nuestro tiempo: Poesía,* with *Nuestro tiempo: Pintura,* by Darío Suro (Madrid: Fareso, 1951);

*El bosque* (Santander: Nieto, 1952);

*Kikiriquí-Mangó* (Madrid: Grifón, 1954);

*Aérolithes,* translated into French by Denise Breuhil (Paris: Rougerie, 1962); published in Spanish as *Aerolitos* (N.p.: Observatorio, 1985);

*Los sonetos* (Madrid: Taurus, 1963);

*Camus y el ateísmo "in extremis"* (Madrid: Nacional, 1964);

*Una exhibición peligrosa* (Madrid: Taurus, 1964);

*Federico García Lorca,* translated into French by Jacques Deretz (Paris: Editions Universitaires, 1967);

*Poemas* (Madrid: Rialp, 1969);

*El alfabeto griego* (Barcelona: Esquina, 1970);

*Música de lobo* (Madrid: Grupo N.O., 1970);

*Poesía 1945–1969,* edited by Félix Grande (Barcelona: Edhasa, 1970);

*Técnica y llanto* (Barcelona: Llibres de Sinera, 1971);

*Mèphiboseth en Onou: Diario de un loco* (Las Palmas: Inventarios Provisionales, 1973);

*Los poemas de 1944,* edited by Joaquín Giménez-Arnau (Madrid: Aguaribay, 1973);

*Poesía abierta (1945–1973),* edited by Jaime Pont Ibáñez (Barcelona: Barral, 1974);

*Basuras (1945–1973)* (Madrid: Júcar, 1975);

*Diario* (Barcelona: Barral, 1975);

*Lee sin temor* (Madrid: Nacional, 1976);

*Energeia (1940–1977)* (Barcelona: Plaza & Janés, 1978);

*Metanoia,* edited by Rafael de Cózar (Madrid: Cátedra, 1978);

*La flauta prohibida* (Bilbao: Zero, 1979);

*Miserable ternura; Cabaña* (Madrid: Hiperión, 1981);

*Eunice Fucata: Diarios* (Madrid: Begar, 1984);

*Soneto vivo* (Barcelona: Anthropos/Hombre, 1988).

SELECTED PERIODICAL PUBLICATIONS – UNCOLLECTED: "Versos de pronto," *Fantasía,* 19 (July 1945): 15–28;

"Caín y Abel no fueron literatos," *Español* (15 December 1945);

"Valor y lógica del postismo," *Hora* (7 May 1948);

"Geografía del postismo," *Lanza* (8 September 1949);

"La comunidad clandestina del arte," *Correo Literario,* 23 (1 May 1951): 12;

"Babel en la capital y entendimiento en las provincias," *Correo Literario,* 40 (15 January 1952): 9;

"Poesía y definición," *Poesía Española,* 26 (February 1954);

"El Surrealismo de par en par," *Índice,* 187–188 (July–August 1964);

"Elogio de la neurosis o felicidad y metafísica," *Cuadernos Hispanoamericanos,* no. 179 (November 1964): 298–302;

"Erotismo y civilización," *Cuadernos Hispanoamericanos,* no. 221 (May 1968): 251–272;

"¿Surrealismo en España?," *Cuadernos Hispanoamericanos,* no. 261 (March 1972): 579–583;

"Marinetti y el futurismo italiano," *Fin de Siglo,* 6–7 (1983).

Since the mid 1940s Carlos Edmundo de Ory has defended his vision of imaginatively wielded language as the key to transcendence over personal anguish and to the creation of poems that illuminate a common humanity. During the first two decades of Ory's writing career his work remained largely unknown; critics considered it an anachronism, interesting primarily because of its link to the ephemeral avant-garde movement called *postismo,* cofounded by Ory, Spanish painter Eduardo Chicharro, and Italian poet Silvano Sernesi in Madrid during the 1940s. Since the 1970s, however, critics undertaking a reappraisal of Ory's work have come to recognize its scope and originality and have deemed it an important precursor of the language-centered poetry which gained critical prominence in Spain during the 1970s and 1980s.

*Carlos Edmundo de Ory*

Ory was born on 27 April 1923 in Cádiz. His father, Eduardo de Ory, a modernist poet, was the founder of the Academia Hispanoamericana de Cádiz and was friends with poets Rubén Darío, Juan Ramón Jiménez, Salvador Rueda, Amado Nervo, and Manuel Reina.

In a poem Eduardo de Ory wrote when his son was four years old, "A mi hijo Carlos" (To My Son Carlos; collected in *Poesía 1945–1969* [1970]), he reflects on the child's melancholy and solitary nature, imagining it as linked to a future poetic vocation:

¡Pobrecito mío
siempre tan callado,
tan meditabundo
tan triste y tan pálido!
. . . . . . . . . . . . . . . . . .
¡Ah! Quizá te inquiete
un enigma, un algo
que allá, en lontananza,
no se ha dibujado;
. . . . . . . . . . . . . . .

Tú serás poeta,
poeta preclaro;
¡serás . . . mi obra magna
y mi mejor lauro!

(My poor child
always so silent,
so abstracted
so sad and so pale!
. . . . . . . . . . . . . . .
Oh! Perhaps an enigma
troubles you, something
which, off in the distance,
is not yet visible;
. . . . . . . . . . . . . .
You will be a poet,
an eminent poet;
you will be . . . my greatest work
and my crowning achievement!)

Reflecting on his childhood years, in his *Diario* (1975), Carlos Edmundo de Ory confirms his father's vision of him as a child, saying: "Yo viví

247

una infancia viva, pero triste en el fondo y angustiosa. Era como perseguido y estaba solo" (I lived a lively childhood, but it was fundamentally sad and anguished. I felt pursued and I was alone).

Beginning in 1930, Ory attended a Marianist elementary school in Cádiz. In 1936 he began studies toward a *bachillerato* (high-school diploma) at the Instituto Provincial and enrolled in the Escuela Náutica there. The outbreak of the Spanish Civil War disrupted Ory's studies, which he never formally resumed. His poetic vocation emerged during these early years, of which he says in his diary: "Mi vida de poeta empieza en aquellos lejanos días, cuando tendido en la cama, casi en plena niñez, pasaba las horas mirando el estante donde estaban los libros de mi poeta preferido. Ese poeta era [Paul] Verlaine" (My life as a poet begins in those distant days, when, stretched out on my bed, still a child, I would spend hours looking at the shelf where the books of my favorite poet were kept. That poet was Verlaine). His father's library was a source of Ory's acquaintance with the works of Darío, Jiménez, Francisco Villaespesa, Gustavo Adolfo Bécquer, Julio Herrera y Reissig, Alfonsina Storni, and Leopoldo Lugones.

In 1940 Ory began to write his first poems. These eventually were typed and gathered into eight leather-bound notebooks, illustrated with drawings by friends and featuring prologues by José María Pemán, Miguel Martínez del Cerro, and Fernando de los Ríos y de Guzmán. Jaime Pont Ibáñez characterizes these poems in his book *El postismo* (1987) as influenced by the modernist aesthetic: they feature colorful, musical metaphors and are generally written in eight-syllable, twelve-syllable, and alexandrine lines. The first of these groupings includes a tellingly effusive dedication to the young poet's father, who had died in 1939: "¡Padre!, en memoria de ti, este libro. Porque te dormiste dejándome tu lira, para que la pulsase como un eco de tu voz" (Father! in your memory, this book. Because you died leaving me your lyre, so that I might pluck it making it yield your voice's echo).

In October 1942 Ory took up residence in Madrid, where he lived until 1956. He made a meager living by working as a librarian for the Parque Móvil de Ministerios Civiles, writing articles for several Madrid magazines, and giving lectures about art. Ory's *Diario* is a valuable source of insights into his day-to-day life during this period – a life marked by material and spiritual difficulties and given over to the alternately anguishing and rewarding pursuit of an identity as a writer.

About the dire financial difficulties he endured, Ory writes, "Estoy viviendo en una pensión donde pago 25 pesetas diarias. No tengo más dinero. Comida mala" (I am living in a boardinghouse where I pay 25 pesetas a day. I have no more money. Bad food) and "Mil preocupaciones de dinero y deudas me asedian. He quemado mi traje nuevo y no tengo calcetines ni ropa interior" (A thousand worries about money and debts besiege me. I have accidentally burned my new suit and I do not have any socks or underwear).

Ory received encouragement during his time in Madrid from the writers Gabriel Celaya, Vicente Aleixandre, Juan-Eduardo Cirlot, and Eugenio d'Ors. He also counted among his acquaintances the artists Darío Suro, Luis Feito, Antonio Saura, Antonio Tàpies, and Angel Ferrant. Of his tendency to form friendships with visual artists, Ory says, "Seguramente se debe a mi desprecio por la vida intelectual, a mi adoración casi mística por la pintura y la escultura o los objetos de arte" (No doubt it is due to my scorn for intellectual life, to my nearly mystical adoration for painting and sculpture or art objects).

Ory's diary leaves little doubt that his emotional state – particularly during nights of insomnia – was often one of a depressiveness verging on the suicidal, as in these passages: "Tengo miedo de mí . . . quiero matarme. . . . De un momento a otro se abrirán las ventanas y entrará el viento, y entrará la muerte y yo desapareceré en los aires montado en mi cama triste" (I am afraid of myself. . . I want to kill myself . . . . At any moment the windows will open and the wind will come in, and death will come in and I will disappear in the air riding my sad bed); "Anoche tuve que dejar a medias esta página y hoy la continúo. Me sentía vigilado en la noche por seres hostiles a los dolores del hombre que escribe a propósito de su cabeza llena de cenizas" (Last night I had to leave this page half-finished, and today I continue it. I felt myself spied upon in the night by beings hostile to the anguish of the man writing to relieve his head filled with ashes); "Siento una ráfaga de locura, un deseo fugaz, instantáneo, fogoso de suicidio. Miedo" (I feel a sudden gust of madness, a fleeting, instantaneous, fiery desire to kill myself. Fear); and "yo mismo soy el infierno, un infierno" (I myself am hell, a kind of hell).

The obsessive self-preoccupation which Ory's diary entries reveal may reflect his anxiety to forge an identity as a young writer. This possibility is articulated by Grande, who says in the prologue to *Poesía 1945–1969* that Ory's diary entries are characterized by "una desmesurada necesidad de genio" (an excessive need to be a genius). By August 1951 Ory's emotional and physical state seemed alarming enough to such friends as Alejandro Busuioceanu, Pedro Laín Entralgo, and Juana Mordó that they were encouraging him to have himself examined for

*Ángel Crespo, Ory, and Eduardo Chicharro at Chicharro's studio in Madrid, 1948*

tuberculosis and committed for a month to a sanatorium.

An examination for tuberculosis came out negative, but, nevertheless, on 19 October Ory checked himself into the Asilo de los Convalecientes de Chamartín de la Rosa, taking with him his writing materials. After a three-day stay Ory – bored, dismayed at the curtailment of his freedom, and saddened by the plight of his fellow inmates – had himself released. On his last evening in the Asilo he wrote: "Aquí no hay más que hombres atristados, muchachos dementes, viejos asmáticos, albañiles desgraciados, ¡pobre gente! y yo, un millonario de sueños, ¿qué hago aquí?" (Here there are only sad men, demented boys, asthmatic old men, construction workers down on their luck, poor unfortunates! and I, a millionaire of dreams, what am I doing here?).

During his years in Madrid, Ory's existential doubt and pessimism were allayed by his reflection on the words and lives of great writers of the past and by his recognition of the anguish they underwent in order to create their work. In a section of his diary in which he considers such writers as Aleksandr Blok, Nikolay Gogol, Charles Baudelaire, Gérard de Nerval, Friedrich Hölderlin, Torquato Tasso, and Giacomo Leopardi, Ory says: "Son unos genios mundiales. . . . Cuando pronuncio sus nombres tiemblo. Ellos asombran y alumbran mi espíritu. . . . Amo esas vidas. Son unos trágicos. . . . Hombres que, en su mayoría, murieron locos" (They are world-renowned geniuses. . . . When I pronounce their names, I tremble. They amaze and illuminate my spirit. . . . I love these lives. They are tragic men. . . . Men who, for the most part, died insane). John Keats, Friedrich Nietzsche, Novalis, Fyodor Dostoyevski, Bernard Shaw, and Franz Kafka also inspired Ory's reflections.

The preoccupation with madness Ory displays in his diary found a creative outlet in his autobiographical novel *Mèphiboseth en Onou: Diario de un loco* (Mèphiboseth in Onou: Diary of a Madman, 1973); begun in 1944, it was finished in 1955. The first-person narrator, the personage of the title, is writing the novel while residing in an insane asylum run by a childhood friend. An entry from Ory's diary, dated 27 October 1951, describes the fictional character as having supplanted the author: "Carlos Edmundo de Ory es un ser imaginario. Yo soy Mèphiboseth, el personaje de mi novela. Yo no existo. Existe mi loco" (Carlos Edmundo de Ory is an imaginary being. I am Mèphiboseth, the character of my novel. I do not exist. My madman exists).

Although Ory cultivated the novel, the short story, and the diary during his Madrid period, it was to the art of poetry that he attached his deepest hopes of transcending his anguished solitude and forging a meaningful life and work: "Mi felicidad está en el canto que oigo en mi interior y elevo a las alturas cuando compongo poemas. Sin escribir poemas estoy más solitario que el pastor sin sus ovejas" (My happiness is in the song that I hear within me and that I raise to the heights when I compose poems. Without the solace of writing poems, I am more solitary than a shepherd without his sheep); and "Mi poesía parte del hombre 'humano.' De la nostalgia y de la angustia, y aspira a ser escuchada por Dios" (My poetry takes humankind as its point of departure. It is grounded in nostalgia and anguish and aspires to be listened to by God).

Recognizing the disparity between his poetic ambition and his lack of an audience, Ory was led to anguished reflection. On finishing "Canto irreal" (collected in *Poesía 1945–1969*), a poem which seemed to him particularly good, he wrote: "Estoy como asustado de mi destino de poeta. Empiezo a comprender mi importancia, mi seria lucha, la evidencia de mi desolación. . . . Y hacer un poema de esta clase me hiere . . . porque soy desconocido" (I am frightened of my destiny as a poet. I am beginning to understand my importance, my serious struggle, the evidence of my desolation. . . . And to write a poem of this kind wounds me . . . because I am unknown).

Although Ory's poetic work was not entirely unknown during his Madrid period – his poems appeared from the mid 1940s in such literary magazines as *Garcilaso, Lanza, Acanto, Estafeta Literaria,* and *Fantasía* – receptivity to his writing was limited. Both Ory's nonconformist, iconoclastic personality and the poetic climate which prevailed in Spain following the civil war were factors in the personal and artistic marginalization he experienced.

The extravagant persona which Ory assumed during his years in Madrid alarmed the staid representatives of the post-civil-war poetic establishment and disinclined them to take him seriously. Ory's friend and collaborator Eduardo Chicharro remembers the Ory of 1944 as a young poet "frenético de su gloria, un neurótico apasionado lector de poetas malditos, de condenados por los amantes de la paz y la normalidad, devorador de biografías siniestras y coleccionador de lo pirográfico, de lo fantasmagórico y ultra-terreno" (frantic to achieve literary fame, an impassioned neurotic who read the "damned poets" and the work of authors condemned by people who loved peace and normality, a devourer of weird and sinister biographies and a collector of anything pyrographic, phantasmagoric, and otherworldly).

Grande (in *Poesía*) remembers the Ory of the 1940s as "cuarenta kilos de disconformidad con ojeras" (forty kilos of rebelliousness with dark circles under his eyes). Grande says, "Su locura cordial, su inocencia, su espectacular torpeza vital – bajo las que alienta una indómita negativa a aceptar como buenos unos valores que suelen añadir prestigio en proporción directa a la espontaneidad que sofocan . . . no cabían en aquel ágora sombría" (His genial madness, his innocence, his spectacular personal awkwardness – under which pulsed an indomitable refusal to accept as valid certain values society "privileges" in direct proportion to their capacity to stifle spontaneity . . . had no place in that somber arena [of Madrid in the 1940s]).

The literary climate in post-civil-war Spain posed significant obstacles to the acceptance of Ory's poetry. During the early 1940s two groups espousing opposing views of poetry, the *garcilasistas* and the *espadañistas,* dominated the poetry scene The *garcilasistas* were associated with the magazine *Garcilaso,* founded in 1943 and named after the well-known Spanish Renaissance poet Garcilaso de la Vega. They cultivated a poetry stressing classical meters, musicality of phrases, beauty of images, and nontemporal, escapist themes. Their poetic stance came under attack in 1944, with the founding of the magazine *Espadaña* by a group of opposition poets in the city of León. The *espadañistas* proposed the need for a committed, rehumanized poetry which could address the harsh realities of life in a nation left devastated by a civil war. Ory's cofounding in 1945 of the avant-garde movement called *postismo* highlighted his disagreements with the poetic tenets of both these other groups.

The *postista* manifestos – written between 1945 and 1949 by Ory, Chicharro, and Sernesi – proposed an assault on *garcilasista* values, and as Pont Ibáñez points out in his definitive study *El postismo,* they did so from a position different from that taken by the *espadañistas.* The *espadañistas* opposed the classical language and timeless themes of *garcilasismo* by advocating the use of colloquial language to portray the sociopolitical reality of present-day Spain; the *postistas* put forward language itself – freed from historical constraints – as the key to challenging the staid *garcilasista* vision. Building on the legacy of European avant-garde movements (particularly surrealism), the *postistas* proclaimed the centrality to poetic creation of humor, whimsy, wordplay, "invented madness," and the artist's conscious ordering of creative elements supplied by the subconscious.

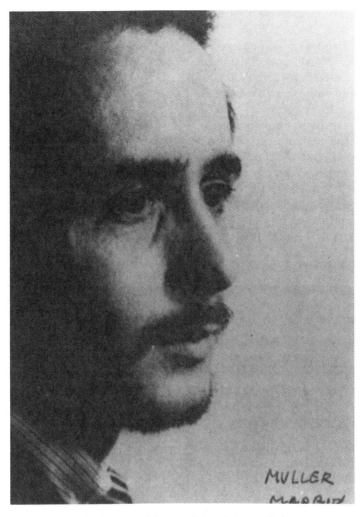

*Ory in 1949 (photograph by Nicolás Muller)*

The *postistas* attacked the world of official culture in both their writings and their actions. Pont Ibáñez characterizes the public response to *postista* pronouncements, happenings, and provocations as ranging from amusement to outrage; by the political and aesthetic Left they were called *evasionistas* (evasionists), and the Right called them "comunistas, rusófilos y frente-populacheros" (communists, Russophiles, and Popular Front supporters). *Postismo* was also deemed politically unacceptable by the Francisco Franco regime: two *postista* magazines, *Postismo* and the *Cerbatana,* were suspended by government order after each had been issued once. Although by 1950 it had failed as a movement, *postismo* bespoke many of the poetic values Ory continued to cultivate throughout his career: experimentation with sound and syntax, imaginative juxtaposition of images, the use of humor and irony, and iconoclastic intent.

In 1951 Ory and his friend Suro set forth the tenets of a new creative mode, "el introrrealismo íntegro" (integral introrealism), in a brief book comprising Ory's *Nuestro tiempo: Poesía* (Our Time: Poetry), and Suro's *Nuestro tiempo: Pintura* (Our Time: Painting). In his part, Ory says that integral introrealism displays "un SUBJETIVISMO pujante, creador . . . un estremecimiento sensual y patético de vida, producido . . . por el amor a la vida y el dolor que entraña la vida" (a pulsating, creative SUBJECTIVISM . . . a sensual and pathetic trembling of life, produced . . . by the love of life and the anguish life entails). Ory rejects poetry clad in pretentious language: "Al fuego con esas pudibundas y groseras ropas finas" (Into the fire with those prudish, unsightly fine clothes). He affirms the poet's imperative as being "escribir con fe y pasión; fe en lo sobrenatural; fe en la POESÍA; fe en la salvación por medio del flujo eterno y verdadero del LENGUAJE poético" (to write with faith and passion; faith in the supernatural; faith in POETRY; faith in salvation through the eternal and true flowing of poetic LANGUAGE).

A poem Ory identifies in his diary as illustrating integral introrealism is his 1948 "Amigo fuma" (Smoke Friend, 1974), which was collected in *Poesía abierta (1945–1973)*. The anecdotal frame of the poem is uncomplicated: an unnamed first-person narrator addresses himself to a friend with whom he sits while the friend reads a book and the two of them smoke. A stream-of-consciousness technique, surprising juxtapositions of imagery, experimentation with sound and rhythm, and the breaking of syntactic norms complicate and transform this simple anecdotal frame, making the poem yield a more broadly allusive commentary on the capacity of friendship and literature to diminish the anguish of solitary existence:

> Todo lo veo yo lo siento yo asustado
> y descubro que vivo de estar animal vivo
> y con otro animal malucho de ser mucho
> Fumamigo que puedes vivir podemos ir
> puedo y puedes en este silencio de poderes
> paralelo a los cantos de los muertos

> (Everything I see I feel it frightened
> and I discover that I live by being a living animal
> and with another animal sick from too much being
> Smokefriend you can live we can go on
> I can and you can in this silence of powers
> parallel to the songs of the dead)[.]

Given the hostility of the Spanish literary world to Ory's provocative personal and aesthetic stance, it is not surprising that by late 1950 he was entertaining thoughts of leaving Spain: "España me está haciendo mucho daño. No sé cómo podré huir de aquí" (Spain is making me suffer. I do not know how I can manage to flee from here). On 23 November 1951 he wrote that, as soon as he had money and a passport, he was "dispuesto a errar, a cambiar radicalmente de vida y de salud y de ambiente y de todo" (ready to wander, to change radically my life, my health, my environment, and everything).

Ory's first trip to Paris, in 1952, was made possible by a scholarship from the French government; his second, in 1955, was funded both by the French government and by the Spanish National Ministry of Education. After a third trip to Paris, Ory – who married Denise Breuhil in 1956 – finally took up residence in the French capital. With the exception of a year spent teaching Spanish language and literature in Peru (1957–1958), Ory remained there for ten years.

During his stay in Paris, Ory taught Spanish at the École Alsacienne and the Institut Catholique. He worked as a journalist, contributing to the French magazines *Nouvelle Revue Française* and *Réalities Secrètes* and collaborating on the Spanish magazines *Ínsula* and *Papeles de Son Armadans*. He served as an editorial con-

sultant with the Buchet/Chastel publishing house. He also held several scholarships granted by the prestigious Juan March Foundation. Pont Ibáñez (in *El postismo*) lists as the French writers whose friendship Ory cultivated Pierre Jean Jove, André Frénaud, Jean Wahl, Jean Cassou, Marcel Béalu, Alain Bosquet, Claude Couffon, and Maurice Nadeu. From Paris, Ory made trips to Belgium, England, Italy, and Morocco. In 1965 and 1966 he gave a series of poetry recitals and lectures in Spain.

In February 1962 *Cuadernos Hispanoamericanos* published the first of several substantial groupings of Ory's poems, the last of which would appear in 1974. Also in 1962 Ory published *Aérolithes,* a collection of aphorisms translated into French by his wife. These fragmentary, elliptic formulations are characterized by linguistic and syntactic playfulness, metaphoric inventiveness, and a tendency to deflate metaphysical pretentiousness.

In 1963 Ory published *Los sonetos,* a collection of sonnets written between 1944 and 1963. While Ory's themes – love, time, despair, and the elusiveness of beauty and meaning – are consistent with those typically configured in the classical sonnet and while he observes the sonnet's traditional stanzaic and metrical structure, he effects a startling transformation of the form's expressive possibilities through his use of surprising images, enjambments, nontraditional syntax, and plays on words, sounds, and meanings.

Some of these qualities are apparent in the second quatrain of the *postista* sonnet "Pozo Calabozo" (Well Jail, 1947), in which the first-person speaker evokes his metaphysical disorientation during a night of insomnia:

> En este pozo en este calabozo
> en este nicho en esta noche en una
> tiniebla en que tal vez llama la luna
> con delicados dedos cuando gozo

> (In this well in this jail
> in this niche in this night in a
> darkness in which perhaps the moon calls
> with delicate fingers when I feel pleasure )[.]

The concluding tercets of another sonnet, "Amo el sueño" (I Love Sleep, 1948) illustrate how plays on sound are elements fundamental to Ory's creation of meaning:

> Amo el sueño porque es señal de una
> más grande seña de la muerte enseña
> igual que la guadaña de la luna

> Y amo el misterio por su semejanza
> con el sueño y la muerte y con la leña
> que engendra el fuego hermano de la danza

*Ory, Félix Casanova de Ayala, and Pedro García Cabrera, 1972*

(I love sleep because it is a signal of a
larger sign of death an emblem
like the scythe of the moon

And I love all that is mysterious for its likeness
to sleep and to death and to the wood
which engenders fire dance's brother)[.]

The sonnet "Lo que siempre digo" (What I Always Say, 1962) demonstrates how Ory grounds the surprising existential revelations of some of his poems in his experimentation with language. His idiosyncratic juxtaposition of forms of the two verbs in Spanish signifying "to be" – *estar,* meaning "to be" in a temporary state or a location; and *ser,* meaning "to be" in an essential or permanent state – enables Ory to evoke effectively the speaker's paradoxical existential status:

Cansado y triste estoy en mi Gran Ser
luego estoy en mi soy sin hoy ni ayer
Soy un muerto seguro en vivo puro

(Tired and sad am I in my Great Being
so I exist in my "I am" without a today or a yesterday
I am a certain dead man purely alive)[.]

In 1967 Ory moved to Amiens, France, taking a job as librarian of the Maison de la Culture. In 1968 he founded the Atélier de Poésie Ouverte (Workshop for Open Poetry). Over a period of two years this group – whose aim was further exploration of a new idea of poetry – brought together a constantly changing roster of mostly student-aged participants for workshops, recitals, dramatic presentations, happenings, and collective experimental poetry writing. Grande reproduces in *Poesía* a partial list of some of Ory's "Proposiciones" for open poetry. Among them are "Arte experimental: no encontrar la cosa definida" (Experimental art: not to find the definitive thing); "Inventar metáforas en una competición de emancipación verbal" (To invent metaphors in a contest of verbal emancipation); "La poesía del juego, de lo gratuíto, de lo humano: el amor, la amistad, la hospitalidad. La nueva inocencia" (Poetry as a game, as a gratuitous exercise, a human exercise: love, friendship, hospitality. The new innocence); "Desconcertar al público es un acto moral de la poesía, de la música, de la pintura" (To disconcert the public is a moral act undertaken by poetry, by music, by painting); and "Autenticidad vivida. El resto es miseria" (Lived authenticity. The rest is misery). The workshop marks Ory's effort to make pursuit of knowledge about poetry a public and collective endeavor.

In December 1969 the Madrid firm Rialp published Ory's *Poemas* in the prestigious "Adonais" collection, thus heralding the critical reappraisal of Ory's work which the decade of the 1970s would bring. The book comprises thirty-one poems, some written in alexandrines and others in blank verse. Nearly all feature a first-person speaker in a state of emotional distress; in some poems this distress is occasioned by difficulties in love. (Ory's marriage was coming to an end during the 1960s.) The editorial piece printed on the book's inner flaps affirms the opportuneness of a critical reappraisal of Ory. Praising Ory's work for its "extraordinaria inquietud" (extraordinary inquiring spirit), its "densidad humana" (human density), its "audacia expresiva" (expressive daring), and its "original estilo" (original style), the piece closes by stating, "este volumen da a conocer en toda su importancia a un poeta hasta ahora más bien marginado, con quien hay que contar en adelante" (this volume discloses in all his importance a poet until now marginalized, one who from now on will have to be taken into account).

Two important anthologies of Spanish poetry, published in 1968 and 1970, provide evidence of the shifting literary climate within which the critical reappraisal of Ory (whose work is not included in either anthology) would take place. The first is José Batlló's *Antología de la nueva poesía española*. In the prologue Batlló states that the unifying characteristic of the poets whose work he features is the strong desire to overcome the divisiveness produced by the civil war. He says that these poets, no longer compelled by sociohistorical circumstance to ally themselves either with a poetry of "esteticismo esterilizante" (sterile aestheticism) or with a poetry of "compromiso político" (political commitment), are animated by their "afán desmitificador" (eagerness to demythify) and by their "lucidez literaria, poética, científica, política y filosófica" (literary, poetic, scientific, political, and philosophical lucidity).

In the appendix to the Batlló anthology, Grande expresses his belief that the diverse poets comprised in this new grouping have in common their desire to explore "nuevas formas expresivas mediante las cuales la carga de rehumanización sea manifestada de un modo más eficaz" (new expressive forms through which the rehumanized thrust may be more effectively manifested). That this group of poets found in the work of Ory a kindred poetic spirit is suggested by the fact that not only Grande but two other antholo-

gized poets – Pere Gimferrer and Joaquín Marco – later wrote articles on Ory's work.

The second anthology indicative of a change in the Spanish poetry scene is José María Castellet's *Nueve novísimos poetas españoles* (Nine Very New Spanish Poets), featuring such writers as Manuel Vázquez Montalbán, Ana María Moix, Guillermo Carnero, Leopoldo María Panero, and Gimferrer. Characterizing both the poets' new orientation and Ory's relevance to their endeavors, critic Andrew P. Debicki says in his *Poetry of Discovery: The Spanish Generation of 1956–1971* (1982), "their writing reveals . . . a more aestheticist and decorative note; playful references to popular culture, film, and music, mixed with literary allusions; a breaking away from philosophical concerns in favor of aesthetic and sensorial ones; a renewed interest in surrealist features and the frequent use of *collages;* and a search for new heroes including authors as diverse as Octavio Paz and Carlos Edmundo de Ory."

Within the newly receptive literary climate attested to by publication of the Batlló and the Castellet anthologies, critical reappraisal of Ory's work proceeded apace. Several diverse collections of Ory's work published during the 1970s contributed to this reappraisal, making Ory's poetry accessible to the Spanish public that had remained largely ignorant of his work. For example, Grande's *Poesía* includes a substantial selection of representative poems written by Ory between 1945 and 1969. It also has a prologue in which Grande critically validates Ory's poetic vision; important prose pieces by Ory about poetry; excerpts from his diary; a bibliography; and a biographical sketch.

In 1973 Joaquín Giménez-Arnau edited Ory's *Los poemas de 1944,* a collection of early poems never before published. Featuring an anguished first-person speaker and focusing on the themes of insomnia, poetry, and love, these poems reveal many of the traits that characterize Ory's later work as well: play with language, surrealistic images, and an intense conviction that language holds the key to human meaning.

In 1974 Pont Ibáñez edited *Poesía abierta (1945–1973)*. This anthology, which the editor intended to complement Grande's, features previously unpublished poems written between 1945 and 1973. Pont Ibáñez, who begins his preface by stating his hope that the volume will erase "la pesadez y desazón de unos años grotescos, regidos . . . por [el] intocable 'poeta funcionario' " (the tediousness and irritation of the grotesque [post-civil-war] years ruled . . . by [the] untouchable 'poet bureaucrat'), ends it by stating his belief that Ory's artistic moment has finally arrived.

*Portrait of Ory by Ginés Liébana*

The edition of Ory's work edited by Rafael de Cózar, *Metanoia* (1978) – containing a prologue, a biographical essay, critical essays, an extensive bibliography, and a selection of Ory's visual collages – features a broad selection of poems written by Ory between 1944 and 1977. Extremely useful for the student of Ory is de Cózar's documentation of the publishing history of each of the poems included.

*Energeia* (1978) presented to the public a selection of Ory's unpublished work written between 1940 and 1977. The 1970s also saw the writing of three Spanish master's theses and one doctoral dissertation on Ory's work. Indicative as well of the new interest in Ory were homages published by two Spanish literary magazines: *Litoral* (April–May 1971) and *Operador* (April 1978). The homages contain poems and prose pieces written in Ory's honor by such prominent and diverse writers as Celaya, Grande, Jesús Cabrera Vidal, Gloria Fuertes, Ignacio Aldecoa, Juan Alcaide Sánchez, and Francisca

Aguirre; they also feature visual material both by Ory and by those who pay him tribute.

During the 1970s Ory published three new books of poetry – *Música de lobo* (Wolf Music, 1970), *Técnica y llanto* (Technique and Tears, 1971), and *Lee sin temor* (Read without Fear, 1976). He also published a collection of earlier poems of social and political protest, *La flauta prohibida* (The Forbidden Flute, 1979), and two volumes of short stories, *El alfabeto griego* (The Greek Alphabet, 1970) and *Basuras (1945–1973)* (Garbage, 1975).

*Música de lobo* is divided into two parts. The first consists of a long poem entitled "Te" (a Confucian word meaning "moral force"), which Ory says was produced using the method of discursive collage and which reveals the influence on Ory of Oriental philosophies. The second, titled "Belleza aquerónica" ("Aquarontic" Beauty), consists of short, discursive poems in which a speaker reflects on the art of poetry as comprising both tragic and transcendent intuitions. Says the speaker in one untitled poem: "Haciendo poesía me elevo a la omnipotencia mágica / de placer por mi propia persona / Pero esto sólo es posible en mis desgarros trágicos." (In making poetry I am elevated to a magical omnipotence / of pleasure in myself / But this is only possible in my tragic throes.)

The poems of *Técnica y llanto* are steeped in the despair Ory felt over the breakup of his marriage. The titles of some of the poems attest to their autobiographical nature: "Ya no está conmigo" (She Is No Longer with Me); "Los amantes" (The Lovers); "Plenitud de desastre" (Fullness of Disaster); "La separación de los amantes" (The Separation of the Lovers); and "La despedida" (The Farewell). In this last poem the speaker says: "Yo soy un hombre auto-peligroso" (I am a self-dangerous man) and "Mi nombre es Carlos Edmundo de Ory / He llegado a los límites extremos / Y no sobrevivo a mi pasión" (My name is Carlos Edmundo de Ory / I have reached the outer limits / And do not outlive my passion).

*Lee sin temor* comprises four short books written by Ory between 1970 and 1971: "Agni"; "Lee sin temor"; "Los poemas de Karl Borromäus"; and "Silencio" (Silence). The poems in this volume are relatively brief and are characterized by stylistic diversity, wordplay, and a preoccupation with the theme of love, which is a constant in Ory's work.

After the flurry of publishing activities which characterized Ory's career during the 1970s, the 1980s represents a period of relatively few publications. In 1981 Hiperión published *Miserable ternura; Cabaña* (Miserable Tenderness; Cabin), poems written in 1971 and 1972. These lyrical love poems abound in natural images and are characterized by a simpler syntax and a less strongly defined speaker than those featured in earlier love poems.

Also during the 1980s Ory published a selection of his diary entries written between 1976 and 1984. The volume's intentionally cryptic title, *Eunice Fucata* (1984), reflects Ory's hope that the reader "se abstenga de atribuirle propiedades de género literario" (will refrain from attributing to it the properties of a literary genre). In the prologue Ory playfully yet seriously invites the reader to share his revelation of "fenómenos íntimos y líricos" (intimate and lyrical phenomena), "relatos de mi experiencia onírica" (stories of my dreamed experience), "niveles de abstracción y de delirio" (levels of abstraction and of madness), and "fantasías discontinuas" (discontinuous fantasies).

*Soneto vivo* (Living Sonnet, 1988) is divided into four sections. The first consists of sonnets writ-

ten between 1970 and 1987; the last three comprise sonnets written between 1941 and 1964, many published previously in *Los sonetos*. The sonnets of the first part feature Ory's preferred themes of love, mortality, solitude, and poetry, and they draw on his favorite techniques of surprising metaphors and experimentation with sound, as in the first quatrain of "Ventrilocua Vates" (Ventriloquial Diviner):

Escribo escribo escribo estoy encita
nazca el hijo enjaulado en la palabra
y la palabra que el silencio labra
se convierta en la estatua de mi tinta

(I write I write I write I am pregnant
may the child be born caged in the word
and may the word which silence forges
become the statue of my ink)[.]

From his beginnings as a writer in the constrained and unresponsive Madrid of the 1940s, to his critical reappraisal in the newly receptive Spain of the 1970s and 1980s, Carlos Edmundo de Ory has shown an unshakable belief in creatively wielded language as the key to transcendence and creation. That Ory never doubted his work would eventually draw the audience he desired is suggested by this 1948 entry from his diary, quoted by Pont Ibáñez in the prologue to *Poesía abierta*:

"¡Jóvenes algo profundos me oiréis! Tarde o temprano saldré yo con mis libros, como ahora salgo con mis barbas. Como mis barbas de fuego turbador serán mis ideas y mis profecías."

(Somewhat deep young people, you will hear me! Sooner or later, I will emerge with my books as I now emerge with my beard. Like my beard of disquieting fire will be my ideas and my prophecies.)

Ory's poetry – more widely appreciated now than it was in the 1940s but still insufficiently read and studied – continues to extend its challenging invitation to readers and critics.

**Interview:**
Jesús Fernández Palacios, "Carlos Edmundo de Ory," *Cuadernos del Norte* (January–February 1984): 23.

**References:**
Eduardo Chicharro, "Carlos Edmundo a machamartillo," *Español* (10 November 1945);
Rafael de Cózar, "Introducción a Carlos Edmundo de Ory," in Ory's *Metanoia,* edited by Cózar (Madrid: Cátedra, 1978), pp. 19–94;

*Ory in 1973 (photograph by Irénée Scalbert)*

Ángel Crespo, "Carlos Edmundo de Ory," *Lanza* (8 May 1947);

Eugenio D'Ors, "A ponerse serio Carlos Eduardo," *Estafeta Literaria,* 39 (30 December 1945);

José L. García Martín, "Textos lingüísticos creativos: La poesía de Carlos Edmundo de Ory," *Cuadernos Hispanoamericanos,* no. 359 (May 1980): 459–471;

Pedro Gimferrer, "Tres heterodoxos españoles," in *30 años de literatura española,* by Gimferrer and Salvador Clotas (Barcelona: Kairós, 1971) pp. 99–106;

Felix Grande, "Carlos, Carlos . . . ," in Ory's *Poesía 1945–1969,* edited by Grande (Barcelona: Edhasa, 1970) pp. 7–17;

Grande, "Instantáneas de Ory," *Cuadernos Hispanoamericanos,* 178 (October 1964): 161–167;

Grande, "Poesía: Carlos Edmundo de Ory," *Cuadernos Hispanoamericanos,* 245 (May 1970): 304–314;

"Homenaje a Ory," special issue of *Litoral,* 19–20 (April–May 1971);

Julio López, "Carlos Edmundo de Ory, uno y vario," *Insula,* 35 (May 1980): 3–4;

Joaquín Marco, "El postsurrealismo de Carlos Edmundo de Ory: Un olvidado," *Vanguardia Española* (February 1971);

Pilar Eugenia Mingote, "Carlos Edmundo de Ory: Poesía Abierta," *Estafeta Literaria,* 558 (15 February 1975);

"Oleaje a Ory," special issue of *Operador,* 1 (April 1978);

José M. Polo de Bernabé, "El universo poético de Carlos Edmundo de Ory y el postismo," *Cuadernos Hispanoamericanos,* no. 335 (May 1978): 305–315;

Jaime Pont Ibáñez, "Carlos Edmundo de Ory o el deseo: Del amor absoluto a lo visionario cósmico," *Cuadernos Hispanoamericanos,* nos. 289–290 (July–August 1974): 238–254;

Pont, *El Postismo* (Barcelona: Mall, 1987);

Pont, "El Postismo: génesis, teoría y obra," *Scriptura,* 1 (1986).

# Blas de Otero

*(15 March 1916 – 29 June 1979)*

Felipe Antonio Lapuente
*Memphis State University*

BOOKS: *Cántico espiritual* (San Sebastian: Grafico-Editora, 1942);

*Angel fieramente humano* (Madrid: Insula, 1950);

*Redoble de conciencia* (Barcelona: Instituto de Estudios Hispánicos, 1951);

*Antología y notas* (Vigo, 1952);

*Pido la paz y la palabra* (Torrelavega: Cantalapiedra, 1955); republished in *Con la inmensa mayoría* (Buenos Aires: Losada, 1960);

*Ancia* (Barcelona: A.P., 1958);

*Parler clair (En Castellano),* translated [into French] by Claude Couffon (Paris: Seghers, 1959); published in Spanish as *En Castellano* (Mexico City: Universidad National Autónoma de México, 1960); republished in *Con la inmensa mayoría* (1960);

*Hacia la inmensa mayoría* (Buenos Aires: Losada, 1962);

*Esto no es un libro* (Río Piedras: Universidad de Puerto Rico, 1963);

*Que trata de España* (Paris: Ruedo Ibérico, 1964; Barcelona: RM, 1965);

*Expresión y reunión: A modo de antología (1941–1969)* (Madrid: Alfaguara, 1969);

*Mientras* (Zaragoza: Javalambre, 1970);

*Historias fingidas y verdaderas* (Madrid: Alfaguara, 1970);

*País: Antología 1955–1970,* edited by José Luis Cano (Barcelona: Plaza & Janes, 1971);

*Escrito para* (Palma de Mallorca: Papeles de Son Armadans, 1974);

*Verso y prosa* (Madrid: Cátedra, 1974);

*Poesía con nombres* (Madrid: Alianza, 1977);

*Todos mis sonetos* (Madrid: Turner, 1977);

*Poemas de amor* (Barcelona: Lumen, 1987).

**Editions in English:** *Twenty Poems,* selected and translated by Hardie St. Martin (Madison, Wis.: Sixties, 1964);

*Miguel Hernández and Blas de Otero: Selected Poems,* edited by Timothy Baland (Boston: Beacon, 1972).

SELECTED PERIODICAL PUBLICATIONS – UNCOLLECTED: "Cuatro poemas," *Albor,* 6 (1941);

"Poesías en Burgos," *Escorial,* 34 (August 1943).

The death of Blas de Otero left an empty space in contemporary Spanish poetry. Though in the vanguard of the so-called social poetry of the 1950s, he does not fully fit under any name tag or in any school. Having followed the avalanche of the three movements of Spanish poetry in the post-civil-war era – religious, *desarraigada* (rooted out), and social – Otero chose a much more personal path.

Blas de Otero Muñoz was born on 15 March 1916 in Bilbao. His infancy was spent in Bilbao and Madrid. In high school he studied with the Jesuits and later, after attending the Universities of Valladolid and Madrid, earned his licentiate degrees in law, philosophy, and letters. After fighting on the Republican side in the Spanish Civil War, Otero taught briefly in Bilbao, then lived for a while in Barcelona, taking time to take a cruise across the Atlantic to the Pacific Ocean. He then moved to Paris, occasionally returning to Bilbao. He traveled across Spain from north to south and from east to west, absorbing landscapes he later incorporated in his poetry. Otero always remained aloof from literary circles, and he seldom collaborated with others in journals of poetry. Although he was not a prolific poet, he demanded a lot from himself, correcting and discarding much of what he created; he gave lectures and poetic recitals throughout Spain and abroad.

His early poems are not well known. They include "Cuatro poemas" (Four Poems), in the jour-

Blas de Otero, circa 1969

nal *Albor* (1941), which was directed in Pamplona by Díaz Jácome; *Cántico espiritual* (Spiritual Canticle, 1942); and "Poesías en Burgos" (Poems in Burgos), published in the journal *Escorial* (August 1943). Although no one has studied these unimportant and obscure works, Otero appears to be groping in his first poetry for a direction. The reader gets the feeling that the poet feels himself called or chosen for some particular mission and that he is searching for the poetic creation by which to accomplish it. Otero says in one of the poems in *Cántico espiritual,* "Tiene que reposar mi pensamiento" (My thought has to repose). After a period of eight years of repose, he published his next collection of poetry.

*Angel fieramente humano* (Fiercely Human Angel, 1950), the title being taken from a line by Luis de Góngora, was followed the next year with *Redoble de conciencia* (Echo of Conscience, 1951), which won the Boscán Prize, a coveted award in poetry. *Redoble* is a continuation and completion of the themes of *Angel,* and the two books may be considered as one; in later editions they are often bound together. The first of the two reveals Otero as a poet of surprising vigor, originality, and ideas, and it earned for him a rank among the top three or four postwar poets. The two collections are typical of Otero's style,

characterized as philosophical poetry, a poetry of much depth, filled with modern themes of anguish and banishment, and reminiscent of Francisco Quevedo and Miguel de Unamuno. Otero's work centers on two great traditional themes – love and death – and humankind is always the center of attention through the relations with these two problems.

In *Angel* and *Redoble* Otero is fully aware of his mission; he is successful in shaking off his dormancy and becoming dynamically alive; he wants Spain and the world to hear his lament, in which he shows his brotherhood toward humankind: all people suffer, all are human, and most of them desire to live. The title *Angel fieramente humano* suggests a type of "angel-man" and further suggests the problems of nothingness, God, and eternity. Indeed, there are many religious implications throughout Otero's first great works.

For Otero at this stage in his development, God is often the terrible God of the Old Testament, in no way human, tender, or charitable as he appears in the New Testament. The question of God and his nature presents a great problem whence arrives a feeling of anguish, according to Otero, for a man feels himself as if in a dark night, fluctuating between nothingness and the hope that he may find God.

The opening poem of *Angel,* "Lo Eterno" (The Eternal), illustrates many of the basic points often repeated and elaborated in Otero's work:

Sólo el hombre está solo. Es que se sabe
vivo y mortal. Es que se siente huir
– ese río del tiempo hacia la muerte – .
Es que quiere quedar. Seguir siguiendo,
subir, a contra muerte, hasta lo eterno.
Le da miedo mirar. Cierra los ojos
para dormir el sueño de los vivos.
Pero la muerte, desde dentro, ve.
Pero la muerte, desde dentro, vela.
Pero la muerte, desde dentro, mata.

(Only man is alone. He knows
he is alive and mortal. He feels he has to flee
– that river of time moving toward death – .
He wants to stay. To continue existing,
to go up against death all the way to eternity.
He is afraid to look. He closes his eyes
in order to sleep the dream of the living.
But death is looking on from inside.
But death is watching from inside.
But death is killing from inside.)

Death acts as the catalyst for anguish. Not only is death a sure event, but its presence is felt throughout life.

The life/death antithesis is a problem humankind must resolve. To Otero, man is a being who seems to be alive only to die; therefore, he rebels against the God who causes death. Man must give to his life some reason for existence. In his search for values, only silence comes from above. God seems to hide from man, and man stands all alone fighting desperately as in this sonnet from *Angel:*

Luchando, cuerpo a cuerpo, con la muerte,
al borde del abismo, estoy clamando
a Dios. Y su silencio, retumbando,
ahoga mi voz en el vacio inerte.
Oh Dios. Si he de morir, quiero tenerte
despierto. Y, noche a noche, no sé cuando
oirás mi voz. Oh Dios. Estoy hablando
sólo. Arañando sombras para verte.
Alzo la mano, y tú me la cercenas.
Abro los ojos: me los sajas vivos.
Sed tengo, y sal se vuelven tus arenas.
Esto es ser hombre: horror a manos llenas.
Ser – y no ser – eternos, fugitivos.
¡Angel con grandes alas de cadenas!

(Fighting, hand in hand, with death,
at the edge of an abyss, I am shouting
to God. And his silence, echoing,
chokes my voice in the senseless emptiness.
Oh God. If I must die, I want to have you
awake. And, night after night, I don't know when
you will hear my voice. Oh God. I am talking
alone. I am scratching shadows in order to see you.
I lift up my hand, and you cut it off.
I open my eyes: you scarify them raw.
I am thirsty, and your sand turns into salt.
To be man is this: hands full of horror.
To be – and not to be – eternally fugitive.
Angel with big chains for wings!)

One might conclude from the last line that man is to some degree divine, a kind of angel. He is given wings (his freedom) to live his life as he wishes; yet the chains (death) always weigh him down. In another sonnet, God is blamed for man's fate and even scorned: "Si pudiese yo matarte, / . . . Quiero cortarte las manos" (If I could kill you, / . . . I want to cut off your hands). The frailty of man and the uselessness of his efforts are underlined. There is likewise a hint of agnosticism and a belief in nothingness after death: "Cuando morir es ir donde no hay nadie, / nadie, nadie; caer, no llegar nunca, / nunca, nunca; morirse y no poder / hablar, gritar, hacer la gran pregunta" (When to die is to go where there is nobody, / nobody, nobody; to fall, never to arrive, / never, never; to die and not to be able / to talk, to shout, to ask the most important question).

At the beginning of *Cántico espiritual* Otero adopted a position analogous to that of the mystic going through the pain of the dark night: "Mis ojos se adelgazan suspirando / la llegada de Dios a mis andenes" (My eyes get thinner and thinner sighing / for the arrival of God to my platforms); and "Soy un arco de Dios que se estremece. / Soy una vana potestad de ausencias" (I am an arch of God that shakes. / I am a futile power of absences). Later in his work (in *Angel* and *Redoble*) the desire for God corresponds to that of mystics who think that God has abandoned them. The poet has suffered "las iras del espíritu" (the madness of the spirit) and is caught between the death pangs of the passing of the river of time and the desire to remain between the dream of life and the inexorable and corrosive coming of death. One must hold on to God, says Otero, to fight with God in order to make sense out of life and assure oneself of the only possibility of survival. Speaking about God in *Angel,* Otero writes: "Quiero tenerte, / y no sé donde estás. Por eso canto" (I want to have you, / and I don't know where you are. Because of that I sing).

*Angel* also contains a section filled with love poems, such as the lyrical "Mademoiselle Isabelle," "Un Relámpago Apenas" (Just a Flash), and "Cieg-

*Otero in 1953 (Foto Archivo Rafael Montesinos)*

amente" (Blindly), poems in which one often forgets the philosophical message that characterizes much of Otero's poetry. But one never forgets that Otero believes woman is on earth for a purpose. Through her love and through her embraces, man can perhaps find salvation and reach the God for which he is aspiring: "Mares, alas, intensas luces libres, / sonarán en mi alma cuando vibres, / ciega de amor, tañida entre mis brazos. / Y yo sabré la música ardorosa / de unas alas de Dios, de una luz rosa, / de un mar total con olas como abrazos" (Oceans, wings, intense and free lights / will sound in my soul when you vibrate / blind with love, played in my arms. / And I will recognize the burning music / of the wings of God, of a pink light, / of a total ocean with winglike embraces).

Since divine love appears impossible, human love is the only recourse. Human and divine love are often intertwined by Otero, and the word *God* is

used in almost every one of Otero's love poems. Erotic passion is, at the same time, an expression of anguish and a thirst for God. Otero's meaning for the word *love* is not the prosaic, erotic one. Love is, rather, the liberator of man from his chains. The body of a woman is greatly praised, for in it there is God: "Cuerpo de la mujer, fuente de llanto / donde, después de tanta luz, de tanto / tacto sutil, de Tántalo es la pena. / Suena la soledad de Dios. Sentimos / la soledad de dos. Y una cadena / que no suena, ancla en Dios almas y limos" (Body of a woman, fountain of tears / where, after so much light, after so much / subtle touch, flows Tantalus-like pain. / The solitude of God is sounding. We feel / the loneliness of the two of us. And a silent chain / links to God both souls and slime); "Cuando te vi, oh cuerpo en flor desnudo, / creí ya verle a Dios en carne viva" (When I saw you, body like a naked flower, / I thought I was seeing God in his own flesh alive). Human love, while appearing to be a consolation, is perhaps an insufficient solution: "Oh Dios, oh Dios, oh Dios, si para verte / bastara un beso, un beso que se llora / después, porque, ¡oh, por qué! no basta eso" (Oh God, oh God, oh God, if in order to see you / a kiss would suffice, a kiss that you weep over / later on, because, oh, why! that is not sufficient).

*Redoble* further develops the theme of human/ divine love: in search of God man embraces the flesh of a woman, and like a shipwrecked person, he clings to her and swallows the salted water. A woman cries tears of blood when she conceives death through love. The attempted union is both crazy and useless; for God cannot be seen or felt. Thus, Otero says, in another powerful sonnet entitled "Es inútil" (It's Useless):

> Cada beso que doy, como un zarpazo
> en el vacío, es carne olfateada
> de Dios, hambre de Dios, sed abrasada
> en la trenzada hoguera de un abrazo.
> Me pego a ti, me tiendo en tu regazo
> como un náufrago atroz que gime y nada,
> trago trozos de mar y agua rosada:
> senos las olas son, suave el bandazo.
> Se te quiebran los ojos y la vida.
> Lloras sangre de Dios por una herida
> que hace nacer, para el amor, la muerte.
> ¡Y es inutil pensar que nos unimos!
> ¡Es locura creer que pueda verte, oh Dios, abriendo,
>     entre la sombra, limos!

> (Each kiss I give, like a blow of a paw
> in the vacuum, is scented flesh
> of God, hunger of God, burning thirst
> being braided in the blaze of an embrace.
> I cling to you, I lay in your lap
> like a cruel shipwrecked person that moans and swims,
> I swallow pieces of the ocean and pink water;
> the breasts are oars, the violent roll to the side is soft.
> Your eyes and your life are broken.
> You cry bloody tears of God through a wound
> which death brings forth in order to love.
> It's useless to think we are united!
> It's craziness to think I can see you,
> My God, opening slime among shadows!)

*Redoble* ends in a somewhat pessimistic tone: "Triste, triste es el mundo" (Sad, sad is the world). Otero describes the sad state of the world, pointing out the wars, failures in diplomacy, the decadence, and the possible future end of the world. "Miradme bien, y ved que estoy dispuesto / para la muerte" (Look at me well, and see that I am ready / for death). But Otero never gives up; he still prefers life to death: "Quiero vivir, vivir, vivir" (I want to live, to live, to live). His hope lies in the present rather than the hereafter: "Esa tierra con luz es cielo mío" (That land with light is my heaven). Human destiny and salvation are the focus of Otero's poetry in his first two major collections.

In 1955, with *Pido la paz y la palabra* (I Ask for Peace and the Word), there begins a more constructive stage in Otero's poetry. He was hurt by the repression of the Francisco Franco regime, by Spaniards being deprived of freedom, condemned to silence, and submitted to tutelage. In *Pido* he sings of hope for the future. Anguish remains a constant in this collection, but it is not further developed. Instead, Otero tries to find serenity and happiness. Here begins a new phase in his work, a step toward social poetry. Up until this point he had only spoken of loving, living, and dying from within; now he speaks of the immense majority in the street. No longer does he blame God for inflicting pain, but he blames social injustices. The combat with God has been lost; the nothingness has been accepted. The poet understands his destiny: he will set up a simple scale of values for a world without values. That scale, that ideal, encompasses a belief in humankind, peace, and the mother country.

Aloneness is no longer important; being a man is enough. Otero's zeal in this collection turns to peace and human solidarity. There is a profound sociopolitical ring to this book, yet the poetry cannot truly be called propaganda.

Spain is the major theme in this collection, and Otero preaches the necessity of love for the mother country. Spain is portrayed as moving backward uncontrollably: "Retrocedida España / agua sin vaso, cuando hay agua; vaso / sin agua, cuando hay sed" (Receded Spain / water without a glass, when there is water; a glass / without water, when there is thirst). There are two features about Spain which Otero treats: first, the nature of Spain – its destiny and its dramatic history; second, the physical Spain – its landscape. Like Unamuno and Antonio Machado, Otero grieves bitterly over Spain. During the Spanish Civil War César Vallejo, the Peruvian poet, wrote a book with the title *España, aparta de mí este cáliz* (Spain, Take This Chalice Away from Me, 1940); Otero writes in his poem "Proal" (Prow): "España, espina de mi alma. Uña / y carne de mi alma. Arráncame / tu cáliz de las manos. / Y amárralas a tu cintura, madre" (Spain, thorn of my soul. Nail / and flesh of my soul. / Pull out / your chalice from my hands / and tie them to your waist, mother). Spain is "madre y maestra" (mother and teacher) but also "madrastra" (step-

*Writers at a 1959 ceremony marking the twentieth anniversary of Antonio Machado's death: front row, Jaime Gil de Biedma, Alfonso Costafreda, Carlos Barral, and José Manuel Caballero Bonald; back row, Otero, José Agustín Goytisolo, Angel González, José Angel Valente, and Alfredo Castellón*

mother). At times the country is an "árbol de sangre" (tree of blood) or an "árbol arrastrado sobre los ríos" (tree dragged over the rivers). Madrid is "el sitio donde enterraron un gran ramo verde" (the place where they buried a big green branch) and is "infestado por gasoil, los yanquis y la sociedad de consumo" (polluted by gasoline, Yankees, and consumer society). But the Spain of which Otero dreams is the Spain of the future. Hope reigns supreme. Otero himself commented on this change in his tone: "Si ahora cambio de tema . . . pues al fin he comprendido que aprovecha más salvar el mundo que ganar mi alma" (If by now I have changed my theme . . . [it is] because I finally have understood that it profits [me] more to save the world than to save my soul).

*Ancia* (Ancient, 1958) is a reworking and reorganization of *Angel* and *Redoble*, plus forty-eight previously unpublished poems treating the same themes as *Pido*. *Ancia* won the Crítica Prize. The titles of many poems from the previous collections have been changed, and the order has been altered. Otero continues to mix concise and curt expressions – achieved by using brief and uneven rhythms and vocabulary – with surprising and shocking syntactic structures. At times he uses colloquial expres-

sions to emphasize rebellion and social protest. Besides the themes of God, death, and solitude, the theme of life as a precipice is often repeated. Thus Otero is close to Quevedo's concept of life and death, as when Otero writes: "Cantil, con un abismo y otro en medio" (Steep rock, with an abyss on each side); "un hombre al borde / de la muerte" (a man on the edge / of death); or "parece como si el mundo caminase de espaldas / hacia la noche enorme de los acantilados" (it seems as if the world were walking backward / toward an enormous night of cliffs). Like Quevedo, Otero says that death is in the center of life and is present from the time of birth. Thus cliffs symbolize life being menaced permanently by death. The poem "Cantil" expresses the idea that man feels dead although still alive: "Ahora canto mis manos / Manos de muerto vivas. Mudas manos de muerto / Moviéndose todavía" (Now I sing for my hands / The alive hands of a dead man. / Mute hands of a dead person / Still moving).

The essential themes of *Ancia* are the search for and fruitless call to God – signified by haughty rebellion and hard demands; the obsessive presence of death, which makes man feel dead although still alive – together with the repeated theme of the silence of God; the anguish of living a fruitless search that precipitates death; and the feeling of solitude of the whole human race flung into nothingness. Thus the reiteration of *Dios, Muerte, Silencio,* and *Nada* (God, Death, Silence, and Nothingness) permeates Otero's metaphysical preoccupations. One by one, all possible roads to transcendence are closed. The last poems of *Ancia* are apocalyptic and terrifying. In "Tabla rasa" (Flat Table), for example, he writes: "Entramos en la Nada / y sopla Dios de pronto, y nos termina. / Aquí la tierra fue" (We enter into Nothingness / and suddenly God comes and finishes us. / Here there was once the earth).

Other less common themes in *Ancia* are solitude, as in the poems "A la inmensa mayoría" (To the Immense Majority) and "Canto primero" (First Song); love as a fruitless search with a sense of failure, as in "Cuerpo de la mujer" (Body of Woman); the desire for life, as seen in "Impetu" (Impetus), "Gritando no morir" (Shouting Not to Die), and "Pido vivir" (I Ask to Live); death as happiness, as in the poem "El ser" (Being), wherein Otero asks, "¿Cómo podríamos reposar y morir, / si la muerte no fuese / otro modo de amor y alegría?" (How could we repose and die / if death were not / another way of love and happiness?); and, finally, death as a mystery, as seen in "Claustro de las sombras" (The Cloister of Shadows).

In 1960 Otero published *En Castellano* (In Castilian), the Spanish version of his bilingual (French/Spanish) edition *Parler clair* (To Speak Clearly, 1959). *En Castellano* is written for the majority; it is a more popular style of verse. Many of the poems are only terse, concise, two-line thoughts, such as the poem "Fuera" (Out): "Terrible, hermosa España / estoy contigo, a contrapirineo" (Terrible and beautiful Spain / I am with you, contradicting the Pyrenees). This example is a continuation of the theme of Spain, as begun in *Pido.* For the first time readers learn of Otero's love for the Communist party, which he eventually would join. In his poem "Poética" (Poetics) he declares: "Apreté la voz. / Como una mano / alrededor del mango de un martillo / o de la empuñadura de una hoz" (I tightened my voice. / Like a hand / around the handle of a hammer / or the hilt of a sickle). Spain is unfavorably compared to France throughout this collection. At the beginning of the book, he writes: "para . . . / borrar / la sangre / y / la iniquidad / del mundo / (incluida / la caricaturesca españa actual)" (to . . . / erase / blood / and / the iniquities / of the world / [including / the present caricature of Spain]). At times, the word *España* is not capitalized, thus ac-

centuating the negative aspects of Spain. The function of the poet, Otero says, is "horadar / dormida piedra, hasta encontrar españa" (to perforate / the sleepy stone, until Spain is found). The theme of two Spains facing each other appears in the poem "La va buscando" (He Is Searching for Her). Otero seems to say that the true Spain of hope, "la verde" (the green one), was lost in the civil war at the hands of the "black" Spain, "la negra." The poem opens with a well-known passage from the *Primera Crónica General de España* (First General Chronicle of Spain, 1289), by Alfonso X el Sabio: "la tierra que tornaron sus espadas en sí mismos unos contra otros" (the land where they turned their swords against themselves) and closes with a quotation from Mariano José de Larra: "Aquí yace media España. Murió de la otra media" (Here lies half of Spain. It died at the hands of the other half). Spanish cities (Turuel, Seville, Baeza, Cádiz, Logroño, Soria, Segovia, and Bilbao), rivers (Ebro and Miño), and writers (Miguel de Cervantes, Quevedo, Antonio Machado, and Gabriel Celaya) are mentioned. In his poem "Bilbao" Otero regrets the negative statements he has made about his native city but confesses that he thought about Bilbao in the sleepless nights he spent in Madrid and in his visits to Moscow, Shanghai, and Havana. He sees his city as a "turbio regazo / de mi niñez, / húmeda de lluvia / y ahumada de curas" (troubled bosom / of my childhood, / wet by rain / and smoked by priests). Bilbao is also a "ciudad de monte y piedra, / con la mejilla manchada / por la más burda hipocresía" (city full of mountains and stones, / with a dirty cheek / because of the most coarse hypocrisy).

In 1962 Otero published *Hacia la inmensa mayoría* (About the Immense Majority), which comprises new versions of *Angel, Redoble, Pido,* and *En Castellano.* He had it published in Buenos Aires because of his difficulties with Franco's censure. From the title, one can deduce that Otero was convinced that the poet must write about the people and for the people.

Another book published abroad, the collection *Esto no es un libro* (This Is Not a Book, 1963), includes few poems that were unpublished before. Only poems prohibited by censure in Barcelona are added to selected, previously published ones.

In 1964 in Paris, Otero published his next collection, *Que trata de España* (Dealing with Spain); it includes poems from *Pido* and *En Castellano,* as well as new poems. Otero says in his introduction that he has written this poetry inside and outside Spain and that the poems are "dirigida por y a la inmensa

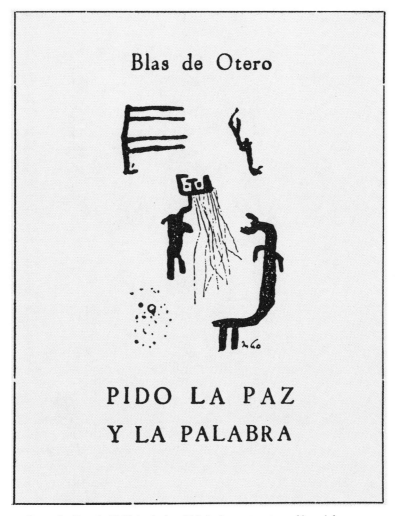

Blas de Otero

PIDO LA PAZ
Y LA PALABRA

*Cover for Otero's 1955 book, in which he began to express his social concerns*

mayoría" (addressed by and to the immense majority). This majority is a "pueblo / roto y quemado bajo el sol, / hambriento, analfabeto / en su sabiduría milenaria" (people / broken and burned by the sun, / hungry, illiterate / with a thousand years of wisdom). Spain is drowning and can only be saved "a golpes de palabra" (strike by strike with words). The poet's vocation is to combat injustices, fight for peace, and make Spain into an image and semblance of purity.

*Que trata de España* is divided into five "chapters." Each chapter has a title and an introductory poem. Preceding the first chapter, Otero asks the book to excuse him for sectioning it and also says he had encountered his country while being driven by "conductores torvos" (grim-looking drivers) who mutilated his lines and burned them with "el hacha de un neotorquemada" (the torch of a new Torquemada). Chapter 1, including nine poems, is ti-

tled "El Forzado" (The Galley Slave), and in the introduction Otero asks the oceans of Spain to erase, with the help of his verse, the memory of years of fratricides and to unite in one wave the solitudes of the Spaniards. Chapter 2, comprising twenty-one poems, has the title "La Palabra" (The Word); in the introduction Otero says that the lost country can be recovered by means of the aesthetic word. Chapter 3, with fourteen poems, is titled "Cantares" (Songs), and in the introductory poem Otero warns that literature has the tendency to overlook the popular vein of the ballads. Chapter 4, including forty-six poems, is "Geografía e Historia" (Geography and History) and is by far the largest section of the book. In the introductory poem Otero addresses the old Spain, connected to Africa, and the young Spain "de uñas grandes, / prestas para el asalto" (with large claws, / ready for assaults). Spain puts a limitation on the poet: "límite de mis días / primeros y fi-

*Drawing of Otero by Alvaro Delgado*

nales" (limit of my days / first and final). This section includes poems about several regions of Spain and its landscapes. At times Otero seems optimistic about the future. In his poem "No te duermas" (Do Not Fall Asleep) he says: "Oh derramada España, / rota guitarra vieja, / levanta los párpados / (canta / un gallo) que viene, / llena de vida, / la madrugada" (My scattered Spain, / old and broken guitar, / lift up your eyelids / [a rooster / sings] for dawn / is coming / full of life). Chapter 5, with twenty poems, is titled "La verdad común" (Common Truth), and in the introductory poem Otero says that oblivion cannot erase the powerful explosion of common truth.

The book closes with the reminder that, although Spain is full of campesinos with dried skin, Otero sees behind their burned faces a firm tree full of wisdom and new sap. *Que trata de España* is not only one of the largest books of poems written by Otero but also the most structured and thematically concentrated. The sonnet is seldom used, but alliteration and metaphors abound. The book is also related to the thematic preoccupations of the "Generation of 1898": the history and geography of Spain, the existence of two Spains, and the psychological study of the Spanish character.

In 1969, and after long journeys to France, Cuba, Russia, China, and North Vietnam, Otero published *Expresión y reunión,* which comprises poems written between 1941 and 1969. But the collection lacks many poems that Franco's censors still saw as polemic.

In 1970 Otero published one collection of poetry, *Mientras* (While), taking the title from the initial sentence of the book: "Mientras haya en el mundo una palabra cualquiera, habra poesía"

*Cover for a 1977 collection of Otero's sonnets*

(While there is any word left in the world, poetry will exist). This phrase is an echo of the refrain of the "Rima IV" (in *Rimas,* 1860–1861), by Gustavo Adolfo Bécquer, which is also used in the last poems of Pedro Salinas's *Confianza* (Confidence, 1955) and Jorge Guillen's *Clamor* (1955–1958). Time and space occupy Otero in *Mientras.* There are remembrances and hopes ("recuerdos y esperanzas") as well as autobiography. He remembers his life in poems such as "Una luz anaranjada" (Orange Light), "Penúltima palabra" (Penultimate Word), "Y you me iré . . . " (And I Shall Depart . . . ), and "Morir en Bilbao" (To Die in Bilbao). Otero always returns in his poetry to his native Bilbao, the city he loved and hated. He says in his poem "Y yo me iré . . .": "Te padecí, hasta el ahogo / Bilbao: tu cielo, tus casas / negras. Y tu hipocresía. / No; no volveré. / Quemaste mi juventud / como un trapo viejo. Un día / me rebelé. Vi y volví. / No; no

volveré" (I suffered you to the point of choking, / Bilbao: your skies, your houses / black. And your hypocrisy. / No; I shall not return. / You burned my youth / like an old rag. One day / I rebelled. I saw, and I returned. / No; I will not and shall not return).

There are other cities that Otero evokes in *Mientras:* the Madrid of his childhood and adolescence; Havana, praised with love; Peking, delicious and terrible; and Moscow. At the end of all these travels he is going to leave a testimonial legacy: his poetry. He says in "Serenen" (They Calm):

Dejo unas líneas y un papel en blanco.
Líneas que quiero quiebren la desesperanza.
Líneas que quiero despejen la serenidad.
Líneas que balanceen el reposo.
Líneas sobrias
como el pan.
Transparentes como el agua.
Cuando me lean dentro de trienta años,

de setenta años,
que estas líneas no arañen los ojos,
que colmen las manos de amor,
que serenen el mañana.

(I leave a few lines and a blank paper.
Lines that I wish would break hopelessness.
Lines that I wish would clear up serenity.
Lines that would balance rest.
Frugal lines
like bread.
Transparent like water.
When they read me thirty years from now,
seventy years from now,
I hope these lines do not scratch the eyes,
that they fill the hands with love
that they calm the dawn.)

*Mientras* is full of literary allusions and borrowings from the poetry of José de Espronceda, Bécquer, Machado, Rubén Darío, and Federico García Lorca. There are numerous examples of what the critic Carlos Bousoño has called "ruptura del sistema en una frase hecha" (interruption of a system in a previously existing phrase); this preexisting phrase usually comes from an earlier literary text. At the end of the book, Otero claims that most of the poems were taken from a yet-unpublished work titled "Hojas de Madrid" (Sheets from Madrid) and that they were written between 1968 and 1970.

*Historias fingidas y verdaderas* (Invented and True Stories, 1970) is mostly a collection of prose. However, Otero also included a bit of poetry in the book. *Escrito para* (Written For, 1974) contains a poem dedicated to Otero's comrade Rafael Alberti — "Historia de una palabra" (History of a Word), in which Otero alternates lines by and allusions to Alberti with civil-war memories: "De pronto, un disparo en la pared / de españa" (Suddenly, a shot in the wall / of Spain). The poem repeats this line: "Nada. Nadie. Canta el agua / azul" (Nothing. Nobody. The blue water / sings), which seems to suggest that, except for the voice of Alberti in Cádiz, Buenos Aires, and Rome, nothing makes sense. The future is being strangled by the boots of *yanquis* (Americans). *Poesía con nombres* (Poetry with Names, 1977) includes seven poems from "Hojas de Madrid" as well as a poem dedicated to Lorca that was read in the homage to him in Granada in 1976. It was a controversial poem in the newly established democracy. Otero concludes by saying there will be no peace until Lorca's bones are resurrected and until the Americans are expelled.

Of the other collections of Otero's poetry that were published in his lifetime, the most notable one was edited by the poet and critic José Luis Cano in 1971 under the title *País* (Country). It comprises poems from 1955 to 1970 dealing with the theme of Spain. The title is taken from a poem originally published in *Historias fingidas y verdaderas*. In the poem, while a Spanish guitar breaks the shadows with its sounds, the white shirt of Francisco José de Goya y Lucientes's painting *Fusilamientos* (Fusillades) comes down from the skies. A bullfight is taking place, with the picador holding one of the lances of Diego Rodríguez de Silva Velázquez's painting *Rendimiento de Breda* (Surrender of Breda). From the rainy region of the northwest, Galicia, comes the ink of Ramon del Valle-Inclán, while Galician immigrants appear. Suddenly marines are firing guns in Vietnam. And up in the skies one can see the eyes of Saturn as Goya had painted them, as Saturn devours his children. Thus, Spain is the symbol of the whole world in chaos.

Struggling with cancer, Otero spent the last years of his life in Madrid in total seclusion. But, in spite of his aloofness, he was an optimist. As a conclusion to his book *Verso y prosa* (1974), he writes:

Gracias doy a la vida por haberme nacido.
Gracias doy a la vida porque vi los árboles y los
ríos y el mar.
Gracias en la bonanza y en la procela.
Gracias por el camino y por la verdad.
Gracias por la contradicción y por la lucha.
Gracias por el asombro y por la obra.
Gracias por morir; gracias por perdurar.

(I thank life for being born.
I thank life because I saw the trees, and the
rivers and the seas.
I give thanks in the calm seas and the tempest.
Thanks for the way and the truth.
Thanks for contradictions and struggles.
Thanks for surprise and for the poetic work.
Thanks for dying; thanks for surviving.)

In one of his rare and last interviews, published in the journal *Reseña,* Otero says, "La poesía es un medio para transformar el mundo, ya directamente, tratando temas relacionados con la situación histórica, ya incidencia en la conciencia individual para, a través de ella, agigantar su propia función colaborando en el desarrollo de la conciencia colectiva" (Poetry is a means to transform the world, either directly, dealing with themes related to the historical situation, or by incidence in individual consciousness so that, through it, it may grow in its own function, collaborating in the development of collective consciousness). In this important interview Otero declares that a sincere poet will need to re-create his technique constantly and that although Otero feels he has influenced poets such as Angel González, José Angel Valente, or Jaime Gil de Biedma, the Spanish poetry of the last decades cannot be divided too much. He sees three groups: the poets immediately after the civil war, the poets of the 1950s, and the new poets. There has not been, in this last group, any unity like there was in the Generation of 1927. Otero confesses that he was influenced by Fray Luis de Leon and Quevedo, among the classics, and by Vallejo, Nazin Kickmet, and Arthur Rimbaud, among the moderns. Finally he does agree with Bousoño that surrealism is an essential part of his poetry and that this is quite evident in the poems of "Hojas de Madrid."

When Otero died in the dawn of 29 June 1979, one of the most curt, powerful, and dramatic voices in modern Spanish poetry was silenced. Yet Otero's characterization of his approaching death, in a letter to his friend the Nobel Prize winner Vicente Aleixandre, had been essentially positive, fueled by his awareness of a continuing collective consciousness: "Llegaré a la muerte deshecho, pero no vencido. . . . Queramos o no, el hoy inmediato y el mañana es del pueblo" (I will arrive at death broken but not beaten. . . . Whether we want it or not, the immediate present and tomorrow belong to the people).

**Letters:**
*Correspondencia sobre la edición de Pido la paz y la palabra* (Madrid: Hiperión, 1987).

**Interview:**
*Reseña* (January 1976).

**References:**
Emilio Alarcos Llorach, *La poesía de Blas de Otero,* second edition (Salamanca: Anaya, 1973);

Geoffrey R. Barrow, *The Satiric Vision of Blas de Otero* (Columbia: University of Missouri Press, 1988);

Felipe-Antonio Lapuente, "El concepto de Dios en la poesía de Blas de Otero," in *LA CHISPA '83: Selected Proceedings,* edited by Gilbert Paolini (New Orleans: Tulane University, 1983), pp. 143–151;

Carlos Mellizo, ed., *Blas de Otero: Study of a Poet* (Laramie: University of Wyoming Press, 1980);

Jesús Tomé, "La poesía de Blas de Otero en su circunstancia," *Revista de Estudios Hispánicos* (Puerto Rico), 7 (1980): 147–152.

# Emilio Prados

*(4 March 1899 – 24 April 1962)*

Roberto Carlos Manteiga
*University of Rhode Island*

BOOKS: *Tiempo: Veinte poemas en verso* (Málaga: Sur, 1925);

*Canciones del farero* (Málaga: Litoral, 1926);

*Vuelta (Seguimientos – Ausencias)* (San Lorenzo: Sur, 1927);

*El llanto subterráneo* (Madrid: Héroe, 1936);

*Llanto en la sangre: Romances, 1933–1936* (Valencia: Españolas, 1937);

*Cancionero menor para los combatientes, 1936–1938,* edited by Manuel Altolaguirre (Barcelona: Literarias del Comisariado del Ejército del Este, 1938);

*Memoria del olvido* (Mexico City: Séneca, 1940);

*Mínima muerte* (Mexico City: Tezontle, 1944);

*Jardín cerrado* (Mexico City: Cuadernos Americanos, 1946);

*Dormido en la yerba* (Málaga: Dardo, 1953);

*Antología, 1923–1953* (Buenos Aires: Losada, 1954);

*Río natural* (Buenos Aires: Losada, 1957);

*Circuncisión del sueño* (Mexico City: Tezontle, 1957);

*La sombra abierta* (Mexico City: Suplemento de Ecuador, 1961);

*La piedra escrita* (Mexico City: Universidad Nacional Autónoma de México, 1961); enlarged edition, edited by José Sanchis-Banús (Madrid: Castalia, 1979);

*Transparencias* (Málaga: Guadalhorce, 1962);

*Signos del ser* (Madrid: Papeles de Son Armadans, 1962);

*Ultimos poemas* (Málaga: Guadalhorce, 1965);

*Diario íntimo,* edited by Angel Caffarena (Málaga: Guadalhorce, 1966);

*Cuerpo perseguido,* edited by Carlos Blanco Aguinaga and Antonio Carreira (Barcelona: Labor, 1971);

*Poesías completas,* edited by Blanco Aguinaga and Carreira (Mexico City: Aguilar, 1975);

*Antología poética,* edited by Sanchis-Banús (Madrid: Alianza, 1978);

*El misterio del agua,* edited by Sanchis-Banús (Valencia: Pre-Textos, 1987).

OTHER: *Homenaje al poeta Federico García Lorca,* edited by Prados (Valencia: Españolas, 1937);

*Romancero general de la guerra de España,* selected and edited by Prados (Valencia: Españolas, 1937);

*Laurel: Antología de la poesía moderna en lengua española,* compiled by Prados (Mexico City: Séneca, 1941);

"Appendices: I–VI" [previously unpublished papers], in *The Poetry of Emilio Prados: A Progression Towards Fertility,* by P. J. Ellis (Cardiff: University of Wales Press, 1981);

Various papers, in *Emilio Prados: La memoria del olvido,* volume 2, by Patricio Hernández Pérez (Zaragoza: Prensas Universitarias, 1988).

A preeminent social and political activist in pre-civil-war Spain who was recognized for his unflagging commitment to the Republican cause, Emilio Prados remains, nonetheless, a relative unknown within the context of contemporary Spanish poetry, and he has been relegated to the lower echelon of writers in the group known as the "Generation of 1927." The lack of critical attention to his work is mostly due to its breadth and complexity. Prados's opus includes almost two dozen published collections of poetry, in addition to several previously unpublished collections included in his *Poesías completas* (1975), and many individual compositions that appeared only in anthologies, newspapers, and journals. The deeply philosophical nature of Prados's poetry makes it difficult to penetrate, and only a few critics have taken the time to study his work in depth.

Unlike many of his generational colleagues, Prados was not born into or nurtured in the kind of artistic environment that often helps determine or define one's aesthetic calling. There were, nevertheless, several pivotal factors in the poet's childhood and adolescence which had a profound effect on his future development as a poet. He was born on 4 March 1899 in Málaga to Emilio Prados Navero, proprietor of a lucrative furniture-making company,

*Emilio Prados*

and Josefa Such de Prados, daughter of a modest Valencian family. Prados Navero was the dominant figure in his son's early childhood. In the tradition of *krausismo,* a powerful liberal movement of the late nineteenth century, he taught the boy to value honesty and generosity, and he instilled in him a sense of respect for the rights of all individuals. Vicente Aleixandre, who was a classmate of the young Prados in grammar school, remembered his friend as a humble, somewhat shy and withdrawn child with an uncharacteristically exaggerated sense of social justice. Despite his own rather diminutive stature, Prados would routinely protect the younger children from the bullies of the school. A chronic bronchial condition accompanied by severe headaches and recurrent nightmares restricted his participation in normal childhood activities and required extended stays in the country. In his solitude Prados began to cultivate a profound love of nature and would spend hours in contemplation of it. He soon grew to prefer the shelter of his own internal

world to the more tumultuous activities of the street or the classroom.

When, in 1915, Prados enrolled in a pilot program known as *los niños de la Residencia* (the children of the Residencia) – a kind of preparatory school under the auspices of the Residencia de Estudiantes of Madrid – he was instinctively drawn to the study of the natural sciences, a discipline he was to pursue later as a student at the University of Madrid. Prados's first assigned readings in philosophy, his friendship with his teacher García Morente, and a chance meeting with Juan Ramón Jiménez were influential in determining the course of his life. He was also influenced by his friendship with Federico García Lorca in 1919–1920. An impressionable young man, prone to erratic behavior, Prados was expelled twice from the university because of confrontations with his teachers. He had switched his major to pharmacy and was well on his way to abandoning his studies altogether when, in 1920, he was diagnosed with tuberculosis and told by one doctor that he had only six months to live. His brother, Miguel, who was studying medicine in London at the time, accompanied him to Switzerland, where he was interned in a special facility in Davos for tuberculates. Prados, in the throes of death, discovered the works of Charles Baudelaire and began writing with a sense of urgency and commitment.

Following his internment, Prados went to Paris and then to Madrid before returning in 1921 to his family home in Málaga. The poet's brief visit to the French capital was enough to awaken his interest in the vanguard movements, whose influence was spreading rapidly throughout Europe. A shattered love affair and a deepening interest in philosophy occasioned a move to Freiburg to pursue his studies in this area. He returned to Madrid in 1922 with a neo-Marxist bent and a heightened sense of social justice. Discouraged by what he perceived as a lack of seriousness and commitment on the part of his generational colleagues, he abandoned a dinner held in his honor and went back to his native Málaga. This move was the first of a series of escapes that, according to Carlos Blanco Aguinaga, became legendary and stigmatized Prados as the black sheep of his generation.

Prados never married. He did, however, adopt in 1942 a young Spanish boy, Francisco Salas, whom he met on the streets of Mexico City. He raised, educated, and cared for the child as though Francisco were his own son.

José Sanchis-Banús, considered by many the foremost Prados critic, sees in Prados three distinct personas. Sanchis-Banús supports Loreina Santos Silva's claim that Prados is a surrealist poet and that this movement had a more indelible effect on his work than either his experimentation with pure poetry or with *Góngorismo* (a baroque style of poetry named after the seventeenth-century poet Luis de Góngora and practiced by the poets of the Generation of 1927). Sanchis-Banús also finds merit in Juan Cano Ballesta's argument that Prados was a precursor of the poetry of social and political commitment popular in Spain during the 1930s. And Sanchis-Banús further believes that Prados was a mystic poet, profoundly influenced by San Juan de la Cruz. Prados was all of these things and more. Notwithstanding, one of the greatest shortcomings in Pradian studies has been the insistence on the part of his critics to place him within a rigid construct established a priori. It is impossible to penetrate the enigmatic world of Prados by aligning him with any one literary source or trying to approach his work from an exceedingly limited perspective. Even the most

cursory study of his manuscripts – which include diagrams, sketches, and notes – reveals a myriad of theological and philosophical influences ranging from Heracleitus, to the Bible, to André Breton. All helped shape Prados's poetry and must be considered when critiquing his work.

Despite the multifarious, often divergent influences on Prados's poetry, it is possible, nonetheless, to synthesize his philosophical digressions into one internalized ideological struggle, which was a constant source of torment for him over the course of his life. This struggle can be defined in terms of two conflicting forces at work on his psyche: his unrelenting search for a kind of Platonic ideal or absolute truth, on the one hand, and his strong sense of commitment to his fellow man and to the betterment of humanity, on the other. This conflict is evident on a textual level as well. *La palabra* (the Word or logos) is the vehicle that transported him toward each of these ends, and it is in the Word where the integration of the two is ultimately realized.

There has been debate among critics concerning the chronology of Prados's work. Carlos Blanco Aguinaga posits four clearly defined literary periods: the first includes Prados's poetry written between 1923 and 1926, which Prados referred to as "la etapa clara" (the clear period); the second comprises the years from 1926 to 1928, a period of great emotional conflict for the poet, during which he wrote the poems in *Cuerpo perseguido* (Besieged Body, 1971); the third period corresponds roughly to the years of the Second Republic and the Spanish Civil War, a period of social and political consciousness for Prados; the fourth commences with his self-imposed exile and includes all of the poetry he wrote during his years in Mexico, up until the time of his death. Some critics, including Harriet K. Greif, believe that *La piedra escrita* (The Written Stone, 1961) deserves to be treated separately from the rest of Prados's work, and, in itself, constitutes a separate literary period. Sanchis-Banús is perhaps more correct in his assertion that Prados's "opus poeticus" needs to be considered as a whole – as a kind of vital organism that developed in a systematic way – and that any attempt to impose an arbitrarily devised system of classification can succeed only in destroying this sense of harmony and homogeneity.

Prados's poetic quest, like that of any metaphysical poet, evolved from a series of ontological and cosmological concerns, of which the most vital was the quest for self-knowledge. Toward this end he directed all his creative energy; this lifelong mission led him along the metaphorical paths of the

*Prados in 1936, when he moved to Madrid to assist the Republican forces in the Spanish Civil War*

subconscious. For Prados *encontrarse* (finding oneself) meant being able to transcend his physical state and ascend to a mythic plane where he could experience a sense of oneness with the cosmos. On this mythic plane he hoped to "ver a Dios cara a cara" (confront God face to face), as he declares in "Tres tiempos de soledad" (Three Stages of Loneliness, in *Poesías completas*). One cannot begin to penetrate the poetic world of Prados without, at least, a perfunctory understanding of the philosophical influences at work in his poetry. The Christian roots of Prados's philosophical meanderings are to be found in Fray Luis de León's *De los nombres de Cristo* (1583): "Consiste, pues, la perfección de las cosas en que cada uno de nosotros sea un mundo perfecto, para que, por esta manera, estando todos en mí, y yo en todos los otros, y teniendo yo su ser de todos ellos y todos y cada uno de ellos teniendo ser mío, se abrace y es-

lavone toda aquesta máquina del universo, y se reduzga a unidad la muchedumbre de sus diferencias" (The perfection of things depends on our being a perfect world unto ourselves, in order that, in this way, all being in me, and I in all, and I having your being, and each and all of you having my being, the entire mechanism of the universe shall become bound and embraced, and the multitude of differences reduced to oneness) — or, perhaps, even earlier, in Saint Augustine's contention that the world, in all its multiplicity, is but a shadow of a divine perfection, a shadow of sufficient beauty to prove the existence of God. Prados's Platonic bent led him to envision the body, in Plotinian terms, as a prison from which the soul must escape in order to achieve a mystical union with the One or Absolute Being. The many biblical references in Prados's notes and sketches attest to his belief that the negation of the physical self is a necessary first step in the quest for the Absolute: "El que quiera venir en pos de mí, niéguese a sí mismo, tome su cruz y sígame" (He who wishes to follow me, deny yourself, take up your cross and follow me).

Although Prados's philosophy was fundamentally Christian, he departed somewhat from Christian theology in his refusal to accept the total scission of the body and soul. It was his belief that the body, like a seed, would someday implant itself once again in the fertile fields of the soul, and there, in the center of being, germinate and bear new fruit. Many of Prados's ideas about nature and God are clearly pantheistic. His perception of the universe as a harmonious body in constant flux recalls the Heraclitean notion of *panta rhei*. His ideas with respect to the concept of the Absolute share a certain similarity with the Jungian notion of the "collective unconscious." And the many symbols he used in reference to the world of dreams lend themselves easily to Freudian interpretation. Notwithstanding the presence of these and other influences on Prados's work, his metaphysics had, above all, Christian-mystical overtones, which account for the parallels that have since been drawn between his poetry and that of San Juan de la Cruz.

Prados believed that his personal search for the Absolute was intimately related to the poetic process. For Prados, attaining a sense of oneness with the cosmos meant discovering one's *nombre verdadero* (true name), or what Greif appropriately has referred to as "the permanent reality of the unique and secret self." Poetry was the creative activity that would permit Prados to name the things around him, thus transforming, through the power of the word, temporal reality and making it eternal. All of the *entes* (bodies) present in the material world were, in this manner, perceived as *signos del ser* (signs of being), mirrors which, in a metaphorical sense, reflected the metaphysical aspirations of the poet. Prados's entire lifework could be described, therefore, as a kind of poetic odyssey or incessant search to find himself in the various "signs of being" that surrounded him, a search that culminated in the discovery of his true name, or sole transcendental identity.

Inspired by his readings of Baudelaire, Prados published in 1925 his first book of poetry, *Tiempo* (Time), a slim volume that comprises twenty poems about the sea. Neither this book nor his *Canciones del farero* (Songs of the Lighthouse Keeper, 1926), *Vuelta* (Return, 1927), "Seis estampas para un rompecabezas" (Six Pieces of a Puzzle, in *Poesías completas*), and "Nadador sin cielo" (Swimmer without a

Sky, also in *Poesías completas*), all written between 1925 and 1927, have been given sufficient critical attention. Sanchis-Banús says of the first three collections that they address exclusively, perhaps obsessively, the themes of the night and the sea and that the poet, persecuted by the light of day, seeks refuge in the darkness of night. Sanchis-Banús adds that Prados, showing good critical insight, later purged these collections, publishing a selection from them in his 1954 *Antología, 1923–1953* under the general heading "Tiempo." Carlos Blanco Aguinaga calls the poems of *Tiempo, Vuelta,* and *Canciones del farero* verses about the sea and the mystery of the Malagueñan nights.

However, these early collections are more than mere poems about the night and the sea. They are the bedrock on which Prados's entire poetic production rests, and they deserve more than the cursory treatment they have received at the hands of the critics. All of Prados's major themes, poetic aspirations, and metaphysical concerns are articulated in these works. Some of his philosophical and theological sources are readily discernible. The binomial ship/sea is the essential metaphorical construct in each of these early works. In a philosophical sense the ship is the body of the poet sailing the sea (the soul) in search of a port (salvation). On a linguistic level the ship becomes a pen and the sea a sheet of paper, as in "Epistola" (Epistle, in *Poesías completas*): "Es fragata mi pluma / de mil timones y una sola ancla, / que fondeó sobre el papel / de cadena cargada" (My pen is a frigate / of a thousand helms and only one anchor, / cast with heavy chain into this sheet of paper). The linguistic ramifications of Prados's metaphors are almost inexhaustible. Already in *Tiempo* Prados demonstrates an appreciation for the power of *la palabra* and an acute awareness of the different nuances that words with similar meanings can have. *Palabra, verbo* (word), *signo* (sign), *nombre* (name), and *voz* (voice) acquire specific meanings in Prados's lexicon. In the tradition of Antonio Machado and Gustavo Adolfo Bécquer, Prados found words delimiting. He considered them mere signifiers with totally arbitrary meanings and likened them in "Memoria de la poesía" (Memory of Poetry, in *Poesía completas*) to "corchos flotando sobre un mar de incertidumbre" (corks floating on a sea of uncertainty), and in "Tres tiempos de soledad" to "hormigas ciegas andando sin rumbo hacia el granero" (blind ants wandering haphazardly toward the granary). Later he wrote in "Canción" (Song, in *Poesía completas*), "Muera pronto lo que aún vive / amarrado a mi garganta, / rompa el collar que la aprieta / y en su sinrazón me ata"

(Let perish that which still lives / tied to my throat, / break the collar that chokes me / and by whose lack of reason I am bound).

According to Prados, only through *pensamiento* (the spirit of ideas or poetic inspiration) can words free themselves from their concretized state and attain a mythical character. In the tradition of the Christian school of philosophy, he believed that *pensamiento* was not tied to reason but derived from a far superior source. In "Constante amigo" (Constant Friend, in *Poesías completas*) he wrote, "Yo canto mi pensamiento, / y el pensamiento no es mío, / sino de quien me lo da" (I sing my inspiration, / and the inspiration is not mine, / but from him who gives it to me). In the complex world of Pradian symbology, the sea is nearly always associated with the soul, and it is there that poetic inspiration has its origin. He speaks in *La sombra abierta* (Open Shadows, 1961) of "el mar de mi pensamiento" (the sea of my poetic inspiration) and of the "orillas de mi pensamiento" (the shores of my poetic inspiration). For Prados, therefore, *pensamiento* is the impetus that drives him in his search of his *nombre verdadero* and toward his ultimate *cita con el Absoluto* (date with the Absolute Being). Prados's treatment of the question of time is significant in his early poetry. In a metaphorical sense, sailing the sea is synonymous with traversing time and space. The symbolic act of casting anchor, therefore, is equivalent to marking one's coordinates, that is, confirming one's presence in time or, in Pradian terms, "clavar su estampa en la pared del Tiempo" (affixing one's stamp on the wall of Time, as he writes in "El Milagro," in *Poesías completas*).

Love and personal communication are prominent themes in his early works. In *Tiempo* Prados addresses the question of amatory dialogue, likening it in "El primer diálogo (The First Dialogue, in *Poesía completas*) to a flower that, when nurtured by the warmth of the sun (amorous passion, or what Prados refers to as "celo"), produces a nectar necessary for the continued germination of the species: "Así nuestro diálogo, / regado por el sol, / abrió sus yemas / y su azucar quemada / cayó en la flor del aire, / desde el rojo pistilo de la lengua" (Thus our dialogue, / sprinkled by sunlight, / opened its buds / and its caramel / fell from the tongue's red pistil, / on to the surface of the air).

In *Vuelta,* a collection of poems written during 1924 and 1925 but not published until 1927, the binomial ship/sea reappears in a mystical context. The ship (the poet) becomes a contemplative Narcissus in repose on a tranquil sea. Enamored of his own reflection in the transparent waters, he sets out

in "Cambio" (Change, in *Poesías completas*) in impassioned pursuit of the unattainable: "En el espejo falso / de mi deseo igual, pulido / y limpio por la trémula esponja / del recuerdo sin mácula, / apareció la imagen impostora / que copio de mi anhelo / tu armonía" (In the false mirror / of my equal desire, polished / and cleaned by the tremulous sponge / of my unblemished memory, / appeared the fraudulent image / that translated my yearning into / your symmetry). In "Seis estampas para un rompecabezas," the ship sinks into the sea, in a symbolic act marking the poet's incursion into the world of the subconscious. Later, in "Nadador sin cielo," Prados writes, "Se entra al sueño como / uno se tira al mar . . . / Así queda guardada / la estirpe de la ausencia, / oculta en transparencia / y en belleza librada" (One enters the world of dreams / in much the same way that one might throw himself into the sea . . . / thus saving the lineage of absence, / hidden in transparency / and in beauty freed).

Between 1926 and 1929 Prados's time was divided between his active publishing career and his more introspective or contemplative moments alone, in harmony with the elements of nature that surrounded him. *Litoral,* the journal Prados edited with Manuel Altolaguirre, was one of the most successful literary publications of its time. It was combined with a publishing house. Luis Cernuda's *Perfil del aire* (Profile of the Air, 1927), Rafael Alberti's *La amante* (The Lover, 1926), and Prados's *Canciones del farero* (1926) were published by the Litoral company. Through this journal Prados was reintroduced to surrealism. He became an avid reader of Breton and the other French surrealist poets, was introduced to Salvador Dalí and Gala Eluard, and spent hours on end discussing the new poetry with Aleixandre. The poetic theories being spoken of by Breton, Guillaume Apollinaire, Vicente Huidobro, and Ramón Gómez de la Serna; the experimental art and musical forms of postsymbolist Europe (those of Dalí, Claude Debussy, Manuel de Falla); and the popularity of the social sciences (in particular, psychology) all helped Prados reaffirm his belief in the transitory nature of things and intensified his desire to seek new and creative ways to transcend his own physical reality. It was during this period that Prados wrote *El misterio del agua* (The Mystery of the Water, 1987) and *Cuerpo perseguido,* two works which, due to a series of unfortunate circumstances, would remain unpublished until much later. Both works are included in his 1954 anthology and were later revised and published separately.

The more significant of the two is *El misterio del agua,* written in 1926. Blanco Aguinaga calls *El*

*Prados (left) with Jorge Guillén, José Moreno Villa, and Manuel Altolaguirre, writers in the group called the Generation of 1927*

*misterio del agua* one of the most extraordinary lyric poems of modern times. Based on the mystery and miracle plays popular in Europe from the ninth to the sixteenth centuries, the book is divided into five parts, or miracles, that follow in chronological sequence the transition from nightfall to dawn. Employing a poetic lexicon reminiscent of that of San Juan de la Cruz or Santa Teresa de Jesús, Prados reenacts the "amada's" (lover's) impassioned quest for a mystical union with "el Amado" (the Loved One or God). Day and night (light and darkness) are the protagonists of the drama, while water, the most mellifluous of the primordial elements, is the medium through which the drama is played out.

In *Cuerpo perseguido* Prados continues his struggle against the delimiting forces of time, a battle he had begun in *El misterio del agua*. Love is again the central theme. The lover's mystical pursuit of "el Amado," which in the poetry of San Juan and in Prados's earlier compositions is depicted in terms of an amatory dialogue, is in "El mismo día al atardecer" (The Same Day at Nightfall, in *Poesía completas*) portrayed as an all-out war: "Por los campos oscuros de la guerra, / huyéndome a mí mismo, / medio flotando y sin memoria vuelo / desolado . . . / solo la muerte me acompaña y sigue / como con-

stante amigo" (Over the dark battlefields, / fleeing from myself, / half floating and without memory I fly / disconsolate . . . / accompanied only by death, who remains / my constant companion). The pessimistic tone and contentious nature of these compositions can be explained by the fact that they were inspired by Prados's precarious, often hostile, relationship several years earlier with a woman named Blanca Nigel or Nagel, who eventually left him to marry another. The paradoxical juxtaposition of the themes of love and death reveals also the influence of Aleixandre, whose *Ambito* (Precinct) was published in 1928 and who was already busy working on some of the compositions that later were collected as *Espadas como labios* (Swords like Lips, 1932). The fact that the poems of *Cuerpo perseguido* sprang from a personal romantic experience is confirmed by the style of the poetry, more corporeal and concrete than that of his previous works and by the poet's vocabulary, which includes words such as *cuerpo, carne, calor, sangre,* and *pecho* (body, flesh, warmth, blood, and breast).

Although carnal love is a central theme in these compositions, Prados's metaphysical concerns are nonetheless readily apparent. He struggles with the question as to whether or not it is possible to concretize love. Sounding like Bécquer, Machado, or even Cernuda, he says in "Al amor" (To Love, in *Poesías completas*), referring to his loved one, "no sé como encontrarte / para hacerte prisionero" (I don't know how to find you / in order to make you my prisoner). Frustrated, he concludes, "Es inútil. El perderte / no tiene forma en mi olvido. / Es inútil. El buscarte / en mi amor no tiene forma" (It is hopeless. Losing you / has no form in my forgetfulness. / It is hopeless. Searching for you / has no form in my love). Following the signs his lover has left imprinted on the wind, the speaker seeks a mystical union with her through this more ethereal medium (air). As an initial step, however, he must shut his door to the physical world and make the air the site for his dreams. In poem number 2 of "Memoria del olvido" he writes:

> Cerré mi puerta al mundo;
> se me perdió la carne por el sueño. . . .
> Me quedé, interno, mágico, invisible,
> desnudo como un ciego.
>
> Lleno hasta el mismo borde de los ojos
> me iluminé por dentro.
>
> Trémulo, transparente,
> me quedé sobre el viento,
> igual que un vaso limpio
> de agua pura,
> como un ángel de vidrio
> en un espejo.

> (I closed my door to the world;
> my flesh became lost in a dream. . . .
> I remained, internalized, magical, invisible,
> naked as a blindman.
>
> Filled to the very brim of my eyes
> I was illuminated from within.
>
> Quivering, transparent,
> I remained on the wind,
> just like a clean glass
> of pure water,
> like a glass angel
> in a mirror.)

In the poem "Resurrección" the speaker's lover (or other self) experiences a similar transformation. Evoking a panorama that recalls the Jungian landscape of the collective unconscious, the speaker invites his lover to enter his dream:

> un día
> te irás durmiendo también
> despacio, y hacia otro sueño
> te saldrás: te irás subiendo,

> perdiendo pie de tus ojos,
> volando, alzándote de ellos
> por fuera de ti, desnuda,
> igual que un aura en el cielo. . . .
> Fuera – cuando seas del aire . . . ¡Qué cristal de vida,
>     eterno!

> (one day
> you too will begin to fall asleep
> and slowly, toward another dream
> you will drift: you will begin to ascend,
> slipping from your own eyes,
> flying, rising above them
> beyond yourself, naked,
> just like a gentle breeze in the sky. . . .
> Out there – when you are of the air . . . What a crystal
>     goblet of life, eternal!)

While surrealism provided Prados with the stimulus for developing his creative talents, it had its negative side as well. Like Louis Aragon, Prados became disillusioned with an art movement he considered escapist and lacking in seriousness or commitment. Following in the footsteps of his French counterpart, Prados solicited the help of Aleixandre and Cernuda in an attempt to organize a more politicized surrealist group among the members of his generation. His inability to convince his friends to join him in this venture, the closing down of the Litoral publishing house because of financial problems, and the discontinued publication of *Litoral* all contributed to a profound emotional crisis leading to a self-imposed isolation that kept him incommunicado for several years. One of the clearest signs of Prados's detachment was his refusal in 1932 to contribute to Gerardo Diego's *Poesía española. Antología. 1915–1931* (Spanish Poetry. An Anthology. 1915–1931). Only after some friendly coercion from his friend Aleixandre did Prados finally agree to collaborate in the effort. His relationship with the group became severely strained after his categorical refusal to be included in Diego's second, expanded *Antología,* published in 1934. Prados spent a great deal of time either by himself or visiting with the local fishermen of El Palo, a district of Málaga, whose own personal hardships appealed to his sense of social consciousness. During these emotionally unsettled times, Prados became a social activist and a champion of the rights of the working class. He helped organize a union for workers in the graphic arts, read and discussed Karl Marx with the fishermen, and taught their children to read and write. Years later, living in exile in Mexico, Prados had photographs and letters of his fishermen friends on the walls of his study.

*Emilio Prados*

Surprisingly, 1930 to 1934 was a prolific period in Prados's life. During these yeas he wrote material for several collections of poetry: "Andando, andando por el mundo" (Wandering, Wandering All over the World), "¡No podréis!" (You Will Not Succeed), "Calendario del pan y del pescado" (Musings on Bread and Fish), and "La voz cautiva" (The Captive Voice). Most remained unpublished until their inclusion in *Poesías completas,* with the exception of a section of "Andando" titled *El llanto subterráneo* (The Weeping from the Underground), which was published by Altolaguirre's publishing house Héroe in 1936, just prior to the outbreak of the civil war. Many of Prados's poems from this period did appear, however, in journals such as Alberti's *Octubre.*

The euphoria that accompanied the victory of the Spanish Republicans in the elections of 14 April 1931 was short-lived. By 1933 Adolf Hitler had assumed power in Germany. In Spain economic conditions were worsening, and the right-wing CEDA party was rapidly gaining support. Prados, like many artists and writers of the time, struggled with the question of whether or not committing oneself to a political cause meant sacrificing one's aesthetic principles. Influenced by his revolutionary predecessors Vladimir Mayakovski and Aragon, Prados decided to put aside his metaphysical pursuits and turn his attention to the harsh reality around him. In "Adónde van, adónde (Where, Where Are They Going, in *Poesía completas*), he writes: "Aquí estoy, / aquí estoy: / nunca niego mi piel amoratada / como existen las aves, / como esa llama permanente que no derrumba / porque mi carne como el corcho no ensordece" (Here I am, / here I am: / I never deny my black and blue skin / just as I would never deny the existence of birds, / like that permanent flame that never dies / because my flesh, unlike cork, never becomes deaf ). But, for Prados, true commitment implied more than a mere sacrifice of aesthetic principles. It also meant divesting oneself of material possessions and learning to experience poverty and suffering firsthand. The verses of the poem "Andando, andando como el mundo" (Wandering, Wandering like the Rest of the World) confirm these convictions: "Andando, andando por el dolor se entiende, / en las ínfimas salas en que crujen sus lechos; / andando andando por las desiertas calles, / en las interminables colas que aguardan en los muelles" (Wandering, wandering through suffering one understands, / in the infamous rooms where their beds creak; / wandering wandering along deserted streets, / in interminable lines that await us at the docks).

In 1933 Prados wrote the heart-wrenching verses of "Calendario del pan y del pescado" that were published in *Llanto en la sangre* (Weeping in the Blood, 1937). In these poems Prados proclaims his indignation for the social injustices he saw all around him. There was neither bread nor fish on people's tables. Only seeds of hunger and death were being sown in the barren Spanish countryside. The *cuchillo* (knife) becomes a recurrent symbol of the violence, hunger, and repression that the campesino was experiencing. A growing sense of impotency begins to surface in the verses. In the poem "¡No podréis!" Prados verbally chastises those who, conscious of the social inequalities of Spanish society, failed to raise their voices in opposition. There is a hint of self-criticism: "Gritad, gritad inutilmente / sangre turbia en las sienes que no podréis limpiar / os marcará de lejos" (Scream, scream to no avail / impure blood on your temples that you will not be able to clean / will identify you from a distance).

In October 1934 a new development shook Prados's social consciousness. Fed up with their low wages and poor working conditions, the Asturian mine workers staged a strike that was immediately and violently repressed by the local authorities. In response to this wanton display of hostility, Prados wrote the poem "Llanto de octubre" (An Anguished Cry in October, in *Poesías completas*). That same year his father died, leaving Prados with a sense of irreparable loss. From this point on he wrote poetry that is markedly more seditious.

In the collection "Andando" several images and symbols emerge which were to become constants in Prados's poetry of commitment. The most significant of these is the voice. In "Hay voces libres" (There Are Free Voices) one of the more memorable compositions from this collection, Prados writes: "Hay voces libres / y voces con cadenas / y hay palabras que se funden al chocar contra el aire /

y corazones que golpean en la pared como una llama" (There are free voices / and voices in chains / and there are words that dissolve when they collide with the air / and hearts that beat against the wall like a flame). In the grouping "La voz cautiva" the poet's voice is the protagonist of several of the compositions. It is an "interno sol" (internal sun), a light engulfed in darkness, a prisoner begging to be chained while the winds of freedom call to him from beyond the bars of his cell. Such an image later reappears as a leitmotiv in Prados's civil-war poetry. For example, in "Elegía" (Elegy, a poem in the collection "Destino fiel" [Faithful Destiny] in *Poesías completas*) Prados's personified voice is seen bowing in pain over a dead comrade. In "El campo" (The Battlefield) the horrors of war transform the voice into a lament, and only Prados's faith gives him the strength to continue singing:

Aquí vivo, cantando la voz que ya me queda,
aquí vivo, y mi canto conduzco por el tiempo,
y si mi voz se nubla por tanta lejanía
que confundida al llanto luce bajo mi angustia,
sólo es dulce nostalgia de la oculta presencia
que el azar de la guerra fugazmente me obliga . . .
Aunque mucho he perdido, no llega a mi derrota,
que más mi fe se anima si más lejano vivo;
a veces, ¡qué fuerte la llamada se escucha!

(Here I live, singing with the voice that is left me,
here I live, and I direct my song through time,
and if distance beclouds that voice
which, in my misery, sounds more like an anguished
    cry,
it is but the sweet longing for a spirit
that the winds of war have temporarily shrouded in
    darkness . . .
While I have lost a great deal, I have not been de-
    feated,
for distance can only strengthen my faith;
and, sometimes, how clearly I hear its call!)

On 18 July 1936 several military officers signed a proclamation of war against the Spanish republic. In August of that year Prados moved to Madrid, determined to commit himself wholeheartedly to the defense of his nation's capital. He worked with the Red Cross, the International Brigades, the Fifth Regiment, and Radio Madrid, over whose airwaves he read his now-legendary "Ciudad sitiada" (City Under Siege), later published in *Llanto en la sangre*. "¡Ay ciudad, ciudad sitiada, / ciudad de mi propio pecho: / si te pisa el enemigo, será para verme muerto! / Castillos de mi razón / y fronteras de mi sueño . . . / ¿Dónde comienzas, Madrid, / o es, Madrid, que eres mi cuerpo?" (Oh city, city under siege, / city of my breast: / if the enemy tramples you, it is, no doubt, to see me killed! / Castles of my reason / and boundaries of my dreams . . . / Where do you begin, Madrid, / or is it, Madrid, that you are my very body?).

In 1937 Prados went to the neutral zone of Valencia. With the help of Altolaguirre he published *Llanto en la sangre;* he also collaborated with María Zambrano on the journal *Hora de España* and received the National Prize for Poetry for his then unpublished "Destino fiel." He edited two collections of poetry: *Homenaje al poeta Federico García Lorca* (Homage to the Poet Federico García Lorca) and *Romancero general de la guerra de España* (A Collection of Ballads about the War in Spain), both published in 1937. The following year, also with the help of Altolaguirre, Prados published his *Cancionero menor para los combatientes 1936–1938* (A Short Collection of Lyrics for Soldiers).

When, in 1939, the Spanish republic was defeated, Prados boarded a cargo train to the Catalonian border with France. He made his way to the small town of Banyuls, where he was met by a few Mexican friends who promptly made arrangements to take him first to Paris and later to Mexico. When he arrived in Banyuls, Prados had with him a nearly completed collection of poetry titled "Diario íntimo de un poeta en la guerra de España" (Intimate Diary of a Poet in the Spanish War). So great were his feelings of loss, resentment, and frustration that he threw the manuscript into the sea.

The rest of Prados's civil-war poetry was later collected and published under the heading "Destino fiel" in *Poesías completas.* Although critics have written off much of this poetry as mere "service to a cause" and of little or no literary merit and Prados himself was, at one point, ready to destroy all he had written during those years, one can recognize the social and historical value of such poetry and the superior artistic quality of at least a handful of the compositions.

With Prados's arrival in Mexico City there commenced what some critics have referred to as his period of "exile and resurrection." Emotionally and financially destitute, Prados lived for a short time in the home of Octavio Paz, worked off and on for the publishing house Séneca, and volunteered his services as a guardian for the children at the Luis Vives School. Thanks to the financial support of his brother, Miguel, and the companionship of his adopted son, Francisco, Prados managed to survive those difficult times. But it was his unwavering devotion to his poetry, to which he dedicated several hours each day until his death in 1962, that gave him a sense of purpose. There is little bio-

graphical information on the poet during the period from 1939 to 1962. Those who had dealings with him described Prados as withdrawn, noncommunicative, and excessively maudlin. From his letters to Sanchis-Banús and his conversations with people who knew him, one can tell that Prados's health was not good, and this problem had an effect on his mental state.

Nostalgia and rebirth are dominant themes in the first three collections he wrote in exile. His body seeming as foreign to him as the new landscape, Prados strives to retrieve, in the grouping titled "Penumbras" (Shadows, in *Poesías completas*), his poetic voice in hopes that it might help him transcend his present condition: "Huella soy de voz desnuda: / mi voz tal vez en tu voz / nació y hoy tu vuelo empuja" (I am but a trace of a naked voice: / my voice in your voice perhaps was / born and today your flight impels). Memory becomes the door to salvation. Retreating into himself, into the dreamworld of his past, he emerges into the light and, in the process, is symbolically reborn: "Otro paisaje en mi pecho / iba encendiéndome el día / también a medio lograr / por mi memoria perdida" (Another landscape in my breast / the day's light was partially revealing / through my lost memory). Over the years Prados would systematically enlarge this collection, which he commonly referred to as his "transitional poetry."

In *Mínima muerte* (Minimal Death, 1944) Prados's *soledad* (loneliness) grows like an apple tree overshadowing him and making him feel as insignificant as a single written word on the otherwise blank page of oblivion: "Mírame diminuto sobre esta blanca página, / sobre esta blanca ausencia tendida en mi memoria, / bajo el blanco desierto fecundo del olvido, / como una letra aislada de la flor de mi nombre" (Look at me so tiny on this white page, / on this white absence that has been spread out over my memory, / under the stark rich desert of oblivion, / like a single letter of the flower that is my name). Alone and despondent, Prados resumed the quest for his true name; a quest that years earlier had been abruptly curtailed by the war. Like a blind ant instinctively led to a granary, the speaker (in the metonymic guise of the letter or word) sets out in "Tres tiempos de soledad" on a journey toward "la honda memoria" (the depths of his own memory): "Tal vez llegue a mi nombre o al nombre de la piedra / o a los nombres del cielo o a los nombres del agua, / que con su antena torpe, mi letra perseguida / no deja cuerpo al mundo que de su tacto libre" (Perhaps it will arrive at my name or at the name of the stone / or at the names of the sky or the

*Prados and Guillén, philosophical poets who went into exile in North America to escape the aftermath of the Spanish Civil War*

names of the water, / for, even with its clumsy antennae, my persecuted letter / will not allow a single object in the world to escape its touch). The search leads Prados to the rose, a new *signo del ser*. In "Trinidad de la rosa" (The Trinity of the Rose), one of the best-wrought pieces of his entire oeuvre, Prados expresses his metaphysical aspirations using as paradigms the New Testament story of the birth, death, and resurrection of Jesus Christ and the normal evolutionary processes of nature.

Published in 1946, *Jardín cerrado* (Confined Garden) has been hailed as Prados's masterpiece. The Old Testament book of Genesis provided the underpinnings on which Prados's allegory was built. The tree and the garden are the essential symbolic figures. On one level the *álamo* (poplar) in the poem "Arboles" (Trees) is the insecure poet transplanted into a foreign soil – "expuesto / por falta de equilibrio / al fácil atropello / del asalto de un grito / o del cruzar de un beso" (vulnerable / because he lacks a sense of balance / and easily toppled by the assault of a scream / or a passing kiss) – and nostalgically recalling his lost garden (Spain). Summoning the elements of nature to assist him, he sets out to find himself within himself. The wind, the birds, and the flowing water all join in an effort to transport the tree's seeds (an extension of the poet himself) to that internal garden (the poet's memory) where they might germinate once more. On another level the tree is the Tree of Life in the primordial Garden of Eden, the very crux of Creation itself, where life and death converge and time becomes eternal. The speaker is drawn into the garden by the voice of God (in reality, his own inner voice) and there, within the confines of the garden, experiences a metaphorical rebirth.

In "El dormido en la yerba" (The Sleeper in the Grass), book 2 of *Jardín cerrado,* the tree in the garden metamorphosizes into the figure of a man who is asleep in the grass and is firm in his resolve to join in total communion with nature and is oblivious to those who come to him offering advice. As he lies there, he perceives the night sky, in all its immensity, as an extension of his soul, and the moon as a reflection of the inner light (God's light) that calls to him from the dark recesses of his subconscious. Part 2 of "El dormido en la yerba," titled "La soledad y el sueño" (Loneliness and Dreams), includes the highly acclaimed "Tres tiempos de soledad" (Three Stages of Loneliness), previously published in *Mínima muerte.*

Book 3 of *Jardín cerrado,* "Umbrales de sombra" (Thresholds of Shadow), includes some of Prados's most poignant and intimate compositions. He assumes an almost nihilistic attitude as he attempts to deal with the question of his sexuality. Emotionally tormented and consumed by loneliness (and perhaps guilt), he escapes, in a Cernudian sense, into his own *olvido* (forgetfulness). In "La voz en el jardín" (The Voice in the Garden), reminiscent in some respects of "Ciudad sitiada," the poet's tormented body is described in terms of a battlefield: "Como una blanca espada, / de golpe por mis ojos / clavó el dolor mi cuerpo. / Bajó por mí pisando en mis ruinas; / colonizando el campo de mi sueño" (Like a white sword, / suddenly as if through my very eyes / pain pierced my body. / It descended over me treading on my ruins; / colonizing the battleground of my dreams). In his darkest despair the poet, feeling his search has been misdirected, symbolically closes the door to his soul: "¿para qué voy a entrar en la alameda / si no llega a lo Eterno?" (why should I enter the poplar forest / if it does not lead to the Absolute?). He discovers that he no longer shares an affinity with the rose and the tree, both of which have feelings, and in "Cuerpo perseguido" (The Besieged Body) he writes, "Y el árbol sigue gimiendo / cuando lo acaricia el aire . . . / la rosa sigue luciendo / y, yo, sin saber de mí" (And the tree continues to sigh / when caressed by the wind . . . / the rose continues to shine / and, I, with no knowledge of myself). Casting these aside, he turns his attention to the insensitive stone in hopes that this new "sign of being" will prove to be a more faithful mirror of his metaphysical aspirations.

*Río natural* (Natural River) and *Circuncisión del sueño* (Circumcision of Dreams), both published in 1957, signal a change in Prados's outlook on life. As unflagging as ever in his determination to attain a greater self-knowledge and a sense of oneness with the universe, he pursues his mission with a renewed optimism. In his system of symbolic expression, germination and proliferation replace barrenness and infecundity; the white of the dawn, the darkness of the Pradian night. In "Nombres del mar" (Names of the Sea, in *Poesías completas*), "la aurora está en mi cuerpo" (dawn is in my body). In "Otoño bueno" (The Good Autumn, in *Poesías completas*), he writes, "blanca es mi voz" (my voice is white). In "La soledad y el sueño" (Loneliness and Sleep, in *Poesías completas*) he likens himself to a butterfly after the cocoon of loneliness has been broken: "Mi piel se abrió, recuerdo, / y rota la crisálida, / desde mi frente, al mundo / salí a nacer de un vuelo" (My skin opened, I remember, / and, the cocoon having

been broken, / from my very forehead, into the world / I was born into flight).

*Río natural* (Natural River) evokes the Heraclitean principal of *panta rhei,* or continuous evolution. The river alluded to in the title of the work is the river of the poet's life, the river of his dreams, ever flowing like his blood. Several new symbols are introduced into the system of expression. The window becomes a means of accessing memory, an opening through which the past can be reexperienced in myth and dream. The *caracol* (snail shell), yet another "sign of being," is symbolic of loneliness. Paradoxically it is also a symbol of wholeness or unity. The empty shell (the poet's body) is a perfectly self-contained environment, simultaneously immersed in and retaining within itself the source of its own salvation, water (consciousness, the soul). The *dídimo* (didymous), a plant organ formed by two symmetrical and exact lobes, represents the split between the poet's self and his other and is an extension of the earlier symbology surrounding the figure of Narcissus. Physically the didymous resembles the female sex organ, from where life springs. In "Corazón e mi historia" (Heart of My Life, in *Poesías completas*), Prados writes: "Dídimo soy de mi mismo; / hijo de mis dos mitades / y esclavo en la soledad / que hoy alimenta mi cárcel" (Didymous I am of my self; / child of my two halves / and slave in the loneliness / that today furnishes my prison).

*Circuncisión del sueño,* dedicated to Prados's father, is – faithful to its source of inspiration, the Old Testament – a panegyric on fertility and procreation. The *germen* (seed) becomes the archetype of centricity, the crux of Creation.

Prados took copious notes and drew sketches that graphically represented the concepts with which he was dealing. This activity increased substantially in his later years as his poetry became more and more complex. The question of time and to what extent man can control it became an obsession with Prados. He envisaged time as a spring which, following a spiral course, moves continually inward and outward toward infinity and the universe as an enormous tapestry being woven by time and composed of individual threads which crisscross at an infinite number of junctures. Man, like all the other entities in the universe, is characterized in a Lockean sense as nothing more than the physical presence of something that has no life, no history – a blank sheet of paper or a tombstone with no epitaph. In Asistencia a un crepúsculo" (Witnessing a Sunset, in *Poesía completas*) time, depicted by Prados as a sculptor, chisels out for man an epitaph, giving him both a future and a past; "Tú que pasas, soy piedra desechada . . . / ven, graba en mí tu nombre, dame espacio, / céntrame arriba, abajo: golpe a golpe se forma en cruz mi vida. Punta en punta, / el cincel de tu tiempo irá encontrándome hueco espacio de acción doble y continua" (You who pass, I am a stone that has been cast aside . . . / come, sketch on me your name, give me a space, / orient me upward, downward: blow by blow my life takes on the shape of the cross. Point by point, / the chisel of time will find for me an empty space of duplicate and continuous motion). The present, the confluence of future and past, or the point at which time crosses over itself, is the moment Prados tried to perpetuate or immortalize in his later works in his unending search for centricity or oneness.

*La piedra escrita,* whose title is of biblical origin, was projected to be Prados's final work, the culmination of a lifetime of soul-searching and poetic labor. A small white stone with the poet's "new" name inscribed on it was to be his ultimate "sign of being" – the symbol he was reserving for his "último diálogo humano de poesía" (final human poetic dialogue), as he explained in a 15 November 1955 letter to Father Alfonso Roig, the cornerstone upon which he would forge a skyscraper or construct a lasting temple. As originally conceived, the book was to be divided into four parts. An 11 December 1959 letter written to Sanchis-Banús makes reference to the completion of the work: "Fin de año, fin de libro y ¿fin de vida? Sí; en realidad un libro es una vida que se va, que se da y que no hay más remedio que dar, porque para eso se está viviendo" (The completion of the year, the completion of a book and, perhaps, the completion of a life? Yes; in reality a book is a life that passes on, that one offers up and has no alternative but to offer up, because for that reason, and for that reason alone we are living). The fact that the definitive version of *La piedra escrita* was not finally published until February 1961 underscores Prados's dissatisfaction with the original version. In its final version the book has seven parts, symbolic perhaps of the seven *moradas* (dwellings) of Santa Teresa's *castillo* (castle), alluded to in some of Prados's poems, or the numerous manifestations of this number in the Book of Revelation from which the title of *La piedra escrita* was drawn. Prados titled the final section of the book "La ciudad abierta" (The Open City), leaving little doubt about his change of heart concerning the nature of the book: instead of a definitive work, it was to be but another piece in a still-incomplete puzzle. Subsequent letters to Sanchis-Banús echo Prados's disillusionment with the book, with poetry in general, and with life itself. The

poems themselves reveal a confused and frustrated individual struggling to gain a sense of equilibrium in a topsy-turvy universe. The first three sections of *La piedra escrita* – "Hora de nacer" (The Hour of Birth), "Jardín en medio" (The Garden in Between), and "Torre de señales" (Tower of Signs) – tell of a retrospective journey through the symbolic landscape of his previous works in search of the light, culminating in the poem "Cambios de estado" (Changes of State) with the realization that he is the light, that the light is in him. His transformation into the prototypal symbol, the Christ figure, and his subsequent metaphorical crucifixion within a circle prefigures his resurrection or ascendance to a higher level of being.

The question of time and space continues to engage Prados's interest in *Signos del ser* (1962). Considered redundant by several Pradian scholars, the book is perhaps the most sincere expression of his fears, shortcomings, and lingering desires.

On 24 April 1962 the bronchial condition that plagued Prados as a child and that had recurred in his later years finally claimed his life. To the day of his death, Prados continued writing poetry. "Cita sin límites" (Unlimited Engagement), which appeared posthumously in *Poesías completas,* includes premonitions of death.

Emilio Prados remains somewhat of an enigma in the context of twentieth-century poetry, in part because of his reclusive nature, in part because of the breadth and complexity of his work. One of the most intellectual and well read poets of his generation, but also one of the most personally troubled, Prados will be remembered primarily for his social and political poetry in defense of the rights of the poor and downtrodden, although he deserves more. Recently there has been a renewed interest in Prados's poetry among literary critics, but there still remains much to be said.

**Letters:**

José Sanchis-Banús, "45 lettres inédites d'Emilio Prados annotées et commentées," Doctoral thesis, Sorbonne University, 1972;

José Luis Cano, "Cartas de Emilio Prados a José Luis Cano," *Insula,* 43 (June–August 1988): 69–72.

**References:**

Carlos Blanco Aguinaga, *Emilio Prados: Vida y obra; Bibliografía; Antología* (New York: Columbia University Press, 1960);

Juan Cano Ballesta, "Poesía y revolución: Emilio Prados," in *Homenaje universitario a Dámaso Al-*

*onso,* compiled by the students of Romance Philology of the University of Madrid (Madrid: Gredos, 1970), pp. 231–240;

Antonio Carreira, "Límites de la poesía y limitaciones de la crítica," *Anales de la Literatura Española Contemporánea,* 15, nos. 1–3 (1990): 203–234;

Andrew Debicki, "Unos procedimientos sintácticos en la poesía de Emilio Prados," in his *Estudios sobre poesía española contemporánea: la generación de 1924–1925* (Madrid: Gredos, 1968), pp. 307–320;

José Luis Del Castillo Jiménez, "Las formas poéticas tradicionales en Emilio Prados: *Mínima muerte,*" *Revista de Literatura,* 47 (January–June 1985): 129–138;

P. J. Ellis, *The Poetry of Emilio Prados: A Progression Towards Fertility* (Cardiff: University of Wales Press, 1981);

Harriet K. Greif, *Historia de Nacimientos: The Poetry of Emilio Prados* (Madrid: Porrúa, 1980);

Patricio Hernández Pérez, *Emilio Prados: La memoria del olvido,* 2 volumes (Zaragoza: Prensas Universitarias, 1988);

Vivien Rose Lombardi, *Estudio sobre "Jardín cerrado"* (Río Piedras: Estudios Hispánicos, University of Puerto Rico, 1974);

Ignacio Javier López, "Larrea y Prados: La poesía como mística y transfiguración," *Nueva Revista de Filología Hispánica,* 37, no. 1 (1989): 221–236;

López, "Repetición e integración en la obra poética de Emilio Prados," *Bulletin of Hispanic Studies,* 62 (October 1985): 373–383;

Roberto Carlos Manteiga, "En torno al binomio barco-mar en la poesía temprana de Emilio Prados," *Anales de la Literatura Española Contemporánea,* 16, nos. 1–2 (1991): 175–191;

Candelas Newton, "Emilio Prados y la dialéctica ontológica: Ser y no ser en *El misterio del agua,*" *Folio: Essays on Foreign Languages and Literatures,* 18 (February 1990): 11–24;

Elena Reina, *Hacia la luz: Simbolización en la poesía de Emilio Prados* (Amsterdam: Rodopi, 1988);

José Sanchis-Banús, *Seis Lecciones: Emilio Prados, su vida, su obra, su mundo* (Valencia: Pre-Textos, 1987);

Loreina Santos Silva, "Envolvimiento socio-político en *Destino fiel* de Emilio Prados," *Revista/Review Interamericana,* 11 (Spring 1981): 37–52;

Fidel Villar, "Lectura de Emilio Prados," *Hora de Poesía,* 14 (March–April 1981): 3–36;

María Zambrano, "Emilio Prados," *Cuadernos americanos,* 127 (January–February 1963): 162–167.

**Papers:**

All of Prados's papers, with the exception of his personal correspondence, were microfilmed by the Library of Congress. They were indexed by Carlos Blanco Aguinaga in *Lista de los papeles de Emilio Prados en la Biblioteca del Congreso de los Estados Unidos de America* (Baltimore: Johns Hopkins University Press, 1967).

# Claudio Rodríguez

*(30 January 1934 – )*

Charles Maurice Cherry
*Furman University*

BOOKS: *Don de la ebriedad* (Madrid: Rialp, 1953; revised and enlarged edition, Madrid: Torremozas, 1989);

*Conjuros* (Torrelavega: Cantalapiedra, 1958);

*Alianza y condena* (Madrid: Revista de Occidente, 1965);

*Poesía, 1953–1966* (Barcelona: Plaza & Janés, 1971);

*El vuelo de la celebración* (Madrid: Corazón, 1976);

*Antología poética,* edited by Philip W. Silver (Madrid: Alianza, 1981);

*Desde mis poemas* (Madrid: Cátedra, 1983; revised, 1990);

*Claudio Rodríguez,* edited by Dionisio Cañas (Madrid: Júcar, 1987);

*Casi una leyenda* (Barcelona: Tusquets, 1991);

*Poesías escogidas,* edited by Angel Rupérez (Madrid: Mondadori, 1992).

OTHER: "Unas notas sobre poesía," in *Poesía última,* edited by Francisco Ribes, (Madrid: Taurus, 1963; revised, 1975), pp. 87–92.

Claudio Rodríguez belongs to what has been termed the "Generation of the 1950s," also known as the "Generation of 1956–1971," the "Second Generation of Post-Civil-War Poets," and the "Rodríguez-Brines Generation." In addition to Rodríguez, this group includes Francisco Brines, Angel González, José Manuel Caballero Bonald, Jaime Gil de Biedma, Carlos Sahagún, and others who succeeded the wave of poets immediately following the Spanish Civil War and whose themes often include social commentary or even social protest. Although such concerns were of interest to many members of the Generation of the 1950s, they were equally motivated by a desire to create an aesthetic. In his interview with José Andrés Rojo, Rodríguez remarked that he saw his generation of writers as being bound by "la amistad" (friendship), and "la importancia que cada uno le daba, en su propio estilo, a la calidad del lenguaje, a la destreza poética" (the importance that each one gave, in his own style, to the quality of the language, to poetic skill).

Born in Zamora on 30 January 1934, just two years before the outbreak of the civil war, Rodríguez recalls little of the war other than the sound of the battle alarms in his hometown – "un recuerdo infantil, confuso, que, sin embargo, no se me olvida" (a confused memory from early childhood which, nevertheless, does not abandon me). His parents were of substantially different socioeconomic backgrounds. María García Moralejo de Rodríguez, his mother, was born into a moderately wealthy family. His father, Claudio Rodríguez Diego, the product of far humbler origins, was nevertheless an intelligent, well-read man who had prepared himself for a career in law.

On 23 March 1947, when the poet was scarcely thirteen years old, his father died suddenly, and young Claudio's life was to change dramatically. His father had published a few poems in the newspapers of Zamora and was recognized locally for his avocation as a poet. Claudio, known among his friends by the nickname Cayin, discovered in his father's library many volumes that influenced him significantly, including the classics of Spanish literature and collections of French poetry, especially the works of Arthur Rimbaud. Because the school he attended did little to encourage reading, these masterpieces proved especially intriguing to him.

Rodríguez was affected in another way by his father's death, for at that time he began to take long walks and breathe the fresh country air. He discovered that he could leave behind the cares of city life and the responsibility of playing the role of father figure to Javier, his younger brother, born in 1939, and his twin sisters, María Luisa and María del Carmen, born in 1945. At the same time he was free to escape the often strained relations he was to maintain for many years with his mother. This diversion provided him both the chance to appreciate nature and to become engaged in conversation with the

*Claudio Rodríguez*

country dwellers. He noted in the interview with Rojo that "esas largas caminatas, días y días, han influido decisivamente, no sólo en mi poesía, sino en mi manera de ser y de entender la vida" (those long strolls, for days and days, have had a decisive impact not only on my poetry, but on my lifestyle and my understanding of life).

In 1944 Rodríguez had begun his studies in his hometown of Zamora at the Instituto Claudio Moyano, where he was especially intrigued by the field of philosophy and also enjoyed the analysis of French, Spanish, and Latin poetic meters. He moved to Madrid in 1951, and in 1957 he completed the master's degree program in romance philology at the Universidad Central.

Among the predominant characteristics of Rodríguez's poetry are a preoccupation with nature and the routines of rural life, an interest in the concerns of the individual, a desire to be nonjudgmental, and a fondness for the reality of the moment. Above all, perhaps, there is a contemplative, often

testimonial quality permeating all of his work. His style is marked by a variety of verse forms, syntactical complexities, enigmatic metaphorical language, and the use of concrete, simple words in unusual ways to create results that are often difficult to comprehend initially.

In 1953 Rodríguez published his first collection of poetry, *Don de la ebriedad* (The Gift of Intoxication), a work he had begun at age seventeen, before he went to Madrid. The nineteen poems in *Don de la ebriedad* are organized into three *libros* (books). With the exception of the two poems that make up the second book, which also happen to be much longer than the others in the collection, all are written in measured hendecasyllables with assonance in every second line, an unusual verse pattern for the period.

In his introduction to the 1989 edition of *Don de la ebriedad,* Rodríguez explains the title. He sees poetry, on the one hand, as the act of handing over or surrendering something ("una entrega") and, on the other, as "un entusiasmo en el sentido platónico de inspiración, de rapto, de éxtasis o, cristianamente, de fervor" (an enthusiasm in the Platonic sense of inspiration, of rapture, of ecstasy or, in Christian terms, of passion). The individual poems are part of a unified vision, a pilgrimage of sorts in which the young writer must, through the contemplation of the world he encounters, define what it is to have poetic insight.

In the opening selection of the book Rodríguez writes of the mysteries of the skies, of the clarity which comes from heaven as a gift, of light and darkness, and of dawn and nightfall. In poem 2 he senses that in the night there will always be

> un fuego oculto,
> un resplandor aéreo, un día vano
> para nuestros sentidos, que gravitan
> hacia arriba y no ven ni oyen hacia abajo.
>
> (a hidden fire,
> an aerial brilliance, an unreal day
> for our senses, which gravitate upward
> and neither see nor hear from down below.)

In such an environment, he says, morning springs eternal, having neither a beginning nor an end.

Typical of Rodríguez's affinity for metaphorical language is poem 3, in which he celebrates the evergreen oak:

> No siente lo espontáneo de su sombra,
> la sencillez del crecimiento; apenas
> si conoce el terreno en que ha brotado.
> . . . . . . . . . . . . . . . . . . . . . . . . . . . . . . . .
> Y con qué rapidez se identifica
> con el paisaje, con el alma entera
> de su frondosidad y de mí mismo.
>
> (It does not sense the spontaneity of its shadow,
> the simplicity of its growth; it scarcely
> knows the terrain from which it has sprouted.
> . . . . . . . . . . . . . . . . . . . . . . . . . . . . . . . .
> And how rapidly it becomes identified
> with the countryside, with the complete soul
> of its luxuriance and of me myself.)

Like the oak, the poet sees himself reaching ever upward, constrained only by elements beyond his control.

In the final poem of book 1 Rodríguez asks that his voice be allowed to float freely in the air. Aware that the wind, the light, and the song of the birds belong to no one, he reminds readers that "la flor vive / tan bella porque vive poco tiempo" (the flower lives / so beautifully because it endures for so short a time).

Book 2 comprises two poems different in form from the others in the collection. Although they, too, are written in hendecasyllables, they are somewhat longer and lack assonant rhyme. In the "Canto del despertar" (Song of Awakening) the speaker says that his senses are challenged by a variety of sights, sounds, and aromas which accompany the dawning of a new day.

The structure of book 3 is almost identical to that of the first. The selections are brief, and the tone is similar. Poem 2, dedicated to Clara Miranda, who later became Rodríguez's wife, is a particularly moving love poem. For two people in love everything seems new, from the rising of the sun, which makes each day like the first morning of creation, to the flight patterns of birds, which never exactly repeat themselves. Such is the power of love that "nunca ve en las cosas / la triste realidad de su apariencia" (it never sees in things / the sad reality of their appearance).

The final poem in the collection provides a fitting ending for the contemplation of the fields, the sea, and the mountains. Rodríguez remains somewhat confused, though, and seeks answers:

> ¿Es que voy a morir? Decidme, ¿cómo
> veis a los hombres, a sus obras, almas
> inmortales? Sí, ebrio estoy, sin duda.
> La mañana no es tal, es una amplia
> llanura sin combate, casi eterna,
> casi desconocida porque en cada
> lugar donde antes era sombra el tiempo
> ahora la luz espera ser creada.
>
> (Is it a fact that I am going to die? Tell me,
> How do you regard men and their works, immortal
> souls? Yes, I am undoubtedly intoxicated.
> Morning is not like that; it is an extensive
> plain free of combat, almost eternal,
> almost unknown, because in each
> place where time was previously a shadow,
> light now waits to be created.)

He realizes that air, sun, fire, and water possess answers to some of his questions, if he will only take advantage of them; and he asks finally, "¿Es que voy a vivir? ¿Tan pronto acaba / la ebriedad?" (Is it a fact that I am going to live? Does intoxication come to / an end so soon?)

The literary world was astounded to discover that such a mature creation had been written by a young man not yet twenty years of age. For this effort Rodríguez received the coveted Adonais Prize for Poetry. Despite his having read widely from his father's library, his acquaintance with contemporary Spanish literature was so limited that when he

*Rodríguez walking along the Paseo Rosales in Madrid, 1951*

was introduced to Vicente Aleixandre, one of those responsible for selecting him for the award, he had no knowledge of the great poet's work or prominence. The two were later to form such close personal ties that the young poet visited Aleixandre two or three times a week; and through these meetings Rodríguez developed friendships with Carlos Bousoño, José Angel Valente, Brines, González, and other figures of the literary establishment. Rodríguez and Aleixandre also initiated a long-term exchange of correspondence, which was to benefit the younger poet for many years.

The reaction spawned by the appearance of *Don de la ebriedad* is captured in the remarks of Bousoño in his prologue to Rodríguez's *Poesía, 1953–1966* (1971): "Aunque han pasado bastantes años, me acuerdo aún del efecto de sorpresa que la lectura . . . del primer libro de Claudio Rodrí-

guez . . . produjo en mí. Me hallaba de pronto frente a un poeta completamente desconocido y sumamente joven . . . que, sin embargo, aparecía en el escenario de la literatura española con arte maduro y personalizado" (Although a sufficient period of time has passed, I still remember the effect of surprise that the reading . . . of the first book by Claudio Rodríguez . . . produced in me. I suddenly found myself face-to-face with a completely unknown and exceedingly young poet . . . who, nevertheless, appeared on the scene of Spanish literature with a mature and personal art). Bousoño was struck by both the originality and perfection of the eighteen-year-old poet's diction, as well as the fact that the style seemed to emanate from a non-Hispanic tradition.

Five years later the collection *Conjuros* (Incantations, 1958) appeared. Dedicated to Aleixandre, whose influence on the development of Rodríguez had been so significant, this volume is generally viewed as a sequel of sorts to *Don de la ebriedad*.

Critic Guillermo Díaz-Plaja notes that the primary shift between the first and second collections represents precisely a replacement of what he terms the relationship of the poet to his world – the "yo-mundo" (I-world) of *Don de la ebriedad* – with a "confrontación yo-hombres" (I-men confrontation), achieved primarily through metaphorical language in *Conjuros*. Díaz-Plaja cites as examples Rodríguez's mentions of the roof beam of a tavern, clothes hung out to dry, an adobe wall, and the flame of a hearth, all of which "anecdotizan y particularizan . . . la visión panorámica de los paisajes para incidir en la pequeña, entrañable, dramática realidad de cada día" (tell a story and particularize . . . the panoramic vision of the countrysides to touch on the small, intimate, dramatic reality of each day).

Convinced that a darker meaning underlies the collection, some critics argue that it would be wrong to interpret *Conjuros* too narrowly as a mere evocation of rural life. It is, nonetheless, impossible to escape the reality of the key words, which figure prominently in the titles of various selections. There are, for instance, poems about the sun, the stars, the clouds, the summer rain, the harvest, the swallows, and a pine grove at dawn. The setting becomes of such vital importance that at times one feels that Rodríguez is creating a modern, sometimes disturbing book of hours in verse. The distinctively bucolic tone, when combined with alternating lines of seven and eleven syllables in many of the selections, has reminded many readers of the works of the Renaissance poet Fray Luis de León.

In the opening selection, "A la respiración en la llanura" (To Breathing on the Plain), Rodríguez offers unconventional advice to his readers:

> ¡Dejad de respirar y que os respire
> la tierra, que os incendie en sus pulmones
> maravillosos!
>
> (Stop breathing and let the earth put its
> breath into you, let it ignite you in its
> marvelous lungs!)

The poet urges the reader to take full advantage of whatever is offered by the natural world, and in "A las estrellas" (To the Stars) Rodríguez asks that his own star not be the one that shines the most, but rather the most distant one.

"Primeros fríos" (The First Cold Days) contains some painful questions about the reality of winter:

> ¿Quién nos calentará la vida ahora
> si se nos quedo corto
> el abrigo de invierno?
> ¿Quién nos dará para comprar castañas?
>
> (Who will warm our lives now
> if our winter overcoats
> turned out to be too short?
> Who will give us money to buy chestnuts?)

In "Lluvia de verano" (Summer Rain) the speaker bids the water to descend from the sky to bind itself to humankind, to the soil, and to the work of the fields. Sadly, however, the rain comes too powerfully and leaves the countryside worse off than before.

In the final selection of the book, "Pinar amanecido" (Pine Grove at Dawn), the poet tells the reader, here viewed as a "traveler," that it will be impossible to forget the clean air and the beauty of the pine grove. There is a call for the solidarity of all people, but the reality of such unity is seen as an almost unattainable goal. The optimistic poet, nonetheless, believes that obstacles can be surmounted:

> ¡Viajero,
> sigue cantando la amistad dichosa
> en el pinar amaneciente! ¡Nunca
> creas esto que he dicho;
> canta y canta! ¡Tú, nunca
> digas por estas tierras
> que hay poco amor y mucho miedo siempre!
>
> ( Traveler,
> keep singing of the blessed friendship
> in the pine grove at dawn! Never
> believe this that I have said;
> sing and sing! Don't you ever
> say in these lands that there is
> little love and always a great deal of fear!)

Through the assistance of Aleixandre and Dámaso Alonso, Rodríguez received a lectureship at the University of Nottingham, England, and taught there from 1958 to 1960. In 1959 he married Clara Miranda, whom he had met six years earlier. In 1960 he was awarded a lectureship at Cambridge, where he and Clara lived until 1964, when they returned to Madrid; Rodríguez devoted much of his time there to university teaching. Among the most positive experiences of his stay in England was the opportunity it afforded him to develop a close personal friendship with Brines, whose visiting lectureship at Oxford coincided with Rodríguez's years at Cambridge.

In "Unas notas sobre poesía" (Some Notes about Poetry), published in *Poesía última,* edited by

*Rodríguez and his future wife, Clara Miranda, in Zaráuz, 1954. They married five years later.*

Francisco Ribes, Rodríguez wrote, "Creo que la poesía es, sobre todo, participación. Nace de una participación que el poeta establece entre las cosas y su experiencia poética de ellas, a través del lenguaje. Esta participación es un modo peculiar de conocer" (I believe that poetry is, above all else, participation. It is born of a participation that the poet establishes between things and his poetic experience of them, through language. This participation is a peculiar means of knowing.)

In 1965 Rodríguez published his third collection, *Alianza y condena* (Alliance and Condemnation), which was to earn for him the coveted Premio de la Crítica. He employs some verse forms not seen previously in his work, and in some ways the selections in this volume are more easily read than those of *Conjuros*. The contrast between the favorable connotation of *alliance* and the negative association one sees in *condemnation* is maintained throughout the collection through the juxtaposition of contradictory objects, emotions, and settings. Many of the poems announce themes of disappointment, denial, and betrayal; yet they do not always offer fitting solutions.

The opening poem, "Brujas a mediodía" (Witches at Noon), creates a bizarre picture of

witchcraft on a September day. Despite the subtitle, "Hacia el conocimiento" (Toward Understanding), there are disturbing, often unrelated images in the poem. The reader learns that all life possesses "un punto de cocción, un meteoro / de burbujas" (a boiling point, a meteor / of bubbles). The speaker searches vainly for some ultimate truth in a world rife with contemptible laws and problems of injustice.

In the poem "Cáscaras" (Outer Coverings) Rodríguez provides an inventory of shells, peelings, and other materials which mask the sometimes insidious reality buried beneath their surface. His metaphorical gift shines in "Espuma" (Foam), where the qualities he associates with seafoam – delicateness, simplicity, and a transitory nature – give rise to reflections of the fundamental images of birth, life, passion, and death.

Other simple objects and forces of nature also inspire him: a spring wind; the sparrow who never really travels far and seems to be constantly searching for something; the rain, strong and unpredictable, which forces all to seek shelter; the sunflower, which moves its head about in a dance, changing its entire posture to respond to external realities; and money, which can buy love, success, and power.

In "Nieve en la noche" (Snow in the Night) natural order is disturbed by the snow, which feigns innocence to disguise its deceptive quality, as it re-creates midday in the middle of the night. Although it possesses an endearing quality on other occasions, the snow can blind people, robbing them of light. As it continues to fall, instead of being gentle, it smothers and suffocates whatever is in its path.

In the opening lines of "Como el son de las hojas del álamo" (Like the Sound of the Poplar Leaves), Rodríguez writes of pain, the manifestation of which can prove surprising:

El dolor verdadero no hace ruido:
deja un susurro como el de las hojas
del álamo mecidas por el viento . . .

( True pain makes no noise:
it leaves a murmur like that of the leaves
of the poplar tree shaken by the wind . . .)[.]

*Poesía, 1953–1966,* including the poems in *Don de la ebriedad, Conjuros,* and *Alianza y condena,* was published in 1971. What distinguishes this collection is the prologue by Bousoño, a valuable assessment of Rodríguez's development. Given Rodríguez's lack of exposure to contemporary Spanish poetry prior to the publication of *Don de la ebriedad,* Bousoño feels that its original quality results from Rodríguez's unusual personality. This feature becomes apparent in the two later collections as well, where, in addition to manifesting a significant change in style in each work, he maintains a highly personal quality. With specific reference to *Alianza y condena,* Bousoño writes, "Cuando terminamos la lectura, una sensación de bienestar nos inunda: un corazón benévolo y un alma limpia nos acompañan, ya para siempre, desde las páginas de un libro" (When we complete the reading, a sensation of well-being engulfs us: a benevolent heart and a pure soul accompany us forever more from the pages of a book).

During the years following the publication of *Alianza y condena,* Rodríguez reacquainted himself with Madrid, and he and Clara became comfortable in their home on Calle Lagasca. Meanwhile, his mother and sisters had also moved to the Spanish capital. Tragedy struck the family on 31 July 1974, when María del Carmen, Rodríguez's beloved sister, was murdered. The following year, on 28 September 1975, his mother died as well.

*El vuelo de la celebración* (The Flight of Celebration), the fourth of Rodríguez's collections of new poetry, was published in 1976. In the introduction to *Desde mis poemas* (From My Poems, 1983) Rodrí-

guez says of *El vuelo* that what he attempts to celebrate is "lo que se abre o lo que se cierra desde todas las posibilidades vitales: la figura de las cosas, el poderío de las sensaciones que pueden desembocar en feracidad y en sequía. Es como una 'animación,' que recrea, fugitivamente, lo que nos sobrecoge y nos camina, y nos pule, y nos mejora. La celebración como conocimiento y como remordimiento" (what is opened or what is closed from among all vital possibilities: the shape of things, the power of sensations which can result in fertility or drought. It is like an "animation," which re-creates, fleetingly, what startles us and affects us, and refines us, and improves us. Celebration as knowledge and as remorse).

As in Rodríguez's earlier collections, there are many references in *El vuelo* to the objects and images one takes for granted until they are scrutinized, often triggering profound emotions of satisfaction or pleasure, yet as often resulting in sadness or despair. In the opening poem, "Aventura de una destrucción" (Adventure of a Destruction), which is one of the poems in the section "Herida en cuatro tiempos" (Injury in Four Times), the sight of a pillow creates profoundly negative associations. The speaker recalls the sobbing, nightmares, and feelings of desertion he experienced in this same bed for a period of fifteen years.

In "La arena" the sand is personified as a naked, forsaken, agile being, capable of flying and singing, and it is implored by the speaker to penetrate his pores, thus becoming a pulsating part of a human body in need of the sand's serenity and tenderness. An essentially paranoid quality marks "Hermana mentira" (Sister Lie), in which the narrator asks why, on a clear day which is otherwise so pleasant, the air is looking at him "con vileza y sin fe" (with vileness and without faith). Rodríguez writes of envy, arrogance, injustice, and desire in the three-part "Elegía desde Simancas" (Elegy from Simancas).

In "Hilando" (Spinning) Rodríguez re-creates visual art through his talent as a writer in a tribute to a painting by Diego Velázquez. In "Perro de poeta" (Poet's Dog) Rodríguez recalls with affection the dog Sirio, the faithful companion of Aleixandre; and in "Noviembre" (November) he welcomes a month that brings him many pleasures and begs it not to desert him. In a well-known poem Rodríguez dedicated to Brines, "Ballet del papel" (Ballet of the Paper), he traces the movements of different types of paper, which variously flutter; perform agile, balletlike movements; and eventually settle on the pavement.

*Vicente Aleixandre, Rodríguez, and José Hierro in Madrid, 1956*

*Antología poética* (Poetic Anthology, 1981) includes approximately half of the poems previously printed in Rodríguez's earlier collections. The book opens with a brief, yet penetrating introduction by the editor, Philip W. Silver, who selected the poems. Resisting the temptation to cover territory already exploited by other critics or to analyze in greater depth Rodríguez's debt to Spanish mysticism, Silver chooses instead to examine other areas, such as the relationship between Rodríguez's art and the surrealist tradition, as well as the automatism that seems to underlie much of his creative process.

*Desde mis poemas,* a comprehensive collection of Rodríguez's published poetry to 1983, includes the poet's introductory essay "A manera de comentario" (By Way of Commentary). He writes that "Si la poesía, entre otras cosas, es una búsqueda, o una participación entre la realidad y la experiencia poética de ella a través del lenguaje, claro está que cada poema es como una especie de acoso para lograr (meta imposible) dichos fines" (If poetry, among other things, is a quest, or a communication between reality and the poetic experience of that reality by means of language, it is clear that each poem is like a type of pursuit to achieve [an impossible goal] such ends).

Rodríguez received the Premio Nacional de Poesía on 31 October 1983. A month before the award ceremony, he discussed *Desde mis poemas* with Curtis Millner (in an interview published in 1984) and insisted that he had faithfully reproduced his original poems, making no changes other than a few incidental modifications of punctuation. Seeing himself as an improviser whose artistic focus is on the concrete reality of the world about him and never on abstract thought, Rodríguez stated that he had always written his poetry strolling about, not seated: "Puede suceder el fenómeno siguiente. Es decir, yo contemplo una realidad o un árbol o un campo, el cielo, etc. Caminando, andando surge la reflexión, y surge sobre todo la sorpresa" (The phenomenon may occur in this way. That is to say, I contemplate a reality or a tree or a field, the sky, etc. Traveling about, walking, the reflection appears, and, above all, surprise springs forth).

For Rodríguez, the composition of poetry must never be regulated by the constraints of time, but rather by natural impulse: "Yo no puedo dejar de ser poeta. Sería una barbaridad. . . . Yo puedo estar mucho tiempo sin escribir, sin escribir nada, absolutamente nada . . . ; mucho tiempo . . . sin escribir ni un solo verso. ¿Por qué? Porque no tenía el impulso – siempre he creído en el impulso – o

Cover for Rodríguez's second book, which, according to critic Guillermo
Díaz-Plaja, particularizes the "dramática realidad de cada día"
(dramatic reality of each day)

digamos, la inspiración, en el sentido griego de la palabra" (I cannot stop being a poet. It would be nonsense. . . . I can spend a great deal of time without writing, without writing anything, absolutely anything . . . ; a great deal of time . . . without writing one single line. Why? Because I had no impulse – I have always believed in the impulse – or let us say, inspiration, in the Greek sense of the word). He admits that his collections have appeared sparsely over the years, citing *El vuelo de la celebración,* which seemingly required almost ten years of preparation, simply because "no tenía cosas que escribir" (I had nothing to write).

In response to a question from Millner concerning what poetry does for him and what it does for his audience, Rodríguez said that only the readers themselves are capable of responding. One reader wrote to him that upon completing one of Rodríguez's collections, he had converted to Catholicism, although Rodríguez insists that he himself is not Catholic. Yet another reacted in a completely contrary manner: "Entonces el efecto que produce en el lector depende del lector" (Thus the effect which is produced in the reader depends on the reader himself).

Rodríguez justified his reputation for keeping his personal life fairly private in a world in which many contemporary writers thrive on publicity: "Cuando me pongo a escribir, a escribir de mí mismo, de mi biografía, mi amor, la alegría, repito . . . me da una especie de pudor" (When I begin to write, to write of myself, of my background, of my love, of happiness . . . it creates in me a type of modesty). His final comments in the interview are especially revealing: "La poesía es vida, si no, no es nada. No es arte, no es literatura. Claro, la misma vida te va llevando a unas posiciones ya de reflexión, de meditación. Cuando uno está con la mano en la mejilla, como dice Rubén Darío, meditabundo, ya la exaltación juvenil se ha perdido. Yo entiendo la poesía como salvación. Yo utilizo la palabra 'celebración.' . . . Parece una cosa religiosa, pero no. Es salvar al hombre en toda su manera de existir." (Poetry is life; if not, it is nothing. It is not art; it is not literature. Of course, the same life goes on transporting you to positions of reflection, of meditation. When one is with his hand on his cheek, as Rubén Darío says, pensive, the youthful exaltation has already been spent. I understand poetry as salvation. I employ the word "celebration." . . . It seems like a religious thing, but it is not. It is to save man in his entire manner of existence.)

The Premio Nacional brought renewed attention to Rodríguez and his poetry and resulted in the appearance of several articles about him in Spanish and North American journals. After Rodríguez received the honor, José Olivio Jiménez, writing in *Cuadernos Hispanoamericanos* (December 1984), recalled his friendship of over thirty years with the poet, whom he first met when the two were university students in Madrid, and congratulated Rodríguez for his well-deserved prize, one which would ensure that his poetry would reach "un plano de atención más objetivo y, a la vez, más solidario — devolviéndole así a este afanoso cantor de la solidaridad, la alianza, la amistad, y la hospitalidad" (a more objective level of attention and, at the same time, a more involved one — thus returning to this hard-working singer of solidarity, alliance, friendship, and hospitality). In 1987 Rodríguez was further honored by having the Premio Castilla y León de Letras bestowed on him.

The publication in 1991 of Rodríguez's *Casi una leyenda* (Almost a Legend) was hardly a surprise to the literary world; he had been working on the book for several years. In his introductory essay for Rodríguez's *Poesías escogidas* (Selected Poetry, 1992) editor Angel Rupérez stresses the fact that *Casi una leyenda* can be understood only within the context of Rodríguez's previous collections. What is most striking to Rupérez about the 1991 book is the inherent tone of serenity he finds lacking in Rodríguez's earlier poetry: "Sí había percibido entusiasmo, fervor, alegría suprema, pero tal vez no serenidad, calma, aceptación de un final revelador y tranquilo, semejante al de una primavera que se prolonga dulcemente en el verano para nunca morir" (I had indeed perceived enthusiasm, passion, supreme joy, but perhaps not serenity, calm, acceptance of a tranquil and revealing conclusion, similar to that of a spring that is sweetly prolonged into summer so as never to die).

The anonymous commentary on the book jacket announces that in *Casi una leyenda* Rodríguez is astonished by all the alterations that complicate his life: "No duran los momentos de plenitud, ni puede sostenerse el instante de la visión, ni permanece constante el conocimiento" (Moments of plentitude do not endure; nor can the instant of vision be sustained; nor does knowledge remain constant). A sense of isolation permeates the introductory selection, "Calle sin nombre" (Street without a Name), in which the speaker confronts not only the unpredictability of the rain and the darkness of night but phenomena he cannot readily interpret — the faceless someone at a window above the street, and a sidewalk trying to communicate with him. Finally dawn arrives, the air clears, and the narrator abandons this place to which he may never return.

The poems in the section "De noche y por la mañana" (At Night and In the Morning) include images and concepts familiar to readers of Rodríguez's earlier work. In "Revelación de la sombra" (Revelation of the Shadow) he asks why it is that "la luz maldice y la sombra perdona" (the light curses and the shadow forgives). In other poems in the same section he seeks order, solitude, and grace. In "Nuevo día" (New Day) he discovers that the new morning brings him clarity and the freedom of contemplation. Despite a few optimistic notes, this section presents disturbing chords; however, in the final selection of this part, "Manuscrito de una respiración" (Manuscript of a Respiration), the speaker seems momentarily to be at ease with himself:

"Y estás sintiendo cómo
la mayor injusticia de la vida
es el dolor del cuerpo, el del espíritu
se templa con espíritu. Y me sanas,
y yo te doy las gracias por venir
tan delicada que casi te veo. . . ."

("And you are feeling how
the greatest injustice in life
is the pain of the body; that of the spirit
is tempered with spirit. And you heal me,
and I thank you for coming
so delicately that I almost see you. . . .")

In *Casi una leyenda* Rodríguez renews his search for answers to the human riddle, a quest symbolized in some of the later selections through the metaphor

*Rodríguez and Francisco Brines in Biarritz, 1963*

of pursuit. He contemplates love, happiness, and truth, and he eventually discovers that death is the eternal verity.

*Poesías escogidas* includes more than half of Rodríguez's published works. Rupérez introduces the selections with an overview of Rodríguez's development throughout his career.

In his interview with Rojo, Rodríguez noted that he has always maintained close ties with his hometown, Zamora, to the extent that he has never been completely comfortable with the rhythm of Madrid and has tried instead to lead a life like one encounters in the provinces: "Mis tabernas, la gente del barrio, el mercado. Nunca he hecho vida literaria" (My bars, the neighborhood people, the market. I have never led a writer's life).

Rodríguez has in recent years expressed a fondness for reading more widely from works of science, including books in the fields of physics, astronomy, zoology, and botany. He also displays an interest in learning how things are made and admits that "Me imagino que todo este sinfín de intereses terminan por impregnar mi poesía. Pero, en principio, lo que me motiva es la curiosidad" (I imagine that all of these endless interests eventually saturate my poetry. But, fundamentally, what motivates me is curiosity).

Rodríguez garnered yet another award on 27 May 1993, when he was named the recipient of the coveted Premio Príncipe de Asturias de las Letras, which included a cash award of five million pesetas (forty thousand U.S. dollars). Because intervals of five or more years have elapsed between the publications of his various collections, it is not surprising that many readers have voiced their disappointment that he has not been more prolific. As Rodríguez explains, because he devotes much of his time to university teaching in Madrid, he has found it difficult to conduct classes on poetry and then return home to write poetry.

In addition to the literary honors he has received, Rodríguez was awarded on 29 March 1992 the seat formerly held by Gerardo Diego in the Real Academia Española . In the speech marking his induction, Rodríguez provided a superb synthesis of his artistic code: "La poesía es rebeldía, es inconformidad esencialmente, es locura armoniosa. . . . El poeta no trata de escribir acerca de algo concreto, porque la vida no es poesía, pero la poesía sí es vida, la poesía es participación, antes que comunicación o incluso conocimiento" (Poetry is rebellion; it is essentially nonconformity; it is harmonious madness. . . . The poet does not try to write about something concrete, because life is not poetry, but poetry is indeed life; poetry is participation, rather than communication or even understanding). He further defined the paradoxical role of the poet, who must be "en permanente libertad y

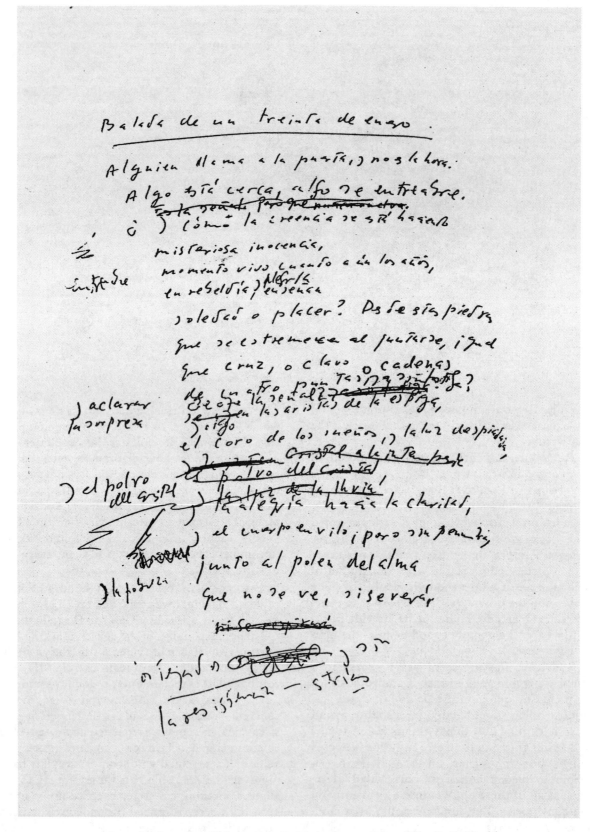

*Manuscript for an unpublished poem by Rodríguez (by permission of Claudio Rodríguez)*

esclavitud, una persona que ha de llegar a la expresión viva y ha de estar en el pulso y cambio del mundo, de la vida, para saber distinguir lo que es valioso de lo que no es valioso, porque es un creador de pensamiento" (in permanent liberty and slavery, a person who is supposed to achieve lively expression and is supposed to exist with the pulse and change of the world, of life, in order to know how to distinguish what is worthwhile from what is not, because he is a creator of thought).

For four decades Claudio Rodríguez has found an enthusiastic audience for his work. Selections from his collections have found their way into various anthologies of contemporary poetry and have been analyzed on both sides of the Atlantic by critics who have been particularly fascinated with his creation of linguistic codes and his affinity for metapoetry. His place in Spanish letters seems secure, though it is constantly undergoing change. Efforts by critics to compare him to the poets of antiquity or to those of the Spanish Golden Age, to his mentor Aleixandre, and to the first generation of post-civil-war poets are intriguing. Such exercises, however, risk diminishing his importance as one who has experimented creatively with new themes and has achieved a highly personal and original style, characterized by an ability to manipulate words by constantly creating new meanings for them and by combining them in unusual ways.

**Interviews:**

Antonio Núñez, "Encuentro con Claudio Rodríguez," *Insula*, 21, no. 234 (May 1966): 4;

Curtis Millner, "Entrevista con Claudio Rodríguez," *Anales de la Literatura Española Contemporánea*, 9 (1984): 285–294;

José Andrés Rojo, "Tabaco, alcohol, y literatura," in "Memoria de una generación," *Prólogo*, 6 (January–February 1990): 32–41.

**References:**

Carlos Bousoño, "La poesía de Claudio Rodríguez," prologue to Rodríguez's *Poesía, 1953–1966* (Barcelona: Plaza & Janés, 1971), pp. 7–35;

Carole A. Bradford, "Francisco Brines and Claudio Rodríguez: Two Recent Approaches to Poetic Creation," *Crítica Hispánica*, 2 (1980): 29–40;

José Luis Cano, "La poesía de Claudio Rodríguez de *Conjuros* a *Alianza y condena*," in his *Poesía*

*española contemporánea: Generaciones de posguerra* (Madrid: Guadarrama, 1974), pp. 153–164;

Andrew P. Debicki, "Claudio Rodríguez: Language Codes and Their Effects," in his *Poetry of Discovery: The Spanish Generation of 1956–1971* (Lexington: University Press of Kentucky, 1982), pp. 40–58;

Guillermo Díaz-Plaja, "*Poesía, 1953–1966*," in his *Al pie de la poesía: Páginas críticas 1971–1973* (Madrid: Nacional, 1974), pp. 188–192;

Joaquín González-Muela, "Claudio Rodríguez," in his *La nueva poesía española* (Madrid: Alcalá, 1973), pp. 59–80;

Irene Belle Hodgson, "The Poetic Works of Claudio Rodríguez," Ph.D. dissertation, Purdue University, 1986;

José Olivio Jiménez, "Claudio Rodríguez entre la luz y el canto: Sobre *El vuelo de la celebración*," *Papeles de Son Armadans*, 87 (1977): 103–124;

Jiménez, "Para una antología esencial de Claudio Rodríguez," *Cuadernos Hispanoamericanos*, no. 414 (December 1984): 92–110;

Jonathan Mayhew, *Claudio Rodríguez and the Language of Poetic Vision* (Lewisburg, Pa.: Bucknell University Press, 1990);

José Méndez, ed., "Memoria de una generación," *Prólogo*, 6 (January–February 1990): 20–41;

Antonio R. Naranjo, "Claudio Rodríguez: 'El poeta tiene que buscar lo secreto y lo sagrado de la vida,'" *ABC* (16 July 1992); reprinted in *Spain: Boletín Cultural*, 120 (July 1992): 22;

Margaret H. Persin, "The Syntax of Assertion in the Poetry of Claudio Rodríguez," in her *Recent Spanish Poetry and the Role of the Reader* (Lewisburg, Pa.: Bucknell University Press, 1987), pp. 68–97;

Pedro Provencio, "Claudio Rodríguez," in his *La generación del 50* (Madrid: Hiperión, 1988), pp. 165–180;

José M. Sala, "Algunas notas sobre la poesía de Claudio Rodríguez," *Cuadernos Hispanoamericanos*, no. 334 (April 1978): 125–141;

Philip W. Silver, *La casa de Anteo: Estudios de poética hispánica: De Antonio Machado a Claudio Rodríguez* (Madrid: Taurus, 1985);

Silver, "Claudio Rodríguez o la mirada sin dueño," introduction to Rodríguez's *Antología poética* (Madrid: Alianza, 1981), pp. 7–22.

# Luis Rosales

*(31 May 1910 – 24 October 1992)*

Felipe A. Lapuente
*Memphis State University*

BOOKS: *Abril* (Madrid: Arbol, 1935);

*La mejor reina de España,* by Rosales and Luis Felipe Vivanco (Madrid: Jerarquía, 1939);

*La poesía hispánica y el sentimiento de la Patria* (Madrid: Asociación Cultural Hispano-Americana, 1940);

*Retablo sacro del nacimiento del Señor* (Madrid: Escorial, 1940; enlarged edition, Madrid: Universitaria Europea, 1964);

*Algunas consideraciones sobre el lenguaje* (Madrid, 1947);

*La casa encendida* (Madrid: Seminario de Problemas Hispanoamericanos, 1949; revised and enlarged edition, Madrid: Revista de Occidente, 1967);

*Rimas, 1937–1951* (Madrid: Cultura Hispánica, 1951);

*Cervantes y la libertad,* 2 volumes (Madrid: Sociedad de Estudios y Publicaciones, 1960);

*Pasión y muerte del Conde de Villamediana* (Madrid: Real Academia Española, 1964, enlarged edition, Madrid: Gredos, 1969);

*El sentimiento del desengaño en la poesía barroca* (Madrid: Cultura Hispánica, 1966);

*El contenido del corazón* (Madrid: Cultura Hispánica, 1969; revised and enlarged, 1978);

*Lírica española* (Madrid: Nacional, 1972);

*Teoría de la libertad* (Madrid: Seminarios & Ediciones, 1972);

*Segundo abril* (Zaragoza: Javalambre, 1972);

*Canciones* (Madrid: Cultura Hispánica, 1973);

*Como el corte hace sangre; Homenaje a Luis Rosales,* by Rosales and others (Cáceres: Encina, 1974);

*Las puertas comunicantes: Primera antología poética* (Salamanca: Alamo, 1976);

*Pintura escrita* (Madrid: Azur/Pliegos del sur, 1978);

*La poesía de Neruda* (Madrid: Nacional, 1978);

*Diario de una resurrección* (Mexico City: Fondo de Cultura Económica, 1979);

*La almadraba* (Madrid: Cultura Hispánica, 1980);

*Verso libre: Antología, 1935–1978* (Barcelona: Plaza & Janés, 1980);

*Poesía reunida,* 2 volumes (Barcelona: Seix Barral, 1981, 1983);

*Un rostro en cada ola* (Melilla, Morocco: Ayuntamiento de Melilla / Málaga: Rusadir, 1982);

*Antonio Machado: Conferencias pronunciadas en la Fundación Universitaria Española los días 3 y 13 de mayo de 1975* (Madrid: Fundación Universitaria Española, 1983);

*Antología poética* (Madrid: Alianza, 1984);

*Oigo el silencio universal del miedo* (Madrid: Visor, 1984);

*El desnudo en el arte y otros ensayos* (Madrid: Cultura Hispánica, 1987).

OTHER: *Poesía heróica del Imperio,* 2 volumes, edited by Rosales and Luis Felipe Vivanco (Madrid: Jerarquía, 1940, 1943);

*Juan de Tassis, Conde de Villamediana,* compiled by Rosales (Madrid: Nacional, 1944);

"Apuntes biográficos," *Anthropos,* 25 (June 1983): 25.

*Abril* (April, 1935), by Luis Rosales, represents some of the innovative tendencies in poetry before the Spanish Civil War. Books published in 1936 by Luis Felipe Vivanco, Juan Panero, and Germán Bleiberg confirmed a conscientious effort by these poets, along with Rosales, to separate themselves from the previous avant-garde movements and to establish a new creative interest in originality and renewal. Rosales's 1992 death, the result of a stroke, brought renewed attention to the importance of his work and the impact he had on modern Spanish poetry.

Born in Granada on 31 May 1910, Luis Rosales completed his primary and secondary studies there. Encouraged by his friend and teacher Joaquín Amigo, a Spanish intellectual later shot in the civil war, Rosales started training for two professions: literature and law. Amigo took him to the University of Madrid to study philosophy and letters in the new *filología románica* department that had opened in September 1932. Rosales's parents were

*Luis Rosales, circa 1961*

Miguel Rosales Vallecillos and Esperanza Camacho de Rosales; they had one daughter, María, and five sons: Miguel, Antonio, Luis, José, and Gerardo. Luis and Gerardo were poets and were never interested in politics; the other brothers, encouraged by their mother, became interested in joining the Falangists. The father, on the other hand, had no interest in politics and was a respected businessman who owned a hardware store. He told Luis to stay away from politics and to treat everyone with respect while defending the rights of the individual and the cause of human freedom; he was also a close friend of Federico García Lorca's father. Federico and Luis were introduced in 1930 by their common friend and mentor Amigo.

In 1933 Luis Rosales was in the second year of his career at the University of Madrid. Four Spanish poets converged in friendship and literary production: Rosales, Vivanco, and the brothers Leopoldo and Juan Panero. Although the Generation of 1927 had an influence in technique on these poets, the Rosales group revealed the philosophical, ethical, and thematic influence of Antonio Machado, and they separated themselves from the dehumanized, surrealist world of such poets as Rafael Alberti, Vicente Aleixandre, and Lorca. Three Catholic thinkers, in particular, had an impact on Rosales and his friends: Xavier Zubiri (whom Vivanco accompanied to Rome when Zubiri got his secularization from the priesthood); José Bergamín, Vivanco's uncle and director of the liberal Catholic journal *Cruz y Raya*; and Jacques Maritain, who published an April 1935 article in *Cruz y Raya* complaining of the existence of an "angelismo pictórico" (pictorial angelic world) of forms that produced a vacuum in the human intellect.

The publication of Rosales's *Abril* marked a new beginning in Spanish poetry. It meant the decline of the cult of the images, after the avant-garde's surrealist influence, and a renewed interest in pure lyrical poetry with a variety of forms and a variety of moods. *Abril* is a long book, carefully divided into three parts with epigraphs from Fernando de Herrera, Lope de Vega, San Juan de la Cruz (Saint John of the Cross), Garcilaso de la Vega, and Lorca. It consists of *romances* (ballads), elegies, eclogues, sonnets, and long poems in hendecasyllables and in free verse. The book reveals a metaphysical, cosmic vision and a search for lost love. The speaker says he feels abandoned, alone, left only with memories of his "abril perdido" (lost April). He suffers from the absence of his loved one, but his naive faith serves as a crutch. He continually appeals to God and insists that his terrestrial love was no more than a reflection of the boundless love that fills his soul. He claims he deserves mercy, and this plea is the theme of the long religious poem "Misericordia" (Mercy): "Tú sabes que yo nunca he negado el presente, / Y el presente eras Tú, cuando yo te buscaba / por los rincones de mis ojos heridos" (You know that I have never denied the present, / And the present was You, when I looked for you / in the corners of my wounded eyes).

The theme of lost love recurs throughout the book. It haunts the speaker, as in the title sonnet: "Bajo el limpio esplendor de la mañana / en tu adorado asombro estremecido, / busco los juncos del abril perdido; / nieve herida eras tú, nieve temprana / tu enamorada soledad humana" (Beneath the limpid splendor of the morning / I look for the rushes of the lost April / in your adored trembling astonishment; / wounded snow you were, early snow / your human solitude in love). The antithetical conception of this love poem is characteristic of the new poets of the mid 1930s. The day in the poem is splendid and vibrant, but the state of the poet's soul is unaffected. His interior landscape is covered with snow, solitude, and darkness, and he can only dream of April: "busco los juncos del abril perdido" (I look for the rushes of the lost April). Readers see in this sonnet some key words used by Rosales – *voz* (voice), *dolor* (pain), *llanto* (weeping), *nieve* (snow), *herido* (wounded) – that recur often in his poetry. He took liberty with the sonnet form and with Spanish syntax and drew the reader's attention to the isolated impression produced by words and word combinations. There is in his poetry, however, the transference of a legitimate emotion caused by the human error of searching for eternity in physical love. Speakers appeal to God, the only recourse, to soothe grief and sadness, but they seem to think that only upon dying would they cease to feel alone. Nevertheless, the emotion is sublimated by a somewhat contrived technical perfection, which does not allow form and content to be in harmony.

The first section of *Abril*, "Vigilia del agua" (The Vigil of Water), presents jubilant songs about the "bien hecho" (well-made) world – songs that center on the search for an "other," a lover. The section comprises sixteen *décimas* (ten-line poems), five *romances*, and ten sonnets. Three poets are imitated: Jorge Guillén, Lorca, and Herrera. The "doncella" (maiden) and the "madre en júbilo de río" (mother in a jubilant river) are surrounded by signs of fecundity: "trigo" (wheat), "agua" (water), "sol mojado" (wet sun), and "naranjo en flor" (blossoming orange tree). There is universal solidarity; everything (wheat, water, dawn, light, spring, the vegetable world, and even the lover) is fused in womanhood, the center and organizer of this paradise: "Tú incorporas el mundo" (You incorporate the world). This paradise is presented as a "maravilla" (marvel), a "cántico" (song), and a "gozo" (joy).

In the second part of *Abril*, "Primavera del hombre" (Man's Spring), Rosales appears to be in search of the transcendence of the senses, the sublimation of love, and the final realization that God is the unifying force of the cosmos in the person of Jesus Christ. Most of this second part is written in free verse.

The third part, "Poemas en soledad" (Poems in solitude), continues the religious theme and portends the triumphant and optimistic world of *La casa encendida* (The Lighted House, 1949). In "Poemas en soledad" Rosales presents all beings as forced by a secret pull, which critic Victor García de la Concha calls (in his *La poesía española de posguerra* [Postwar Spanish Poetry]) "el ansia metafísica de totalidad" (the metaphysical desire for totality). The speaker searches for love, and when he finds love in a woman, they are both pulled toward an "ascensión hacia el reposo" (an ascension toward rest), according to García de la Concha. God is the last cause and call for unity, and creation finds a new order with the incarnation of Christ, as Rosales writes: "¡Ay, plenitud divina de amor en lo disperso!" (Oh divine plenitude of love in the dispersed!). God as unifying and pure is symbolized by "nieve" (snow), as in "nieve absoluta y primera" (absolute and first snow); by "luz" (light); and by "número" (number), as in "número sencillo" (simple number) and "número tan divino" (such a divine number). God also appears as "Total forma gozosa" (The total joyful form); "Presencia sin instante" (A presence without instant); "Amor sin determinaciones" (Love without resolve); "Advenir sosegado" (Quiet advent); and "Sosiego de mis ojos" (Tranquillity of my eyes).

The contrast of two dialectically opposed poles should be noted in Rosales's verse – a contrast also prevalent in the mystical love poetry of San Juan de la

los ojos juntos y apretados como dentro de un beso.
como dentro de un labio que estuviera estremeciéndoles
bajo una frente nueva cada día.
y vi que despertaba de algún dolor o de algún sueño
con la mirada titilante aun y restregándose los ojos
y entrecruzando la mirada con aquella sonrisa
que se borraba entre sus labios, que se escuchaba sonar aun sobre
　　　　　　　　　　　　　　　　　　　　　　　　sus labios.

igual que un paso que se aleja
y que se pierde al ser　~~sobre~~　la llusia.
Y la volví a mirar, y comprendí al mirarla.
que tras de su desnuda extensión de las aguas　todo estaba
　　　　　　　　　　　　　　　　　　　　　　　desierto

todo estaba vacío lo mismo que una máscara　que se empieza
　　　　　　　　　　　　　　　　　　　　　a dormir

y vi que el corazón parecía sonámbulo
y un poco más pequeño que la tristeza de un os
que la inútil que es anterior al hombre
que la inútil en que el muelle desierto comenzaba a vivir
　　　　　　　　　y se extendía

　　　　　¿Sabes?
　　　　~~Me~~ llamo Luis

Y todo se hacía, oral con su tristeza obra y ~~_____~~ huma-
　　　　　　　　　　mente canta mal del año nuevo

y todo se hacía lugo y hacía la juventud
de esas flores antiguas.
que al nombrarse despiertan súbitamente con aroma;
hacia la juventud de aquellos nombres que son tan solo nom
　　　　　　　　　　　　　　　　　　　　　bres
y sin embargo
al contemplarse juntos se encienden y se queman.

*Manuscript for a poem by Rosales (by permission of the Estate of Luis Rosales)*

Cruz (1542–1591). The bipolarities of opposites are designed to convey the integrating force of God: form without forms, presence without absence, light without shadows, and the present with no past. Above all, God is the symbol of perfection: the number one, the key to everything, the beginning and the end. Human love and religious wanting are fused in *Abril*.

Rosales's return to classical stanzas was more than a rebellion against the chaos of surrealism; it was accompanied by a refreshingly clean style of description. *Abril* was a dazzling milestone, the culmination of the battle between words and images. Rosales's visual poetry is loaded with flashes of sensuality: "Tengo una voz que se cubre de yerba donde / vuelan alondras y palabras y lágrimas" (I have a voice that is covered with grass where / larks and words and tears fly); "Ahora quiero decirte: / vivir es asombrarse / ante el cielo y la espiga y la brizna de hierba" (Now I want to tell you: / to live is to be amazed / in the presence of the sky and the spike and the grass string). After paying attention to the presence of small things, Rosales gives in to faith, which produces a certitude of contemplation: "Para tener confianza en mis sentidos, / para saber que escucho, siento, veo. / Sólo el milagro la fe transida" (In order to have trust in my senses, / in order to know that I listen, I feel, I see. / Only the miracle of torn faith).

The formal structure of *Abril* was studied by Antonio Sánchez Zamarreño. He has pointed out the predominance of adjectives describing amazement, sweetness, tenderness, religious experience, the external senses, and human emotions. Alliterations, transpositions, similes, and metaphors are plentiful and daring in *Abril*.

When he wrote *Abril*, Rosales was studying romance philology at the University of Madrid, and, like his friend Lorca, he returned to Granada in the summers. On 12 July 1936 Rosales's mother, after leaving his sister in a convent in Turin, Italy, traveled with him from Madrid to Granada. On that same day, the Republican guard José Castillo was shot in Madrid, and when Esperanza and Luis arrived in Granada, they found out that Antonio and José Rosales, Falangists since 1934, were fully involved in the approaching revolt. Their father never belonged to the party; their brother Miguel became a member of the party after the civil war started. The younger brother, Gerardo, a poet like Luis and the closest to his heart, did not join the Falangists, but Luis was later forced to join the party by the circumstances surrounding Lorca's death in August.

When Rosales arrived in Granada with his mother, he found the city in the fervor of the pre-civil-war revolution. On 13 July Lorca decided to travel to Granada, against the advice of his friends in Madrid. That night the monarchist Joaquín Calvo Sotelo was shot. On 20 July the revolt extended to Granada, and Lorca's brother-in-law, Manuel Fernández-Montesinos, who was the mayor of Granada, was taken prisoner along with other socialists. On 9 August a group of armed Nationalists broke into Lorca's house, insulted and beat him, and ordered him not to move from his house. Frightened by this violence, Lorca telephoned Rosales to come to his aid. Between 10 and 15 August, Lorca stayed at Rosales's house. He lived on the second floor and spent time correcting his sonnets, playing the piano, and reading poetry to the women of the house. During these days the Nationalists searched Lorca's house, looking for him. They destroyed his piano while searching for a clandestine radio transmitter. On 15 August the chief of police threatened to kill Lorca's father, and Lorca's sister, Conchita, told the chief that Lorca was at the home of Rosales. On 16 August, at dawn, Fernández-Montesinos was shot to death. In the early afternoon, after a huge showing of troops under the command of rightist leader Ramón Ruiz Alonso, Lorca was taken into custody.

When Rosales found out, he went to the civil governor's office with some of his brothers and a few armed Falangists to protest Lorca's detention. Rosales had a serious confrontation with Ruiz Alonso, who claimed that he alone was responsible for Lorca's plight. Rosales's father communicated to Lorca's father what had happened and suggested that he get a lawyer. That night Luis's brother José went to talk to the civil governor, Col. José Valdés Guzmán. The next day José Rosales obtained an order to free Lorca and went back to Valdés Guzmán, who told him that Lorca had already been executed (an apparent lie) and that Luis's life was also in danger. Lorca's servant, Angelina Cordobilla, claimed that she visited Lorca on 17 and 18 August and brought some food to him. According to her, Lorca was shot on 19 August in the early dawn near the road to Córdoba.

Between 17 and 27 August, Luis Rosales lived under house arrest and in danger of being shot until he was saved by Narciso Perales, a chief Falangist from Seville. Rosales was exonerated from all charges and offered a desk job with the Falangist party. He did not accept it. Instead he volunteered for the Falangist/Nationalist front in Pamplona. According to his friend Pedro Laín Entralgo, Rosales went to Pamplona to put a distance between himself and the assassination of Lorca.

*Luis Rosales*

In Pamplona, Rosales took refuge in his literary creativity. Between 1936 and 1940 he worked on poems that were to appear later in his books *Rimas* (Rhymes, 1951) and *Segundo abril* (Second April, 1972). The first poem he wrote after Lorca's death was "La voz de los muertos" (The Voice of the Dead, 1936). This long poem was conceived when Lorca was at Rosales's house in August. Lorca was thinking about their writing together an elegy to all the dead people of Spain; Lorca planned to write the music to accompany it. Rosales's poem, in Alexandrine verses without rhyme, appeared first in the journal *Jerarquía* (October 1937). The poem was popular during the war but was excluded from his books until it was revised and published in *Las puertas comunicantes* (The Communicating Gates, 1976), *Verso libre* (Free Verse, 1980), and the first volume of *Poesía reunida* (Collected Poetry, 1981, 1983). The poem is full of allusions to the devastation

of the war: "Es la voz de los muertos por la unidad del hombre, / tierra firme y promesa donde descansa España" (It is the voice of the dead for the unity of man / the firm ground and the promise where Spain rests).

In 1937 Rosales wrote the following poems: "Viento en la carne" (Wind in the Flesh), "Despertar en el frente" (Awakening on the Front), and "Ofrecimiento" (Offering). Of these only the last one appeared in the journal *Vértice* (August 1938). The other two were eventually published in *Rimas*. At the end of 1938 the collection "Los versos del combatiente" appeared. As a joke, Rosales put as the author the name of his brother José Rosales Camacho. Two-thirds of the thirty-nine poems were written by Luis Rosales; the rest were by Manuel Machado, Agustín de Foxá, José María Pemán, Vivanco, and Dionisio Ridruejo. Rosales also collaborated at this time on a sonnet to Falangist-party founder José Antonio Primo de Rivera: "Soneto a José Antonio que descubrió, expresó y defendió la verdad de España. Murió por ella" (A Sonnet to José Antonio Who Discovered, Expressed and Defended the Truth about Spain. He Died Because of It). At the end of this poem, Rosales speaks of the personal search for religious values and the defense of hope during difficult daily existence, themes he was to pursue in his later poetry.

Immediately after the civil war Rosales was involved in the foundation and direction of the journal *Escorial* (1940–1950) in Madrid. He was the secretary of a group led by Ridruejo and Laín Entralgo. They tried in the journal to revive the works of the Generation of '98 (especially those of Antonio Machado) and to translate into Spanish the poetry of Percy Bysshe Shelley, John Keats, Novalis, Rainer Maria Rilke (who greatly influenced the *Escorial* group), Gerard Manley Hopkins, and Friedrich Hölderlin. Although at times the journal seemed to ignore reality by negating history, in general the poets of this journal persisted in creating a personal, profound, and existential view of the world by using classical forms such as the sonnet. Rosales published most of the poetic prose of *El contenido del corazón* (The Content of the Heart) in *Escorial* during 1941 and 1942; the book itself was not published until 1969.

In December 1940 Rosales's second book of poems was published: *Retablo sacro del nacimiento del Señor* (Sacred Altarpiece of the Birth of Our Lord). Initially having only fifteen poems, it was revised to have thirty-one in 1964 and was again changed in 1981 (when included in *Poesía reunida*) to add eight more poems. In the first two versions, Rosales uses the theme of Christmas as a pretext to expand on existential preoccupations such as time and humankind's searching at night and finding nothing but grief:

> Somos hombres, Señor, y lo viviente
> ya no puede servirnos de semilla;
> entre un mar y otro mar no existe orilla;
> la misma voz que te canto miente ...
> Llegaremos de noche, y el helor
> de nuestra propia sangre te daremos.
> Este es nuestro regalo: no tenemos
> más que dolor, dolor, dolor, dolor

> (We are men, Lord, and living things
> cannot serve us by now as seed;
> between one ocean and another there are no shores;
> the same voice that I sing for you is lying ...
> We will arrive at night, and the smell
> of our own blood we shall give you.
> This is our gift: we do not have
> more than grief, grief, and grief upon grief )[.]

In the third version of the book more poems were included on the themes of death and time, as well as social preoccupations: the world was stricken by lies, by hate, by grief, and by material and spiritual poverty: "La tierra siente un profundo / estertor mortal y eterno. / No puede más. Hace invierno / y hace dolor sobre el mundo" (The earth feels a profound / mortal and eternal death rattle. / It cannot hold it any longer. It is winter / and there is nothing but grief all over the world).

With the publication of his next poetry collections, *Rimas* and *La casa encendida,* Rosales achieved the height of his fame and accomplishment. He started writing *Rimas* in 1937. It comprises forty-two poems, preceded by quotations from Antonio Machado, Miguel de Unamuno, Dámaso Alonso, Leopoldo Panero, and Vivanco. The first part of the book is based on a line from Garcilaso: "Juntos los dos en la memoria mía" (The two of us together in my memory). The second part is titled "La palabra del alma es la memoria" (The Word of the Soul Is Memory). The world appeared to Rosales to be floundering in ruins. Memories of the Spanish Civil War and of World War II forced him to appeal to Christ to restore order. In *Rimas* the symbol of the shipwreck alternates with the theme of the loss of childhood innocence, a paradise lost. Hence Rosales returns to the memory of his mother: "porque sólo me siento hombre cuando recuerdo su sonrisa" (I only feel like a man when I remember her smile). His mother is the umbilical cord that unites him with the outside world. The unity of the family is symbolized by the house: "La casa está mas junta que una lágrima" (The house is more together than a tear). Many of the poems are thematic variations of later ones collected in *La casa encendida.* In *Rimas* there are also apocalyptic visions of resurrected dead people holding hands and forming a chain around the world: "Y quizá irán creciendo unos dentro de otros, hasta formar un bosque silencioso, / un bosque de raíces que formarán un árbol único, / cuando llegue la noche" (And maybe they will grow some inside others, until they make a silent forest / a forest made out of roots that will form only one tree / when the night comes).

*La casa encendida* is made up of Rosales's condensation of thoughts that had appeared in *Rimas* and *El contenido del corazón.* Critics have been unanimous in pointing out that *La casa encendida* is one of the most important books of poetry published in Spain after the civil war. The book comprises a long poem (revised and enlarged in 1967), written without rhyme and with absolute freedom of form.

*Guests at a 1954 dinner honoring Jorge Guillén (seated fourth from left). Rosales is standing directly behind Guillén. Other guests include Gerardo Diego (seated on Guillén's right), Vicente Aleixandre (seated on Guillén's left), Luis Felipe Vivanco (standing on far right), and Dámaso Alonso (seated on far right).*

Time and memory take the poet back to his childhood in Granada, his house, his brothers, and his friends. The poem ends with hope and with the presence of a lover and the house illuminated by her.

The poem is divided into five parts. In the first one, by way of introduction, Rosales places humankind in a radical state of loneliness in which boredom, disintegration, and the awareness of fugacity crisscross to give the reader a vision of chaos. The influence of Rilke in this section is obvious. In the next three sections Rosales forms a unity with his memory (the past) and his hope (the future). A series of persons dear to him, dead and alive, appear in the poem.

In the epilogue (section 5) the house is presented with the lights on in all the rooms: "y al mirar hacia arriba, / vi iluminadas, obradoras, radiantes, estelares/ las ventanas / – sí, todas las ventanas – / Gracias, Señor, la casa está encendida" (And upon looking above / I saw the illuminated, working, radiant, stellar / windows / – yes, all the windows – / Thanks, Lord, the house is lighted). According to Rosales, only the light of love, family

memories, and God can console humankind and offer hope.

*Canciones* (Songs, 1973) includes ballads, songs, and popular sayings from Andalusia. This collection was written at Rosales's house in Cercedilla (1968–1972) and dedicated to Antonio Machado and Ramón Gómez de la Serna. There are 148 songs interspersed with long, somber poems about time, memory, violence, sickness, and death.

In the spring of 1979 Rosales's *Diario de una resurrección* (Diary of a Resurrection) was published. The thirty-seven poems are divided into two unequal sections (twenty-two in the first and fifteen in the second). Most of the poems were written in the summers of 1976, 1977, and 1978. All the themes of his poetry are represented in the book – humankind is surrounded by negative destructive forces: "Y no hay nada en la vida, / nada, / nada" (And there is nothing in life, / nothing, / nothing); death approaches as time passes (symbolized by a series of travels). Love and death are dialogical and interchangeable. Lovers in an embrace search for perpetuation but sense a communication with death: "¿No

*Rosales, circa 1987 (photograph by M. Duran)*

sientes tu presencia? / ¿no la oyes? / Se ha quedado sentada entre nosotros; / tal vez ya no se marche, / tal vez sólo podamos definirnos en su desolación" (Don't you feel its presence? / Don't you hear it? / It has stayed seated between us; / maybe it will not go away, / perhaps we will only be able to complete ourselves in its desolation). In another poem Rosales calls himself "un muerto prematuro" (a premature dead man) and later says he expects a normal death: "un beso para luego, / una mitigación bisbiseante, / una mano que me arregle la almohada" (A kiss for later on / a muttering mitigation / a hand that will fix my pillow). He wants to confront God face-to-face; God "es como un perro que me lame y me limpia la vida y las palabras" (is like a dog that licks me and cleans my life and my words).

Another theme is humankind's inability to live in peace. Violence, slander, indifference, corruption, and the pursuit of money are the big sins: "Seguimos andando durante toda nuestra vida para encontrar el Banco" (We continue walking throughout our whole life in order to find the Bank). Personal innocence should replace this collective evil, and love should be the spark that starts a resurrection. To Rosales, a woman's love was "agua originaria / la trama de los días" (primitive water / the weft of my days). Woman also represented a bridge he needed to establish harmony: "Trigo es mi voz cuando te nombra, trigo, / puente es mi cuerpo al abrazarte, puente" (Wheat is my voice when it mentions you, wheat, / bridge is my body upon embracing you, bridge).

Rosales also believed that freedom came from within and could preserve one's dignity. In his "Apuntes biográficos" in the journal *Anthropos* (June 1983) Rosales says, "Uno de los problemas capitales de nuestro tiempo: no hay libertad, no nos dejan elegir, sólo podemos optar, y nuestra libertad se encuentra presionada por la política, el poder, la prensa y todos los sistemas de presión, de opresión y de información. Nuestra vida es la resultante de esta interferencia" (One of the capital problems of our times: there is no freedom, they do not allow us to choose, we can only opt, and our freedom is pressed by politics, power, the press, and all kinds of pressure, oppression, and information. Our life is the result of that interference). The last lines of *Diario* warn the reader: "estas palabras ateridas, / estas palabras dichas en una calle inútil . . . / Si nadie las escucha, / paciencia" (These frozen words / these words spoken in a useless street . . . / If nobody listens to them / have patience).

In 1943 Rosales had participated in poetic recitals organized by the Aula de Cultura of the Delegación Provincial de Educación de Madrid for poets residing in the capital, a group that also included Gerardo Diego, Leopoldo Panero, Adriano del Valle, Vivanco, and others. Rosales's impact on the Generation of 1936 and post-civil-war poetry can be partially seen by the high level of his participation in literary journals, such as *Escorial, Sí, Estafeta Literaria, Cuadernos Hispanoamericanos* (which he directed from 1958 to 1965), *Garcilaso, Cuadernos de Agora, Espadaña, Isla, Platero, Ilíberis,* and *Molino de Papel.* His impact on these journals and on the younger generations of poets was substantial.

Rosales was elected to the Real Academia in 1962. During his career he received the following prizes: the Bonsoms (1960), the Nacional Miguel de Unamuno (1972), the José María Lacalle de Poesía (1975), the Mariano de Cavia, the Nacional de Literatura, and, finally, the Cervantes (1982). Two Latin-American Nobel Prize winners praised his poetry: Pablo Neruda and Octavio Paz.

In 1984 Luis Rosales had a stroke that left him almost unable to speak. His wife, María Fouz de Rosales, and his son, Luis Cristobal, took care of him during the last years of his life. On 20 October 1992 Rosales suffered a second stroke. He died on 24 October. He was buried in the town cemetery of Cercedilla, where he lived during his last years and of which he had written:

> Las noches de Cercedilla
> las llevo en mi soledad,
> y son ya la última linde
> que yo quisiera mirar.
> Quisiera morir un día
> mirando este cielo, y dar
> mi cuerpo a esta tierra que
> me ha dado libertad.
> Quisiera morir un día
> y ser tierra que pisar
> tierra en la tierra que sueño
> ya para siempre jamás.

> (The nights of Cercedilla
> I carry them in my solitude,
> and they are the last boundary
> that I would like to look at.
> I would like to die someday
> looking at these skies, and give
> my body to this land that
> has given me freedom.
> I would like to die someday
> and be land to be walked on
> land in the land I dream about
> now and forever more.)

## References:

Luis Joaquín Aduriz, "El contenido del corazón: Su significación filosófica," *Cuadernos Hispanoamericanos,* nos. 257–258 (May–June 1971): 542–552;

Dámaso Alonso, "Luis Rosales, la lírica barroca y los desengaños de imperio," in his *Del Siglo de Oro a este siglo de siglas* (Madrid: Gredos, 1962), pp. 78–89;

Alonso, "Unas palabras para Luis," *Cuadernos Hispanoamericanos,* nos. 257–258 (May–June 1971): 341–355;

José Luis Cano, "Carta de España. Un poeta en la Academia: Luis Rosales," *Asomante,* 3 (1964): 80–82;

Guido Castillo, "La poesía última de Luis Rosales," *Cuadernos Hispanoamericanos,* no. 299 (May 1975): 453–465;

Victor García de la Concha, "Luis Rosales: *Rimas* y *La casa encendida,*" in his *La poesía española de posguerra* (Madrid: Prensa Española, 1973), pp. 159–169;

Ian Gibson, *The Death of Lorca* (Chicago: J. Philip O'Hara, 1973);

Félix Grande, "Autobiografía: una biografía de Luis Rosales," *Anthropos,* 25, no. 3 (1983): 33–39;

Grande, *La Calumnia. De cómo a Luis Rosales, por defender a Federico García Lorca, lo persiguieron hasta la muerte* (Madrid: Mondadori, 1987);

Pedro Laín Entralgo, "Carta a Luis Rosales, amigo sesentón," *Cuadernos Hispanoamericanos,* nos. 257–258 (May–June 1971): 360–366;

Antonio Sánchez Zamarreño, *La poesía de Luis Rosales (1935–1980)* (Salamanca: Universidad de Salamanca, 1986);

Luis Felipe Vivanco, "La palabra encendida," *Cuadernos Hispanoamericanos,* 9 (May–June 1949): 723–733.

# Pedro Salinas

*(27 November 1891 – 4 December 1951)*

Kathryn G. McConnell
*Point Loma Nazarene College*

BOOKS: *Presagios* (Madrid: Indice, 1923 [i.e., 1924]);

*Víspera del gozo* (Madrid: Revista de Occidente, 1926);

*Seguro azar* (Madrid: Revista de Occidente, 1929);

*Fábula y signo* (Madrid: Plutarco, 1931);

*La voz a ti debida* (Madrid: Aguirre, 1933); translated by Willis Barnstone as *My Voice Because of You* (Albany: SUNY Press, 1976);

*Razón de amor* (Madrid: Cruz & Raya, 1936);

*Error de cálculo* (Mexico City: Fábula/Lira, 1938);

*Literatura española, siglo XX* (Mexico City: Séneca, 1941; revised edition, Mexico City: Antigua Librería Robredo, 1949);

*Poesía junta* (Buenos Aires: Losada, 1942);

*Aprecio y defensa del lenguaje* (Río Piedras: Universidad de Puerto Rico, 1944);

*El contemplado: Tema con variaciones* (Mexico City: Stylo, 1946); translated by Eleanor L. Turnbull as *Sea of San Juan: A Contemplation* (Boston: Humphries, 1950);

*La poesía de Rubén Darío* (Mexico City: Séneca, 1946; revised edition, Buenos Aires: Losada, 1948);

*Jorge Manrique; o, tradición y originalidad* (Buenos Aires: Sudamericana, 1947);

*El defensor* (Bogotá: Universidad Nacional, 1948);

*Todo más claro, y otros poemas* (Buenos Aires: Sudamericana, 1949);

*La bomba increíble* (Buenos Aires: Sudamericana, 1950);

*El desnudo impecable y otras narraciones* (Mexico City: Tezontle, 1951);

*Teatro: La cabeza de Medusa: La estratoesfera: La isla del teatro* (Madrid: Insula, 1952);

*Poemas escogidos,* edited by Jorge Guillén (Buenos Aires: Espasa-Calpe, 1953);

*Confianza: Poemas inéditos (1942-1944),* edited by Guillén and Juan Marichal (Madrid: Aguilar, 1955);

*El romancismo y el siglo XX* (Paris: Espagnoles, 1955);

*Poesías completas,* edited by Juan Marichal (Madrid: Aguilar, 1955); enlarged edition, edited by Soledad Salinas de Marichal (Barcelona: Seix Barral, 1971; enlarged again, 1981);

*Teatro completo,* edited by Marichal (Madrid: Aguilar, 1957);

*Volverse sombra y otros poemas,* edited by Marichal (Milan: Scheiwiller, 1957);

*Ensayos de literatura hispánica, "Cantar de Mío Cid" a García Lorca,* edited by Marichal (Madrid: Aguilar, 1958);

*Amor, mundo en peligro* (Milan: Scheiwiller, 1958);

*La responsabilidad del escritor,* edited by Marichal (Barcelona: Seix Barral, 1961);

*Futuros* (Boston: Salinas & Marichal, 1962);

*Poemas* (Medellín: Horizonte, 1963);

*Poesía* (Havana: Consejo Nacional de Cultura, 1966); revised by Julio Cortázar (Madrid: Alianza, 1971);

*La poesía,* edited by Julio García Morejón (São Paulo: Universidade de São Paulo, 1969);

*Narrativa completa* (Barcelona: Barral, 1976);

*La realidad y el poeta* (Barcelona: Ariel, 1976);

*Aventura poética* (Madrid: Cátedra, 1980);

*Ensayos completos* (Madrid: Taurus, 1983).

**Editions in English:** *Lost Angel and Other Poems,* translated by Eleanor L. Turnbull (Baltimore: Johns Hopkins Press, 1938);

*Reality and the Poet in Spanish Poetry,* translated by Edith Fishtine Helman (Baltimore: Johns Hopkins Press, 1940);

*Truth of Two and Other Poems,* translated by Turnbull (Baltimore: Johns Hopkins Press, 1940);

*Zero,* translated by Turnbull (Baltimore: Contemporary Poetry, 1947);

*To Live in Pronouns: Selected Poetry,* translated by Helman and Norma Farber (New York: Norton, 1974).

OTHER: Juan Meléndez Valdés, *Poesías,* edited, with a prologue and notes, by Salinas (Madrid: Lectura, 1925);

Fray Luis de Granada, *Maravilla del mundo,* selected, with a prologue and notes, by Salinas (Mexico City: Arbol/Séneca, 1936);

San Juan de la Cruz, *Poesías completas,* edited, with a prologue and notes, by Salinas (Madrid: Signo, 1936).

TRANSLATIONS: Alfred de Musset, *Los caprichos de Mariana y otras comedias* (Madrid: Clásica Española, 1920);

Marcel Proust, *A la sombra de las muchachas en flor* (Madrid: Espasa-Calpe, 1922);

El Cid Campeador, *Poema de mío Cid* (Madrid: Revista de Occidente, 1926);

Proust, *En busca del tiempo perdido* (Buenos Aires: Rueda, 1944).

Though a renowned literary critic, essayist, university professor, translator, fiction writer, and dramatist, Pedro Salinas is best remembered as the eldest and most versatile member of the acclaimed "Generation of 1927," a group of poets who flourished in Spain from 1920 to 1936. The ultimate goal of the group was to renovate the poetical scene by fusing current European literary trends with Spain's literary heritage. In the 1920s that task was accomplished by poetry with complex images, metaphors, and synesthesia and by postulating a bias for a pure conceptual art lacking in emotional overtones — such as that espoused by the ultraists and French symbolists. The group of poets who idolized the Spanish baroque poet Luis de Góngora, regarded as an exponent of excessively ornate poetry, further provided the impetus for the creation of a "pure poetry" based on concrete reality and for the adaptation of classical and popular forms characteristic of Spain's Golden Age. The 1930s saw a significant change in the generation's philosophical tone: there was a loss of optimism; an inward withdrawal intended to balance the external world; and, with the signs of imminent civil war, a need to deal with humankind in its historical circumstances.

Born in Madrid on 27 November 1891, Salinas lived on Don Pedro Street near the main square and mercantile center of the city. Close by, his father, Pedro Salinas Elmas, ran a small general store on Esparteo Street. Young Pedro's delicate health and the premature death of his father in 1899 forced him into a sheltered and solitary life-style, during which his mother, Soledad Serrano Fernández de Salinas, overprotected him and allowed him little time with other children, thus inadvertently planting the seed for the development of his imaginative and creative abilities. His formal education began in 1897 at the Colegio Hispano-Francés, where he learned French and from which he graduated in 1903. In 1908 he earned his secondary degree from the Instituto San Isidro and then enrolled in Madrid's Central University as a law student, but he later changed direction and graduated with a licentiate in letters in 1913.

In his early university years Salinas attended Madrid's Ateneo library to spend long hours reading, where he met Enrique Díez-Canedo, a modernist poet from the "Generation of '98," who probably first introduced him to modern French literature. That experience, coupled with the 1911 appearance of Salinas's first poems in *Prometeo* — a literary magazine directed by Ramón Gómez de la Serna — and a short stay in Paris in 1912 to study art history, began to impress upon Salinas his literary calling. Shortly thereafter he began translating works by various French poets, and his versions were included in a 1914 volume edited by Díez-Canedo: *La poesía francesa moderna* (Modern French Poetry). While working on his doctorate, Salinas taught as a lecturer in Spanish literature at the Sorbonne (1914–1917), where he met French Hispanists Mathilde Pomés and Jean Cassou and the symbolist and proponent of pure poetry Paul Valéry. This period also included his 1915 marriage to Margarita Bonmatí — whom he had met in Santa Pola, a small Mediterranean Spanish village — and the completion of his doctoral thesis, "Las ilustraciones del 'Quijote'" in 1916.

Shortly after his return to Spain, Salinas accepted a professorship at the University of Seville in 1919; he remained there until 1928. It was there that he firmed up friendships with two members of his generation: Jorge Guillén, whose inti-

mate friendship with Salinas lasted thirty years and who replaced Salinas both at the Sorbonne and at Seville; and Luis Cernuda (then a student at Seville), for whom Salinas provided advice and professorial tutelage. Years later, after Salinas's death, Guillén fondly remembered his friend as a gentle and modest man whose zest and fascination for life was contagious. Guillén once called Salinas the "niño-poeta" (child-poet) because of his affinity for toys and gadgets, his natural curiosity that caused him to surround himself with quotidian life, and his childlike exuberance demonstrated when it was announced that dessert would be served at the end of a meal. That profile has been reiterated by Salinas's daughter, Solita, born in 1920, who has said that he showered her and her younger brother, Jaime (born in 1925), with toys with which their father would play for hours. She also notes his modesty, in that he never spoke about his work while at home, and even though many members of his generation would come to the house for poetry readings, she was not aware as a young girl that her father himself was a poet.

A flurry of activity always seemed to accompany Salinas during the Seville era, for among other things, he collaborated with the literary magazines, *España, La Pluma,* and the *Revista de Occidente,* did translations of works by Alfred de Musset and Marcel Proust, and completed his first novel, *Víspera del gozo* (On The Eve of Joy), in 1926. Most important, however, Salinas initiated his first major poetical phase, which lasted from 1923 through 1931 and was crystallized in three major works: *Presagios* (Presages) in 1924, *Seguro azar* (Steadfast Chance) in 1929, and *Fábula y signo* (Fable and Sign) in 1931. These first books form a unit, fundamentally experimental in nature, that deals progressively with Salinas's philosophy on the proper function of poetry and its relationship to the poet and to humankind. For him, the poet must transform external reality by internalizing and reshaping it into a newer and purer vision so that it may be preserved within a collective unconsciousness for present and future generations.

While on leave from his professorial duties at Seville and lecturing as a visiting professor of Spanish literature at England's Cambridge University, Salinas published his first book of verses, *Presagios,* the culmination of a work begun in 1915. The title suggests an allusion to the false appearance of reality and a prediction of a deeper significance behind superficial appearances. It also alludes to themes that were to grow and blossom into more mature ideas in later works by Sali-

*Federico García Lorca, Salinas, and Rafael Alberti in 1927*

nas. Loosely structured and without individual titles, the most characteristic trait of the book is that
the poet is always on the edge of the inner and
outer worlds of reality. Although he sees that tan-
gible reality and awareness of its temporal and
spatial circumstances are the basic ingredients for
a work of art, the appearances of the material
world are illusive and confusing. Thus it is tempting for the poet to remain in his inner world,
where reality is not constantly changing, but he
must break out in order to link material objects
into a chain forming a meaningful and creative
whole.

Presagios reflects some of the most varied stylistic techniques gleaned from Spanish literary
heritage. Evident are the themes and forms employed by Spanish Golden Age poets such as
Góngora, Pedro Calderón de la Barca, and Fray
Luis de León and more-modern poets, including
Gustavo Adolfo Bécquer and Juan Ramón Jimé-

nez. However, in contrast to the poetry of his colleagues, Salinas did not depend as much on tradition and has been viewed more as a poet who
avoided, to a great degree, the baroque influences
of complex imagery and metaphorical composition and the modernist emphasis on rhyme and musicality.

As examples of early literary tradition Presagios includes nine poems from the popular romantic mode depicting unobtainable love, a
theme that is more dominant in Salinas's mature
works of the 1930s. Stylistically simple and expressed in a conversational style, the frustration
of unrequited love is expressed in the fifth poem,
where the speaker accuses his lover of coming and
going at her whim and says that her presence and
absence are merely shadows of each other. Physical possession of the beloved is an impossibility,
and images of darkness show a sense of emptiness
and confusion.

Whereas in *Presagios* Salinas grapples mainly with the discovery and understanding of objects in their environment, in *Seguro azar,* written between 1924 and 1928, he begins to suggest the possibility of a metamorphosis of material matter into what he called a "transrealidad" (transreality). The potential transformation takes place within the imagination and is demonstrated in the poem "Vocación." Worldly perfection, seen with one's eyes open, seems complete in itself, but it is ruled by secrets which are deceptive and illusive, whereas closing one's eyes reveals an imperfect and somewhat chaotic scene waiting for someone to give it order. The poet, then, chooses to close his eyes so he can transform and enrich the world by giving it his new perspective, which ultimately enters into the collective unconscious.

Many of the poems in *Seguro azar* were inspired by modern inventions and evoke the spirit of the generation in terms of its ultraist tendencies during the 1920s. Because of Salinas's love of progress and his natural interest in the technology of machines and gadgets, several of his verses take commonplace objects and present them in new and unusual ways. The result is a poetry that is, at times, ironic but that is essentially upbeat. The objects are reduced to pure geometric lines, as in a cubist painting, so that only their essential properties are revealed, and the use of conjugated verbs and connectives is limited, thus further accentuating the static quality of the objects.

Three poems exhibiting these characteristics are "Navacerrada, abril" (Navacerrada, April), "35 bujías" (35 Candelas), and "Cinematógrafo" (Cinematograph). The first two of these exhibit a strong sense of irony: an automobile and a light are personified as the poet's lovers. "Navacerrada, abril" begins with the line "Los dos solos" (The two of us alone). Subsequent verses lead the reader through the description of a mountain pass and the adventure and exhilaration inspired within the speaker by the natural beauty he sees. That ineffable experience is abruptly contrasted with the prosaic reality of the starting of the car engine, the "aventura de arranque eléctrico" (the adventure of an electrical impulse). With the speaker's spirit and the physical strength of the car's twelve-horsepower engine, the abstract and concrete are joined so that a great endeavor is shared. Equally ironic is "35 bujías," in which the speaker describes his lover, a light, as an artificial princess imprisoned in a crystal castle above him; he can free her by turning on the light switch. She then surrounds him with her warm seductive rays while doubling as a poetic muse who illuminates him in the darkness of the night.

"Cinematógrafo" has a more serious tone and leads readers into the imaginary world of the cinema. The poem is divided into two sections — "Luz" (Light) and "Oscuridad" (Darkness). The first delineates the limited world of the protagonists, circumscribed by the precise measurements of the movie screen. In geometrical terms the screen is described as four straight lines, two horizontal and two vertical, into which is shone the light of the projector. The images reveal a false and deceptive reality, one that lasts only as long as the machine projects its image. Hope returns in the second part, when the light is extinguished and the protagonists are left in pure darkness, where they are released from the strictures of time and space imposed by the screen and the image it reflects. Consistent with Salinas's philosophy, outward appearances are not what they might seem, while darkness provides the opportunity for each individual to become a kind of cameraman in the creation of his own reality.

In 1928, three years before the publication of *Fábula y signo,* Salinas decided to vacate his post at the University of Seville to take a position as a researcher for Madrid's Center for Historical Studies, where he headed the summer-school program for foreign-exchange students. He also accepted a professorship in 1930 at the Central School for Languages, where he remained until his 1936 departure for the United States. In the spring of 1931 he published the last book of his experimental phase. The material object reaches its least stable form in *Fábula y signo,* and the implied message of the title is manifested as Salinas interprets the material world and recreates it with more-imaginative overtones by utilizing his intuitive process, thereby creating new myths and rendering life with less exactitude.

Fluctuating between the real and the imagined are three poems dealing with El Escorial, an austere and ominous monastery/palace built in the sixteenth century by King Philip II. "Escorial I" emphasizes the building's stability by referring to its dimensions, age, and strong granite composition. The dreams and memories of the past are frozen and unable to escape from within its severe lines of formation. "Escorial II" defines the proportions; there is nothing left to the imagination with regard to accurate measurements, the number of windows, and the time of day that the

*Pedro Salinas*

speaker is observing the building. Time is symbolized by the striking of twelve bells. Consequently both time and space are reduced to mathematical formulas. However, in "Jardín de los frailes" (Garden of the Friars) the building is transformed by a new picture emerging from a nearby pool. A mirror image is not produced because the gentle summer breezes ripple the water, changing the straight lines of the walls to lines that are more curved and subtle like a living body, thus destroying the rigidity and adding a magical and human touch to the scene. The speaker commends the building for having escaped its geometrical destiny and for releasing its soul from its cadaverous frame by way of the reflecting pool.

In addition to treating themes related to the creative process, Salinas also shows his interest in modern technical progress, as well as touching on themes of unrequited love. Machines, such as a radiator in "Radiator y fogata" (Radiator and Bonfire) and a telephone in "El teléfono," share in the experi-

ences of the poet, while the typewriter in "Underwood Girls" is hailed for its partnership in the creative process of writing. Ironically Salinas finds that love is more compatible with machines than with human lovers. His basic message about love in many of the poems is one of total disillusionment, separation, and estrangement from the beloved. He becomes more hopeful in his next stage of writing.

Salinas's second cycle of poems encompasses the years 1933 to 1938, and critics have agreed that this period represents the high point of his career. Not only had he achieved his best poetical style, but he continued to occupy important administrative university positions. In 1933 he inaugurated the International Summer University at Santander, a school supported by the government of the Second Spanish Republic. Salinas conceived of this school as a university whose goals were not particularly utilitarian but whose international professoriat would seek to attend to the spiritual needs of its two hundred students. The experiment came to a sud-

*Drawing of Salinas by Gregorio Prieto (from Prieto's* Lorca y la generación
del '27, *1977)*

den end in 1936, when the Spanish Civil War began, forcing him to embark for the United States. Erroneously believing the war would last only a year, he accepted a position at Wellesley College in Massachusetts for the fall of 1936 and a visiting professorship at Johns Hopkins University in Baltimore for the spring of 1937. At Johns Hopkins he occupied the distinguished Turnbull Chair of Poetry, an honor previously bestowed upon only one other Spaniard: Ramón Menéndez Pidal.

Amid the turmoil leading to the war and his exile, Salinas began his great epoch of love poetry. Within six years he produced a trilogy of books, which, considered as a whole, form a spiritual unit outlining the various stages of love. The first book, *La voz a ti debida* (1933; translated as *My Voice Because of You,* 1976), presents some of the most lyrical, subjective, and intimate expressions of love in Spanish love poetry. Such emotional depth shocked the public and critics alike, for his previous works had not

prepared the public for the disarming and touching myriad of personal revelations that abounded. *Razón de amor* (Love's Reason) was published in 1936, and "Largo lamento" (Long Lament) was completed in 1938 but not published until its inclusion in the 1971 edition of Salinas's *Poesías completas.* These three collections made a significant contribution, along with the works of Vicente Aleixandre, Rafael Alberti, and Cernuda, to a modern resurgence of traditional love themes within Spanish literature.

Some of the first poems of *La voz a ti debida* appeared in February 1933 under the title "Amor en vilo" (Love Unbound) in *Los Cuatro Vientos,* a literary magazine edited by Salinas and some of his friends. The subsequent publication of the completed text that same year and of the following work, *Razón de amor,* three years later has created divergent opinions concerning the meaning and structure of the love cycle manifested in the two books.

Perhaps the biggest questions focus on the narrative structure, the veracity of the love experience itself, and the authenticity of the speaker's beloved. Early critics such as Leo Spitzer and Pierre Darmangeat argued that the poems are merely meditations on love and that the experience is a conceptualized mind game in which the beloved functions as an alter ego for the poet. However, more-recent critics, including R. G. Harvard and Julian Palley, have disagreed, stating that a love narrative exists and that the beloved is verisimilar but that discretion on the part of Salinas makes the poetry transcend his personal experience, thus making a general statement on the perplexing and delicate nature of love.

In the first and most important book of the trilogy, *La voz a ti debida,* the narrative structure can be divided into four parts tracing the different stages of a love story. It begins with the discovery of love, followed by the fullness of the experience as expressed in part 2. Readers witness the lovers' estrangement and separation in the third section, and, to conclude, the speaker examines his lost paradise while seeking to resolve his pain by internalizing his grief. As a consequence, he reappraises the situation and finds new meaning in the power of love by redefining it as a Platonic ideal and eternal force which, when coupled with the poet's pen, forges its own reality.

The beloved is a human being, a poetic muse, and a medium through which the poet's ideas are symbolized. She is described in the vaguest terms with no mention of names; she is only referred to by the intimate second-person-singular pronoun *tú* (thou). Physically she is sensuous and alluring, and Salinas emphasizes her "tierno cuerpo rosado" (tender rose-colored body) and states that "me sobran los ojos y los labios" (your lips and eyes overwhelm me). Youth as an archetypal symbol of power is established in the early stages of the story, when the beloved is described as a young woman of boundless light and energy whose vitality contrasts with the older speaker, portrayed as "sombra" (darkness), who is invisible and stagnant. He is acutely aware of his vulnerability when he refers to her age as an "arma de veinte años" (twenty-year-old weapon). Nevertheless, her tender age also underlines her imperfect development, impulsiveness, lack of experience, and insensitivity, which the speaker resents and criticizes during the departure scene. His age and maturity contrast sharply with her immaturity, but, fearing he might offend her, he apologizes for looking for more depth in her character, for his only intention is to discover the best she has to offer. As an older mentor and lover, he vacillates

in his attitude toward her, at times captivated by her youth and provocative beauty and then censorious of her levity.

One of the central metaphors is attained by the juxtaposition and blending of the beloved's antithetical powers. As a positive force, she represents both universal and personal creativity. Universally she symbolizes the mother of life in an Edenic garden on earth. In "¡Qué gran víspera del mundo!" (On the Eve of the Great Creation!) the beloved becomes a cosmic force in the creation of the world: at her whim all comes into being, and she literally provides and sustains life. Personally her love is the power behind the poet's inspiration; it is a catalyst unleashing his creative impulses and leading him out of his darkness. On the contrary, when estrangement and separation occur, his perception changes so that she becomes a threatening universal force and personally does not meet his specific needs, nor is she capable of true love. Consequently she exists on two planes, as a universal symbol of love, creation, and destruction but, at the same time, as a creature who offers herself physically, effecting a blending of concrete and abstract symbols. In the final moments he realizes that the dream as it existed is dead and that all that is left is the shadow of love, but, contrary to Salinas's earlier works, hope remains in his ability to re-create through his poetry a new and positive reality in the midst of his personal darkness.

*Razón de amor* cannot be totally seen as a separate work, for it continues many of the same themes and resolves some of the issues introduced in the first book of the trilogy, but it never gains the intensity of *La voz. Razón de amor* is divided into two parts and is narratively linked to the first book. While the Garden of Eden myth is repeated, the garden is closed to the two lovers, and the alternation between Salinas's positive attitude toward love and his sense of loss and grief persists. However, the lover's power now transcends present reality, and she imbues even the most trivial objects with new meaning. Living in her "transreality," he gains a new perspective on life. In turn, his poetry takes on new significance as it is assimilated by a "great silent love" symbolized by the water and the sea. Ultimately he finds the salvation of his love for her, for he sacrifices his individual happiness just as a single river flows into the ocean, bonding all waters together and subsequently creating a perfect, harmonious whole. As a result he regains his lost paradise by sacrificing his personal love to a more meaningful and lasting experience, one which will en-

*A group of writers: (in front) Salinas, Ignacio Sánchez Mejías, and Jorgé Guillén; (in back) Antonio Marichalar, José Bergamín, Corpus Barga, Vicente Aleixandre, García Lorca, and Dámaso Alonso*

dure for future generations. Similar themes are reiterated and summarized in the second part of *Razón de amor* so that what is attained at the end is a humanitarian philosophy founded on love and sacrifice. Indeed, the use of the symbolic elements of water as salvation foreshadows themes in his latter poetry.

Salinas's last cycle of works coincides with his years of exile in the United States, 1936–1951. These were his most productive years as a writer, during which he generated poetry, literary criticism, a novel, short stories, and several plays. His most important literary criticism is *Reality and the Poet in Spanish Poetry* (published in English in 1940). Gleaned from lectures at Johns Hopkins University, the work elucidates Salinas's ideas on the poet's duty with regard to the function of poetry. To illustrate, he demonstrates the themes of six major Spanish works and the attitude that each author displays toward reality. Although a lucrative time professionally, this exile was a difficult time for Salinas, for although he was with his family, he suffered immense loneliness and isolation from his friends and homeland. As a personal catharsis, Salinas expressed his nostalgia in his plays, and, on a practical

level, he gathered with many of Spain's expatriates at Vermont's Middlebury College, where, beginning in 1937, he directed an exceptional center for language studies during the summer months.

Ten years elapsed in the United States before Salinas began publishing his last major poetry volumes: *El contemplado* (1946; translated as *Sea of San Juan: A Contemplation,* 1950), *Todo más claro* (All Things Clearer, 1949), and *Confianza* (Confidence), published posthumously in 1955. These three works attest to his basic affirmation of life but also to his disappointment with modern society.

Perhaps Salinas's happiest years in the United States were at the University of Puerto Rico in Río Piedras, where he taught from 1943 to 1946. This small island provided him an illusion of his homeland, for it alleviated his sense of linguistic isolation and allowed him to renew old friendships. It also reminded him of vacations spent on the Spanish Mediterranean coast during his early married years. Cheerfully he passed his afternoons teaching and his mornings at the Afda Club, where he was able to contemplate the beautiful ocean while writing *El contemplado*. In this work Salinas sees the poet and the ocean as a symbiotic pair, with humankind look-

*Pedro Salinas*

ing to the ocean for the secret of existence. Through this balance of the outer and inner worlds of reality — vision followed by introspection — a person can find his or her true essence and connect with those who have contemplated the ocean in past generations. The sea serves as a guide, a mentor, and a substitute for the physical lover in *La voz a ti debida;* the sea is the ultimate confidant, symbolic of a spiritualized salvation.

Structurally *El contemplado* is composed of fourteen titled sections characterizing different views of the ocean and two main protagonists, the poet and the sea. However, the sky and light perpetuate a poetic miracle, too. Light makes vision possible, while the interplay and fusion of colors of the heavens and water blend them into a cosmic unity. Within this articulated whole can be found four planes. The first level is the concrete, which includes the clouds, waters, waves, and beaches. The second plane is composed of a metaphorical reality, transforming the material objects of the first into a magical and

atemporal world. The third is that of man's interior world, manifested through a series of links between the ocean and conscience; and the fourth is represented by a spiritual reality in which the ocean symbolizes eternity.

Within the second level is included a poem rich in metaphorical material — "Primavera diaria" (Daily Spring) — in which the dawn of each day represents a continuous spring. Dawn is a symbolic worker whose planting is rewarded daily by a beautiful garden. Concrete objects, such as the foamy waves, are transformed by twilight's blush so they appear like red flower petals washing up on the beach. The idea of this magical and atemporal garden is further exemplified by words such as *florecer* (to flower), *campos* (fields), and *tallos impacientes* (impatient stems). Typical of the third level of poetry is "Todo se aclara" (Everything Becomes Clearer), in which there are links between dawn's darkened horizon and vague thoughts within the speaker's mind. Momentary clarity appears symbolically in the form of lightning flashes, but with the rising of the sun the conscience becomes illuminated. Thus the ocean provides intuition, a function the narrator had previously assigned to himself. "Presagio" is characteristic of the fourth level. By contemplating the sea, the poet arrives at a kind of mystical union in which one becomes the other. This intertwining foreshadows the spiritual salvation alluded to in the last poem, "Salvación por la luz" (Salvation by Light), which summarizes Salinas's ultimate profession of faith in the sea as a repository joining human feelings with the beauty of nature. The poem's speaker finds that he can bond all humanity and find salvation by accepting the perfection of the sea's reality.

With his return to Johns Hopkins, Salinas found that his depression increased, and his preoccupation with modern society's mechanization overwhelmed him, especially when coupled with the tragic events of the Spanish Civil War and World War II. As a consequence, in *Todo más claro* readers witness the tragedy of contemporary man, whose moral blindness, produced by technology, ultimately manifests itself in the destruction of humanity. These themes are later reiterated in Salinas's 1950 novel, *La bomba increíble* (The Incredible Bomb).

Thirteen sections make up *Todo más claro*, with some broken into smaller parts. The technology and gadgetry with which Salinas was fascinated in his first poetic works have taken on a nightmarish quality, so that material objects become stumbling blocks to the perception of a true reality and create feelings of alienation and despair. Cars streaming by in "El inocente" (The Innocent One), in New York's frenetic metropolis, terrify the protagonist, while revelations into the world of the drivers disclose evidence of economic enslavement. In "Pasajero en museo" (Museum Passenger) there is a slight relief for the speaker when he takes refuge in the aesthetic corners of the city, the museums. Like the sea, the beauty of the works of art is interpreted as a way of transcending material existence, time, and space by bonding with those who have previously viewed the works. Aside from this small retreat, all has become transitory and base.

The culminating blow is the disaster of war, as seen in "Cero" (translated and published separately as *Zero*, 1947) – the longest poem in the text. First published in 1944 in the Mexican magazine *Cuadernos Hispanoamericanos*, it offers an unsettling prophecy of the Hiroshima bombing, which occurred only a few months later. The poem, di-

vided into five sections, describes the bombing of a fictitious city by a pilot who, having been victimized by a mechanized society, is indifferent to the suffering he causes. The result of the bombing is a *cero* which settles over the *nada* (nothingness), and dust rises from the forest of ruins. The speaker, symbolically a shadow of what existed, looks for some salvation but finds none. The material things, the basis for poetry, have been obliterated along with nature's beauty and humankind's connection to the past, and all that is left is the howling sound of a dog looking for his master.

In *Confianza* Salinas returns to his faith in humankind's continuance. The book was actually one of the first ones he wrote in exile, in 1942, but for some reason it was left untitled and unpublished until after Salinas's death, and, because the order of the poems was not arranged by the poet, some of its critical merit has been overlooked. However, the overall effect of the poems, mostly made up of nature poetry, expresses Salinas's final acceptance of the material world in communion with nature. The role of poetry, again, offers a spiritual solution to the problems of mechanized society. The final poem, "Confianza," attests to Salinas's basically positive outlook on life and his acceptance of reality by stating, "Mientras hay lo que hubo ayer, lo que hay hoy, lo que venga" (As long as there is something of what was yesterday, what there is today, will be what may come tomorrow).

Those hopeful lines express Salinas's desire to continue to create and redefine reality so that something will be left for future generations. Even in the last few months of his life, after his bone cancer was diagnosed, he moved to a flat overlooking the Charles River in Boston, Massachusetts, where he continued to write until he lost the use of his right arm. On 4 December 1951 he died in Massachusetts General Hospital, after which his body was taken to his beloved Puerto Rico and interred in the Santa Magdalena Cemetery in San Juan, next to the endearing ocean that gave him so many hours of happiness. His life was an integrated whole, for he knew how to fuse life, destiny, vocation, acts, and works, a veritable hallmark of a great artist.

**Letters:**
*Cartas de amor a Margarita,* edited by Solita Salinas de Marichal (Madrid: Alianza, 1984).

**References:**
Dámaso Alonso, "Con Pedro Salinas," in his *Poetas españoles contemporáneos* (Madrid: Gredos, 1978), pp. 189–200;

José Luis Cano, *La poesía de la generación del 27* (Madrid: Guadarrama, 1973), pp. 11–24, 52–58;

Joaquín Casalduero, "La creación poética de Pedro Salinas," *Cuadernos Hispanoamericanos,* 431 (May 1986): 103–117;

Gustavo Correa, "*El Contemplado,*" *Hispania,* 35 (May 1952): 137–142;

Olga Costa Viva, *Pedro Salinas frente a la realidad* (Madrid: Alfaguara, 1969);

John Crispin, *Pedro Salinas* (New York: Twayne, 1974);

Carlos Feal Deibe, *La poesía de Pedro Salinas* (Madrid: Gredos, 1965);

Joaquín González Muela, "Poesía y amistad: Jorge Guillén y Pedro Salinas," *Bulletin of Hispanic Studies,* 35 (1958): 28–33;

Jorge Guillén, "Elogio de Pedro Salinas," in *Pedro Salinas: Colección el escritor y la crítica,* edited by Andrew P. Debicki (Madrid: Taurus, 1976), pp. 26–33;

R. G. Harvard, "Pedro Salinas and Courtly Love. The 'amada' in *La voz a ti debida*: Woman, Muse, and Symbol," *Bulletin of Hispanic Studies,* 56 (1979): 123–144;

Juan Marichal, *Tres voces de Pedro Salinas* (Madrid: Taller de Ediciones, 1976);

Kathryn G. McConnell, "The Poet in 'La voz a ti debida': A Life in Transition," *Mester,* 14 (Spring 1985): 20–28;

C. B. Morris, *A Generation of Spanish Poets 1920–1936* (Cambridge: Cambridge University Press, 1969), pp. 1–44, 84–170;

Julian Palley, "*Presagios* de Pedro Salinas," in *Pedro Salinas: Colección el escritor y la crítica,* pp. 99–107;

Palley, "*La voz a ti debida*: An Appreciation," *Hispania,* 40 (December 1957): 450–455;

Angel del Río, "El poeta Pedro Salinas," in *Pedro Salinas: Colección el escritor y al crítica,* pp. 15–23;

Solita Salinas de Marichal, "Recuerdo de mi padre," in *Pedro Salinas: Colección el escritor y la crítica,* pp. 35–40;

José Vila Selma, *Pedro Salinas* (Madrid: Españoles, 1972).

# Ramón del Valle-Inclán

*(28 October 1866 – 5 January 1936)*

Kathryn G. McConnell
*Point Loma Nazarene College*

BOOKS: *Femeninas: Seis historias amorosas* (Pontevedra: Landín, 1895);

*Epitalamio: Historia de amores* (Madrid: Marzo, 1897);

*Cenizas* (Madrid: Rodríguez y Perma, 1899);

*Sonata de otoño: Memorias del marqués de Bradomín* (Madrid: Pérez, 1902);

*Corte de amor: Florilegio de honestas y nobles damas* (Madrid: Marzo, 1903);

*Jardín umbrío* (Madrid: Rodríguez Serra, 1903);

*Sonata de estío: Memorias del marqués de Bradomín* (Madrid: Marzo, 1903);

*Flor de santidad: Historia milenaria* (Madrid: Marzo, 1904);

*Sonata de primavera: Memorias del marqués de Bradomín* (Madrid: Marzo, 1904);

*Sonata de invierno: Memorias del marqués de Bradomín* (Madrid: Archivos, Bibliotecas y Museos, 1905);

*Jardín novelesco: Historias de santos, de almas en pena, de duendes y de ladrones* (Madrid: Archivos, Bibliotecas y Museos, 1905; enlarged edition, Barcelona: Maucci, 1908);

*Aguila de blasón: Comedia bárbara dividida en cinco jornadas* (Barcelona: Granada, 1907);

*Aromas de leyenda: Versos en loor de un santo ermitaño* (Madrid: Villavicencio, 1907);

*El marqués de Bradomín: Coloquios románticos* (Madrid: Pueyo, 1907);

*Historias perversas* (Barcelona: Maucci, 1907);

*Romance de lobos: Comedia bárbara dividida en cinco jornadas* (Madrid: Pueyo, 1908);

*El yermo de las almas: Episodios de la vida íntima* (Madrid: Balgañón & Moreno, 1908);

*Los cruzados de la causa* (Madrid: Balgañón & Moreno, 1908); republished in *La guerra carlista*, 3 volumes (Madrid: Suárez, 1909);

*El resplandor de la hoguera* (Madrid: Pueyo, 1909); republished in *La guerra carlista*;

*Gerifaltes de antaño* (Madrid: Suárez, 1909); republished in *La guerra carlista*;

*Cofre de sándalo* (Madrid: Suárez, 1909);

*Una tertulia de antaño* (Madrid: Cuento Semanal, 1909);

*Cuento de abril: Escenas rimadas en una manera extravagante* (Madrid: Pueyo, 1910);

*Las mieles del rosal* (Madrid: Marzo, 1910);

*Voces de gesta: Tragedia pastoril* (Madrid: Alemana, 1911);

*Obras completas,* 19 volumes, edited by Perlado Páez (Madrid: Renacimiento, 1912–1928);

320

*Cover for Valle-Inclán's 1919 book of poetry. The drawing of the pelican is by*
*Angel Vivanco.*

*La marquesa Rosalinda: Farsa sentimental y grotesca* (Madrid: Alemana, 1913);

*El embrujado: Tragedia de tierras de Salnés* (Madrid: Perlado & Páez, 1913);

*La cabeza del dragón* (Madrid: Perlado & Páez, 1913); translated by May Heywood Broun as *The Dragon's Head,* in *Poet Lore,* 29, no. 5 (1918): 531–564;

*La lámpara maravillosa: Ejercicios espirituales* (Madrid: Helénica, 1916);

*Eulalia* (Madrid: Novela Corta, 1917);

*La media noche: Visión estelar de un momento de guerra* (Madrid: Clásica Española, 1917);

*Rosita* (Madrid: Novela Corta, 1917);

*Mi hermana Antonia* (Madrid: Blass, 1918);

*Cuentos, estética y poemas,* selected by Guillermo Jiménez (Mexico City: Cultura, 1919); translated by Robert Lima as *Autobiography, Aesthetics, Aphorisms* (N.p., 1966);

*La pipa de Kif* (Madrid: Sociedad General Española de Librería, 1919);

*Divinas palabras* (Madrid: Yagües, 1920); translated (London: Heinemann/National Theatre, 1977);

*Farsa de la enamorada del rey: Dividida en tres jornadas* (Madrid: Sociedad General Española de Librería, 1920);

*El pasajero: Claves líricas* (Madrid: Yagües, 1920);

*Zacarías el cruzado* (Madrid: Artística Saez Hermanos, 1920);

*Farsa y licencia de la reina castiza* (Madrid: Artes de la Ilustración, 1922);

*Cara de plata: Comedia bárbara* (Madrid: Renacimiento, 1923);

*La rosa de papel y La cabeza del Bautista: Novelas macabras* (Madrid: Prensa Gráfica, 1924);

*Luces de Bohemia: Esperpento* (Madrid: Cervantina, 1924); translated by Anthony N. Zahareas and

Gerald Gillespie as *Lights of Bohemia* (University Park: University of Pennsylvania Press, 1969);

*Opera omnia* (Madrid: Rivadeneyra, 1924–1933);

*Cartel de ferias: Cromos isabelinos* (Madrid: Prensa Gráfica, 1925);

*Los cuernos de don Friolera: Esperpento* (Madrid: Cervantina, 1925);

*Ecos de Asmodeo* (Madrid: Novela Mundial, 1926);

*El terno del difunto* (Madrid: Novela Mundial, 1926);

*Las galas del difunto* (Madrid: Rivadeneyra, 1926);

*Ligazón: Auto para siluetas* (Madrid: Novela Mundial, 1926);

*Tablado de marionetas para educación de príncipes* (Madrid: Rivadeneyra, 1926);

*Tirano Banderas* (Madrid: Rivadeneyra, 1926); translated by Margarita Pavitt as *The Tyrant* (New York: Holt, 1929);

*La corte de los milagros: El ruedo ibérico* (Madrid: Rivadeneyra, 1927);

*Estampas isabelinas: La rosa de oro* (Madrid: Novela Mundial, 1927);

*La hija del capitán* (Madrid: Novela Mundial, 1927);

*Retablo de la avaricia: La lujuria y la muerte* (Madrid: Rivadeneyra, 1927);

*Fin de un revolucionario: Aleluyas de la Gloriosa* (Madrid; Moderna, 1928);

*Las reales antecámaras* (Madrid: Atlántida, 1928);

*Teatrillo de enredo* (Madrid: Moderna, 1928);

*Viva mi dueño: El ruedo ibérico* (Madrid: Rivadeneyra, 1928);

*Otra castiza de Samaria* (Madrid: Novela de Hoy, 1929);

*Claves líricas* (Madrid: Rivadeneyra, 1930);

*Martes de carnaval: Esperpentos* (Madrid: Rivadeneyra, 1930);

*Flores de almendro* (Madrid: Bergua, 1936);

*Opera lírica* (Madrid: Rua Nueva, 1943);

*Obras completas de Don Ramón del Valle-Inclán,* 2 volumes (Madrid: Rivadeneyra, 1944);

*Publicaciónes periodísticas anteriores a 1895,* edited by William L. Fichter (Mexico City: Colegio de México, 1952);

*Baza de espadas* (Barcelona: AHR, 1958);

*Obras escogidas* (Madrid: Aguilar, 1958);

*Teatro selecto* (Madrid: Escelicer, 1969);

*El trueno dorado* (Madrid: Nostromo, 1975);

*Artículos completos y otras páginas olvidadas* (Madrid: Istmo, 1987).

**Edition in English:** *The Pleasant Memoirs of the Marquis de Bradomín: Four Sonatas,* translated by May Heywood Broun and Thomas Walsh (New York: Harcourt, Brace, 1924).

OTHER: Almagro San Martín, *Sombras de vida,* prologue by Valle-Inclán (Madrid: Marzo, 1902);

Victoriano García Martí, *De la felicidad (Eternas inquietudes),* prologue by Valle-Inclán (Madrid: Mundo Latino, 1924);

Ricardo Baroja, *El Pedogrée,* prologue by Valle-Inclán (Madrid: Caro Ragio, 1926);

S. J. Sender, *El problema religioso en México,* prologue by Valle-Inclán (Madrid: Cénit, 1929).

TRANSLATIONS: José Maria Eça de Queirós, *El crimen del padre Amaro* (Barcelona: Maucci, 1901);

Paul Alexis, *Las chicas del amigo Lefèvre* (Valencia: Pueblo, 1902);

Eça de Queirós, *La reliquia* (Barcelona: Maucci, 1902);

Eça de Queirós, *El primo Basilio* (Barcelona: Maucci, 1904);

Matilda Serao, *Flor de pasión* (Barcelona: Maucci, 1907).

Although a writer of poems, essays, short stories, plays, and novels, Ramón del Valle-Inclán is most renowned as the prose stylist of the "Generation of '98" whose works most clearly approach the modernist mode. For him there was no clear demarcation between prose and poetry, so his earlier critics argued about whether he should be classified as a modernist or as one of the members of the Generation of '98, who analyzed and dissected Spain's internal problems in their writings. Though these writers also experimented with aesthetics, they were more motivated to inspire a national consciousness. Because Valle-Inclán exhibited both characteristics in his writings, recent criticism has placed him within both literary camps. With his considerable emphasis on poetic style, it is ironic that only a few collections of poetry appear in his long list of credits. However, these works fit both thematically and stylistically within his overall literary production.

Don Ramón, as he was affectionately called by his contemporaries, has been described by them as a strong-willed, insolent, sarcastic, violent, explosive, yet timid person. He was probably as colorful and bizarre as the complicated protagonists he created. He was born on 28 October 1866 in the small town of Vilanueva de Arosa, in the Galician province in the northwest part of Spain. His parents, Ramón del Valle-Inclán Bermúdez and Dolores de la Peña y Montenegro del Valle-Inclán, had him christened Ramón José Simón del Valle y Peña in a local parish church. His father, who was a poet and journalist of limited success, was an intellectual and exerted con-

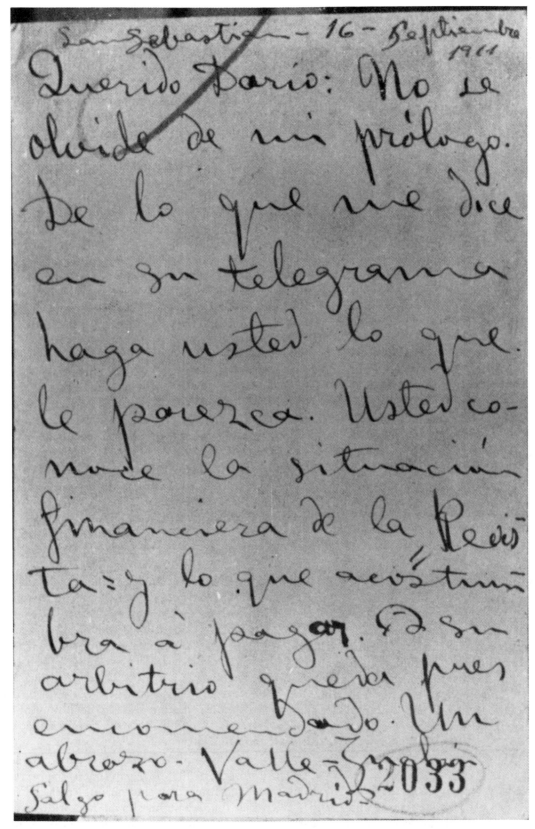

*Letter from Valle-Inclán to Nicaraguan poet Rubén Darío (Comisión Nacional Nicaragüense de Homenaje a*
*Rubén Darío; by permission of the Estate of Ramón del Valle-Inclán)*

*Valle-Inclán with sculptor Sebastián Miranda and writer Ramón Pérez de Ayala in 1914 (Collection of Don Carlos del Valle-Inclán)*

siderable influence over his son's literary training. During his formative years the young Valle-Inclán was a sickly child who loved to read, and he spent many hours listening to the family maid, Micaela la Galana, relate mysterious tales of Galician folklore. Those early influences – combined with his formal secondary education at the Instituto de Santiago de Compostela, uncompleted law studies at the University of Santiago de Compostela (1887–1889), and long hours spent reading in the personal library of Jesús Muruais, a family friend – provided the seed for the flowering of one of Spain's most prolific writers.

Artistically Valle-Inclán went through various phases. His early works are sensual and erotic but stylistically artificial and archaic. Progressively he centered his works more on the popular spirit until, in the last phase, his works reflect a mocking and disdainful attitude toward Spanish society. Stylistically his early works heavily reflect the modernist technique, concentrating on the use of musical words, cadence, harmony, and rhythm. Themes focus on Galician tradition, including its primitive, superstitious ambience and the mystical miracles of its folklore. Political themes are presented in his trilogy of novels on the Carlist wars (*La guerra carlista,* 1909), and decadent sensuality informs his best-known works, the *Sonatas* (1902–1905), a series of four books collected and translated as *The Pleasant Memories of the Marquis de Bradomín* (1924). Beginning around 1920, Valle-Inclán published several works that clearly illustrate his *esperpento* mode of writing, which he defined as a deformation of human figures and action. Such a style has its roots in the writings of Francisco de Quevedo and the paintings of Francisco José de Goya. Spanish life, Valle-Inclán felt, was deformed as is a concave mirror, and Spain was a grotesque deformation of European civilization. Although these works exhibit the most absurd and grotesque aspects of society, they never depart from human or historical realities. The modernist and *esperpento* styles and various themes appear and recur in novelistic, theatrical, and poetic productions throughout his career but with varying degrees of intensity. They complement one another, forming and refining a myriad of sensations, moods, and ideas.

Valle-Inclán was a seasoned writer by the time he produced his major poetry volumes – *Aromas de leyenda* (Aromas of Legend, 1907), *La pipa de Kif* (The Hashish Pipe, 1919), and *El pasajero* (The Passenger, 1920). He had published articles in the Spanish newspapers *Globo* and *Diario de Pontevedra* in the 1880s, but it was not until an 1892 trip to Mexico that he decided to make writing his vocation. His tenacity won him the opportunity to publish in the Mexican newspapers *Correo Español* and *Universal,* but it also plunged him into a potential public duel when he challenged the editor of the *Tiempo,* who had released an offensive article against Spaniards. After various deliberations all parties seemed satisfied, and the duel did not occur, but this confrontation was the beginning of a lifelong trend of public disturbances created by Valle-Inclán.

After his return to the Pontevedra area in the spring of 1893, he began to join the literary circles that gathered in the various cafés. With flowing hair that lay on his shoulders, a wide-brimmed hat, a beard that reached his chest, horn-rimmed spectacles, and a long black cape, he spent hours in conversation with the local intelligentsia.

*Cover, with Moya de Pino's caricature of Valle-Inclán and a poem in his honor by Ruben Dario, for the 1913 issue of*
El Cuento Galante *that includes the first publication of Valle-Inclán's* Mi hermana Antonia

Two years after the publication of his first book, *Femeninas* (Females, 1895), he decided to go to Madrid, where he led a rather bohemian existence. In that same year he published his second book, *Epitalamio* (Epithalamium, 1897), a resounding flop, and his financial situation became precarious. Poverty did not inhibit him from frequenting the many literary circles of Madrileño society. He became acquainted with the writers who were later to become known as part of the Generation of '98. There he also met Rubén Darío, the great Nicaraguan modernist and author of *Prosas profanas* (Profane Writings, 1896). They remained close friends until Darío died in 1916. However, not everyone liked Valle-Inclán, and one night at the Café de la Montaña in 1899 his explosive temper led to a brawl with the literary critic Manuel Bueno. Having thrown a bottle of water at Bueno, Valle-

Inclán received a blow on the left arm from Bueno's cane. Soon afterward a potentially deadly infection set in and necessitated an amputation at the shoulder. Reportedly Valle-Inclán refused to take an anaesthetic and thus witnessed his own operation with resignation and without fear. After this incident many fantastic stories arose about how he lost his arm.

Concerned about his unstable financial situation, his friends produced his first play, *Cenizas,* in 1899 at the Teatro de Lara in Madrid, but it was short-lived. To survive, Valle-Inclán translated several works by the Portuguese author José Maria Eça de Queirós, who had a decisive influence on Valle-Inclán's modernist creations. With the new century came works heavily evoking modernism, such as his *Sonatas* and *Flor de santidad* (Flower of Holiness, 1904), echoes of which were

*Ramón del Valle-Inclán*

short verse quoted in the Galician dialect. There is a great appeal to the senses, with imagery focusing on the aromas of the countryside, the pealing of the church-tower bells, and the visualization of an idyllic paradise lost. To create that vision, impressionistic pictorial elements play a key role in the poetry. Colors appear in their purest forms. A luminous radiance is achieved by the use of white and gold, symbolizing the harmonious purity of the ideal and somewhat exotic Galician world. Blue, a favorite color of modernists, is seen in the azure sky and, for Valle-Inclán, is an expression of universal religiosity. Naturally, green is used for the countryside, while red has decorative value, and black and other dark colors contrast with the luminous colors. Phrases such as "azul cristal" (crystal blue), "vacas bermejas" (bright red cows), "por la senda roja" (by way of the red path), and "linos de luz" (linen of light) are only a few examples of his use of color and light.

In *Aromas de leyenda,* Galicia is a timeless garden filled with the poorest and most humble people, whose defects become idealized beauty. Beggar bands wandering on the dusty roads, pilgrims making their way to religious shrines, and shepherds tending their flocks are the main protagonists of this verse, and the themes of Christian miracles or human adversity surround these characters. Metaphors, such as the ones in which birds watch the passing of time and a fountain symbolizes the origin of life and eternal life, aid in achieving atemporal effects. In the poem "Flor de la tarde" (Afternoon Flower) the "fontana late como un corazón" (spring beats like a heart), and in "No digas de dolor" (Do Not Talk about Pain) "¡La fuente arrulla el sueño del jardín señorial!" (The fountain lulls to sleep the dream of the stately garden!). Critics agree that *Aromas de leyenda* is fully modernist in style, but its popular tone, the use of traditional Spanish meters, and the lack of Parnassian overtones has placed it closer to the spirit of the Generation of '98 than to the more cosmopolitan movement called modernism.

With his first poetry volume complete, the memories of his boyhood home seemed to fade as Valle-Inclán began to concentrate more on the theater. In 1909 his wife began a tour of Latin America with her theatrical troupe. He decided to accompany her, but while en route, in the Canary Islands, he locked her in a hotel room to prevent her from performing in a play he did not like. It was a scandalous scene with both the police and the governor intervening in the domestic dispute, and it ended with the cancellation of the play.

to be heard later in his poetry. These years also marked his increased interest in joining elite theatrical circles and his acquaintance with Josefina Angela Blanco, an actress at the Teatro Español. They were married in Madrid on 24 August 1907, and in the ensuing years six children were born to them.

Valle-Inclán's first volume of poetry, *Aromas de leyenda,* is a representative modernist work connected both stylistically and thematically to his fiction works *Flor de santidad* and *Jardín umbrío* (Shady Garden, 1903). Only recently have critics begun to look seriously at Valle-Inclán's poetry. *Aromas de leyenda* closely utilizes modernist techniques and is his only poetry collection devoid of *esperpento* ingredients.

Comprising fourteen poems with a variety of rhyme schemes and meters, the collection was inspired by nostalgia for the idealized virtues and traditions of Galicia. Though the poems are written primarily in Castilian, eleven of them end with a

The Valle-Incláns were involved in a flurry of activities in the succeeding years: his unsuccessful attempt at entering politics, the publication of several new books, and a 1912 move back to Galicia, where their second son later drowned. Both parents were traumatized by the incident. After World War I began, Valle-Inclán and other intellectuals signed a pro-Ally declaration in June 1915; he became a war correspondent for the *Imparcial* and spent time on the French front. Later he wrote his impressions of the war in *La media noche: Visión estelar de un momento de guerra* (Midnight: Starry Vision of a Moment of War, 1917). Inspired by his residence in Galicia, he wrote *La lámpara maravillosa* (The Marvelous Lamp, 1916), followed by his second poetry volume, *La pipa de kif.*

*La pipa de kif* is a clear break both stylistically and thematically from his earlier poetry. Although some modernist tendencies remain, the *esperpento* aesthetic also appears: these poems represent Valle-Inclán's transition from the modernist to the *esperpento* mode. Juxtaposed with the playful tone characteristic of modernist works, bitter sarcasm and a focus on the grotesque are manifested. Certain poems exhibit dehumanization techniques and the manipulation of puppet figures or actors, which were to become pronounced features of the major works of Valle-Inclán's *esperpento* period. Thus critics have linked this book to his *esperpento* works *Luces de Bohemia* (1924; translated as *Lights of Bohemia,* 1969) and *Los cuernos de don Friolera* (The Horns of Don Friolera, 1925), as well as to the farces *Farsa de la enamorada del rey* (Farce of the King's Sweetheart, 1920) and *Farsa y licencia de la reina castiza* (Farce and License of the Chaste Queen, 1922).

The first poem, "La pipa de kif," has many modernist characteristics: musicality, allusions to exotic places and mythological figures, and the sense of playfulness that smoking hashish creates; furthermore, the drug was the poetic muse that inspired the poetry. The second poem, "Aleluya" (Hallelujah), is more representative of Valle-Inclán's aesthetic. He announces that his verses will be funambulous and that purists will call them grotesque. The caravan of humble characters in *Aromas de leyenda* is here replaced by contemporary figures who are satirized and demystified: "La gran caravana académica saludo con risa ecuménica." (I salute the great academic caravan with ecumenical laughter). While the modernists emphasized and refined beauty, Valle-Inclán went to the opposite extreme in stressing the most deformed and absurd.

The country setting of *Aromas de leyenda* is abandoned for an urban space, and three of the poems — "La pipa de kif," "La tienda del herbolario" (The Herbalist Shop), and "Rosa de sanatorio" (The Sanatorium Rose) — focus on the hallucinatory drugs to which Valle-Inclán was addicted. Readers note the burlesque and sordid tone and the theme of drug use as an escape from reality. Social themes emanate from various poems, including "Fin de carnaval" (The End of Carnival), where masks employed by carnival figures only serve to hide the *esperpento* puppets they really are. A mocking tone is evident: "Absurda tarde. Macabra mueca de dolor" (Absurd afternoon. Macabre painful grimace). The theme of crime surfaces in "El crimen de Mendinica," in which religiosity, avarice, and the puritanism of the reigning social class are satirized. This poem, like all those in the *esperpento* mode, ridicule the characters' actions by making them a part of a great and absurd dramatic spectacle, but the confines of reality, as seen in "Rosa de sanatorio," can be pleasantly breached by the soothing effects of hallucinatory drugs.

Perhaps the dependence on drugs had its roots in Valle-Inclán's poor health: in 1920 he suffered his third major cancer surgery. That same year saw the publication of his last complete volume of original poetry, *El pasajero.* Several of the poems had been published earlier, in 1911 and 1914, so they are stylistically linked more closely with *Aromas de leyenda* than with *La pipa de kif.* In imagery, vocabulary, and content *El pasajero* includes the most modernist of Inclán's poetry, and it is linked thematically with the nonfiction philosophy book *La lámpara maravillosa.* Twenty-six of the thirty-three poems in *El pasajero* refer to roses in their titles, though the flower is not represented in a physical way but rather in a metaphysical sense with a myriad of hidden meanings.

The title of the book suggests the general theme — Valle-Inclán's itinerant search for thematic variety, techniques, and aesthetics, as well as his search for meaning in life. In those poems that deal with stylistics, he presents a meditation on the aesthetics of the poetry. For example, in "Rosa del sol" (Sun Rose) he points to the necessity for unity in his creations as he searches for the absolute, and in "Rosa métrica" (Metric Rose) the symbolist style is affirmed.

Several of the poems offer autobiographical memories of his infancy and youth. In "Rosa hipérbole" (Hyperbole Rose) Valle-Inclán remembers his travels abroad: "fui peregrino sobre la mar, y en todas partes pecando un poco, dejé mi vida como un cantar" (I was a pilgrim on the ocean, and I sinned a little everywhere, left my life like a song.)

In contrast to *Aromas de leyenda,* and to *La pipa de kif,* in which the setting is the country and the city, respectively, the passenger's travels take the reader to a variety of places: to Castile in "Rosa matinal" (Morning Rose) and León in "Rosa de caminante" (The Traveler's Rose) and to Latin America in "Rosa de túrbulos" (Rose of Trouble) and "Alegoría" (Allegory). Readers see reflections of Galicia in "Rosa matinal" and "Rosa vespertina" (Evening Rose).

The last seven poems of *El pasajero* deal with the meaning of existence. The passenger's search leads him to the magical qualities of the zodiac in "Rosa de zoroastro" (Zoraster Rose) and to a nontraditional approach to Christianity in "Rosa gnóstica" (Gnostic Rose). He laments the difficulty of life and his journey toward death when he states in "Rosa de Job" (Job's Rose) that "¡Todo hacia la muerte avanza de concierto, toda la vida es mudanza hasta ser muerto!" (Everything advances harmoniously toward death, all of life is movement until death!). The final poem, "Karma," describes the kind of house the traveler/poet will finally build for himself at the end of his journey: "sea labrada de piedra; mi casa . . . / y un día decore la hiedra, sobre el dolmen de Valle-Inclán" (it may be made of rock, my house . . . / and one day Valle-Inclán's dolmen will be decorated with ivy).

The last sixteen years of Valle-Inclán's life included his increasing his political activity, apparent in his writings. He did not miss an opportunity to criticize the political regime, and, after demonstrating against the government of Miguel Primo de Rivera in 1929, he was fined, imprisoned, and publicly censured by the dictator. In addition, these years also saw his further concentration on the *esperpento* works for which he is well known. However, his personal life did not go well: he divorced his wife in 1932 and endured continuing financial difficulties and a constant battle with his bad health. The intertwining of his life and works was strong, and near the end of his life he suffered a scandalous Roman love affair similar to those experienced by the fictional Marquis de Bradomín.

On 5 January 1936 Ramón del Valle-Inclán died of bladder cancer. On his deathbed he had denied his opportunity to confess and had seemed resigned to take what came in the hereafter without special absolution, asking for a nonreligious funeral. He was buried in Boisaca the next day. While lowering the coffin, Modesto Pasín, a family friend, noticed a crucifix atop the casket and insisted it be removed. He tripped, knocked the coffin into the grave, and fell beside it. This virtual *esperpento* scene ended Valle-Inclán's life on a macabre, flamboyant note.

References:

Guillermo Díaz-Plaja, *Las estéticas de Valle-Inclán* (Madrid: Gredos, 1965);

Gaspar Gómez de la Serna, Prologue to Valle-Inclán's *Obras escogidas* (Madrid: Aguilar, 1958);

Obdulia Guerrero, *Valle-Incán y el novecientos* (Madrid: Magisterio Español, 1977);

Pedro Salinas, *Literatura española del siglo XX* (Madrid: Alianza, 1970);

José Severa Baño, *Ramón del Valle-Inclán* (Madrid: Júcar, 1983);

Verity Smith, *Ramón del Valle-Inclán* (New York: Twayne, 1973);

Anthony N. Zahareas, ed., *Ramón del Valle-Inclán: His Life and Works* (New York: Las Américas, 1968).

# Manuel Vázquez Montalbán

*(July 1939 - )*

Samuel Amell
*Ohio State University*

BOOKS: *Informe sobre la información* (Barcelona: Fontanella, 1963; revised and enlarged edition, 1975);

*Una educación sentimental* (Barcelona: Bardo, 1967);

*Reflexiones ante el capitalismo* (Barcelona: Cultura Popular, 1968);

*Antologia de la nova cançó catalana* (Barcelona: Cultura Popular, 1968);

*Recordando a Dardé y otros relatos* (Barcelona: Seix Barral, 1969);

*Movimientos sin éxito* (Barcelona: Bardo, 1969);

*Manifiesto subnormal* (Barcelona: Kairós, 1970);

*Crónica sentimental de España* (Barcelona: Lumen, 1971);

*Cancionero general, 1939–1971* (Barcelona: Lumen, 1972);

*Cien años de deporte* (Barcelona: Difusora Internacional, 1972);

*Yo maté a Kennedy* (Barcelona: Planeta, 1972);

*Joan Manuel Serrat* (Madrid: Júcar, 1973);

*El libro gris de la televisión española* (Madrid: Ediciones 99, 1973);

*La via chilena al golpe de estado* (Barcelona: Saturno, 1973);

*A la sombra de las muchachas sin flor* (Barcelona: Ediciones Saturno, 1973);

*Coplas a la muerte de mi tía Daniela* (Barcelona: Ediciones Saturno, 1973);

*Guillermota en el país de las Guillerminas* (Barcelona: Anagrama, 1973);

*Happy End* (Barcelona: Gaya Ciencia, 1974);

*Cien años de canción y Music Hall* (Barcelona: Difusora Internacional, 1974);

*Cuestiones marxistas* (Barcelona: Anagrama, 1974);

*La penetración americana en España* (Madrid: Cuadernos para el Diálogo, 1974);

*1974: España se queda sola* (Barcelona: Punch, 1974);

*El libro de la pena de muerte* (Madrid: Sedmay, 1976);

*Mil novecientos setenta y cinco: El año del Ay, Ay, Ay* (Madrid: Sedmay, 1976);

*Qué es el imperialismo* (Barcelona: Gaya Ciencia, 1976);

*Tatuaje* (Barcelona: G.P./D.L., 1976);

*L'art del menjar a Catalunya* (Barcelona: Edicions 62, 1977);

*Cómo liquidaron al franquismo en dieciséis meses y un día* (Barcelona: Planeta, 1977);

*Diccionario del franquismo* (Barcelona: Dopesa, 1977);

*La soledad del manager* (Barcelona: Planeta, 1977);

*La cocina catalana* (Barcelona: Peninsula, 1979);

*Los mares del Sur* (Barcelona: Planeta, 1979);

*La palabra libre en la ciudad libre* (Barcelona: Gedisa, 1979);

*Historia y comunicación social* (Barcelona: Bruguera, 1980);

*Asesinato en el Comité Central* (Barcelona: Planeta, 1981); translated by Patrick Camiller as *Murder in the Central Committee* (London: Pluto, 1984; Chicago: Academy Chicago, 1985);

*Praga* (Barcelona: Ocnos, 1982);

*Los pájaros de Bangkok* (Barcelona: Planeta, 1983);

*Tres novelas ejemplares* (Barcelona: Bruguera, 1983);

*Mis almuerzos con gente inquietante* (Barcelona: Planeta, 1984);

*La rosa de Alejandria* (Barcelona: Planeta, 1984);

*Crónica sentimental de la transición* (Barcelona: Planeta, 1985);

*El pianista* (Barcelona: Seix Barral, 1985); translated by Elisabeth Plaister as *The Pianist* (London: Quartet, 1989);

*El balneario* (Barcelona: Planeta, 1986);

*El matarife* (Madrid: Almarabú, 1986);

*Memoria y deseo: Obra poética (1963–1983)* (Barcelona: Seix Barral, 1986);

*Los alegres muchachos de Atzavara* (Barcelona: Seix Barral, 1987);

*Asesinato en Prado del Rey y otras historias sórdidas* (Barcelona: Planeta, 1987);

*Historias de fantasmas* (Barcelona: Planeta, 1987);

*Historias de padres e hijos* (Barcelona: Planeta, 1987);

*Historias de política ficción* (Barcelona: Planeta, 1987);

*Pigmalión y otros relatos* (Barcelona: Seix Barral, 1987);

*Tres historias de amor* (Barcelona: Planeta, 1987);

*Manuel Vázquez Montalbán*

*El delantero centro fue asesinado al atardecer* (Barcelona: Planeta, 1988);

*Cuarteto* (Madrid: Mondadori, 1988);

*Rafael Ribó* (Barcelona: Planeta, 1988);

*Escritos subnormales* (Barcelona: Seix Barral, 1989);

*Las recetas de Carvalho* (Barcelona: Planeta, 1989);

*Galíndez* (Barcelona: Seix Barral, 1990); translated by Carol and Thomas Christensen (New York: Atheneum, 1992);

*El laberinto griego* (Barcelona: Planeta, 1991);

*Pero el viajero que huye* (Madrid: Visor, 1991);

*Autobiografía del general Franco* (Barcelona: Planeta, 1992).

VIDEOTAPE: *Manuel Vázquez Montalbán,* Madrid, Autores Españoles Contemporáneos, 9, Centro de las Letras Españolas, Ministerio de Cultura, 1988.

Manuel Vázquez Montalbán is a prolific writer who has cultivated diverse genres: essay, novel, poetry, short story, and drama. He is mostly known as a novelist, particularly as the creator of a series of detective novels with Pepe Carvalho as the protagonist. The Carvalho books have reached high sales numbers, and some of them have been adapted for cinema and television. His other novels have also been well received. His novel *Autobiografía del general Franco,* published in 1992, was on the best-seller lists for many months. The success of his narrative has been proven by many literary awards: the Planeta Prize, 1979; the French International Detective Literature Prize, 1981; the German Critics' Bunche Prize, 1988; the City of Barcelona Prize, 1989; the Italian Recalmare Prize, 1989; the Spanish National Literature Prize, 1991; and the Italian Raymond Chandler Prize, 1992. On the other hand, his constant work as an active journalist (with *Interviú, Mundo Diario, El País, Por Favor, TeleXprés,* and *Triunfo*) has made his essays – especially on sociopolitical issues – very well known. His success as a novelist and essayist, however, has obscured his work in poetry. His poems are much less known by the public than his other publications. Even most literary critics have not given his poetry the attention it deserves. Santos Sanz Villanueva's opinion in this respect is a good example: "Manuel Vázquez Montalbán se ha dispersado en numerosos géneros y la poesía no se ha convertido en el más sobresaliente, aunque no carezca de interés" (Manuel Vázquez Montalbán has spread himself thin over numerous genres, and his poetry, though interesting, is not his most outstanding feature).

Vázquez Montalbán was born in July 1939 in El Raball, a popular Barcelona neighborhood close to the ancient walls and historically inhabited by Catalans. At the time of Vázquez Montalbán's birth the neighborhood had started to change, and the autochthonous popular classes were joined by proletarians from other regions of Spain. Neither of Vázquez Montalbán's parents is Catalan. Due to social circumstances, the inhabitants of El Raball were among the losers of the Spanish Civil War. This neighborhood and its atmosphere during the post-civil-war years appear in one way or another throughout Vázquez Montalbán's work. In this aspect, as well as in his socioeconomic background, there are distinct parallels with another author of the same period. In both Vázquez Montalbán's and Juan Marsé's works the neighborhood in which they lived plays an essential part.

Although Vázquez Montalbán planned to be a car mechanic, he took advantage of the opportunity to go to college and thus better his economic and social status. He studied humanities at the University of Barcelona and journalism at the Official School of Journalism in Madrid. As a student he became involved in organized politics. He became a member of the Frente de Liberación Popular and later joined the Catalan Communist party, the PSUC (Unified Socialist Party of Catalonia). During this time he had to make a living through varied jobs, from tutoring to collecting insurance payments. After he lived in Madrid for a year in order to finish his degree in journalism, his continuous political activities caused him to be arrested and sentenced by a military court to three years in prison. After he was released from prison he had a difficult time finding a job in journalism because his criminal record impeded his access to first-class publications,

and he had to resign himself to writing for home-decoration and gardening journals and doing articles for encyclopedias and translations.

His poetry production started in the 1960s, and his first published collection of poems was *Una educación sentimental* (An Education in Feelings, 1967). This was followed in 1969 by *Movimientos sin éxito* (Fruitless Movements), for which he received the Vizcaya Award. In 1968 José Batlló included Vázquez Montalbán in the *Antología de la nueva poesía española* (Anthology of New Spanish Poetry), and in 1970 Vázquez Montalbán was the first poet included in the anthology edited by José María Castellet, *Nueve novísimos poetas españoles* (Nine of the Newest Spanish Poets).

José María Alvarez, one of the poets represented in Castellet's anthology, has written that "La poesía española de hoy nace de una antología que, compendiada por José María Castellet, publicada por Carlos Barral y bajo el título *Nueve novísimos,* lanzó en 1970 a unos poetas que, aún llegados de aventuras diferentes y con los ojos puestos en metas más diferentes aún, significaron una decidida voluntad de ruptura, no solamente con el verso anterior sino con el mundo cultural reinante hasta aquel momento" (Today's Spanish poetry comes forth from an anthology edited by José María Castellet, published by Carlos Barral, and entitled *Nueve novísimos,* which in 1970 launched some poets who, though coming from different backgrounds and with even more different goals, showed a determination of rupture, not only with previous poetry, but also with the ruling cultural world of that moment). What Alvarez has stated is confirmed by Castellet, who in the works of these poets sees a rupture with previous aesthetics, and among them "una serie de coincidencias, de elementos comunes, junto con una serie de contradicciones" (a series of coincidences, of common elements, together with a number of contradictions).

Two of the *novísimos,* Vázquez Montalbán and Antonio Martínez Sarrión, wrote their first verses within the aesthetics of social poetry. But only Vázquez Montalbán has continued throughout his career to use elements that are similar to some aspects of social poetry. Critics as diverse as Sanz Villanueva and Kay Pritchett recognize that fact, even though they emphasize the differences between Vázquez Montalbán and the poets of the previous generation. Sanz Villanueva states that, due to its critical aspects, the poetry of Vázquez Montalbán "entronca, en cierto sentido, con la poesía de la promoción que le precede, aunque le alejen de ella sus procedimientos expresivos" (links him in a certain way to the poets of the previous generation, although his expression distance him from them). When discussing Vázquez Montalbán and two other *novísimos* – Pere Gimferrer and Guillermo Carnero – Pritchett maintains that "Vázquez Montalbán is the only one who, by reason of social and political affinities, may be linked with the social realist aesthetic of many other postwar poets. Nonetheless, his literary personality, both as novelist and poet, is so much the reverse of the social realist." The subject of his poetry relates Vázquez Montalbán to the social poets, while his modes of expression distance him from them. One could say that Vázquez Montalbán's work means for social poetry what Luis Martin Santos's *Tiempo de silencio* (Time of Silence, 1962) meant for the social novel.

An aspect that somewhat differentiates Vázquez Montalbán from the other *novísimos* and ties him to previous generations of poets are his literary influences. According to Vázquez Montalbán, these are Pío Baroja, the social poets, and those he calls the poets of experience, especially Jaime Gil de Biedma – and most of all an Italian author, Cesare Pavese.

Martínez Sarrión has observed that the first book of poetry of Vázquez Montalbán, *Una educación sentimental,* "[está] en el límite extremo del social-realismo, cuyas actitudes ideológicas comparte el autor" (borders on social realism, the ideologies of which coincide with the author's). Martínez Sarrión also points out that what characterizes *Una educación sentimental* is "un discurso en donde memoria y paisaje urbano, emoción controlada por la ironía y abundantes referentes de la cultura popular de masas se utilizan en ambiguo y riquísimo registro. El libro de Vázquez Montalbán arrumbaría para siempre la rigidez y estereotipia de los epígonos de la poesía social" (a discourse in which memory and urban landscape, emotion controlled by irony, and abundant references to mass culture are used in a both ambiguous and rich repertoire. Vázquez Montalbán's book does away forever with the rigidity and stereotypes of the followers of social poetry).

The elements pointed out by Martínez Sarrión, memory, urban landscape, irony, and references to mass culture, are present not only in this first book by Vázquez Montalbán but in his whole poetic production. One of the most interesting aspects of the poetry of Vázquez Montalbán is the influence of the mass media. He says that "cine y canción se han alimentado de literatura. Hora es ya que la literatura se alimente de cine y canción. Los programadores de divorcio entre cultura de *élite* y

cultura de masas morirán bajo el peso de la masificación de la cultura de *élite*" (film and song have been nourished by literature, and now it is time that literature be nourished by film and song. Those who program the divorce between elite and popular culture will succumb under the weight of the mass production of elite culture). Another characteristic of Vázquez Montalbán's work and one that also distinguishes it from that of the other *novísimos* is its sociopolitical, critical, and even denunciatory nature.

Vázquez Montalbán's poetic world, like his narrative, contains definite autobiographical aspects and presents a critical portrait of contemporary Spanish society. All these elements are present in his first work, *Una educación sentimental*. In the poem "Conchita Piquer" there are references to popular songs (such as "Tatuaje," which later became the title of one of the novels of his Carvalho cycle), as well as to political anthems (including the Carlist anthem "Oriamendi"). Other poems take their titles from well-known films such as Alfred Hitchcock's *The Man Who Knew too Much* (1934). There are also poems with the titles of other literary works, for example F. Scott Fitzgerald's *Tender Is the Night* (1934). One of the last poems of the book is dedicated to the French painter Paul Gauguin and harbors the seed of one of the best novels in the Carvalho series, *Los mares del Sur* (The South Seas, 1979). At the same time, the poems of this collection contain strong criticism of post-civil-war Spanish society. Perhaps the most obvious one in this respect is the poem titled "SOE" (Seguro Obligatorio de Enfermedad – Required Health Insurance).

Since the appearance of his poems in Castellet's anthology – because of the great success of his other literary works, especially his novels – critics seem to have forgotten Vázquez Montalbán the poet. Although Batlló included poems by him in *Poetas españoles poscontemporáneos* (Postcontemporary Spanish Poets, 1974) and Gustavo Correa did the same in his *Antología de la poesía española (1900–1980)* (Anthology of Spanish Poetry [1900–1980], 1980), Vázquez Montalbín's work does not appear in many other contemporary anthologies. There is no comparison between the attention critics have paid to other *novísimos,* for example Guillermo Carnero and Pere (Pedro) Gimferrer, and that given to Vázquez Montalbán, who in many cases barely has been mentioned.

Nevertheless Vázquez Montalbán has often published poetry as well as novels and essays. In 1973, for example, two collections of his poems appeared: *Coplas a la muerte de mi tía Daniela* (Verses on the Death of my Aunt Daniela) and *A la sombra de las muchachas sin flor* (In the Shadow of the Flowerless Girls). His next collection of poems was *Praga* (Prague, 1982), and in 1986 his complete poetry was gathered in a volume titled *Memoria y deseo: Obra poética (1963–1983)* (Memory and Desire: Poetic Work [1963–1983]). In 1991 Vázquez Montalbán published a new collection of poems, *Pero el viajero que huye* (But the Traveler He Flees). He explains in an introductory note that this book "cierra el ciclo iniciado por *Una educación sentimental*" (closes the cycle initiated by *Una educación sentimental*). Critic Joaquín Marco has written in this respect that "*Pero el viajero que huye* puede entenderse como el fin de un ciclo. Sin embargo, en la creación poética no existen ciclos cerrados, progresivos o definitivos. En sus poemas encontramos el sustrato de un escritor polifacético que torna una y otra vez a un mundo – su paisaje – que busca compartir. Son los escenarios de la infancia en el viaje hacia el pasado o la fidelidad a una ética comprometida. Son también los motivos que impelen hacia el exterior, a la búsqueda de una identidad que perdura más allá de la geografía y de la Historia" (*Pero el viajero que huye* may be conceived as the end of a cycle. In poetic creation, however, there are no closed, progressive, or definite cycles. In his poems we find the background of a multifaceted writer who again and again turns to a world – his land – that he wishes to share. It is the scene of his childhood on his journey into the past or his faithfulness to the ethics of com-promise. It is also his quest for an identity that lasts beyond geography and history).

In a statement regarding his detective novels, but which is equally applicable to his other work, including his poetry, Vázquez Montalbán has affirmed that almost everything in his work "es paisaje social y sentimental, es decir, crónica moral de una colectividad en un tiempo determinado" (is a social and emotional landscape, that is, a moral chronicle of a collectivity in a specific time period).

## References:

José María Alvarez, "Poesía española actual," in *Nos années 80: Culture hispanique* (Dijon: Université de Bourgogne, 1990), p. 229;

José María Castellet, *Nueve novísimos poetas españoles* (Barcelona: Barral, 1970), pp. 38, 40;

Joaquín Marco, "*Pero el viajero que huye,* de Manuel Vázquez Montalbán," *Insula,* 48 (June 1993): 20–21;

Antonio Martínez Sarrión and Antonio Ramos Gascón, "La poesía española en el último cuarto de siglo," in *España hoy, II: Cultura,* edited by Ramos Gascón (Madrid: Cátedra, 1991), p. 58;

Kay Pritchett, *Four Postmodern Poets of Spain* (Fayetteville: Arkansas University Press, 1991), p. 66;

Santos Sanz Villanueva, *Literatura actual* (Barcelona: Ariel, 1984), p. 443.

# Luis Antonio de Villena

*(31 October 1951 -   )*

Jerry Phillips Winfield
*Mercer University*

BOOKS: *Sublime solarium* (Madrid: Azur, 1971);

*La revolución cultural: Desafío de una juventud* (Barcelona: Planeta, 1975);

*Hymnica,* edited by Angel Caffarena (Málaga: Guadalhorce, 1975; revised edition, Madrid: Hiperión, 1979);

*El viaje a Bizancio* (León: Diputación Provincia, 1978);

*Conocer Oscar Wilde y su obra* (Barcelona: DOPESA, 1978);

*Dados, amor y clérigos* (Madrid: Cupsa, 1978);

*Catulo* (Madrid: Júcar, 1979);

*Para los dioses turcos* (Barcelona: Laertes, 1980);

*Huir del invierno* (Madrid: Hiperión, 1981);

*Un paganismo nuevo* (Zaragoza: Olifante, 1981);

*Ante el espejo: Memorias de una adolescencia* (Barcelona: Argos Vergara, 1982);

*Poesía (1970–1982)* (Madrid: Visor, 1983); enlarged as *Poesía, 1970–1984* (Madrid: Visor, 1988);

*Aubrey Beardsley* (Barcelona: Lumen, 1983);

*Amor pasión* (Barcelona: Laertes, 1983);

*Corsarios de guante amarillo* (Barcelona: Tusquets, 1983);

*La muerte unicamente* (Madrid: Visor, 1984);

*El razonamiento inagotable de Juan Gil-Albert* (Madrid: Anjana, 1984);

*En el invierno romano* (Barcelona: Plaza & Janés, 1986);

*José Emilio Pacheco* (Madrid: Júcar, 1986);

*La tentación de Icaro* (Barcelona: Lumen, 1986);

*Máscaras y formas del fin de siglo* (Madrid: Dragón, 1988);

*Chicos* (Madrid: Mondadori, 1989);

*Yo, Miguel Angel Buonarroti* (Mexico City: Planeta Mexicana, 1990);

*Como a lugar extraño* (Madrid: Visor, 1990);

*Fin de siglo: El sesgo clásico en la última poesía española* (Madrid: Visor, 1992);

*Fuera del mundo* (Barcelona: Planeta, 1992);

*Leonardo da Vinci* (Barcelona: Planeta, 1993).

OTHER: Antonio Prieto, ed., *Espejo del amor y de la muerte,* includes poems by Villena (Madrid: Azur, 1971), pp. 105–132;

*Antología general e introducción a la obra de Manuel Mujica Laínez,* selected, with a prologue, by Villena (Madrid: Felmar, 1976);

Vicente Aleixandre, *Pasión de la tierra,* includes notes and commentary by Villena (Madrid: Narcea, 1976);

Luis Cernuda, *Las nubes; Desolación de la Quimera,* edited by Villena (Madrid: Cátedra, 1984);

*Postnovísimos,* selected, with an introduction, by Villena (Madrid: Visor, 1986);

Porfirio Barba Jacob, *Rosas negras: Antología poética,* edited by Villena (Valencia: Mestral, 1988);

"El paganismo nuevo," poems by Villena, in *Sobre un pujante deseo,* edited by Jesús García Sánchez, *Litoral,* no. 188 (1990): 81–130.

TRANSLATIONS: Oscar Wilde, *Cartas a Lord Alfred Douglas,* translated, with a prologue and notes, by Villena (Barcelona: Tusquets, 1987);

Pietro Arentino, *Sonetos lujuriosos,* translated, with a prologue and notes, by Villena (Madrid: Visor, 1991).

Luis Antonio de Villena is one of the most respected contemporary Spanish poets, as well as a versatile writer of literary criticism, translations, novels, and articles in newspapers and periodicals. He is identified with the group of poets known as the *novísimos* (very new ones), also called the "Generation of 1970" or the "Generation of Language." He shares with these poets a faith in the capacity of language to mirror experiential reality, the definition of poetry within the creative act (metapoetry), *culturalismo* (culturalism), and intertextuality – the poetic integration of other literary texts. As others of this movement are, he is drawn to the cosmopolitan, the exotic, the hermetic, and occasionally what

*Luis Antonio de Villena*

is known as "camp." Like the celebrated poet Luis Cernuda, he has openly pursued the motif of homosexual love. In Villena's work this motif occurs within the larger context of his dominant theme – the relationship of beauty, love, and desire. Yet, his poetry is highly individualistic and innovative; it resists rigid confinement to the questionable classification of the *novísimos* or any singular literary movement. The poetry of Villena is at once rebellious, elitist, erudite, brilliant in imagery and metaphor, and gifted in originality. It is also difficult and esoteric in the complexity of its language and multiplicity of its cultural references.

Villena was born in Madrid on 31 October 1951 and later received his licentiate in romance philology. He has engaged in intense literary activity in publishing books as well as in such newspapers and journals as *El País, Insula, Papeles de Son Armadans,* and *Quimera.* His considerable critical studies include those focusing on such diverse fig-

ures as Honoré de Balzac, Catullus, Cernuda, and Oscar Wilde. In addition to his novels Villena has written several short stories. The details of Villena's life are something of a mystery, largely because Villena wishes it so. There is great difficulty in separating the "legend" of the personality from Villena the person and Villena the poet. In Villena's *Sobre un pujante deseo* (On a Powerful Desire, 1990), editor Jesús García Sánchez offers a simple but sentient portrayal of Villena as "caring, a loyal friend, intelligent, and extremely cultured." He also describes Villena's public debuts as a performer of popular songs (who made a recording), a television personality, and a *charlatán* (fast talker).

Villena has made scant effort in his works to conceal his delight in describing nocturnal visits to bars and cafés of dubious reputation or his fascination for those who frequent them. The life-style and the poetry are defiantly provocative in their passion and intense demand for personal freedom. Both his life and its reflection in his creative work are theatrical because he believes both are inherently deceptive – *máscaras* (masks) existing between reality and falsehood. In *Sobre un pujante deseo* the poet Francisco Brines published his presentation of Villena at the Ateneo de Valencia on 18 December 1986. Brines accurately portrays Villena as one who sees himself as the inheritor of a way of life grounded in ethical freedom and a lineage of heterodoxy – "una especie de humanista muy particular" (a very special kind of humanist). Brines performs what he refers to as "demythification" in opposing Villena's public image of elitism, a certain coldness, narcissism, and frivolity. Antithetically he calls attention to Villena's moral strength, the courage of his search for an existential and personal freedom in society, and his disguised, but essential, modesty.

Certainly no one is more gratified witnessing these contradictory responses than Villena himself. Yet, certain suggestions in his works – including the semi-autobiographical *Ante el espejo: Memorias de una adolescencia* (Before the Mirror: Memories of an Adolescence, 1982) – offer reasonably accurate insights, despite the impossibility of separating life and works or fantasy and objective reality.

Readers of *Ante el espejo* are introduced to an extremely precocious adolescent who reads a great many books in several disciplines and genres from the classical to the contemporary. His insatiable desire to create seems to come at an early age and is accompanied by the gradual adolescent discovery of a divergent sexual orientation. Finally, the image emerges of a young man with strength, vitality, talent, and pride.

The publication of Villena's first poetry occurred in the anthology *Espejo del amor y de la muerte* (Mirror of Love and Death), edited by Antonio Prieto in 1971. The work signaled a substantial rupture in the poetry of the period and includes a presentation of the young poets by the Nobel Prize laureate Vicente Aleixandre. The majority of these poems by Villena, written between October 1970 and June 1971, were included in his first published collection of poetry *Sublime solarium* (1971). Villena, commenting on the book – in *Las voces y los ecos* (Voices and Echoes, 1981), by José Luis García Martín – describes the poetry as "un esteticismo querido, amalgamado con *flashes* surrealistas, cultistas y decadentes. Un libro de intensidad adolescente" (a beloved aestheticism, mixed with surrealistic, cultured, and decadent flashes. A book of adolescent intensity). It is also a book that the poet lived, yet this experience is distanced from the poetry by the nature of its images, allusions, and metaphors. The poems of *Sublime solarium* were written when Villena was only nineteen years old; interestingly he was more versed in the classics of Greco-Roman literature than in those of his contemporaries in Spain. There is a constant and pressing current of allusions, which include such disparate influences as the poetry of ancient China and baroque Spain and the songs of the troubadors.

Villena's interest in the poetry of the Italian Nobel laureate Salvatore Quasimodo and the Greek poet Constantine Cavafy, and his attraction to French literature and *decadentismo* have continued throughout his career. In *Ante el espejo* Villena describes the persistent feeling that his adolescence was stolen from him and that, in reading, he first experienced the bond among beauty, desire, and life; his reading then became a sort of theater for self-exploration. In *Sublime solarium* the young poet welcomes excess and the exotic amid sumptuous verses and cultural profusion. Distancing himself from the reader, Villena, in a display of verbal ostentation, joins his colleague Guillermo Carnero in the belief that poetic language is autonomous – aesthetic and not communicative. The "I" of the poet is concealed and masked, a process of "impersonalization" in Villena which Carlos Bousoño found implicit in poetry following the Parnassians and Charles Baudelaire. In *Sublime solarium* the dissenting ethical position of Villena is not as evident as it is in his more mature verse.

In his introductory notes to the book, Villena indicates a double signification in the title. A Spanish translation could represent all that "nos tienta en su oculta voz, que nos atrae, y que es al mismo tiempo palacio de nuestro refugio y de nuestra duda" (touches and tempts us with its hidden voice, and which is at the same time the palace of our refuge and our doubt). The second reading of the title could be Latin, pointing to the writings of the Mozarabic martyr Eulogio de Córdoba, who told of the Emir Abd Al-Rahman II. Persecuted by Christians, the Emir ascends to the highest *terraza* (floor) of his palace to await death. His waiting is a symbol of the acceptance of death in serenity and beauty. Villena fuses past and present in the prose poem "Muere Abd Al-Rahman II" (Abd Al-Rahman II Dies) with a dazzling inventory of jewels, lights, colors, and "el filo de una rosa" (the cutting edge of a rose): "Una mano había traído la muerte. Y el desierto habitó entonces en los ojos del emir, en sus grandes anillos, en su cárdena oriflama, y todo fue ya para siempre" (A hand had brought death. And the desert lived then in the eyes of the emir, in his great rings, in his purple oriflamme, and all was forever).

The emir is surrounded by beauty but also by silence and disillusionment. The designed and exuberant artificiality of the poetry, as well as its exoticism, musicality, and agitated rhythms, continues the *modernismo* of the first part of the twentieth century in Spanish poetry. To many readers grown accustomed to realism or social humanism, Villena's emphatic aestheticism proved surprising if not perplexing. Such baroque images of decadent and opulent life were not easily understood by those with a taste for ordinary poetry.

The intent behind this imagery and culturalism is to confront the reader with an opposing lifestyle, like that of the dandy in the poem "Tango" who reminisces of Maxim's restaurant while a crystal glass of kirsch is balanced between his fingers and the orchestra plays "Hernando's Hideaway." The poem "Marilyn norma dulcis amatrix" (Marilyn Norma Sweet Lover) includes mentions of not only Marilyn Monroe but Joe DiMaggio, Marc Antony, Petrarch, Norman Mailer, Chevrolets, and the Nevada desert, in a surrealistic mixture of symbolism and verbal play.

José Olivio Jiménez, in his perceptive introduction to Villena's *Poesía (1970–1982),* published in 1983, indicates that the identification of beauty, death, and love presages an intense nostalgia and sadness, an "añoranza eterna" (eternal longing) in Villena's later works; it is clearly a Platonic commitment to idealism. In the prose poem "Un monje en los atrios de la noche copia un poema mitológico" (A Monk in the Atria of the Night Copies a Mythological Poem), the protagonist Allan de Lille is a sad idealist who, tired of the world, Plato, and his own life, seeks death: "con envidia escuchó el sistro de la noche, y he aquí que solo, triste y viejo, sin púrpuras ni joyas, pone fin al poema" (with envy he listened to the sistrum of the night, here it is that alone, sad and old, without purple raiment or jewels, he ends the poem). Seeking transcendent beauty, according to Villena, is an attempt to escape the existential pain of time and separation; this beauty may be synonymous with death. *Sublime solarium* is the work of a very young poet, yet the essential themes and style of his later works are in place.

*El viaje a Bizancio* (The Voyage to Byzantium, 1978) includes poems written between 1972 and 1974. The title is adapted from "Sailing to Byzantium," a poem by William Butler Yeats. The mythic Byzantium is a city which celebrates the beauty of young bodies and where youth is eternal, "mito donde la vejez no es posible" (a myth where old age is impossible); it is Paradise and the lost Eden, as Villena indicates in his introduction and in the prose poem dedicated to F. Scott Fitzgerald, "The Beautiful and Damned." In *El viaje a Bizancio* Villena initiates the theme of the young nude body as a symbol of beauty and desire – a symbol which will remain consistent in his later poetry but within a variety of metaphors. The poem "Piscina" (Swimming Pool) fuses nature and the body in an imagery of danger and of solitude which seems outside of time:

Y al regresar al sol, nos miras en la orilla,
mientras, toda codicias sexuales,
el agua deseosa, se goza solitaria en tu cintura

(Returning to the sun, you watch us on the edge
while, wholly as sexual desire,
the anxious water alone enjoys itself upon your waist)[.]

Jiménez, in his introduction to *Poesía,* says that Villena in his myth of desire employs both intellectual and physical descriptions of the splendor of the body and its ultimate fall. There is both the mental activity of memory and imagination as well as actual physical contemplation. In "The Beautiful and Damned" the first section creates a world of mirrors, and touch as desire is initiated by the contemplation of pure physical beauty; yet, in the third section readers discover that the splendor is short and the fall is long: "La belleza es una perenne derrota que triunfa. Hierba y no arbol" (Beauty is a perennial defeat which triumphs. Grass and not a tree). The victory of beauty is within memory and its inventive force. In the case of a poet, it is the word which preserves remembrance, despite the fleeting nature of physical beauty. To Villena, desire is the most prized gift of existence, and the joys of language, desire, and possession are synthesized in "Navíos en verano" (Ships in Summer): "La alegría del lenguage es nuestro único señor / La alegría de la posesión nuestro único objeto" (The joy of language is our only master / The joy of possession our only purpose).

José Luis Cano, in his article "Luis Antonio de Villena: *El viaje a Bizancio,*" finds in the book a perfect harmony between the theme of the naked body and seduction, and the luminous and baroque nature of the style – the sensuality of desire corresponds with the sensuality of the poetry describing it. The celebration of sensual pleasure fuses language, image, and metaphor. In the poem "Páginas sobre un pujante deseo" (Pages on a Powerful Desire), Villena writes, "La palabra es el signo del cuerpo. / El poema es el deseo mismo de la sangre" (The word is the sign of the body. / The poem is de-

*Cover for Villena's 1981 collection, which won the prestigious Premio
de la Crítica award*

sire itself from the blood). Nature provides a source for the images and metaphors of *El viaje a Bizancio:* the eyes of the desired one become a "negro río" (black river) or "aves maravillosos" (marvelous birds); sexual energy is infused with "el río esbelto y bello de tus piernas" (the slender and beautiful river of your thighs). These surrealistic tones, with the synesthesia of chromatic, auditory, olfactory, and tactile imagery, evoke a changing ambiance of secrecy and danger in sexual desire.

The poem "Reseña de estatuaria griega" (Outline of Greek Statuary) recalls the "Archäischer Torso Apollos" (Archaic Torso of Apollo) by Rainer Maria Rilke in its evocative use of *claroscuro* (use of light and shadow). In such poems as "Navíos en verano," "Labios bellos, ámbar suave" (Beautiful Lips, Soft Amber), and "Páginas sobre un pujante deseo" (Pages on a Powerful Desire), Villena creates the leitmotiv of summer as the identity of desire in warmth and light, elements that are recurrent in his later poetry.

The *culturalismo* of Villena's first work is continued in *El viaje a Bizancio,* but with more clarity and relevance. He openly cites his influences: Yeats, Charles Baudelaire, Paul Valéry, Giacomo Leopardi, Wallace Stevens, Ezra Pound, and the myth of Siegfried. Yet this culturalism is more than simply a pedantic exercise; it lends force to the basic themes of pleasure, desire, the young body, and beauty. The final prose poem of the volume, "Monumento en honor de Lord Byron," offers insight into the aesthetic system of Villena. He invites the participation of the reader in a vertiginous current of images. The celebration of desire and the body is tainted only by a repressive society. The summer will end; yet, for this instant the bodies are real:

(Es necesario hablar del cuerpo, derrocar el tabú de la mano que palpa, del herboso confín del abrazo y la lengua. . . . Hablar de la vibración del momento, de todo el inmenso zumbido de las manos y los labios, del torrente oscuro, del agua nocturno de los sexos.)

([It is necessary to speak of the body, to demolish the taboo of the hand that touches and feels, the grassy limits of embrace and tongue. . . . To speak of the vibration of the moment, of all the immense buzzing of hands and lips, of the dark torrent of sex.])

*Hymnica* (Hymnal) was first published in 1975, with a second and definitive edition in 1979. This second edition includes poems written between June 1974 and April 1978. As the title indicates, it is a book of hymns, which praise the young body which creates its own song – a celebration of physical love in the manner of ancient Greece. Critic Marcos-Ricardo Barnatán characterizes the work as a new stage in Spanish poetry because of its explicit exhibition of eroticism and homosexual love, coinciding with a new personal and social freedom in Spain following the 1975 death of Francisco Franco. Moreover, the book seems a ritual of paganism. While the thematics evolve from Villena's earlier poetry, a new vitalism emerges from the experiences of the poet, although this autobiographical slant is shadowed by symbolism. The culturalist tendencies continue and become more synergistic with the voice of Villena. Ancient myths, songs of the troubadours, oriental works with semblances of the haiku, and Greek and Arabic poetry contrast with the contemporary figures of hustlers, vampires, and "night people." Yet these personae are more than artifice and decoration; even the historical decadents represent real identities and are as contemporary as the nameless young men of the streets. In *Hymnica* there is a clear and consistent rebellion by Villena against a shallow, moralistic, and artificial world. Ogata Kirin, the Japanese artist portrayed in "El ciruelo blanco y el ciruelo rojo" (The White Plum Tree and the Red Plum Tree), was called an eccentric, a dandy, and an aesthete; yet, he dedicated himself with audacity to art and pleasure. Dressed in the finest silk, "Gozó del esplendor de la juventud en / los barrios de licencia" (He enjoyed the splendor of youth in / the districts of license). He asked for no more than "Sensación por sensación. / Vivir, sentir, gozar. Sin más problemas" (Sensation for sensation. / To live, to feel, to have pleasure. Without more problems).

Jiménez, in his introduction to *Poesía,* finds a strong Hellenic archetype in *Hymnica* in the presence of Platonic and Neoplatonic thought; in addition to the theme of homoerotic love in Greek philosophy, it also implies a metaphysics. If Socrates found beauty as eternal, then the multiplicity of young and beautiful bodies form, according to Jiménez, a certain intuition of unity in the poetry of Villena – a

transcendental progression of idealism. Yet, in the temporality of lives and the failure of desires, people aspire to the ideal and progress toward it without ever reaching it. In the poem "Otros querubes" (Other Cherubs) the speaker marvels at the deceptive beauty of young men whom he cannot believe are real: "No tocas realidad aunque los labios besen, / luz, tal vez, en imagen de cuerpos que no existen" (You do not touch reality although your lips may kiss, / light, perhaps in an image of bodies which do not exist).

In the poem "Omnibus de estética" (Omnibus of Aesthetics) love surges from desire, and desire from beauty: "La belleza evoca imágenes / lejanas. Acentúa la realidad; el deseo / la modifica. El amor la acrece" (Beauty evokes images / far away. It accentuates reality; desire / changes it. Love increases it). Love as possession creates images of a new reality, and the process of poetry is a mirrored but distorted reflection of experience: "Un brazo / sugiere una espada radiante. Un ojo verde / el muro vegetal de un jardín persa" (An arm / suggests a radiant sword. A green eye / the green growth on the wall of a Persian garden). The identification of the body with poetry is intensified in this collection to a degree of mysticism; yet, the mysticism is pagan rather than Christian. It embraces a personal ethic with which Villena separates himself from society – a kind of fin de siècle dandyism. In the poem "Desnudez breve de la carne" (Brief Nudity of the Flesh) Villena demonstrates his admiration for the poet Cavafy in praising the empty night and prostitutes: "la estricta moral condenará" (strict morality will condemn); yet, desire's moment of opportunity and freedom is "agua vital" (water of life).

The mystification in Villena's previous poetry is less apparent in *Hymnica* because he provides a clearer presence of his own experiences in the poetry, but there is ironically an increased component of surrealistic free association. In a note to *Poesía (1970–1982)* Villena indicates that *Hymnica* is not his favorite work but is the one which gives him the most intimate pleasure. The poetry in *Hymnica* is emotionally charged and egocentric and has imagery of bars, discos, and alcohol; the scenes of night and the streets offer multiple metaphors of disillusionment and increasing pathos in such poems as "Hustler," "Desnudez breve de la carne," "Bares," and "Beau Satán." As have others of his generation, Villena has chosen to live his rebellion as well as writing of it. In the poem "Nuestra señora de la noche" (Our Lady of the Night) the speaker seeks the promised pleasure of the night and joins those he would despise during the day: "Aún perdura el silencio en las calles mojadas. / Y renegamos entonces de la noche – tan solos – / con el cansancio ese, tan viejo y cotidiano, de la vida" (The silence in the wet streets still remains. / And then we give up the night – so alone – with that weariness, so old and everyday, of life).

*Huir del invierno* (To Flee from Winter) is among the best collections of Villena's poetry. First published in 1981, it was later included in *Poesía (1970–1982)* and, with the exception of four poems, comprises poetry written between early 1978 and 1981. The book has four parts: "Odas" (Odes), "Epigramas" (Epigrams), "Efigies" (Effigies), and "Elegías" (Elegies). For this work Villena received a grant from the Fundación Juan March and was awarded the prestigious Premio de la Crítica. In an interview with Rosa María Pereda (*Insula,* January 1984), Villena subtly distinguished the work from his earlier poetry. *Hymnica* presents the joy of desire and the possibility of realizing it, but Villena finds in *Huir del invierno* the emptiness of desire unfulfilled.

In a preliminary note to the book, Villena introduces its symbolic structure as being based on the antithesis of winter (north) and summer (south), recalling such works of the German novelist Thomas Mann as *Death in Venice* (1912; translated, 1925) and *Mario and the Magician* (1930; translated, 1931). Winter and the north symbolize detested realism, the vacuum of coldness, and the morality of puritanism: "vino que debe diliurse . . . vejez, el miedo, la mansedumbre, el no atreverse" (wine to be diluted . . . old age, fear, meekness, and not daring). Summer represents a vital resistance inspired by Greco-Roman paganism and Arabic culture – a search for the heat and perfume of dark, young, beautiful bodies. The voyage in fleeing winter is the escape from an intolerant God to a polytheism which finds the sacred in many things: "La búsqueda de todo lo que la luz y el meridiano representan" (The search for all that the light and the meridian represent). Yet, as Jiménez notes in *Poesía,* in the final section of *Huir del invierno,* "Elegías," this idea of paradise and the south is questioned by Villena himself. "Inmensas tierras amarillas / donde el sol estival danza con su piel de leopardo" (Immense yellow lands / where the summer sun dances in its leopard skin), described in the poem "Viento del sur" (Southern Wind), become threatened by loneliness and alienation.

With a new clarity of language and complexity of rhythm in *Huir del invierno,* Villena seeks his essential self; he is conscious of time and more aware of a brotherhood of those who desire and suf-

fer. The contemplation of beauty is primary, and the act of seduction through desire is effaced as it reveals itself deceptive and transitory. Villena creates a meditative register in this collection, and although the work is more narrative than his earlier ones, he seems acutely aware of his own masquerade in the coexistence of language and desire – poetry and life. In the poem "Giovanni Antonio Bazzi, Il Sodoma" the Italian painter Bazzi realizes that it is his desire that is real, even if cruel and transitory, and not his art:

> Soy un ladron de realidad,
> y creo bien que todo arte es rapto.
> Por eso importa más el vivir,
> finalmente.
>
> (I am a thief of reality,
> and I truly believe that all art is abduction.
> Because of this living matters most,
> finally.)

The section "Odas" includes poems that celebrate the beauty of the body and desire, recalling Villena's earlier poetry, while "Epigramas" is a stage in the progression toward melancholy and loss seen in the final section, "Elegías." Barnatán has observed that the epigrams are bitterly ironic, with tones of iniquity never before seen in the works of Villena. They represent a distancing in preparation for "Elegías." In the elegies Villena intensifies the culturalist mode with references to great mosques and to Novalis, Brunetto Latini, Desiderius Erasmus, Maurice Ravel, and Coco Chanel, as well as to the arcane and nameless, such as some ancient Arabic perfumist or a great actress now anonymous. What may seem to be arcane, pedantic descriptions of these exotic figures and places shows Villena's faith in a tragic community of those who join him in the failure to preserve desire and love; mysterious shadows represent a new despair in paradise.

Thus this final section of *Huir del invierno* evokes a sustained level of disillusionment and despair new to the poetry of Villena. There is the radiance of summer and the harmonious beauty of the young body, but there is also the presence of cold, silence, deceit, and prostitution. The coming of this "winter" was already apparent in the "Odas" section in such poems as " 'David' por Donatello" ("David" by Donatello), in which the slayer of Goliath incorporates "La más bella maldad en el cuerpo más núbil" (The most beautiful evil in the most nubile body), and "Extrarradial" (On the Outskirts), in which the young and golden gods of

*Cover for the special issue of* Litoral *(no. 188, 1990) that includes Villena's "El paganismo nuevo"*

Olympia, now fond of symbolist art and the music of Felix Mendelssohn-Bartholdy, have fallen. There are other gods huddled in the suburbs: "mal-hablados . . . estatuillas de oro y vanila . . . diamante y chewing-gum" (foul-mouthed . . . little statues of gold and vanilla . . . diamond and chewing gum). In the poem "Esa querida atmósphere de tango hacia las tres" (That Beloved Atmosphere of Tango around Three), in "Elegías," the speaker leaves a bar aware that the gift of desire may be solitude: "¡Hasta mañana, señor! La soledad está servida" (Until tomorrow, sir! Loneliness is served). In such poems as "Bares," "Four Roses," and "Endimión," Villena enters the world of *vicio* (vice) and homosexual love more openly than did the poet Cernuda, whose influence is strongly reflected, or Wilde, whom Villena admires. The use of the first person in this section increases the potential for the participation of the reader who is sensitive to the destruction of the dream in social reality.

In one of the most skillful and sentient poems of the book, "Experience du gouffre" (Experience of the Abyss), love and desire become sterilized, mer-cenary, and threatening, yet the thirst for them is unabated because it is vital:

> Saber que buscas sólo extorsionarme,
> que te finges amable por dinero,
> que vas, entre caricias, a estafarme,
> a pedirme, a robarme, a sacar cuanto
> puedas de mi; saberlo todo claramente,
> y buscar sin embargo la llama de tu cuerpo;
> adorarte como a un pequeño dios bello
> y cruel . . .
>
> (To know that you intend only to extort me,
> that you pretend to be friendly for money,
> that, between caresses, you are going to cheat me,
> to ask from me, to steal from me, to take all you can
> from me; to know it all clearly,
> and nevertheless to search for the flame of your body;
> to adore you as a small beautiful
> and cruel god . . .)[.]

There is an increasing need to communicate the Fall and Villena's own vital experience. The confrontation between beauty and the sense of loss in physical love mirrors the conflict between art and reality.

From the center of the antithesis he voices an ambiguous hope in the poem "Adveniat tuum regnum" (May Your Kingdom Come): "Sácame del invierno. Tu rostro de dios joven / es luz de mi desierto. / Mira cómo te espero" (Take me from winter. / Your face of a young god / is light in my desert. / Look how I wait for you).

José David Pujante cites Villena as one of the first Spanish poets in many years to create a new poetic world. Pujante claims that *Huir del invierno* includes one of the richest lexicons in contemporary poetry. Villena merges the colloquial language of the street with cultured and refined speech. As in his previous work, there is a remarkable synesthesia of sight, sound, touch, and color. In 1981 Villena also published *Un paganism nuevo* (A New Paganism), which includes thirty poems from his earlier collections, the majority of the poems coming from *Huir del invierno*.

The poems of *La muerte unicamente* (Death Alone, 1984) were written between September 1981 and May 1984. In his interview with Pereda, Villena described this book as being the result of all he had written and as presenting the idea that all the plenitude the senses proclaim is found in death. The title is based on a poem by Cernuda, "La gloria del poeta" (The Glory of the Poet, 1935), in which "la muerte unicamente / puede hacer resonar la melodía prometida" (death alone / can cause the promised melody to resound). As Villena indicated in the interview, the motivating force behind *Hymnica* was the joy of desire and its potential realization; in *Huir del invierno* unfulfilled desire became emptiness and alienation. In *La muerte unicamente* the concept of desire reaches a new plane, which includes the Platonic and Petrarchan idea of merging with the universe. Yet, Villena would go beyond the metaphysical to include all desire, from the sexual and sensual to the metaphysical – forming a kind of "metafísica de las sentidos" (metaphysics of the senses). In the integration of love, life, and death, all become synergistic and interdependent. Poetry becomes the interior search for the interrelationship of desire.

To Villena, the only truth is an ironic one – that the temporal world admits no permanent beauty or desire, and that there is no truth. According to Villena in his introduction to *La muerte unicamente,* people can only seek that which Plato and Fray Luis de León sought in the interior of the self. The traveler in the poem "El paso de la laguna Estigia" (The Passing of the Lagoon of the Styx) encounters a naked old man, an oracle, of whom he asks what he should have served or sought in life.

The lost oracle replies "Cualquier cosa que hicieras, es lo mismo. / No hay verdad aquí. Nada es verdad segura" (Whatever you did, is the same. / There is no truth here. Nothing is certain truth). The moment is the only truth, and the traveler is led wading to a boat while there appears in the background a strange and cold sun, which, in its redness, "parecía la sangre cuando mana" (seemed as blood flowing).

This association of life with death is present in the first works of Villena and by increment intensifies during his career, becoming a vital symbol in *La muerte unicamente*. As Jiménez writes in an essay in *Sobre un pujante deseo* (On a Powerful Desire, 1990), the need for transcendence in death appears parallel to the existence of the physical beauty of the body and the celebration of this world, both coalescing in time and place just as the emotions of the poet merge with the mythical. In some concluding remarks to *La muerte unicamente* Villena states that "La muerte es solución, metáfora, puerta hacia una diferente realidad perfecta" (Death is a solution, metaphor, door leading to a different, perfect reality).

The cards of the tarot provide titles for the three progressive stages of the book: "La Maison-Dieu" (The House of God) represents a destroyed tower evocative of the Fall of Man and the erosion of hope; "Le Soleil" (The Sun), the title of the second section, represents splendor and luminescence; and "Les Etoiles" (The Stars) closes the work with faint glimpses of transcendence – flickering and transient. Throughout the poetry of *La muerte unicamente* Villena creates a tension between the inquietude of the need for beauty and love, and the deceit of time, which steals hope. In the unusually lengthy poem "Tractatus de amore" (Treatise on Love) there is a contrast between visualization and the changing identities of love within time. For Villena love is magical: "Queremos romper / el cuerpo para encontrar el cuerpo" (We wish to break / the body in order to find the body). Love is desire and not possession; it is the betrayal of the soul by the senses, the need for warmth in companionship, and finally the naming of all that is desire. Yet this nominalism is ultimately without meaning, for in the same poem Villena speaks to love: "Sombrío dios sin devotos, les presta tu mirar a todos ellos, / pero ninguno eres" (dark god without worshipers, you lend your semblance to all, / but you are none of them).

This heuristic strain of interrogation recalls the *Diálogos del conocimiento* (Dialogues of Knowledge, 1974) of the Nobel laureate Aleixandre, yet the voice of Villena seems directed toward something beyond existentialism or human consciousness. In his poem "Sobre un tema de Berkeley (On a Theme of Berkeley) a dialogue occurs between time and the poet's desire, in a profusion of images; a reverie of golden bodies, squares of light, and Bacchanalian dances promise fulfillment, yet are destroyed by time. Images are created only to break apart, as does reality in time: "De pronto una garganta juvenil, / y el mundo se forma, se ordena, y se deshace" (Suddenly, a young throat, / and the world is formed, is ordered, and is broken apart). The masques of death are innumerable, and, critic Leopoldo Alas writes, death (in Villena's work vicious, beautiful, warm, caressing, blond, and absolute) offers the greatest freedom in the escape from time. Yet, if the poet is tempted to flee a deceptive and miserable world in death, he simultaneously yearns for the dance – the celebration of life and poetry.

In the poem "Villamediana," Villena confronts the pull of death with a transcendence within suffering:

¿Caer? ¡Qué importa caer! El impulso es la vida.
Morir al acercarse al sol, tocarlo con las manos,
y precipitarse al hondo chillando jubiloso en la agonía.
Pues que nadie quitará al saturnal intento,
la gloria, con caer, y el bello honor de haber subido.

(To fall? What does it matter to fall! The impulse is life.
To die on approaching the sun, to touch it with our hands,
and to throw ourselves to the bottom screaming joyfully in agony.
Because no one will take from the Saturnian intent,
the glory, with falling, and the beautiful honor of having ascended.)

The work of the poet – the word – offers the impetus to survive. *La muerte unicamente* reveals a poetry of deep structure and is a transition through metaphysics, rather than metaphysical. Villena, in his concluding comments to the work, rejects the description of the book as poetry of experience. Rather, the complex symbols of the work create, as do the cultural referents, a system of myths. The thematic depth, the variety and clarity of the poetic structures, and the intense imagery of *La muerte unicamente* insure the position of Villena as a major poet.

In 1990 Villena published *Como a lugar extraño* (As to a Strange Place), including poetry written between January 1985 and July 1989. The sixteenth-century Spanish humanist and poet Fernán Pérez de Oliva inspired the title of the book: he described hu-

mankind as going into the world "como a lugar extraño, llorando y gimiendo" (as to a strange place, crying and wailing). Villena, in his introduction, describes a type of exile in the coexistence of people and the world: "Pertenecemos al mundo, y no somos de él" (We belong to the world, and we are not of it); it is a description of alienation, recalling the existential philosophy of Albert Camus.

Life is a strange place because people seem exiled from desire, beauty, and perfection. This idea of exile is also evident in Villena's novel *En el invierno romano* (In the Roman Winter, 1986) and is an organic element of his later poetry. People are exiled in their intellects as well as their emotive responses. The myth of Byzantium and the beauty of eternal youth in *El viaje a Bizancio,* and the escape in the potential realization of desire in the radiant sun and gold bodies of *Huir del invierno* led to the fusion of death, life, and celebration in *La muerte unicamente. Como a lugar extraño* shows a new confrontation with reality and pain. The Platonic ideal of the previous two works is threatened with fracture. Although Villena senses a reflection of beauty in the core of humankind, it is momentary and mutable. In the poem "En el invierno romano" Villena seeks refuge in the past ideal of beauty: "Aquí, entre los libros, es muy grato quedar, amigo mío" (Here, among my books, it is very pleasant to remain, my friend). Yet the world is treacherous, cold, dirty, and filled with mottled hordes from afar, bellowing in search of plunder: "Y en covachas infectas ejercen ambidextro placer / con crueldad: Rueda la cerveza por un suelo / de goma, y en las paredes hay huellas de patadas" (And in infected small caves they practice ambidextrous pleasure / with cruelty: Beer encircles a filthy floor, / and on the walls are footprints from kicks).

In the poem "Et omnia vanitas" (And Vanity in All), the poet who seeks refuge in a rustic cabin as he reads works by Arthur Schopenhauer, T. S. Eliot, Theocritus, or the Spanish Renaissance poet Francisco de Medrano – like the scholar in the poem "En honor de un sabio solitario" (In Honor of a Learned Recluse) – cannot evade what seems to Villena a barbarous siege from without. Villena's own experience is allegorized in the poem "En el invierno romano," as he fears that he will not feel again the harmony and symmetry of adolescent beauty: "¡Grandes dioses, que no / llegue el verano, nunca llegue – les pido – porque entonces, / ciertamente entonces, vendrá nuestro final!" (Great gods, let not / the summer come – I beg of you – because then, / certainly then, will come our end!). It is useless to evoke the summer because all that *was*

*Luis Antonio de Villena (photograph by Aleyo Lorén)*

is lost, as in "Hermosos rostros del pasado" (Beautiful Faces From the Past):

> Tú y yo pudimos haber sido amantes muchos años;
> nuestra noche fue breve, pero larga la dicha. . . .
> ¿Qué queda de vosotros,
> espectros de aquel río donde un gran sol brillaba. . . ?

> (You and I could have been lovers for many years;
> our night was brief, but our happiness long. . . .
> What remains of all of you,
> shadows of that river where a great sun was shining. . . ?)

The "beautiful faces from the past" image is a collective metaphor in an imagery of fleeting time and death. People cannot escape themselves, nor the world; they are condemned to fall. In the poem "Cervantes," Villena joins the madman of La Mancha in the faith that victory is in the struggle: "la sombra / es luz para quien siente la carne y la totalidad del sentimiento. / No habló de la ex-periencia, más su vivir" (the shadow / is light for one who feels the flesh and the totality of feeling. / He did not speak of experience, but its living). As in *La muerte unicamente* such cultural references are based on real people and are vital symbols of living and desiring.

María del Pilar Palomo believes that *Como a lugar extraño* represents the most mature work of Villena because of the increased variance in style and clarity, as well as a new fusion of the mystic and aesthetic. The lexicon includes the colloquial, classical, and pure jargon in a continuing antithesis of the ideal and real. The transcendent ideal, Platonic or Neoplatonic, becomes increasingly distant. The book is a portrait of life as *felt,* Villena indicates in his introductory remarks, and the center of one's "lugar extraño" is made up of erotic desire, joy, and celebration, as well as failure and alienation.

The created illusion of this center is poetry. In "Encomio a un amigo, en su total renuncia" (Praise of a Friend, on His Total Renunciation), Villena writes:

Y ha de ser my posible que la fe no importe tanto.
(Aunque hermoso sería aceptar casa, premio, y bandera. . . .
y saber que el dolor, gota a gota,
se transmuta en gema, y sentir
que cada movimiento y cada voz, poseen significado.)
Mas quizá la fe no importe tanto.

(And it has to be very possible that faith does not matter so much.
[Although it would be beautiful to accept a house, prize, and banner . . .
And to know that pain, drop by drop,
is changed into a precious stone, and to feel
that each movement and each voice, possesses meaning.]
However perhaps faith does not matter so much.)

The poetry of Luis Antonio de Villena places him in the forefront of contemporary Spanish verse writers. The striking imagery and intricate complexity of his symbolism lend energy to a style that has constantly evolved. Creating a gallery of historical personae, he invites the reader to participate in the emotive tension of past and present. Villena is a product of his age, yet his *culturalismo* unites his experiences with those of history and art. His life and his poetry are synthesized in the quixotic thirst for beauty, given life through love and desire. In a world which is often deceitful and mean, this quest in his verse is increasingly shadowed by disillusionment and alienation. His pursuit of the controversial themes of eroticism and homosexual love courageously advocate a personal and social freedom and divergent ethics which some would reject. Yet he has earned the respect of Spain's most eminent critics and poets, and he continues to exert a considerable influence on younger poets. Despite the inherent difficulty of interpreting his complex verse, he reveals the marrow of contemporary poetry in self-confrontation, and he speaks to all humankind – as the speaker does in a deserted bar in the poem "Esa querida atmósfera de tango hacia las tres," where

poca gente queda bailando ya a esas horas,
y en esos días últimos de enero, tan fríos como
un lunes permanente. . . . Sientes, frente al espejo,
el orgullo tan duro de estar solo.

(few people remain dancing now at those hours,
and in those last days of January, as cold as
a permanent Monday. . . . You feel, coldly in front of
the mirror,
the pride so hard of being alone.)

**Interview:**

Rosa María Pereda, "Conversación con Luis Antonio de Villena," *Insula,* 39 (January 1984): 14.

**References:**

Leopoldo Alas, "Luis Antonio de Villena: La realidad como nostalgia y como deseo," *Insula,* 41 (April 1986): 10;

Marcos-Ricardo Barnatán, "La belleza hechizada por Luis Antonio de Villena," *Insula,* 37 (September 1982): 3;

Francisco Brines, "La heterodoxia generacional de Luis Antonio de Villena," *Insula,* 34 (September 1979): 11–12;

Brines, "Presentación de Luis Antonio de Villena," in *Sobre un pujante deseo,* edited by Jesús García Sánchez (Torremolinos: Litoral, 1990), pp. 29–33;

José Luis Cano, "Luis Antonio de Villena: *El viaje a Bizancio,*" *Insula,* 33 (October 1978): 8–9;

José Luis García Martín, *Las voces y los ecos* (Madrid: Júcar, 1981), pp. 109–123;

José Olivio Jiménez, "Hacia el último horizonte. Sobre *La muerte unicamente,*" in *Sobre un pujante deseo,* pp. 65–72;

Jiménez, "La poesía de Luis Antonio de Villena," introduction to Villena's *Poesía (1970–1982)* (Madrid: Visor, 1983), pp. 9–56;

Emilio Miró, "La búsqueda de la belleza del cuerpo, en Luis Antonio de Villena," *Insula,* 39 (April 1984): 7;

Concepción G. Moral and Rosa María Pereda, *Joven poesía española* (Madrid: Cátedra, 1979);

María del Pilar Palomo, "El ocaso de Bizancio," *Insula,* 534 (1991): 16–17;

José David Pujante, "Algunas apreciaciones a *Huir del invierno* de Luis Antonio de Villena," *Estudios de Lingüística de la Universidad de Alicante,* 3 (1985–1986): 325–332;

Jaime Siles, "Sobre la poesía última de Luis Antonio de Villena," *Insula,* 31 (January 1976): 12.

# Checklist of Further Readings

Alonso, Dámaso. *Ensayos sobre poesía española.* Buenos Aires: Revista de Occidente Argentina, 1946.

Barella, Julia. *Despúes de la modernidad: Poesía española en sus distintas lenguas literarias.* Barcelona: Anthropos, 1987.

Baur, Carlos, ed. and trans. *Cries from a Wounded Madrid: Poetry of the Spanish Civil War,* bilingual edition. Athens, Ohio: Swallow Press, 1984.

Bousoño, Carlos. *Teoría de la expresión poética,* revised, definitive edition. Madrid: Gredos, 1976.

Brihuega, Jaime. *Manifiestos, proclamas, panfletos y textos doctrinales: Las vanguardias artísticas en España, 1910–1931.* Madrid: Cátedra, 1979.

Cano, José Luis. *Poesía española contemporánea: Generaciones de posguerra.* Madrid: Guadarrama, 1974.

Carreño, Antonio. *La dialéctica de la identidad en la poesía contemporánea: La persona, la máscara.* Madrid: Gredos, 1982.

Castellet, José María. *Nueve novísimos poetas españoles.* Barcelona: Barral, 1970.

Chander, Richard E., and Kessel Schwartz. *A New History of Spanish Literature,* revised edition. Baton Rouge & London: Louisiana State University Press, 1991.

Cobb, Carl W. *Contemporary Spanish Poetry (1898–1963).* Boston: Twayne, 1976.

Concha, Victor G. de la. *La poesía española de 1935 a 1975,* 2 volumes. Madrid: Cátedra, 1982.

Concha. *La poesía española de posguerra: Teoría e historia de sus movimientos.* Madrid: Española, 1973.

Connell, Geoffrey N. *Spanish Poetry of the "Grupo Poético de 1927."* Oxford & New York: Pergamon, 1977.

Daydí-Tolson, Santiago. *The Post–Civil War Spanish Social Poets.* Boston: Twayne, 1963.

Debicki, Andrew Peter. "New Poets, New Works, New Approaches: Recent Spanish Poetry," *Siglo XX/20th Century,* 8, nos. 1–2 (1990): 41–53.

Debicki. *Poetry of Discovery: The Spanish Generation of 1956–1971.* Lexington: University Press of Kentucky, 1982.

Debicki, ed. *Contemporary Spanish Poetry: 1939–1990.* Manhattan, Kans.: Studies in Twentieth-Century Literature, 1992.

Díez de Revenga, Francisco Javier. *Panorama crítico de la generación del 27.* Madrid: Castalia, 1987.

*Espadaña: Revista de poesía y critica.* Volumes 1–48 (1944–1951); republished, León: Espadaña, 1979.

Ferrán, Jaime, and Daniel P. Testa, eds. *Spanish Writers of 1936: Crisis and Commitment in the Poetry of the Thirties and Forties: An Anthology of Literary Studies and Essays.* London: Tamesis, 1973.

Geist, Anthony J. *La poética de la generación del 27 y las revistas literarias: De la vanguardia al compromiso (1918–1936)*. Barcelona: Labor/Guadarrama, 1980.

Gullón, Ricardo. *Direcciones del modernismo,* revised edition. Madrid: Gredos, 1971.

Hamer, Louis, and Sara Schyfter. *Recent Poetry of Spain: A Bilingual Anthology*. Old Chatham, N.Y.: Sachem, 1983.

Havard, Robert G. *From Romanticism to Surrealism: Seven Spanish Poets*. Totowa, N.J.: Barnes & Noble, 1988.

Ilie, Paul. *The Surrealist Mode in Spanish Literature*. Ann Arbor: University of Michigan Press, 1968.

Jiménez, José Olivio. *Cinco poetas del tiempo (Vicente Aleixandre, Luis Cernuda, José Hierro, Carlos Bousoño, Francisco Brines),* revised edition. Madrid: Insula, 1972.

Jiménez. *Diez años de poesía española: 1960–1970*. Madrid: Insula, 1972.

Jiménez and Dionisio Cañas. *Siete poetas españoles de hoy*. Mexico City: Oasis, 1983.

Jiménez, Juan Ramón. *El modernismo*. Madrid: Aguilar, 1962.

Jiménez Fajardo, Salvador, and John C. Wilcox, eds. *At Home and Beyond: New Essays on Spanish Poets of the Twenties*. Lincoln, Nebr.: Society for Spanish and Spanish-American Studies, 1983.

Ley, Charles David. *Spanish Poetry Since 1939*. Washignton, D.C.: Catholic University Press, 1962.

Manrique de Lara, José Gerado. *Poetas sociales españoles*. Madrid: EPESA, 1974.

Mantero, Manuel. *Poetas españoles de posguerra*. Madrid: Espasa-Calpe, 1986.

Marco, Joaquín. *Poesía española siglo XX*. Barcelona: Edhasa, 1986.

Moral, Concepción G., and Rosa María Pereda. *Joven poesía española: Antología*. Madrid: Cátedra, 1979.

Morris, Cyril Brian. *A Generation of Spanish Poets: 1920–1936*. London: Cambridge University Press, 1969.

Palomo, María del Pilar. *La poesía en el siglo XX: Desde 1939*. Madrid: Taurus, 1988.

Paulino Ayuso, José. *La poesía en el siglo XX: Desde 1939*. Madrid: Playor, 1982.

Pérez Bajo, Javier. *La poesía en el siglo XX: Hasta 1939*. Madrid: Playor, 1984.

Persin, Margaret H. *Recent Spanish Poetry and the Role of the Reader*. Lewisburg, Pa., & Cranbury, N.J.: Associated University Presses, 1987.

Pont, Jaume. *El postismo: Un movimiento estético-literario de vanguardia*. Barcelona: Mall, 1987.

Pozanco, Victor. *Nueve poetas del resurgimiento*. Barcelona: Linosa, 1976.

Pritchett, Kay. *Four Postmodern Poets of Spain: A Critical Introduction with Translations of the Poems*. Fayetteville & London, U.K.: University of Arkansas Press, 1991.

Rosenthal, David. *Postwar Catalan Poetry*. Lewisburg, Pa.: Bucknell University Press, 1991.

Rubio, Fanny. *Revistas poéticas españolas: 1939–1975.* Madrid: Turner, 1976.

Rubio and José Luis Falcó. *Poesía española contemporánea: Historia y antología, 1939–1980,* revised edition. Madrid: Alhambra, 1982.

St. Martin, Hardie, ed. *Roots and Wings: Poetry from Spain, 1900–1970: A Bilingual Anthology* New York: Harper & Row, 1976.

Salinas, Pedro. *Literatura española: Siglo XX,* revised edition. Mexico City: Robredo, 1949.

Sanz Villanueva, Santos. *Historia de la literatura española actual.* Barcelona: Ariel, 1984.

Soufas, C. Christopher. *Conflict of Light and Wind: The Spanish Generation of 1927 and the Ideology of Poetic Form.* Middletown, Conn.: Wesleyan University Press, 1989.

Videla, Gloria. *El ultraísmo: Estudios sobre movimientos poéticos de vanguardia en España,* revised edition. Madrid: Gredos, 1971.

Villena, Luis Antonio de. *Postnovísimos.* Madrid: Visor, 1986.

Vivanco, Luis Felipe. *Introducción a la poesía española contemporánea,* revised and enlarged edition, 2 volumes. Madrid: Guadarrama, 1974.

Wright, Eleanor. *The Poetry of Protest under Franco.* London: Tamesis / Dover, N.H.: Longwood, 1986.

Young, Howard T. *The Victorious Expression.* Madison: University of Wisconsin Press, 1964.

Zardoya, Concha. *Poesía española del siglo XX: Estudios temáticos y estilísticos,* 4 volumes. Madrid: Gredos, 1974.

Zuleta, Emilia de. *Cinco poetas españoles (Salinas, Guillén, Lorca, Alberti, Cernuda),* revised edition. Madrid: Gredos, 1981.

# Contributors

Ana María Alfaro-Alexander ..............................................................*Castleton State College*
Samuel Amell ...................................................................................*Ohio State University*
Patricia J. Boehne ...................................................................................*Eastern College*
Alan S. Bruflat ...............................................................................*Wayne State College*
Susana Cavallo ..................................................................*Loyola University of Chicago*
Charles Maurice Cherry ..................................................................*Furman University*
Peter Cocozzella ........................................*State University of New York at Binghamton*
J. Eric Diehl ...............................................................................*Collège Montmorency*
Niza Fabre ...........................................................................*Ramapo College of New Jersey*
Xoan González-Millán ........................*Hunter College of the City University of New York*
Salvador Jiménez-Fajardo ..................*State University of New York at Binghamton*
Dona M. Kercher ...........................................................................*Assumption College*
Felipe A. Lapuente ...............................................................*Memphis State University*
Mary Makris ..........................................................................*University of Louisville*
Roberto Carlos Manteiga ...............................................*University of Rhode Island*
Patricia E. Mason .................................................................*University of South Carolina*
Kathryn G. McConnell ...........................................*Point Loma Nazarene College*
Linda D. Metzler ..............................................................................*Kenyon College*
Martha LaFollette Miller ..................*University of North Carolina at Charlotte*
Glenn Morocco ...........................................................................*La Salle University*
Candelas Newton .....................................................................*Wake Forest University*
Janet Pérez .................................................................................*Texas Tech University*
Susan Rivera ..........................................................................*University of Oklahoma*
Sylvia R. Sherno .....................................*University of California, Los Angeles*
Stephen J. Summerhill ...............................................................*Ohio State University*
Jerry Phillips Winfield ...............................................................*Mercer University*
Eleanor Wright ........................................................................*Birmingham, Alabama*
Howard T. Young .........................................................................*Pomona College*

350

# Cumulative Index

*Dictionary of Literary Biography,* Volumes 1-134
*Dictionary of Literary Biography Yearbook,* 1980-1992
*Dictionary of Literary Biography Documentary Series,* Volumes 1-11

# Cumulative Index

**DLB** before number: *Dictionary of Literary Biography*, Volumes 1-134
**Y** before number: *Dictionary of Literary Biography Yearbook*, 1980-1992
**DS** before number: *Dictionary of Literary Biography Documentary Series*, Volumes 1-11

## C

Cumulative Index

## H

# Q

ISBN 0-8103-5393-8

## *Documentary Series*

## *Yearbooks*